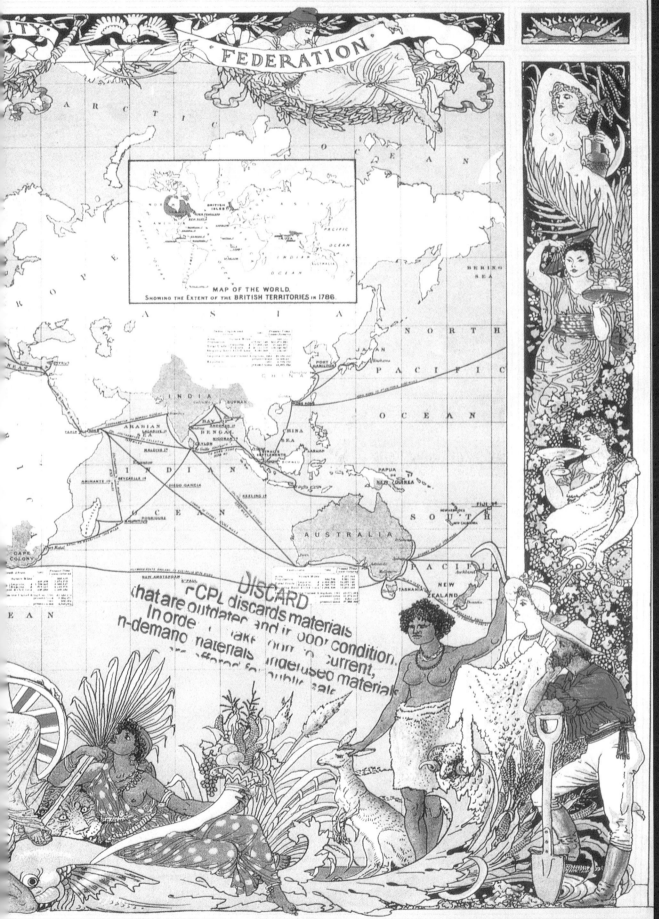

FEDERATION

MAP OF THE WORLD.
SHOWING THE EXTENT OF THE BRITISH TERRITORIES IN 1786.

T OF THE BRITISH EMPIRE IN 1886.
RLY R M A ——— BRITISH TERRITORIES COLOURED RED

ENCYCLOPEDIA OF THE
VICTORIAN ERA

Encyclopedia of the

VICTORIAN ERA

Editorial Board

James Eli Adams • Editor in Chief
Cornell University

Tom Pendergast • Editor

Sara Pendergast • Editor

Advisory Board

ENCYCLOPEDIA OF THE
VICTORIAN ERA

James Eli Adams, Editor in Chief
Tom Pendergast and Sara Pendergast, Editors

Volume 4
SPIR – ZOOL

Grolier Academic Reference, an imprint of
Scholastic Library Publishing, Inc.
Danbury, Connecticut

Published by Grolier Academic Reference, an imprint of Scholastic Library Publishing, Inc.
Danbury, Connecticut

Cover image: Two scenes from Queen Victoria's reign: her coronation, 1837; and her Golden Jubilee procession, 1887, with elaborate border. Illustrated London News, 1897.
©Mary Evans Picture Library

Library of Congress Cataloging-in-Publication Data

Encyclopedia of the Victorian Era/James Eli Adams, editor in chief;
Tom Pendergast, Sara Pendergast, editors.
p. cm.
Includes bibliographical references and indexes.
ISBN 0-7172-5860-2 (set)
1. Great Britain--History--Victoria, 1837-1901--Encyclopedias.
2. Great Britain--Civilization--19th century--Encyclopedias.
I. Adams, James Eli. II. Pendergast, Tom. III. Pendergast, Sara.
DA550.E527 2003
941.081'03--dc22

2003057101

Printed and Manufactured in the United States of America.

1 3 5 4 2

⊖ The paper used in this publication meets the minimum requirements of the American National Standard for Information Sciences—Permanence of Paper for Printed Library Materials, ANSI Z39.48-1984.

ENCYCLOPEDIA OF THE
VICTORIAN ERA

(CONTINUED)

SPIRITUALISM

Victorian spiritualism was based on the belief that spirits of the deceased were able to communicate with the living through a medium. Its wide popularity was due not only to the spectacular nature of the manifestations: spiritualism tapped into and exploited the Victorian obsession with death and the afterlife and (as with MESMERISM) fears about the erasure of the individual's will and autonomy. The spirit communications typically were manifested in sounds and table tilting but were most valued when touch or visual apparitions took place.

The séance (a spiritualist meeting or, literally, "sitting"), which usually took place in a domestic setting, could also involve more dramatic manifestations such as levitation and automatic (or passive) writing. The medium would typically have a spirit control or guide who channeled the communications of other spirits: this is an ingenious way for the medium

to disassociate him- or herself from improper manifestations. Sometimes the spirits of famous literary and historical figures would materialize, although more frequently, the spirits were simply those of the deceased relatives of the séance participants, especially children.

Spiritualism was popular and controversial from its inception in the late 1840s into the twentieth century, when the slaughter of World War I would rekindle the need for consolation in the spirits. As a practice it was arguably the most successful American export to Europe in the nineteenth century. Spiritualism has its origins in Rochester, New York. In 1848 Margaret and Kate Fox heard knocking and rappings in their home. By means of a simple code, the sisters learned to communicate with the spirit, who unveiled himself as a peddler who had been murdered and buried in the cellar of the residence. The "Rochester rappings" became a national sensation, particularly on the East Coast, spurred on by Christian reviv-

1

alism and millenarianism (belief in the millennium of Christian prophecy).

CROSSING THE ATLANTIC

In October 1852 the arrival of the American medium Mrs. Hayden in LONDON signaled the start of spiritualism's popularity in Britain. Soon NEWSPAPERS began advertising the services and prices of mediums (Mrs. Hayden charged upwards of half a guinea). Some leading London PERIODICALS, such as *Atlantic Monthly*, declared the new imported mediums to be propagating "an essentially American plot" to spread "their own religious and political views." Often the fear of spiritualism was linked to snobbery about Americans; in *Blackwood's Edinburgh* magazine in 1853, W. E. Aytoun pronounced, "These Transatlantic ghosts are superlative idiots." Nevertheless, despite dissenting voices, the craze for spiritualism spread throughout the nation, and many significant figures attempted to communicate with the spirits, including QUEEN VICTORIA. As an apparently democratic practice (anybody, regardless of class, could discover their mediumistic powers), spiritualism became linked to dissenting religion and radical politics, and the socialist ROBERT OWEN "converted" to it. For some intellectuals, for example William and Mary Howitt, spiritualism was an extension of the thinking of the Swedish philosopher and religious writer Emanuel Swedenborg. Journals devoted to the subject of the spirit manifestations sprang up, in particular the *Spiritual Magazine* (1859–1877).

Throughout the 1850s controversy about spiritualism raged in British newspapers, which often carried information about American manifestations. The craze had by now spread to the cities and provinces of Britain, and prominent scientists investigated the phenomenon. On July 2, 1853, for example, MICHAEL FARADAY wrote a letter to the *Athenaeum* with the results of his experiments into table tilting, which concluded that unconscious muscular action of those touching the table was the cause.

In the spring of 1855 another American visitor caused a further wave of excitement. Daniel Dunglas Home (1833–1886) arrived in England on April 9. He was born in Scotland but moved to America as a child, where from 1850 he had made a modest name for himself as a successful medium. Home was distinctive because he did not charge for his mediumship (although he accepted gifts) and because his séances were often illuminated. His séances took place in the private homes of the upper classes and intelligentsia, where his charisma and talent made him famous. Despite the suspicions of many and several investigations, he was never uncovered as a fraud. One of the most famous incidents involving Home was the Ealing séance on July 25, 1855. Present were ELIZABETH BARRETT BROWNING (1806–1861), who was crowned with a wreath by spirit hands, and ROBERT BROWNING (1812–1889), and their accounts of the evening are dramatically different. In Browning's dramatic monologue "Mr. Sludge, 'the Medium'" (1864), he characterized Home as a fraud. His wife, who was dramatically and painfully deceived by American medium Sophie May Eckley (as described in Browning's "Where's Agnes?"), persisted in her belief in the spirits, even if mediums might disappoint. Of the spirit manifestations, she wrote to friend Fanny Haworth in 1861, "As far as I am concerned, I never heard or read a single communication which impressed me in the least: what does impress me is the probability of there being communications at all. I look at the movement. What *are* these intelligences, separated yet relating and communicating?"

WOMEN MAKING A CAREER OUT OF MEDIUMSHIP

In the 1870s spiritualism changed dramatically in style. Young, beautiful women (often of working-class or uncertain background) made a career out of mediumship, with a newly theatrical and daring style of spirit communication. These mediums produced what was seen as the dangerous height of mediumistic powers: a fully formed materialized spirit. Notable in this regard was Florence Cook, whose spirit control was "Katie King." The women mediums who thus gained notoriety were often investigated by medicine's new specialists in insanity, who correlated mediumship with hysteria. While the woman medium usually conformed to the conventions of her GENDER and society (and femininity was seen to be innately gifted with visionary and healing powers), in the séance room those norms were dramatically transgressed: according to Alex Owen, "Spiritualist mediumship not only colluded with the feminine ideal but also undermined it. What the séance promised was the ritualised violation of cultural norms."

While the spirits were taking on a particularly fleshly manifestation, experiments began in Cambridge, England, in 1874 into telepathy, or communication (both of bodies and minds) at a distance. The researchers, who included F. W. H. Myers, formed the Society for Psychical Research (SPR) in 1882. Pamela Thurschwell argues that the interest in telepathy discloses a shift in the concept of intimacy and that newly heightened anxieties about contamination of the will by another person were linked to the development of tele-technologies such as the TELEGRAPH and TELEPHONE.

Associated with excessive and threatening intimacy was also, of course, the excitement of transgressive erotic desires. Literature of the fin de siècle (showing a world-weariness and fashionable despair characteristic of the late nineteenth century) frequently worked through questions of intimacy and will, such as RUDYARD KIPLING's "Wireless," BRAM STOKER's *Dracula*, OSCAR WILDE's *The Picture of Dorian Gray*, George du Maurier's *Trilby*, and HENRY JAMES's "In the Cage." The sexual significances of intimate relationships between two subjects was also, at this time, theorized by Sigmund Freud, who was indebted to the work of the SPR but who was always careful to separate psychoanalysis from telepathy.

See also MESMERISM.

FURTHER READING

Barrow, Logie. *Independent Spirits: Spiritualism and English Plebeians, 1850–1910.* London: Routledge and Kegan Paul, 1986.

Goldfarb, Russell M., and Clare R. Goldfarb. *Spiritualism and Nineteenth-Century Letters.* London: Associated University Presses, 1978.

Kenyon, Frederic G., ed. *The Letters of Elizabeth Barrett Browning.* 2 vols. London: Smith, Elder, 1897.

Moore, Laurence R. *In Search of White Crows: Spiritualism, Parapsychology and American Culture.* Oxford: Oxford University Press, 1977.

Owen, Alex. *The Darkened Room: Women, Power and Spiritualism in Late Victorian England.* London: Virago, 1989.

Thurschwell, Pamela. *Literature, Technology and Magical Thinking, 1880–1920.* Cambridge: Cambridge University Press, 2001.

ALISON CHAPMAN

SPORTING NOVEL

Although games and pastimes of all kinds are encountered in the pages of Victorian novels, the widely popular subgenre known as sporting fiction is overwhelmingly preoccupied with foxhunting and horse racing. Throughout the Victorian era sizable numbers of (largely male) writers established successful literary careers by purveying evocative descriptions—generally strung together with the flimsiest of plots—of exhilarating mornings in cross-country pursuit of the foxhounds, of close finishes at regimental steeplechases, and of betting triumphs and catastrophes at the racecourses of Ascot or Epsom. The taste for such reading matter was not confined to the privileged circles whose recreations it depicted: at his death in 1919 Nat Gould, author of more than 100 formulaic

novelettes about horse racing aimed at the newly literate lower classes, was reckoned by one obituarist to have been the English-speaking world's best-selling writer.

NIMROD

In common with other genres evolving in early nineteenth-century England (the NEWGATE NOVEL, for example), sporting fiction had its origins in topical JOURNALISM. In 1822 Pittman's *Sporting Magazine* began to publish a series of articles by Nimrod (Charles James Apperley), an impecunious but well-connected member of the exclusive group of upper-class foxhunters known as Meltonians (from Melton Mowbray in Leicestershire, the center of their activities). Nimrod's sketches of fashionable sporting life, combining snobbery (his florid prose is resonant with dropped names) and the excitements of the chase, proved enormously popular and were regularly reprinted in book form. Their success suggested the potential marketability of fictionalized accounts of sporting activity, and in 1842 Nimrod himself produced *The Life of a Sportsman*, his only NOVEL.

SURTEES

It was Robert Smith Surtees (1803–1864), Nimrod's successor at the *Sporting Magazine*, who explored and developed the possibilities of the nascent genre. In *Jorrocks's Jaunts and Jollities* (1838) he grouped a series of HUNTING episodes around the character not of a GENTLEMAN (as Nimrod had done) but of a brash Cockney grocer with an unquenchable enthusiasm for sport. In subsequent novels (*Handley Cross*, 1843; *Hillingdon Hall*, 1845), Jorrocks reappears as a master of foxhounds and the proprietor of a country estate, two roles from which his lowly background and dropped *h*'s conventionally should have barred him, but for which he turns out to be better suited than the established landowning gentry. Surtees deploys the coarse but shrewd Jorrocks partly as a vehicle for exposing the petty snobberies and meannesses of provincial society, which inevitably won him detractors as well as admirers among the hunting fraternity. This vein of cynically observant satire is more extensively mined in his two finest novels, *Mr. Sponge's Sporting Tour* (1853) and *Mr. Facey Romford's Hounds* (1865). The protagonists of both books are seedy confidence tricksters who exploit the credulity and social ambition of their rural hosts by impersonating WEALTHY sportsmen. Sponge and Romford are thoroughgoing rogues, but they are redeemed, like Jorrocks, by their genuine love of hunting, and so contrast favorably with most of their victims, who ride to hounds either because it is expected of them or because it enables them to rub shoulders with the ARISTOCRACY.

WHYTE-MELVILLE AND SMART

Surtees's wonderfully engaged accounts of foxhunting were extensively imitated by his successors, but his abrasive social commentary (much admired by WILLIAM MAKEPEACE THACKERAY) was not. The two best-known sporting novelists of the second half of the century, George John Whyte-Melville (1821–1878) and Henry Hawley Smart (1833–1893), both former army officers who had seen service in the CRIMEAN WAR, generally describe hunting and riding with reminiscent nostalgia and set their action in the past decades of their own youth. Whyte-Melville's earliest novel, *Digby Grand* (1853), is the rambling autobiography of a young aristocrat who takes to all sports with equal facility but who comes temporarily to grief through improvident GAMBLING. For Grand, as for the characters in much of Whyte-Melville's subsequent fiction, hard riding is a pleasurable adjunct to a desirably affluent lifestyle rather than an overmastering passion. Only in *Market Harborough* (1861), a comic account of the sporting exploits of a hard-drinking and not overscrupulous country squire, does he approach either the infectious enthusiasm or the irony of Surtees.

Whereas Whyte-Melville was independently wealthy and donated the considerable proceeds of his writing to charity, Hawley Smart, having early gambled away his money on the racecourse, wrote novels to make a living. In his plots, sporting incidents tend to be integrated with the familiar devices of SENSATION NOVELS (bigamy, forged wills, mistaken identities, and so on) and with accounts of military life in peace and war (the stock-in-trade of yet another nineteenth-century fictional subgenre). Smart's attempts to amalgamate several different sources of audience appeal generally result in ramshackle but lively narratives. In *Hard Lines* (1883), for example, the hero is unjustly suspected not once, but twice, of cheating in regimental steeplechases, but he lives to redeem his honour in the Crimea and to reclaim his sweetheart in England.

USE OF SPORT IN OTHER FICTION

Smart's clearly market-driven decision to use hunting and racing as single ingredients in a heady brew concocted of various stimulants is representative of a broader tendency. Although many mediocre nov-

els with an exclusive focus on sport continued to appear in the second half of the century, most professional writers (always excepting the prodigious Gould, who targeted a specific audience) incorporated equestrian activity in their fiction as only an incidental part of the narrative interest. ANTHONY TROLLOPE, for example, regularly includes hunting scenes in his novels, where they operate as microcosmic displays of the virtues of Tory rural England. Collaborative writers Edith Somerville and Martin Ross (Violet Martin) use sport both as a source of comedy and as a focus for their penetrating fictional accounts of Anglo-Irish social life.

SOURCES OF POPULARITY

The popularity of sporting fiction with Victorian readers had a number of sources. First, an enthusiasm for horses in general and foxhunting in particular was increasingly regarded as a distinctively English trait, and its fictional celebration therefore contributed to the definition of a positive national identity in which qualities like courage and fair play were paramount. Moreover the specific variety of Englishness displayed in the chase or even (despite its moral dangers) on the racecourse was associated with the countryside and with tradition, so that the sporting world readily became a version of the pastoral, an idyllic and conservative counterbalance to the urban world of getting and spending. Surtees's Jorrocks, of course, is an intruder on the rural scene from commercial LONDON (which is why many early readers found him distasteful), but nevertheless he can be assimilated into the milieu of the foxhunt because sport, being typically English, is also democratic and rewards stamina and enthusiasm rather than accidents of birth. In fact as the historian Raymond Carr demonstrated, foxhunting became increasingly exclusive as the century progressed, but for the reader of sporting novels it was less the reality than the myth that counted— the myth of an immemorial and aristocratic tradition that was nevertheless open to mettlesome outsiders, of a national pastime in which one might hobnob with dukes if only one could sit one's mount with the requisite panache.

See also NOVEL; SENSATION NOVEL; SPORTS.

FURTHER READING

Blain, Virginia. Introduction to *Mr. Sponge's Sporting Tour,* by R. S. Surtees. St. Lucia: University of Queensland Press, 1981.

Carr, Raymond. *English Fox Hunting: A History.* London: Weidenfeld and Nicolson, 1976.

Gash, Norman. *Robert Surtees and Early Victorian Society.* Oxford: Oxford University Press, 1993.

Welcome, John. *The Sporting World of R. S. Surtees.* Oxford: Oxford University Press, 1982.

ROBERT DINGLEY

SPORTS

The Victorians did not invent sports so much as they modernized, regulated, and popularized them and invented new activities under their general umbrella. Much of this transformation of sports is credited to the British and, much more so, to the English, who expanded the role of sports in a form of cultural imperialism that extended far beyond the physical boundaries of the British EMPIRE and the anglophone world. During the Victorian era traditional popular activities such as animal baiting, which had threatened the respectable sensibilities of the new industrial culture, were largely suppressed and older sports such as foxhunting and CRICKET were given new roles and codes of etiquette to better suit them to the needs and expectations of new social groupings. This was by no means an even process, involving as it did tensions along hazy class boundaries, arguments over the use of time and money, gender identities, and assumptions about ethical and moral hierarchies attached to particular activities. There were also issues concerning the role of the collective and the individual, the team and the place of the hero in it.

The development of sports in the Victorian era may be divided into three loosely overlapping periods. The first, until the mid-1860s, saw the development and codification of team games, largely in reformed PUBLIC SCHOOLS, as a means of inculcating manliness and channeling male adolescent urges into disciplined activities. The second, from the later 1860s to the 1880s, was a period of consolidation, bureaucratization, the clarification of some class-related pursuits, and the introduction of new ones. The last decade or so saw a massive expansion at all levels in most activities, as sports became a recognizable commodity for which time and money were widely available; it also saw the voicing of a growing number of concerns about its social effects in the light of social Darwinian arguments about the long-term viability and survivability of British industrial supremacy and the empire. Within the whole process, social and sporting elites were defined and values designed for upper-class males were given a much wider currency. Toward the end of Victoria's reign, the latter were challenged by a growing argument about the place of women, almost invariably from the upper and middle classes, in sports.

PUBLIC SCHOOL SPORTS

The key element in the changes in sports lay in the public schools, which were designed to equip upper-class males for roles of social leadership. Whether old and reformed or newly founded, these schools emerged as the forcing grounds of a limited number of activities, principally RUGBY football (SOCCER, the Association game, soon became a distinctly second-level activity), cricket, ROWING, track and field, and a variety of racquet games with local roots. These sports also developed in the older UNIVERSITIES as well as their nineteenth-century imitators, to which many of the boys progressed. It was Uppingham School's headmaster, Edward Thring (1821–1877), who set the model under which sport became the heart of MUSCULAR CHRISTIANITY. The greatest emphasis in this development was on team play, ranging from the necessary uniformity of the rowing eight to the use of individual skills in the ball games, as long as they were subordinated to the team's interests. Where star performers showed skills, as in cricket or football, they were expected to meld them into broader examples of leadership and service. Competition was usually as much intra- as intercollegiate, and provision was made in teaching timetables for substantial periods to be devoted to play, something still reflected in those many British universities that devote Wednesday afternoons to games. Teachers and tutors were supposed to join in as well, a self-replicating process since most of them had been taught in such institutions. Games were held to foster moral cleanliness, but they were also prophylactics against the infectious DISEASES with which such enclosed communities were threatened frequently.

Most of the games grew rapidly outside collegiate environments by the 1860s, often fostered by young men who carried their enthusiasms into the adult worlds of the professions and business. Doctors and clergymen had a particularly important role in this, concerned as they were with physical and moral health among their charges, as well as continuing to seek exercise themselves. Such enthusiasts found a ready following in the many middle-class men and the growing number of white-collar males who had been educated outside the public-school world but who wished to emulate its essential features. Local cricket, football, and athletic clubs were reformed or started in towns and villages all over Britain and eventually organized into local leagues for competition. Friendly informality ran side-by-side with a growing level of bureaucracy and codification. The Marylebone Cricket Club (founded in 1787) offered a broad ethical supervision of the game that relied heavily on local custom, reinforced by the development of county-level play and the need for dedicated playing space. The various forms of football developed distinctly, not just with separate codes of play but also along class as well as regional lines. The formation of the Football Association in 1867 marked the emergence of soccer from the shadow of rugby and the beginning of its eventual numerical, if not social, domination of winter games. Rugby itself split, into Union (the game of the amateur middle classes, except in Wales where its appeal remained much wider) and League, predominantly northern and working-class in following; their respective associations, the Rugby Football Union (RFU), founded in 1871, and Rugby League, which split from the RFU in 1895, were divided by much more than playing codes.

SPORTS AND SOCIAL CLASS

Such strenuous sports were only part of the story. During the second stage of growth, the traditional field sports of foxhunting and shooting attracted a huge increase in followers as the once largely exclusive pursuits of the landed classes were democratized by the addition of newly monied groups anxious to establish their place alongside the established hierarchies. Foxhunting, which had once seemed likely to disappear with fading agricultural fortunes, revived and doubled its following after 1870. New syndicates were formed for the increasingly popular driven-game shooting, whose enthusiasts were able to rent shooting rights and estates from impecunious landowners. On a smaller but more prestigious scale was the rapid development of deer stalking in Scotland, part of the broader interest in that country's role as a holiday destination after QUEEN VICTORIA and PRINCE ALBERT built their COUNTRY HOUSE at Balmoral. All these activities venerated the healthiness of outdoor activities in a country lacking real wilderness; they also claimed to develop the fieldcraft skills deemed essential to an officer class whose fitness for leadership had been honed by its collegiate sports.

FISHING boomed as well, but without such a justification. Although it was broadly held to encourage healthy outdoor recreation it was also divided strongly on class lines, with the prosperous upper and middle classes seizing control of access to such game fish as trout in the Hampshire chalk streams and salmon on Scottish rivers, while humbler men were restricted to ordinary coarse or bottom fish wherever they could find them. Again, there were strong regional as well as class differences. Upper-class fishing was largely portrayed as an individual engagement with nature, while most working-class angling involved competitive matches symbiotic with a PUBLIC HOUSE culture and involving hundreds of people at a time.

The 1870s and 1880s saw the popularization of new middle-class sports, which extended the age range of those who could safely participate and opened new demands for investment and space. Croquet, which had been enjoyed since the 1840s, gave way to lawn TENNIS, invented in 1874. Although it was a game that could be played on a suitably large domestic lawn, its main attraction was that it encouraged a rapid growth of clubs in middle-class urban areas where it could be played by small groups of varying levels of skill as an ancillary to other social activities, including courting. Although largely localized in organization, tennis soon enjoyed national prestige when it effectively ousted croquet at the All England Club at Wimbledon and provided a stage for new sporting heroes such as the Renshaw twins in the 1880s.

Rather more land-hungry and socially aggressive was GOLF, originally derided as "Scottish Croquet," but imported from Scotland with growing enthusiasm during the later 1870s and 1880s; there had been two clubs in England in 1850, and there were around 1,000 by 1910. As technologies and skill levels increased, the game absorbed an increasing amount of marginal urban and rural land and demanded levels of investment from its members, whose clubhouses often became palatial. This revealed a singular tension between the need to widen membership for economic reasons and a desire for social exclusivity, which led to the emergence of a social hierarchy of clubs as well as ethnic tensions, noticeably between JEWS and Anglo-Saxons in some cities. The game was never formally organized as such, maintaining an uneasy deference to its spiritual home, the Royal and Ancient Golf Club at St. Andrews, Scotland, whose committee was asked frequently to adjudicate on rules, etiquette, and the impact of new implements of play.

EXPANSION AND DIFFERENTIATION

The last decade of Victoria's life saw the expansion of sports, both established and new sports. The leader was probably soccer, with the development of large working-class followings for local clubs dominated by professional players and the league system. The growth of soccer demanded an increasing level of investment by local businesses, and the sport became increasingly easy to follow and organize in competitive terms as leisure time and RAILWAY travel reached a Victorian peak. Crowds at matches were numbered in thousands, with an increasing number of attendances around the 10,000 mark at single games by the 1890s. By contrast the popularity of BICYCLING boomed across the social spectrum in the mid-1890s, both as a locus for professional competition and as a means of exploring the countryside. The burgeoning of manufacturing companies, mass production, and the popularity of the inflatable tire all contributed to a widespread enthusiasm among both individuals and various cycling clubs. The bicycling craze soon peaked but the considerable residual popularity meant that the activity, whether sporting or merely recreational, was firmly established in the British athletic pantheon. One other event had only a marginal immediate impact but a virtually incalculable long-term import.

The revival of the Olympic Games in Athens in 1896 attracted a casual British amateur input. The revival had been fostered by an enthusiastic Frenchman, Pierre de Coubertin (1863–1937), whose adulation of the English public school athletic spirit led him into the singularly mistaken belief that sports could be exported as an antidote to international political and military rivalries. De Courbertin was soon proved wrong by the clash of nations during World War I, but the notion of British innovation and excellence reinforced an effective hegemony in the popularization of sport.

A great deal of the growth of sports had its roots in the social class structure of British society, and sports offered a whole range of subtle new indicators for aspiration and achievement. Sports were quite carefully graded into affordability as well as accessibility, and membership at certain clubs, as much as playing skill itself, became a criterion of social status. This was more than just a mechanism for differentiation; it was underpinned by a playing snobbery based on assumptions about class morals. The greatest divide, as much ethical as remunerative, was be-

Sports such as rowing taught teamwork and appropriate male social roles. Pictured here is an Oxford University crew from 1894.

tween amateur and professional, distinctions often fudged in practice. Older upper-class sports such as foxhunting had almost always relied on the assistance of servants, though these servants were often honored for their skills. By contrast, the huge expansion in team games raised issues of division and exclusion.

Victorian sports leaders elevated the cult of the amateur to almost ridiculous heights, based not so much on performance as on supposed moral and intellectual superiority. To be paid for play was to sink into moral turpitude. It was assumed that almost any working-class player would be attracted by either wages or financial prizes, as well as probably showing physical superiority because of muscle developments fostered by employment. So, in theory, middle-class sports either avoided prizes altogether or created a culture of honorific rewards. In fact, this was frequently breached by "shamateurs," always a source of concern. The most eminent of these was the cricketing hero Dr. W. G. Grace (1848–1915). Such athletes were able to hide their incomes as expenses, or operate in the grey area represented by the huge market for writing that accompanied the growth of sports. To preserve purity many sports were structurally divided between amateurs and professionals. County cricket eventually became notorious for its divisions between Gentlemen and Players, rugby eventually split between Union (amateur) and League (professional). The most obvious distinction emerged in rowing where, under the Henley Rules of 1879, any amateur who rowed against or with a manual worker was held to have lost status and was banned from future events; despite their being a number of working-class amateur rowing clubs, these were held to be ethically impure.

THE CULTURE OF SPORT

Around the playing of sports, and as key parts of their attraction, there grew a whole range of supporting inventions that boosted players' identities and developed either a sense of exclusiveness or wider support. The paradox was that the latter two were not mutually prohibitive. The best example of this was the annual Oxford-Cambridge Boat Race, held on the Thames and founded in 1829. Although essentially a competition between the leading rowing eights of the two ancient universities, the race was not only supported by other university athletes and their friends and families but also by a very large range of spectators of all classes, who usually claimed to be supporters of one of the sides but had no actual links with

either university. Where leading cricket or football clubs developed they frequently became agents of county or urban identities, fostering local and regional pride.

More generally sports developed a whole apparatus of distinctive traditions, some with their roots in older etiquettes, such as foxhunting, others invented to suit the new situations. Colored uniforms and badges not only identified different teams, they became part of the broader symbols of membership or support. By the century's end many middle-class men wore plain or colored blazers, often emblazoned with fanciful new heraldry, to mark their membership of exclusive bodies; humbler clubs had enameled metal badges. To master the language of individual sports was to enter a world of arcane knowledge. School and club songs were composed to help bonding; the best known was the "Eton Boating Song" (1878). Sports clubs not only played games, they surrounded them with an increasingly elaborate range of social activities, dinners, concerts, and so on, by far the most elaborate of which were held in increasingly palatial golf clubhouses. With the exception of the almost aristocratic Hurlingham Club, founded in 1867 on the edge of London, there were virtually no British equivalents of the contemporary boom in country clubs that surrounded major U.S. cities.

In addition a huge sporting press grew, ranging from well-established popular papers, such as *Bell's Life*, founded in 1822, to specialist journals such as the *Fishing Gazette*, which first appeared in 1877. These were accompanied, particularly in the last 15 years of Victoria's reign, by pamphlets and books, designed to foster a taste for and some knowledge of particular sports. The cheapest were simple instruction manuals, such as those produced by Ward Lock; the most prestigious were those in the *Badminton* series, begun in 1885 and concentrating on elite sports, including MOUNTAINEERING. In turn the popularity of sport generated a considerable manufacturing boom in which traditional craft firms, such as hunting-boot makers, increased alongside new specialists mass-producing playing equipment. Among the latter were such key firms as Jaques, which dominated the croquet market after exhibiting playing equipment at the GREAT EXHIBITION OF 1851; Slazenger, formed in midcentury and leading tennis production; and Raleigh, floated on the stock exchange in 1896 as a major bicycle manufacturer. In an environment where British industrial leadership was widely held to be declining, sporting goods manufacturers were often a distinctive exception in leading economic modernization.

EXPORTING SPORTS

One key aspect of the growth of Victorian sport was its export from Britain both to the empire and elsewhere. The moral ideals that underpinned the Olympic revival were far less significant than the actual playing of games. Cricket and the varieties of football established their strongest roots in the warmer white dominions such as AUSTRALIA AND NEW ZEALAND. Although cricket was also widespread in the Indian subcontinent, where it was used in copies of public schools created to provide an indigenous subordinate local elite; it had a more popular following in the Caribbean. CANADA benefited rather more from Scottish settlers, with curling and other winter games. The empire also became an extended playground for expatriate British civil servants and soldiers, opening up big-game HUNTING for elephants and rhinos in Africa and tigers in INDIA, where resident Britons also went pig-sticking, riding with lances after wild boar. Where sporting targets did not exist, they were often imported, such as in Kashmir, where the local rivers were stocked with Scottish trout. Foxhunting was introduced into Canada and Australia and copied in the UNITED STATES.

There was also a reverse flow of such activities as badminton and polo, brought back from the Indian subcontinent. Other Britons extended mountaineering from the Lake District to the Swiss Alps, where Edward Whymper (1840–1911) made the first ascent of the Matterhorn in 1865, and then to the Himalayas. Another invasion of Switzerland followed on a late Victorian winter sports boom, particularly when skiing was transferred from Norway and made competitive by the English, as was bobsleighing, invented in 1890 by British visitors to the resort of St. Moritz in the Swiss Alps. They also opened up the wilder regions of Norway for game fishing and shooting. More widely, wherever there were British settlers, golf courses began to appear, from semiarctic to desert sites. The sport found a ready market among the aspiring middle classes of the United States, where it was linked with burgeoning country clubs, as did lawn tennis, which also took root in FRANCE, alongside rugby football, introduced by British expatriates in the wine trade and developing eventually into a sport with a mass following.

WOMEN IN SPORTS

The process of diffusion was not without tensions, and the most significant of these, apart from class issues, emerged by the 1880s with growing pressures for women to participate in at least some sporting activities. Upper-class women had been appearing on the foxhunting field with increasing daring since midcentury, but it was the new activities that caused problems. While rugby remained an exclusively masculine arena for many decades and cricket was occasionally played semiseriously by women, croquet and lawn tennis encouraged their participation from the beginning. In those games women competed alongside men as well as separately; the problem came when matches moved from the domestic arena, for which they were initially intended, into public view. Inevitably the involvement of women raised doubts as to whether some games could be treated as serious contributions to masculinity or whether women's participation would essentially feminize men. There were sharp disagreements about the desirability of developing healthier mothers for the empire versus damaging women's physique by over-activity and ruining their morals by exposing them to too much male company. These were battles often fought very hard at the local level, most obviously in golf clubs, which often either kept women out altogether or banned intersex play, keeping women segregated in separate clubs or courses, or restricting access severely. Female athletes became the butt of many humorous articles and cartoons in both the specialist and general presses. Yet the examples of such elite models as Queen Victoria, who fished in Scotland in the 1850s, Empress Elizabeth of Austria, who hunted English foxes strenuously in the 1870s, and Lady Margaret Scott, who dominated women's golf in the 1890s, provided incentives for participation lower down the social scale.

There were other battles, in which the hegemony of sporting ideals was achieved amid hard contests. The values play was supposed to enshrine—including good behavior, abiding by the rules, treating opponents decently, and developing the mutual respect implicit in team spirit—were often threatened by individual misconduct. Perhaps the best-known expression of virtue came with the much-repeated, and probably frequently ignored, chorus of Henry Newbolt's poem of 1897, *Vitai Lampada*: "Play up, play up, and play the game." The poem's links between the last innings of a minor public school's cricket match and the heroism of British troops beleaguered in a desert battlefield illustrate only too well the dilemmas that the late Victorian sporting boom created. Linked as it was with cleanliness of spirit and the supposed team spirit of an expansionist empire, sport frequently fell foul of its own internal contradictions. Not only were there such domestic crises as those over amateurism, these extended increasingly into international play when British teams found themselves beaten by their supposedly cultural descendants, white colonials and Americans. The latter played not so much with genteel restraint as with a determination to win.

As British competitive dominance faltered, the process became a metaphor for wider issues, a reflection of an increasingly alarmist social Darwinism. The failure of British competitors seemed to indicate a wider social and economic crisis as the country's predominance as the world's greatest manufacturing and trading nation faced challenges from Germany and the United States, not least when American oarsmen started to win at the Henley Regatta in the 1890s. Worse still, the supposed obsession of the entrepreneurial groups with activities such as lawn tennis and golf, whose capacity for developing manliness was questionable, was widely held to be a major contributor to national entropy. Such claims ignored sport's role as a major generator of new industries, not least in the rubber trades, which had to meet huge demands for tennis and golf balls as well as bicycle tires, although they hardly replaced those sectors that were stagnant. Perhaps the greatest long-term problem came because the exaltation of amateurism fostered a culture whose worst feature was the assumption that war could be characterized as a game in which it was as important to lose in the right spirit as it was to win by devious means. Many British paintings and stories encouraged a social narrative of honorable defeat and amateur heroism, that were finally exposed for their inadequacies in the battlefield carnage of the World War I.

Sport was not entirely successful as an agent for modernizing social relationships and culture; it was occasionally exploited cynically and there were plenty of examples of cheating and dubious, or even villainous, practice at all levels of society. Yet, having taken that into account, the experience of Victorian sports remained a remarkable history of reform, innovation, social reorganization, and attempts to impose values of order and decency that both challenged and mirrored the wider changes of a complex society.

See also EMPIRE; PUBLIC SCHOOLS.

FURTHER READING

Cox, R., G. Jarvie, and W. Vamplew, eds. *Encyclopedia of British Sport.* Oxford: ABC-CLIO, 2000.
Lowerson, J. *Sport and the English Middle Classes, 1870–1914.* Manchester: Manchester University Press, 1993.
Mackenzie, J. M. *The Empire of Nature: Hunting, Conservation, and British Imperialism.* Manchester: Manchester University Press, 1988.
Mangan, J. A. *Athleticism in the Victorian and Edwardian Public School.* Cambridge: Cambridge University Press, 1981.
Mason, T. *Association Football and English Society, 1863–1915.* Brighton: Harvester, 1980.
Mason, T., ed. *Sport in Britain: A Social History.* Cambridge: Cambridge University Press, 1989.
McCrone, K. E. *Sport and the Physical Emancipation of English Women, 1870–1914.* London: Routledge, 1988.
Mrozek, D. J. *Sport and American Mentality, 1880–1910.* Knoxville: University of Tennessee Press, 1983.
Sandiford, K. A. P. *Cricket and the Victorians.* Aldershot: Scolar, 1994.
Tranter, N. *Sport, Economy, and Society in Britain, 1750–1914.* Cambridge: Cambridge University Press, 1998.
Vamplew, W. *Pay Up and Play the Game: Professional Sport in Britain.* Cambridge: Cambridge University Press, 1988.

JOHN LOWERSON

SPURGEON, CHARLES HADDON

Born: June 19, 1834; Kelvedon, England
Died: January 31, 1892; Menton, France

Charles Haddon Spurgeon was the most popular preacher of mid- to late-Victorian LONDON and well known throughout the world as the People's Pastor. Soon after becoming a Baptist in 1850, Spurgeon gave his first sermon in a cottage at Teversham, Cambridgeshire. In January 1852 he accepted a pastorate at Waterbeach, near Cambridge, and by 1854 the so-called boy pastor could draw 400 to hear his sermons. His published sermons later brought him international fame.

Spurgeon took on a trial pastorate at the invitation of the congregation of London's New Park Street Baptist Chapel in early 1854. His impassioned sermons drew increasingly larger crowds to the Southwark chapel, which had been in decline owing to encroaching industry and slum housing. He accepted a permanent appointment there several months later, only to watch as his congregation quickly exceeded Park Street's 1,200-seat capacity. During a sermon later that year, while pointing to the back wall of the overcrowded chapel, Spurgeon famously declared, "By faith the walls of Jericho fell down, and by faith we shall have this wall down too!" The chapel was expanded, but even with 1,800 seats was insufficient. Over the next five years Spurgeon and his congregation shifted between Exeter Hall and the Music Hall at Royal Surrey Gardens, where weekly attendance reached 10,000. By 1859 construction had begun on the 6,000-seat Metropolitan Tabernacle in south London; after it opened in 1861 Spurgeon preached there until his death.

Spurgeon's fame was sudden and complete. He was somewhat disingenuous when, in March 1854, he wrote to an uncle, "You have heard that I am now a Londoner, and a little bit of a celebrity." Unique among London preachers of the time, he used a conversational style, serious but lacking the complexity of his university-trained peers. His style embodied his provincial upbringing and education and drew sneers from critics throughout his career. Spurgeon was an aggressive Calvinist who believed in the truthfulness of the Bible and rejected philological BIBLICAL CRITICISM. Although he became known as The People's Preacher, his combative conservatism left him increasingly isolated among nonconformists from the 1860s on. He finally withdrew from the Baptist Union in 1887, accusing its members of unorthodoxy and "gross disloyalty to Christ."

Spurgeon began publishing his weekly sermons in 1855. They circulated widely in the English-speaking world and were translated into 40 languages. He soon drew a weekly readership of 25,000. From 1865 Spurgeon also edited *The Sword and Trowel*, a monthly magazine, and he was known for *The Treasury of David*, his seven-volume commentary on the Psalms (1869–1885). He founded a pastor's college in 1856, a Bible society in 1866, and an orphanage in 1867. In February 1892 over 100,000 mourners attended funeral services for Spurgeon in London and one eulogist regretted that "our country has lost its greatest living preacher." Spurgeon's wife, who was also his personal secretary, later compiled from his writings a four-volume autobiography (1897–1900).

See also BIBLICAL CRITICISM; RELIGIOUS LITERATURE.

FURTHER READING

Bacon, Ernest W. *Spurgeon: Heir of the Puritans.* London: George Allen and Unwin, 1967.

Bradstock, Andrew. "A Man of God Is a Manly Man: Spurgeon, Luther, and 'Holy Boldness.'" In *Masculinity and Spirituality in Victorian Culture,* edited by Andrew Bradstock et al. New York: St. Martin's, 2000.

Ellison, Robert H. *The Victorian Pulpit: Spoken and Written Sermons in Nineteenth-Century Britain.* Selinsgrove: Susquehanna University Press, 1998.

Murray, Iain H. *The Forgotten Spurgeon.* London: Banner of Truth Trust, 1966.

JOHN E. LUEBERING

STAINER, JOHN

Born: June 6, 1840; Southwark, England
Died: March 31, 1901; Verona, Italy

Often characterized in the twenty-first century as the archetypal Victorian church musician, owing principally to his authorship of *The Crucifixion*, a popular musical depiction of the Passion (and still regularly sung throughout the English-speaking world at Eastertide), Sir John Stainer was a man of many parts. A remarkable leader and facilitator, he dedicated his energies and influence to the consolidation of music as an essential part of artistic and intellectual life in nineteenth-century Britain.

Stainer's career in church music was forged early in his life as a chorister at St. Paul's Cathedral, and his abilities as an organist and improviser, which developed rapidly while he was still at the choir school, were noticed by Frederick Ouseley, the founder of St. Michael's College, Tenbury, the first collegiate foundation built in England after the Reformation of the sixteenth century. At the invitation of Ouseley, who was to all intents and purposes his mentor, Stainer moved to Tenbury in 1857 where, as he later acknowledged, he spent his three most crucial and formative years as Ouseley's assistant. Twelve years at Oxford (1860–1872), where he was organist at Magdalen College, and another 16 in the same capacity at St. Paul's Cathedral (1872–1888) established him as a leading musical figure in Britain. This reputation was supported by distinguished anthems such as "I Saw the Lord" (1858); "Drop Down Ye Heavens from Above" (1866); and "Lead Kindly Light" (1868); services; hymn tunes; two cantatas; and *The Crucifixion* (1887), a Passiontide cantata, that was an instant success, owing to its practical accessibility by parish church choirs.

Stainer's elevated position was enhanced by his other diverse activities. In 1874 he and William Pole assisted Ouseley in founding the Musical Association (later the Royal Musical Association) "for the investigation and discussion of subjects connected with the art, science and history of music." After Ouseley's death in 1889, Stainer was elected president, a post he held until his death. As an organist known for his powers of improvisation, he was appointed a teacher of the instrument at the National Training School of Music in 1876 and succeeded Arthur Sullivan as principal of the institution in 1881. A preoccupation with musical instruction was also reflected in the energy Stainer devoted to standards of teaching in music. In 1883 he was appointed her majesty's inspector of music in elementary schools and colleges (succeeding John Hullah), a highly exacting form of employment (as attested by Frederick Bridge in his autobiography *A Westminster Pilgrim*) that, in his capacity as examiner, took to him to many parts of the British Isles.

Stainer resigned from St. Paul's in 1888 owing to failing eyesight (he was knighted the same year), but in recognition of his work, he was appointed professor of music at the University of Oxford the following year, after Ouseley's death. A notable academic and musicologist, he did much to improve the lecture courses in music at the UNIVERSITY and delivered a number of important public lectures including "Music in Relation to the Intellect" (1892). His interest in early music—he was president of the Plainsong and Medieval Music Society and the London Gregorian Association—was also evident in his late edition *Dufay and His Contemporaries* (1898).

See also CATHEDRAL AND CHURCH MUSIC; HYMNS AND SACRED SONGS; MUSIC PROFESSION; ORATORIO AND CHORAL MUSIC.

FURTHER READING

Caldwell, John. *From c. 1715 to the Present Day.* Vol. 2 of *The Oxford History of English Music.* Oxford: Oxford University Press, 1999.

Charlton, Peter. *John Stainer and the Musical Life of Victorian Britain.* Newton Abbot: David and Charles, 1984.

Edwards, F. G. "John Stainer." *Musical Times* XLII (1901): 297.

Howes, Frank. *The English Musical Renaissance.* London: Secker and Warburg, 1966.

Temperley, Nicholas, ed. *The Blackwell History of Music in Britain: The Romantic Age 1800–1914.* Oxford: Basil Blackwell, 1981.

JEREMY DIBBLE

STANFORD, CHARLES

Born: September 30, 1852; Dublin, Ireland
Died: March 29, 1924; London, England

The reputation of composer Charles Villiers Stanford has rested for many years on his prowess as a teacher and academic. His list of pupils—among them Samuel Coleridge-Taylor, Ralph Vaughan Williams, Gustav Holst, Frank Bridge, Rutland Boughton, Edgar Bainton, James Friskin, Ivor Gurney, Herbert Howells, Arthur Bliss, and E. J. Moeran—are testimony to his remarkable magnetism and abilities exercised at the Royal College of Music (RCM), where he was professor of composition from 1883 until his death in 1924 (though his teaching diminished appreciably in his last years), and at Cambridge University where he was professor of music from 1887 until 1924. He was, however, a composer of great versatility; the author of seven symphonies, concertos, chamber music, and songs, he aspired to be a composer for the stage, though, with the exception of *Shamus O'Brien* (1896), a palpable hit in Britain, the United States, and Australia, success in this genre largely eluded him. His most enduring and original achievement lay in his anthems and services for the Anglican liturgy, which are still sung widely today, and in the extraordinary part-song setting of Mary Coleridge's "The Blue Bird."

Educated in Dublin, where he studied the piano, violin, and organ, Stanford later entered Queen's College, Cambridge, as an organ scholar in 1870. From Queen's he migrated to Trinity in 1873 and remained there as ORGANIST until 1892. After three six-monthly periods of study in Leipzig (1874–1875) and Berlin (1876), he returned to Cambridge where he did much to transform music-making in the university as conductor and performer. In addition to the performance of his own works, he promoted the music of Johannes Brahms (whose First Symphony received its first English performance in Cambridge on March 8, 1877, and with whom he was on friendly terms), Richard Wagner, Antonin Dvořák (who visited Cambridge in 1891 to receive an honorary degree), and HUBERT PARRY, and enjoyed the close friendship of Hans von Bülow, Hans Richter, and his mentor, Joseph Joachim, who annually visited Cambridge. He was also instrumental in bringing Piotr Ilyich Tchaikovsky, Arrigo Boïto, Max Bruch, and Camille Saint-Saëns to Cambridge for the society's Golden Jubilee in 1893, and Edvard Grieg (who was not well enough to come that year) in 1894. Besides his activities at Cambridge, Stanford conducted the London Bach Choir (1885–1902), and after settling in LONDON in 1893 he directed the Leeds Philharmonic Society (1897–1909) and the Leeds Festival (1901–1910). He actively campaigned for OPERA in English, a policy put into practice through his pioneering opera class at the RCM, and by his agitation to establish a national opera house in London. He also did much to reform the music degrees at Cambridge, and was at the forefront of the crusade to give composers greater rights in the field of copyright.

Proud of his Irish roots, he published several collections of Irish FOLKSONGS and included traditional melodies in his "Irish" Symphony (1887), his comic opera *Shamus O'Brien* (1896), and his seven Irish Rhapsodies. A Protestant Unionist, he identified closely with his British heritage, as is evident from the patriotic *Songs of the Sea* (1904) and *Songs of the Fleet* (1910) and the dedication of several works (notably his first oratorio *The Three Holy Children* of 1885) to QUEEN VICTORIA. He vigorously opposed HOME RULE for Ireland and allied himself with the cause of Ulster articulated by Sir James Craig and Sir Edward Carson, a sentiment he later expressed in his Fourth Irish Rhapsody (1914), based on Ulster tunes.

See also MUSICAL EDUCATION; MUSICAL INSTITUTIONS.

FURTHER READING

Caldwell, John. *From c. 1715 to the Present Day.* Vol. 2 of *The Oxford History of English Music.* Oxford: Oxford University Press, 1999.

Dibble, Jeremy. *C. Hubert H. Parry: His Life and Music.* Oxford: Oxford University Press, 1992; rev., 1998.

Dibble, Jeremy. *Charles Villiers Stanford: Man and Musician.* Oxford: Oxford University Press, 2002.

Greene, H. Plunket. *Charles Villiers Stanford.* London: Edward Arnold, 1935.

Howes, Frank. *The English Musical Renaissance.* London: Secker & Warburg, 1966.

Temperley, Nicholas, ed. *The Blackwell History of Music in Britain: The Romantic Age 1800–1914.* Oxford: Basil Blackwell, 1981.

JEREMY DIBBLE

STANLEY, ARTHUR PENRHYN

Born: December 13, 1815; Alderley Rectory, England
Died: July 18, 1881; London, England

Arthur Penrhyn Stanley was an ecclesiastical historian, a leader in the BROAD CHURCH movement, a courageous advocate for religious tolerance, and, during the last years of his life, at QUEEN VICTORIA's pleasure, he served as dean of Westminster Abbey. The second of four sons born to Edward Stanley, later bishop of Norwich, Arthur was educated first at a private school at Seaforth, where he early earned a reputation among his schoolfellows as a storyteller, and then at Rugby (1829), where he fell under what would be the lifelong influence of its famous headmaster, THOMAS ARNOLD. At Rugby, while not athletic, Stanley was distinguished by his brilliant scholarly achievement and entered Balliol College, Oxford, in 1834, on scholarship. Here he first encountered the brewing religious controversy of the time, the pull of the "Romanism" of JOHN KEBLE and JOHN HENRY NEWMAN, which would later erupt into the Oxford Movement (TRACTARIANISM); however, he remained true to the Broad Church theology so strongly instilled in him by Arnold.

During his Oxford career he won many prizes, including the coveted Newdegate Prize (1837) for English verse with his poem "The Gypsies"; he took a first class in classics; and was elected a fellow of University College in 1838, where he lived and was a tutor for the next 12 years. In December 1839 he was ordained by the bishop of Oxford. An 1840 tour to Switzerland, Italy, Greece, and Sicily first revealed his love of TRAVEL and his talent as a travel writer, which remained with him throughout his life.

Although his years at Oxford were frustrating because of religious controversy, Stanley was momen-tarily cheered by the appointment of Arnold as chair of modern history in 1841 but then devastated by his unexpected death in 1842. Arnold's wife commissioned Stanley to write *The Life and Correspondence of Dr. Arnold* (1844), possibly his best work in a long career and a book that established his literary reputation, not only in Oxford but also in the world beyond.

ADOPTING AN INCLUSIVE VIEW OF CHRISTIANITY

As "select preacher" at Oxford from 1846 to 1847, Stanley offered a series titled Sermons on the Apostolical Age, which marked a crisis in his thinking and was the first outward manifestation of his ecumenical views on church matters, a philosophy that would remain with him throughout his career. He acknowledged the truths of Arnold's teaching and of German theologians and also called for free inquiry in biblical studies.

Stanley's father died in 1849, followed almost immediately by the death of two of his brothers, leaving Arthur to head the family and also to publish, in 1850, his *Memoir of Bishop Stanley.* In 1851 he was named a canon at Canterbury Cathedral, an appointment that brought him much joy. The illustrious his-

THE GRANGER COLLECTION

Broad Church leader and dean of Westminster Abbey, Arthur Penrhyn Stanley.

tory of the cathedral stirred his passion for the past and for the building itself, which he termed "the cradle of English Christianity," and which he wrote about in *Memorials of Canterbury* (1854). The appointment also left him with the leisure to travel; he visited Egypt and the Holy Land, gathering materials for what would become *Sinai and Palestine* (1856), the most widely known of his books.

On his appointment as professor of ecclesiastical history at Oxford in 1856, which also carried with it a canonry at Christ Church, Stanley returned to UNIVERSITY life, an event that marked the beginning of his steady rise through the Episcopal hierarchy. He enjoyed renewing old friendships, relished both the lecture hall and the pulpit, and engaged in pleasant society with students and colleagues. His lectures were issued as books: *The Study of Ecclesiastical History* (1857); *The History of the Eastern Church*(1857); (1861); and *The History of the Jewish Church* (part l, 1863; part 2, 1865; part 3, 1876).

Stanley continued to champion free inquiry into religious matters, which led him into fierce controversy over his support for Bishop (of Natal) John William Colenso's publications, *St. Paul's Epistle to the Romans* (1861) with its denial of eternal punishment, and *The Pentateuch and the Book of Joshua* (1862–1870), which challenged the traditional historical accuracy and authorship of these books. Although he did not necessarily agree with these ideas, Stanley demanded a fair hearing for them, a view that enraged both the High Church and Evangelical factions of the church.

From February to June 1862, at the invitation of Queen Victoria, Stanley toured the East and the Holy Land with EDWARD, PRINCE OF WALES, and a party; despite original misgivings he gained respect for the prince, and it strengthened his ties to the royal court, to the queen, and led to his marriage to one of her favorite ladies-in-waiting, Lady Augusta Bruce (1822–1876) the fifth daughter of the 7th earl of Elgin. They were married on December 22, 1863, in Westminster Abbey, and on January 9, 1864, he was consecrated as dean.

Now occupying a position of great influence, Stanley took the broadest view of the vow made at his installation for "the enlargement of the Christian church," which he took to mean a policy of inclusion. His pulpit was open to good men of all faiths, and he never hesitated to preach to others, such as the nonconformists, Dissenters, Wesleyans, and Scottish Presbyterians, a practice that brought him much severe criticism. Always he sought for the high moral ground that could unite people of all faiths. As with Canterbury Cathedral, he was fascinated by the physical features of the abbey, which he termed "the royal and national sanctuary."

Oddly, despite his liberal views, Stanley could be quite firm on doctrinal matters; for example, when he denied burial in the abbey's Poet's Corner to George Eliot in 1880, because of her irregular relationship with George Henry Lewes. This omission was rectified in 1980 when the George Eliot Fellowship successfully dedicated a plaque to her memory in that location.

In addition to his books, Stanley wrote widely for secular periodicals, including the *Contemporary Review*, the EDINBURGH REVIEW, FRASER'S MAGAZINE, the *North British Review*, and particularly for MACMILLAN'S MAGAZINE, where he had a warm and long-standing friendship with the editor, GEORGE GROVE. From 1868 to the time of his death, Stanley contributed 14 major articles and 14 substantial pieces of verse, the latter largely devotional and remarkable for their depth and intensity of faith.

When Stanley's wife preceded him in death in 1876, he was inconsolable; he died, diagnosis erysipelas, July 18, 1881, and was buried in Westminster Abbey by her side. Despite the hostility and angry criticism that his views attracted, Stanley was courageous in dedicating his deanship to unity and tolerance among people of all faiths.

See also BROAD CHURCH.

FURTHER READING

Dark, Sidney. *Five Deans: John Colet, John Donne, Jonathan Swift, Arthur Penrhyn Stanley, William Ralph Inge.* New York: Harcourt Brace and Co., 1928.

Hare, Augustus J. C. *Biographical Sketches; Being Memorials of Arthur Penrhyn Stanley, Henry Alford, Mrs. Duncan Stewar.* London: G. Allen, 1895.

Prothero, Rowland E. *The Life and Letters of Dean Stanley.* London, New York: T. Nelson, 1909.

ROSEMARY T. VANARSDEL

STANLEY, EDWARD

Born: March 29, 1799; Knowsley, England
Died: October 23, 1869; Knowsley, England

Edward George Geoffrey Smith Stanley, better known as lord Derby (pronounced DAR-bee), was three times prime minister of the United Kingdom, in 1852, 1858–1859, and 1866–1868. He led the Conservative Party through its years of least electoral success but kept its hopes alive through realistic accommodation and a willingness to form minority governments that lasted longer in each case than most observers expected.

A Life of Privilege

The Stanleys were one of the wealthiest ancient families of England. Their Lancashire estate, Knowsley, and the family's notoriety—the horse race at Epsom was named for the 12th earl—helped to secure parts of that industrial region as an unexpectedly Conservative bastion long into the Victorian era. The 14th earl's reputation as a habitué of the track gradually proved to be a barrier to broader support for his party. But his splendid oratory gained him the epithet "the Rupert of Debate," in reference to the prince-general of the seventeenth-century civil wars who defended the royalist position.

Stanley was educated at home, at Eton, and at Christ Church, Oxford (without taking a degree), and was marked out as brilliant from an early age, excelling in Latin and Greek; he published a translation of Homer's *Iliad* in 1864. His father employed the painter EDWARD LEAR (1812–1888), who soon took to penning

HULTON/ARCHIVE BY GETTY IMAGES

This 1869 *Vanity Fair* caricature of Edward Stanley bore the caption: "It is his mission to stem the tide of democracy."

nonsense verse and limericks for the children. Thus Edward Stanley learned irony and spark.

His father was a Whig, and the family effectively bought Edward a seat in Parliament at age 21, in 1820. He joined George Canning's ministry in 1827 and lord Grey's in 1830 as chief secretary for IRELAND. He improved Irish schools and reduced the scope of the (Anglican) Church of Ireland, despite being a staunch defender of the established church. This reduction incensed some clergy, and helped spawn the Oxford Movement.

The Making of a Conservative

As colonial secretary in 1833, he penned the Slave Emancipation Bill, enraging member of Parliament (M.P.) WILLIAM GLADSTONE and others with West Indian investments. Unlike most political leaders of his generation, Stanley had seen the UNITED STATES, in travels from 1824 to 1825, and disliked how slavery contorted both the white and the black worlds. He was present in the House of Representatives when John Quincy Adams was elected president over Andrew Jackson in the "corrupt bargain," and may here have developed his lifelong aversion to the secret ballot and to democratic politics.

Stanley joined and then quit the cabinet and the Whig party in 1834 when some of the Irish church revenues were set to be diverted to nonreligious ends. He joined Sir ROBERT PEEL's Conservatives and fought to maintain grain-price supports—the CORN LAWS—for farmers and landowners. Much needed in the Lords for his speaking ability, Stanley was raised to the peerage in his own right in 1844, but when Peel's ministry came out in support of FREE TRADE in 1846, he resigned and leagued himself with BENJAMIN DISRAELI and the protectionists. On his father's death in 1851 he inherited the earldom.

At this time the Conservative Party's leaders were Lord George Bentinck and Benjamin Disraeli. Bentinck was a die-hard, holding out for a new arrangement of capitalism that would help the aristocracy retain primacy. Derby came to see that this would never work, and, on Bentinck's sudden death in 1851, he became leader in the Lords. The next year, admitting the Corn Laws could not be revived, Derby was able to form a minority government that lasted ten months. Of this ministry the duke of Wellington famously said "Who? Who?" when read the names of each member, and by that appellation it has been known. Yet Derby's willingness to choose newcomers and unknowns signaled a break with the past. This helped the party avoid any parallel to the disasters that befell the British army two years later in the CRIMEAN WAR when its corps of generals were mostly leftovers from Wellington's campaigns against Napoleon. Against the next, Peelite, ministry, Derby spoke out for its ineffectiveness in conducting the war, although declined to form a ministry in 1855.

CONSERVATIVES IN POWER AND OUT

The danger from radical movements on the Continent was one of the few serious issues on which leading politicians disagreed during the 1850s, and Derby's Conservatives defended some of the old regimes. When in early 1858 Lord Palmerston lost support for appearing to give British refuge to a French gunman (the Orsini affair), Derby did seize the chance to take the reins of government. Gladstone and other ex-Conservatives gave him tacit support, and he remained prime minister for 16 months, until June 1859.

Disraeli was now clearly his second-in-command. Their chief measures were the end to civil disabilities for Jews and the Government of INDIA Act, formally depriving the EAST INDIA COMPANY of suzerainty in the subcontinent and vesting power in the crown.

Derby's opposition to parliamentary or franchise reform gradually led backbench supporters to depart, and again Palmerston took over in mid-1859, despite the Conservatives' slightly improved showing at the polls in a general election. While Palmerston had his way for six years, a few younger Conservatives began to rise, replacing some of the old nobility. Their next chance came amid chaos in June 1866. Called on by QUEEN VICTORIA, Derby faced a nation hot-tempered over the question of parliamentary reform. It was his suggestion (though some historians credit Disraeli) that household suffrage be the basis of their bill, and this standard prevailed. Derby led Conservatives in the Lords to a grumpy acceptance of the merits of being part of a progressive measure. Though three cabinet members resigned in protest, the rest held, and his party gained the lion's share of credit for the Second Reform Act of 1867, which enfranchised most middle-class men living in boroughs. The ministry lasted 30 months.

Also notable was Derby's policy toward Abyssinia (Ethiopia). There a mad emperor kidnapped 50 Europeans after the Liberal governments ignored his demands for three years. Derby sent a huge Anglo-Indian rescue (and scientific) mission in 1867–1868, while holding the line against some of his cabinet colleagues who wanted to annex the mountain kingdom. It would fall to later Conservatives to strike the imperialist chord. Suffering from age and gout, Derby

retired in February 1868, handing the government to his obvious successor, Disraeli.

Derby's heir, Edward, lord Stanley, thought by many to be a Liberal at heart, attracted enough other talent to his father's ministries of the 1850s to help make them possible. The two disagreed on much, particularly the father's resistance to parliamentary and church reform. In 1878 the son resigned from Disraeli's ministry and soon switched to the Liberal party. The 15th earl's diaries are an invaluable source of knowledge about his father as well as about the politics and society of 30 years.

Derby rebuilt the notion that the Conservatives, even without the free-trade Peelites, could still credibly govern. Usually in the political wilderness after 1846, he hoped that a new Conservative majority could be forged with moderate Liberals who shunned the radicalism of Gladstone, the Irish, and the republicans. By the time of his retirement this shift looked imminent, but he was never cruel or shrewd enough to carry off the realignment. Disraeli and Salisbury would reap what Derby had so patiently sown.

See also DISRAELI, BENJAMIN; PARLIAMENTARY GOVERNMENT.

FURTHER READING

Hawkins, Angus. *Parliament, Party and the Art of Politics in Britain, 1855–59.* London: Macmillan, 1987.
Jones, Wilbur Devereux. *Lord Derby and Victorian Conservatism.* Athens: University of Georgia Press, 1956.
Smith, F. B. *The Making of the Second Reform Act.* Melbourne: Melbourne University Press, 1966.
Stewart, Robert. *The Politics of Protection: Lord Derby and the Protectionist Party, 1841–1852.* Cambridge: Cambridge University Press, 1977.
Vincent, John, ed. *Disraeli, Derby and the Conservative Party: Journals and Memoirs of Edward Henry, Lord Stanley, 1849–1869.* Hassocks, U.K.: Harvester, 1978.

JAMES M. CORNELIUS

STANLEY, HENRY MORTON

Born: January 28, 1841; Denbigh, Wales
Died: May 10, 1904; London, England

Sir Henry Morton Stanley achieved international fame as a journalist, explorer, and empire builder in Africa. He initially gained notoriety in 1871, when he led an expedition into central Africa and successfully located the missionary DAVID LIVINGSTONE, who had been feared lost or dead. Stanley then made his reputation as an explorer by mapping the Congo River in a three-year expedition between 1874 and 1877. He was a prolific writer who advanced his reputation through numerous publications, including several best-selling books on his adventures in Africa. His career was,

British explorer and journalist Henry Morton Stanley is best remembered as the man who found Dr. Livingstone after years of searching in Africa.

vessel bound from Liverpool to New Orleans, where he promptly jumped ship. His fortunes took a positive turn when he found work in New Orleans with a prosperous merchant, Henry Morton Stanley, who became fond of Rowlands and offered to adopt him and give him his name in token of his affection. Having never enjoyed the love and care of a parent, Rowlands accepted this surrogate father and took the name that he would make famous. The elder Stanley died in 1861, but his adopted son was unable to claim an inheritance because his adoption had never been made legal.

Henry Morton Stanley, now 20 years old, resumed a wayward existence under his new name. He fought for and deserted both the Confederacy and the Union in the American CIVIL WAR, but his dishonorable military record notwithstanding, service as a ship's writer for the Union navy pointed him toward a vocation as a journalist. In 1867, after the war's end, Stanley broke into journalism as a special correspondent for the *Missouri Democrat*, covering a United States government expedition to negotiate treaties with Native American cultures. The New York *Herald* subsequently hired Stanley to cover a British military expedition in Abyssinia and, impressed by his resourcefulness, next commissioned him to conduct one of the most remarkable publicity stunts in the NEWSPAPER industry to date—the search for David Livingstone in the heart of Africa.

DR. LIVINGSTONE, I PRESUME?

Stanley had no experience as a leader of men when he began to organize his expedition in Zanzibar, which is an island kingdom off the east coast of Africa, in January 1871. Two months later, he set off with 191 men into the African interior, guided by a rumor that Livingstone was at Lake Tanganyika. In the ensuing months, Stanley and his expedition, in what was often called the "dark continent," were severely tested by having to fight a great many battles with hostile tribes, overcome a mutiny, and survive starvation as well as 23 attacks of fever. In the course of these trials, the fledgling explorer exhibited three attributes that proved essential to his success. He exercised remarkable judgment and patience in negotiating peaceful settlements with potential adversaries; he did not hesitate to take violent action when he deemed it necessary; and he displayed a resilient constitution.

Thus, at Ujiji between late October and early November 1871, Stanley discovered the whereabouts of David Livingstone, greeting him with the now well-

however, dogged by controversies that focused on the validity of his geographical discoveries and his brutal methods of leadership in the bush. In the end his discoveries were validated, and the controversies over his brutality did not undermine his fame, which was marked by honorary degrees from prestigious universities, awards from governments around the world, and by popular recognition as a preeminent explorer in the Victorian era.

Stanley was born to another name under circumstances of poverty and neglect. Elizabeth Parry gave birth to the illegitimate boy in Wales on January 28, 1841, and baptized him with the name of his father, John Rowlands. She left the boy in the care of her family, who eventually deposited him at the St. Asaph Workhouse, where he endured a regime of strict discipline and physical abuse until, at age 15, he fled the WORKHOUSE after beating a schoolmaster unconscious in retaliation for an unwarranted punishment. In 1858 the youth took work as a deck hand on a known words, "Dr. Livingstone, I presume?" This historic encounter not only made Stanley's name as a journalist, but also directed him toward his future goals as an explorer. Livingstone was determined to prove his theory that the Lualaba River was the source of the Nile, a theory that Stanley would actually test after Livingstone's death in 1873. In the meantime, the meeting of the two men created a sensation in Britain, Europe, and the UNITED STATES, fueled by Stanley's publication in 1872 of his book *How I Found Livingstone*.

THE DARK CONTINENT

Stanley returned to East Africa in 1874 to lead an exploratory expedition under the joint sponsorship of the *Herald* and Britain's *DAILY TELEGRAPH*. He departed from the coast with 359 people under his command and became the first person to circumnavigate both Lake Tanganyika and Lake Victoria, before turning to the Lualaba River. Geographers had long disputed whether the Lualaba was the source of the Nile, the Niger, or the Congo rivers. Stanley mustered a reluctant expedition to settle this debate, purchasing the additional support of a powerful slave trader, Tippu Tib, who accompanied him with 1,000 men as he began his journey down the Lualaba in November 1876. Stanley's riverine exploration proved to be an epic, and often horrific, experience. Tippu Tib's forces withdrew after several weeks, leaving the explorer and his followers to face untold dangers from hostile tribes, disease, and the river itself. Having determined that the Lualaba flowed into the Congo River, Stanley miraculously navigated the Congo to the European outpost at Boma on the west coast of Africa in August 1877. Of the 359 people who had set off with him 1874, only 82 returned. Stanley chronicled his exploration in *Through the Dark Continent*, which became an international best-seller on its publication in 1878.

Stanley traveled back to the Congo one year later as an employee of King Leopold II of Belgium, who intended to build an empire in central Africa. Over the next five years, he secured the south bank of the Congo River by a combination of negotiation and force, building stations and trading networks by order and by example. He was nicknamed "Bula Matari" ("breaker of rocks") by the African laborers who watched him swing a hammer in road construction. Stanley left King Leopold's service in 1884, having laid the foundation of the Congo Free State, which Leopold established in 1885.

Following a series of British military setbacks in the Sudan, Stanley led a British expedition in 1887 to rescue a provincial governor named Emin Pasha. Although this two-year expedition became a debacle of needless casualties, Stanley made a significant geographical discovery by locating the fabled "mountains of the moon," which were rumored to be the source of the Nile. Following the controversy over this ill-fated relief expedition, Stanley found himself mentally and physically exhausted. Consequently, at age 49 he gave up exploration and, for the first time, directed his energies to a home life.

In July 1890 Stanley married Dorothy Tennant, the daughter of a prominent aristocratic family. With his wife's encouragement, he won election to Parliament as a Liberal-Unionist in 1895 but led an undistinguished political career and declined to contest the general election of 1900. He had been knighted by QUEEN VICTORIA in 1899 and was subsequently content to retire to an estate in Purbright, Surrey, where he enjoyed the unfamiliar life of a country gentleman. He died in London on May 10, 1904, and his remains were returned to Purbright for burial in the village churchyard. His epitaph, inscribed in granite, read simply: "Henry Morton Stanley/Bula Matari/1841–1904/Africa."

See also AFRICAN COLONIALISM; EMPIRE; EXPLORATION; JOURNALISM; LIVINGSTONE, DAVID; NEWSPAPERS.

FURTHER READING

Farwell, Byron. *The Man Who Presumed: A Biography of Henry M. Stanley.* New York: W. W. Norton and Co., 1989.
McLynn, Frank. *Stanley: The Making of an African Explorer, 1841–1877.* New York: Cooper Square Press, 1989.
McLynn, Frank. *Stanley: Sorcerer's Apprentice, 1877–1904.* Oxford: Oxford University Press, 1992.
Stanley, Henry Morton. *How I Found Livingstone.* New York: Scribner, Armstrong, and Co., 1872.
Stanley, Henry Morton. *Through the Dark Continent.* New York: Harper and Brothers, 1878.
Stanley, Henry Morton. *The Congo, and the Founding of Its Free State.* Vols. 1 and 2. New York: Harper and Brothers, 1885.
Stanley, Henry Morton. *The Autobiography of Sir Henry Morton Stanley.* New York: Houghton Mifflin Co., 1909.

KEVIN GRANT

STATISTICS

In its modern usage the word *statistics* refers to the methodology for presenting quantitative data about aggregates or variable mass phenomena, as well as to the data themselves and their collection. In the nineteenth century, by contrast, the definition of this word was not fixed, but the various practices called statistics were considered so useful that they were applied to a wide range of social, moral, and scientific subjects. During the course of the century, statistical analysis was primarily used in three areas, each of which allowed for a development within the ensemble of practices called statistics. These included the analysis of social and moral phenomena governed by laws of numerical regularity, such as populations and criminality; theoretical attempts to conceptualize probability; and applied mathematics. While statistics was initially regarded as a way to extend scientific certainty into domains whose phenomena previously had resisted exact knowledge, by the end of the century, it was viewed as a tool for establishing probable knowledge about phenomena that were considered inherently uncertain or irregular.

The discovery that aggregate social entities obey the principles of numerical regularity dates back to the seventeenth century. In 1661 William Petty (1623–1687), building on the work of John Graunt, discovered in the London Bills of Mortality certain demographic regularities: the excess of male over female births, the approximately equal number of males and females in the adult population, and the high rates of mortality in urban, as opposed to rural, areas. Petty championed his new science of "number, weight, and measure" as an instrument for enhancing government efficiency. The Victorians who followed Petty in applying numerical analysis to social phenomena also stressed bureaucratic efficiency, but they did so in the name of social reform. During the first half of the nineteenth century, developments within social and moral statistics occurred through a mixture of closely related government and private initiatives. These included the Statistical Department of the Board of Trade, founded in 1832 to collect information about trade and provincial manufacturing; the General Registrar's Office, created in 1837 to gather data about births, deaths, and marriages; and a number of statistical societies founded to garner numerical information on subjects ranging from sanitary conditions to the incidence of crime in specific areas. Among the latter, the most important were the Manchester Statistical Society (1833) and the Statistical Society of London (1834); the latter was an offshoot of the Statistical Section of the British Association for the Advancement of Science (the BAAS), which was created in 1831 by mathematicians Charles Babbage (1791–1871) and Adolphe Quételet (1796–1874). In the 1860s this twin program of enhancing bureaucratic efficiency and improving social conditions through the collection of statistical data was extended to British INDIA, largely through the efforts of FLOR-

ENCE NIGHTINGALE (1820–1910), who promoted statistics throughout her long nursing career.

Even though the first half of the nineteenth century was distinguished by many Britons' belief that numerical data would lead to social improvement, the word *statistics* was neither stable in its definition nor always associated with the use of numbers. The word was probably first used in English in 1770 in a translation of a German book by J. F. von Bielfeld. In German *Statistik* had initially been used to refer to the collection and political arrangement of knowledge about states; by the end of the eighteenth century, *staatenkunde* had become a serious academic discipline in Germany, although practitioners quarreled over whether information should be presented in narrative and tabular form or numerically. In England the word *statistics* began to be used in the last decade of the eighteenth century, as in Sir John Sinclair's *Statistical Account of Scotland*, which defined statistics as the "view or survey of any kingdom, county, or parish." While statistics continued to be associated with description and the collection of data useful for government and for social reform, it was still possible in the 1840s for a proponent of statistics to reject the idea that this data had to be expressed numerically.

The systematic collection of data about social and moral phenomena followed from and helped refine Petty's idea that social aggregates obey principles of regularity. In the 1830s Adolphe Quételet, a Belgian astronomer with a strong commitment to social reform, introduced the ideas that social regularities expressed statistical laws and that the useful facts Britons were collecting could anchor a social science devoted to these laws. Inspired by the recognition that both nature and society contained periodic phenomena, Quételet set out to found a social physics, which was intended to promote social improvement by showing legislators how the law, like regularities of society, could be enhanced. Quételet's observations challenged the eighteenth-century interpretation of these regularities, which had attributed them to divine will or design, for he argued that statistical regularity was simply a natural property of all aggregates, which would embody this inherent lawfulness if freed from artificial restraints. The heyday of this conviction was the 1850s, when British lawmakers invoked the idea that statistical laws governed social phenomena to justify the adoption of laissez-faire (free trade) legislation. In 1860 Henry Thomas Buckle (1821–1862) began to publish his influential *History of Civilization in England*, which argued that statistical laws could also be discovered in historical events, thus proving that past government interference had foolishly impeded England's growth.

Neither Quételet nor Buckle used mathematics in their observations about statistical regularities, nor did they question the certainty of the knowledge they derived from data. The mathematical component of statistics was initially elaborated in relation to probability theory. Classical probability theory had focused on the perception of regularity—on degrees of belief—not on the measurable frequency of phenomena. Beginning in 1840s four writers working independently broke from this tradition. John Stuart Mill (1806–1873), Richard Leslie Ellis, A. A. Cournot (1801–1877), and Jakob Friedrick Fries (1773–1843) all offered ways to explain probability in terms of the regularities generated by chance phenomena, which could be captured in statistics. They drew on the probabalistic method of least squares, which was used by astronomers and in the mathematics of insurance to calculate error in cases involving multiple observations and irregular variables. This mathematical calculation reduced multiple observations or instances to a single curve that minimized the sums of the squares of deviations of the individual measurements from the curve. This curve is called the Gaussian curve, after Carl Friedrich Gauss (1777–1855), who helped develop this method in the eighteenth century, or, for its characteristic shape, the bell curve. By the 1830s this curve was also applied to the distribution of individual errors, and in 1844 Quételet finally liberated the curve from error analysis when he declared that it also applied to human features like height and weight.

Building on Quételet's observations, James Clerk Maxwell (1831–1879), Ludwig Boltzmann (1844–1906), and Francis Galton (1822–1911) applied the mathematics of variation to natural phenomena like the dynamics of gases (thermodynamics) and heredity (eugenics). Unlike their predecessors, Maxwell, Boltzmann, and Galton sought to capture and analyze the variation that appeared in nature, not to neutralize it. In their adaptations of the Gaussian curve, Quételet, Maxwell, Boltzmann, and Galton helped transform probability from the study of degrees of belief to the analysis of variation, and they helped make statistics a study of phenomena that could not be measured directly, not just the collection of useful facts.

Like Quételet before him, Galton transferred the statistical analysis of regularities and variation from one kind of phenomenon to another because he saw that behaviors in one domain could be expressed in terms of behaviors in the other, as a simile or figure of speech. In other words, Galton could describe the hereditary process of transmitting traits in terms that Quételet and Buckle had used to describe social processes because they intuitively seemed similar, and, with this analogy in hand, he could argue that the principle of statistical regularity, which could be demonstrated for social phenomena, also applied to heredity, where regularity was harder to measure. Galton did not derive the similarity between hereditary transmission and social phenomena from probability theory, nor did he characterize this relationship mathematically. Once he had introduced the similarity as a simile, however, he was able to invoke the mathematical principle of the Gaussian curve to describe the regularities of hereditary transmission mathematically. Such descriptions helped make his arguments about heredity credible and palatable to the public, for the prestige statistics had acquired in reformers' analysis of social phenomena carried over to more controversial areas, such as Galton's contention that the bell curve defines normative types as well as regularities. Thus, in his *Hereditary Genius* (1869), Galton supported his notorious thesis that excellence in a variety of fields, from statesmanship to wrestling, was inherited with statistics that conformed to the characteristic bell curve.

Galton's use of statistical units to capture objects that could not be directly measured provided an important contribution to the mathematical development of statistics. Beginning in the 1860s the field of mathematical statistics was also expanded by other Englishmen, including Francis Edgeworth (1845–1926), William Jevons (1835–1882), and Karl Pearson (1857–1936), as they sought to capture and express the irregularities in phenomena as various as insurance, currency valuations, and biological variation. From this work, especially the analyses of index numbers and statistical series, the key mathematical concepts of regression and correlation were elaborated. The publication of Galton's *Natural Inheritance* in 1889 and his simultaneous formulation of the method of correlation can be said to mark the beginning of the modern period of statistics. This period is characterized by the separation and professionalization of the two fields that were fused in the early nineteenth century (sociology and statistics), the incorporation of mathematical principles into the practice of statistical analysis, and the acceptance that statistical analysis brings order to phenomena that are inherently indeterminate or uncertain.

See also CENSUS; FREE TRADE; SANITATION.

FURTHER READING

Cole, Joshua. *The Power of Large Numbers: Population, Politics, and Gender in Nineteenth-Century France.* Ithaca: Cornell University Press, 2000.

Cullen, Michael J. *The Statistical Movement in Early Victorian Britain: The Foundations of Empirical Social Research.* New York: Barnes and Noble, 1975.

Daston, Lorraine. *Classical Probability in the Enlightenment.* Princeton: Princeton University Press, 1988.

Hacking, Ian. *The Taming of Chance.* Cambridge: Cambridge University Press, 1990.

Patriarca, Silvana. *Numbers and Nationhood: Writing Statistics in Nineteenth-Century Italy.* Cambridge: Cambridge University Press, 1996.

Poovey, Mary. *A History of the Modern Fact: Problems of Knowledge in the Sciences of Wealth and Society.* Chicago and London: University of Chicago Press, 1998.

Porter, Theodore M. *The Rise of Statistical Thinking, 1820–1900.* Princeton: Princeton University Press, 1986.

Porter, Theodore M. *Trust in Numbers: The Pursuit of Objectivity in Science and Public Life.* Princeton: Princeton University Press, 1995.

Stigler, Stephen M. *The History of Statistics: The Measurement of Uncertainty before 1900.* Cambridge, Mass.: Harvard University Press, 1986.

MARY POOVEY

STEAD, W. T.

Born: July 5, 1849; Embleton, England
Died: April 15, 1912; at sea

William Thomas Stead was an important figure in late-Victorian JOURNALISM and national politics. He became editor of the *Northern Echo* in Darlington in 1871, at the age of only 22, and brought to his journalism a crusading spirit that derived from his nonconformist values. He first came to national prominence in 1876 during WILLIAM GLADSTONE'S (1809–1898) election campaign. In contrast to BENJAMIN DISRAELI'S (1804–1881) geopolitically motivated cooperation with the Ottoman Empire, Gladstone's campaign and Stead's paper emphasized the immorality of Turkish atrocities in Bulgaria, and Stead's crusade was instrumental in helping Gladstone to win the 1877 election and in establishing Stead as a significant voice in Liberal politics. Stead was also a journalistic entrepreneur who helped to introduce the concept of headlines and interviews into the British daily press and who, in 1890, founded the *Review of Reviews*, a digest of the leading magazines and journals of the day.

Stead's journalism brought the melodrama of the mid-Victorian Sunday popular press and the muckraking style of the American press to the British daily NEWSPAPER. The universe on which he reported was populated by evildoers who preyed on the weak and powerless, and he saw himself as a latter-day Oliver Cromwell, exposing corruption in high places by means of his journalism. Following the Bulgarian atrocities campaign, Stead displayed his crusading style most prominently as editor of the *Pall Mall Gazette*, a low-circulation London evening paper aimed at the "influential" classes. In a series of sensational articles in 1885 called "The Maiden Tribute of Modern Babylon," Stead presented LONDON as home to an extensive white slave trade. In order to make his case, he "purchased" an underage virgin, thereby showing how easy it was to do so. The young girl was entrusted to the SALVATION ARMY and taken to FRANCE, but his action made Stead technically guilty of kidnapping, and his political enemies ensured that he served time in prison for the offense. Nonetheless, Stead's crusade led to the passing of a Criminal Law Amendment Bill in 1885 that raised the age of consent. Of more lasting significance, it seemed to legitimate a new style of political journalism in which the daily press came to serve as the conscience of the nation. In a bombastic article published in 1886 and entitled "Government by Journalism," Stead argued that the newspaper was a more democratic institution than Parliament and that the daily press should govern the country by forcing the political agenda through publicity. During the BOER WAR (1899–1902), Stead became one of the leading champions of the antiwar cause, publishing a newspaper called *The War against the War in South Africa* and pamphlets with titles such as *Shall I Slay My Brother Boer?*

Perhaps fittingly for a master of publicity, W. T. Stead became part of one of the biggest news stories of the early twentieth century, losing his life aboard the ill-fated *Titanic* in 1912.

See also JOURNALISM.

FURTHER READING

Baylen, J. O. "The 'New Journalism' in Late Victorian Britain." *Australian Journal of Politics and History* 18, no. 3 (1972): 367–385.

Baylen, J. O. "W. T. Stead as Publisher and Editor of the Review of Reviews." *Victorian Periodicals Review* 12, no. 2 (1979): 70–84.

Schults, Raymond L. *Crusader in Babylon: W.T. Stead and the Pall Mall Gazette.* Lincoln: University of Nebraska Press, 1972.

Stead, W. T. "Government by Journalism." *Contemporary Review* 49 (May 1886): 653–674.

Stead, W. T. *A Journalist on Journalism.* Edited by Edwin H. Stout. London: John Haddon, 1892.

MARK HAMPTON

STEPHEN, JAMES FITZJAMES

Born: March 3, 1829; London, England
Died: March 11, 1894; Ipswich, England

An authority on nineteenth-century criminal law, James Fitzjames Stephen was the author of the criminal code adopted by many British colonies, including CANADA. Besides the codification, he is best known for his *History of the Criminal Law of England* (1883). Stephen was the son of Sir James Stephen (1789–1859), who served as colonial undersecretary, and a brother of scholar LESLIE STEPHEN (1832–1904). He was educated at Eton (an expensive boarding school) and Cambridge University, where he was a member of the Apostles, and then studied law.

Stephen became a barrister (a trial lawyer) in 1854 and at the same time developed a secondary career as a journalist, writing articles and reviews for the periodical press. His articles appeared in the *Morning Chronicle*, the *SATURDAY REVIEW*, the *EDINBURGH REVIEW*, *FRASER'S*, the *London Review*, and *CORNHILL MAGAZINE* in the 1850s and early 1860s. From 1858 to 1861 Stephen served on a royal commission to investigate the state of popular education. He then began work on *A General View of the Criminal Law of England*

Legal authority James Fitzjames Stephen wrote the criminal code used in many colonies of the British Empire, including Canada.

(1863), a lucid analysis of the tradition of English criminal law in the context of other systems, particularly the French. From the 1870s he wrote for the *Fortnightly*, the *Contemporary Review*, and *Nineteenth Century*.

PHILOSOPHICAL BACKGROUND

From its establishment in 1865 until 1878, Stephen wrote more than 600 articles for the *Pall Mall Gazette*, including an attack on JOHN STUART MILL (1806–1873) that was published in book form as *Liberty, Equality, Fraternity* (1873). Stephen started out as a utilitarian, following the PHILOSOPHY of JEREMY BENTHAM (1748–1832), who felt that the state should act in the interest of the greatest number of its citizens. Though Stephen considered himself a liberal, he resisted the wave of democratic liberalism that culminated in the second Reform Bill (1867). In *Liberty, Equality, Fraternity* Stephen took issue with the emphasis on individualism expressed in *On Liberty* (1859), in which Mill argued that, in order to develop, society needed new ways of looking at things. This meant replacing the tradition of rational and benevolent government with a more representative, responsive, and humane approach. Mill thought that government should encourage not only the physical well-being but also the personal development of men and women of all classes. Above all, the state should encourage, rather than impose itself on, its citizens.

Stephen had been sympathetic to some of Mill's ideas but objected to his dismissal of the English governing class. In Stephen's opinion, authority and enforcement by a small inner group were essential to the infrastructure of any civilized society. Mill, on the other hand, argued that there should be no interference with the freedom of an individual except in certain dangerous circumstances. Mill believed that experiment and eccentricity should be encouraged, whereas Stephen saw conformity to tradition and authority as central to the enrichment of society.

Liberty, Equality, Fraternity also attacked the views on equality of the sexes put forth in Mill's *Subjection of Women* (1869). Unlike Mill, Stephen believed in the strong authority of the state over the rights of the individual. Similarly, in relations between the sexes he believed in the authority of the partner stronger in mind and body. In most cases, for Stephen this meant the male; he felt that marriage obliged men to lead and women to obey. This was not an unusual view for that time, but it was an unpopular one, especially coming after Mill's arguments for equality. In Stephen's view there was nothing oppressive about the unequal position of husbands and wives; it was simply a practical arrangement that conduced to harmony and efficiency.

For similar reasons he dismissed the novels of CHARLES DICKENS (1812–1870) as mere sentimental sensationalism. He recognized the validity of some of Dickens's political criticism but pointed out that he offered nothing in the way of concrete suggestions for improvement. The personal suffering of Dickens's characters is usually relieved not by state intervention or reform, but by acts of individual kindness. It was not that Stephen did not agree that the social injustices exposed by Dickens should be addressed, but rather that he did not find Dickens's approach practical.

PUBLIC OFFICE AND LEGAL CAREER

From 1869 to 1872 Stephen served as a legal member of the Viceroy's Council in INDIA, taking on the massive task of redrafting the penal code and the code of criminal procedure. The idea of structuring and recoding legal procedures fits well with Stephen's approach to government intervention and his distrust of individualism; codes would provide structures and limit eccentric decisions and behavior in the legal system. He also redrafted Indian acts on the law of evidence, the limitations of suits, and contract law. Stephen ran for Parliament as a Liberal in 1873 but was not elected. He served on the Criminal Code Commission (1878–1879) and was made a criminal court judge in 1879.

When he returned from India Stephen tried to get the English to accept codification and succeeded to the extent that he was asked to draw up an evidence code, though it was not passed by Parliament. The same fate met a bill he designed to define the offense of murder. Working alone, Stephen then codified English law in the form of two publications, *A Digest of the Criminal Law (Crimes and Punishments)* (1877) and *A Digest of the Law of Criminal Procedures in Indictable Offences* (1883). After the first *Digest* he was asked to draft a bill for a criminal code, but it too died on the order paper. Nonetheless, the codes adopted by Canada (in 1892), New Zealand (1893), Queensland (1899) and other parts of AUSTRALIA, and many other crown colonies are based largely on his *Digest* and draft code.

STRONG VIEWS ON CRIMINALS AND JUSTICE

During his legal career there was continuing controversy about the effectiveness of the justice and prison systems in the deterrence of crime. Stephen was a vociferous defender of the tradition that promoted public hatred and harsh, vengeful punishment of criminals. He was a strong opponent of efforts to abolish CAPITAL PUNISHMENT. He did not claim that all criminals were caught, but he insisted that those tried and found guilty under the English system had the benefit of the fairest way that could be devised of establishing criminality. Therefore, their punishment needed to satisfy the public. Furthermore, he argued, relentless punishment deterred crime by others by producing fear of social censure.

Perhaps the most memorable of the criminals Stephen defended as a barrister was George Victor Townley, who in 1863 was sentenced to death for the murder of a young woman who had jilted him. Townley was not certifiably insane at the time of the murder, but Stephen, against his better judgment, found a legal loophole that prompted the home secretary (the government minister in charge of the justice system) to respite him and commit him to a lunatic asylum. After a public outcry Townley was removed to an ordinary prison, whereupon he demonstrated his insanity by bashing his brains out against a wall.

As a judge Stephen had a reputation for severity driven by righteous indignation. In two high-profile cases over which he presided, the defendants, Israel Lipski (1887) and Florence Maybrick (1889), were found guilty and sentenced to death, largely on the strength of strong moral disapproval communicated by Stephen to the jury in his summing up. Lipski was temporarily reprieved and then executed; Maybrick was reprieved and imprisoned for 15 years for a crime that was never proved. Both cases, especially the latter, aroused public indignation, and it was suggested that Stephen was no longer mentally competent, having suffered a stroke in 1885. He suffered another stroke in the spring of 1890, and in 1891 after doubts were expressed in the press and in Parliament about his fitness for the bench, he resigned. That same year he was made a baronet in recognition of his lifetime achievement.

See also CAPITAL PUNISHMENT; CRIME AND PUNISHMENT; LAW AND LEGAL REFORM; UTILITARIANISM.

FURTHER READING

Fawcett, Millicent Garrett. *Mr. Fitzjames Stephen on the Position of Women.* London: Macmillan, 1873.

Hostettler, John. *Politics and the Law in the Life of Sir James Fitzjames Stephen.* Chichester: Barry Rose, 1995.

Mill, John Stuart. *On Liberty.* 1859. Vol. 18, *Collected Works.* Toronto: Toronto University Press, 1963.

Radzinowicz, Sir Leon. *Sir James Fitzjames Stephen, "Selden Society Lecture."* London: Bernard Quaritch, 1957.

Smith, K. J. M. *James Fitzjames Stephen: Portrait of a Victorian Rationalist.* Cambridge: Cambridge University Press, 1988.

Stephen, James Fitzjames. *Liberty, Equality, Fraternity.* London: Smith, Elder, 1873.

Stephen, Leslie. *The Life of Sir James Fitzjames Stephen.* London: Smith, Elder, 1895.

JUDITH KNELMAN

STEPHEN, LESLIE

Born: November 28, 1832; London, England
Died: February 22, 1904; London, England

Sir Leslie Stephen was a historian of ideas and first editor of the *Dictionary of National Biography*. He was heir to the twin traditions of English EVANGELICALISM and British rationalism, from which he constructed a critical method of skeptical optimism designed to meet the challenges of the post-Darwinian era.

FROM PRIEST TO AGNOSTIC

Stephen's father, barrister and historian Sir James Stephen, was a leading member of the Clapham Sect, a group of activist evangelicals within the CHURCH OF ENGLAND opposed to the slave trade and dedicated to social reforms. Stephen grew up in a household where the abolitionist Wilberforce had been a frequent guest, the historian Macaulay and the economist Nassau Senior were regular visitors, and John Stuart Mill's works were read with admiration. He fulfilled one of his father's ambitions for him when, after graduating from Trinity Hall, Cambridge, he became a fellow of that college and in 1859 a priest in the Church of England (the conditions of his fellowship required that he be in holy orders). The evangelical tradition in which he was raised required each individual to follow the dictates of conscience as informed by right reason and by scripture interpreted through personal judgment. By 1862 Stephen had begun his lifelong study of philosophy and literature, and in the light of his reading, scripture seemed to him a collection of contradictions and absurdities; reason disclosed that Christianity rested on cruel and impossible dogmas, and conscience instructed him to become an agnostic, which he did (the term *agnostic* was coined by THOMAS HENRY HUXLEY in 1869 to describe a rigorously skeptical view toward religious beliefs; Stephen quickly adopted the label as his own). He stopped participating in chapel services, was asked to resign his position as tutor, and left both Cambridge and the priesthood.

In 1863 Stephen visited the battlefields of the American CIVIL WAR. In an age when CHARLES DICKENS and Mrs. Trollope disparaged the manners of Americans and Lord JOHN RUSSELL contrived to support the Confederacy against the Union, Stephen, true to his evangelical roots, abominated the slave-holding South, supported President Abraham Lincoln (whom he met on his tour), and found sense and sanity in the UNITED STATES. His first published work, *The Times on the American War* (1865), was a refutation of the English establishment's pro-Confederate views as expressed in its most prominent newspaper.

By 1865 he had begun a new career as a freethinking scholar and author, contributing essays and reviews to the *Pall Mall Gazette*, the *Nation*, the SATURDAY REVIEW OF LITERATURE, and CORNHILL MAGAZINE, of which he became the editor in 1871. His editorial judgment—he nurtured and published ROBERT LOUIS STEVENSON, THOMAS HARDY, W. E. Henley, HENRY JAMES, and MATTHEW ARNOLD—tells as much about his literary tastes as his own voluminous criticism, published as *Hours in a Library* (3 vols.; 1874, 1876, 1879). During these years Stephen also published a collection of his essays elaborating his AGNOSTICISM (*Essays on Freethinking and Plain Speaking*; 1873) and his masterwork, *History of English Thought in the Eighteenth Century* (2 vols.; 1876, 1881).

THE GRANGER COLLECTION

Leslie Stephen's *Dictionary of National Biography* remains a classic work of Victorian scholarship.

THE DICTIONARY OF NATIONAL BIOGRAPHY

Under Stephen's direction, circulation at the *Cornhill* fell from 25,000 to 12,000, and the proprietor, George Smith, found another job for Stephen as editor for a dictionary of biography, which Smith originally envisioned as international in scope. Stephen persuaded him to confine the project to what could be done well—a compendium of lives of all prominent, influential, or remarkable persons (excluding those still alive) within the British Isles from Boadicea to Parnell—and by 1882 the *Dictionary of National Biography* (*DNB*) was in progress, a project second only to the OXFORD ENGLISH DICTIONARY among the monuments of Victorian scholarship. The first volume of the *DNB* (Abbadie to Anne) was published on January 1, 1885, and successive volumes appeared quarterly without interruption until the dictionary reached Zuylestein in 1900. The project embraced 29,120 lives of British men and women. Stephen contributed 378 entries, enough to fill two volumes of the work. His predilection for grand poetry (much of which he could recite from memory), empirical philosophy, and serious novels is revealed by a partial list of his entries: CHARLOTTE BRONTË, Burns, Carlyle, Coleridge, Defoe, Dickens, George Eliot, Fielding, Gibbon, Hobbes, Hume, Dr. Johnson, Locke, Milton, Pope, Scott, Adam Smith, Swift, and Wordsworth. Stephen turned over the editorship of the project to his assistant Sidney Lee in 1891 but continued to contribute to every volume. In the last decade of his life, he expounded his religious skepticism in *Agnostic's Apology and Other Essays* (1893), collected a series of miscellaneous biographical sketches under the title *Studies of a Biographer* (1898), and complemented his survey of eighteenth-century intellectual history with *The English Utilitarians* (1900), a study of JEREMY BENTHAM and the Mills.

For Stephen the modern world had been born, at least in the British Isles, from vast but confused social upheavals most easily traced in the history of the ideas generated as people struggled to comprehend what was happening to them. In Britain this revolution in human affairs manifested itself in the deist controversy of the late seventeenth and early eighteenth century, during which the traditional Christian world view succumbed to the forces of skepticism and reason. The contest had often been petty, vicious, and illogical, and Stephen delighted in larding his biographies and histories of the period with revealing anecdotes and ironic asides: the fact that in his old age the philosopher David Hume "had grown very fat, and was once rescued by an old woman from a bog into which he had fallen on condition of repeating the Creed and the Lord's Prayer" captured for Stephen something essential about the often absurd confrontation between complacent rationalism and stubborn belief out of which the age of industry and progress had evolved.

In Stephen's view, Hume had acted out the roles of both hero and villain in the historical drama of the eighteenth century: hero, because he had taken the empirical tradition of Bacon, Hobbes, Locke, and Berkeley to its logical conclusion in a scientific skepticism that denied the validity of Christianity, its miracles, and all superstitious creeds; and villain, because, having deprived the world of its beliefs, Hume had left it to founder in a moral void that he did nothing to fill with any thought that might give humans a reason to live. Stephen had followed the rationalists into skeptical agnosticism, but he was repulsed by the "degenerate" eighteenth century's descent into self-centered ethical vacuity. In his *Science of Ethics* (1882), Stephen hoped to demonstrate that altruism and social cooperation are human instincts developed by evolution. Stephen's own moral imperative was that humans should try—and that they were biologically programmed to make the attempt—to leave the world a better place than it was when they came into it.

Contemporary philosophy frequently dismisses Stephen's insights as superficial. Reservations about his methods usually amount to the observation that he was not Marx, Comte, or Weber. He propounded no sweeping theory of ideas. In part, he could not (his one attempt at original philosophical speculation, the *Science of Ethics*, was dismissed even by his twentieth-century champion Noel Annan as the work of an amateur); in addition, he temperamentally disliked dogmas and believed that none was possible in the state of knowledge at the time he wrote. For Stephen, the best service he could render was to amass empirical data on which another generation could erect a science of history and sociology based on facts; the *DNB* and the *History of English Thought in the Eighteenth Century* share this common purpose.

Stephen was much honored in life and death (he was knighted in 1902), but his greatest memorial is the portrait of Mr. Ramsey, modeled on him, in his daughter Virginia Woolf's novel *To the Lighthouse* (1927), where he is depicted, often with ridiculous incident and always with insight devoid of sentiment and cant, as a complete human in all his imperfections. "The book should be the man himself speaking or acting, and nothing but the man," Stephen had said of biography. His ironic empiricism found its full expression in his daughter's prose and fiction.

See also AGNOSTICISM, ATHEISM, AND FREE THOUGHT; PHILOSOPHY.

FURTHER READING

Annan, Noel. *Leslie Stephen: The Godless Victorian.* Chicago: University of Chicago Press, 1986.

Bicknell, John, ed. *Selected Letters of Leslie Stephen.* Columbus: Ohio State University Press, 1996.

Gross, John. *The Rise and Fall of the Man of Letters.* London: Weidenfeld and Nicolson, 1969.

Maitland, Frederic L. *Life and Letters of Leslie Stephen.* London: Duckworth, 1906.

Woolf, Virginia. *To the Lighthouse.* New York: Harcourt, 1927.

Woolf, Virginia. "Leslie Stephen." In *The Captain's Death Bed and Other Essays.* New York: Harcourt, Brace, 1950.

ROBERT PATTISON

STEPHENSON, GEORGE

Born: June 9, 1781; Wylam, England
Died: August 12, 1848; Chesterfield, England

Though the Industrial Revolution began in England in the eighteenth century, its rapid acceleration during the Victorian era produced some of its greatest triumphs in engineering technologies, changing people's connection to the landscape and to each other through new forms of transportation, communication, and manufacturing. Among the engineers who achieved near-heroic status in the new industrial economy was George Stephenson, who skillfully adapted James Watt's and Thomas Newcomen's steam engines for use as locomotives in the railroad systems that began crisscrossing England in Victoria's reign. Railroads during this period had a tremendous impact on the landscape. They fundamentally altered the relation between city and countryside, topographically, economically, and psychologically, and expanded a new commercial middle class by helping forge new movements of people and goods. If any one man helped usher in this new culture, it was George Stephenson.

Born near Newcastle, one of the boomtowns of the Industrial Revolution, Stephenson had an early training in the mechanical and industrial arts. At the age of 14 he became an assistant to his father, a fireman in a local coal mine, and worked his way up to colliery engineer by his early 20s, all the while studying at night school. His hands-on familiarity with many types of steam engines, and his expertise with the Newcomen engine in particular, made him a prized asset, and he was put in charge of all the engineering at the Killingworth colliery in 1812. There

he invented a safety lamp for miners around the same time that Sir Humphry Davy had patented his in 1815; some historians now believe that Stephenson deserves more credit for the innovation.

Stephenson's lasting place in history, however, rests in his development of a practical steam locomotive for the Stockton and Darlington railway, which opened in 1825. Building on his experience with steam technology at Killington, where he had also experimented with new valve, spring, and piston refinements, he and his son Robert created a superior locomotive called the *Rocket*. This model, with its more efficient boiler configuration using a water-jacketed firebox and vertical chimney, became the prototype of the modern locomotive. In 1826 Stephenson became chief engineer of the Liverpool and Manchester Railway, which pressed the *Rocket* into service and easily outshone its competitors in becoming the world's first railway to rely entirely on steam locomotion. Over the next two decades Stephenson helped engineer much of Britain's railway network and also developed coal-mining interests. Despite his significant contributions to the economic development of Britain, he refused to accept honors or titles from his sovereign. He did, however, accept the Order of Leopold from the king of Belgium in 1835. In 1847, the year before his death, Stephenson founded the Institution of Mechanical Engineers.

Although an acknowledged genius in his field, Stephenson occasionally—and sometimes justly—faced harsh criticism from investigators for blunders resulting from his scant attention to detail, but his legacy, and that of his son Robert, is inscribed for all time in the railway system that helped propel Great Britain into the first rank of industrial hegemony.

See also ENGINEERING; RAILWAYS.

FURTHER READING

Rolt, L. T. C. *The Railway Revolution: George and Robert Stephenson.* New York: St. Martin's, 1962.

Smiles, Samuel. *The Life of George Stephenson: Railway Engineer.* 4th London ed. Columbus, Ohio: Follett, Foster and Company, 1859.

EDWARD MORAN

STEVENSON, ROBERT LOUIS

Born: November 13, 1850; Edinburgh, Scotland
Died: December 3, 1894; Samoa

Robert Louis Stevenson was a Scottish writer of adventure stories, essays, travelogs, poetry, literary criticism, and novels. He is best known for *Treasure Island* (1883), a children's adventure story, and the

MANSELL/TIMEPIX/GETTY IMAGES

An illustration from *Treasure Island* (1883), a popular book by Robert Louis Stevenson.

case his profession of choice, writer, fell through. Thus began a lifetime of unconventionality.

Suffering ill health since his childhood, Stevenson spent much of his life traveling; the climate of Scotland and England was detrimental to his respiratory difficulties. While traveling on the Continent in 1876, he met Fanny Osbourne and fell in love with her. Fanny, a NEW WOMAN from America who was ten years Stevenson's senior, had come to France with her two children while separated from her husband; she was hardly the sort of woman of whom Stevenson's family would approve. Nevertheless, when she finally divorced her husband two years later after returning to America, Stevenson journeyed to California to be with her, and they were married there. The trip across the UNITED STATES took a heavy toll on Stevenson's already fragile constitution, and he was near death for some time after his arrival. This was exacerbated by his and Fanny's POVERTY, fitfully supplemented by the small articles that Stevenson was able to publish.

Throughout all these travels, romances, and struggles with sickness and poverty, Stevenson was writing. He published two travelogs, *An Inland Voyage* (1878) and *Travels with a Donkey in the Cevennes* (1879), along with short stories such as "A Lodging for the Night" (1877) and "Providence and the Guitar" (1878). These stories and others were collected as *Virginbus Puerisque* (1881) and *New Arabian Nights* (1882). In addition, Stevenson was writing essays and criticism, slowly building a reputation as a writer of note.

In 1880 Stevenson's father gave him assurance of an annual income of £250 a year, allowing the family to move back to England and Stevenson to concentrate on writing without looming financial worries. In 1883 he published his first novel, an adventure story begun when he and his stepson created an imaginary pirate's treasure map to pass the time on a rainy day. *Treasure Island* was immediately successful and was followed by *Kidnapped* (1886), another adventure story set in Scotland, and *Strange Case of Dr. Jekyll and Mr. Hyde* (1886). This last, a short Gothic novel set in London and dealing with the divided inner self of the Victorian psyche, was inspired by a nightmare and written at a white heat over a period of three intense days. He was horrified by the final product and burned the manuscript. At Fanny's insistence he then rewrote it over three more days, adding the psychological elements that complicate the novel's message. All three of these novels sold well (*Jekyll and Hyde* sold over 40,000 copies in the first six months alone), and Stevenson at last

Gothic novella *Strange Case of Dr. Jekyll and Mr. Hyde* (1886). Although he was only 44 when he died, Stevenson published 25 novels and collections, not including uncollected stories, essays, and poems, and there exist parts of at least 10 unfinished novels. His writings were extremely popular during his time with both critics and the general reading public; his reputation, which suffered in the early part of the twentieth century owing to his dismissal by the modernists (notably the Woolfs), has slowly been reestablishing itself.

Born Robert Louis Balfour Stevenson in 1850 to strict Presbyterian middle-class parents in Edinburgh, Stevenson originally went to Edinburgh University to study science, following in his father's footsteps toward a career as an engineer. Stevenson's dreamy, artistic demeanor, nourished by Walter Scott's historical romances and expanded by frequent sojourns in Edinburgh's bohemian Old Town districts, rendered him unfit for a scientific life. As a compromise with his parents, Stevenson read for the bar in found success as a popular novelist. He wrote other children's novels (among them *Catriona* [1893], a sequel to *Kidnapped*), as well as adventure fiction set in imaginary countries (1885's *Prince Otto*) and straightforward novels (*The Master of Ballantrae*, 1889). Stevenson also wrote a number of works set in and around the South Seas: *The Wrecker* (1892), *The Ebb-Tide* (1894), and "The Beach of Falesà" (1892) among them.

The disparate genres, settings, and subject matter of Stevenson's works makes the task of discerning common thematic threads a daunting one. There are, however, some recurrent ideas. Stevenson was fascinated throughout his life with the atmosphere of place, possibly because of his extensive travels. As a result, his works, especially the novels and stories, exhibit a strong sense of place; whether set in the northern climes of Scotland, on the foggy gas-lit streets of London, or on the beaches of a South Pacific island, Stevenson's novels vividly evoke the physical geography and esoteric flavor of their settings. Another common theme for Stevenson is that of the doppelgänger, or double, explicitly explored in *Jekyll and Hyde* but also appearing in stories such as "Markheim" (1885). The relationship between a son and a domineering father, a theme that struck fairly close to home for the author, is also often in evidence, notably in Stevenson's final, unfinished novel, *The Weir of Hermiston* (published posthumously in 1896).

After his father's death in May of 1887, Stevenson took his wife, his mother, and Fanny's 12-year-old son to America for most of the year before they set sail for the South Seas in May of 1888. Stevenson's fascination with the sea and the island cultures of the South Pacific had always been strong, and additionally he felt that the different climate would have a positive effect on his continuing ill health. In December of 1889 the Stevenson entourage settled on Samoa, where the writer would spend the remainder of his life.

The climate was indeed beneficial, and Stevenson's health and happiness were at their peak during his years in Samoa. Stevenson managed a large estate and was treated as a patriarch by the Samoans, all the while continuing his prodigious literary output. When he died, it was not from his lifelong respiratory problems—the tuberculosis he had always feared never manifested itself. A cerebral hemorrhage seems to have been the cause of Stevenson's death; he collapsed on December 3, 1894, in the kitchen after bringing a bottle of wine up from the cellar. He was 44 years old.

See also CHILDREN'S LITERATURE; NOVEL.

FURTHER READING

Calder, Jenni. *RLS: A Life Study*. London: Hamish Hamilton, 1980.

Callow, Phillip. *Louis: A Life of Robert Louis Stevenson*. London: Constable Robinson, 2001.

Chesterton, G. K. *Robert Louis Stevenson*. London: Hodder and Stoughton, 1927.

Hammond, J. R. *A Robert Louis Stevenson Companion: A Guide to the Novels, Essays, and Short Stories*. London: Macmillan, 1984.

Hammond, J. R. *A Robert Louis Stevenson Chronology*. New York: St. Martin's, 1997.

JAMIESON RIDENHOUR

STOCK MARKETS

Stock markets are institutions that organize the purchase and sale of transferable securities, also known as shares. In nineteenth-century Britain, stock markets took two forms: official stock exchanges and less-regulated stock markets. Stock exchanges are closed institutions where specialist intermediaries—such as brokers—buy and sell securities under a common set of rules. In less-regulated markets securities were bought and sold more informally. Such markets were either excluded from participation in the period's more formalized exchanges, or sought to compete with institutions like the London Stock Exchange. While the nineteenth century witnessed a dramatic increase in the importance of all British stock markets, and in the volume of securities traded, most investors before the 1880s preferred to invest directly either in businesses or in private companies that were not listed on an exchange.

THE LONDON STOCK EXCHANGE

The most important stock market in nineteenth-century Britain and the world was the London Stock Exchange. This exchange, which had existed in a rudimentary form since the late-seventeenth century when the government created a permanently funded national debt, was expanded during the French Revolution to absorb the business that fled the disrupted securities markets in Amsterdam and Paris. The London Stock Exchange was formally established in March 1801. Members of the London Exchange were either brokers, who conducted transactions for clients, or jobbers, who bought and sold securities for their own accounts, for resale, or acted as intermediaries between brokers. The distinction between jobbers and brokers, established by rule in 1847, 1877, and 1903, is one example of the numerous regulations by which the London Stock Exchange sought to govern its members in order to inspire public trust and prevent abuses by its members.

In 1802 the London Stock Exchange had 363 members. By 1851 membership had increased to 906, and by 1877 to 2,000. This expansion partly reflects the increased opportunities for investment created by new company legislation. Adopted in 1844, 1856, and 1862, these laws all encouraged the formation of joint-stock companies (companies owned by many shareholders rather than a few partners), the last two by conferring LIMITED LIABILITY on shareholders. The increased number of securities specialists reflects the expansion of the kinds of securities quoted on the London Stock Exchange. Whereas the national debt, in the form of securities called consols, dominated the activities of the London Stock Exchange at the beginning of the century, the relative importance of the consols began to decrease after the end of the war with FRANCE in 1815. By the end of the century, the exchange also listed foreign government bonds, overseas railway companies, other foreign enterprises such as MINING, coffee, and rubber companies, as well as domestic corporate securities.

As a company, the London Stock Exchange was owned by a group of shareholders, some of whom were also brokers or jobbers. Throughout the century the tension between the exchange's proprietors

and its members generated repeated struggles over the institution's rules. The proprietors, for example, who wanted to transact as much business as possible each day with as many dues-paying members as they could attract, favored longer hours of operation and lax principles for membership. The brokers and jobbers, by contrast, wanted to limit both the competition with rivals and the amount of time they worked. They sought to shorten the hours of operation and to establish stringent criteria for admission to the exchange. In 1876 the tension between the two groups was diminished by a resolution that required all future purchasers of shares in the exchange to be members. By 1914 shareholders in the London Stock Exchange numbered 2,366 individuals, up from 268 in 1876.

SHARE TRADING OUTSIDE THE LONDON EXCHANGE

The London Stock Exchange dominated the securities market in LONDON, but it did not hold a monopoly over securities trading. Before 1823 the London Stock Exchange did not handle foreign securities. This business was conducted outside the exchange in Capel Court, in the streets, or in the Royal Exchange. Until 1834 securities were also traded in the rotunda of the Bank of England, and even after that date some securities were exchanged in other sites long associated with the securities market, including coffee houses such as Garraways. Throughout the century there were also intermittent attempts to establish rivals to the London Stock Exchange, such as the Open Stock Exchange (1886), the Union Stock Exchange (1893), and the Investors Exchange (1893). These exchanges tended to be relatively short-lived and listed more speculative shares than did the London Stock Exchange. But their very existence points to the relatively small number of companies quoted on the London Stock Exchange, up from 500 in 1853 to 5,000 in 1913.

The London Stock Exchange also had British rivals outside of London. In addition to the Dublin Stock Exchange (established 1799), the first half of the century witnessed the creation of ten provincial stock exchanges, all of which were founded during the century's two railway booms in 1836 and in 1845–1846. Only one exchange, the Dundee Stock Exchange (1879), was established between 1846 and 1885, but by 1900 there were 21 provincial exchanges. In 1890 these exchanges coordinated their activities through the Council of Associated Stock Exchanges. Provincial exchanges tended to list domestic, primarily industrial securities, and they catered to local inves-

HULTON/ARCHIVE BY GETTY IMAGES

Interior of the London Stock Exchange, circa 1854.

tors seeking long-term, rather than speculative INVESTMENTS. Because the provincial exchanges were less prestigious, jobbers and brokers did not feel the same pressure to join them as did their London counterparts, and as a consequence considerable trading continued to take place outside the formal exchanges. Despite their informality, the provincial exchanges were important vehicles for drawing capital into home industrial companies and for attracting investors into the securities market.

COMMUNICATIONS AND INVESTORS

The complex relationship between the provincial exchanges and the London Stock Exchange during the nineteenth century reflects in part the tension between London investors and those in the provinces. London investors tended to be interested in riskier foreign or speculative investments, while provincial investors preferred the security of consols or familiar enterprises closer to home. These differences can be explained to some extent by the changing nature of TECHNOLOGY in the period. In the 1820s it took five days for news to travel from London to Dublin, and this discouraged Irish investors from using the London Stock Exchange. The invention of the TELEGRAPH in 1837 sped up the transfer of information, and by 1840 London was connected by wire to all the major cities of Britain. By the 1890s information could be telegraphed from London to Glasgow (some 400 miles, or 640 kilometers) in two-and-a-half minutes, while the TELEPHONE allowed for even more rapid, two-way communication. The first submarine telegraph cable was laid under the English Channel in 1851, linking Britain to continental Europe. The first London-to-New York cable was in use by 1866 and allowed connection to the active New York Stock Exchange, founded in 1792.

The ability to transfer information rapidly between two markets dramatically expanded the connections between the London Stock Exchange and other exchanges in Britain as well as other financial centers. Among these connections was the practice of arbitrage, which entails buying at a low price in one market and immediately selling high in another, and the specialization called shunting, by which provincial brokers directed local business to London from clients located in outlying cities. At the beginning of the nineteenth century, stock markets were risky, unregulated, and crude. As the Victorian era ended they had become sophisticated, formalized, and technologically advanced.

See also BANKING, MONEY, AND CREDIT; BUSINESS AND CORPORATE STRUCTURE; INVESTMENTS; LIMITED LIABILITY.

FURTHER READING

Jeffreys, James B. *Business Organization in Great Britain, 1856–1914.* 1938. Reprint, New York: Arno Press, 1977.
Kynaston, David. *A World of Its Own, 1815–1890.* Vol. 1, *The City of London.* London: Chatto and Windus, 1994.
Michie, Ranald C. *The London Stock Exchange: A History.* Oxford: Oxford University Press, 1999.
Thomas, W. A. *The Provincial Stock Exchanges.* London: Frank Cass, 1973.

MARY POOVEY

STOKER, BRAM

Born: November 8, 1847; Dublin, Ireland
Died: April 20, 1912; London, England

Abraham "Bram" Stoker, the prolific Irish-born novelist, journalist, and theater manager, is largely remembered as the author of *Dracula* (1897), the most celebrated and enduring tale to emerge from the Gothic horror novels of the Victorian age. Indeed, so popular did *Dracula* prove with the public of the day, and ever afterward, that it quite overshadowed any other achievements of its creator, who published 17 other books as well as his classic of vampirism.

Stoker spent much of his early youth suffering from a mysterious malady that kept him bedridden until he was seven. By his teenage years he had recovered sufficiently to become a proficient athlete—so much so that he was named University Athlete during his student years at Trinity College in Dublin, where he earned a mathematics degree in 1867. While at Trinity he began a lifelong affair with the theater, attending numerous performances and often writing reviews for the *Evening Mail*.

It was at Trinity that Stoker met the great Shakespearean actor HENRY IRVING (1838–1905), a legend of the Victorian stage and the first member of his profession to receive a knighthood. Irving proved a major influence in Stoker's life, responding to the young man's extravagant praise of his genius by offering him the dual post of his personal manager and manager of the Lyceum Theatre in London in 1876. For the next 25 years Stoker worked tirelessly in both capacities.

Despite the often overwhelming nature of Stoker's theatrical duties (he once claimed to have written almost half a million words on Irving's behalf), he was able to hone his craft as a novelist. Although he had to give up journalism because of the other demands on his time, he began writing fiction in earnest. In 1882 he published *Under the Sunset*, a collection of eerie children's stories; however, it was not until 1891 that he published his first novel, *The Snake's Pass.*

That same year Stoker began the seven-year odyssey that would result in the publication of his most famous work, *Dracula* (1897). He based the title character Count Dracula on the Balkan legend of the vampire and is thought possibly to have also modeled him after the sixteenth-century Transylvanian prince, Vlad Tepes—Vlad the Impaler. *Dracula* is a classic Gothic horror novel, a genre that had its origins in mid-eighteenth-century English fiction, and became a popular (if not overwhelming) seller when first released. The novel attracted far greater initial interest in America where, owing to a mistake in copyright, Stoker never received royalties. Stoker's later fiction, including *The Jewel of Seven Stars* (1903) and *The Lair of the White Worm* (1911), never came to close to replicating the appeal of *Dracula.*

In 1878 Stoker had married Florence Balcombe, who became caretaker of her husband's literary estate after his death. She was extremely protective of the Dracula franchise and, in 1922, famously won a copyright lawsuit against the great German movie director F. W. Murnau, who filmed a version of the Dracula story as the silent *Nosferatu.* Owing in large part to Florence's zeal (she licensed numerous motion pictures), Count Dracula remains one of the most recognized literary creations in history and has become a cultural icon of the cinema throughout the world.

See also GOTHIC NOVEL.

FURTHER READING

Belford, Barbara. *Bram Stoker: A Biography of the Author of Dracula.* New York: Alfred A. Knopf, 1996.
Farson, Daniel. *The Man Who Wrote Dracula: A Biography of Bram Stoker.* New York: St. Martin's Press, 1976.
Haining, Peter, and Peter Tremayne. *The Un-dead: The Legend of Bram Stoker and Dracula.* London: Constable and Company Limited, 1997.
Hughes, William. *Beyond Dracula: Bram Stoker's Fiction & Its Cultural Context.* New York: St. Martin's Press, 2000.
Ludlam, Harry. *A Biography of Dracula: The Life Story of Bram Stoker.* London: W. Foulsham and Co., 1962.
Miller, Elizabeth, and Clive Leatherdale. *Dracula: Sense & Nonsense.* Westcliff-on-Sea: Desert Island Books, 2000.
Stoker, Bram. *Personal Reminiscences of Henry Irving.* New York: The Macmillan Co., 1906.

TODD E. A. LARSON

STREET PERFORMERS

Performers of many types formed a prominent part of the large number of people making their living on Victorian streets. LONDON was the center of the trade, and street entertainers there reached a peak of activity in the 1850s and 1860s. The rise of commercialized entertainment such as the MUSIC HALLS greatly reduced the number of street performers by the end of the century, but the musicians among them remained a lively and ubiquitous presence, despite campaigns for their suppression.

From interviews with London street performers in the 1850s, the journalist HENRY MAYHEW (1812–1887) noted "a predilection for dexterous and dangerous feats," including acrobatics, juggling, stilt walking, and sword and snake swallowing. Among other shows were Mr. Punch, marionettes, galantee or shadow theater, various animal acts, and the exhibition of monster models of Guy Fawkes (involved in the "Gunpowder Plot" to blow up the Houses of Parliament in 1605) and other demonized figures of the day, from the pope to the Russian emperor. Some of Mayhew's "wandering tribes" of predominantly male performers were peripatetic. They took their acts into PUBLIC HOUSES (pubs), penny gaffs (cheap entertainment houses), and THEATERS, going on the road to fairs, horse race meetings, or touring the Continent. SEASIDE towns such as Brighton on the south coast were also profitable stopovers for traveling entertainers. Some street performers made good money providing entertainment for genteel private house parties, but the trade was precarious and there were complaints of increased competition from casuals and foreign immigrants.

The largest general category of entertainers was musicians. They played a wide range of instruments, from bagpipes to street pianos. Many were highly proficient performers, but there were a substantial number, many blind, whose instrument was simply a cover for begging. Bands of English string players were angry at recently arrived German BRASS BANDS stealing their business. Other continental newcomers were refugees from the 1848 revolutions, but the earliest and most numerous competitors were Italian. Italian organ boys arrived in large numbers in the 1820s, often accompanied by dancing bears or monkeys. Most were indentured, which meant their parents were paid an up-front fee in exchange for a number of years' service to a "master." So-called Ethiopian serenaders were actually locals playing the new American music then called "nigger." Singing ballad sellers provided more traditional English fare, though they and the political commentary they offered were fast disappearing with the onset of mass-produced sheet music. All street performers were liable to charges of vagrancy. Arrests were infrequent, but as

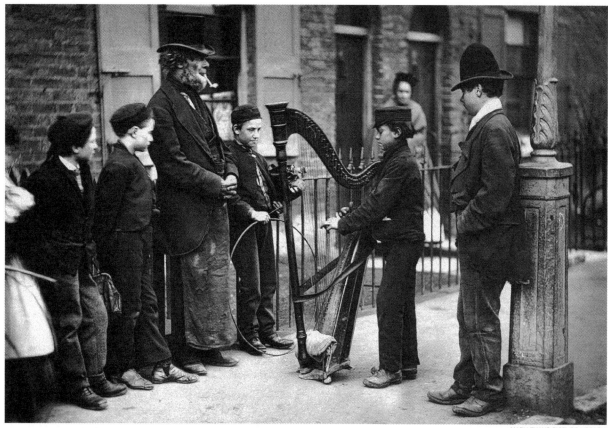

Italian street musicians perform for onlookers in this photograph from *Street Life in London* (1877).

streets became busier the POLICE increasingly ordered them to move on.

In the late 1850s the mathematician CHARLES BABBAGE (1792–1871), supported by other intellectuals and the member of Parliament (M.P.) Michael Bass (1799–1884), campaigned against the nuisance of street musicians disturbing his studies and holding householders to ransom. Crowds gathered at Babbage's door in defense of the bands and popular pleasures. Tougher laws in 1864 and a home office order to suppress the traffic in Italian child musicians in 1877 proved ineffective. Other performers were absorbed into new entertainment sites such as the music hall, but the street musician, typically the Italian organ grinder, remained a familiar and mostly welcome figure until World War I (1914–1918).

See also MUSIC HALLS; MUSIC PROFESSION; PUBLIC HOUSES; SEASIDE.

FURTHER READING

Mayhew, Henry. *London Labour and the London Poor.* 1861–1862. Reprint, London: Frank Cass, 1967.

Winter, James. *London's Teeming Streets, 1830–1914.* London: Routledge, 1993.

Zucchi, John E. *Little Slaves of the Harp: Italian Child Street Musicians in Nineteenth Century Paris, London and New York.* Montreal: McGill-Queen's University Press, 1993.

PETER BAILEY

SUBURBIA

Suburbs have existed, in various forms, as long as cities themselves. The Victorian era, however, witnessed the rise of suburbs in the modern sense: low-density residential areas geographically marginal to—yet economically and socially dependent on—an urban center. Although they emerged outside LONDON in the eighteenth century, and expanded most dramatically in Britain between World War I (1914–1918) and World War II (1939–1945), it was during Victoria's reign that suburbs shifted from exclusive enclaves for the WEALTHY to commonplace communities for the masses. Indeed, as historian John Burnett suggests, suburban expansion represented "perhaps the greatest single change in the living habits of the English people since the industrial revolution." A notable phenomenon by 1840, suburban development exploded between 1861 and 1901, when the size of London's outer ring grew about 50% each decade. Victorian suburbs varied greatly in status and style—from picturesque and grand to dull and ramshackle. But the term *suburbia*, popular since the 1880s, became synonymous with architectural monotony, social conformity, and cultural barrenness. Despite this reputation, suburbs transformed everyday life throughout Britain and the English-speaking world, especially North America and AUSTRALIA.

Located on the outskirts of medieval and Renaissance London, "suburbes" were often reviled as quarters of pollution and CRIME. Their standing improved during the eighteenth century, however, as aristocrats and merchants began to establish *urbs in rure*, country retreats close to London. John Shaw's Eyre Estate and John Nash's Regent's Park, both of which took shape in the early nineteenth century, are now considered the first true suburbs. Shaw's innovation lay in adapting the congruous Georgian terrace to rural environs, while Nash designed the earliest community of semidetached villas. Concealing a mirrored pair of separate dwellings under one roof, the semidetached house gave the appearance of a single large residence in its own grounds. This compromise between the fully detached country villa and the urban town house came to symbolize the suburban ideal, offering an alternative to the city's overcrowding and pollution and reinforcing Victorian domestic values such as the sanctity of family and the separation of public and private life. By midcentury semidetached houses were springing up north and south of the Thames.

While the fashionable "semi" epitomized suburban life for the middle classes, the petit bourgeoisie and working classes began moving into more affordable suburban terraces from the 1870s onward. The four places in Britain with the greatest population increase during the 1880s—Leyton, Willesden, Tottenham, and West Ham—were London suburbs inhabited largely by laborers, artisans, clerks, office workers, and shopkeepers. Legislation such as the Public Health Act of 1875 sought to improve building standards in such areas but often resulted in drearily uniform bylaw architecture. Other suburbs were reputed for dwellings that went up quickly and decayed soon after—hence the popular disdain for the so-called "jerry," or speculative builder, whose supposedly questionable skills and inferior materials contributed to suburbia's declining social status. Although parliamentary acts in 1890 and 1900 made cheap LAND available for working-class HOUSING, affordable options would remain limited for laborers hoping to settle in the suburbs.

SPRAWLING SUBURBS

Unchecked sprawl during the second half of the nineteenth century led to rural despoliation on a massive scale, undermining the benefits of suburban life and making it, as many feared, a source of social degeneration. At the same time, the suburb's low POPULATION and proximity to nature continued to offer the most obvious antidote to urban overcrowding and blight. Thus the last decades of the century witnessed some innovative attempts to reinvent the suburb by limiting its drawbacks (isolation, unsystematic growth, unsightliness) and reviving its ideals (privacy, comfort, health). Bedford Park, an influential estate begun by Jonathan Carr and Norman Shaw in 1875, integrated houses in the new Queen Anne style with the area's existing landscape and foliage. The result, a fashionable haven for bohemian and bourgeois residents alike, influenced suburban development for decades to come.

More revolutionary, however, was the garden city concept outlined by Ebenezer Howard (1850–1928) in his 1898 book *To-morrow*. Howard proposed building hygienic new rural towns of limited size and population, to be owned and governed by residents from all SOCIAL CLASSES. Drawing on a variety of sources—anarchists, colonists, and the industrial villages of Titus Salt, William Lever, and George Cadbury—Howard intended to produce a utopian alternative to suburban segregation and sprawl. Although garden cities were built at Letchworth (1903) and Welwyn (1920), financial problems would force Howard to compromise his goals of class mixing and communal ownership. Nevertheless, the garden city concept had a profound impact on later suburban development. Howard's followers initiated the discipline of town planning and popularized the more modest garden suburb, whose prototype, begun in Hampstead in 1907, was the brainchild of Henrietta Barnett, Raymond Unwin, and Barry Parker. The New Towns that went up throughout Britain after World War II also constitute part of Howard's legacy.

A number of factors contributed to Victorian suburban expansion: rising population and income rates, the increasing availability of agricultural land and capital for building, and an evolving network of mass TRANSPORTATION. During the 1830s the reliable if expensive coach service between London and the inner suburbs gave way to the more popular horse-drawn OMNIBUS. It was not until the second half of the nineteenth century, however, that transportation became accessible to the masses. RAILWAYS began to develop suburban lines for the middle classes in the 1860s, and, in the decades that followed, cheaper train fares and horse trams made suburban commuters of working- and lower-middle-class Londoners. The last decade of the century saw the introduction of the tube (the London subway system called the UNDERGROUND) and motorbus. The age of the automobile was not far behind.

CRITICISM OF SUBURBIA

Literary critic John Carey has demonstrated a pervasive scorn for suburbia among twentieth-century artists and intellectuals. However, the suburbs were a target of mockery and condemnation much earlier—in poetry by William Cowper, architectural criticism by JOHN RUSKIN, and fiction by CHARLES DICKENS. During the 1890s, when the suburb overtook the slum as a subject of social investigation, a distinct literature of suburbia came into its own. Central to the genre is George and Weedon Grossmith's 1892 novel *The Diary of a Nobody*, a comic story of a hapless clerk; other examples include fiction by once popular but now forgotten writers such as Jerome K. Jerome, Edwin Pugh, Barry Pain, Shan Bullock, William Pett Ridge, and Keble Howard. Suburbia also figures prominently in the work of more famous late Victorians and Edwardians: latter-day "CONDITION OF ENGLAND" novels by GEORGE GISSING and E. M. Forster, detective stories by ARTHUR CONAN DOYLE, social comedies by H. G. WELLS, and mystical fantasies by G. K. Chesterton. Largely snubbed by the modernists, suburbia nonetheless appears in fiction by early-twentieth-century writers such as Rebecca West, D. H. Lawrence, and George Orwell.

See also HOUSES AND HOUSING; LIVING STANDARDS; SOCIAL CLASSES; URBANIZATION.

FURTHER READING

Burnett, John. *A Social History of Housing: 1815–1985.* 2d ed. London and New York: Methuen, 1986.
Carey, John. *The Intellectuals and the Masses: Pride and Prejudice among the Intelligentsia, 1880–1939.* London and Boston: Faber and Faber, 1992.
Dyos, H. J. *Victorian Suburb: A Study of the Growth of Camberwell.* London: Leicester University Press, 1961.
Edwards, Arthur M. *The Design of Suburbia: A Critical Study in Environmental History.* London: Pembridge, 1981.
Olsen, Donald J. *The Growth of Victorian London.* New York: Holmes and Meier, 1976.
Silverstone, Roger, ed. *Visions of Suburbia.* London and New York: Routledge, 1997.
Thompson, F. M. L., ed. *The Rise of Suburbia.* London: Leicester University Press and St. Martin's, 1982.

TODD KUCHTA

SUGAR

A remarkable but somewhat neglected feature of the Victorian era was the phenomenal increase in British sugar (sucrose) consumption per capita, with the United States not far behind and only outstripped by British Australasia, both in absolute terms and in comparison to the expanding per capita consumption of other European countries. When Victoria succeeded to the throne in 1837, sugar was still a luxury, with annual per capita consumption less than 10 pounds (5 kilograms) a year. By the time of her death in 1901, per capita consumption had increased to over 85 pounds (39 kilograms) and sugar was an article of mass consumption providing over 10% of the average Briton's calorie intake, in a diet that had considerably improved over the course of her reign in quantity and energy supply for the masses.

In the early nineteenth century sugar was particularly sold as a medicine. It was considered a "cure all" for a host of ailments, especially those involving fevers. The product was even recommended as a remedy for the common cold. Sugar was presumed to strengthen the liver, kidneys, and stomach. As late as 1852 a leading Italian physician recommended it as an antiseptic for cuts, and in the late twentieth century, the application of sucrose directly to wounds, as well as to damaged skin areas to aid the healing process, was still supported by some medical research. Belief in the medicinal properties of sugar also survived the nineteenth century in some quarters as a cure for fevers, and the product continued to be recommended by some medical practitioners as a digestive aid for weak stomachs. From at least around the middle of the century, however, sugar was essentially considered to be a sweetener. Its relationship to pharmacology became that of a means of disguising the unpleasant taste of most medicines in the liquid and tablet forms.

Although subject to high import duties into the nineteenth century, the social widening of cane sugar consumption, approaching an addiction only constrained by price, was promoted by periodic crises of overproduction having a "ratchet effect" on consumption. These resulted in periodic significant falls in prices that broadened consumption, before output was curtailed and consumers lower down the social order endeavored to maintain an acquired taste as prices rose. As a monoculture and a perennial crop, usually grown for six to seven years before replanting, in numerous tropical areas by the eighteenth century, such downward adjustments in cane sugar output were not easy to achieve.

Into the nineteenth century, as what was an imported good, in an era when earlier mercantilist/protectionist economic thinking still held some sway, the duties on sugar remained high and contributed around a third of all state revenue. Apart from the product being perceived to be a luxury, it possessed the desirable characteristic from a revenue-raising item for a fiscal imposition, in that demand was relatively inelastic in response to price increases. For the well-to-do sugar accounted for a small proportion of household budgets. And for the masses a taste acquired during price slumps was reluctantly denied. Over the second half of the century, with a trend decline of sugar prices, demand for the product proved to be highly price- and income-elastic. In other words, each decline of prices or increase of real incomes brought a disproportionately high increase in sugar consumption.

A TASTE FOR TEA

As a complementary good, sales of sugar increased with those of infusion beverages. In Victorian Britain this was principally tea (although consumption only overtook that of coffee during the 1850s), on which import duties were drastically reduced in 1784, in the wake of the American War of Independence. The tea was the relatively expensive "green" tea from China, which still accounted for over 90% of sales in Britain in the mid-1860s. To an extent consumption was promoted by a "trickle-down effect" whereby, as in fashion, subordinate imitated superordinate groups. Rather in the manner of the second-hand market and the "hand-me-down" process in the diffusion of clothing styles, a taste for tea was also diffused down the social order by the upper classes presenting their used tea leaves to favored domestic servants. According to the census of 1851, over 10% of the British labor force was employed in domestic service. For most servants, especially females, it was an occupation before marriage. And females particularly became more or less addicted to tea, and the sugar that usually accompanied it. In Australia as early as the 1820s, the weekly rations of convicts, as well as indentured servants, commonly included a quarter of a pound of tea and a pound of sugar, as incentives to labor.

Although "black" tea from the Assam first arrived in Britain in 1838, consumption of the variety did not take off until the later 1860s, with the rapid expansion of cultivation of the tea plant in India and Ceylon. Along with a falling sugar price, cheaper black tea formed the basis of the expansion of grocery chains such as Lipton's, with over 300 stores by the 1890s and its own tea trademark, and what eventually became the A&P supermarket chain in the United States (originally the Great Atlantic & Pacific Tea Company). British annual per capita tea consumption of 2 pounds (1 kilogram) in 1800 increased to over 10 pounds (5 kilograms) by 1900. This expansion was influenced by growth of the temperance movement. Infusion beverages also possessed a capacity for sale in small quantities. By the later nineteenth century doses of a teaspoon of tea with sugar were widely sold in working-class districts. These doses, and tea in general, came to be commonly purchased by the working class and taken with condensed milk, with sugar accounting for as much as half of ingredients. Sales of condensed milk were promoted by the widespread adulteration of fresh milk and the acquired knowledge of the role of the latter in the spread of the feared DISEASE of tuberculosis, or consumption.

SWEETENED FOOD

While the Victorian era in Britain saw the rapid growth of direct consumption of sugar with that of infusion beverages and household baking, indirect demand in processed foodstuffs and beverages, over which households had control limited to the power to purchase or not, expanded at an even faster pace. Among these sources of demand, biscuits appeared in grocery stores from the 1820s, with firms such as Huntley & Palmer of Reading experiencing rapid growth from later in the century on the basis of cheap grain as well as cheap sugar. Unlike that of bread and cakes, the storage quality of biscuits widened the market for firms geographically and, with improvements in communications, thereby enhanced their ability to exploit economies of scale. This, as well as brand control and resale price maintenance, was further enhanced around the turn of the twentieth century by the appearance of prepackaged biscuits, rather than their delivery in large tins for grocers to weigh out to customers. Manufacturers quickly became aware that a high sugar content promoted sales.

In addition to expanding sales of cocoa as an infusion beverage, to which sugar was commonly added, consumption of confectionery became a substantial indirect source of demand for sugar in the latter part of Victoria's reign. From the end of the 1870s, milk chocolate, which the Swiss chemist Henri Nestlé developed using condensed milk, became the form of the product favored by the British palate. The firm of Cadbury began to market "Milk Tray" chocolate in the mid-1890s. However, it was not until 1904, that, contrary to the qualms of the firm's technicians, the proportion of sugar in the product was increased sufficiently for it to become the market leader and the basis of the company's fortunes in the twentieth century.

The mid-Victorian boom brought high malt prices, and in response British brewers began to use increasing quantities of sugar to enhance fermentation of, and partially replace, barley in the manufacture of beer. By the late 1860s over 175,000 tons of sugar were used for the purposes. By the turn of the century that amount had more than doubled. German breweries, on the other hand, adhered to the so-called purity law (*Reinheitsgebot*), whereby beer was made only from water, barley, and hops. Jam production, containing up to 75% sugar, emerged in Britain as a major source of indirect demand for sugar from the 1880s and was especially consumed by the working class. By the early twentieth century British jam manufacturers purchased over 400,000 tons of sugar a year, or around a quarter of total demand.

CHEAP SUGAR

Underlying the enormous expansion of British sugar consumption from the 1850s was the declining price of the commodity. Here the reduction of import duties on the product played a part, as with the equalization of British colonial and foreign duties at a lower level in 1846, before the establishment of free trade in the commodity from 1874. The repeal of the mercantilist Navigation Acts in 1849 contributed, through enhancing competition in the sugar trade by allowing it to be landed by foreign ships. The major factor in stimulating demand, however, was the growing competition cane sugar faced from the chemically identical beet sugar produced on the continent of Europe. When Victoria became queen, British sugar imports consisted entirely of cane sugar from British colonies, mostly from those in the Caribbean. By the time of her death in 1901, the West Indies colonies supplied about 1% of sugar imports, and beet sugar dominated what was the only significant free market in the world.

The nineteenth-century transformation of the labor system in cane-sugar-producing areas, from slavery to indentured labor, created problems of adjustment and increased production costs. Slavery was abolished in Britain's Caribbean colonies in 1834, in those of France in 1848, in the United States as an outcome of the Civil War, and, last of all, in Brazil in the 1880s. More significant, however, was the competi-

tion of beet sugar. In the protectionist United States, cane-growing Louisiana faced serious competition from the spread of beet cultivation in the states with a temperate climate from the mid-1890s. In the British market, which overwhelmingly dominated international trade in sugar, the threat came much earlier from the expanding acreage of beet on the continent of Europe.

The initial impetus to the growth of the beet-sugar industry on the Continent occurred during the French Revolutionary and Napoleonic Wars of 1793 to 1815, with the British naval blockade of Europe and the state bounties afforded beet-sugar production under Napoleon's Continental System introduced in 1806. The industry collapsed in 1815 with the return of peace and cane sugar to the Continent, surviving only on a small scale in France.

European beet-sugar exports to Britain were subsidized in the form of bounties. The latter had their origins in the long-established export rebate on refined cane sugar adopted by all European countries, involving a differential import duty on raw and refined sugar. It was impossible to establish precisely the actual sucrose content of sugar before the later 1860s, and the adoption of the polarimeter, an instrument measuring the polarization of light to distinguish sucrose from nonsugar residues. The arrangement adopted from the later 1830s was known as the Dutch color system, whereby sugars were allocated into 21 grades (reduced to 18 in 1840), from white, assumed to have the highest sucrose content, to dark brown, presumed to have the highest proportion of molasses. This encouraged customs and excise fraud by artificially whitening raw sugar, with lime and even with the poison Prussic acid, to claim the maximum export rebate.

In 1840 the states of the German customs union (the *Zollverein*) led by Prussia, out of concern for their revenue from imported raw cane sugar, applied a tax to the beet product. This was levied as a percentage on the tonnage of washed beet entering mills, which was weighed anyway to calculate payments to individual growers, on the basis of a notional sugar yield. This provided a stimulus to the activity to raise the actual sugar content of beet above the notional yield, which was maintained by periodic upward adjustments of the sugar percentage on which the levy was based. By the mid-1860s the customs union area was self-sufficient with regard to sugar, behind a tariff barrier, and the authorities faced the decision as to whether or not to permit the continued expansion of the industry on the basis of a rebate of duty on exports. This was decided in the affirmative, so that an absolute stimulus to production was added to the relative one of the rebate of beet taxation.

On the basis of the disguised bounty derived from the export rebate, German sugar exports boomed, with Britain as the major market by far. Owing to improvements in productivity, the German sugar import duty became as much a barrier to exports to Germany from other European beet-sugar producers adopting an open bounty, most notably Austria-Hungary and France, as a device to protect a source of state revenue. The continued existence of the import duty among beet-sugar producers encouraged the emergence of sugar cartels, to subsidize exports through raising domestic prices to a higher level than those on the world market. Briefly in the late 1890s, with the Spanish-American War of 1898, Germany became the largest sugar exporter in the world. Even after the Brussels Convention of 1902, whereby the bounties were abolished, Germany remained the world's largest sugar producer and third largest exporter, after Cuba and Java. German sugar continued to dominate the British market, so much so that the United Kingdom experienced a sugar supply crisis from late 1914 with the outbreak of World War I. Germany, along with Austria-Hungary, ceased to be a supplier and the major war front soon stabilized to

straddle and devastate the major beet-growing areas of French Flanders and southern Belgium. German sugar exports to Britain, increasingly in the refined form, had been assisted earlier by relatively low shipping rates, with the commodity providing a ballast return cargo for colliers carrying British coal to Hamburg.

In Britain in the later nineteenth century, subsidized beet-sugar imports stimulated the appearance of a division within the ranks of those espousing the dominant free-trade ideology. Advocates of "fair trade" denounced sugar bounties, with a Fair Trade League being established in 1881 with the support of the sugar-refining industry. Remaining and still predominant free traders were of the view that if beet-sugar producing countries wished to subsidize British sugar consumers then they should be encouraged to do so. Political opinion really shifted from the later 1890s, with the Boer War (1899–1902) and a Conservative government in which the dominant figure was Joseph Chamberlain, the advocate of empire free trade. On account of the Boer War, between the British army and the settlers of Dutch descent in South Africa, Britain became isolated among the major powers that sympathized with the Boers (or farmers), occasioning increased dependence on the support of the em-

Raw sugar was processed in mills such as this one in St. Thomas, West Indies, circa 1870s.

pire. The beet-sugar bounties, therefore, came to be more widely accepted as threatening Britain's sugar colonies, especially in the Caribbean. This forms the background to British support for an effective means of eliminating the bounties, which was realized with the Brussels Convention of 1902. Earlier efforts to achieve this objective had failed on account of British unwillingness to levy countervailing duties of bounty-fed beet-sugar exports.

SUGAR CONSUMPTION LINKED TO OBESITY

The expanding consumption of sugar was not without its critics. From the 1850s the commodity was attacked in tracts by a number of medical practitioners, a profession in the process of acquiring scientific respectability, as the cause of obesity. Earlier in the century stoutness had been considered a sign of prosperity and the public paid to view exceptionally fat men at fairground sideshows and other venues. The most famous of these was Daniel Lambert of Leicester, after whom several public houses were named.

Born in 1770, at the time of his death in 1836, Danny Lambert weighed nearly 742 pounds (53 stone), with a girth of 90 inches (230 centimeters). By the 1850s obesity was becoming identified as a disease. With publicity surrounding the discovery in 1889 that removal of the pancreas occasioned the development of diabetes in dogs, and undigested sugar in the bloodstream, the disease came to be widely ascribed to the consumption of sugar. The affliction was commonly known as in "sugar diabetes," or "sugar disease" (Zuckerkrankheit) in Germany. Sugar also came to be viewed by the dentists, another profession acquiring respectability in the Victorian era, as the cause of rotting teeth and toothache, which was "proved" by depositing teeth for days in a sugar solution.

Saccharin derived from coal tar, with 300 times the sweetening power of sugar, posed a threat to the latter commodity and was promoted as an alternative for diabetics. The German beet-sugar lobby managed to contain that threat on the domestic front, other than through smuggling from Switzerland, by limiting sales of saccharin to pharmacies on presentation of prescriptions from medical practitioners. Otherwise, sales were limited by the unpleasant aftertaste of saccharin and its limited suitability for industries requiring sugar for the manufacture of their products, where heat was required in the processing.

Although declining price and improving real incomes were the major factors in the rapid expansion of demand for sugar over the Victorian era, other influences cannot be totally ignored. Contemporaries noted the relatively low per capita consumption in wine-drinking areas. In Germany, where coffee became the popular infusion beverage over the course of the second half of the nineteenth century, consumers became accustomed to the somewhat bitter taste of the beverage with a limited addition of sugar. In the neighboring Austro-Hungarian Empire, where sugar was just as expensive, the acquired taste was for coffee with a large addition of sugar and milk. Living standards were lower in Austria-Hungary as compared with Germany, and consumption of coffee was limited for the masses initially to special occasions. It was notable, however, that as the beverage became diffused down the social order, the preference was for the highly sweetened version.

See also AGRICULTURE; EMPIRE; FREE TRADE; INTERNATIONAL TRADE.

FURTHER READING

Clarence-Smith, W. G. Cocoa and Chocolate, 1765–1914. London and New York: Routledge, 2000.
Deerr, N. The History of Sugar. London: Chapman and Hall, 1950.
Fitzgerald, Robert. Rowntree and the Marketing Revolution, 1862–1969. Cambridge: University Press, 1995.
Mintz, Sidney. Sweetness and Power: The Place of Sugar in Modern History. New York: Penguin, 1985.
Munting, Roger, and Tamas Szmrecsanyi., eds. Competing for the Sugar Bowl. St. Katharinen, Germany: Scripta Mercaturae, 2000.
Pettigrew, Jane. A Social History of Tea. London: National Trust, 2002.
Woloson, Wendy A. Refined Tastes: Sugar, Confectionery and Consumers in Nineteenth-Century America. Baltimore: Johns Hopkins University Press, 2002.

JOHN PERKINS

SULLIVAN, ARTHUR. *See* GILBERT AND SULLIVAN.

SUNDAY SCHOOLS

The Sunday school was the most pervasive educational institution of the early Victorian era. In 1833 enrollment in English Sunday schools was some 1.36 million people, or almost half of the population aged 5 to 14; this was 20% larger than weekday school enrollment. Almost all English working-class children in the early nineteenth century would have spent time in a Sunday school, and for many this would have been their only exposure to formal schooling. For many religious denominations, Sunday schools were essential to replenishing the ranks of believers from the young.

Sunday schools may have been in operation in England by the early seventeenth century. However, Robert Raikes (1735–1811) is often credited with providing the initial impetus to the English Sunday school movement with the four schools he founded in the city of Gloucester in the 1780s. Raikes viewed schooling on the Sabbath as an antidote to the disorderly behavior he perceived among children employed in factories during the week. As Sunday schools spread nationally in subsequent decades, they tended to predominate in areas with high demand for child labor.

Both Anglican and dissenting religious groups contributed to the explosive growth of Sunday schools in the late eighteenth and early nineteenth century. But while religious teaching featured prominently, instruction in basic literacy skills was also common. Surveys of Sunday school curricula in the 1830s and 1840s indicate that virtually all students attended Sunday schools in which reading was taught and about a fifth were in schools in which writing was taught as well. Sunday schools also commonly sponsored recreational activities such as picnics, teas, and sports.

Historians have differed in their assessments as to whether elite and middle-class or working-class groups initiated the establishment of Sunday schools and whether their educational objectives were primarily those of social control and promoting orderly behavior among the working classes or whether they reflected genuine working-class efforts to promote self-improvement.

In the second half of the nineteenth century, the religious and recreational functions of Sunday schools increased relative to that of literacy instruction as weekday schooling became pervasive. And the proportions of students under the age of five and over the age of fifteen rose as well. Enrollment as a percentage of the British population peaked in the 1880s, although absolute numbers enrolled in British Sunday schools rose until the early twentieth century.

The Sunday school movement rapidly spread from England in the late eighteenth and early nineteenth century to other English-speaking areas, while its influence on the European continent was far more limited. In Scotland and IRELAND, Sunday schools largely developed along English lines; however in Ireland the impact was limited owing to the hostility of Catholic clergy to the Protestant-sponsored Sunday school. Compared with England, Sunday schools in Wales had a larger proportion of adult students and were known for their emphasis on literature, music, and singing. In the UNITED STATES and CANADA, Sunday schools in the early nineteenth century initially followed the English pattern of serving as substitutes for day schools and offering generic religious instruction. However, in the United States from the 1830s, Sunday schools became increasingly associated with evangelical Protestantism focusing more narrowly on tasks of conversion and doctrinal nurturing with close connections with particular churches and congregations. After the CIVIL WAR (1861–1865), the temperance movement provided an important impetus to the growth of U.S. Sunday schools, an influence that spread to Canada and Britain in the early twentieth century.

The Sunday school remains a pervasive feature of modern religious life. Although considerably changed in character, it can trace its origins back to the early-nineteenth-century English Sunday school movement.

See also CHILDHOOD; PUBLIC SCHOOLS.

FURTHER READING

Boylan, Anne M. *Sunday School. The Formation of an American Institution. 1790–1990.* New Haven and London: Yale University Press, 1988.

Laqueur, Thomas. *Religion and Respectability. Sunday Schools and Working Class Culture 1780–1850.* New Haven and London: Yale University Press, 1976.

Malcolm, Dick. "The Myth of the Working-Class Sunday School." *History of Education* 9 (1980): 27–41.

McMillen, Sally G. *To Raise Up the South. Sunday Schools in Black and White Churches, 1865–1915.* Baton Rouge: Louisiana State University Press, 2001.

Snell, K. D. M. "The Sunday-School Movement in England and Wales." *Past and Present* no. 164 (August 1999): 122–168.

DAVID MITCH

SWINBURNE, ALGERNON CHARLES

Born: April 5, 1837; London, England
Died: April 10, 1909; London, England

Both in his life and his poetry, Algernon Swinburne shocked his Victorian contemporaries with his flagrant disregard of contemporary standards of morality and decorum. But he was among the greatest poets of his age and was influential in establishing the doctrine of aestheticism, or "art for art's sake," in England, in separating the aesthetic realm from the ethical, and in maintaining the Romantic tradition inherited particularly from William Blake (1757–1827) and Percy Bysshe Shelley (1792–1822).

British poet Algernon Swinburne helped establish the doctrine of aestheticism, or "art for art's sake."

Swinburne's notoriety was based mostly on the paganism and frank eroticism of his early publications, particularly *Atalanta in Calydon* (1865) and *Poems and Ballads* (1866), but his POETRY was also an expression of other lifelong passions: a fierce worship of elemental forms of nature (sun, wind, and sea) fostered by his childhood on the Isle of Wight, and a rabid REPUBLICANISM engendered by a family tradition of Jacobite political rebellion. Jacobite sympathies—allegiance to the deposed Stuart royal line—could easily lead to political conservatism, but Swinburne was drawn less to the cause of the Stuarts than to the general stance of rebelliousness; to FRANCE as the romantic land of the exiled Stuarts; and, especially, to the tragic and, in his mind, lurid figure of Mary, Queen of Scots, who inspired a trilogy of plays, *Chastelard* (1865), *Bothwell* (1874), and *Mary Stuart* (1881). While still a child Swinburne not only developed his love of nature and rebellion, he also developed a precocious passion for literature. Even before going to school at Eton in 1849, he had read extensively in Shakespeare and other Renaissance drama-

tists and immersed himself in the works of CHARLES DICKENS. He had, too, learned French and Italian from his mother, and at age 12 was already mastering the literature of southern Europe and nurturing the Francophilia that made him the Victorian age's greatest advocate for Victor Hugo, Théophile Gautier, Charles Baudelaire, and the doctrine of *l'art pour l'art* (art for art's sake).

EARLY INFLUENCES

Eton had a disproportionate effect on Swinburne's temperament and his poetry, partly because his education there in the Greek and Latin classics instilled in him both a love of classical form and a kind of intellectual elitism that enabled him to defy the strictures of his less-educated critics and to pursue his own course. In addition, the tradition of flogging as part of the discipline at Eton had a powerful effect on the youth's libidinal development, producing a flagellation fetish and contributing to the masochistic temperament apparent in his notorious poetic representations of sadistic, overpowering female sexuality. Swinburne proceeded from Eton to Oxford University, where he studied classics under the tutelage of one of the age's greatest classicists, BENJAMIN JOWETT (1817–1893).

By far the most important influence of Swinburne's Oxford years, however, was his acquaintance with the artistic avant-garde, led by DANTE GABRIEL ROSSETTI (1828–1882) and including WILLIAM MORRIS (1834–1896) and EDWARD BURNE-JONES (1833–1898). Immediately swept up into their circle, Swinburne devoted himself to their aesthetic interests, which focused at the time on the conflict between the ascetic ideals of medieval Christianity and robustly sensual, erotic paganism—in the words of WALTER PATER, the characteristic medieval choice between Christ and a rival lover.

At this time Morris was working on the poems for his volume *The Defence of Guenevere and Other Poems* (1857), possibly the defining volume of what Pater called the "aesthetic school" of poetry, and Swinburne adapted Morris's style and concerns in a verse-drama called *Queen Yseult* (1857–1858). More generally, Rossetti's circle encouraged Swinburne's tendencies toward art for art's sake, which defined the development of the AESTHETIC MOVEMENT and frank representations of eroticism. Rossetti, Morris, and Swinburne all chose the rival lover, positioning their poetry in opposition to prevailing Christian morality and positioning art in general in opposition to conventional values, drawing battle lines between avantgarde art and middle-class culture. For them the function of art was always to serve beauty, not social duty.

EXTRAVAGANT BOHEMIANISM

When Swinburne left Oxford in 1860 to join with Rossetti and his circle in London, he immediately threw himself into a remarkably productive period of writing, accompanied by an extravagantly bohemian way of life. In addition to drunken sprees with the adventurer-explorer RICHARD BURTON (1821–1890), scandalous behavior at London clubs, and unconventional living arrangements with Rossetti, Swinburne launched attacks on conventional culture on several fronts, including a hoax in which he invented two scurrilous French poets and wrote "excerpts" from their work in order to review them and parody the moral bias of English criticism.

More important work of the time included a splendid but overlooked epistolary novel, *Love's Cross-Currents* (pseudonymously serialized much later, in 1877), and another novel, *Lesbia Brandon*, never completed. But Swinburne was essentially a poet, and his most significant work of the early 1860s included *Chastelard*, the brilliant Aeschylean tragedy *Atalanta in Calydon* (1865), and the remarkable lyrics of his most notorious book, *Poems and Ballads* (1866). All of these works expressed a preference for the rival lover of sensual paganism over ascetic Christianity, most conspicuously in "Laus Veneris," in praise of the pagan Venus; "Hymn to Proserpine," which denigrated the pallid morality of Christ, the "pale Galilean"; and "Dolores," addressed to *"notre dame des sept douleurs,"* substituting a hymn to a dominatrix—"our lady of the seven pains"—for a hymn to the Virgin Mary, "our Lady of the seven sorrows."

The poet was writing from genuine convictions and proclivities, but his poetry was also intended to shock the Victorian audience, and it succeeded spectacularly. He was variously denounced as a satyr and a dirty-minded schoolboy, but his poetic virtuosity forced his contemporaries to take him seriously and sparked a critical debate over the social obligations, if any, of the artist.

Under the cover of classicism, the chorus in *Atalanta* attacked "the supreme evil, God," while "Anactoria" in *Poems and Ballads* vividly presented lesbian and sadistic eroticism in the voice of Sappho. Swinburne's Hellenism was a far cry from the usual Victorian characterization of classical serenity, far closer to Nietzsche's views than to MATTHEW ARNOLD's, and enabled him to attack contemporary Christian ethics from within the high cultural establishment. He

responded to his critics in the press with a lofty assumption of intellectual and scholarly superiority, ultimately unassailable because the plays and poems he had produced were sufficiently powerful and beautiful to command the respect of the highest literary authorities.

MAKING THE CASE FOR AESTHETICISM

The frontal assault on Victorian pieties was most effectively conducted by the blasphemies and eroticism of Swinburne's poetry, but his most profound presentation of the case for aestheticism was offered in his critical writing. This is especially so in his remarkable *William Blake: A Critical Essay* (1868), the first full statement in English of the doctrine of art for art's sake, and Swinburne's fullest statement of his own form of rebellious romanticism, his allegiance to the "church of Blake and Shelley."

Swinburne will always be best remembered for his sudden and shocking attack on conventional values in the early and mid-1860s, for his masterpiece, *Atalanta in Calydon*, and for his substantial influence on late-century aestheticism, but he had a long and distinguished career as a poet and critic and was widely regarded as the greatest living English poet after the deaths of ROBERT BROWNING in 1889 and ALFRED, LORD TENNYSON in 1892. After *Poems and Ballads* Swinburne devoted himself primarily to radical republican poetry in the cause of the establishment of an Italian republic (*A Song of Italy*, 1867; *Songs before Sunrise*, 1871; *Songs of Two Nations*, 1875), to critical essays, to many volumes of brilliant nature poetry, and to his tour de force of Arthurian narrative poetry, *Tristram of Lyonesse* (1882).

See also AESTHETIC MOVEMENT; POETRY.

FURTHER READING

Louis, Margot K. *Swinburne and his Gods: The Roots and Growth of Agnostic Poetry*. Montreal: McGill-Queen's University Press, 1990.

McGann, Jerome. *Swinburne: An Experiment in Criticism*. Chicago: University of Chicago Press, 1971.

Riede, David. *Swinburne: A Study of Romantic Mythmaking*. Charlottesville: University Press of Virginia, 1978.

Rooksby, Rikky. *A. C. Swinburne: A Poet's Life*. Brookfield, Vt.: Ashgate Publishers, 1997.

DAVID RIEDE

SYMONDS, JOHN ADDINGTON

Born: October 5, 1840; Bristol, England
Died: April 19, 1893; Rome, Italy

John Addington Symonds was a prolific historian, critic, poet, and translator and a major cultural arbiter of the Victorian period who wrote hundreds of articles, thousands of letters, and biographies of playwright Ben Jonson, the poet aristocrat Sir Philip Sidney, and Percy Bysshe Shelley. He translated from the Greek, Latin, Italian, German, and French and produced his greatest work, a study of the *Renaissance in Italy* (1875–1886) in seven magisterial volumes, as well as a monumental, still important biography of Michelangelo. He is best remembered today, however, as a fervent believer in a "new chivalry" based on romantic love between men, an idea developed in his classical studies, in *A Problem in Greek Ethics* (1883), and in a more direct treatment of modern HOMOSEXUALITY, or "inversion," as a collaborator with HAVELOCK ELLIS on the important and influential *Studies in the Psychology of Sex, Volume 1: Sexual Inversion* (1896). Much of Symonds's work, and his own life, were dedicated to promoting the concept that homosexuality was not only normal but also a Platonic ideal that should be accepted by society at large.

His adherence to much conventional Victorian morality made Symonds deeply ambivalent about his homosexuality: he had an almost stereotypical upper-middle-class Victorian upbringing, complete with tutors, servants, and education at Harrow and Oxford. His energetic grandfather began teaching him Latin before he was five years old, and his father, a physician, cultivated his son's love of Italian art and Greek sculpture. With his combination of conventional values and aspirations on one hand, and of highly developed intellectual inclinations on the other, Symonds dutifully studied law in London but devoted his best energy to writing for the *SATURDAY REVIEW* during the early 1860s. Thanks to an independent income, he could afford to spend much of his time composing poetry, while fretting that everything he wrote was "grossly autobiographical." During the middle of the 1860s Symonds contributed many articles on the Elizabethan dramatists to prestigious journals such as the *CORNHILL MAGAZINE* and *The Pall Mall Gazette,* and he was recognized as a promising essayist. Married and the father of several daughters, Symonds abandoned all pretense at trying to do anything other than be a literary man and immersed himself in the study of Greek poets, Renaissance artists, philosophy, ethics, poetry, and languages. An inveterate hypochondriac, he was able to cite reasons of health for his decision to live more or less permanently on the Continent, in Switzerland and Italy, for most of his adult life.

CODED HOMOSEXUALITY

Symonds was often ambivalent about his poetry. He felt that the *illus cacoenthes poetandi* ("the craze for writing poetry") alternately overwhelmed him and disappeared throughout his life. He writes in his *Memoirs* (finally published in 1984) that his poetry is highly autobiographical, that homosexual passions are the "preoccupation" of his life, that "literature takes the second place," and that he has "never been able to regard it very seriously." The title of one poem, "Phallus Impudicus," indicates his poetic theme. The poem is filled with words such as *obscenity, mouldering, unwholesome, shame, rude, unlovely, poisonous,* and *loathsome,* yet such words are balanced by the romantic and celebratory: *melodiously, tremulously, aflame with beauty, rapture, splendour,* and *sweetness.* His poetry revels in masculine beauty and depends on coded or "subterranean" phrases and the "cunning falsification of the sexes." He published vol-

Prolific historian, critic, poet, and translator John Addington Symonds.

umes of verse at a furious rate: *Many Moods* appeared in 1878, followed by *New and Old* (1880), *Animi Figuri* (1882), and three volumes in 1884, *Wine, Women, and Song* (translations from *Carmina Burana*, medieval drinking songs), *Fragilia Labilia*, and *Vagabunduli Libellus*. All of these volumes were received with various measures of scorn, dismay, puzzlement, apathy, or revulsion from reviewers, who may have been less than responsive to the "code" of Symonds's covert subject: homosexual love. As a translator of sonnets by Michelangelo and Campanella (1878) and works of Sappho (1885, 1893), Symonds had a sensitive and lyrical voice. Perhaps his most successful translation, though, was not poetry but *The Life of Benvenuto Cellini* (1888), which quickly sold out and went into a second and then a third edition by 1889.

Despite the coded language of his poetry, Symonds could be outspoken about homosexuality and composed two polemical volumes. *A Problem in Greek Ethics* (written in 1873; published in 1883) is the first study in the English language about homosexuality and its history. *A Problem in Modern Ethics* (1891) argued eloquently for the reform of British sodomy laws and posited the theory that "inverts" represented a "third sex," a normal, reasonable, congenital state that should not be considered degenerate. The third sex joined the genders of man and woman as a normative developmental outcome, a "creature healthy and well organized."

In 1892 Symonds approached Havelock Ellis to suggest that they might publish a book together on sexual inversion, a term for homosexuality. Ellis agreed to provide the psychological analysis while Symonds would include a historical study, the conclusion, and some case studies. The men disagreed about the neurotic basis for inversion: Symonds argued for the inclusion of people such as Shakespeare, James I, and Frederick the Great, while Ellis seemed more cautious. Symonds died before the project was completed, but the book was published, first in German and then in English, as a collaborative project. Horatio Brown, Symonds's literary executor, purchased almost the entire English edition in 1897 to avoid embarrassment to the Symonds family. Later that year the book was republished as *Studies in the Psychology of Sex: Vol. 1: Sexual Inversion* by Havelock Ellis. Ellis had expunged some of Symonds's contribution, which he considered insufficiently scientific, but approximately a third of the volume was written by Symonds, although his formal authorship was not revealed publicly.

Today John Addington Symonds might perhaps be best remembered for his memoirs, which were not published during his lifetime; indeed, they were not published without great bowdlerization until 1984. His candid account of a lifelong obsession with the difficulties of being homosexual during the Victorian era casts an important light on a period in which most autobiographies were characterized by reticence and omissions. Symonds seems to have regarded his memoirs as "confessions" akin to those of Rousseau, and they have become a major resource for students and scholars of the history of homosexuality. He hoped that they would ultimately help others who, like himself, struggled with homosexuality. Described by their editor as a "hybrid, falling somewhere between literature and a psychological case history," the *Memoirs* are muddled by Symonds's own contradictions as he oscillates between praising the happiness of his married life, for example, and lamenting the fact that he ever married at all. He changes the names of some people, yet does not obscure the identity of others. He even uses real names at times but asserts that they are not real. Symonds concludes that the "bewildering contradictions, tending to madness" of his life are both an "incurable malady" and a "joy in living" that probably are "commoner than I imagine."

See also ELLIS, HAVELOCK; HOMOSEXUALITY.

FURTHER READING

Grosskurth, Phyllis. *John Addington Symonds: A Biography.* London: Longmans, 1964.

Smith, Timothy d'Arch. *Love in Earnest: Some Notes of the Lives and Writings of English "Uranian" Poets from 1889–1930.* London: Routledge and Kegan Paul, 1970.

Symonds, John Addington. *The Memoirs of John Addington Symonds.* Edited by Phyllis Grosskurth. London: Hutchinson, 1984.

Weeks, Jeffrey. *Coming Out: Homosexual Politics in Britain from the Nineteenth Century to the Present.* London: Quartet Books, 1977.

DAVID RIEDE

SYMONS, ARTHUR

Born: February 28, 1865; Milford Haven, Wales
Died: January 22, 1945; Wittersham, England

As a prominent poet, the most important spokesman for aestheticism in the 1890s, a major influence on the generation of William Butler Yeats (1865–1939) and T. S. Eliot (1888–1965), and editor of the avantgarde literary magazine *The Savoy*, Arthur Symons was among the most important men of letters of the Victorian fin de siècle. He is probably best known as the critic who introduced French symbolism into English letters in *The Symbolist Movement in Literature*

(1900), which was called a "revelation" by T. S. Eliot, and contributed importantly to the modernist aesthetic. Yeats called Symons "the best critic of his generation."

AN UNLIKELY AESTHETE

Symons was an unlikely person to emerge at the head of the literary elite, especially at a time when literature was conspicuously celebrating the freedom of art from moral restraints. As the pious son of a Wesleyan clergyman, Symons was provided with limited educational opportunities and no influential connections. His formal education ended when he left school at the age of 17 in 1882 to educate himself in English literature, a subject not available in the curriculum of the High Street Classical and Mathematical School in Bideford. Very early in life Symons had independently developed a passion for literature, though his earliest literary effort, a poem called "God is good," written at the age of five, did not accurately forecast the development of his talents. While still very young, however, he developed a taste for the poetry of Lord Byron (1788–1824) and then for his own prominent contemporaries, ALGERNON SWINBURNE (1837–1909), ALFRED, LORD TENNYSON, (1809–1892), and ROBERT BROWNING (1812–1889). When the Browning Society was first formed, in 1881, Symons joined immediately and became connected for the first time to the literary life of London. His first publication, an appreciation of Browning's Christian principles, appeared in the *Wesleyan-Methodist Magazine* in 1882. It was a modest beginning but led quickly to further writing projects and led him into acquaintance with many of England's major literary figures, including Browning himself and the age's greatest aesthetic critic, WALTER PATER (1839–1894). At the age of 21 he published his first book, *An Introduction to the Study of Browning* (1886).

Even as he was establishing himself as a critic, Symons was beginning an effective career as a poet in his own right, combining Browning's dramatic technique with Pater's interest in experiencing and rendering intense impressions of fleeting moments. His first collection of poems, *Days and Nights* (1889), established the young Symons as a major poet at the cusp of the fin de siècle. Throughout the following decade Symons was at the center—almost was the center—of literary activity in London. A member of the famous Rhymer's Club, Symons contributed to its two volumes of verse. He also wrote for *The Yellow Book*, but when that magazine determined to purge itself of decadent influences and styles in 1896, Symons founded and edited *The Savoy*, a short-lived

THE GRANGER COLLECTION

Poet Arthur Symons was the era's most important spokesman for aestheticism.

but important journal that brought together the work of exciting young artists such as Yeats, Ernest Dowson (1867–1900), George Moore (1852–1933), and AUBREY BEARDSLEY (1872–1898). Symons was himself responsible for the entire content of the final issue: two essays, a short story, some translations, a poem, and a final selection entitled "A Literary Causerie: By Way of Epilogue," which states that *The Savoy* will discontinue its publications because of lack of financial support and that "art cannot appeal to the multitude. It is wise when it does not attempt to."

THE IMPACT OF FRENCH DECADENCE

Symons's writing during this period included several more books of poetry, *Silhouettes* (1892), *London Nights* (1895), and *Amoris Victima* (1897) and some of his most important critical books. All of this work drew heavily on a three-month stay in Paris in 1890, where Symons explored the culture of museums, cafés, and more dubious establishments and also met the most outstanding French writers of the time, Paul

Verlaine, Stephane Mallarmé, Remy de Gourmont, and Joris Karl Huysmans. His poetry is an illustration of his own critical elaborations of French symbolism—he intended to record the "religion of the eyes" and was, therefore, more intrigued with nuances, impressions, and subtlety than with any kind of polemics, aside from his successful attempts to break from Victorian tradition and imitate the style of the French symbolists.

Symons's poetry from this period fits his own description of Verlaine's: "It is the poetry of sensation, of evocation; poetry which paints as well as sings." The poetry attempts "to fix the last fine shade, the quintessence of things; to fix it fleetingly, to be disembodied voice and yet the voice of a human soul: that is the ideal of Decadence." Also reflecting the French influence, this poetry is erotic, Bohemian, world-weary, and presents such strong images as "The Opium-Smoker," "Javanese Dancers," and female sexuality through women as diverse as a prostitute and a nun. His "Juliet of a night" and his affectionate portraits of other prostitutes caused a good deal of moral disapprobation, and one disgruntled critic inquired, "Why should poetic art be employed to celebrate common fornication?" Despite what Symons termed the "singular unanimity of abuse" that greeted his poetry, he remained interested in "the infernal fascination of Sex." As a critic Symons drew on his knowledge of French literature in the important essay "The Decadent Movement in Literature" (1893), which established him as the leading English authority on French literature and the leading English spokesman of symbolism and DECADENCE.

Symons consolidated his critical prestige and influence with *Studies in Two Literatures* (1897), and especially with *The Symbolist Movement in Literature* (1900), celebrating Verlaine, Mallarmé, Maeterlinck, and others active during the last 30 years of the Victorian era. Influenced by Baudelaire and Poe, these writers revolted against realism to examine sensual evocations, the deepest recesses of the human psyche, and sometimes obscure and personal symbols and metaphors. Symons's attention to their work in his criticism, and his translations and use of their methods in his own poetry, influenced Yeats, Eliot, and the twentieth-century novel.

Symons's career was abruptly halted by a psychotic breakdown in September 1908. Although he continued to publish prolifically, most of his ideas were revisions of earlier works and lacked the lucid brilliance of his younger years. His *Confessions: A Study of Pathology* (1930), an exploration into his own psyche and that of other artists and a study of his break-

down and treatment, is, perhaps, the most notable work he published after his confinement in the cells of jails and mental institutions. He commenced work on a fuller autobiography, but *The Memoirs of Arthur Symons* found a publisher only posthumously in 1977.

Symons lived until 1945, but his most important work was done by the time of his breakdown. In addition to the poetry and criticism of the 1890s, he wrote a book of short stories, *Spiritual Adventures* (1905), and several more volumes of poetry and criticism in the first decade of the twentieth century, but he remains best known as the spokesman of the decadent movement and the French symbolists.

See also DECADENCE; FRANCE; LITERARY CRITICISM; POETRY.

FURTHER READING

Beckson, Karl. *Arthur Symons: A Life.* Oxford: Clarendon Press, 1987.
Dowling, Linda. *Language and Decadence in the Victorian Fin de Siecle.* Princeton: Princeton University Press, 1986.
Markert, Lawrence W. *Arthur Symons: Critic of the Seven Arts.* Ann Arbor, Michigan: UMI Research Press, 1988.

DAVID RIEDE

SYMPHONIES

An increasing number of British composers wrote symphonies during the nineteenth century, but Britain was in no sense a major center of the development of the symphony. British composers worked in the context of a largely Germanic musical aesthetic, and as a consequence British symphonies were successively modeled on Franz Joseph Haydn, Ludwig von Beethoven, Felix Mendelssohn, Robert Schumann, and Johannes Brahms. British composers drew inspiration from both recent and older Germanic music. Thus Sir Julius Benedict's Symphony in G minor of 1873 has several passages where the wraith of Benedict's teacher, Carl Weber, can be heard from long before.

THE PHILHARMONIC SOCIETY

The symphony's history reflects the development and growth of CONCERT LIFE. The pioneering concert-giving organization, the Philharmonic Society in LONDON, founded in 1813, heard symphonies by William Crotch in 1814 and Lord Burghersh in 1818. Five symphonies by Cipriani Potter (1792–1871) were played in 1826–1836 and another two in the 1850s. Potter's pupil George A. Macfarren had a symphony played in 1845, and another of Potter's pupils, William Sterndale Bennett, became conductor of the Society in the 1850s and began playing his own symphonies. Gen-

London's Philharmonic Society, the nation's premier concert-giving organization, performs in 1843 at the Hanover Square Concert Rooms, London.

erally the society did not actively favor British composers, a fact later resulting in the formation of competing organizations such as the Society of British Musicians (1834–1865), which provided a platform for many British composers, though many of the works have not survived. Some of the symphonies performed there have been documented by Simon McVeigh, including examples by William Sterndale Bennett, James Calkin, Thomas Cooke, Charles Lucas, Macfarren, Thomas Molleson Mudie, William Lovell Phillips, Cipriani Potter, and Henry John Westrop.

BRITISH COMPOSERS

The first to produce a significant symphonic oeuvre was Cipriani Potter, who visited Beethoven in Vienna and gave the first performances in England of piano concertos by Mozart and Beethoven. Potter gave up composition at the age of 40, but before then he had composed at least ten symphonies. In 1855 Richard Wagner conducted Potter's tenth symphony in London. Potter's pupil Sir George A. Macfarren composed nine symphonies, but his reputation did not survive

his death; until his fourth and seventh symphonies were issued on compact disc in 1999, he had been completely forgotten.

Possibly the most successful British composer of the midcentury was Sir William Sterndale Bennett. Like his teacher Potter, Sterndale Bennett wrote most of his music when young, spending much of his time later in administration at the Royal Academy of Music. The first four of his five symphonies date from the 1830s; the early Symphony in G minor was warmly commended by Mendelssohn in 1836. His later Symphony in G minor, Op. 43 (1864–1867), was the first British symphony to find a regular place in concert repertoires. Its later success (it was, for example, given 12 times by Dan Godfrey at Bournemouth between 1893 and 1916) was probably due to the fact that it was published in full score and parts, in the days when purchase of a set of parts gave rights of performance. During this time other British composers whose symphonies were given a hearing included William Baly (1847), John Barnett (1837), Charles Edward Horsley (1844), John Lodge Ellerton (two of six,

1845, 1849), and Henry Charles Banister (four symphonies—1847, 1848, 1850, 1853). In 1855 Wagner also conducted Charles Lucas's third and last symphony. Other than the organists Horsley and Ellerton, these were all senior staff members at the Royal Academy. Not all these symphonies survive.

PLAYING AT THE CRYSTAL PALACE

The Crystal Palace became a popular venue for concert life starting in 1885 in its new location at the south London suburb of Sydenham. For 41 years the Saturday Concerts conducted there by August Manns introduced British audiences to most of the romantic orchestral repertoire by the leading composers of the day and premiered an increasing number of new British works. The only British symphony from the midcentury still regularly played, however, is Sir ARTHUR SULLIVAN's *Irish Symphony*, first heard at Crystal Palace in 1865 when he was 23. Less well remembered symphonies from this time include those by Alice Mary Smith (1863), John Francis Barnett (1864), and the teenage Frederic Cowen, whose first two symphonies are now lost. Cowen had a notable success with his Third Symphony, *The Scandinavian*, in 1880. Other British symphonies from the 1870s include two by James Hamilton Clark Smee, two by Sir Julius Benedict, an example by Charles Stephens, and the first two (both at Crystal Palace) of four by the pedagogue Ebeneezer Prout.

Before the rise of the symphonies of Brahms, Antonín Dvořák, and Tchaikovsky, British composers responded to the all-pervasive example of Beethoven, whose stature was promoted by Sir GEORGE GROVE in his Crystal Palace program notes, while Mendelssohn and Schumann framed the tradition in which many of them wrote. In the 1870s Joachim Raff, too, became a potent example, though he was not a model widely followed stylistically. In February 1876 the Alexandra Palace in North London announced a competition for a new symphony, attracting 46 entries. The winner was Frances William Davenport, later professor of harmony and composition at the Royal Academy of Music; Charles Villiers Stanford won second prize with his First Symphony, a score in debt to Schumann, though its first performance at Crystal Palace three years later was its only hearing until it was recorded over a century later.

Stanford and Sir Hubert Parry are the most notable British writers of symphonies in the 1880s and 1890s, Stanford's Third, *The Irish* (1887), being soon published and going literally round the world. It was the British symphony chosen by Gustav Mahler for New

York in 1911. Parry wrote four symphonies in the 1880s, with a fifth in 1912. Similarly, Stanford produced five by 1895, while a sixth appeared in 1906 and a seventh in 1912. The 1880s saw a gathering of strength in the achievement of British symphonies, those by Cowen and Stanford achieving performance and recognition abroad, particularly in Germany. Examples heard at Crystal Palace include the celebrated choral conductor Henry Leslie's (1822–1896) *Chivalry* Symphony; Thomas Wingham's (1846–1893) Fourth (Wingham, professor of piano at the Royal Academy was musical director at the Roman Catholic Brompton Oratory); the last of Macfarren's symphonies, in E minor; Prout's Third and Fourth; Henry Gadsby's *Festal Symphony*, and a solitary example by Barclay Jones, Wingham's successor at Brompton Oratory, whose Symphony in C minor was in memory of his predecessor. The most striking new symphony from this period is the Symphony in C minor by Frederick Cliffe, the professor of piano at the Royal College of Music, by a composer with no previous history of composition. One cannot explain why Cliffe's colleagues at the Royal College of Music never acknowledged his achievement, but he had a remarkable press coverage and enjoyed a brief career as a composer with a widely played Second Symphony in 1892, though only the First was published.

THE END OF THE ERA

The 1890s saw the gradual appearance of a new generation of British composers, notably focused on the teaching of Stanford at the Royal College of Music, which had been established in 1883. These included the Scottish pianist Edward Lamond, whose Symphony in A appeared in 1890, Edward German, whose two symphonies date from 1887 and 1893, and one by Stanford's favorite pupil, the black composer Samuel Coleridge-Taylor (1896). Two earlier grandees of Victorian music, Sir William Cusins, Master of the Queen's Music, and the organist of Chester Cathedral, Joseph Cox Bridge, produced symphonies in 1892 and 1894, respectively.

The young generation of the 1890s presaged the immense stylistic changes that were to come, and scores such as William Wallace's *Creation Symphony* (1898), W. H. Bell's *Walt Whitman Symphony*, Op. 8 (1899), Gustav Holst's *Cotswolds Symphony* (1899–1900), and Cyril Scott's First Symphony (1900) must have seemed very new then, but did not reflect the mature style of their composers' later works. The brilliance and personality of Sir EDWARD ELGAR's First Symphony in 1908, immediately followed by the stylistic changes attendant on impressionism and the Russian ballet, were such that most of the Victorian symphonies, even the few that were then remembered, were forgotten for the next 70 years, their revival on compact disc or in broadcasts only gradually beginning in the 1990s.

See also CONCERT LIFE; MUSIC PROFESSION; ORCHESTRAL MUSIC.

FURTHER READING

Brown, James D., and Stephen S. Stratton. *British Musical Biography: A Dictionary of Musical Artists, Authors and Composers Born in Britain and Its Colonies.* Birmingham: S. S. Stratton, 1897.

Foreman, Lewis, ed. *Music in England 1885–1920 as Recounted in Hazel's Annual.* London: Thames Publishing, 1994.

Foster, Miles Birket. *History of the Philharmonic Society of London 1813–1912.* London: John Lane, The Bodley Head, 1912.

Lloyd, Stephen. *Sir Dan Godfrey: Champion of British Composers.* London: Thames Publishing, 1995.

McVeigh, Simon. "The Society of British Musicians (1834–1865) and the Campaign for Native Talent." In *Music and British Culture, 1785–1914: Essays in Honour of Cyril Ehrlich.* Edited by Christina Bashford and Leanne Langley. 145–168. Oxford: Oxford University Press, 2000.

Temperley, Nicholas. "William Sterndale Bennett 1816–1875 Three Symphonies." In *The Symphony 1720–1840.* 60 vols., Editor-in-chief, Barry S. Brook. New York and London, Garland Publishing, 1982.

Young, Percy M. *A History of British Music.* London: Ernest Benn, 1967.

Young, Percy M. "Orchestral Music." In *The Athlone History of Music in Britain.* Edited by Nicholas Temperley. 358–380. Vol. 5 of *The Romantic Age 1800–1914.* London: Athlone Press, 1981.

LEWIS FOREMAN

TAILORING

In an era when people's lives were being transformed by the impacts of INDUSTRIALIZATION, URBANIZATION, and British imperial expansion, tailoring underwent substantial changes in social, cultural, and technological terms. In a time of radical change in class and gender relations, the tailor became an essential ally in the creation of a socially acceptable appearance. The tailoring industry played a major role in the formulation of the visual identity of British IMPERIALISM both in its military and more subtle, but equally influential, "civilizing" role. Technological improvements facilitated the tailoring industry and made possible mass production and standardization of garments.

Almost all men's clothing in the Victorian era was made by tailoring methods, including that worn for a wide range of informal, formal, sporting, and military occasions. Women's dress was much less reliant on tailoring throughout most of the nineteenth century; however from the 1860s ladies increasingly wore tailored suits or "costumes." Tailoring is therefore crucial to an understanding of changing social identities. By the late nineteenth century the image of the English GENTLEMAN clad in a deftly tailored suit or blazing red imperial military uniform came to epitomize the international spread of civilized ways of life, values, and norms. New stylistic developments in tailoring of this period, in particular the emergence of the modern business suit and the tuxedo, have continued to influence the male and recently the female wardrobe through the present day.

BRITISH TAILORS LEAD THE INDUSTRY

Britain was at the forefront of the international tailoring industry from the late eighteenth century through the early twentieth century. The preeminence of British tailors was to a large extent owing to their superior ability to work wool cloths by steam, stitching, and hand manipulation into the plain, closely fitting styles that remained popular throughout the reign of QUEEN VICTORIA. By the mid-nineteenth century LONDON was established as the international center for men's FASHION. This was primarily due to the rise of Savile Row in the West End of London as an area of tailoring of unrivaled quality and style. The international popularity of British tailored styles and the acceptance of the London-based tailoring industry as an arbiter of taste are indicative of the considerable cultural, social, and political influence of Britain at this period. The best London tailoring establishments were patronized by a truly international clientele, as indicated by the sales records of the leading Savile Row tailors, Henry Poole and Company.

The Victorian era saw the development of the fashionable male wardrobe from one dominated by the formal dress codes associated with the English aristocratic lifestyle to a new, more democratic and informal way of dressing based upon the lounge or modern business suit, a style that was derived from sporting dress. The lounge suit had by 1900 been adopted by British society from the lower levels of the middle class downward as everyday wear. Its adoption at the level of elite international society was widespread, but also more complex, in that codes of social formality still existed but in a more relaxed form. This meant that a short jacket was now acceptable on an increasing number of occasions. For example the tuxedo, which was initially only worn in male company, was worn at informal mixed dinners by 1900. However a frock coat (knee-length and usually double-breasted), morning coat (worn for more formal occasions during the morning or early afternoon), and evening dress coat were still essential purchases for elite gentlemen from American bankers to minor European aristocrats. Jo Barraclough Paoletti identified that the wider American market for menswear between 1880 and 1910 was entirely based upon the occasion-specific British styles noted above. However she also stated that the increasing popularity of the modern, informal lounge suit indicated a shift toward a less elitist and "more American" ideal of masculinity.

TECHNOLOGICAL INNOVATION AND INDUSTRY EXPANSION

The period from 1837 to 1901 was one of substantial change in the design, production, and consumption of tailored clothing. New technological developments at the turn of the nineteenth century, such as the invention of the tape measure and "scientific" cutting systems, facilitated change at all levels of the international tailoring industry. This included tailoring made by custom, made-to-measure, and mass production methods. These different categories primarily refer to the way in which the garments are cut and have major implications as to the price levels and clientele involved. In the Victorian era the British custom tailoring industry was much larger than it is in the twenty-first century as almost all upper- and most middle-class men had their clothes custom made. The growth of the international markets for ready-to-wear tailoring was largely determined by a combination of technological and social factors. For example the middle sections of American society had less resistance to the adoption of this type of clothing than their more class-conscious British equivalents.

The tape measure, which came into common usage in the early nineteenth century, enabled drastic improvements in pattern drafting methods, whereby estimates of a whole series of bodily measures could be taken based on a few basic ones, such as that of the chest, waist, and hip. The development of these scientific cutting methods made it possible to create tailoring that was mass-produced in a series of standard sizes. The sewing machine, invented in the 1840s, further stimulated growth in the ready-made tailoring industry when it came into common usage in the 1850s. The rise of the ready-to-wear industry was also facilitated by the exploitation of tailors at the lower end of the trade, a phenomenon often referred to as *sweating*. This involved a middleman who did no work but employed others out of the payments he received from the tailor's shop. People employed by sweaters had to work longer hours for lower rates than those who worked on the tailor's premises. In Britain many of these "outdoor" workers were immigrants and female workers, who could not get jobs "indoors."

The British tailoring trades underwent a major expansion in the late nineteenth century. In London the number of tailors grew from 34,678 in 1861 to 64,993 in 1911, an increase of 87.4% (compared to an 81% growth for the same period for England and Wales together). This growth was partly linked to developments in the international, colonial markets for civilian and military tailoring, and also to a relative increase in the spending power of the British middle classes during that period.

Throughout the early nineteenth century women's outer garments and riding habits were made by male tailors. However from 1842 to 1881 British establishments such as Charles Creed and John Redfern, which specialized in women's tailoring, opened in London and Paris. Initially only the most emancipated of women wore masculine-influenced tailored suits or "costumes," which consisted of a jacket worn with a long skirt. However by the 1890s ladies' tailored costumes had achieved wide popularity as sporting, leisure, and work attire.

See also FASHION AND CLOTHING; GENTLEMAN; SOCIAL CLASSES; UNIFORMS AND LIVERIES.

FURTHER READING

Anderson, Fiona. "Fashioning the Gentleman: A Study of Henry Poole and Co. Savile Row Tailors 1861–1900." *Fashion Theory: The Journal of Dress, Body and Culture* 4 (2000): 405–426.

Breward, Christopher. *The Hidden Consumer: Masculinities, Fashion and City Life 1860–1914.* Manchester: Manchester University Press, 1999.

Breward, Christopher. "Manliness, Modernity and the Shaping of Male Clothing." In *Body Dressing,* edited by Elizabeth Wilson and Joanne Entwhistle, 165–213. Oxford: Berg, 2001.

Honeyman, K. *Well Suited: A History of the Leeds Clothing Industry 1850–1990.* Oxford: Oxford University Press, 2000.

Kidwell, C., and M. Christman, eds. *Suiting Everyone: The Democratization of Clothing in America.* Washington, D.C.: Smithsonian Institution Press, 1974.

Paoletti, J. B. "Ridicule and Role Models as Factors in American Men's Fashion Change 1880–1900." *Costume* 29 (1985): 121–134.

Schmiechen, James. *Sweated Industries and Sweated Labour.* London: Croom Helm, 1984.

FIONA ANDERSON

TALBOT, WILLIAM HENRY FOX

Born: February 11, 1800; Melbury, England
Died: September 17, 1877; Lacock Abbey, England

Despite his skills as a linguist, botanist, mathematician, Egyptologist, philologist, and scholar of the classics, William Henry Fox Talbot is remembered chiefly for his discovery of a process based on the light sensitivity of silver salts that allowed him to fix photographs from images he achieved with a camera. Although the resulting pictures were less impressively detailed than the crisply defined images of Louis Daguerre (1789–1851), Talbot's work was ultimately to

HULTON/ARCHIVE BY GETTY IMAGES

William Henry Fox Talbot, shown at right in front of his studio near Reading, England, is considered the inventor of photography.

prove the more significant in its development of a negative/positive process that provided the foundation for modern PHOTOGRAPHY. That process—cheaper by far than the process used to render DAGUERREOTYPES and heralding the mass reproduction of the image—eventually permitted photography to become an expressive medium for the middle classes and a powerful agent and symbol of the rise of realism.

Talbot's initial interest in photography grew out of frustration at his inability to sketch scenery while on a honeymoon visit to Lake Como in ITALY. Drawing instruments, such as the camera lucida, and earlier experiments with the camera obscura left him dissatisfied with the inability of his pencil to do justice to the transient images thrown upon the paper by the camera—"fairy pictures," as he recalled in the *Pencil of Nature* (1844), "creations of a moment, and destined as rapidly to fade away. . . . "

During the spring of 1834, he began to experiment with paper, table salt, and silver nitrate, and later that year worked on fixing images with washes of potassium iodide. On sunny days he left small box cameras about the grounds of his home, Lacock Abbey, for half-hour exposures: "when opened," he wrote, "there was in each a miniature picture of the objects before which it had been placed." Surprise news in early 1839 of Daguerre's invention caused him to rush somewhat prematurely to publish his work and display images made from his own method, but when the details of Daguerre's work were made public some seven months later, they proved utterly unlike Talbot's in principle and results.

In September 1840 Talbot developed the calotype, a new negative process that allowed exposure times to be counted in seconds, as opposed to minutes or even hours, and between 1844 and 1846 he published a series of original photographs as examples of his process. But his accomplishment was soon overshadowed by problems with the uneven quality of prints; like the "fairy pictures" at Lake Como, many of the early calotypes began to fade away. Moreover, the complexities of the paper process, coupled with the continuing appeal of the daguerreotype's exquisite details and silvery surface, meant that Talbot's work was of little interest commercially and, though taken up as a hobby by leisured amateurs, who enjoyed working outdoors making pictures of landscapes and architecture, it was initially too expensive and time-consuming for most people.

Significant modifications to both cost and practice, however, such as the introduction of the wet-plate process by Frederick Scott Archer in 1851, led to a virtual explosion of photographic printing from the mid-1850s. While today we may think of formal daguerreotype portraits when we imagine the Victorians, it is to Talbot's early work in the photographic print process that we really owe our sense of visual intimacy with them. His summation of his own contribution to photography is as modest as it is accurate: "I do not profess to have perfected an art but to have commenced one, the limits of which it is not possible at present exactly to ascertain."

See also PHOTOGRAPHY; DAGUERREOTYPE.

FURTHER READING

Buckland, Gail. *Fox Talbot and the Invention of Photography.* Boston: David R. Godine, 1980.

Schaaf, Larry J. *The Photographic Art of William Henry Fox Talbot.* Princeton, N.J.: Princeton University Press, 2000.

Talbot, William Henry Fox. *The Pencil of Nature.* London: Longmans, Brown, Green & Longmans, 1844–1846. Reprint, with essay by Beaumont Newhall, New York: Da Capo Press, 1969.

Weaver, Mike. *Henry Fox Talbot: Selected Texts and Bibliography.* Oxford: Clio Press, 1992.

SELECTED WEB SITE

University of Glasgow. *The Correspondence of William Henry Fox Talbot.*
http://www.foxtalbot.arts.gla.ac.uk/project/project.html

JENNIFER GREEN-LEWIS

TAXATION

The burden of taxation in Victorian Britain was, by today's standards, relatively small. However, taxation was an important concern of the times and the nature and purpose of government revenue formed a significant area of political controversy. At the dawn of the Victorian era, which ushered in an age of ever-expanding industry that had begun with the Industrial Revolution, more than two-thirds of the British government's tax revenue came from the customs and excise duties levied on imported raw materials. Although the tax system was often plagued by lax and inefficient administration, such duties ensured, at least in theory, a secure source of income.

NATIONAL TAXATION

At the beginning of the Victorian era, the central government raised revenues from a number of sources. The introduction of a protective duty on corn imports in 1816 served both as a revenue-raising measure and as protection for domestic agriculturists.

The central government raised 15 percent of tax revenue from stamp duties, augmenting a diverse range of taxes on land and assessed taxes dating back to the seventeenth and eighteenth centuries. These included the Inhabited House tax, a tax on the employment of servants, and the Window tax, which provided around a tenth of tax income. The bricked-up windows that are still seen today in many English period buildings are the legacy of the Window tax.

An income tax had been introduced in 1799 to help fund the war with FRANCE. A much-hated measure, it had been repealed in 1816; however, the 1820s and 1830s brought a consistent campaign for its reintroduction, led by the political economist David Ricardo among others. At this time, too, pressure from the Anti-Corn Law League helped to turn government attention to the possibility of increasing direct at the expense of indirect taxation (an income tax is a direct tax, while a duty on imported goods is an indirect tax). However, it was not until 1842, in the context of an economic crisis and the simultaneous reduction of customs duties on 750 articles, that income tax was reintroduced by Sir ROBERT PEEL's government. The rate was set at seven pence to the pound (2.9 percent) on incomes that were more than £150 a year and, as Martin Daunton has pointed out, "the introduction of the income tax [in 1842] appears in retrospect to be a precursor to Peel's abolition of the CORN LAWS in 1846, although this was not the intention at the time. There was widespread opposition to the income tax in subsequent decades, and attempts by WILLIAM GLADSTONE as Chancellor of the Exchequer, and subsequently Prime Minister, to abolish it, which saw it drop as low as twopence to the pound (0.8 per cent) by 1874—a level that barely justified the cost of collecting it."

Nevertheless, income tax never formed a particularly significant proportion of tax revenue in the Victorian era. In the period between 1871 and 1875, income tax accounted for just 10.3 percent of tax revenue, compared with 71.4 percent from customs and excise duties, and from 1891 to 1895 the respective proportions were 17.2 percent and 60.3 percent. Moreover, only a very small proportion of the population was liable to pay the income tax—approximately 200,000 people at the end of the nineteenth century—whereas indirect taxes also affected working-class consumers, a considerable number of whom had been enfranchised by the REFORM ACTS of 1867 and 1884. The growth of popular political activity in the wake of these extensions to the franchise encouraged the airing of proposals for tax-funded social reform, which would bear legislative fruit in the Edwardian period.

LOCAL TAXATION

Social welfare in the Victorian period, however, was largely the responsibility of local authorities, and the most important element of English local government finance was the poor rate (tax). The NEW POOR LAW of 1834 had confirmed the existing principle that poor relief should be provided at a local level, and although the reform brought parishes together to form Poor Law Unions in the interests of improved administrative efficiency, the responsibility for meeting the cost of PAUPERISM remained with the parishes. This obviously unfair system, whereby the poorest parishes were burdened with paying the highest poor rates, was modified in 1865 by the Union Chargeability Act, which laid down that rate assessments would be carried out at the level of the Union rather than the individual parish. Further changes to the burden of local taxation included the EDUCATION ACT OF 1870, which established local school boards empowered to levy a rate to support the establishment and running of schools.

TAX REFORM

Despite these modifications to the system of taxation and rating, by the late nineteenth century both central and local government finances were in crisis. The introduction of union chargeability failed to remove significant inequalities in the rate burden of different Poor Law Unions, and the increasing demands of supporting the poor had caused local government costs to swell. Poor law expenditure increased at a significant rate in the 1880s and early 1890s, and local authorities grew increasingly reliant on central government subsidies. A combination of these increasing subsidies and the heavy cost of financing the ROYAL NAVY caused a crisis of central government expenditure. This was further intensified by the expense of the second BOER WAR (1899–1902), to the extent that annual government expenditure, which had stood at £83 million in 1880, rose to a peak of £195 million during the war.

One response to increased government spending was the reform of death duties in Sir William Harcourt's budget of 1894. This measure introduced the principle of graduation—not yet extended to the income tax—thus substantially raising the revenue available from this source. The 1894 budget has been viewed as a landmark in the history of British taxation: it also introduced a surtax on very large incomes, thus embodying, albeit unwittingly, the principle that the state has a moral right to a share in the wealth of the nation. Harcourt told the House of Commons that "the title of the state to a share in the accumulated property of the deceased is an anterior title to that of the interest to be taken by those who are to share in it." It can be argued that this budget marked a decisive shift in the balance between direct and indirect taxation in Britain, although it was not until the early 1910s that direct tax revenue finally outstripped customs and excise income.

However, in the late Victorian period there were also growing calls for a reintroduction of protection through increased import duties. These calls for "Fair Trade," which ultimately led to JOSEPH CHAMBERLAIN'S Tariff Reform campaign of 1903, resulted from the experience of the Great Depression that began around 1873 and brought a relative decline to the British economy. Protectionists focused on the use of tariffs to protect British industry and AGRICULTURE, but campaigners also justified protection as a revenue-raising measure. Joseph Chamberlain hoped to use import duties to support a scheme of old-age pensions, for example.

Revitalized radicalism and the emergence of the Independent Labour Party during the 1880s and 1890s highlighted the extent to which taxation could be used as a social instrument. The insistence on the part of Liberals, and many Unionists, on the maintenance of FREE TRADE encouraged social reformers on the left of British politics to look to direct taxation, especially land taxes and the income tax, for the support of social reform. Despite its continuing unpopularity, income tax has remained a continuous feature of British financial life ever since Peel reintroduced it and, by 1900, a series of late century increases brought the rate of taxation to 14 pence to the pound (5.8 percent) in 1900.

FURTHER READING

Daunton, Martin. *Trusting Leviathan: The Politics of Taxation in Britain 1799–1914.* Cambridge: Cambridge University Press, 2001.

Harris, Jose. "The Transition to High Politics in English Social Policy 1880–1914." In *High and Low Politics in Modern Britain: Ten Studies.* Edited by Michael Bentley and John Stevenson. Oxford: Clarendon Press, 1983.

Sabine, B. E. V. *A Short History of Taxation.* London: Butterworths, 1980.

Sabine, B. E. V. *A History of Income Tax.* London: Allen and Unwin, 1966.

MARK FREEMAN

TAYLOR, TOM

Born: October 19, 1817; Bishop-Wearmouth, England
Died: July 12, 1880; London, England

Best known to his contemporaries as a prolific playwright and an editor the famous magazine *PUNCH*, Tom Taylor was also a journalist, art critic, lawyer, and bureaucrat. Born near the northern industrial city of Sunderland, Taylor arrived in London in 1844 after attending the University of Glasgow and Trinity College, Cambridge. His B.A. (1840) and M.A. (1843) degrees from Cambridge qualified him for his appointment in 1845 as professor of English literature and language at London University, a post he held for two years. Taylor also studied law at the Inner Temple from 1844. He was called to the bar (qualified as a barrister, a trial lawyer) in late 1846 and practiced on the northern circuit of local courts for four years.

During his first two years in London, Taylor established himself as a writer of light stage entertainments. From 1844 to 1845 he collaborated with the minor dramatists Albert Smith, Charles Kenney, and others on a farce and three burlesques staged by Mary and Robert Keeley at the Lyceum Theatre. He also turned to JOURNALISM, publishing in NEWSPAPERS such as the *Morning Chronicle* and the *Daily News* and PERIODICALS such as the *Illuminated Magazine* and *Puck*. He made his first contribution to *Punch* in 1844. And in 1848 he became an art, literature, and THEATER critic for *THE TIMES*.

Taylor returned to live and work in London year-round in 1850, when he accepted the position of assistant secretary to the Board of Health, newly created under the Public Health Act of 1848. He was named secretary in 1854 and held the position until he retired in 1871. He also continued to contribute to *Punch*, *The Times*, and (as an art critic) the *Graphic*. He compiled a biography of Benjamin Robert Haydon (1786–1846) from the artist's papers in 1853, edited the historical painter Charles Robert Leslie's autobiography in 1860, and finished Leslie's biography of the painter Joshua Reynolds in 1865. From 1874 until his death, he was editor of *Punch*.

But Taylor's primary focus remained the stage. During his thirty-six-year career he wrote or collaborated on more than 75 plays, from burlesques to verse dramas. His *The Ticket-of-Leave Man* (1863) is considered his best, but in adapting Édouard Brisebarre and Eugène Nus's play *Léonard* (1862) by infusing it with a gritty London realism, Taylor also created one of the earliest English stage DETECTIVES, Hawkshaw. Although much of the play is standard mid-Victorian MELODRAMA in its plot and characters, theater historian Michael R. Booth argues that "Taylor shaped a drama refreshingly different in spirit and humanity from the mass of its contemporaries." The play had 407 consecutive performances at the Olympic Theatre in 1863-1864 and was revived in London at least four times before 1890.

Taylor's plays show a surprising range and most—from the comedy *Masks and Faces* (1842) to the historical verse drama *Lady Clancarty* (1874)—were commercial successes. He also adapted several contemporary novels for the stage, including CHARLES DICKENS's *A Tale of Two Cities* in 1860 and, with Mark Lemon, Harriet Beecher Stowe's *Uncle Tom's Cabin* in 1852. In the twenty-first century however his work draws little critical interest. Beyond *The Ticket-of-Leave Man*, Taylor is perhaps best known for his popular comedy *Our American Cousin* (1858), largely because American president Abraham Lincoln was shot during a performance of the show in Washington, D.C., in 1865.

See also MELODRAMA; THEATER.

FURTHER READING

Booth, Michael R., ed. *English Plays of the Nineteenth Century. II: Dramas 1850–1900.* Oxford: Clarendon Press, 1969.

Price, G. G. *A History of Punch.* London: William Collins, 1957.

Taylor, Tom. *Plays.* Edited by Martin Banham. Cambridge: Cambridge University Press, 1985.

Tolles, Winton. *Tom Taylor and the Victorian Drama.* New York: Columbia University Press, 1940.

JOHN E. LUEBERING

TEA

Tea—indelibly associated with the temperament and habits of the English, who were renowned for promoting "a nice cup of tea" as the panacea for all ills, a source of strength in a crisis, a thirst-quencher, and a social accessory—became firmly established as the national drink of England during the course of the nineteenth century. Cheering but non-inebriating, tea carried significant associations of respectability, moderation, and civilized conviviality, in tune with the outwardly restrained moral climate of QUEEN VICTORIA's reign. Tea became an item of mass consumption to be enjoyed by all classes and generated new institutions and social practices. As a common ritual of everyday life and an adjunct to the DIET of both rich and poor, this widely popular beverage developed into a high-volume commodity that was in the forefront of late-nineteenth-century innovations in mass marketing.

THE PEOPLE'S DRINK

Tea appears to have been first introduced into England in the early seventeenth century as an exotic import from China. Originally an expensive luxury for the indulgence of the rich and fashionable, the new drink was rapidly popularized during the eighteenth century as part of a general boom in consumption. Adopted by the middle classes as a sign of aspirant gentility, the beverage then became an affordable extra for working people. By the early 1800s tea was replacing beer at breakfast, and what had been an occasional pleasure was soon transformed into a regular ingredient of the popular diet. It fortified and refreshed workers, exhausted by the severe demands of a new industrial work discipline and the privations of the new manufacturing towns. In the same period tea became a staple among the Irish peasantry, another beleaguered class. Brewed by infusing its leaves in boiling water (which offered protection from polluted water supplies), hot tea relieved fatigue and warmed the body in cold conditions such as unheated buildings and bad weather.

Depressed wage levels and a high tax on tea reduced consumption in the first decades of the nineteenth century, but there was a marked rise in the 1840s when, despite the label of "the hungry Forties," there was some improvement in economic conditions. In 1853 WILLIAM GLADSTONE, an advocate of both temperance and FREE TRADE and a confirmed tea drinker, initiated lower taxes on the commodity. This, combined with better wages for the working class, contributed to the most dramatic and sustained leap in tea consumption, which rose from an annual two pounds per head in 1851 to six pounds in 1900, greatly outstripping its competitor, coffee.

SUGAR, a cheap import from Britain's Caribbean colonies, now became the automatic additive to the cup of tea (as to much else). While sugar added appeal to the taste of tea and proved a source of energy, it also contributed to the bad teeth that became a conspicuous feature of the English—one of several indicators of the extent to which the tea-drinking habit had become embedded in the national way of life at home, and in factories and offices where the "tea break" became a more regular feature of the working day.

However comforting the beverage was found to be, a great deal of the tea sold in the general market in the first half of the century was of inferior quality, subject, like many other foodstuffs, to gross adulteration. Reformer HENRY MAYHEW reported several factories in London that recycled tea leaves—"facing" them, as the trade term put it, with black lead and other toxic chemicals. (A perquisite of poorly paid domestic servants employed in the big houses was the sale of used tea leaves from the back door.) Tea substitutes were compounded from the leaves of trees and plants, curled and colored on copper plates, and tea of whatever kind might be stretched with sand, iron filings, or licorice. During hard times, the poor devised their own substitute by pouring boiling water over burnt crusts of bread. Working people established some defense against adulteration in the 1840s with the founding of the Cooperative movement, whose grocery stores assured the purity as well as the cheapness of their provisions and became leaders in the tea trade.

Commonly sold loose, tea was first marketed in brand-named packages in the 1820s by Hornimans the Quakers, a practice that was widespread by the 1850s and afforded some guarantee of quality. There was a further and general improvement in the trade with the implementation of the Food and Drugs Act of 1875.

By the late nineteenth century new sources of supply and mass marketing assured consumers of an abundance of cheap, better-quality tea. From the 1870s the home market was dominated by the products of the EMPIRE, as the tea industry opened up in INDIA and Ceylon. The delicate green teas of China were supplanted by the darker, more robust, and fuller-flavored teas of the subcontinent, which were taken with milk. By the 1880s large new grocery chains boosted tea sales by employing extensive advertising of brand names and nationwide distribution. Scottish merchant Thomas Lipton (1850–1931), who was a pioneer in such retailing innovations, advertised tea from his own plantations as "Rich, Pure and Fragrant" and discreetly exploited his appointment as official purveyor to Her Majesty the Queen. By 1990 Lipton had a hundred stores selling a million packets of tea a week.

Tea, the great British drink, was advertised heavily late in the nineteenth century. In this 1893 advertisement the united forces of Chinese, English, and Scottish workers bring tea to a fatigued lady.

TEA AND TEMPERANCE

Another strong promoter of tea was the TEMPERANCE MOVEMENT that emerged in the 1830s. Tea and coffee were served at meetings as healthy and rational alternatives to ALCOHOL, and the new teetotalers claimed to have invented the soirée, or evening tea party, designed to supersede the drunken rituals of the upper class dinner party. In the 1860s reformers opened temperance PUBS and MUSIC HALLS, attempting to retain the conviviality of the originals while substituting tea and coffee for their traditional fuel of strong drink. Though these experiments mostly failed, they identified the need for new resorts of cheap, popular refreshment for the increasing social traffic of the big cities and the growing armies of commuters. By the 1880s catering entrepreneurs had turned the idea into commercial success with the establishment of the tea shop. Like the new grocery stores, the tea shop multiplied in chains such as the Aerated Bread Company (ABC) and the Lyons Corner House—or "Joe Lyons" as it was affectionately called—which had nearly a hundred tea shops in London alone by 1910. In the music halls, popular songs that had long celebrated the pleasure of strong drink now enthused about tea shops and the pretty girls among their waitresses and customers. Tea was thus romanticized as well as purified, for the tea shop or café, like the new department store, was one of the few places of public resort in the Victorian city where women could go without compromising their respectability. By the 1880s London's West End boasted a number of tea shops, genteel environments generally owned and managed by women, and catering primarily or exclusively to female customers.

The strong domestic and feminine associations that tea had carried from its earliest days had given birth in the 1840s to a new social custom: afternoon tea. Its appearance was (perhaps apocryphally) credited to a duchess, but it was not until 1868 that the queen instituted the royal garden party (continued by her successors to the present day), which was in effect a tea party. Afternoon tea began as a stopgap for the upper classes in the increasingly lengthy interval between the times of luncheon and dinner, and was served with dainty snacks. Beginning as a private occasion among women, its ritual ceremony elevated the function of the hostess and reaffirmed the fashionable over the homely status of tea drinking. By the end of the century, however, afternoon tea, while retaining vestiges of gentility, was commonly available to all in tea shops and restaurants. Similarly well established on the menu by then was "high tea,"

served in the late afternoon and a more substantial affair approximating a main meal. Taken most often on Sundays and holidays by the better-off members of the working and lower-middle classes in the industrial North, high tea became an almost sacramental tribute to good living in what has come to be regarded as a traditional working-class way of life. The simple designation "tea" also came to denote the main evening meal in many humbler households, with dinner eaten at midday—a further example of the extent to which one simple commodity had transformed the patterns of everyday life and been absorbed into the discourse and practice of British culture.

See also DIET; INTERNATIONAL TRADE; TEMPERANCE MOVEMENT.

FURTHER READING

Burnett, John. *Liquid Pleasures: A Social History of Drinks in Modern Britain.* London: Routledge, 1999.
Mennell, Robert O. *Tea: An Historical Sketch.* London: E. Wilson, 1926.
Willson, K. C., and M. N. Clifford, eds. *Tea: Cultivation to Consumption.* London and New York: Chapman and Hall, 1992.

PETER BAILEY

TECHNOLOGY

In the early industrial Victorian decades, the 1830s to the 1850s, the advent of technology meant the multiplying and the enhancing of human power, replacing what had been done by hand and even by the human intellect by the machine. Waterwheels gave way to the steam engine; the hand loom was supplanted by the power loom, the stagecoach by the RAILWAY, and the sailing ship by the steamship. Calculating by human "computers" could now be done by a calculating engine. Machine technology meant bobbins and looms operating automatically, self-acting machines in Victorian parlance, tended by men, and women and small children; the steam hammer shaping huge pieces of metal with power and precision; steam-powered lathes able to turn metal into exact interchangeable forms and to carve wood into delicate designs with tireless repetition. Primarily, technology meant the railway—the smoky train moving across the pastoral landscape and dashing through storms; locomotives racing over city streets on viaducts; the passenger train peacefully carrying commuters from SUBURB to city. Through the power of ELECTRICITY words were flashed over telegraph wires throughout England.

To the early Victorians technology also meant the degradation of daily life, the erasure of the natural and of the authentically human. The system of industrial capitalism that organized the power of the new technologies generated an entirely new class, the urban INDUSTRIAL WORKER or proletariat, who had moved from the countryside to the city to live in overcrowded HOUSING and to die from DISEASES caused by the lack of SANITATION. The release from the social constraints of traditional village life appeared to generate sexual anarchy in the manufacturing towns. These men, women, and children worked long hours six days a week in the textile mills where the air was filled with cotton dust or "fluff." Adults and children tending unfenced machinery were, in the words of an article in CHARLES DICKENS's *Household Words*, "Ground in the Mill." The smoke from steam engines settled over the great manufacturing towns dirtying the air and obliterating light; the rivers turned a sullen color from industrial waste; the enclosed carriage of the speeding train cut off contact with the natural world. Mechanical reproduction eliminated the craft of the hand and the skill of the eye. Even the intellect was supplanted by a calculating engine and even a thinking machine, an Analytical Engine. In the periodic unemployment produced by the business cycle, workers and their families starved since there was no relief provided by government. In an often violent struggle with the owners of the new machines, the workers organized, engaged in strikes.

In these decades, technologies that had been gestating through the late eighteenth and early nineteenth century fused synergistically into a system that initiated a continuing surge of technological innovation. Powering this transformation was the steam engine, the dominant technology of the first industrial era. The steam engine, whose first function had been as a stationary pumping engine in rural coal mines and whose efficiency had been continuously improved by such figures as James Watt (1736–1819), was increasingly applied to the spinning of the bobbins, the pulling back of the looms as the repetitive movements of improved textile machinery were linked to the reliable power of steam. Then, too, the steam engine itself became mobile, pulling carriages along a track; the first railway to use only steam-powered locomotives began operation between MANCHESTER and Liverpool in 1830. By 1850 England had over 6,000 miles of track. The railway transported coal to the steam engines of the city, moved finished goods to markets and to seaports. With the coming of the railway, cotton mills no longer needed to be near waterfalls nor iron foundries near coal seams. The sites of production moved from the cottages of hand-loom weavers and large workshops on the banks of fast-moving streams to the city, thus creating the centralized technological efficiency of the FACTORY. There arose, quite suddenly, the great industrial cities of Manchester and Birmingham, Sheffield and Leeds. Between 1801 and 1831 the population of Manchester doubled.

PUBLIC FASCINATION WITH TECHNOLOGY

The response to this world created by these new technologies was astonishment at the extent and wonder at the velocity of the transformation. The vocabulary of fantasy and magic came readily to the imagination as if genie or enchanter had called up railways and cities and automatic machines from nothingness. And with this amazement, there came fascination, a desire to view, to examine, and to report on the great cities of the Midlands, now a short railway journey northward from London. The Black Country, as the industrial areas were termed, became the destination of middle-class techno-tourists. Dickens traveled from London to gather information on striking workers in Preston for the writing of *Hard Times* (1854). Friedrich Engels (1820–1895), who traveled from Germany, recorded the appalling conditions of life in Manchester in *The Condition of the Working Class in England* (1845). For the inquisitive middle-class reader there emerged a vast literature of periodical articles, fiction, and treatises devoted to explaining, illustrating, and commenting on the new technologies. Those who could not travel to the Midlands could see advance technology at exhibitions in LONDON, shows that culminated at the midpoint of the century in the GREAT EXHIBITION OF 1851, "The Industry of All Nations" held in an iron and glass building, the Crystal Palace. There the departments devoted to machinery saw thousands of visitors of all classes gathered around such technological marvels as a marine steam engine of 700 horsepower and the Great Hydraulic Press.

The stream of books and periodicals in the Victorian period was itself a manifestation of the new technological age that was so often its topic. The application of steam power to the printing press, new mechanical processes for making paper from wood pulp, stereotyping, and improvements in printing machinery, such as rotary printing, multiplied the mechanical reproduction of the written word, enabling the astonishing scale of the print culture that defines the period. The monthly numbers of a Dickens novel reached as much as 50,000 copies.

The print culture of the Victorians both recorded and shaped the deep controversies over the uses of the new technologies. Some early Victorian commentators were intensely hostile to what THOMAS CARLYLE (1795–1881) called "the Mechanical Age, the Age of Machinery, in every outward and inward sense of that term." Led by Carlyle and BENJAMIN DISRAELI (1804–1881) some social critics called for factory owners to adopt a paternalism modeled on the pre-industrial past, on the ties of mutual responsibility exemplified in the monasteries and the feudal system of medieval England. Such ties of loyalty and duty between industrialist and worker would replace a POLITICAL ECONOMY where profit was the only value and wages for labor the only social tie, and that rejected any government regulation of wages and hours, working conditions, or pollution.

Some industrialists, such as ROBERT OWEN (1771–1858) at New Lanark in the first decades of the century and Lord Lever at Port Sunlight at the end of the century did build model communities providing high-quality housing, schools, and health care for their workers. But, generally speaking, the Victorians did not put paternalism into practice. Nor were the Victorians Luddites, opponents of technological innovation named after a movement of craft workers in the North at the initiatory moment of mechanization, the 1810s, who killed mill owners and smashed the new textile machinery that was displacing the hand-loom weavers. Rather the dominant Victorian ideology that engaged what was termed the machinery question, the problem of how to deal with the unprecedented social effects of steam-powered self-acting machines, sought not to impede but to stimulate technological innovation while meliorating such destructive phenomena as child labor and unfenced machinery.

The dominant Victorian response to the relation of technological innovation to social change was grounded in two interrelated assumptions that have continued into our own time. The first was technological determinism, the notion that technological development is autonomous rather than shaped by social priorities, driven by its own internal logic. The evolution of machinery is seen as inevitable and will move at maximum pace only if government does not interfere with inventors. However, one government regulation was ardently advocated, a patent system that would encourage innovation by allowing the inventor to retain the profits of his enterprise. Technologists often pointed to the rapid pace of technological progress in England where freedom for individual genius was encouraged, as compared to the Continent, where science and technology were under centralized government control.

Linked to this determinism was the assumption that the growth of technology is ultimately beneficial to the population. Social problems, such as unemployment caused by the replacement of human workers by machines, are only transitory. Although some commentators, such as Peter Gaskell in *Artisans and Machinery: The Moral and Physical Condition of the Manufacturing Population Considered with Reference to Mechanical Substitutes for Human Labour* (1836) pointed to the suffering of the displaced hand-loom weavers and other victims of technological unemployment, others justified the new machinery under unfettered laissez-faire as eventually increasing employment and human happiness. CHARLES BABBAGE's enormously popular *On the Economy of Machinery and Manufactures* (1832) explained and celebrated the benefits of the new industrial technology to a large, eager, and sympathetic reading public, as did Andrew Ure's *The Philosophy of Manufactures: or, An Exposition of the Scientific, Moral, and Commercial Economy of the Factory System of Great Britain* (1835) and HARRIET MARTINEAU's *Illustrations of Political Economy* (1832–34).

As the Victorian literature of technology in books and in popular periodicals demonstrates (the *Illustrated London News* is itself a fine illustration) for the middle class, if not for the machine-tenders themselves, the latest technologies were a source of pleasure and delight. The Victorians conceived of locomotives, looms, printing presses, and steamships as prostheses, mechanical additions to the human body that enabled enormous enhancements of human force and of human intellect. Although indicating a lack in the human body, as in a prosthetic or artificial limb, the notion of technology as prosthesis primarily signified to the Victorians the augmentation of bodily powers, as exemplified in a favorite Victorian example, the steam hammer whose metal arm acting with enormous power and great delicacy seemed spliced with the arm of the human operator. Thus the Victorians represented sophisticated machinery as a fusion of the mechanical and the human. Victorians such as Ure imagined the factory itself, and even the entire English factory system, as an immense entity made of machines and human beings, "a vast automaton, composed of various mechanical and intellectual organs."

LIVING MACHINES

From the earliest encounters with power looms and steam engines operating tirelessly and regulating themselves without human interference, the Victorians perceived technology in a way familiar, if not overly familiar, to the modern view. They saw sophisticated machinery as somehow animate, as if it had a kind of vitality, an aliveness akin to the human. There emerged, then, in the literature of technology and in industrial fictions such as Dickens's *Hard Times*, the sense of the living machine, the self-acting machine as an entity situated between the animate and the purely mechanical. If the Victorians did not feel the intense fear of the intelligent machine that is the staple of science-fiction nightmares and instead saw the automatic loom as a wonder and an enhancement of the human, it was because they did not conceive of the self-acting machine as self-generated but rather as an entity that had been fashioned by and could remain under the direction and control of human intellect.

The creation of what seemed to be living machines destabilized the traditional boundary or distinction between the uniquely organic or human and the nonliving or mechanical. With the automatic action of the power loom, particularly of the Jacquard loom where the weaving of varied designs was programmed by punched-paper cards, the idea of the human as sentient automaton, a mechanical apparatus of bones and muscles powered by a brain, seemed to have been given material form. But as the century progressed, the notion of the mechanical body gave way to a reconceptualization of the body modeled on the steam engine and the electric motor, an entity that ingests fuel or food and whose work or activity requires an expenditure of this fuel. Thus the laboring body was reimagined as endangered by energy depletion or fatigue as fuel is consumed. With this new view of worker as engine emerged a labor policy that sought to regulate or govern work so as to maximize the productive expenditure of energy. For the human being as human motor, in the factory and in life outside, fatigue became the central malaise of the industrial age.

The epitome of Victorian technology replicating what had traditionally been understood as exclusively human was Babbage's Difference Engine and Analytical Engine, machines of gears and spinning rods that duplicated the operation of human intellect. In the never-completed Difference Engine, Babbage applied industrial methods to human mental processes in order to, in his words, "calculate by steam." Making mechanical what had been mental, the Difference Engine was self-acting; once started the Difference Engine continued to calculate without the need for human intervention. The never-built Analytical Engine, a general thinking machine, was designed on the model of the Jacquard loom as a proto-computer, its memory programmed by punched-paper cards to perform a variety of intellectual functions.

Widely known and widely admired for his calculating and thinking machines, Babbage exemplifies the Victorian ideal of the technologist, "mechanist" to use the nineteenth-century term, as hero. The admiration of technology generated a multitude of such celebrated figures, true heroes within the historical narrative of the English nation's rise to greatness. Among the venerated men within this pantheon were James Watt, considered to be the inventor of the steam engine; Richard Arkwright (1732–1792) who developed water-powered spinning and carding machines as well as establishing early textile mills; GEORGE STEPHENSON (1781–1848), known as the inventor of the steam locomotive and developer of the first railways; ISAMBARD KINGDOM BRUNEL (1806–1859), the builder of the Great Western railway and of such ocean-crossing steamships as the *Great Western*. These men, and they were all men, were transformed into secular saints within the Victorian imagination, for the inventor was imagined as manifesting the divinity of man by imitating the divine power residing within men, creating living machines in a manner corresponding to God creating living beings in Eden.

CRITICISM OF TECHNOLOGY

There was, of course, a powerful Victorian counterargument to the pervasive admiration of machine technology, a set of beliefs articulated in the writing of John Ruskin and put into practice by WILLIAM MORRIS and his followers in the ARTS AND CRAFTS MOVEMENT late in the century. In this view, automatic machinery such as the Jacquard loom had not enhanced, but rather destroyed what is uniquely human, that is, the divine creative power expressed through handwork and made visible in the irregularity of the handmade product. For the Ruskinians, the truly human and the true manifestation of the divinity of man is exemplified in the irregular carved forms on the facades and capitals of Gothic cathedrals chiseled by ordinary working men, rather than in the regular, repetitive products of the power loom and mechanical lathe that body forth the transformation of machine-tender into machine. Thus, from the capacity of the machine for exact replication emerged, as a reaction, the cultural validation of the inexact, the imperfect, the unique, the handmade. To employ Walter Benjamin's influential formulation, the age of mechanical reproduction brought about the validation of the work of art as a unique object informed by an "aura." More generally, to cite the influential work of Raymond Williams, what we now called "culture," as the term refers to the arts and to a humanist definition of the self as articulated in the writing of MATTHEW ARNOLD, validates activities by their difference from industrial practices, notably the work of the scientist and the technologist. For most Victorians, then, fine art and ARCHITECTURE considered as a high art came to be associated with preindustrial eras. MUSEUMS and public buildings in the manufacturing towns were dignified by being built with the columns and pediments of classical architecture. The polychrome, turreted, highly decorated facades of what came to be called Ruskinian or Victorian Gothic were seen as providing religious resonance to public structures, of which the Albert Memorial, QUEEN VICTORIA's monument to her late husband, is the prime example.

MARRIAGE OF ART AND INDUSTRY

As influential as the Victorian definition of high culture as the opposite of the industrial and the technological has been down to modern eras, there also emerged in the period from what might be termed the Victorian culture of technology a contrasting and equally influential set of ideas, a view that saw beauty and value in the machine and in its products. The enormous admiring crowds at the departments of machinery at the Great Exhibition and the mechanists in their writing saw specific forms of beauty in the technologies of their time. Massive engines bodied forth the intellect of the designer and the Platonic beauty of mathematics. The quick, accurate interlocking movement of gears and rods was likened to a dance, to dancing metal. The great iron and glass hall, the Crystal Palace, that rose so swiftly in London's Hyde Park seemed a piece of magic, employing the industrial practices of accurate mass reproduction and interchangeable parts. If the Ruskinians inveighed against such buildings as mere engineering, the Crystal Palace, along with the similar iron and glass train sheds of metropolitan railway stations, exemplified to an appreciative public the rationality that designed the sophisticated technologies of the nineteenth century and prefigured the functionalist machine aesthetic of our time.

Victorian practice, however, saw the coexistence of the opposed visual and aesthetic cultures generated by technology. In factories, stationary steam engines were often supported by fluted classical columns. The great railway stations of London had facades in Egyptian or Gothic style through which passengers moved to the vaulted iron and glass train sheds supported by prefabricated cast-iron columns crowned with cast-iron Corinthian capitals. The Oxford University Museum of Natural History completed in 1859 fused an interior iron and glass exhibition hall with a Gothic facade; the stonework was hand-carved by Irish craftsmen.

Along with the self-acting machine and steam power, the electric TELEGRAPH appeared as another technological wonder. Invented in the late 1830s in both England and America, the telegraph instantaneously transmitted words as coded electrical impulses over a constantly expanding network of wires The effects were transformative, and widely admired. The telegraph was crucial to the functioning of the railway, for only electricity could convey information more quickly than the speeding steam locomotives, another example of Victorian technology considered as a system rather than as single isolated devices. With the fusion of the railway and the telegraph, time itself, formerly varying by locality, became standardized through the nation in what was termed "railway time." The Victorians themselves likened the network of wires to the nerves of the body politic. News—financial, political, and personal—could be transmitted quickly, widely, accurately. The telegraph announced the birth of Queen Victoria's second son at Windsor in August 1844. By the 1850s sending telegrams was commonplace among the general public. In the late 1860s, cable was laid under the Atlantic linking England and the UNITED STATES, a technological feat celebrated for binding together the two great Anglo-Saxon nations. Telegraph lines spread outward from England in the 1870s in a complex net of underground and undersea cable connecting the metropolitan center with such imperial outposts as EGYPT and INDIA and allowing greater centralized control of the empire. If "What Hath God Wrought" was the first intercity telegraph message sent by Samuel Morse in America, the answer might be that this technology wrought a worldwide system of communication long before the Internet.

Since the telegraph was a clean technology and except for the wires overhead almost invisible, opposition was muted. The telegraph operator, with his or her skill with the telegraph key, linked to others in a mysterious web became a technological elite, the operation of telegraphy seen, too, as almost magical. The literary response to telegraphy was complex as writers assimilated this new modality of communication at a distance. Some, such as Dickens, saw in the web of the telegraph a manifestation of the invisible ties that linked the high and the low in English society in a social web that has no center. Writers saw in the crisp, unadorned language of the telegram a model for a transparent realist prose. Other texts found in the electric impulses flowing through copper wire and between lovers an analogy for erotic feelings flowing through the nerves of the body.

Early in the nineteenth century, electricity had been imagined as the vital energy of the organic, the galvanism that animates Frankenstein's creature. As the century drew on, electricity came gradually to become the benevolent energizing force for technologies. By the end of the century the electric motor had come to replace the steam engine in many sites, even in the railway locomotive. With the invention of the filament incandescent bulb in the 1870s and advances in the mass transmission of power over distance, by the last decades of the nineteenth century electric energy brilliantly lit city streets, public buildings, and even the private home. If the early technology had annihilated space and time, electric LIGHTING had eliminated not only gaslights but also darkness itself.

See also LIGHTING; FACTORIES; PROGRESS; TELEGRAPH, THE.

FURTHER READING

Benjamin, Walter. "The Work of Art in the Age of Mechanical Reproduction." *Illuminations.* New York: Schocken, 1969.

Berg, Maxine. *The Machinery Question and the Making of Political Economy, 1815–1848.* Cambridge: Cambridge University Prcss, 1980.

Cardwell, Donald. *The Norton History of Technology.* New York: Norton, 1994.

Freeman, Michael. *Railways and the Victorian Imagination.* New Haven: Yale University Press, 1999.

Kern, Stephen. *The Culture of Space and Time 1880–1918.* Cambridge: Harvard University Press, 1983.

Mayr, Otto. *Authority, Liberty & Automatic Machinery in Early Modern Europe.* Baltimore: Johns Hopkins University Press, 1986.

Noble, David F. *The Religion of Technology: The Divinity of Man and the Spirit of Invention.* New York: Knopf, 1997.

Rabinbach, Anson. *The Human Motor: Energy, Fatigue, and the Origins of Modernity.* Berkeley: University of California Press, 1992.

Schivelbusch, Wolfgang. *The Railway Journey; The Industrialization of Time and Space in the 19th Century.* Berkeley: University of California Press, 1986.

Spufford, Francis, and Jenny Uglow, eds. *Cultural Babbage: Technology, Time and Invention.* London: Faber and Faber, 1996.

Sussman, Herbert. *Victorians and the Machine: The Literary Response to Technology.* Cambridge: Harvard University Press, 1968.

Williams, Raymond. *Culture and Society, 1780–1950.* New York: Columbia University Press, 1983.

Wosk, Julie. *Breaking Frame: Technology and the Visual Arts in the Nineteenth Century.* New Brunswick: Rutgers University Press, 1992.

HERBERT SUSSMAN

TELEGRAPH, THE

The electric telegraph was widely hailed by the Victorians as one of the greatest inventions of their age. In many ways for contemporary commentators it seemed to epitomize the nineteenth century's status as a period of unprecedented PROGRESS. Social commentators waxed lyrical about the way the telegraph appeared to exceed "even the feats of pretended magic and the wildest fictions of the East."

Despite the apparently universal regard in which the telegraph was held later on in the century, the technology's beginnings were surrounded with difficulties. When the English inventor Francis Ronalds (1788–1873) attempted to interest the British Admiralty in a scheme for electrical telegraphy in 1816, he was informed that the existing system of semaphore was quite adequate to their needs. Similarly, during the late 1830s the telegraph inventors Charles Wheatstone (1802–1875) and William Fothergill Cooke (1806–1879) were told that pneumatic systems of signalling were preferable for use on the RAILWAYS. By the 1830s electrical experimenters such as the Princeton professor Joseph Henry (1797–1878) were showing that electricity could be used to convey signals over large distances as part of their classroom demonstrations. Relatively few people believed that such demonstrations had any practical use, however.

The first English patent for an electric telegraph was signed on June 10, 1837, by an ailing King William IV. The patent holders were Charles Wheatstone, Professor of Natural Philosophy at King's College, London, and his business partner William Fothergill Cooke, a former officer in the East India Company's army. Their system worked by means of an arrangement of needles that could be made to point toward different letters of the alphabet when an electrical circuit was closed. The partners succeeded in persuading the directors of a number of railway companies to consider adopting the electric telegraph as a means of signaling on their lines. An electric telegraph system was deployed along the section of the Great Western railway line built by ISAMBARD KINGDOM BRUNEL (1806–1859) between Paddington station in London and Slough. The telegraph hit the headlines in 1845 when a suspected murderer fleeing from the scene of the crime to London was apprehended on arrival after a description had been signaled ahead by means of the electric telegraph.

During the early years of their patent, Cooke and Wheatstone faced competition from a number of sources as rival inventors attempted to patent their own versions of an electric telegraph. A telegraph system developed by the Scotsman William Alexander was exhibited at the Adelaide Gallery in 1838. Another competitor, Edward Davy (1806–1885), was granted a patent for his invention in 1838 despite strong opposition from Wheatstone and Cooke. In 1845, having bought out Wheatstone's share of the patent, Cooke set up the Electric Telegraph Company to develop the telegraph as a commercial proposition. The Electric Telegraph Company maintained an effective monopoly on British telegraphy until the 1850s when it started facing increasing competition from rival companies such as the British Electric Telegraph Company. It bought out the patents of rival inventors such as Alexander Bain (1818–1903) to prevent their being used in competing networks. Between 1851 and 1855 the Electric Telegraph Company's telegraphic network expanded from 2,122 to 5,228 miles. The British telegraph network was eventually nation-

alized under the jurisdiction of the POSTAL SERVICE in 1868.

In the UNITED STATES the first patent for an electric telegraph was awarded to Samuel Morse (1791–1892) in 1837. Morse, an impoverished artist and professor of art at the University of the City of New York, had come across the possibility of signalling over long distances by means of electricity during a trip to Europe in the early 1830s. Throughout the second half of the decade he worked at developing his ideas and by 1837 was in a position to mount public exhibitions of his prototype invention. He consulted physicist Joseph Henry (1797–1878) among others on electrical matters and joined into partnership with Leonard Gale, Professor of Chemistry at the university, and Alfred Vail, the son of a wealthy New Jersey industrial family, to help develop his invention. His finished telegraphic apparatus worked by using an elec-

THE EIGHTH WONDER OF THE WORLD.
THE ATLANTIC CABLE.

This 1866 illustration celebrates the linking of London and New York by telegraph cable.

tromagnet to cause a succession of dots and dashes (the famous Morse code) to be inked onto a strip of paper. In 1843 Morse succeeded in gaining a grant of $30,000 from the U.S. Congress to construct a telegraph line between Washington, D.C., and Baltimore.

Morse completed his line between Washington and Baltimore in 1844, sending the famous message "What has God wrought?" down the line. In 1845 he and others founded the Magnetic Telegraph Company to license use of Morse's invention. In 1846 the first commercial telegraph line in the United States was established between Washington, D.C., and New York by the company. By the 1850s there were more than fifty rival companies operating telegraph lines in the United States. Many of them were licensed to use the Morse patent but others used competing telegraph systems such as the one developed by the Scottish inventor Alexander Bain, Wheatstone and Cooke's old adversary from Britain. In 1851 a number of the companies were amalgamated into the New York and Mississippi Valley Printing Telegraph Company, which, following a number of further amalgamations, was renamed in 1856 as the Western Union Telegraph Company; it was eventually to dominate the telegraph industry in the United States.

Both in Britain and in North America, controversy surrounded the issue of just who had invented the clcctric tclcgraph. In thc Unitcd Kingdom thc partncrship of Cooke and Wheatstone soon fell out over precisely this issue. Cooke complained that Wheatstone was ignoring his own claims to a share in the invention and published a number of vitriolic pamphlets attacking his former partner. Others such as the rival inventor Bain similarly accused both Cooke and Wheatstone of unfairly appropriating the telegraph's invention. In the United States Morse was also embroiled in a series of highly litigious court cases over his claims to be considered as the inventor of the telegraph. His rivals even hauled in Joseph Henry, by then secretary of the Smithsonian Institution, to argue that all the technical requirements for a working telegraph system predated Morse's invention. Part of the motivation for these controversies on both sides of the Atlantic was, of course, purely financial. But they were also controversies over the question of just what was involved in laying claim to the invention of a new technology like the telegraph.

By the late 1850s telegraph networks were spreading across the United Kingdom, the rest of Europe, and the United States. The first underwater cables laid been laid linking Dover and Calais in 1851. In 1858 the first attempt was made to lay a telegraph cable across the Atlantic, instigated by the Ameri-

can industrialist Cyrus Field (1819–1892). The first attempt failed, as did the second one. The first successful Atlantic cable was laid however in 1866. Excited commentators viewed this as an unprecedented event. It was tantamount to the annihilation of time and space. Information that would previously have taken weeks to travel from LONDON to New York could now do so in a matter of minutes.

By the end of the nineteenth century telegraphy was a key tool of imperial government. Through a worldwide network of telegraph cables, largely controlled by British companies, the British EMPIRE could keep its distant colonies under constant surveillance. Protecting the so-called "All-Red Route" was a key goal of imperial foreign policy. Telegraphy was a major industry in its own right. Among other things it provided new employment opportunities for Victorian women. The electric telegraph had come a long way from its fragile origins.

See also TECHNOLOGY; POSTAL SERVICES; PROGRESS; RAILWAYS.

FURTHER READING

Headrick, Daniel. *The Invisible Weapon: Telecommunications and International Politics, 1851–1945.* Oxford: Oxford University Press, 1992.
Kieve, J. L. *The Electric Telegraph: A Social History.* Newton Abbot: David and Charles, 1973.

IWAN RHYS MORUS

TELEPHONE

The telephone revolutionized communication. Now considered so essential to daily life that many people carry cellular phones wherever they go, the telephone seemed little more than an entertaining luxury to people and businesses on its introduction during the Victorian era. Soon the power of transmitting the human voice over vast distances struck the public, and the telephone forever changed the way people communicated.

INVENTING THE TELEPHONE

The origins of the telephone are complex, involving scientific quandaries, philanthropic concerns, and commercial ambitions. This fact is clearly illustrated in the life of ALEXANDER GRAHAM BELL (1847–1922). Bell came from a Scottish family in which his grandfather and his father had made careers out of teaching elocution, curing stammering, and helping deaf people to learn to speak. Bell, whose education included a few courses at the University of Edinburgh in 1864 and the University of London in 1868 to 1869, followed the lead of the older generation of his family. Even after he gained international fame for his work with the telephone, Bell would list "teacher of the deaf" as his profession—perhaps not a surprising fact given that his mother and his wife Mabel both suffered from impaired hearing.

After his two brothers had died of tuberculosis, Bell in 1870 emigrated with his parents to CANADA in search of a healthier climate, and the next year he moved to Massachusetts where he would in 1873 take up a post as professor of vocal physiology at Boston University. During the next years Bell pursued several lines of enquiry, including experimenting with the simultaneous transmission of several messages along the same line of a "harmonic" TELEGRAPH and investigating patterns of airwaves in the human ear when speech was uttered.

In taking up such research, Bell joined a number of scientists and inventors who had worked in the same area. As early as 1861 the German scientist Johann Philipp Reis (1834–1874) had designed instruments that could transmit sound electrically, but which could only reproduce a simple tone, not the complex wave patterns of speech. In America Elisha Gray (1835–1901), who was cofounder of Western Electric Company, was also hard at work on the transmission of speech at the same time as Bell. Bell's research in this area was spurred on by Gardiner Greene Hubbard, a Boston entrepreneur and Bell's future father-in-law, who grasped the commercial promise of the telephone. By June 1875 Bell, working with Thomas A. Watson (1854–1934), had constructed a very rough version of the telephone, which transmitted "speechlike" sound—although not intelligible speech.

On February 14, 1876, Hubbard filed a patent application for Bell's telephone with the Patent Office in Washington, D.C. Only a few hours later Gray filed a proposal for an untested idea for a telephone with the same office. Although Gray would later challenge Bell's claim to be the inventor of the telephone, the patent issued in support of Bell's application, often called history's most valuable patent, was ultimately upheld by the United States Supreme Court.

On March 10, 1876, three days after the patent was issued, Bell, working in Boston on his concept of variable electrical resistance to communicate speech, transmitted the telephone's first intelligible sentences "Mr. Watson, come here. I want you." Because there was no receiving telephone at Bell's end of the wire, Watson could not verbally reply to Bell's request for help—Bell had spilled battery acid on his clothes—but that moment was nonetheless a fundamentally important one in the larger history of nineteenth-century science and society. As Thomas Alva Edison (1847–1931), who himself contributed to the

Central Telephone operators answering calls at St. Paul's Churchyard, London, 1901.

later development of the telephone by introducing a carbon transmitter remarked, Bell indeed had "brought the human family in closer touch."

ADOPTION OF THE TELEPHONE THROUGHOUT THE WORLD

The impact of the telephone varied considerably from country to country. By the mid-twentieth century the UNITED STATES, Canada, Sweden, and New Zealand, for example, had much higher per capita numbers of telephones than Spain, Japan, Poland, and Czechoslovakia. Britain also lagged behind in its use of the telephone, in part the result of the relatively slow start that the invention made there in the late nineteenth and early twentieth centuries.

Even though the invention of the telephone was enthusiastically publicized, it was not readily embraced by Britons. William Thomson (1824–1907), the future Lord Kelvin, had been impressed by the telephone's potential when Bell demonstrated one at the Centennial Exposition in Philadelphia in April 1876, and Thomson introduced the telephone to Britain the following September at a meeting of the British Association in Glasgow. The next months saw numerous articles on the telephone in the press, including a report in *The Times* on a demonstration that Bell presented for QUEEN VICTORIA in January 1878. Nevertheless the telephone experienced limited success in Britain for two main reasons. First, the country already had the most efficient system of communication in the world. With the establishment of a Penny Post in 1840, the British post office emerged as a model government department, conveying millions of letters efficiently and frequently. Accordingly, to some observers in Britain the telephone was a luxury item, perhaps suitable for some business uses, but certainly not to be regarded as a basic necessity such as water or gas. Second, the government was reluctant to give support to a policy for telephone use. In 1870 the post office had nationalized the telegraph industry. Although the move led to a greatly expanded

and much more utilized telegraph system, there were serious revenue deficits in its operation, partly because of high labor costs. Therefore, when officials at the post office, such as S. A. Blackwood (post office secretary, 1880–1893), proposed to operate the telephone system under governmental management, doubts arose at the Treasury and in the public mind as to the wisdom of the proposal.

As a result, telephone development in Britain was characterized by a series of fits and starts. In 1884 the government opted to allow private companies to promote the invention in a competitive market. Unfortunately, this policy failed when a private monopoly emerged in the late 1880s. As a result, two piecemeal remedies were applied—the trunk lines were nationalized under post office control in 1896 and local telephone development under the direction of individual municipalities was promoted in the late 1890s. Neither remedy provided a solution to the basic problem, the need for a unified, national system with reasonable rates and efficient service. When all other options seemed to have been tried and found wanting, the post office in 1912 nationalized the entire telephone industry for £12.5 million. The post office continued to direct the telephone system until 1981 when a separate corporation was established. The government of Prime Minister Margaret Thatcher opposed the idea of state-managed industries, and in 1984 51% of the stock of the telecom corporation was sold to private investors, ending nationalization of the industry.

See also BELL, ALEXANDER GRAHAM; TELEGRAPH, THE.

FURTHER READING

Baldwin, F. G. C. *The History of the Telephone in the United Kingdom.* London: Chapman and Hall, 1925.

Briggs, Asa. *Victorian Things.* Chicago: University of Chicago Press, 1988.

Bruce, Robert V. *Bell: Alexander Graham Bell and the Conquest of Solitude.* Ithaca: Cornell University Press, 1973.

Kieve, Jeffrey. *Electric Telegraph A Social and Economic History.* Newton Abbot: David and Charles, 1973.

Perry, C. R. *The Victorian Post Office: the Growth of a Bureaucracy.* Woodbridge: The Royal Historical Society, 1992.

Pitt, Douglas C. *The Telecommunications Function in the British Post Office.* Westmead: Saxon House, 1980.

Pool, Ithiel de Sola, ed. *The Social Impact of the Telephone.* Cambridge: MIT Press, 1977.

CHARLES R. PERRY

TELEPHONE INCREASE, 1890–1920		
Year	Number of Telephones in Great Britain	Number as Percentage of British Population
1890	45,000	0.12
1895	99,000	0.25
1900	210,000	0.51
1905	438,000	1.02
1910	662,500	1.48
1915	817,500	1.85
1920	985,000	2.11

TEMPERANCE MOVEMENT

During the nineteenth and early twentieth centuries a social reform crusade known as the temperance movement flourished throughout the English-speaking world. At first, temperance signified a refusal to drink spirits but not necessarily a refusal to drink beer or wine. During the Victorian period temperance became identified with individuals who refused to consume any kind of alcoholic beverage. They were called teetotalers or total abstainers. Some teetotalers consumed ALCOHOL as communion wine and as MEDICINE and served alcoholic beverages to guests and customers. In contrast the most militant opposed these compromises; they regarded alcohol as a poison or sin. Most (but not all) temperance reformers were evangelical Protestants and belonged to the middle class or the skilled artisan working-class elite. Women comprised a majority of all teetotalers.

Not content with their own sobriety, teetotalers organized societies that tried to convert others. Most of them later moved from moral suasion to coercion. Temperance societies demanded that government make it difficult to buy alcoholic beverages or even ban its sale altogether. Temperance reformers joined with Sabbatarians in agitating for Sunday closing of businesses that sold drink. Even people who personally enjoyed alcoholic drink supported some temperance proposals, especially when they were directed against the sale of alcohol to groups that they con-

sidered dangerous—such as workers and immigrants and people of color—or kept drink sellers out of respectable neighborhoods.

THE EVILS OF ALCOHOL

Most temperance reformers were modernizers who denounced alcoholic drink as an obstacle to progress. Reformers and their sympathizers among moderate drinkers blamed alcoholic drink at least in part for serious problems that confronted their times: POVERTY and CRIME, squalor and disorder, disease and fecklessness. Anger toward drink extended to those who manufactured and sold alcoholic beverages. Allegedly the "drink traffic" corrupted political life at elections and legislative sessions.

Temperance first achieved prominence in the UNITED STATES, and it was there that temperance developed the greatest power as a social and political movement. It also quickly became influential throughout the United Kingdom and its white settler colonies such as CANADA and AUSTRALIA.

In England the first antispirits societies were organized at the beginning of the 1830s. Moving beyond the antispirits pioneers, Joseph Livesey led a handful of Lancashire workingmen in signing a total abstinence pledge in 1832. The industrial north and the southwest stood out as the strongholds of the English temperance movement. In the early Victorian phase, teetotalism often appealed to extreme radicals, including some Chartists. It also was a self-help movement for ambitious members of the working class. In the mid- and late Victorian period teetotalism became increasingly respectable, identified with intensely religious middle-class men and women. Often temperance reformers were active in other reform movements as diverse as peace societies, WOMEN'S SUFFRAGE, and vegetarianism. Typically they belonged to Nonconformist denominations, but theologically diverse Anglican clergy also supported temperance reform, as did a few prominent Roman Catholics.

The temperance movement was stronger in Scotland, Wales, and for a short time, IRELAND, than it was in most of England. Revealingly, Parliament enacted Sunday closing legislation: first for Scotland, next for Ireland other than its biggest cities, and finally for Wales, but never for England, where the PUBLIC HOUSE or pub was idealized as the workingman's club. Ireland, a predominantly Roman Catholic country, experienced a brief enthusiasm for teetotalism in the late 1830s and early 1840s when a Father Theobald Mathew convinced most of the Irish to give up their whiskey and beer.

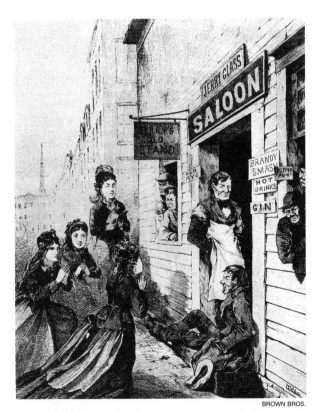

BROWN BROS.

The most determined temperance advocates took their crusade directly to drinkers in this saloon, circa nineteenth century.

TEMPERANCE ORGANIZATION

The English temperance movement operated at several levels. There were local organizations whose meetings provided occasions for sociability, Bands of Hope that fostered a commitment to teetotalism among children, moral suasionist MISSIONARIES who tried to save wretched drunkards and even visited them in jail, and a variety of national organizations, many of which published their own weekly or monthly NEWSPAPERS. Some of the national organizations were denominational, the most powerful being the CHURCH OF ENGLAND Temperance Society. Some, like the London-based National Temperance Society, were educational. Some were fraternal insurance societies such as the Rechabites. Some were political in their objectives. The United Kingdom Alliance was founded in 1853 to promote legislation for prohibition.

The alliance borrowed the idea of prohibition from the New England state of Maine. The centralized constitutional structure in the United Kingdom made impossible the experimentation that prevailed in America. The alliance quickly retreated from its original goal of statutory prohibition for the entire United Kingdom to a new policy: a referendum by local voters called Direct Local Veto. Sir Wilfrid Lawson, a wealthy landowner with a knack for writing humorous verse, served as alliance president for many years.

The prohibitionist wing of the temperance movement became a political pressure group. It functioned as an ally of the Liberal Party, although virtually no Liberal leaders were teetotalers and most—like WILLIAM GLADSTONE—lacked enthusiasm for Direct Local Veto. By the end of the Victorian period, the Liberal leadership decided that, even in the form of Direct Local Veto, prohibition was politically impractical.

Restrictive legislation was enacted for the various parts of the United Kingdom and in the white settler colonies, but the British parts of the English-speaking world did not emulate the United States where statewide prohibition was enacted in some states and local option prohibition in many parts of the country. Where prohibition existed in the British Empire, it prevented the sale of alcohol to black Africans and other nonwhite indigenous peoples.

Temperance stands out as the most widely supported international moral reform movement of the nineteenth and early twentieth centuries. Particularly in English-speaking countries, ideas and tactics, publications and speakers traveled freely. Father Mathew worked for teetotalism on both sides of the Irish Sea and on both sides of the Atlantic. John Gough, an English-born reformed drunkard who became cel-ebrated as a temperance speaker in the United States, visited his home country on successful lecture tours. Temperance organizations such as the Good Templars and the Woman's Christian Temperance Union (WCTU) had affiliates in all English-speaking countries and beyond. For example Joseph Malins joined the Good Templars fraternal society while a young immigrant in Philadelphia and then returned to England where he planted lodges. The American leader of the WCTU, Frances Willard, spent part of her last years in England, and Bessie Lee Cowie, an Australian missionary for the WCTU, campaigned for sobriety around the globe. Bonds of fellowship and friendship grew throughout the English-speaking world, uniting reformers in their common fight against alcoholic drink.

See also ALCOHOL; BREWING AND DISTILLING; LOCAL GOVERNMENT.

FURTHER READING

Blocker, Jack S., Jr., Ian R. Tyrrell, and David M. Fahey, eds. *Alcohol and Temperance in Modern History: An International Encyclopedia.* 2 vols. Santa Barbara: ABC-Clio, 2003.

Dingle, A. E. *The Campaign for Prohibition in Victorian England: The United Kingdom Alliance, 1872–1895.* London: Croom Helm, 1980.

Harrison, Brian. *Drink and the Victorians: The Temperance Question in England, 1815–1872.* 2d ed. Staffordshire: Keele University Press, 1994.

Quinn, John F. *Father Mathew's Crusade: Temperance in Nineteenth-Century Ireland and Irish America.* Amherst: University of Massachusetts Press, 2002.

Shiman, Lilian Lewis. *Crusade against Drink in Victorian England.* New York: St. Martin's, 1988.

Tyrrell, Ian. *Woman's World, Woman's Empire: The Woman's Christian Temperance Union in International Perspective, 1880–1930.* Chapel Hill: University of North Carolina Press, 1991.

DAVID M. FAHEY

TEMPLE, HENRY JOHN

Born: October 20, 1784; Broadlands, England
Died: October 18, 1865; Broadlands, England

Henry John Temple, 3d viscount Palmerston, was one of four British prime ministers of the nineteenth century to merit an eponymous "Age of" (alongside Lord Liverpool, ROBERT PEEL, and WILLIAM GLADSTONE); the "Age of Palmerston" spanned 1846 to 1865. Embodying the patriotic "John Bull" policy overseas, he held in domestic affairs variously progressive and standpat positions. A Whig of the old school, he was the last premier to straddle the pre- and post-Reform eras, and among the first to recognize the new primacy of public opinion. This dexterity helped him to hold office over the widest span of years of anyone except Gladstone—most of the years from 1807 to 1865. His double tenure at 10 Downing Street (1855–1858; 1859–1865) merely capped his ever-rising dominance over political affairs.

Of an ancient Irish family, Palmerston carried its vivacity and prejudices to Westminster. One ancestor was speaker of the Irish House of Commons, and that man's son gained an Irish viscountcy in 1723. About half of the Temple estates were near Sligo, IRELAND, where hardship was great from the 1840s. A rare public attack on him occurred when some immigrants to the UNITED STATES from his estates perished in unseaworthy boats from his docks; yet he was absolved of direct guilt. He was suspected of Irish political ambitions but did not necessarily support an enlarged British electorate; as a rule he opposed most efforts at franchise reform, vowing never to allow a reprise of the storms of 1830 to 1832.

Palmerston attended the Harrow School and inherited his title upon his father's death in 1802. He went first to the University of Edinburgh, studying with the famed moral philosopher and political economist Dugald Stewart (as had Walter Scott, James Mill, and WILLIAM LAMB [Lord Melbourne]). Stewart's support of the French Revolution did not alter his pupil's

INP/TOPHAM/THE IMAGE WORKS
British statesman Henry John Temple, 3d viscount Palmerston.

aversion to it, who as a child had witnessed horrors in FRANCE. He finished his studies at Cambridge University.

In 1807, aged 22, by virtue of rank and ability (some Irish lords were eligible to sit in the Commons), he became a Member of Parliament and was made a junior lord of the Admiralty. From 1811 to 1831 he represented Cambridge University. He was secretary-at-war for the last six years of the Napoleonic wars, managing the BRITISH ARMY's finances, and kept the post till 1828. His Tory beliefs fading, he became a follower of George Canning, leader of the liberal Tories and a supporter of Catholic Emancipation and of FREE TRADE. For most of his later career he represented the borough of Tiverton, in Somerset.

When in 1830 the Whigs took office under Lord Grey, Palmerston became foreign secretary. He held that office in 1830–1834, 1835–1841, and 1846–1851, and is more identified with it than any other Briton. Pressing constitutional reform on the English model overseas, he also built up the naval and commercial primacy Britain had already begun to achieve, and combated the slave trade. Greece gained independence from the Turks in 1832 with his aid, but when the Egyptian pasha tried to weaken Turkish control on the Nile, Palmerston struck him down. His Straits Convention of 1841, considered a watershed in European diplomacy, closed the Black Sea to Western navies in peacetime, in order to protect Ottoman Turkey from Russian and other encroachment. By the forcible opening of Chinese trade in 1839 to 1842 for a lower tariff, he brought Hong Kong into the British EMPIRE. A treaty of 1830 averted war by creating a buffer Kingdom of Belgium free of Dutch and French domination; a follow-up treaty in 1839 required Britain and France to guarantee Belgium's sovereignty. Palmerston on his deathbed asked that the Belgian treaty be read to him (rather than Scripture), so proud of it was he. This commitment to Belgium led Britain to declare war in 1914 when German armies crossed its ally's border. His famous "Don Pacifico" speech of 1850, over four hours long, defended Britain's right to protect every British subject everywhere; in it his phrase "civis Romanus sum"—"I am a Roman citizen"—likened Britain to the greatest of the ancient empires.

The CRIMEAN WAR (1853–1856) annealed his reputation, just as World War II would fix Churchill in the historical record. At the war's outset in 1853 Palmerston was home secretary. Criticism of others' maladministration of the war grew until it became obvious that this man who had long been so indelicate, so bumptious, must take charge. Palmerston fast brought the war to a successful end in part through luck and his adept relations with Britain's ally, France. This crest in his acclaim continued into the elections of 1857, when his Radical critics were routed for opposing his belligerence against CHINA. He later invited some of them into his cabinets.

Bluff conduct ebbed slightly in his last years, and relations with France benefited. He was unable to back up his verbal support for Polish rebels against Russia in 1863, or for Danish interests against Prussia the next year. His barely concealed support of the Confederacy in the American CIVIL WAR (1861–1865) was better contained than Gladstone's, and Palmerston's native caution probably kept Britain officially neutral in that historic contest. His worry was that an overmighty United States would aid the Fenians, encroach upon Canada, and upset the European balance of power he always endeavored to sustain.

His most notable legislation at home was the Matrimonial Causes Act of 1857, the first measure to liberalize and cheapen divorce in more than a century. At the time no one was quite sure why Palmerston held so fiercely to his course in pushing the bill through Parliament during that hot summer, when the stench from the River Thames forced all windows to be closed and the tenor of debate to become rancorous. Churchmen had always questioned his religious faith and now were sure of his immorality; yet he knew of the public support for such a realistic move, which let divorce actions be made in civil COURTS and not just through Parliament.

His reputation as a *bon vivant* (a person with sophisticated taste in food and drink) drew criticism from some and the admiration of many more. In writings of his day and since, the word most often used to describe him is "jaunty"; his nicknames were Lord Cupid and Pam. He rode, danced, talked, and conducted amorous affairs into old age. These were the outer signs of tremendous energy; he usually worked at a tall lectern, writing and reading late into the night. In his last years he was named co-respondent in a divorce case involving a much younger Mrs. O'Kane and was dubbed "Lord Able" (from the biblical story of Cain and Abel). His profile among the public shone. He was very happily married from 1839 until his death to Emily Cowper, sister of then prime minister Lord Melbourne. Lady Cowper, a widow, had probably born their children while still in her first MARRIAGE. She made their manse (large residence) on Piccadilly and their country estate the chief political salons for a quarter-century, an office that appreciably assisted her husband's Whigs in maintaining the upper hand in his lifetime.

Deft with a pen, he wrote or inspired scores of pieces for the *Morning Post*, the *Standard*, and the *Globe*. BENJAMIN DISRAELI (1804–1881), for one, sought unsuccessfully to copy this route to influence. The *Standard* grew conservative, and the vacuum left in the Whig party after Palmerston's death was perhaps best shown when the *Globe* soon became a conservative organ as well.

More consequentially, Palmerston sometimes dodged proper channels in carrying out his work. He once sounded out some Russians about a new English envoy before discussing the matter with Windsor or his fellow Whigs. For this he earned a royal reproach; QUEEN VICTORIA and PRINCE ALBERT ever remained wary of him. He loathed NAPOLEON III of France yet saw him as a bulwark against revolution, and approved the coup d'état of 1851. For this he was dismissed from the cabinet of his party rival Lord JOHN RUSSELL (1792–1878). Palmerston took "tit-for-tat" revenge the next year in voting down a ministerial bill, bringing down Russell's government. Thereafter his leadership of the Whigs was unquestioned, and the effect was, in the slightest way, the beginning of the end of royal control over ministerial affairs.

Greater effect in European affairs came from his support for Italian unification. In 1859 the Austro-Italian war looked to drag Britain into fighting against the erstwhile ally France, but Palmerston executed another minor diplomatic revolution by abandoning the old ally, Austria, and supporting both Italian and French interests. This issue also, for nearly the only time, brought him and Gladstone into common cause, and sealed the latter's allegiance to the incipient Liberal party.

Only in recent decades have historians found some real principles in Palmerston's actions, which his critics long denied. Palmerston was an unabashed nationalist and a liberal-internationalist, as ready to smite foreign autocrats as to dash the hopes of radicals at home, if it kept the peace and balanced the powers of Europe.

See also ANGLO-FRENCH RELATIONS; CHINA; CRIMEAN WAR.

FURTHER READING

Bourne, Kenneth. *Palmerston, the Early Years, 1784–1841.* New York: Macmillan, 1982.

Bourne, Kenneth, ed. *The Letters of the Third Viscount Palmerston to Laurence and Elizabeth Sulivan, 1804–1863.* Camden 4th series, Vol. 23. London: Royal Historical Society, 1979.

Chamberlain, Muriel. *Lord Palmerston.* Cardiff: GPC, 1987.

Guedalla, Philip, ed. *Gladstone and Palmerston: Being the Correspondence of Lord Palmerston and Mr. Gladstone, 1851–1865.* London: Gollancz, 1928.

Southgate, Donald. *"The Most English Minister": The Policies and Politics of Palmerston.* London: Macmillan; New York: St. Martin's, 1966.

Steele, E. D. *Palmerston and Liberalism, 1855–1865.* Cambridge: Cambridge University Press, 1991.

JAMES M. CORNELIUS

TEN HOURS MOVEMENT

The Ten Hours Movement occupies an interesting place in the history of labor struggles in the Victorian era. Exploitative child labor, with pauper children working for more than 12 working hours with only a 40-minute break for a meal, was a by-product of the laissez-faire policy of the Industrial Revolution. Early attempts at reform, such as the Health and Morals of Apprentices Act of 1802, restricting pauper apprentices to 12 hours' daily labor, and ROBERT PEEL's 1819 Act to limit "free" child labor to 12 hours, failed because they were not strictly enforced. In the 1830s the demand for reduced hours was renewed with the lengthening of hours in textile mills in the first three decades of the nineteenth century. Cotton workers who had been active in Short Time committees in the late 1820s now began large-scale agitations in England and Scotland. The demand for a ten-hour working day focused primarily on reducing the working hours for children and women, but it was understood that it would extend to the male workers as well, as children far outnumbered the adults in the factory. Factory workers also hoped that the reduction of child labor would lead to higher employment and increased wages.

The movement brought together various groups with different interests and motivations. For the textile workers, who were often the agents of exploitative child labor, the Ten Hours Movement was a pragmatic attempt to gain control over working conditions. By contrast the middle-class leadership that played a central role was defined by a sense of Christian morality. One of the main leaders, Richard Oastler, a Methodist and a Tory steward of a Yorkshire landowner, upon learning about the condition of factory children in Yorkshire from his manufacturer friend John Wood, wrote a series of letters to the *Leeds Mercury* entitled "Yorkshire Slavery" in which he declared that "thousands of our fellow creatures . . . the miserable inhabitants of a Yorkshire town are this very moment existing in a state of slavery, more horrid than are the victims of that hellish system 'colonial slavery.'" Interestingly, men such as John Fielden of Todmorden (who had already instituted a ten-hour day in his factories) and Joseph Brotherton of Sal-

ford who financed the movement were themselves wealthy factory owners.

The Factory Act of 1833 was passed after a commission headed by EDWIN CHADWICK and Southwood Smith was appointed by the Parliament to investigate into the issue. The act prohibited children below nine from factory work; those between the ages of 13 and 18 years could work up to 12 hours a day, and for children between 9 and 13 years the labor was limited to eight hours a day. This act was more successful than the earlier ones as it created a staff of inspectors that ensured its workability. A fixed working day for the children came only with HENRY JOHN TEMPLE's (Viscount Palmerston's) 1853 act and a genuine Ten Hours Act only in 1874.

See also CHILDHOOD; CHILD LABOR; INDUSTRIAL WORKERS.

FURTHER READING

Cole, G. D. H., and A. W. Filson. *British Working Class Movements: Select Documents 1789–1875.* New York: St. Martin's, 1965.

Wright. D. G. *Popular Radicalism.* London: Longman, 1988.

ARUNA KRISHNAMURTHY

TENNIS

Tennis, or lawn tennis, emerged during the late Victorian era as a popular pastime for the middle and upper classes. Its forerunner was real (royal) tennis, which had been played on an indoor, enclosed, wooden court by English and French royals for centuries, as well as by monks and aristocrats. To the French, it was called *jeu de paume* ("game of the hand"). In the second half of the nineteenth century, the consumer and leisure society produced by British INDUSTRIALIZATION made for increased participation in and organization of all manner of sports. Accordingly, tennis became popular, in part too because women played the game. By 1900 tennis had spread throughout the British EMPIRE and to the UNITED STATES, spawning various tournaments as well as international competitions.

THE FIRST TENNIS GAMES

Modern tennis can be traced back to 1872 and the establishment of the first dedicated club by a racket-sports enthusiast, Major T. H. Gem, at the fashionable English resort town of Leamington Spa. At Christmas of the next year another military man, Major Walter C. Wingfield, entertained his guests by introducing them to a racket game of his own design, which he called inexplicably "sphairistike." Wingfield's

71

game was played on an outdoor hourglass-shaped court with a narrow net, and it proved to be the direct antecedent of modern tennis. The new game caught on extraordinarily quickly, especially at influential public schools around the country such as Harrow and Eton. LONDON's Marylebone Cricket Club (MCC) was the national governing body for rackets and real tennis and in 1875 it drew up a set of rules for lawn tennis. From there it wasn't long before the All England Croquet Club based in the London suburb of Wimbledon inserted Lawn Tennis into its title (and duly expanded its facilities) and sponsored the first tennis championships for men in 1877. The Gentlemen's Singles, as the event was called, was contested by 22 amateur players. The final match was watched by a crowd of some 200 spectators, each of whom paid one shilling to see Spencer Gore, an Old Harrovian rackets player, win the title. The All England Club modified and codified the MCC's provisional rules, including the instituting of tennis's unique scoring system: 15, 30, 40, and game, which was probably based on clock quarters, though its origins are obscure. The popularity of tennis among women prompted the All England Club to start a competition for female players beginning in 1884. The first Ladies' Singles championship attracted 13 amateur competitors and was won by Maud Watson. That

same year Gentlemen's Doubles began, as did the construction of permanent stands at Wimbledon.

The 1880s saw tennis grow spectacularly, helped in part by the prowess and popularity of Ernest and William Renshaw, British twins. From 1881 to 1889, separately and as doubles players, they won the Wimbledon Championships 13 times. The "Renshaw Rush," as the press dubbed these years, cemented the hold Wimbledon had over British tennis and by extension over tournament tennis itself. After 1888 the recently formed Lawn Tennis Association became the sport's governing body. Tennis made it onto the roster of events for the first modern Olympiad in Athens 1896 and in 1900 the Davis Cup was instituted for competition between British and American men. In 1905 May Sutton of the United States became the first overseas Wimbledon champion when she won the Ladies' Singles tournament, a feat matched two years later on the men's side by Norman Brookes of Australia. These two victories sealed the internationalization of the game. The growth of tennis had been remarkable: over the course of some 30 years it had gone from its modern founding to a significant international sport.

QUICK POPULARITY

The popularity of tennis was symptomatic of the value placed on sports of all kinds by the Victorians. The linkage between the playing of sports—especially team sports—and the maintenance of civil society was one that was made repeatedly by institutions of various kinds. The PUBLIC SCHOOLS in large part were responsible for inculcating this way of thinking in upper-class boys, who in turn carried it into the worlds of business, government, the military, and the church. Edward Lyttleton, for example, headmaster of Eton, an accomplished preacher, and one of two famous Victorian CRICKET-playing brothers, confessed that he never walked up the nave of a church without bowling an imaginary ball.

Industrialization with its expanded urban face spawned new sports organizations and a standardization of rules. Important too, was the "MUSCULAR CHRISTIANITY" of Evangelicalism, perhaps the most dominant religious force in early Victorian Britain. Evanglicalism's emphasis on sobriety and moderation, and its exaltation of the body as God's holy temple, led easily to a linkage between sports and Christian duty. For Victorian women, however, working from within rigid ideas of what was appropriate gendered behavior, this link was not so easily made until the middle years of the nineteenth century and

WALLACE G. LEVISON/TIMEPIX

The popularity of tennis spread rapidly among women after 1870, although comfortable tennis attire was still years off.

grew out of the sustained movement to improve educational opportunities for women. The betterment of body and mind went hand in hand for Victorian educators, and as women's education began to really expand after about 1870, so too did women's sports. The engine for this change was the newly established schools and colleges for women. As the latter developed at both Oxford and Cambridge universities, team SPORTS played a major role in socialization and recreation. Field hockey was a major game at women's colleges by the 1890s, as was golf. Both of these sports benefited also from their wide popularity in the form of private women's sports clubs and associations. In 1895, for example, the All England Women's Hockey Association was formed, which oversaw the development and expansion of this field game into the team sport of choice for British women. Despite the growth of hockey and GOLF, as well as other sports in which women participated such as swimming, ice-skating, and croquet, the most popular game for women remained lawn tennis.

Wimbledon may have led the way in allowing women to participate at the highest levels of organized tennis, but much of the game's popularity among Victorian women resulted from its easy accessibility. By 1900 there was scarcely a village or town in England that lacked grass courts and a ladies' tournament. To this can be added the obligatory court at country houses, both grand and middle class.

Tennis captures well the Victorian era with its vigorous action reined in by an overarching social respectability. Only cricket, it may be argued, is more defining of the leisure pursuits of the age's middle and upper classes. And in its early acceptance of both sexes as legitimate players, tennis became emancipationist, helping to herald the growth of women's participation in sports of many different kinds in the future. For the Victorian era's NEW WOMAN—a term coined in 1894 to describe the emerging independence of women at the time—tennis was one of a handful of games that mattered most. Conversely, for the Victorian man, tennis was just one more arena in which to demonstrate physical prowess, something that his era demanded of its men.

See also SPORTS.

FURTHER READING

Baltzell, E. Digby. *Sporting Gentlemen: Men's Tennis from the Age of Honor to the Cult of the Superstar.* New York: Free Press, 1995.

Gillmeister, Heiner. *Tennis: A Cultural History.* New York: New York University Press, 1997.

Haley, Bruce. *The Healthy Body and Victorian Culture.* Cambridge, Mass: Harvard University Press, 1978.

Mangan, J. A. *Sport in the Victorian and Edwardian Public School: The Emergence and Consolidation of an Educational Ideology.* London: Frank Cass, 2000.

McCrone, Kathleen E. *Sport and the Physical Emancipation of English Women, c. 1870–1914.* London: Routledge, 1988.

Walvin, James, and John K. Walton, eds. *Leisure in Britain, 1780–1939.* Manchester: Manchester University Press, 1983.

C. BRAD FAUGHT

TENNYSON, ALFRED

Born: August 6, 1809; Lincolnshire, England
Died: October 6, 1892; Surrey, England

The poet laureate of England from 1850 until his death in 1892, Alfred, Lord Tennyson was by far the most prominent poet of his age and enjoyed fame and prestige unrivaled, perhaps, by any poet in any age. Tennyson sometimes expresses Victorian attitudes in very direct ways, but he was far from being a spokesperson for the conventional pieties of his time. As T. S. Eliot said, "the surface of Tennyson stirred about with his time," but the depths of his poetry, expressed with unparalleled prosodic (versification style) mastery, express idiosyncratic, deeply personal emotional states more often in conflict than in accord with current social values, and expressive of the undercurrents of anxiety and alienation beneath the surfaces of Victorian attitudes. As "the saddest of all English poets," Eliot said, Tennyson was also "the most instinctive rebel against the society in which he was the most perfect conformist."

Tennyson claimed his personal melancholy as a birthright, the "black blood of the Tennysons," inherited from a stormy, alcoholic father, bitter over his seemingly arbitrary disinheritance and his limited prospects as a clergyman with a very modest income and a family of 12 children. Growing up in such a family, Tennyson owed as much to nurture as to nature for his melancholy, but in any case the mood became characteristic of his precocious poetry so early in his life that some of his best critics describe his poetic temperament as fully formed in early childhood, if not in infancy.

Tennyson's poetic efforts began in childhood with precocious imitations of Alexander Pope, Sir Walter Scott, and Lord Byron, and his work began to appear in print as early as 1827 with his contributions to *Poems of Two Brothers.* But his public career was more effectively entered upon after enrolling at Cambridge in 1827, when he returned to an early exercise in visionary ROMANTICISM, *Armageddon*, revising

Alfred Tennyson was one of the greatest and most popular poets of the nineteenth century.

"The Ballad of Oriana," exhibit Tennyson's technical mastery and newfound ability to represent heightened states of feeling in symbolic description, and almost justify the hyperbolic praise in Hallam's enthusiastic review for the *Englishman's Magazine* in 1831. They fully justify Hallam's placement of his friend with Shelley and Keats as a "poet of sensation." Tennyson's poetry achieved a measure of fame, or at least, of notoriety, less for its own merits or Hallam's praise than from an abusive review in *Blackwood's Magazine*, which advised Tennyson to abandon his cockney pretensions to art.

Despite the abusive review, and the greater blow of his father's death in 1831, Tennyson proceeded with another volume, *Poems* (1832), in which he demonstrated yet greater virtuosity of craftsmanship and a much stronger grasp of his characteristic themes, especially his concern with the role of the poet and of art in uncongenial times. Like "Mariana," many of the poems in this volume, notably "Oenone," "The Palace of Art," "The Hesperides," "The Lotos Eaters," and, especially, "The Lady of Shalott," became classic symbolic representations of artistic sensibility struggling in a Philistine age, but the book made little immediate impact after publication.

THE GREATEST LIVING POET

Discouraged by the weak reception of *Poems* and devastated by the sudden death of his much loved Hallam in September 1833, Tennyson entered into a decade of public silence before emerging with a new publication in 1842, *Poems*, in two volumes. Although emotionally shattered by Hallam's death, Tennyson was productive in the following years. Drawing on previously unknown emotional depths, he masterfully revised the poems of 1830 and 1832 and composed many more. The new compositions included the masterpieces "Ulysses" and "Break, Break, Break"; many lyrics that would eventually be woven into his elegy for Hallam, *In Memoriam* (1850); "Morte D'Arthur," the first of what would become the *Idylls of the King*; "Oh! That 'Twere Possible," the poem that eventually became the germ of his monodrama *Maud* (1855); and some of the poems of contemporary life that established his popularity in his own day, especially "Locksley Hall" and "Dora," English idylls that anticipated the hugely successful "Enoch Arden" (1864).

The success of the 1842 poems made Tennyson recognized as the greatest of living poets, and gave him the confidence to see his poetic enterprise as central to contemporary life rather than aesthetically

it and incorporating it into *Timbuctoo* (1829), which won the Chancellor's Prize at Cambridge, established his reputation, at least locally, validated his vocation as a poet, and established a lifelong commitment to POETRY combining visionary Romanticism with modern thought in the form of "keen *Discovery*." Tennyson's prize poem and his official studies at Cambridge, however, pale into insignificance compared with his intense involvement with his fellow students in the Cambridge Conversazione Society, better known as the "Apostles." Among them, Tennyson found eager intellectual inquiry into the most advanced thought of the age, enthusiasm for the arts, and especially, intimate friendship and encouragement. Tennyson's closest friend among them, and the greatest single influence on his life and poetry, was the gifted, charismatic Arthur Henry Hallam, who inspired, encouraged, and even helped market the first volume to appear under Tennyson's name, *Poems, Chiefly Lyrical* (1830). The best of the poems, "Mariana," "Recollections of the Arabian Nights" and to a lesser extent estranged and to take on the most volatile contemporary issues in ambitious longer works. The first of these, *The Princess* (1847), concerned with emergent feminism and with the higher education of women, met with a mixed reception and is now chiefly appreciated for the beautiful songs set within the tale.

Tennyson was far more successful with *In Memoriam: A.H.H.* (1850), an elegy for Hallam consisting of 131 lyrics written over a period of 17 years and arranged in a sequence with a prologue and epilogue to suggest, as Tennyson put it, a kind of divine comedy, beginning with deep grief and ending with a wedding and reintegration into the life of society. The sudden and shocking death of Hallam had shaken Tennyson's faith in a benevolent deity and led him to examine the grounds of faith in an age made increasingly skeptical by wider knowledge in the fields of geology, evolutionary science, MEDICINE and BIBLICAL CRITICISM, so the elegy spoke directly to the most fundamental Victorian anxieties as Tennyson struggled to justify the ways of God to man. The poem impresses most modern readers more as an expression of deep grief than of consolation and more as a testament of doubt than of faith, but Tennyson's contemporaries were deeply moved and comforted by the work. QUEEN VICTORIA herself said that next to the Bible, *In Memoriam* was her greatest consolation in her mourning for PRINCE ALBERT.

In *Maud* (1855) Tennyson again experimented with genre, creating a monodrama consisting of individual lyric poems expressive of the melancholy madness of a sensitive individual alienated from the commercial spirit of the Victorian age. *Maud* was to some extent autobiographical, but like *In Memoriam*, it spoke not simply of Tennyson's anxieties but also those of the age. Tennyson addressed the concerns of the age almost as directly in his medievalist allegory of the modern British kingdom and EMPIRE, the immensely popular epic-length cycle of Arthurian tales, *Idylls of the King*, written over a 40-year period beginning with "Morte D'Arthur" in 1833 and finishing with "Balin and Balan" in 1874 (published 1885).

Inevitably, as Tennyson aged rising generations of poets challenged his supremacy, but he remained a brilliant writer to the end, publishing frequent collections of lyric poetry in addition to his longer works. He remained to the end of his life the poet whom WALT WHITMAN designated the "boss of us all," and posthumously he remained a major influence on the poetry of the late nineteenth and the early twentieth century.

See also POETRY; ROMANTICISM.

FURTHER READING

Ricks, Christopher. *Tennyson*. 2d ed. London: Macmillan, 1989.
Tucker, Herbert. *Tennyson and the Doom of Romanticism.* Cambridge, Mass.: Harvard University Press, 1988.

DAVID RIEDE

TERRY, ELLEN

Born: February 27, 1847; Coventry, England
Died: July 21, 1928; Smallhythe, England

Ellen Terry was one of the most celebrated actresses of the British THEATER in the second half of the nineteenth century. During her career of over 50 years, she was most renowned for her portrayal of Shakespearean heroines opposite the popular actor HENRY IRVING (1838–1905), at London's Lyceum Theatre. Terry's tenure as a child player, supporting young lady, and leading actress coincided with a dramatic shift in the status and range of the British theater, which had been dominated mostly by burlesque and pantomime because of royal restrictions placed on the theater in the eighteenth century. When these bans were partially lifted in the 1840s, actor-managers such as Charles Kean (1811–1868), the Bancrofts (Sir Squire [1841–1926] and Marie Wilton [1840–1921]), and Henry Irving, each of whom in turn hired Terry, revitalized the spoken drama.

Kean and Irving mounted elaborate productions of Shakespeare with a unified stage design that endeavored to achieve historically accurate detail in set and costume design. Productions such as these brought middle-class audiences into the theater, although there were still serious debates about its respectability, and some members of the middle class continued to believe that the theater was immoral in principle. Actors in the first half of the century did not have a high social standing in British culture and most actors came from the lower end of the class system. As the theater became more legitimate, so too did the status of the actor. Acting was also one of the few professions in which women could earn their living. Ellen Terry's own class background was unstable as the child of theatrical parents. She received no formal education, sometimes led a scandalous life, and for most of her life, supported herself and her family. It is symbolic of the rise of the actor's status that in 1925, at the end of her illustrious career, Terry was made a Dame Grand Cross.

Terry was the second daughter of a large theatrical family. Her father and mother were itinerant actors, and they raised their seven children for the stage. Kate Terry, the eldest, was the first success in the

British actress Ellen Terry in costume for her role as Cordelia.

family. Before she retired in 1867 to marry the businessman Arthur Lewis, Kate Terry was for a brief period the leading actress of the London stage at Charles Kean's theater. Terry debuted on the stage in 1856 as the boy Mamilius in Charles Kean's production of Shakespeare's *The Winter's Tale*. She acted with Kean at the Princess's Theatre until 1859, receiving critical acclaim for her performances as Puck in *A Midsummer Night's Dream* and Prince Arthur in *King John*. Afterward, the Terry parents took Terry and her elder sister Kate on a tour of the country performing two plays. Terry then successively joined a number of different companies, including a Bristol stock company where she took part in burlesques as well as drama.

Unlike her sister Kate, Terry's life was unconventional, at times defying the moral codes of nineteenth-century Britain. As an adult, her social milieu not only included other theatrical professionals, but also artistic and literary London. At the age of 16 she left the stage to marry the painter George Frederick Watts (1817–1904), whom she had met when she and her sister Kate posed for his painting, *The Sisters*. At this time, in addition to posing for Watts, Terry also posed for the photographer JULIA MARGARET CAMERON (1815–

1879). The marriage to Watts would only last a year, and the two separated with Terry returning to her parents' house. She met C. L. Dodgson (LEWIS CARROLL [1832–1898]), and he, too, photographed her. After three years of inactivity, Terry returned to the stage in 1866. Soon after, she eloped with the architect and designer E. W. Godwin (1833–1886), disappearing from public view for six years. She had first met Godwin before her first marriage while performing in Bristol. She had not yet divorced Watts, so she and Godwin set up house in Harpendon without being married. The couple had two children, Edith, born 1869, and Edward, born 1872. They would later take the surname Craig: Edith Craig and Edward Gordon Craig became distinguished in their own right, both as theater directors, producers, and designers. Terry and Godwin suffered from financial difficulties, so Terry again returned to the stage in 1874. She would continue her theatrical career uninterrupted and soon became the most prominent actress on the British stage.

Terry joined the Bancrofts at the Prince of Wales Theatre in 1875. There she played Portia in *The Merchant of Venice* in a production designed by Godwin. Godwin was an advocate of historicism in stage design, and he staged the play with realistic, archaeologically based dress and sets. Although the play flopped after three weeks, Terry was a huge success. Like Kean, the Bancrofts hold an important place in theater history. In addition to Shakespeare, they had successfully mounted light, middle-class "cup-and-saucer" comedies, in which Terry was to play, and shifted acting styles away from the declamatory to the more realistic and, in staging, toward the use of more realistic sets.

Not long after Terry's return to the stage, she and Godwin separated. When Terry obtained a divorce from Watts in 1877, she married the actor Charles Wardell (stage name Charles Kelly) in 1878, but this marriage only lasted for a few years before they too separated. With a successful performance at John Hare's theater in a production of *Olivia*, which was based on Oliver Goldsmith's *The Vicar of Wakefield*, Terry came to the attention of Henry Irving, who had just leased the Lyceum Theatre. Irving invited Terry to be his leading lady at the Lyceum, and the two are generally thought to have been lovers. She would play at the Lyceum and tour America several times with him for the next 24 years. He mounted the highest quality productions in LONDON, mostly of Shakespeare and historical dramas or sentimental comedies. Terry's most famous roles at the Lyceum included Ophelia, Beatrice, and Lady Macbeth.

In 1892, Terry began an intimate correspondence that continued for 30 years with the critic and playwright, GEORGE BERNARD SHAW (1856–1950), although the two seldom met in person. Shaw was at odds with Irving. He saw Irving's love of Shakespeare and large-scale dramatic stagings of plays as antiquated compared to the intimate, realistic dramas of Henrik Ibsen (1828–1906) and those he himself was to write. Nevertheless, Irving stuck to the same repertoire throughout the Lyceum's history even as the number of permanent theater companies expanded and the theatrical scene changed with the advent of plays by Shaw and others, including OSCAR WILDE, J. M. Barrie, ARTHUR WING PINERO, and Henry Arthur Jones. As the theatrical landscape changed, Irving's Lyceum Theatre company could not sustain itself and its doors closed in 1902. After Irving's death, Terry performed in *Alice Sit-by-the-Fire* in a role written for her by J. M. Barrie in 1906. She was also to appear in one Shaw play, *Captain Brassbound's Conversion*, in the same year. Through this production she met her third husband, the American actor, James Carew, 25 years her junior. They, too, separated after a few years. With increasing blindness, Terry's career effectively ended. She retired to a farmhouse in Kent (now the Ellen Terry Memorial Museum) and died there in 1928.

See also THEATER.

FURTHER READING

Auerbach, Nina. *Ellen Terry: Player in Her Own Time.* New York and London: W. W. Norton, 1987.
Craig, Edward Gordon. *Ellen Terry and Her Secret Self.* London: Sampson Low, Marston, 1931.
Manvell, Roger. *Ellen Terry.* New York: G. P. Putnam's Sons, 1968.
St. John, Christopher, ed. *Ellen Terry and Bernard Shaw: A Correspondence.* New York: G. P. Putnam's Sons, 1931.
Terry, Ellen. *Ellen Terry's Memoirs.* Preface, Notes, and Additional Biographical Chapters by Edith Craig and Christopher St. John. New York: G. P. Putnam's Sons, 1932.

DIANE WAGGONER

TEST ACTS

In 1673 and 1678, Parliament passed a set of acts, commonly referred to as the Test Acts, that required various displays of allegiance to the Anglican church. The legislation was the climax of a series of conflicts with King Charles II (1630–1685; ruled 1660–1685) over royal authority and initiative. Anglican gentry in Parliament—worried that the king would seek to form a coalition of Roman Catholics, Protestant Dissenters, and others in favor of religious toleration, and would attempt to govern independent of

Parliament—exacted a price for financial support for the king's foreign policy by focusing on issues of religious identification. The Test Acts were not repealed until 1828, but their intent remained an issue long afterward.

The first Test Act declared that every holder of every office, civil or military, or those in the service of the monarch or of his brother the duke of York (who had declared himself a Roman Catholic in the previous year), had to take the Lord's Supper according to the rules of the Church of England and take an oath against transubstantiation (the religious doctrine that holds that the bread and wine taken at the Eucharist are transformed into the body and blood of Jesus). Punishment for not doing so included loss of office, inability to be guardian of any child, and forfeiture or fine of 500 pounds. Some minor civil offices were excluded from these requirements. The second act applied similar requirements of Roman Catholics sitting in either house of Parliament. The Corporation Act (1661) had required the same sacramental test of all municipal office holders.

Despite such strictly worded legislation, two practices gradually developed by which Protestant Dissenters could evade the penalties and participate in politics, although mainly at the local level. One was "occasional conformity," whereby persons could receive the Lord's Supper in an Anglican parish church once a year and thus satisfy the law. Second was the passage of annual "Indemnity Bills," beginning in 1727, which abolished the penalties and enabled a few Dissenters to serve in Parliament.

Because of these common practices, repeal of the Test and Corporation acts removed what had become largely a formal grievance for Protestant Dissenters. In the eighteenth century the Protestant Dissenting deputies had lobbied for repeal and garnered some support. However, the French Revolution in 1789 and the conservative reaction in England put an end to serious efforts for repeal until agitation in Ireland made Roman Catholic disabilities a focus of attention in the 1820s.

The repeal of the Test Acts, together with Catholic emancipation from civil disabilities in 1829, substituted for the sacramental test a declaration that a person would not injure or weaken the established church. By the time of repeal most people regarded the question of religious identification as irrelevant to any person's participation in political life, and that transition from the seventeenth century marked an important shift in the understanding of the relation between religion and politics. While membership in Parliament was still denied to Jews and atheists, repeal sent a more subtle signal: the foundation for understanding the close relationship between church and state had begun to erode.

See also ROMAN CATHOLICISM; DISSENT.

FURTHER READING

Clark, J. C. D. "England's Ancien Regime as a Confessional State." *Albion* 21, no. 3 (1989): 450–474.

Davis, Thomas W., ed. *Committees for Repeal of the Test and Corporation Acts: Minutes 1786–90 and 1827–28.* Chatham, Kent: London Record Society, 1978.

Grant Robertson, C., ed. *Select Statutes, Cases and Documents to Illustrate English Constitutional History, 1660–1832.* New York: G. P. Putnam's Sons, 1904.

Sparkes, Douglas C. "The Test Act of 1673 and Its Aftermath." *Baptist Quarterly* 25, no. 2 (April 1973): 74–85.

DALE A. JOHNSON

THACKERAY, WILLIAM MAKEPEACE

Born: July 18, 1811; Calcutta, India
Died: December 24, 1863; London, England

Next to CHARLES DICKENS (1812–1870), William Makepeace Thackeray was the most popular novelist of the Victorian era. His satirical novel *Vanity Fair* became a huge success a few months after it began appearing in serial installments in 1847, prompting one newspaper to suggest that Thackeray was supplanting Dickens as the leading novelist of the day. Though this never quite happened, *Vanity Fair* placed Thackeray, as he put it, "at the top of the tree . . . having a great fight up there with Dickens." In the minds of readers and critics of the day, the names of Dickens and Thackerey were inextricably intertwined as the most important authors of the era.

The two were very different sorts of writers, however. Dickens's novels are sentimental and idealistic, and contain sympathetic heroes. *Vanity Fair*, according to its subtitle, is "A Novel without a Hero," and in it Thackeray mocks and criticizes almost all of the characters as a means of humorously illustrating the follies and shortcomings of mankind.

Also, whereas Dickens and other writers of the day focused on social problems such as WORKHOUSES, FACTORIES, and the unjust legal system, Thackeray focused on the more timeless failings of human nature, such as hypocrisy, snobbery, and greed. In fact, just as the first installments of *Vanity Fair* were being published, a whole series of Thackeray's essays on snobbery was completing its run in *PUNCH*, the famous humor magazine.

THE VIEW FROM OUTSIDE

Thackeray had always been a bit of an outsider. Although his family was wealthy, its wealth came from INDIA. The family was held in high esteem by the British community in India, but in less high esteem in England. Moreover, soon after inheriting his part of the family fortune at the age of 21, Thackeray managed to lose almost all of it through some extravagant gambling, a banking collapse, and some money-losing investments in such things as the magazine *The National Standard*. Without an inheritance and with a wife and two young daughters to support, he took to earning a living as a JOURNALIST, but because this profession was considered less than respectable and because of his Indian background, he found himself excluded from good society. This may account for his satirical attacks on it and also for his tendency to write sympathetically about characters, like the wickedly appealing Becky Sharp in *Vanity Fair*, whose main aim is to enter society.

Curiously, Thackeray's satirical attacks earned him praise from the very group of people he had most specifically attacked: the fashionable lords and ladies of England. Thackeray found himself invited to dinners given by dukes and duchesses, and once his

William Makepeace Thackeray became a full-time writer after the success of *Vanity Fair* in 1847.

fame had earned him entrance into good society, his satirical attacks on it faded. His novels after *Vanity Fair* tended to express sympathy for upper-middle-class characters, such as Colonel Newcome in *The Newcomes* (published serially from 1853 to 1855) and Major Pendennis in *Pendennis* (published serially from 1848 to 1850). These two novels, along with *The History of Henry Esmond* (1852), also feature conventional Victorian heroes.

Some readers of the day preferred these later, mellower novels to *Vanity Fair*. Thackeray's protégé ANTHONY TROLLOPE (1815–1882), for instance, thought that *Henry Esmond* was Thackeray's greatest achievement. However, in the twentieth century these later novels fell from favor, perhaps because they seemed too much an expression of outmoded Victorian values. Only *Vanity Fair*, the novel in which Thackeray satirized those values, retained its popularity, and by the end of the twentieth century Thackeray was essentially a one-book author whose general reputation no longer compared to that of Dickens.

AN EARLY REALIST?

Thackeray is sometimes considered a forerunner of twentieth-century realism in literature. He criticized the exaggerations in Dickens and said it should be the aim of novels to "represent Nature" and to "convey as strongly as possible the sentiment of reality." He also made it a point to mock unrealistic notions about love, military adventures, and criminals. In other ways, however, Thackeray looks not so much forward to the twentieth century as he does backward to the eighteenth. He was always a great admirer of the eighteenth-century novelist Henry Fielding (1707–1754), and his novels, like Fielding's, contain a great deal of intrusive commentary and digressions by the narrator, who is prone to addressing the "dear reader" and referring to the characters in the novel as puppets. This destruction of the illusion of reality in his novels is the sort of thing condemned by the later American writer HENRY JAMES (1843–1916), who singled out Thackeray's *The Newcomes* as an example of the "large loose baggy monsters" of the Victorian era.

See also NOVEL; SOCIAL CLASSES.

FURTHER READING

Ferris, Ina. *William Makepeace Thackeray.* Boston: Twayne, 1983.

Peters, Catherine. *Thackeray's Universe: Shifting Worlds of Imagination and Reality.* New York: Oxford University Press, 1987.

Ray, Gordon N. *Thackeray: The Uses of Adversity, 1811–1846.* New York: McGraw-Hill, 1955.

Ray, Gordon N. *Thackeray: The Age of Wisdom, 1847–1863.* New York: McGraw-Hill, 1957.

Shillingsburg, Peter. *William Makepeace Thackeray: A Literary Life.* Basingstoke: Palgrave, 2001.

Williams, Ioan M. *Thackeray.* London: Evans, 1968.

SHELDON GOLDFARB

THEATER

The Victorian era was a time of a great deal of change in the Western theater. INDUSTRIALIZATION caused huge increases in urban populations and, for the first time, many working-class people had money to spend on leisure-time pursuits. The theater was one of the establishments to benefit from the increased market for entertainment. In fact, for most of the nineteenth century theater was the principal medium of entertainment for both the literate and illiterate populations of Europe and the UNITED STATES. QUEEN VICTORIA herself occasionally attended the theater and she also staged theatricals at Windsor Castle. The queen's support helped to make the theater more respectable among all classes of people in Great Britain. Although the clergy and religious conservatives still viewed the theater as a magnet for the immoral and indecent elements of society, most of the population patronized local theaters and helped to create one of the most productive and transitional times in all of theater history.

THEATRICAL VENUES

The largest and most prestigious theaters in Victorian England were Drury Lane and Covent Garden. Until 1843 these theaters held royal patents that gave them the exclusive rights to perform "legitimate" theater in LONDON. Full-length plays such as comedies, tragedies, farces, and Shakespearean plays could only be presented at these large patent theaters. The rest of the theatrical establishments were relegated to presenting VAUDEVILLE, burlesque, MELODRAMA, and other musical entertainments. These regulations began to have a negative effect on the theatrical establishments in England. Attendance declined and many of the theater buildings became extremely rundown. In order to counteract this trend, the Theatre Regulation Act was passed in 1843, abolishing the patent houses' privileged position and opening the way for other venues to offer a wider variety of theater. In FRANCE the national theaters were of importance, particularly the Comédie Française, which had been established by Louis XIV in 1680. The theater's mission was the preservation of the heritage of French drama, and therefore, the offerings were in large part classical and traditional.

Respectable Victorian families expected to attend theatrical performances that were free of vulgarity and controversial subject matter. They also wanted to attend theaters that were not situated in crime-ridden neighborhoods. During the early part of the century the theatrical neighborhoods were often teeming with prostitutes and other unsavory characters. As theater managers discovered that they could make more money by appealing to the respectable middle classes, however, they began to remodel and clean up the theaters. During his tenure as theater manager, for example, WILLIAM CHARLES MACREADY (1793–1873) banished prostitutes from the precincts of Drury Lane, thus making it a safer place for the middle class. Theaters also worked to make the advance booking process simpler and increased the foyer space. All of these improvements made the theaters a more attractive place for Victorian families. Most of these improvements and renovations took place after the 1860s, and they precipitated a real boom in theater attendance.

Other theatrical entertainments could be found in MUSIC HALLS patronized by boisterous crowds who liked to be able to drink and smoke during their entertainment. MUSEUMS, lecture halls, and TRAVELING FAIRS presented magicians, mesmerists, freaks, and other unique performers.

INSIDE THE THEATER

The physical layout of the larger Victorian theaters was fairly standard. The auditorium was U-shaped with benches lining the ground floor or pit. The pit was surrounded on all sides by tiers of boxes. Above the boxes in the back of the auditorium were the galleries. The stage jutted out into the floor of the auditorium so that the closest audience members in the pit surrounded it on three sides. As the century progressed, however, this jutting part of the stage, also known as the apron, was gradually reduced in size. By the end of the century, the apron had virtually vanished, and almost all of the stage space was now located behind the proscenium arch. This created the classic picture-frame stage that many are familiar with today. The layout of the seating area reflected the class divisions that were present in London society at the time. Aristocratic audience members sat in the boxes. These were the most expensive seats in the house, even though they did not always offer the best view of the production. In fact, sometimes the view from the boxes was quite terrible, but these seats were

sought after because of the prestige they bestowed. When sitting in the boxes, the purpose was not to see the play, but to be seen. The pit area was usually peopled with students and craftsmen and members of the new middle class. The galleries were the area in which the lower class audience members sat. Each section of the seating had a separate entrance so that the upper classes would not have to mingle with those that were of a lower station in society.

Audiences in Victorian theaters were often rowdy and boisterous, and they didn't hesitate to let the performers know if they were pleased or dissatisfied. It was common for audience members to carry on loud conversations during productions, making it very difficult for the plays to be heard. Many editorials were written complaining about bad audience behavior during the period. In the early part of the century, the lights in the audience remained on during the entire play. After the advent of gas lighting, however, actor-manager HENRY IRVING (1838–1905) began the practice of turning off the houselights and doing scene changes in the dark. At first audiences protested, because this meant they could no longer be the center of attention. After a time, however, the practice of darkening the theater was widely adopted and still remains in place today.

The stage lighting during the Victorian era changed from oil to gas. This gave theater producers a great deal more control over lighting effects because the gas jets could be controlled from a single source. Fantastic sunrises and spectacular lighting displays have been recorded from the period. The cleaner-burning gas fuel also made the theater environment more comfortable, with less heavy smoke hanging in the building than had previously been present with oil lighting. Gas-jet footlights—a series of lights that ran along the front edge of the stage—were used in most theaters to light the actors' faces from below. Limelight was also a popular lighting effect in use at the time. Limelight was created by heating a piece of lime with a flame of oxygen and hydrogen. This process would produce a very bright beam of light that could be focused to form a type of spotlight effect. In 1881, the first completely electric theater, The Savoy, was built in England, but many theaters continued to use gas lighting well into the next century. During most of the century, while theaters continued to use oil and gas lighting, theater fires were a major problem. A disastrous one at the theater in Exeter in September 1887 killed 150 people.

At the beginning of the Victorian period theaters still primarily used a scenic system known as the wing-and-groove. A series of grooves were cut into the stage floor running parallel to the front edge of the stage, and flat scenic pieces made out of wood and canvas—the wings—slid along the tracks created by the grooves. These scenic pieces were affixed to an elaborate system of pulleys and counterweights used to move them into place. There was also a large amount of open space or "fly space" above the stage. This allowed some scenery (and actors) to be flown in from above. Large numbers of stagehands were needed to execute the most elaborate scene changes. For the Christmas pantomimes in the larger theaters, the stagehands often numbered in the hundreds.

At the beginning of the century, all scene changes were accomplished in full view of the audience at the command of bells and whistles. The various sounds were used to coordinate the complex moves needed to get all of the scenery properly in place. This bells and whistles system is the reason it is still believed to be bad luck to whistle backstage at a theater. If you did it during the Victorian era, you might find a piece of scenery flying down on your head. The stage floor also contained a number of holes or traps that could be used to make objects appear and disappear quickly. The larger Victorian theaters were even fitted with mechanized platforms that could rise up to create multiple levels of staging.

Smaller details of stage settings became a focus for some managers as the century progressed. A trend toward historical accuracy in properties and costumes began to take hold, particularly for Shakespearean

An engraving of the interior of the Drury Lane Theatre, from *Old and New London: The City Ancient and Modern* (vol. 3, 1897).

plays. Charles Kean (1811–1868) was famous for his productions of Shakespeare featuring authentic period detail. As a result of this trend, theaters started to hire designers to research historical periods and to oversee the accurate reproduction of the time period being portrayed. As the century progressed, scenic conventions continued to change. Realism not only influenced the props, costumes, and storylines but also the entire way in which plays were staged as well. Some producers began to experiment with the box set. This theatrical convention uses three walls joined together to create an actual room instead of using painted flats to create a stage setting. Real furniture and three-dimensional objects were used to finish the set, making them much like what is seen on stages today. Madame Vestris (1797–1856), theatrical manager of the Olympic theater, was said to have introduced the box set to London audiences around 1832. It remained a novelty, however, until much later in the century.

ATTRACTING THE CROWDS

Spectacle was a common element in most Victorian theater. When people attended a performance, they wanted to see something that would really amaze them. Because of the opportunity for spectacle that they offered, the yearly Christmas pantomimes were extremely well liked by all strata of British society. Pantomimes were built around a fantastical or fairy-tale theme, and they featured lavish sets and elaborate costumes. The productions were musical and comic extravaganzas that typically featured woman in breeches playing the "best boy" and a man in female drag playing the "dame." Many actors of the time made their name by playing these unique types of characters. The highlight of the pantomime was the transformation scene, in which the entire stage underwent a magic metamorphosis. Set pieces would rise up out of the floor and some performers might be flown in on trapezes. The purpose was to amaze and bedazzle the audience. Some of the most lavish pantomimes of the period featured hundreds of performers and almost as many stagehands working backstage to help make the transformation take place.

The traveling panorama was also in use during this period. A traveling panorama was a large stretch of canvas or muslin on which was painted a continuous backdrop scene. The panorama was hung at the back of the stage on two large spools and rolled from one spool to another so it looked like the horizon was moving. The traveling panorama was often coupled with treadmills to create spectacular stage

effects. This was the method that was used to stage the chariot race from *Ben-Hur*; while horses galloped on the treadmills a traveling panorama of the crowds in the stands moved behind them. Real large-crowd scenes were also popular at this time. Extras called "supernumeraries" or "supers" were frequently used to fill the stage space and make a production seem bigger.

PERFORMANCE TYPES

There were a wide array of theatrical offerings during the Victorian era. Melodrama was the most prominent form of theater throughout Europe and the United States, largely due to its appeal for the uneducated masses. The stock characters of the hero, the villain, and the damsel in distress were easily recognizable and understandable to audience members who did not have a lot of previous experience attending the theater. The action and special effects of such plays were also very appealing. Irish playwright DION BOUCICAULT (1820–1890) became famous during the period by writing melodramas featuring spectacular scenes of fires and explosions. Another reason melodrama was so popular in England was that, prior to the passing of the Theatre Regulation Act in 1843, it was one of the few genres that most of the minor theaters were permitted to perform. Melodramas were written in three acts and accompanied by a musical score. Companies often made regular plays into melodramas by dividing them into three acts and adding some music. This loophole caused some fairly bizarre productions to occur. As Oscar Brockett notes, "*Othello* is said to have been performed as a melodrama with the mere addition of a chord struck on the piano every five minutes." Farce was also an extremely popular form of entertainment during the Victorian era, as was Shakespeare. OPERA was a favorite of the cultured classes.

In addition to the well-known theatrical genres, there were also numerous other types of popular theatrical entertainments during the Victorian era. In the 1840s in America, for example, the minstrel show came into vogue. Minstrel shows were productions in which working-class white men portrayed black plantation slaves as comic fools. The performers blackened their faces with burnt cork or greasepaint and parodied black music, dance, and dialects. The performances included ballads, comic songs, jokes, and instrumentals and featured three stock characters—Mr. Bones, Mr. Tambo, and Mr. Interlocuter—as the main performers in the show. Other demeaning black characters such as Jim Crow and Old Zip

Coon were also often part of the production. The minstrel show was an indigenous form of American entertainment that perpetuated negative black stereotypes well into the next century.

Overall, the late nineteenth century was an incredibly productive time for drama, and many influential plays came out of the period. Toward the end of the century, realism became a driving force in the theaters across Europe and eventually in the United States. In the 1870s, Norwegian playwright Henrik Ibsen (1828–1906) created a sensation in northern Europe with his realistic, hard-hitting dramas that dealt with somber, controversial subjects. His groundbreaking play *A Doll's House* premiered in 1879. A social drama in which a woman refuses to obey her husband and walks out on her marriage, the play eventually toured Europe and America, causing a sensation on both continents. In 1891 *Ghosts* premiered in London, further pushing Ibsen's influence upon the English stage. While his subject matter angered many conservatives, Ibsen's vision of real people discussing real problems ushered in a new type of theatrical writing that is still prominent today. His works became the standard by which other socially conscious playwrights were judged, and he influenced the first great playwright of the modern era, George Bernard Shaw (1856–1950).

PERFORMERS

At the beginning of the nineteenth century, most of the theaters housed resident repertory companies that consisted of a group of players who would appear in almost all of the plays presented at that theater. Companies were formed from performers who had a special type of role in which they specialized. This specialty was known as their line of business. Actors were expected to furnish their own costumes and props in accordance with their line of business. For example, an actor who specialized as a tragedian would need to have costumes for all of Shakespeare's major tragic characters, as well as swords, boots, hats, wigs, and so on. This practice diminished later in the century when some managers began to hire designers to create authentic period costumes and properties. Theaters constantly rotated plays so that local audiences kept coming back. Plays might change weekly, or even nightly. This system was very taxing on the performers. They had to quickly memorize numerous roles and be able to play them in succession. By the end of the century, the repertory company was vanishing, however. Increases in population and tourism afforded theaters the opportunity to offer longer runs of popular shows. If a production was a hit, there were now enough people around to keep the seats filled for several weeks. Some of the most popular shows had runs that lasted for hundreds of performances, a phenomenon unheard of at the beginning of the century. Because of the phenomenon of the long run, by the end of the century the repertory company was almost obsolete.

The acting style of the Victorian era was quite histrionic by today's standards. Actors used large gestures and exaggerated body postures to convey the emotional life of their characters. Some built their career on a loud voice alone. Some actors studied the Delsarte system of acting that dictated a specific code of hand gestures and body positions that were to be struck and held for each emotional state. This mode of acting was begun in Paris by French drama teacher François Delsarte, and it was one of the first efforts at formulating a standard for the craft of acting. It gradually went out of vogue, however, and toward the end of the century realism in drama began to have an influence on acting styles. Although they still had a long way to go to reach the realistic style that is familiar today, actors in the latter part of the century moved considerably toward adopting more natural interpretations of their characters' voices and movements.

As the theaters themselves improved, so did the reputation of theater artists. By the end of the century many theater professionals had been welcomed into high society. Many actors elevated their status by becoming actor-managers, whereby they controlled every aspect of their own theatrical productions. This allowed them to position themselves as the star of a company and to cast themselves in the best roles. It also made them fiscally responsible for the productions, however. The actor-manager rarely owned his own theater, but leased it from the owner of the building. Most of the better-known names of the day were performers who took on the difficult role of actor-manager, including Henry Irving, William Charles Macready, Edwin Booth, and Herbert Beerbohm Tree. Several actor-managers were admitted to prestigious GENTLEMEN'S CLUBS, and in 1895 Irving received the first knighthood ever bestowed upon an actor.

The phenomenon of the actor-manager helped to deeply entrench the star system during the Victorian era. Because the principal actors were responsible for promoting themselves, they made sure their names were well known to the public. These celebrities became a major audience draw, and it became a common practice to feature the performer's name in big bold letters on publicity handbills and posters. Often the audience members were not even aware of what production they were going to see, but they certainly knew who would be performing. Star billing became of prime importance.

TOURING

Touring was also an important part of any major theatrical enterprise. After the 1860s a large number of theaters were built, many in the provinces, and these theaters often brought in the most popular plays from London. Touring groups featuring well-known actors would play these provincial circuits during the summer months when the large London theaters were closed. The towns missed by the circuit tours were visited by strolling companies whose repertoire consisted of melodrama, farce, pantomime, and some Shakespeare. These companies would perform at fairs and other venues, offering truncated versions of the most popular productions of the day. Productions that were popular in London would also make their way to other cities in Europe and eventually to the United States. The ease of steamship travel made this a possibility. As Michael Booth notes, "The big companies, led by star actor-managers, profited most from steamships. Henry Irving's Lyceum company, for instance, crossed to North America eight times between 1882 and 1903." French productions also toured extensively. For example, at the end of 1897, *Cyrano de Bergerac* premiered and was an immense success in Paris. Not long after it became a sensation throughout Europe and America. Another very important touring troupe during this period was that put together by Georg II, duke of Saxe-Meiningen (1826–1914) in Germany. He is often considered to be one of the first theater artists to take on the role of what we now recognize as the theater director. The duke made great strides in the theatrical arts by emphasizing ensemble playing among his company. He shunned the star system because he was unable to pay the prices of the most popular players. Instead he concentrated on making sure all performers and other elements in his production worked together to create a unified artistic statement. He also insisted on using authentic fabrics for costumes in place of the cheap substitutes that were often used by other companies. The Meiningen players toured nine countries between 1874 and 1890 and gained the best reputation of any touring company in the world.

CENSORING PLAYS

Throughout the entire nineteenth century, all plays in England were subject to the approval of the lord chamberlain's office. Before it could be produced, a play had to be submitted to the examiner of plays. This office served as a censoring agency for plays that contained subject matter deemed to be offensive or immoral. This system of CENSORSHIP prohibited many playwrights from writing pieces dealing with controversial religious, political, or social themes. The Licensing Act, which gave the lord chamberlain's office this power, remained on the books until 1968.

Overall, playwrights had a somewhat difficult time in Victorian England. In addition to being subjected to censorship by the lord chamberlain, their plays were often stolen and produced by other companies without permission or payment. This remained a major problem until the final decades of the century when the International Copyright Act of 1887 and the American Copyright Act of 1890 were passed. These acts legally recognized a playwright's right to control and be paid for his or her work. While they did not totally eliminate theatrical piracy, they helped to curb it a great deal.

Some outstanding playwrights made their debut during the Victorian era. In 1895 OSCAR WILDE (1854–1900) premiered a play that is still considered to be one of the greatest comedies of all time, *The Importance of Being Earnest*. It opened at London's St. James Theatre on February 14, 1895. George Bernard Shaw (1856–1950) also began his playwriting career in the nineteenth century.

See also ACTORS AND ACTING; MELODRAMA; MUSIC HALLS.

FURTHER READING

Booth, Michael R. *Theatre in the Victorian Age.* New York: Cambridge University Press, 1991.

Booth, Michael R. *Victorian Spectacular Theatre, 1850–1910.* Boston: Routledge and Kegan Paul, 1981.

Brockett, Oscar G. *History of the Theatre.* 3d ed. Boston: Allyn and Bacon, 1977.

Cockrell, Dale. *Demons of Disorder: Early Blackface Minstrels and Their World.* New York: Cambridge University Press, 1997.

Finkell, Alicia. *Romantic Stages: Set and Costume Design in Victorian England.* Jefferson, N.C.: McFarland, 1996.

Foulkes, Richard, ed. *Shakespeare and the Victorian Stage.* New York: Cambridge University Press, 1986.

Frow, Gerald. *"Oh, Yes It Is!": A History of Pantomime.* London: British Broadcasting Corporation, 1985.

Jackson, Russell, ed. *Victorian Theatre: The Theatre in Its Time.* New York: New Amsterdam Books, 1989.

Jenkins, Anthony. *The Making of Victorian Drama.* New York: Cambridge University Press, 1991.

Powell, Kerry. *Women and the Victorian Theatre.* New York: Cambridge University Press, 1997.

Rowell, George. *The Victorian Theatre: A Survey.* New York: Oxford University Press, 1956.

Shattuck, Charles H., ed. *Bulwer and Macready: A Chronicle of the Early Victorian Theatre.* Urbana: University of Illinois Press, 1958.

Walker, Robert H. *Everyday Life in Victorian America, 1865–1900.* Malabar, Florida: Krieger Publishing, 1994.

Woodfield, James. *English Theatre in Transition, 1881–1914.* Totowa, N.J.: Barnes and Noble, 1984.

BETH A. KATTELMAN

THOMSON, WILLIAM

Born: June 26, 1824; Belfast, Ireland
Died: December 17, 1907; Largs, Scotland

William Thomson, professor of natural philosophy at the University of Glasgow from 1846 to 1899, was one of the outstanding physicists of the Victorian period. In 1892 he became the first scientist to be elevated to the peerage as Baron Kelvin of Largs and to sit in the House of Lords.

The son of a respected mathematician, Thomson was born in Belfast and soon distinguished himself as a child prodigy. He began attending lectures at the University of Glasgow, where his father was a professor, at the age of eight, and he entered the university at age ten. He pursued graduate work at Cambridge and in Paris while still in his teens, and in 1846, at the age of 22, he was appointed professor of natural philosophy at the University of Glasgow. During his 53 years as a professor he carried out a wide-ranging program of research. Perhaps his best remembered work was in the field of thermodynamics: he collaborated with James Joule (1818–1899) to illustrate the Joule-Kelvin effect, which describes the cooling of gases as they are expanded, an effect that has implications for refrigeration and other techniques. Most important, Thomson defined the absolute temperature scale and the concept of absolute zero: the temperature unit known as the kelvin is named after him. He also made a significant contribution to electromagnetics, working with MICHAEL FARADAY (1791–1867) on the concept of electromagnetic fields, and developed the theory of electric oscillations. Through this and other work Thomson gained a worldwide reputation. The celebration of his fifty years in the chair of natural philosophy was attended by representatives of universities worldwide, including many from the United States, and yet remained an essentially Glaswegian occasion, reflecting his lifelong association with the city.

Thomson was concerned above all things with the practical use of his many scientific discoveries, and he designed a variety of scientific instruments, including range finders and compasses. As a practical scientist and a director of the Atlantic Telegraph Company, he was involved with the laying of the first transatlantic cable, which after many difficulties was completed in 1866 (as a result of which Thomson was knighted). He patented his Improved Mariner's Compass in 1876, and in association with James White supplied many compasses to Royal Navy ships and to other countries' ships of war in the 1880s. Again his association with the city of Glasgow, easily the world's largest producer of ships, was an important element of this commercial success, which brought Thomson considerable personal wealth. His commercial and political activities did not always endear him to the British scientific establishment, although he was elected president of the Royal Society in 1890.

Politically Thomson was a Liberal and had been offered the Liberal candidacy for one of the Scottish university seats in 1880, but the importance of his Irish background was reflected in his opposition to WILLIAM GLADSTONE'S HOME RULE Bill in 1886 and his subsequent alignment with the Liberal Unionist party. As Crosbie Smith and M. Norton Wise show in their biography of Thomson, his energetic opposition to home rule in the following years played an important part in his elevation to the peerage by ROBERT CECIL'S (Lord Salisbury's) government in 1892. To his death he remained an ardent imperialist, supporting JOSEPH CHAMBERLAIN'S imperial policy and the second BOER WAR.

See also INVENTIONS; PHYSICS.

FURTHER READING

Sharlin, Harold I., with Tiby Sharlin. *Lord Kelvin, the Dynamic Victorian.* University Park: Pennsylvania State University Press, 1979.

Smith, Crosbie, and M. Norton Wise. *Energy and Empire: A Biographical Study of Lord Kelvin.* Cambridge: Cambridge University Press, 1989.

Thompson, Silvanus P. *The Life of William Thomson, Baron Kelvin of Largs.* 2 vols. London: Macmillan and Company, 1910.

MARK FREEMAN

TIMES, THE

The London-based daily NEWSPAPER *The Times* was the single most prestigious and influential paper in Britain during the nineteenth century. Nicknamed "the Thunderer" for its uncompromising expression of independent opinion, its influence prompted leading politicians from all political parties to court its favor.

The paper originated in the late eighteenth century as *The Daily Universal Register,* founded in 1785 by coal merchant John Walter and published under that name until 1788. Walter's son, also John, brought *The Times* to prominence in the early nineteenth century, when government bribes provided a key source of funding for newspapers. John Walter, Jr., used the superior Koenig steam press for the production of his paper, and by putting *The Times* on a sound commercial footing was able to avoid this tacitly accepted form of corruption. Thus free from political obligations, the newspaper proceeded to build its reputation for absolute independence.

THE PAPER OF RECORD

Two editors, Thomas Barnes (1817 to 1841) and John Thaddeus Delane (1841 to 1877), presided over *The Times* for much of the nineteenth century. It was under Barnes that *The Times* moved into the front rank of British newspapers. As the first English paper to send special correspondents abroad, it offered the most comprehensive foreign news coverage and, thanks to its acknowledged independence of opinion, became for many the paper of record. The perception of *The Times* as an unassailable source of truth not only gave it enormous influence but also made it many enemies, particularly in the Tory ranks

A newsboy sells the Sunday edition of England's premier newspaper, *The Times*.

when the paper supported the 1832 Reform Bill. By the mid-century, with QUEEN VICTORIA firmly ensconced on the British throne, *The Times* had become by far the best-selling LONDON newspaper, particularly among the middle-class readership.

The paper's preeminent position of influence continued under Barnes's successor, John Delane. During the 1840s, the first decade of Delane's editorship, *The Times* opposed the repeal of the CORN LAWS until it became clear that there was a groundswell of opinion in favor of the measure. Delane's close friendship with JOHN CAMPBELL GORDON (Lord Aberdeen), a member of the cabinet, provided him with the information that enabled *The Times* to scoop other papers with news of the repeal. The most significant journalistic coup under Delane's stewardship, however, was the paper's revelation of the appalling conditions endured by British soldiers in the Crimean War (1853–1856). The reportage was the work of special correspondent WILLIAM HOWARD RUSSELL (1820–1907), and it led to an inquiry into the war's prosecution that helped to bring down the Aberdeen government. In addition, *The Times* offered key support to FLORENCE NIGHTINGALE as she pursued reforms in the organization of military hospitals.

AN EXCESS OF INFLUENCE?

This manifestation of *The Times*'s power sparked an intense debate in the mid-1850s. To some, the paper embodied the notion of the press as a "fourth estate," there to keep governments in line and thus protect English liberties; for others, it exercised its influence to a dangerously irresponsible degree. ANTHONY TROLLOPE famously satirized *The Times* in his novel *The Warden* (1855), in which a baseless allegation against the warden of an almshouse appears in *The Jupiter* (a fictional representation of *The Times*) and threatens to destroy the warden's reputation. Here, the power of the press amounts to a tyranny that even an elected Parliament cannot contain. In describing Tom Towers, the editor of *The Jupiter*, Trollope wrote: "He could speak out withering words, and no one could answer him: ministers courted him, though perhaps they knew not his name; bishops feared him; judges doubted their own verdicts unless he confirmed them; and generals, in their councils of war, did not consider more deeply what the enemy would do, than what the *Jupiter* would say."

Even before the Crimean War, *The Times*'s influence was a cause for alarm in some quarters. As early as 1841, writes Alan Lee, *The Times* sold twice as many copies as the *Morning Post*, *Morning Herald*, and *Morning Chronicle* combined; by 1850, it sold four times as many. Many observed that the paper threatened to become a monopoly, but there was no easy solution. Not only did *The Times* enjoy superior editing and production values, but it had a decisive lead in ADVERTISING revenues and was the only daily paper to have achieved a truly national circulation. The campaign in the early 1850s against newspaper taxes, often called "taxes on knowledge," was partially aimed at destroying the predominance of *The Times*. By reducing newspaper production costs, it was believed that rival papers could more easily compete with the undisputed leader. Indeed, following the repeal of the newspaper stamp tax in 1855, not only did a daily press emerge in the provinces, but circulation figures of *The Times* were soon overtaken by a successful new rival, the London-based *DAILY TELEGRAPH*.

Thus *The Times* slid from the position of number one seller, but not from its position as the most influential newspaper. The paper's owners, the Walter family, grew more politically conservative during the latter half of the Victorian era, but the paper's independence of any political allegiance remained intact. In addition, *The Times* continued to offer the most comprehensive parliamentary reports and foreign news and, with the *Telegraph* and its imitators diluting these items in favor of lighter, human interest features, *The Times*'s reputation for truth and consequence remained paramount. Selling at twopence a copy as against a penny for the majority of the other daily papers, *The Times*'s reputation was based more than ever on the quality rather than the quantity of its readers.

Following Delane's retirement in 1877, Thomas Chenery (1877 to 1884) and George Earl Buckle (1884 to 1912) presided over the paper for the remainder of the century and beyond. Early in Buckle's tenure, an event occurred that seriously undermined *The Times*'s reputation for accuracy. In 1887, a series of articles alleged that CHARLES STUART PARNELL, leader of the Irish HOME RULE movement, had been involved in the assassinations of the chief secretary of state for Ireland and his undersecretary. Correspondent Richard Pigott, who had supplied the information to *The Times*, admitted under cross-examination by a parliamentary commission that he had manufactured his evidence; he later fled to Spain and shot himself. The legal proceedings cost the paper approximately £200,000 and led it almost to the edge of bankruptcy. In the long term, however, the paper recovered its reputation.

The Walter family remained in control of *The Times* until 1908 when the struggle with daily circulation that had fallen below 40,000 led them to relinquish it. They sold the paper to Lord Northcliffe, one of the pioneers of the "new journalism," causing many observers to fear the cheapening of this venerable national institution. To his credit, however, Northcliffe was very cautious in making selective changes to the paper's presentation and ensured that it retained its integrity.

According to American president Abraham Lincoln, *The Times* possessed a power that was second only to that of the Mississippi River. Although its influence clearly waned during the second half of the nineteenth century, this was only a relative decline from absolute dominance to a position better described—like the position of prime minister—as "first among equals." By maintaining its independence of party, as well as its full coverage of political and foreign news, it remained the most influential and respected paper in Britain well beyond the nineteenth century.

See also DAILY TELEGRAPH, THE; NEWSPAPERS.

FURTHER READING

Cook, Sir Edward. *Delane of the Times*. London: Constable and Company, 1916.

Dasent, A. I. *John Delane, 1817–1879*. 2 vols. London: John Murray, 1908.

Hudson, Derek. *Thomas Barnes of The Times*. Cambridge: Cambridge University Press, 1943.

Lee, Alan J. *The Origins of the Popular Press in England, 1855–1914*. London: Croom Helm, 1976.

Times, The. *History of the Times*. Vols. 1–3. London: *The Times*, 1935, 1939, 1947.

Trollope, Anthony. *The Warden*. 1855. London: Penguin, 1986.

Woods, Oliver, and James Bishop. *The Story of the Times. Bicentenary Edition 1785–1985*. London: Michael Joseph, 1985.

MARK HAMPTON

TOBACCO

Victorian males across the English-speaking world really knew how to smoke. Not for them the quick easy fix of the machine-made cigarette. They surrounded themselves with a variety of smoking accoutrements, from the tools of their habit—clay pipes, briar pipes, meerschaums, churchwardens, cleaners, matches, holders, cases, ashtrays, lights, spills, spittoons, pouches, jars, snuffboxes, racks—to the more general objects that completed the smoking experience—armchairs, tables, slippers, jackets, hats—all ideally stored in that vast monument to bourgeois masculine consumption, the smoking room. In so doing they not only made smoking into an art but also projected an image of themselves to the rest of the world.

VARIETIES OF TOBACCO PRODUCTS

Smoking was also a far more varied practice than it would become with the rise of the cigarette. In a period when the larger part of tobacco consumed was sold loose in amounts of one ounce for threepence, tobacco preferences differed enormously across the country. For example, Welsh miners were known to prefer strong shag tobaccos and rolls, dock laborers were associated with thick twists, and cabmen with Irish roll, while the better-paid LONDON workers preferred the lighter and more finely cut Virginian flake tobaccos, which were ready to smoke. Cavendish, which came in the form of a cake, required much manipulation before being ready for smoking, and it gave way in popularity—especially in IRELAND and the north of England—to more manageable rolls such as nailrod and twist, which had the dual advantage of being ready for chewing. Chewing tobacco was even more popular in the UNITED STATES, where users frequently bit off the hard manufactured tobaccos of twist and plug, which were sold both for pipes and for grating into snuff. Briar pipe smokers of the later nineteenth century preferred mixtures where the lighter Virginian "bright" tobacco leaves were blended with the stronger flavors of latakia, perique, or Turkish tobacco, though the vast majority of smokers still used clay pipes, which varied from the short "cutty" of Scotland to the "dudeen" of Ireland to the "alderman" of rural England.

For those who could afford them, cigars also offered a range of tastes, though preferences were more highly structured. At the top were the cigars of Cuba, followed by others from around the Caribbean, and down through a number of fine gradations to top-quality British cigars (made with Cuban leaf in British factories), and then to cheap penny cigars such as Pickwicks.

Smokers' tastes were catered to by a tobacco industry equally diverse in its local production and by a retail trade fiercely proud of its independence and skill in the manipulation of different blends and mixtures designed to match the individual tastes of its well-informed customers. Middle-class smokers in particular celebrated their refinement of taste and individual discernment. Countless pamphlets, books, poems, and periodical articles acted as etiquette guides for the aspiring connoisseur. Various anecdotal "whiffs" and "pipefuls" were presented as amus-

ing relief for busy city gentlemen who sought solace in their tobacco in the smoking rooms of clubs, hotels, and bars in the great metropolitan centers of London, New York, and Montreal. Smokers learned of the HISTORY, ANTHROPOLOGY, ritual, literary heritage, production, manufacture, and pharmacology of tobacco, knowledge necessary if the mere smoker were to be transformed into a true aficionado. Amusing eulogies either feminized tobacco into the "Lady Nicotine" or "Diva Nicotina," anthropomorphized it into a "trusty companion," or deified it to a level equal with the gods. A man was said to be somehow lacking in character if he did not practice a particular smoking habit or possess his own "paraphernalia of smokiana." And in literature many of the protagonists in the works of THACKERAY, DICKENS, TROLLOPE, GISSING, Ouida, and COLLINS were made distinct through their tobacco consumption.

Most celebrated and idiosyncratic of all was Sherlock Holmes, SIR ARTHUR CONAN DOYLE'S (1859–1930) literary detective who came to exemplify the "philosophy" of smoking. This most singular detective kept his cigars and pipes in the coal scuttle and his tobacco "in the toe-end of a Persian slipper." Buying his "strongest shag tobacco" from a tobacconist named Bradley, he was known to smoke both an everyday briar pipe and an "old and oily clay pipe," as well as a "long cherrywood" when in a "disputatious rather than a meditative mood." He lit his pipe using a glowing cinder held by a long pair of tongs and would collect "all the plugs and dottles left from his smokes of the day before" for his pre-breakfast pipe.

THE RISE OF THE CIGARETTE

It is no surprise then that such smoking individualists looked down upon the machine-made cigarette with great disdain. Although handmade, expensive, and often individually tailored cigarettes had been enjoyed by an urban elite of the smoking fraternity since the end of the CRIMEAN WAR (1854–1856), the mass-manufactured items of the late nineteenth century were felt to be an "unmanly" indulgence. But cigarette manufacture was to be revolutionized by the patenting of the Bonsack machine in the United States in 1880. This could produce up to 300 cigarettes a minute and was quickly put into use by the dynamo of the modern cigarette industry, James Buchanan Duke, who set about transforming the tobacco industry in the 1880s. Through aggressive sales techniques "Buck" Duke ruined, took over, and beat most of his rivals. In 1889 the greater portion of the cigarette industry merged to form the American Tobacco Company (ATC), with Duke firmly at its helm. In 1901 Duke entered the British market where Wills of Bristol has also been using the Bonsack machine since 1883, manufacturing such household names as Three Castles, Cinderella, Gold Flake, and Wild Woodbine, selling at five for one penny. A resulting tobacco war ensued, and Wills was forced into the Imperial Tobacco conglomeration in 1902 with the United Kingdom's other leading tobacconists such as Player's of Nottingham, Lambert & Butler of London, and Mitchell's of Glasgow. Agreement was only reached in 1902 when the ATC retreated to America, the home market was left to Imperial, and together they formed British American Tobacco, which was to achieve spectacular success in INDIA and the dominions.

Opposition to the new cigarette, however, came from the smoking elites as well as from a fervid anti-tobacco movement. Although one had been in existence in Britain since 1853, the message of this non-conformist sect and extremist wing of the TEMPERANCE MOVEMENT went largely unheard until its rhetoric against juvenile smoking coalesced with wider fears about national degeneration in the 1890s. Following the report of the Royal Commission on Physical Deterioration (1904), cigarettes were identified as the most visible manifestation of the "boy labor problem" and a principal cause of the physical weakness of Britain's military recruits. Smoking not only stunted growth and produced a host of minor ailments but also led to a moral and spiritual collapse as well. The medical arguments were comparatively weak and had been readily dismissed prior to the 1890s when applied to adult smokers, but they were regarded as sufficiently convincing to lead to the prohibition of juvenile smoking in the 1908 Children's Act. Here Britain followed similar legislative efforts in AUSTRALIA and CANADA, though it was in the United States, where the anticigarette movement was spearheaded by the more influential Women's Christian Temperance Union, that a greater move to prohibition occurred. By the outbreak of World War I, in 1914, whereas most states had banned juvenile smoking, several had also attempted to stop the sale of cigarettes as a whole.

Ironically much of the antitobacco propaganda focused on the importance of the individual maintaining his independence from a habit that enslaved him to an entity other than the divine. Yet likewise the pro-smoking culture within the Victorian era also emphasized the classic liberal virtues of independence and individuality, though here it was to be from fashion or the influence of others. Smoking for these men was never about simply consuming tobacco. Mobi-

lizing the virtues of manliness and national identity, these smokers refused the dictates of the mass market and stamped their mastery and individuality upon the "majestic leaf." Smoking became a purposeful act, stimulating the creative, intellectual, and entrepreneurial talents of the great gentlemanly amateur and thereby saving the EMPIRE from the same ruin that had befallen the weak and demoralized Turks and Spaniards who had become enslaved to the enervating influence of the indistinguishable cigarette. Smoking in this culture was thus political and ideological, despite its apparently ephemeral and self-indulgent excesses. It mirrored the concerns of Victorian Liberalism and would remain entrenched in the smoking culture of the English-speaking world well beyond the nineteenth century, such that independent-minded smokers of the twentieth century were unwilling to accept the overbearing concerns of the medical professionals who first linked cigarettes to lung cancer in the 1950s.

See also TEMPERANCE MOVEMENT.

FURTHER READING

Alford, B. W. E. *W. D. & H. O. Wills and the Development of the U.K. Tobacco Industry.* London: Methuen, 1973.
Corti, E. C. *A History of Smoking.* London: Harrap, 1931.
Goodman, Jordan. *Tobacco in History: Cultures of Dependence.* London: Routledge, 1993.
Hilton, Matthew. *Smoking in British Popular Culture, 1800–2000.* Manchester: Manchester University Press, 2000.
Kiernan, V. G. *Tobacco: A History.* London: Hutchinson, 1991.

MATTHEW HILTON

TRACTARIANISM

The Victorian era bubbled with religious movements and controversies. The movement now called Tractarianism grew in the 1830s as a response to a new liberalism in theology, and it sought to return to the CHURCH OF ENGLAND a sense of history, reverence, and authority. Tractarianism was most vital in the 1830s and early 1840s, although in later decades its ritualist focus spread through the church and influenced art and literature. Tractarianism had many names. It was also known as Anglo-Catholicism, as it sought to emphasize the catholicity of the Church of England (even calling into question the value of the Reformation). Puseyism was another popular and rather disrespectful label, adapting the name of a leading Tractarian figure, the mild-mannered Oxford don EDWARD BOUVERIE PUSEY (1800–1882). Because the movement was centered at Oxford University, it was also (and continues to be) known as the Oxford Movement. The term *Tractarianism* itself refers to the 90 *Tracts for the Times*, a series of published essays arguing doctrinal, theological, and devotional points often startlingly at odds with accepted church practice.

The Roots of Tractarianism

Victorians might apply names to the movement, and very often had a marked prejudice against it, but they did not always have a strong understanding of the theological and aesthetic beliefs that marked Tractarianism. The movement had profoundly political as well as spiritual roots, because of the close links in nineteenth-century England between CHURCH AND STATE. Tractarianism grew out of the response to a number of constitutional changes that seemed to threaten the disestablishment of the church, as well as the increasing popularity of dissenting Protestant denominations and a surge in anti-Roman Catholic sentiment. Churchmen who wanted to show the Church of England's true and unassailable authority claimed that the church's grounding beliefs were those of the ancient Fathers of the undivided (pre-Reformation) Christian faith, and its bishops were part of the apostolic succession, tracing their office directly back to the original apostles of Christ's time. These churchmen argued that because the Church of England truly represented the teaching of the Fathers and thus true catholicity, it provided a via media, or middle way, between ROMAN CATHOLICISM and "popular Protestantism," or DISSENT. (For these men, the source of complete and unquestionable doctrinal authority was that of the pre-Reformation, undivided church, and this meant that they used the term "catholic" approvingly, although in the 1830s few others in England did.)

Because the Tractarians perceived a dangerous and increasing laxness in the pastoral care and spiritual reverence offered in many churches, they called for reform, emphasizing Pre-Reformation ideas about the importance of the sacraments, the authority of bishops, and the value of celibacy and self-denial. Together with this, Tractarians suggested the reintroduction of reverential rituals and practices that were generally identified with Roman Catholicism. All of these ideas were passionately voiced by a small group of charismatic young men at Oxford University. In 1833 the clergyman JOHN KEBLE preached the Assize Sermon at Oxford, which he entitled "National Apostasy," and which is held to mark the beginning of the Oxford Movement.

Major Figures of the Oxford Movement

After the sermon, Keble and his group began publishing tracts. The *Tracts for the Times* appeared between 1833 and 1841, and they debated many complicated religious topics such as the role of the priesthood and the observance of communion. Several Oxford professors and clergymen contributed to the writing of the Tracts, and it is important to note that there were considerable differences of opinions among the Tractarians themselves; no consideration of the movement would be complete without examining the major figures. JOHN HENRY NEWMAN (1801–1890) was the charismatic leader of the group, the intellectual firebrand, and the most impassioned writer. He wrote 24 of the *Tracts*, edited the whole series, and his published sermons (he was the vicar of St. Mary's) were widely disseminated and debated throughout the country. But Newman was continuously and bitterly criticized for papist tendencies and for shaking the minds of impressionable undergraduates. *Tract 90*, which argued for a liberal interpretation of the Thirty-nine Articles (a standard for all Anglicans) was so controversial that the bishop of Oxford asked that the *Tracts* cease. Desperately disillusioned by the resistance of the church he loved, Newman retreated to Littlemore, a semimonastic community he founded, and battled with whether his convictions would permit him to remain in the Church of England. In 1845 he took the step that most of the country had long been waiting for: he was received into the Roman Catholic Church. Many Tractarians would follow him, causing many opponents of the movement to claim that they had been right, and "Puseyism" had always been a slippery slope toward Rome.

Newman's closest friend was Richard Hurrell Froude (1803–1836), who influenced the movement profoundly even after his early death. Between 1838 and 1839 Newman published Froude's *Remains*, which the public found so scandalous (Froude had bitterly criticized the Reformation, and praised practices such as self-flagellation) that they seriously damaged the credibility of the movement. A far milder figure was that of E. B. Pusey, whose name was commandeered for the movement. A retiring Oxford professor, he practiced strict austerities and was more a hermit than a leader. John Keble was in many ways the senior member of the movement and its poet. He held the post of professor of poetry at Oxford from 1831 to 1841, and thought that poetry worked to reveal truth to the human mind in a very similar way to how the church revealed truth to the Christian. His collection of poems written for all the observances and liturgical dates of the church calendar, *The Christian Year*, expressed these ideas, and it was the runaway best-seller of the nineteenth century. While all these men had diverse strengths, after Newman's defection the movement's fire dimmed for lack of a strong leader.

THE IMPACT OF TRACTARIAN THINKING

While the publication of the *Tracts* continued until 1841, and each one was greeted by more or less virulent criticism, the tenets of the movement spread slowly and unevenly throughout the nation. Some clergymen attacked Puseyism from the pulpit, claiming that Tractarian ideas were pure "popery." A number of politicians, including the Tory prime minister ROBERT PEEL, feared and denounced the movement. There were also extreme reactions; in Exeter riots took place because the curate Mr. Courtenay insisted on wearing a surplice (an ecclesiastical garment of knee length with large open sleeves). On the other hand, many Anglicans enjoyed a renewed, Tractarian-influenced emphasis on the sacraments and the dignity of the priestly role, and adopted bronze candlesticks, flowers on the altar, and new observances in services with no outcry.

After Newman's conversion, the Tractarian debate diminished from a boil to a simmer. While the main force of the movement ended in the early 1840s, the effects of the movement were longstanding. In church observance, it slowly became clear that the Tractarian emphasis on increased reverence, formality, and regularity had, to an extent, won the day. Historians observe an increase, by 1850, in the devotion and character of clergymen inspired by Tractarian emphasis on the sanctity of worship and ministry. Further, the ritualistic aspect of the movement was broadly influential. By the 1860s, congregations had generally adopted more frequent and more formal observances: there was more genuflection, more church ornament. Tractarianism also stimulated a resurgence of interest in the devotional life, with many monastic and conventual communities founded. Some scholars argue that the women's devotional communities inspired by Tractarianism opened up the Church of England to women in important new ways. And finally, the artistic life of the nation was undoubtedly stimulated by the aesthetic repercussions of Tractarian doctrine. The movement's emphasis on the devotional life encouraged poets like CHRISTINA ROSSETTI (1830–1894) to rediscover a spiritual mystery and awe in nature and in the practices of religion. Church historian Owen Chadwick declares that while the Tractarians "weakened the Church of England in politics and popular esteem . . . [t]hey strengthened the Church of England in its soul."

See also ANTI-CATHOLICISM; CHURCH AND STATE; CHURCH OF ENGLAND; DISSENT.

FURTHER READING

Chadwick, Owen. *The Victorian Church.* 3d ed. 2 vols. London: Adam & Charles Black, 1970.

Chapman, Raymond. *Faith and Revolt: Studies in the Literary Influence of the Oxford Movement.* London: Weidenfeld and Nicholson, 1970.

Fairweather, Eugene R., ed. *The Oxford Movement.* New York: Oxford University Press, 1964.

Reed, John Shelton. *Glorious Battle: The Cultural Politics of Victorian Anglo-Catholicism.* Nashville: Vanderbilt University Press, 1996.

F. ELIZABETH GRAY

TRADE UNIONS

Among the many significant social and political developments of the Victorian era, the rise of the trade union movement both reflected, and came to influence, the working practices of the industrial age. Trade unionism highlighted the appalling inequities of the economic divide between rich and poor, leading to the growth of British socialism and the liberation of the working classes from grinding poverty.

FROM SMALL SOCIETIES TO UNIONS

When QUEEN VICTORIA came to the throne in 1837, Britain was entering what was to be the deepest economic depression of the nineteenth century and the bargaining position of most groups of workers was weak. The eighteenth century had seen the emergence of trade societies, formed by groups of craftsmen to try and obtain better pay, and of mutual aid societies that provided support at times of sickness and unemployment, and points of contact for journeymen traveling from town to town in search of work. On numerous occasions, however, justices of the peace were required to arbitrate between these craftsmen and their employers and, in an effort to exercise control over worker demands, at least 20 pieces of legislation were enacted in the eighteenth century. These culminated in the General Combination Acts of 1799 and 1800, which forbade any worker combinations that interfered with trade and manufacture or in the management of firms, or those that attempted to instigate strikes. Trade societies operated under these restrictions until the acts were repealed in 1824, although in reality the effectiveness of the acts in halting the spread of workers' organization had proved very limited.

Most of these early trade societies were small and local, but with the repeal of the Combination Laws there were moves to link them into larger unions. The word *union* began to be widely used in the 1820s, applying in most cases to a union of workers in the same craft. In the 1830s, influenced by the ideas of ROBERT OWEN (1771–1858) and others, there was talk of general unions that would unite workers in different trades. Some of these were local committees such as the Metropolitan Trades' Union in London; however, in 1834 a Grand National Consolidated Trades' Union was formed to act as a federation of existing trade unions, but it had limited success beyond the capital. Nonetheless, the formation of the union indicated a new sense of class division as opposed to trade division. Outside London, an attempt by farm workers in the southwest of England to form a trade union linked to the new general union led to the famous trial of the "Tolpuddle Martyrs"—six laborers who were sentenced to seven years' transportation to Australia after trying to form a union in 1833 (they were pardoned in 1836). In London, 40,000 unionists demonstrated against the harshness of the punishment. Elsewhere, too, there were localized general strikes by different groups of workers. The complaints generally sprang from the changes that were being wrought by the advance of capitalism, but protest was less about wages than about the effects of what was called the "competitive system." The majority of the organized workers were handcraftsmen such as tailors, shoemakers, and handloom weavers, but unions were also beginning to form among the factory-based cotton spinners in Lancashire and Scotland. With the economy expanding rapidly in the early 1830s, employers were frequently willing to make a few concessions, but with the economic downturn later in the decade, attitudes hardened and employers began forcing employees to sign the "document"—a declaration renouncing trade-union membership.

Such measures failed to prevent major strikes in the coal, steel, and textile industries of the North during the early 1840s. Some workers were attracted by the political campaign for the People's Charter and there was what came very close to a general strike in parts of Lancashire in 1842, when steam boilers were sabotaged in the so-called plug riots. The first attempt to unite the miners in a union, also in 1842, was made with the formation of the Miners' Association of Great Britain and Ireland. The particular grievances of the miners included being forced to buy most of their provisions at the company truck shop and the yearly hiring contract or bond under which they worked.

ORGANIZING SKILLED WORKERS

The upturn in the economy in the late 1840s and the rapid expansion of the RAILWAY network and the POSTAL SERVICES system gave new encouragement to the formation of regional and national unions. There were various efforts among engineers, iron molders, and boilermakers—groups who were gaining most from industrialization because of demand for their skills—to make their unions more effective by appointing full-time officials and taking more central control of branches. It was not easy, because local areas jealously guarded their autonomy, but the efforts began to bear fruit and, by the early 1850s, some quite powerful national unions had been formed. Among the best known and most effective of these was the Amalgamated Society of Engineers (ASE) formed in 1851 and the United Society of Boilermakers and Iron Shipbuilders in 1852. The prominent socialists Sidney and Beatrice Webb, who were the first historians of the trade union movement, recognized these unions as a "new model," centrally controlled, efficiently run, and generally seeking to avoid conflict with employers while, at the same time, keeping tight control on membership. While the Webbs may have exaggerated the novelty of many aspects of the ASE's organization, and while many groups of workers rejected it as a model, its sheer size and power could not help but influence others. From 5,000 at its inception, membership rose to 40,000 by the mid-1870s. Members were the skilled fitters and turners, the builders and repairers of machine tools who were crucial in all manufacturing industries.

Past evidence, particularly strong among handloom weavers, demonstrated that the entry of too many workers into a trade led to wages being undercut by newcomers. Thus, uncontrolled entry was seen as the single most destructive threat to the workers' standard of living. The engineers and other skilled workers were determined that this would not happen to them and made it their priority to regulate their number by laying down rules for admission to their union. They insisted that members either had to have served a five-year apprenticeship, or to have received the recognized wage for a skilled worker for several years. Since the success of this "closed shop" strategy depended upon employers taking on only those whom the union recognized as skilled, they took steps to avoid confrontation with the bosses, encouraging negotiated agreements that came to be known as collective bargaining. The unions also recognized that their fledgling predecessors had suffered from a high turnover of members, with men joining the union when an industrial dispute was pending and abandoning it soon afterwards. The ASE and others now sought to maintain stability by having membership of the union linked to FRIENDLY SOCIETY benefits, thus providing payments to those laid off by sickness or unemployment, compensation for loss or damage of tools, and burial funds.

BACKLASH AND LEGAL RECOGNITION

As the economy boomed in the 1850s and 1860s, the union movement as a whole made major advances. Concessions were squeezed from employers anxious not to lose any share of the lucrative worldwide demand for British manufactured goods, and national unions of carpenters and cabinetmakers, builders, miners, and textile workers all flourished. The backlash came with the economic downturn of 1866–1867 when employers began resisting what they saw as the excessive power of the unions. A press campaign led to the establishment of a Royal Commission to enquire into their operation. At the same time, a judgment given in the case of *Hornby v. Close* (1867), threatened the funds of the large trade unions by declaring that they could have no legal recourse against dishonest officers because they were,

according to common law, illegal organizations, being "in restraint of trade."

In this atmosphere the leaders of a number of the most powerful unions headquartered in London joined forces to ensure that the most favorable case possible was presented to the Commission of Enquiry. They emphasized the extent to which their unions were indeed new and different from previous organizations, that they generally avoided strikes, and that the skilled working class, sometimes referred to as the "labor aristocracy," was now thoroughly respectable. They succeeded in getting an influential minority of the commission to produce a report sympathetic to the trade union position. At the same time, the MANCHESTER trade unions summoned a national conference in June 1868 to launch an annual Trades Union Congress, which would discuss outstanding issues affecting unions and act as a pressure group on Parliament. A parliamentary committee of leading unionists was formed both to act as a watchdog and to maintain pressure on Parliament between meetings.

All these efforts bore fruit in the 1870s when, by acts of Parliament in 1871 and again in 1876, trade unions were recognized as having legal rights and

MANSELL/TIMEPIX/GETTY IMAGES

During the Victorian era, workers united in order to secure better working conditions and wages. They gathered for meetings such as this one held by gas workers at Peckham Rye railway station in London on Sunday, December 8, 1889.

their funds were granted protection through the courts. However, hostility to trade unions remained, particularly among smaller employers and in sections of the press. In 1872 a Criminal Law Amendment Act imposed extensive restrictions on effective strike action. Trade unions reacted to the legislation by becoming more politically active and they succeeded in having the measure substantially modified by a Conservative government in 1876. Meanwhile, the traditional labels that referred to "master and servant" were replaced with the more egalitarian employer and worker.

Renewed Labor Activism at the End of the Century

Most trade union members were skilled workers who used the concept of skill to control who could work at their trade. From time to time there were signs that less-skilled workers were attempting to form themselves into a union: an economic boom at the start of the 1870s, for example, brought the first national organization of agricultural workers, but it was only in the 1880s that groups such as dock laborers, seamen, gas workers, and female workers began to organize. This culminated in an outburst of strikes and protests between 1888 and 1890 and the London dockers, assisted by a group of young socialists, won the "docker's tanner" in 1889, a minimum rate of sixpence per hour. According to the eminent twentieth-century Marxist historian Eric Hobsbawm, 80 percent of the strikes in 1889 brought some measure of success to the strikers. Once again, however, a backlash occurred in the form of hostile reaction. Many employers of unskilled workers were experiencing trade unionism for the first time. Although initially caught off balance, they recovered and set out, with much determination and considerable success, to smash the "new unions" by means of strikebreakers and the victimization of activists.

During this period of the late nineteenth century, there were signs, too, of rising militancy among skilled craftsmen. New technology, more cost-conscious attitudes among employers facing increasing foreign competition, and reorganization within the workplace were all threatening the security of these men and motivating them into readiness for confrontation. They joined in demands for the reduction of the working day from what had become a standard nine hours to eight, and were ready to go to law if necessary. The government was showing a readiness to intervene in industrial relations and 1893 brought the introduction of a Labor Department to collect statistics on

aspects of labor. Another royal commission encouraged further state intervention and the Conciliation Act of 1896 gave the Board of Trade power to appoint a conciliator in industrial disputes. The courts, however, were reflecting the general animosity to the recent union militancy in passing some hostile judgements, and many trade unions once again felt the need for a means of exerting political pressure. Encouraged by the spread of socialist ideas among numbers of younger trade unionists, the Trades Union Congress decided to summon a meeting of trade unions and political groups in February 1900 to press for better representation of workingmen in Parliament. The outcome was the historic formation of the Labour Party.

In 1901, from a workforce of 17 million people in Britain, just over two million workers belonged to trade unions. It has been calculated that the ratio of membership to potential membership was just over 13 percent. In other words, only a very small minority of workers, concentrated in particular industries, was actually unionized, but they included the most highly skilled. More than 60 percent of coal miners were in unions affiliated to the Miners' Federation of Great Britain; around 30 percent of metal and engineering workers and printers were organized, and about 20 percent of textile and construction workers. A number of the larger employers of metalworkers and engineers negotiated with union officials over wages, work hours, and workplace practices. On the other hand, other large groups such as the railway companies adamantly refused negotiation. There were many employers who looked to work practices in the United States for ways of breaking union influence, but governments and most significant employers accepted that there was a place for unions within the system of industrial relations.

See also FACTORY LEGISLATION; LABOR, ORGANIZATION OF.

FURTHER READING

Clog, A., A. Fox, and A. F. Thompson. *A History of British Trade Unions since 1889.* Vol. 1. Oxford: Clarendon Press, 1964.
Fraser, W. Hamish. *Trade Unions and Society. The Struggle for Acceptance.* London: George Allen and Unwin, 1974.
Fraser, W. Hamish. *A History of British Trade Unionism 1700–1998.* London: Macmillan, and New York: St. Martin's, 1999.
Mommsen, W. J., and H.-G. Husung, eds. *The Development of Trade Unionism in Great Britain and Germany, 1880–1914.* London and Boston: German Historical Institute and Allen and Unwin. 1985.
Pelling, H. *A History of British Trade Unionism.* Harmondsworth and New York: Penguin Books, 1987.
Ward, J. T., and W. H. Fraser, eds. *Workers and Employers. Documents on Trade Unions and Industrial Relations in Britain since the Eighteenth Century.* London: Macmillan, 1980.

Webb, Sidney, and Beatrice. *The History of Trade Unionism.* London: Longmans, Green, 1920.

Wrigley, C. J., ed. *A History of British Industrial Relations, 1875–1914.* Amherst: University of Massachusetts Press, 1982.

W. HAMISH FRASER

TRANSCENDENTALISM

Transcendentalism was a philosophical movement that flourished primarily in New England from about 1836 to 1860. It exerted a profound influence on American culture and shaped the direction of American literature. Although as a movement it is difficult to define, it centered on a group of writers, philosophers, and intellectuals residing in Concord and Boston, Massachusetts, during the middle of the nineteenth century. This group, which reacted against many of the tenets of the Unitarian Church and the orthodoxy of Calvinism, developed a new kind of religion based on their faith in the mysticism of nature, the primacy of the human soul, and the divinity of humankind. Although transcendentalism never had a systematic PHILOSOPHY, as a movement it espoused certain beliefs: that God exists in people and nature, that individual intuition comprises the highest source of knowledge, and that the soul opens the pathway to God. These beliefs, in turn, led to an emphasis on individualism, self-reliance, and a rejection of conventional authority.

EUROPEAN ORIGINS

Despite the American character of the movement, transcendentalism had European origins. To a much lesser extent, its mystical aspects were also influenced by Indian and Chinese religious teachings. In particular, transcendentalism drew heavily from romantic German philosophy, notably that of Immanuel Kant (1724–1804). Kantian idealism held that a moral law within people shaped their impressions of the world around them, and that an innate set of principles within the mind interpreted life experiences. Kantian idealism thus proposed that people could experience reality in a different (and higher) way than simply through reason or the physical senses alone.

Kantian reason diverged sharply from the dominant values of the time, which stressed neoclassical Enlightenment values such as rationality, science, and a mechanistic worldview. The Romantic movement in art and literature developed in response against these Enlightenment values. ROMANTICISM, particularly as it pertained to literature, began in England with authors such as THOMAS CARLYLE, Samuel Taylor Coleridge, and WILLIAM WORDSWORTH, writers who celebrated the mysticism of nature and the divine human spirit. In contrast to Enlightenment values, Romanticism stressed emotion and imagination. In general, Kantian reason and Romanticism privileged feeling and intuition over hard reason.

THE INFLUENCE OF ROMANTICISM

Romanticism, however, was not exclusively a European movement. In the United States, Romanticism developed in tandem with the British Romantic movement—but also as a reaction against Unitarian and Calvinist orthodoxy. In New England in the mid-nineteenth century, Puritans and Unitarians began to question their religious underpinnings. Many believed that their inherited tradition of faith, as reinvented by the region's first English settlers, provided few spiritual rewards. As many Unitarians became aware of Kantian idealism, they began to adopt a new approach toward spirituality. They strove to develop a religion where people could enjoy an authentic spiritual experience, not through reason and dogma, but rather through intuition and imagination. One major influence on the incipient transcendentalist movement derived from the eloquent sermons of the Unitarian Reverend William Ellery Channing (1780–1842) of Boston, who argued for humanitarianism and tolerance in religion. Although he never allied himself with the abolitionists, his humanistic opposition to slavery appealed to many progressive thinkers. Indeed, the reverend anticipated many of the great philosophies of transcendentalism, and certainly influenced Ralph Waldo Emerson (1803–1882) and his colleagues, including Margaret Fuller (1810–1850), Henry David Thoreau (1817–1862), and William Cullen Bryant (1794–1878), among others.

The transcendental movement started in September 1836, when Emerson; George Ripley, a Unitarian minister from Boston; and Frederic Henry Hedge attended a celebration at their alma mater, Harvard. Discovering their common interest in Kantian philosophy, they decided to form a group that met to discuss literature, philosophy, and religion. The group, of which Emerson and Thoreau were original members, initially called itself the Hedge Club after its "founding" member, who came down from his church in Maine to attend the meetings. Other members included George Ripley, Bronson Alcott, Margaret Fuller, and Theodore Parker. The first meeting took place at the home of George Ripley, and later—for the next eight years—at Emerson's home in Concord. Only later did outsiders describe them as the "Transcendental Club" for their discussion of Kant's transcendental ideas. The club was informal, and its membership varied from meeting to meeting. For many years, much of this group's writing was published in a journal edited by Emerson and Fuller, *The Dial* (1840–1844).

BROOK FARM

If *The Dial* epitomized the intellectual nature of the group, the Brook Farm experiment represented the stress it placed on communal, physical living. The group's major collective experiment, a cooperative community at Brook Farm, lasted between 1841 and 1847 and grew out of their ideas on social reform. Brook Farm, which was located in West Roxbury, Massachusetts, was founded by George Ripley (1802–1880). He believed that Brook Farm, a utopian microcosm of society, would form the prototype for a new social order. Like transcendentalism as a whole, Brook Farm was inspired by European ideas. Ripley drew on the ideas of Charles Fourier (1772–1837), a French utopian socialist. Fourier believed that a faulty social order produced most of the world's suffering, and that human beings were inherently good. Fourier developed small planned communities that recreated socially harmonious units on a small scale, hoping to facilitate humankind's progress from a primitive, economically driven civilization to a higher state.

Ripley founded Brook Farm in April 1841 with his wife, Sophia, and about fifteen other members. An outgrowth of Unitarianism, the purpose of the experiment was to produce individual freedom, harmonious relationships, common values, and the merging of mind and body. Ripley believed that achieving these goals—particularly the latter—relied on the exertion of physical labor. All members, including the writers and poets, were expected to spend at least part of the day in manual labor. This served the purpose of mixing together the different SOCIAL CLASSES, which then promoted the free development of the individual. Ripley wished to end the division between the educated and the laboring classes, and mixing their labor provided one means to do so. The members sold their milk, vegetables, and hay in order to expand production. Yet though Brook Farm espoused equality in education and labor, one divide kept it a rigid society: membership in the association depended on the ownership of property. Those who couldn't buy property paid for their board in cash. All, however, could participate in the intellectual life on the community. Between 1841 and 1847, members included NATHANIEL HAWTHORNE, John S. Dwight, Charles A. Dana, and Isaac Hecker, and visitors such as Ralph Waldo Emerson, Margaret Fuller, Horace Greeley, and Orestes Brownson. Unfortunately, agriculture did not profit from the sandy soil, and Brook Farm did not survive the financial crisis that hit it in 1846.

EMERSON, THOREAU, AND FULLER

Although many thinkers, writers, and philosophers shaped the transcendental movement, a few key figures defined it: Ralph Waldo Emerson, Henry David Thoreau, and Margaret Fuller. Emerson, whose long essay "Nature" (1836) expounded upon all of the philosophical, literary, and religious ideas behind transcendentalism, lay at the center of the movement.

The son of a minister of the First Unitarian Church of Boston, Emerson spent his early years among his studies and books. He attended Harvard and then Harvard Divinity School, but poor eyesight and ill health forced him to leave. Nonetheless, in 1829 he became a Second Unitarian pastor in Boston. He retired only three years later over conflicts between his and his constituents' beliefs. That year he took a trip to Europe, where he met many of the English Romantic poets, including Coleridge and Wordsworth, who helped inspire his incipient transcendental thought. Emerson returned home in 1834 and settled in Concord, Massachusetts. He met and married his second wife, Lydia Jackson, and together they had four children.

During this time Emerson began to write and lecture for a living. "Nature," which was published anonymously and based on some of his early lectures, first espoused his beliefs about transcendentalism. In it Emerson grappled with many issues, including the meaning of the world and nature and humankind's role in it. Emerson was not a philosopher per se, and presented his ideas simply as a person who had experienced daily life. He formulated three interrelated postulates in "Nature." The first was the primacy of the soul, divine in all people and the key to all knowledge and God. The second idea related to nature, whose mysticism allowed people to unlock their spirit. The third concerned the immediacy of God. Together, this triad formed the foundation of Emerson's transcendental thought. "Nature," along with his lectures and other essays (published as *Essays* in 1841, with the second collection published in 1844), elicited general interest in transcendentalism. In particular, "The Over-Soul" and "Self-Reliance" reflected his belief that individuals could find redemption only within their own souls. These works, however, also incited anger because of what was perceived as his rejection of Christianity.

In 1840 Emerson joined the efforts of Margaret Fuller and began to publish *The Dial*, the leading magazine of transcendental thought. In the 1850s Emerson became interested in abolitionism and aligned his sympathies with the North in the Civil War, a sentiment embodied in *The Conduct of Life* (1860) and *Society and Solitude* (1870). By the time of his death, Emerson was revered as one of America's great influential thinkers.

One of Emerson's early protégés was Henry David Thoreau, who came into acquaintance with Emerson's "Nature" while a student at Harvard. Thoreau, who lived with Emerson and his family between 1841 and 1843 and helped edit and contribute to *The Dial*, decided to put his own ideas into action. In 1845, at the age of 28, Thoreau decided to go to Walden Pond to deny the materialism and social conformity of daily life. He built a small cabin on land owned by Emerson, and devoted his time to observing nature, reading, and penning his memories of a river trip he had taken with his brother, *A Week on the Concord and Merrimack Rivers* (1849). Thoreau also began a journal that recorded his observations and thoughts, which became the inspiration for his posthumously published *Excursions* (1863), *The Maine Woods* (1864), *Cape Cod* (1865), and *A Yankee in Canada* (1866).

Thoreau returned to Concord after a little more than two years, having completed his book and his experiment in natural living. Unfortunately, few people were interested in his writing, and he spent the next nine years making pencils and revising his works. He finally published *Walden* in 1854, which recounts his experience at Walden Pond. In it he discusses his interest in nature and ecology, and expresses his desire for himself and all of humankind to achieve integrity, inner freedom, and the ability to shape the direction of their lives. As he writes in the second chapter of *Walden*: "I went to the woods because I wished to live deliberately, to front only the essential facts of life, and see if I could not learn what it had to teach, and not, when I came to die, discover that I had not lived. . . . I wanted to live deep and suck out all the marrow of life, to live so sturdily and Spartan-like as to put to rout all that was not life . . . to reduce it to its lowest terms."

Although *Walden* is considered to be Thoreau's masterpiece, his most politically influential essay was "On the Duty of Civil Disobedience" (1849), which he wrote after an overnight stay in prison. Thoreau had refused to pay a poll tax in support of the Mexican War, which he believed supported slavery. His civil disobedience derived from his belief that individuals must protest government actions they believe to be unjust. The lasting influence of "Civil Disobedience" cannot be overestimated. In this essay Thoreau expounded upon his ideas of individual autonomy, resistance to unfair laws, and a defiance of government encroachment into society. Thoreau did not oppose government in general, but rather laws he believed made the individual incapable of living with a good conscience, like slavery. Like Emerson, Thoreau did not believe in violence, and opposed the Mexican War on the grounds that people could resolve their differences peacefully. The essay influenced modern day leaders including Martin Luther King, Jr., and Mahatma Gandhi. It also inspired the Danish resistance in the 1940s and opponents of McCarthyism in the 1950s, as well as the passive resistance to racial segregation in the 1960s.

Another prominent figure in the transcendentalist movement and close colleague of Emerson and Thoreau was Margaret Fuller. A resident of Boston, she initiated formal conversations for women on different social and literary topics. She then befriended Emerson, whom she taught German. From 1840 to 1842 she worked with Emerson as editor of *The Dial*. She never, however, supported the Brook Farm experiment, though she was identified as a supporter in her friend Nathaniel Hawthorne's fictional account of Brook Farm, *Blithedale Romance* (1852). (Hawthorne, incidentally, examined the flaws of practical utopianism in a fictional setting in New England.) Fuller also wrote *Summer on the Lakes in 1843* (1844), which recorded her travels by train, steamboat, carriage, and foot to the Great Lakes as well as her internal spiritual travel during that time. Fuller was also an ardent feminist, and in many ways presaged the modern-day women's liberation movement. She first called for women's equality in an article published in 1843 in *The Dial*, "The Great Lawsuit: Man versus Men, Woman versus Women." She later expanded this essay into *Woman in the Nineteenth Century* (1845), which became a cornerstone of feminist thought and helped to inspire the SENECA FALLS CONVENTION three years later.

Fuller left the Boston area for New York City in 1844 when she was invited by the publisher Horace Greeley to join the staff of his newspaper, the *New York Tribune*, as a book review editor. Two years later, she became the *Tribune*'s foreign correspondent. She traveled to Europe and sent back articles about life in European cities, which were published in *At Home and Abroad* (1856). Arriving in Italy in 1847, she fell in love with Marchese Giovanni Angelo d'Ossoli, a younger nobleman involved in revolutionary activities. She became involved in the Revolution of 1848 and, when Rome fell in 1850, the two fled back to America, only to die when their ship sank off the coast of New York.

Transcendentalism, while a relatively fleeting movement, left a profound impact on American cultural, political, and literary society. It infused old ideas and religious orthodoxy with new intellectual and spiritual fervor, and affected the course of future literary, political, and social movements.

See also PHILOSOPHY; ROMANTICISM.

FURTHER READING

Barbour, Brian M. *American Transcendentalism: An Anthology of Criticism.* Notre Dame, Ind.: University of Notre Dame Press, 1973.

Boller, Paul F. *American Transcendentalism, 1830–1860: An Intellectual Inquiry.* New York: Putnam, 1974.

Buell, Lawrence. *Literary Transcendentalism; Style and Vision in the American Renaissance.* Ithaca: Cornell University Press, 1973.

Francis, Richard. *Transcendental Utopias: Individual and Community at Brook Farm, Fruitlands, and Walden.* Ithaca: Cornell University Press, 1997.

Gura, Philip F., and Joel Myerson, eds. *Critical Essays on American Transcendentalism.* Boston: G. K. Hall, 1982.

Rose, Anne. *Transcendentalism as a Social Movement, 1830–1850.* New Haven, Conn.: Yale University Press, 1981.

Welleck, Rene. *Confrontations: Studies in the Intellectual and Literary Relations between Germany, England, and the United States during the Nineteenth Century.* Princeton: Princeton University Press, 1965.

JESSICA TEISCH

TRANSPORTATION

The Victorian era was pivotal in the history of transportation. The combination of the power of the steam engine and the reduced resistance of smooth metal rails in the world's first national RAILWAY system in Britain balanced up the longstanding disparity in cost between land and water transportation. Transport innovations were also bound up with radical social change that took place during the reign of QUEEN VICTORIA. In the 1830s urban dwellers were a minority in the POPULATION as a whole; however, by 1900 they had swelled to an overwhelming majority. By then the everyday lives of most urban dwellers involved some form of cheap, frequently mechanized public transport.

MANSELL/TIMEPIX/GETTY IMAGES

Improvements in transportation completely changed the way people traveled and goods were shipped by the end of the Victorian era. This picture of a woman whipping her horse in an attempt to outrun an oncoming train captures the changes of the era.

STEAM POWER AND THE MECHANIZATION
OF TRANSPORT

Inexorable as the mechanization of travel might appear in retrospect, in fact the Victorian transport system did not develop steadily. Although the steam engine made its mark early in the Industrial Revolution as a stationary power source in MINING and FACTORIES, engineers soon realized its potential to drive transportation on land and water. The first such applications predated the Victorian era, but they were as yet localized phenomena. The most noteworthy of these were the paddle steamers on the River Clyde in Glasgow and the River Thames in LONDON, three unconnected steam railways in the north of England and London, and steam carriages on the New Road in North London. Victoria's accession to the throne in 1837 coincided with a brief boom in railway investment. Soon railways linked London with the main ports and industrial centers of England and, by the end of the "railway mania" of 1844–1847, engineers and navvies (laborers who worked on civil engineering projects) had constructed the main lines of a national railway network. From then on railways became the main carriers of passengers and goods over medium and long distances. In just a few years the horse-drawn stagecoach and the canal barge had been superceded in cases where speed was an important consideration.

The steam railway locomotive also competed with other applications of steam power. It ended the brief midcentury heyday of the paddle steamer, which in the early Victorian period served on the rivers Thames and Clyde for commuting and for pleasure trips. The coastal steam packet (cargo ship) was better able to meet the challenge of the railways as a carrier of low-value bulk goods like coal and grain, and remained a bigger carrier by volume throughout Victoria's reign. In the Victorian era the British shipbuilding industry dominated world production and the design and scale of oceangoing ships changed radically. The controllable, reliable power of the improving steam engine gradually prevailed over wind power. Iron and steel displaced wood as the principal structural material for shipping.

The spreading railway network also helped limit the success of passenger-carrying steam carriages on British roads. These first automobiles were in any case accused of tearing up the roads and frightening the horses that were still present in large numbers. An alternative interpretation is that the Victorian AUTOMOBILE was priced off the road by struggling coaching interests through punitive road tolls and then the restrictive legislation of 1865 that allowed automobiles on the road only if a man carrying a red warning flag walked in front.

But if steam traction was in some way unwelcome on Britain's roads, steam railways also struggled to meet the growing demand for travel within Britain's expanding cities, especially where RAILWAY STATIONS were close together and trains could not reach competitive speeds. London was the biggest British settlement and was a notable exception. Steam railways were better suited to its special low-density pattern of settlements, and its unusually high proportion of white-collar workers could better afford the fares. According to T. C. Barker and Michael Robbins, during the third quarter of the nineteenth century a well-developed suburban railway network carried more passengers in the capital than OMNIBUSES (horse-drawn buses) and horse-drawn trams. In 1863 the Metropolitan Railway (known in the twenty-first century as the Metropolitan Line of the UNDERGROUND) began operating in tunnels beneath London's streets to become the world's first underground railway. Tunnels had large vents and later steam locomotives were designed to collect their exhaust gases for release in the open air, but the Victorian UNDERGROUND was certainly an unpleasant place.

ALTERNATIVES TO STEAM

The degree of mechanization of urban transportation placed London well ahead of other cities. Horse-drawn transportation was far from eclipsed in the Victorian period. It has been estimated that the numbers of horses not on farms rose from little more than 500,000 in 1851 to nearly 1.8 million in 1901. There were three times as many horse-drawn vehicles in 1900 than 1830. This was partly because carters' losses to the railway on long-haul trips were more than made up by increased short-haul traffic from railway stations. It was also partly because the horse remained the main mover of urban passenger traffic throughout Victoria's reign. First, the horse-drawn omnibus, introduced to London in 1829, spread to larger provincial cities during the first half of Victoria's reign. The omnibus, however, had limited capacity. It took the reduced rolling resistance of metal rails laid in the streets to increase the return on the horses' labor.

Horse tramways were widespread in the United States by the 1850s, but their adoption was delayed in Britain, partly because of the American George F. Train's (1829–1904) determined use in the early 1860s of a rail that projected above the street surface and imperiled the axles of British wagons. A new design of rail flush with the road surface led to the successful revival of horse tramways in Liverpool in 1868 and in 1870 the passage of a Tramways Act heralded a national boom in tramway investment. The horse tram had twice the capacity of the omnibus for each pair of horses and it offered passengers a smoother ride with safer access. Its patrons were still drawn from the better-off minority, though some local authorities insisted that the operators offered reduced workmen's fares.

But horses remained problematic as the motive force for urban transportation. The sight of suffering and even dying animals undoubtedly upset many Victorians, as did the dung that piled up on city streets, keeping employed an army of crossing sweepers and shoeblacks. Perhaps more to the point, horses accounted for more than half the tramway companies' running costs. Various mechanical alternatives were tried, including electric batteries, compressed air, and clockwork. In the first commercially successful mechanized tramway, the vehicles were attached to a network of moving cables in underground conduits, powered by a stationary steam engine. Although nearly every major American city operated cable trams by early 1890s, they were far less successful in Britain. Two lines on London hills were short-lived, though a full urban cable network proved viable in Edinburgh, where there are more hills. Steam trams ran in some parts of the country, such as the industrial Midlands, where the inhabitants were perhaps more inured to the noise and weight of the vehicles.

The arrival of electric traction soon made it unnecessary to choose between the intrusive steam tram and the inflexible, sometimes unstable cable tram. The electric motor offered a most effective way of translating the power of the steam engine into the rapid stopping and starting needed for a mass transit network. It made daily use of public transportation affordable for the working classes for the first time. The electric tram was invented in Germany and developed in the United States, where it spread rapidly during the 1890s. Adoption in the United Kingdom was slower, probably because a clause in the 1870 Tramways Act allowed local authorities to purchase lines from companies at cost after 21 years, though this is a matter of debate.

A few electric tramways were opened in the United Kingdom during the 1880s, including the first urban electric service at Blackpool. The electrification of the Bristol tramways in 1895 began an upswing of mainly municipal investment in the new TECHNOLOGY, though the conversion of London's extensive system began

only in the year of Victoria's death. However, the capital's transportation engineers led the world in applying electric traction to a new generation of deep underground railways, constructed by tunneling through London's clay substratum. The first was the City and South London Railway, which opened in 1890. The Liverpool Overhead Railway, the world's first surface electric railway, followed in 1893.

PERSONAL TRANSPORTATION

BICYCLING occupies a unique place in the history of Victorian transportation. The development of the bicycle is closely identified with the new materials and mass-production techniques of the Industrial Revolution. Although its direct ancestor was the French velocipede or "boneshaker" of the 1860s, the modern mass-produced bicycle was a product of the British bicycle industry. In 1870 James K. Starley (1830–1881) designed the ordinary or "penny-farthing" bicycle, favored by young sporting males. In 1885 Starley's nephew John Kemp Starley (1854–1901) designed the Rover safety bicycle. Combined with the pneumatic (air-filled) tire produced by Scottish inventor John Boyd Dunlop (1840–1921) in 1888, J. K. Starley's design triggered a middle-class bicycle craze in the final decade of Victoria's reign. It remains the basis for standard bicycle frame designs in the twenty-first century.

The last years of the Victorian period also saw the introduction of the INTERNAL COMBUSTION ENGINE and the automobile, a development that owed something to both consumers and producers of the bicycle. Middle-class cyclists pressed for the improvement of country roads neglected during the railway boom, and for the lifting of the speed limit. Several cycle manufacturers turned their mechanical know-how to automobile production, including Rover, a company that continues to produce cars in 2003. The first British vehicle was built in 1895 and the automobile's well-heeled patrons were rewarded by the Locomotives on Highways Act of 1896, raising the speed limit to 12 miles per hour. In 1898 the motorbus made its first appearance in Edinburgh and in London a year later. These pioneering vehicles were heavy and unreliable and they only started to replace horse-drawn CABS AND OMNIBUSES in the capital during the decade leading up to the outbreak of World War I (1914–1918).

The Victorian transportation revolution was inextricably bound up with other radical changes in the social, economic, and physical structures of Victorian Britain. New railway installations changed the face of towns and cities, both by their presence and because their expansion required the demolition of many buildings. The railway network and its stations had the effect of concentrating businesses and activity in town centers, speeding up the process of URBANIZATION. In the largest cities transportation hubs became victims of their own success, causing unprecedented urban congestion. Successive urban transportation innovations facilitated the outward spread of towns and cities, a process that caused several new problems. For example in compact pre-Victorian cities the rich and powerful lived at the center, with the poor residents on the periphery. In the new industrial city, successive rings of housing and industry developed around a central business district, with the richest now living furthest away. This process of suburbanization, made possible by mechanized transport links, brought with it notable changes in the design of houses and neighborhoods. No longer did the houses of the WEALTHY abut a central square or street, with stabling and the poor in nearby back streets. Instead the better off sought increasingly remote, socially segregated suburbs of detached and semidetached villas, and they no longer needed to keep horses.

TRANSPORTATION AND SOCIAL CHANGE

Transportation innovations played a major role in dietary change by altering the ECONOMICS of food production and distribution. They also underpinned a more general shift from home production to shopping. Multiple grocery stores and large DEPARTMENT STORES presupposed that the buyer would trade some expense on transportation for savings on purchases. Transportation developments also went hand in hand with an increasing diversification of leisure pursuits and not only for the well off. Although the working classes generally still walked to work, their traditional Easter and Whitsuntide excursions on foot or by open cart gave way to tram and steamboat excursions and return rail trips to SEASIDE RESORTS on Sundays. But there was no simple causal relationship between these changes in leisure activities and transportation innovations. The change also depended on rising incomes and a reduction in working hours, freeing up Saturday afternoons and bank holidays.

The relationship between transportation innovations and social and cultural change was always complex. New transportation modes helped challenge existing class boundaries and GENDER roles, but they also reflected and could even reinforce them. Class distinctions were literally built into early trams and railway carriages. Private transportation companies concerned with their balance sheets often resisted legislators' demands for cheap trains and trams for workers. As transportation improved the increased distances people were prepared to travel to work increased class segregation. According to some, transportation also contributed to greater isolation for women in domestic roles. Others argued that the suburbs promoted family life since the middle-class male was less distracted by the urban world of the club, restaurant, and THEATER.

Public transportation raised other issues about gender roles and stereotypes. So-called modesty guards were attached to staircases on horse omnibuses and trams in case women revealed too much in ascending. But transportation could also be liberating. It became acceptable for middle-class women to travel alone and to eat alone in restaurants and hotels attached to railway stations. Toward the end of the period the bicycle helped women break free from the restrictions of traditional dress. The same was also true of the automobile, though much less so in Britain than in the United States.

However, social and cultural change did not flow automatically from the adoption of transportation innovations. In INDIA, for example, British engineers constructed one of the largest railway systems in the world. But the "iron cow," as it was known, tended to be used mainly by white colonists and had little effect on the indigenous population except as a major source of employment for the unskilled. Comparative transportation history remains a relatively unexplored area in 2003. More work is needed in order to understand the links between technological, social, and cultural change and their political and economic contexts.

See also AUTOMOBILE; BICYCLING; SHIPPING; RAILWAYS.

FURTHER READING

Bagwell, Philip S. *The Transport Revolution from 1770.* London: B. T. Batsford, 1974.
Barker, T. C., and Michael Robbins. *The Nineteenth Century.* Vol. 1 of *A History of London Transport: Passenger Travel and the Development of the Metropolis.* London: George Allen and Unwin, 1963.
Derbyshire, Ian. "The Building of India's Railways: The Application of Western Technology in the Colonial Periphery 1850–1920." In *Technology and the Raj: Western Technology and Technical Transfers to India 1700–1947,* edited by Roy MacLeod and Deepak Kumar, 177–215. New Delhi, Thousand Oaks, Calif., and London: Sage Publications, 1995.
Freeman, Michael J., and Derek H. Aldcroft, eds. *Transport in Victorian Britain.* Manchester and New York: Manchester University Press, 1988.

Ochojna, A. D. "The Influence of Local and National Politics on the Development of Urban Passenger Transport in Britain 1850–1900." *Journal of Transport History* (new series) 4 (1978): 125–146.

Thompson, F. M. L. "Nineteenth-Century Horse Sense." *Economic History Review* (2d series) 29 (1976): 60–81.

COLIN CHANT

TRAVEL AND TOURISM

Commerce, conquest, and pilgrimage were the principal goals of travel for centuries before the Victorian era. During the nineteenth century, however, tourism grew enormously popular as a result of advances in the speed, ease, comfort, and affordability of traveling for pleasure. Travel abroad in pursuit of cultural refinement, further education, or mere relaxation—once mainly the privilege of aristocrats participating in the ritual known as the GRAND TOUR—was increasingly available to the middle classes. By the end of the Victorian era, all but the most impoverished workers could at least enjoy the pleasure of a HOLIDAY at the SEASIDE.

The Industrial Revolution equipped sailing ships with steam propulsion and sturdy iron and steel hulls of ever-increasing size, thus rendering sea voyages safer and more reliable. Meanwhile, improved roads and turnpikes facilitated the growth of travel by stagecoach and later the rapid development of RAILWAYS, which followed the opening of the Liverpool and MANCHESTER line in 1830, culminated in the building of transcontinental rail networks in North America, Europe, Asia, and AUSTRALIA. Other major ENGINEERING projects also facilitated travel, such as the Suez Canal, which opened in 1869, thus eliminating the long voyage around Africa to reach INDIA and the Far East, and the St. Gotthard Tunnel, completed in 1882, which provided readier access by rail to northern ITALY and the Adriatic.

Regularly scheduled service and reliable connections by land and sea shrank distances and made travel both more comfortable and affordable. The three-week journey from LONDON to Rome was reduced to three days, and the north Atlantic passage to New York City, which could take weeks by sailing ship, was cut to less than a week. Improvements in the preservation of food—by canning and, later, by mechanical refrigeration—raised the culinary standards on ocean voyages. Provisioners, such as the London firm of Fortnum and Mason, gained fame for supplying both tourist excursions and exploring expeditions. The growth of tourism in the nineteenth century stimulated the further development of service industries to provide advice and guidance, accommodations, and diversions. Travel agencies were established to sell tickets, arrange itineraries, and organize conducted tours. Hotels, RESORTS, and spas grew in popularity and enjoyed an increase in numbers. Victorian publishers produced a plethora of guide-

HULTON/ARCHIVE BY GETTY IMAGES

Victorian travelers trek across the Chamonix Glacier in France's Savoy Alps, circa 1867.

books and timetables, in addition to personal travel diaries, letters, journals, and narratives.

ENTREPRENEURSHIP IN THE TOURISM INDUSTRY

Capitalizing on these developments, THOMAS COOK (1808–1892) founded a new industry by chartering a train in 1841 and selling one-shilling, round-trip tickets to a temperance meeting. Meanwhile in the UNITED STATES, Henry Wells (1805–1878) established a BUSINESS that evolved into the American Express Company to accommodate freight and, later, passengers. Cook was soon promoting pleasure excursions to the English and French seashores as "rational recreation" for the working class. He also organized rail excursions to the GREAT EXHIBITION OF 1851 and to the Paris Exhibition in 1855, and, in the 1860s, he offered three-day excursions to Paris, including hotel room and meals, for £5/7s (U.S.$27). In addition to pioneering such travel aids as reduced-price return fares, travel vouchers, hotel coupons, and travelers' checks, Thomas Cook and Son inaugurated regularly scheduled tours of Switzerland in 1863, of the United States in 1867, of EGYPT and the Holy Land in 1869, and "around-the-world" tours in 1872. Cook and Son also promoted their travel business by publishing a PERIODICAL. *Cook's Excursionist and Home and Foreign Tourist Advertiser* first appeared in 1851 and was produced in both British and American editions.

When the increasing ease of travel led the working class to adopt the seaside holiday, the upper classes sought the enhanced status and exclusivity represented by foreign travel across Europe and to the exotic East. Tourism to the MIDDLE EAST grew especially popular after 1870, when Cook and Son became the Egyptian government's official agents for passenger traffic up the Nile River, of which they gained exclusive control in 1880. A conducted tour from Cairo to Aswan, including the return fare from England, cost £46 ($230), or, for as little as £120 ($600), Cook offered affluent tourists a 90-day tour of Palestine, lower Egypt, and the Upper Nile. By 1872 Cook had dispatched 400 passengers to Egypt and 230 to Palestine. About 200 people booked tours up the Nile in 1873; and 5,000 people had taken Cook's tour of Palestine by 1882.

In 1884 Cook's chartered steamers provided TRANSPORTATION for the military expedition up the Nile to relieve General CHARLES GORDON at Khartoum. The damage they suffered as a result prompted Cook to build a flotilla of larger Nile steamers, the first of which, the *Prince Abbas*, was launched in 1886. The following year Cook opened a luxury hotel at Luxor in Upper Egypt to accommodate his wealthy clients. The world's largest and best-known travel organization, Cook's become synonymous with travel under the leadership of John Mason Cook (1834–1899), the son of the founder, who personally guided the German Kaiser Wilhelm II (1859–1941) on a tour to Jerusalem in 1898.

Railway travel over long distances was greatly improved by the introduction of the "palace" car, with seats that converted into sleeping berths, invented by the American, George Pullman (1831–1897). In 1876 Georges Nagelmackers (1845–1905) of Belgium founded the Cie Internationale des Wagons-Lits to emulate the success Pullman enjoyed in America. By the following year he had negotiated contracts with 20 European national rail companies to provide transcontinental service employing his 58 luxuriously appointed Pullman sleeping cars. In 1882 Nagelmackers added DINING car service and in the following year inaugurated the famous Orient Express from Paris, which in 1889 became a through service to Constantinople. Other routes followed, including the so-called "Blue Train" to FRANCE's Côte d'Azur, where Nagelmackers's company built and operated the Riviera Palace hotel in Nice. Additional luxury hotels were constructed by the Wagons-Lits Company in Brindisi, Luxor, and Beijing (Peking), and former royal palaces were converted into hotels in Constantinople and Cairo, where the company also acquired Shepheard's hotel, a favorite with travelers in Egypt, for its impressive 300 rooms, electric lights, and bathrooms with plumbing.

Luxury hotels began to appear in major American cities following the CIVIL WAR. These catered to the needs of wealthy American travelers, as well as increasing numbers of foreign visitors. Although Europeans often confined their tours to a well-traveled loop through Boston, New York City, Niagara Falls, Toronto, and Montreal, steamboat service on the Ohio and Mississippi rivers and the completion of transcontinental rail lines in both the United States and CANADA opened up the further West to tourism, where big-game HUNTING was a particular attraction for wealthy sportsmen.

While natural hot springs and spas had attracted visitors for centuries, European resorts such as Baden-Baden, Marienbad, and Wiesbaden gained enormous success in the later nineteenth century by entertaining an international clientele of wealthy tourists who came to "take the cure" by bathing in the hot springs and to gamble in the adjacent casinos. Further south, at Monte Carlo and Biarritz, casinos also became major attractions. A more energetic class of tourists was attracted to hiking and the new SPORT of climbing mountains; the Alpine Club was formed in London by British MOUNTAINEERING enthusiasts in 1857. Switzerland was thus an increasingly popular destination with British tourists, many of whom journeyed there on Cook's 21-day tours, which cost as little as £20 ($100). Although Switzerland had a POPULATION of fewer than 3 million, it boasted more than 14,000 inns and hostelries and was widely promoted both by Cook's and by books such as *The Playground of Europe* (1871) by LESLIE STEPHEN (1832–1904) and *Alps and Sanctuaries* (1881) by SAMUEL BUTLER (1835–1902). Alpine skiing later became popular in the 1890s, but already by 1877 the actress Fanny Kemble (1809–1893) was complaining that Switzerland was being "ruined" by mass tourism.

THE GENRE OF TRAVEL LITERATURE FLOURISHES

It was against this background that the production and sale of travel literature flourished as never before, a genre so numerous that no comprehensive bibliography or catalogue of it exists. One of the oldest and most popular forms of literature, travel books provided information and vicarious pleasure to stay-at-home readers, as well as stimulating in others the urge to travel. The ever-increasing number of nineteenth-century travel books both reflected and contributed to the growth of tourism and travel that characterized the Victorian era. Many prominent and successful authors published accounts of their travels. WILLIAM WORDSWORTH'S (1770–1850) *Description of the Scenery of the Lakes in the North of England* (1822), prompted many tourists to visit England's remote Lake District, while travel accounts by J. W. von Goethe (1749–1832), CHARLES DICKENS (1812–1870), and JOHN RUSKIN (1819–1900) encouraged many others to visit Italy. Even extremely hostile accounts of travel, such as *Domestic Manners of the Americans* (1832) by FRANCES TROLLOPE (1780–1863) and Dickens's *American Notes* (1842), appear to have had little effect in discouraging others from following in their footsteps. The exploits of Lord Byron (1788–1824) in Greece helped popularize travel to the eastern Mediterranean, and inspired several generations of travelers who published accounts of their journeys in that region. They included artist and poet EDWARD LEAR (1812–1888), who recorded his frequent Mediterranean journeys in works such as a *Journal of a Landscape Painter in Greece and Albania* (1851).

Some Victorian travel writers were less inclined than their predecessors to document their itineraries by describing and cataloguing almost everything they observed, but instead adopted a more personal, even introspective style. *Voyage en Orient* (1835; trans. as *Travels in the Holy Land*, 1837) by French poet Louis Lamartine (1790–1869) is an early example. Alexander William Kinglake (1809–1891), who declared that he wrote "precisely upon those matters which happened to interest me, and upon none other," provided the British archetype of this newer, more impressionistic, and anecdotal style. His *Eothen, or Traces of Travel Brought Home from the East* (1844) is one of the most successful and enduringly popular of Victorian travel books. *The Crescent and the Cross* (1846) by Eliot Warburton (1810–1852) and *Visits to Monasteries in the Levant* (1849) by Robert Curzon (1810–1873)—an account of his search for rare manuscripts—are similar in style and are still held in high esteem.

Quite apart from the travel accounts of tourists, however intrepid, many of the era's most popular travel books were explorers' accounts of little-known, exotic, and often dangerous regions. Readers relished tales of hardship, heroism, survival, and exoticism, elements common to those books, which were reprinted in many successive editions. Publishers, fully conscious of this, often subjected travel narratives to heavy editing to supply or enhance these desired ingredients. Comparing explorers' field notes and diaries with the formal folio and quarto accounts of voyages and expeditions issued by publishers such as Richard Bentley and John Murray reveals major changes and embellishments. Increasingly, the publication of scientific exploring expeditions and field surveys, which lacked the elements of adventure and ROMANCE expected by readers, was confined to the imprints of governments and LEARNED SOCIETIES. Britain's ROYAL GEOGRAPHICAL SOCIETY, founded in 1830 to promote EXPLORATION and discovery, had many counterparts in Europe, America, and elsewhere. By 1890, more than 100 geographical societies had been established in 21 countries, and they were publishing 130 different geographical journals.

At the same time, the demand for books of exotic travel and exploration continued to grow. While only a wealthy elite could purchase elaborate, large format editions, cheaper reprint editions in smaller formats and less-detailed, narrative versions sold in large numbers, and informed an increasingly democratized audience of readers about parts of the world that they were never likely to visit. The ethnographic content of these books introduced readers to alien cultures and frequently titillated them with erotic details. The expansion of European EMPIRES in the nineteenth century is reflected in much of the literature of travel and exploration, whose authors tended to view the world from a Christian as well as imperialist perspective and who generally took for granted the superiority of all things European. Numeroous professional soldiers, explorers, and imperial administrators—British, French, Dutch, Russian, and American—drew on their personal experiences to produce a vast literature of travel in the service of their respective countries.

THE ROYAL GEOGRAPHICAL SOCIETY ENCOURAGES EXPLORATION

Under the presidency of geologist Sir Roderick Murchison (1792–1871), the Royal Geographical Society employed its sponsorships, publications, and gold medals to promote scientific inquiry hand-in-glove with British imperial aspirations. The society also fed the public's thirst for heroes and heroics by promoting and supporting the work of African MISSIONARY and explorer DAVID LIVINGSTONE (1813–1873), whose *Missionary Travels and Researches in South Africa* (1857) enjoyed almost unprecedented success and elevated its author to secular sainthood. HENRY MORTON STANLEY (1841–1904) was of a totally different character; the apotheosis of the explorer as ruthless empire-builder, Stanley achieved enormous popular success with books such as *How I Found Livingstone* (1872), *Through the Dark Continent* (1878), and *In Darkest Africa* (1890).

The Royal Geographical Society also funded expeditions by the flamboyant and controversial explorer and ethnographer Sir RICHARD BURTON (1821–1890), author of more than 20 travel accounts, of which his *Personal Narrative of a Pilgrimage to El-Medinah and Meccah* (1855–1856) proved to be the most popular with readers. His career as a soldier, explorer, diplomat, and author covered an astounding geographical range, including India, Arabia and Syria, East and West Africa, as well as North and South America. Burton's candor in describing indigenous sexual practices tarnished his reputation in polite Victorian society, while undoubtedly increasing the sale of his books. A later traveler in Arabia, Charles Doughty (1843–1926), produced one of the most challengingly idiosyncratic books on that region; his *Travels in Arabia Deserta* (1888), though never popular with readers, is regarded by many as a literary masterpiece among travel accounts.

The society collaborated with the British admiralty in the sponsorship of polar exploration—a particular Victorian obsession—and the majority of the scores of Arctic expeditions yielded published accounts. The reading public naturally preferred those written in a "through-hell-to-latitude 90" style, especially the numerous accounts of the rescue expeditions that searched in vain for Sir John Franklin (1786–1847) and his ill-fated men. Rivaling the popularity of the numerous polar narratives were the accounts of naturalists, such as CHARLES DARWIN's (1809–1882) account of his research voyage aboard *H. M. S. Beagle* (1839), *The Naturalist on the River Amazon* (1863) by Henry Walter Bates (1825–1892), *The Malay Archipelago* (1869) by ALFRED RUSSEL WALLACE (1823–1913), and *The Naturalist in Nicaragua* (1874) by Thomas Belt (1832–1878).

Accounts of archaeological exploration and discovery also captured the imagination of the reading public and produced a large number of best-selling books about the ruins of lost civilizations, such as *Ninevah and Its Remains*(1849) by Austen Henry Layard (1817–1894), an account of his excavation of ancient Assyrian ruins; and *Incidents of Travel in Central America, Chiapas, and Yucatán* (1841) by John Lloyd Stephens (1805–1852), which aroused interest in Mayan culture. Stephens, an American lawyer, had already enjoyed success with his account of *Incidents of Travel in Egypt, Arabia Petraea, and the Holy Land* (1837), which was but one example of a flourishing genre that helped popularize new discoveries in the field of Egyptology.

FEMALE WRITERS' CONTRIBUTIONS TO TRAVEL LITERATURE

The Victorian era also produced numerous accounts of foreign travel by women travelers, including many titles of enduring interest. Lucy Atkinson (circa 1820–1863) recorded her *Recollections of Tartar Steppes and their Inhabitants* (1863) following five years of adventurous travel in Russia and Siberia. Amelia Edwards (1831–1892) sailed *A Thousand Miles up the Nile* (1877), and Ella Sykes (d. 1939) rode *Through Persia on a Side-Saddle* (1898). Lady Anne Blunt (1837–1917) traveled with her husband among *The Bedouin Tribes of the Euphrates* (1879) and became only the second European woman to visit central Arabia on *A Pilgrimage to Nejd* (1881). Florence Dixie (1855–1905) ventured *Across Patagonia* (1880), while her fellow American Carrie Strahorn (1854–1925) traveled *Fifteen Thousand Miles by Stage* (1911) to traverse much of the western half of North America "from Alaska to Mexico." American cyclist Fanny Workman (1859–1925) published her *Algerian Memories: A Bicycle Tour over the Atlas to the Sahara* (1895) and later wrote of her cycling tours in Spain, India, and the Himalayas.

Two of the most popular and widely read Victorian women authors of travel books were also perhaps the most widely traveled. Austrian-born Ida Pfeiffer (1797–1858) only began her travels at the age of 45, but spent the following 15 years circling the globe twice; she produced a much-translated series of books recording her visits to numerous countries. Although Pfeiffer's works were admired by no less an authority than Alexander von Humboldt (1769–1859), much better remembered and more highly regarded are the nine major travel books produced by ISABELLA BIRD (1831–1904). In these books she recorded her lengthy and solitary travels in Australia, East and South Asia, the North and SOUTH PACIFIC, North America, and the Near East, beginning with *The Englishwoman in America* (1856), *The Hawaiian Archipelago* (1875), and *A Lady's Life in the Rocky Mountains* (1879). Finally, Mary Kingsley revealed herself in her *Travels in West Africa* (1897) and *West African Studies* (1899) as the one woman traveler, explorer, and author who—like Sir Richard Burton—combined the naturalist's curiosity and powers of observation with an ethnographer's cultural objectivity and had a tolerance (or even an actual relish) for the hardships of travel through equatorial swamps and jungles.

THE PROLIFERATION OF THE GUIDEBOOK

While numerous Victorian explorers and tourists maintained the tradition of editing their journals and letters for publication, a more humble but utilitarian form of travel literature also grew in numbers. The tourist guidebook, a genre with both ancient and medieval antecedents, became an indispensable aid for the well prepared Victorian tourist. Instead of presenting a narrative account and description of a specific journey, they ranged from books of homely advice for the comfort and protection of the would-be traveler, to books with information about specific places, such as where to stay, what to see, and what and where to eat.

Guidebooks were generally singular publications dealing with a particular country or region, such as the anonymously published *Hints to Travellers in Italy* (1815) by Richard Colt Hoare (1758–1838). The playwright Mariana Starke (circa 1762–1838) enjoyed considerable success with her more comprehensive *Travels on the Continent, Written for the Use and Particular Information of Travellers* (1820), which had gone through numerous editions before her death in 1838. Other guidebooks targeted special audiences, such as *Hints to Lady Travellers at Home and Abroad* (1889) and *Handbook for Lady Cyclists* (1896) by Lillias Campbell Davidson. Those travelers seeking to restore their health could consult Augustus Granville (1783–1872) on the *Spas of England and Principal Sea-Bathing Places* (1841), many of which were then becoming accessible by train. Still later, the medicinal benefits of travel to the Middle East were detailed in *Egypt as a Health Resort, with Medical and Other Hints for Travellers in Syria* (1873) by Archibald Walker.

The London publishing house of John Murray had long issued accounts of voyages and travel, including guidebooks, but with *A Handbook for Travellers on the Continent* (1836) the firm inaugurated an enormously successful and long-running series of national and regional handbooks for travelers. The series grew in scope and numbers to cover most parts of the world amenable to English-speaking tourists. One volume, the *Handbook for Travellers in Spain* (1845) by Richard Ford (1796–1858), and the author's sequel, *Gatherings from Spain* (1846), continue to be held in the highest regard by students of that country. Another contributor to Murray's *Handbook* series, Augustus J. C. Hare (1834–1903), launched his own highly successful series of guides to the cities and byways of Europe with his *Walks in Rome* (1871), which went through more than 20 editions over the following half-century.

Murray's innovative format for the *Handbooks* and the organization of their contents were soon imitated by the German publisher and bookseller Karl Baedeker (1801–1859), who issued his guide to the Rhineland in 1839. With Teutonic thoroughness, Baedeker was soon outdoing Murray in the scope and detailed content of his guidebooks and he produced dense, reference compendia of information that were unrivaled for their detail and accuracy. In 1854 Baedeker also began imitating Murray's bright-red binding design. A French translation of the guide to the Rhine was issued in 1846, followed in 1861 by an English translation. These books found a ready market over the next two decades, during which 800,000 passengers a year took steamer cruises on the Rhine. All subsequent Baedeker guidebooks were issued in separate German, French, and English-language editions, and Baedeker's name became synonymous with "guidebook."

OTHER TRAVEL PUBLICATIONS EMERGE

The expansive development of railroads and steamship companies created a large demand for printed timetables. Numerous *Railway Companions* were published, such as one for *The Grand Junction, and the Liverpool and Manchester Railway*, which appeared in 1837. But with 400 separate lines built or under construction in Great Britain alone, something more comprehensive was required. In 1839 George Bradshaw (1801–1853) published the first edition of *Bradshaw's Railway Timetables*, which he later serialized as *Bradshaw's Monthly Railway and Steam Navigation Guide for Great Britain, Ireland, and the Continent*. This publication immediately dominated the market and overshadowed *Cook's Continental Time Tables and Tourist's Handbook*.

Although Victorian readers faced no shortage of genuine travel works, fictionalized travel accounts also enjoyed considerable popularity. These ranged from NOVELS of bourgeois manners, such as Frances Trollope's *The Robertses on their Travels* (1846), to exciting tales of foreign adventure typified by *King Solomon's Mines* (1885) by H. Rider Haggard (1856–1925), and, most notably, the *Voyages extraordinaires* of Jules Verne (1828–1905). Extremely popular, even in awkward English translations, Verne's stories captivated readers by combining the wonders of modern science with exotic tales of travel. His best-selling *Le Tour du monde en quatre-vingts jours* (1873, trans. as *Around the World in Eighty Days*) was fiction, but the itinerary and schedule of its eccentric English hero, Phileas Fogg, was soundly factual; indeed, it was borrowed almost literally from the introduction to an 1871 issue of *Bradshaw's*.

See also COOK, THOMAS; EXPLORATION; GRAND TOUR; RAILWAY LITERATURE; RAILWAYS; SEASIDE; TRANSPORTATION.

FURTHER READING

Assad, Thomas. *Three Victorian Travellers: Burton, Blunt, and Doughty*. London: Routledge, 1964.
Brendan, Piers. *Thomas Cook: 150 Years of Popular Tourism*. London: Secker & Warburg, 1991.
Clark, Ronald. *The Victorian Mountaineers*. London: Batsford, 1953.
Croutier, Alev. *Taking the Waters*. New York: Abbeville, 1992.
Fedden, Robin. *English Travellers in the Near East*. London: Longmans, 1958.
Lambert, Richard S. *The Fortunate Traveller: A Short History of Touring and Travelling for Pleasure*. London: Melrose, 1950.
Leask, Nigel. *Curiosity and the Aesthetics of Travel Writing, 1770–1840*. Oxford: Oxford University Press, 2002.
Middleton, Dorothy. *Victorian Lady Travellers*. London: Routledge, 1965.
Pimlott, J. A. R. *The Englishman's Holiday: A Social History*. London: Faber, 1947.
Pratt, Mary Louise. *Imperial Eyes: Travel Writing and Transculturation*. London: Routledge, 1992.
Raby, Peter. *Bright Paradise: Victorian Scientific Travellers*. London: Chatto, 1996.
Ring, Jim. *How the English Made the Alps*. London: Murray, 2002.
Schivelbusch, Wolfgang. *The Railway Journey: Trains and Travel in the Nineteenth Century*. Oxford: Blackwell, 1979.
Stevenson, Catherine. *Victorian Women Travel Writers in Africa*. Boston: Twayne, 1982.
Tinling, Marion. *Women into the Unknown: A Sourcebook on Women Explorers and Travellers*. Westport: Greenwood, 1989.
Turner, Louis, and John Ash. *The Golden Hordes: International Tourism and the Pleasure Periphery*. London: Constable, 1975.

MERRILL DISTAD

TRAVELING FAIRS

The network of traveling fairs was an essential component of popular culture in nineteenth century Britain. These popular events had their origins in charter fairs that were linked to a market-trading past, religious festivities, or statute fairs based on the Statute of Labours passed as early as 1351. Traveling fairs were held in villages, towns, and cities throughout the United Kingdom and lasted anywhere between four and eight days in one particular location. The fair was a venue for a variety of SHOWS, exhibits, and goods for sale that tempted and titillated the public who attended these gatherings. However, the Victorian fair was one of fluctuating fortunes and the golden age of traveling entertainment only came into being in the later half of the century.

The fairground shows of the early to mid-nineteenth century are perhaps the best documented of all the amusements on offer until the introduction of steam-powered roundabouts, and enjoyed their heyday during the first 50 years of the century. By the beginning of the nineteenth century attractions such as theatrical booths, waxworks, and freak shows began to dominate the fairground landscape. The middle of the century saw the emergence of the wild beast shows known as menageries, which began to take precedence over rival attractions.

The showmen of this period developed ingenuity and style, and the gullible public flocked to see not just the great waxworks and menagerie shows but also the peep shows, illusionists, and FREAK SHOWS exhibiting such unedifying spectacles as bearded ladies or the Elephant Man. The life of a traveling showman was hard but the rewards could be high, and some of those who became rich during this period left the fairground altogether. Others, generally families, who were financially successful remained in the fairground communities and laid the foundations of the great shows of the late nineteenth century. The most successful became well-known personalities and adopted extravagant titles—George Sanger, for example, gave himself the prefix "Lord."

CHANGES AT MID-CENTURY

By the 1850s, with the great changes wrought by the Industrial Revolution that brought a migration from rural towns and villages to the ever-expanding industrial cities, the trading element on which fairs had been built had been superseded by entertainment, but the fairs themselves appeared to be in decline. Many of the famous London fairs were abolished at this time, among them Bartholomew Fair, which had lent its name and setting to a famous play by Ben Jonson, disappeared in 1855 together with Camberwell. Greenwich Fair had gone by 1857 and 1860 brought the demise of the fair at Stepney. As the public grew increasingly sophisticated, the attraction of fairground shows diminished and showmen such as David Millar, whose theatrical presentations and Punch and Judy shows had achieved great success in the early decades of the century, could barely survive by 1849. During the same period many of the famous names of the first part of the nineteenth century also seemed to desert the traveling fairs. Lord George Sanger, for example, bought the permanent site of Astleys in 1871 as a circus exhibition and stopped traveling. Although Bostock and Wombwell's Menagerie continued its connection with the fairground industry for another 50 years, the death of the founder George Wombwell in 1850 and the disposal of his show in 1872 would seem to indicate that the nation had outgrown its need for such entertainment.

Fairs throughout the country seemed in danger in the 1860s and 1870s, not only as a result of the Fairs Acts of 1868, 1871, and 1873, but also because of the loss of traditional sites in town centers. The 1871 act had allowed local authorities or "owners" of fairs the right to petition for their abolition, and the further amendments introduced in the 1873 act created the possibility of changing the days when the event could be held. Historians of the time warned against the loss of such events; Amery Fabyan in his paper on "Country Fair and Revels," published in 1878, predicted that "the relics are fast dissolving; soon the generation of fair and revel-goers will disappear also, and with it a rich mine of folklore, traditions, and customs will also be lost."

However, fairs could only face abolition if no public pressure was applied to prevent such an order being carried out. If the notice of abolition was greeted with public protest and pressure, then the secretary of state had the power to rescind the request from the local authorities. In order to prevent such notices taking effect, traveling fairs needed to meet the recreational needs of the populace again. But traveling fairs faced a great deal of competition from MUSIC HALLS, THEATERS, and traveling EXHIBITIONS such as panoramas and lantern shows that presented their attractions in town centers. Thomas Frost described the future of fairs as bleak when he wrote in 1874, "what need then, of fairs, and shows? The nation has outgrown them, and fairs are as dead as the generations which they have delighted, and the last showman will soon be as great a curiosity as the dodo." Despite this prophecy, fairs continued to survive and indeed flourish in the industrial North of England and the rural communities. The Wakes fairs associated with workers' holidays became affirmations of community identity, both past and present, where people expressed themselves through uninhibited pleasure seeking. The fairs themselves began to adapt to changing conditions and embraced the new and the different. Although the audience had changed and events had become increasingly unpopular with the urban bourgeoisie, the appeal of such fairs was on the increase among the working-class members of the populace. Large urban events had died out, but new fairs replaced them and were held in association with Wakes, agricultural shows, and church festivities such as Whit Sunday on the feast of Pentecost and celebrated seven weeks after Easter.

STEAM-POWERED ROUNDABOUTS SAVE FAIRS

In 1863 an event occurred that revolutionized the Victorian fair and laid the foundations for the modern traveling amusement business: the introduction of steam-powered roundabouts at the Midsummer Fair at Halifax. This was soon followed by the founding of Frederick Savage's firm in King's Lynn, Norfolk, for the construction of mechanized roundabouts. A range of rides and designs emerged from the 1870s onward, culminating in 1891 when Savage produced the classic style for the English "Gallopers" or, as it was to become known in Europe and America, the carousel.

The innovation of mechanization on the fairground came at a most opportune time in its history; it revitalized the once glorious fairs and created a hierarchy of businessmen on the fairgrounds. Fairs became a feature of the holiday calendar, both in rural and urban communities. This increased prosperity and respectability resulted in government becoming increasingly tolerant toward the holding of fairs and showing little interest in enforcing the legislation introduced in the previous decade.

Mechanization moved the emphasis away from the shows, which were rooted in the past, toward the rides, thus giving showmen complete freedom to keep in step with the technological advancements of a revolutionary age. The golden age of the fairground roundabouts was yet to come, but the seeds had been planted and continued to grow. By the end of the Victorian era, the landscape of the fairground was populated by rides of all kinds: steam yachts, switchbacks and of course the galloping horses. Mechanization made the fairground appear modern and futuristic and the latest attractions of the age such as the ghost shows, the cinematograph, and X-ray photography were fully exploited by the fairground showmen, who advertised their attractions as being patronized by all classes of people. The showmen achieved prestige and prosperity through investing in new rides when they were unveiled each year in February at the King's Lynn Valentine's Day Fair, which marked the beginning of the traveling season. The golden age of the fairground had arrived and this did not merely refer to the gold leaf decoration on the rides. By the end of the nineteenth-century fairs were no longer in decline in the United Kingdom, where 200 events took place every weekend from Easter through November.

See also SHOWS; FREAK SHOWS; EXHIBITIONS.

FURTHER READING

Braithwaite, David. *Fairground Architecture.* London: Hugh Evelyn, 1968.

Cameron, David Kerr. *The English Fair.* Stroud: Sutton Publishing, 1998.

Fabyan, Amery. "Country Fairs and Revels." *Annual Reports and Transactions of the Plymouth Institute* 7 (1878): 64–83.

Frost, Thomas. *The Old Showmen and the Old London Fairs.* London: Tinsley Brothers, 1874.

Sanger, "Lord" George. *Seventy Years a Showman.* London: Arthur Pearson, 1908.

Weedon, Geoff, and Richard Ward. *Fairground Art.* London: White Mouse Editions, 1981.

VANESSA TOULMIN

TREVELYAN, CHARLES

Born: April 2, 1807; Taunton, England
Died: June 19, 1886; London, England

Although Sir Charles Edward Trevelyan has become fixed in the historic memory as the cruel mismanager of the Irish potato FAMINE, his PHILOSOPHY and career mirror the progression of major reform movements of the Victorian era. Trevelyan began his religious life as a moderate evangelical Anglican who forged ties with the Clapham sect. This group was composed of bankers, business leaders, and civil servants who advocated good works jointed with civic activism. Trevelyan reflected these ideals throughout his public life, no matter how unfeeling his version of good works may seem to later generations. He thought of himself as a man of unswerving principle, although the consequences of his well-intentioned reforms were sometimes startlingly harsh.

Trevelyan began his professional career with entry into the EAST INDIA COMPANY's Bengal CIVIL SERVICE at age 19; he served in INDIA for 12 years until 1838. In his professional role he first addressed the internal tariffs that burdened trade within India and then centered attention on the Indian educational system. Trevelyan married Hannah Moore, sister of Lord THOMAS BABINGTON MACAULAY, and the marriage cemented a political alliance as well as a personal one. In 1835 both men led arguments calculated to influence the British government to stress European literature and science among Indians, at the expense of indigenous languages. After this victory Trevelyan addressed one of the favorite themes: substitution of the Roman for the Arabic alphabet in Indian languages. Trevelyan truly believed that the replacement of Indian cultures with a Christian civilization would solve all of the resistance and difficulties in the subcontinent.

HULTON/ARCHIVE BY GETTY IMAGES

Reformer Charles Trevelyan is best remembered for his mismanagement of the Irish potato famine of the 1840s.

THE POTATO FAMINE

In 1840 Trevelyan was appointed the assistant secretary to the Treasury, and it was in this capacity that he made his historic decisions about the Irish. Trevelyan was a conscientious public servant, but he was severely restrained by his Liberal views. Classic Liberal philosophy decreed laissez-faire economic policies and championed minimal government intervention; above all, Liberals felt that the government should never interfere with nor constrain property rights in any way. Liberalism also set great store on individual hard work, on thrift, and on self-help. The Liberal view on charity was that dispensing handouts was harmful in that it only encouraged indolence and dependence.

These views informed Trevelyan's strategy for dealing with the failure of the Irish potato crop beginning in 1846 and continuing for several years after. Trevelyan refused to restrict the exportation of food from IRELAND, nor would he involve the government in the importation or sale of inexpensive grain to the starving Irish millions. He wrote of Ireland in 1848: "It provides no part of the functions of government to provide supplies of food. . . . [I]t falls to the share of government to protect the merchant and the agriculturist in the free exercise of their respective employments."

Instead of providing food and medical care for the millions of Irish who depended exclusively upon POTATOES for survival, the emphasis was on public works schemes that would have the Irish working for the food that they received. Trevelyan subscribed to the prevalent stereotype of the Irish character, and he believed that by making them work for the help that they received, habits of industry and self-reliance would be taught to the lazy and feckless Irish. In place of indiscriminate handouts Trevelyan devised a strategy whereby the needy Irish would labor in projects, mainly road building or repair, which would be financed by loans to be repaid at 3.5% interest. Through the Irish Employment Act of 1846, the Irish would pay for the assistance controlled solely by the British government.

By 1847 half-starved men were forced to walk miles through dreadful weather in order to perform hard outdoor labor. In return they received money that was inadequate to buy food for their families. Distress was too widespread and severe to be controlled by strict adherence to a political and economic philosophy, and Irish society was in chaos. In the end the insistence on relying on public works projects cost far more than food handouts would have; more important the ill-will and resentment fostered among the Irish by this calculating approach produced long-term political consequences.

Trevelyan genuinely believed that dependence on others was a moral disease that must be eradicated. Furthermore he felt that the Irish famine was a punishment from God sent to teach the Irish a lesson. Trevelyan was very concerned that the right lessons be learned from this disaster, and he worried most that aid "not turn into a curse what was intended for a blessing." Trevelyan did not believe that the cause of the famine was the potato blight or fungus. He felt certain that land tenure, overpopulation, and the backward state of Irish agriculture were all to blame, and he wished to force landlords to reform the rural economy. When this was done and the Irish character was changed to reflect the Victorian values of self-reliance and thrift, IRELAND would be a better place and one that reflected God's economic and social plans.

It is perhaps important to note that Trevelyan had visited Ireland for a short time before the famine in 1843, but he felt it necessary to visit only Dublin for one week in October of 1847. Theory dominated the formulation of his Irish policy, not personal observations; nonetheless during the Irish crisis he took no leave and worked very long hours. He personally donated a substantial sum to the British Association for the Relief of Extreme Distress in Ireland and Scotland. His dedication was rewarded by a grateful government when he was given the equivalent of a year's salary for his "solution" to the Irish potato difficulty. Trevelyan was never the uncaring bureaucrat as he has sometimes been portrayed; he simply wanted to create a better society in Ireland without disturbing property rights, and he believed, moreover, that God sent the potato blight in order to provide him with this opportunity.

OTHER CIVIL SERVICE

Back on the domestic front Trevelyan, along with Sir Stafford Northcote, undertook an inquiry into the state of the British civil service. The famous Northcote-Trevelyan report published in February of 1854 recommended that appointments in the civil service be determined by competitive examinations instead of patronage and aristocratic influence. This report reflected Trevelyan's strong sense of public duty and reform, but an inability to impartially apply his strict standard surfaced when an attempt was made to abolish patronage within the Indian civil service. Haileybury College graduates had long dominated appointments to India, and Trevelyan, a graduate himself, saw no contradiction in recommending Haileybury graduation as the best requirement for holding office in the Indian service.

In 1859 Trevelyan returned to India as the governor of Madras, where he threw himself into various reform projects including the reorganization of the POLICE, but he ran afoul of powerful government opinion when he dared to openly oppose a TAXATION plan. His opposition was viewed as subverting British authority and supporting insurrection; greater store was set on loyalty because of the recent Indian Rebellion in 1857. It is interesting that Liberal views on unnecessary taxation paled in importance when confronted with issues of power and colonization. Trevelyan was recalled after only fourteen months in Madras, although he was able to redeem himself with a reappointment to India in 1862 as finance minister. He occupied himself mainly with public works during this tour of duty and in 1865 returned home. Not one to rest in comfortable retirement, Trevelyan threw himself into the controversy over the purchase of commissions in the BRITISH ARMY. Later his name was associated with a wide variety of social questions, as, for example, the investigation of charities. He remained a staunch Liberal to the end of his life and continued to use his Liberal principles to determine all of his reform proposals.

See also CIVIL SERVICE; FAMINES; IRELAND; POLICE; POTATOES.

FURTHER READING

Hart, Jenifer. "Sir Charles Trevelyan at the Treasury." *English Historical Review* 75 (1960): 92–110.
McRae, Malcolm. "Sir Charles Trevelyan's Indian Letters, 1859–1865." *English Historical Review* 77 (1962): 706–712.
Trevelyan, Charles E. *The Irish Crisis.* London: Longman, Brown, Green and Longmans, 1848.

CYNTHIA CURRAN

TROLLOPE, ANTHONY

Born: April 24, 1815; London, England
Died: December 6, 1882; London, England

Over a century after his death, the novelist Anthony Trollope still sustains voracious readers of Victorian fiction. Of his 47 NOVELS, at least three dozen are well worth reading. He is best known for two sequences of related novels, with interlocking plots and characters: The Chronicles of Barset, comprised of *The Warden* (1855), *Barchester Towers* (1857), *Doctor Thorne* (1858), *Framley Parsonage* (1861), *The Small House at Allington* (1864), and *The Last Chronicle of Barset*

(1867); and the Palliser novels, including *Can You Forgive Her?* (1864), *Phineas Finn* (1869), *Phineas Redux* (1874), *The Prime Minister* (1876), and *The Duke's Children* (1880). Though not a series in the same sense as the linked sequences, a subset of texts with Irish settings, which include his first two novels, reflect Trollope's long-term fascination with both the people and politics of IRELAND, where he lived from 1841 through 1859.

STEADY WORK

Trollope's work in Ireland established his "other" career, in the POSTAL SERVICE, which he joined as a junior clerk in 1834. He is best known as a postal official for introducing the pillar post-box to England. This day job, from which he retired a distinguished senior official in 1867, did not interfere with Trollope's prolific output as a novelist, for as he reported in his posthumously published *Autobiography* (1883), he simply got up early and wrote his quota of words before breakfast. Trollope's work habits mirrored those of his mother; Frances Milton Trollope, a famous novelist and travel writer, rose between four

MANSELL/TIMEPIX/GETTY IMAGES
British novelist Anthony Trollope's work ethic helped him write 47 novels while holding a full-time job in the postal service.

and five o'clock in the morning in order to write before breakfast.

Trollope's frank admission about his regular writing habits, in combination with his reports of sales figures and earnings, may have temporarily damaged Trollope's reputation by making him appear crass, materialistic, and workmanlike. Writing so many books may have also contributed to his reputation as a novelist of the second tier. During his own lifetime he wrote so much that he often had several novels in the drawer: in those circumstances he delayed publication lest he flood the market with his own work. However, Trollope never lost his regular readers, and at the turn of the millennium all of his novels were in print.

Lasting Appeal

Some critics have suggested that as the Victorian worlds Trollope imagined faded from memory, his novels functioned as escapist romances for nostalgic readers longing for a lost time of moral certainties and relishing the minor troubles of characters who usually reach happy endings. The spike in Trollope's popularity during World War II (1939–1945) has lent support to this view. Nevertheless, in his own time Trollope was considered a realist novelist. In his *Autobiography*, he proudly quotes his contemporary NATHANIEL HAWTHORNE's (1804–1864) assessment of Trollope's accomplishment in crafting fictional worlds to seem "just as real as if some giant had hewn a great lump out of the earth and put it under a glass case, with all its inhabitants going about their daily business, and not suspecting that they were being made show of." Trollope's character-centered art does respond to a range of influences: he was widely read in Renaissance drama; he knew the classics; and although he disliked the mechanical plotting of the popular novelist WILKIE COLLINS (1824–1889), Trollope shares with Collins a taste for sensational effects in stories about moral dilemmas.

Trollope's characteristic social satire is best exemplified, according to many readers, by his story of a crooked financier, *The Way We Live Now* (1875). This novel offers a portrait of a society pervaded by dishonesty of virtually every kind. Trollope's talent for short, compelling melodramas comes through in both *Cousin Henry* (1879) and the passionate *An Eye for an Eye* (1878–9). He made a minor specialty of bittersweet romances, of which *Ayala's Angel* (1881) stands out. Some readers prefer the "darker" Trollope, whose interest in PSYCHOLOGY shows in his study of the monomania of an obsessive husband in *He Knew He Was Right* (1869). (Trollope's father suffered from incapacitating mental illness, and Trollope wrote well and sensitively about characters suffering depressions or what Victorians called "mania.") His description of lived moral ambiguities in *Orley Farm* (1862) and of legal and ethical quandaries in *Mr. Scarborough's Family* (1883) deserve attention. Of this abundance of narrative, only a few novels disappoint the avid reader. Even the most wretched among them, such as Trollope's historical novel *La Vendée* (1850), or his futuristic dystopia, *The Fixed Period* (1881–1882), retain interest for specialists looking for representations of revolutionary FRANCE or euthanasia, respectively. Though Trollope's novels are often situated in the middle-to-upper-class social worlds of the landed gentry and the clerical and political establishment, he was an acute observer of new figures moving through the contemporary social scene—we can catch glimpses of American arrivistes (one who is new to a place or endeavor) and vocal feminists and some of the character types more familiar to readers of HENRY JAMES (1843–1916).

Well-known for his depictions of ministers and politicians in the Barset and Palliser novels, Trollope deserves praise for his handling of female characters, whose desires he depicted with more subtlety than any of his male contemporaries. Many of Trollope's novels feature plots of love choice, with the complications introduced by illegitimacy, jilting, bigamy, and barriers of SOCIAL CLASS, nationality, or religion.

His novels, taken as a whole, make encyclopedic reference to Victorian issues: ADVERTISING, disinheritance, EVANGELICALISM, faith and doubt, forgery, fraud, GAMBLING, High and Low Church controversies, JOURNALISM, lost wills, INSANITY, murder, perjury, politics, private detection, PROSTITUTION, suicide, theft, traveling salesmen, and the "woman question." One of the central figures of the Palliser novels sustains a career-long interest in decimalization. Even the Civil Service exams make an appearance, to be lampooned, in the partially autobiographical novel *The Three Clerks* (1857). As many critics have noted, Trollope's enthusiasm for foxhunting results in numerous set pieces describing the experience of HUNTING.

In virtually every case, Trollope's investigation of social problems or contemporary practices is anchored in a small set of characters with whom his narrator exhorts the reader to sympathize. Balancing these characters are Trollope's villains: dissolute aristocrats, men and women on the make, and oily men of indeterminate Mediterranean ancestry. This last detail has been interpreted as anti-Semitism on

Trollope's part. (Yet he treats no character with more affection than his Madame Max, a main character in the Palliser novels and one who is clearly Jewish.) For every unsavory Jew in Trollope's novels, there are quantities of debauched or dissipated Englishmen, invariably aristocrats. One of them, Sir Syph, bears the name of his infectious DISEASE, and conveys the strength of Trollope's animus to the entitled. Trollope grew up in genteel poverty and never forgot his humiliations as a day-boy at Harrow in 1822. Although he has been taken to task by later critics for his focus on the comfortably well-off classes, he did occasionally depict the poor, including the starving Irish, whose suffering he witnessed during his years in Ireland.

While Trollope was involved in politics through magazine work and even ran for office in 1868 as a liberal candidate (he lost), his success as a man of letters did not extend to the political sphere. This was not for want of trying. During the Irish FAMINE, he wrote an ambitious series of letters to the *Examiner* expressing his views about public policy and administration of poor relief in Ireland. They made no splash, to Trollope's evident regret. A few years later the failure of his Carlylean tract about English society (*The New Zealander*, written in 1855, but not published until 1972) coincided with the success of *The Warden*, a humorous novel of ecclesiastical struggles that includes satires of letters to the editor. Trollope had found his form. With *Barchester Towers*, he embarked upon the Chronicles of Barset that would make his name.

FURTHER READING

ApRoberts, Ruth. *Trollope: Artist and Moralist.* London: Chatto and Windus, 1971.

Glendinning, Victoria. *Anthony Trollope.* London: Hutchinson, 1992.

Hall, N. John. *Trollope: A Biography.* New York: Oxford University Press, 1991.

Herbert, Christopher. *Trollope and Comic Pleasure.* Chicago: University of Chicago Press, 1987.

Kendrick, Walter M. *The Novel-Machine: The Theory and Fiction of Anthony Trollope.* Baltimore: Johns Hopkins University Press, 1980.

Kincaid, James R. *The Novels of Anthony Trollope.* Oxford, England: Clarendon Press, 1977.

Trollope, Anthony. *An Autobiography.* 1883. New York: Oxford University Press, 1950.

SUZANNE KEEN

TROLLOPE, FRANCES

Born: March 10, 1779; Heckfield, England
Died: October 6, 1863; Florence, Italy

Frances Milton Trollope is perhaps best known as the mother of ANTHONY TROLLOPE (1815–1882), but she was a popular and groundbreaking author in her own right, publishing 34 novels and six travel narratives between 1832 and 1856. She first came to the public's attention with *Domestic Manners of the Americans* in 1832. By including a polemical conservative preface condemning American-style democracy, Trollope and her publishers positioned the volume to capitalize upon the furor generated by the debates over the first Reform bill. This strategy worked; the volume was an immediate and overnight success. Throughout her prolific career, Trollope continued to shock and scold her audiences, producing sharp, entertaining, and moving critiques of entrenched social problems before other authors dared touch them.

Domestic Manners arose from its author's combination of opportunism, literary skill, sharply critical vision, and financial exigency. *Domestic Manners* was the result of a trip to the United States by which Trollope had aimed to recuperate the family finances by starting a business in Cincinnati, Ohio (her barrister husband, Thomas Anthony Trollope, proved unable to support the family). She succeeded, but not in the way she had anticipated; the business she started failed. Trollope continued to write almost continually for the rest of her life, serving as the primary financial support for her family through the 1850s.

Trollope turned increasingly to novels after 1838, after one travel narrative failed to recoup the costs of the journey it described. This partially financial decision allowed her to give freer rein to her talent for satire. In the late 1830s and 1840s, Trollope primarily wrote novels of social commentary, satirizing problems in contemporary Britain: the hypocrisy of Evangelical clergy (*The Vicar of Wrexhill* [1837]); the conditions of factory children (*The Life and Adventures of Michael Armstrong* [1839–1840]); the cruelties of the New Poor Law (*Jessie Phillips* [1842–1843]); and London literary life (*Charles Chesterfield* [1841]). She rivaled CHARLES DICKENS (1812–1870) in popularity, and she learned from his technique of using serial publication to increase the financial return of novel writing.

Trollope's prolific output during the 1830s and 1840s is especially impressive because she wrote these novels and travel narratives while caring for her husband and her children during often fatal illnesses. (Three of Trollope's five children died of tuberculosis as adults). Her work ethic is legendary, in part because it inspired that of her son, Anthony: she would get up between four and five o'clock in the morning in order to write before breakfast. She continued this habit throughout her writing career, amidst travel, trouble, and change.

Contemporary critics condemned some of Trollope's topic choices as vulgar. Preoccupied by the financial pressures on her, modern critics have overlooked the daring with which she chose these topics, and the censure she received for that daring. She stretched the range of topics acceptable in British fiction as surely as Dickens or ELIZABETH GASKELL—often in advance of either—while drawing particular attention to the struggles and perspectives of women of all social classes and ages.

See also NOVEL.

FURTHER READING

Heineman, Helen. *Mrs. Trollope: The Triumphant Feminine in the Nineteenth Century.* Athens: Ohio University Press, 1979.
Heineman, Helen. *Frances Trollope.* Boston: Twayne, 1984.
Trollope, Frances Eleanor. *Frances Trollope: Her Life and Literary Work from George III to Victorian.* London: Bentley, 1895.

DARA ROSSMAN REGAIGNON

TUBERCULOSIS

Tuberculosis is an infectious, communicable disease that was endemic in Victorian Britain, the English-speaking world, and continental Europe. Its symptoms included fever, night sweats, weight loss, and the spitting of blood, and the disease could take various forms. The chief and most dangerous of these was respiratory or pulmonary tuberculosis, otherwise known as pthisis or consumption, which was contracted when bacilli from an existing sufferer gained entry into the lungs via the inhalation of droplets produced by coughing, sneezing, or spitting. Over a period of, typically, two to five years the lungs were gradually destroyed; this form of tuberculosis commonly affected young adults in the age range of 15 to 34. One variant was scrofula, featuring the appearance of abscesses in the lymph nodes of the neck; and another, bovine tuberculosis, to which infants and young children were particularly susceptible, was caused by the ingestion of tainted cows' milk, which ravaged the intestinal tract.

People at all social levels were vulnerable to infection and sufferers with substantial means might overcome or at least arrest attacks with rest and good diets in salubrious (favorable to promoting health)

settings, such as Torquay, the Isle of Wight, Switzerland, Cannes, and Nice; or, in the case of the UNITED STATES, the Adirondacks (well removed from New York City) and, later, Colorado and New Mexico. Even so, tuberculosis claimed some notable victims including Fredric Chopin, John Keats, Niccolò Paganini, Emily and Anne Brontë, and Henry David Thoreau. Some indeed have concluded that tuberculosis may have nourished literary and artistic genius by heightening emotion, sharpening perception, and quickening the creative impulse.

THE INFECTED MASSES

Be that as it may, the disease affected primarily the masses and occasioned millions of deaths, particularly among the relatively impoverished living in overcrowded urban conditions. In such circles, consumption affecting the chief breadwinner was something to be dreaded and if possible concealed, for dire privations were likely to follow from his inability to work during the period of his "decline." True, the disease was not invariably mortal, for in any individual case much depended on the balance between the seriousness of the infection, the sufferer's powers of resistance, and the general state of his or her health. Yet, the Annual Reports of the Registrar General reveal that tuberculosis accounted for some four million deaths in England and Wales across the Victorian period and, more specifically, for an annual rate of 350 deaths per 100,000 population in the 1850s. In the highly industrialized county of Lancashire this figure was noticeably higher, running at over 400, a level that was matched in the cities of the eastern seaboard of the United States. Most vulnerable of all were indigenous populations whose traditional lifestyles were disturbed and who had little in the way of inbred immunity. In 1880, 2,000 Sioux were made prisoners of war by the United States Army and in their barrack-style accommodation soon succumbed to tuberculosis. Among this group in 1903 the rate of mortality from the disease was ten times higher than the United States norm, even in the great cities. Still more destructive was the outbreak among Indians of the Qu'Appelle Valley reservation in western CANADA where, three decades after they had been obliged to abandon their free way of life on the prairie, the annual tuberculosis death rate reached 9,000 per 100,000 at risk, the highest figure ever recorded.

Despite such disasters, in the round mortality rates from tuberculosis started to decline during the second half of the nineteenth century, from various starting dates and at different speeds. Clear-cut reductions occurred, for example, in the United States from about 1870 and in New Zealand from 1880, while a range of European countries followed suit in the 1890s or in the first decade of the new century. Within the British Isles, progress was delayed for some decades in Ireland, especially in overcrowded Dublin and Belfast: but in Scotland from 1870 and elsewhere in mainland Britain from as early as the mid-century, there were clear signs of amelioration. In England and Wales, the mortality associated with tuberculosis fell between the 1850s and 1901 to 1910 by no less than 46% for males and 60% for females.

MEDICAL HELP?

Accounting for this improvement is notoriously difficult, in the English or indeed any other case. There is a consensus of opinion that the role of medical intervention can be discounted until well into the twentieth century. True, the identification of the tubercle bacillus by Robert Koch in 1882 was a major scientific landmark and one that helped to erode, gradually, the belief that tuberculosis simply ran in families, but no effective cure followed from his finding. Likewise, the penetrating power of X rays, discovered in 1895 by Wilhelm Conrad Roentgen, made possible the earlier detection of tuberculous lesions, but the technique was little used before the 1930s and 1940s. Nor were sanatoria, places of rest and recuperation, very effective in influencing tuberculosis mortality as a whole. These institutions had been pioneered in Germany and Switzerland from the 1860s and they spread quite rapidly in the English-speaking world toward the close of the nineteenth century. The United States acquired 34 by 1900 and Britain about 80, in addition to others attached to NEW POOR LAW infirmaries, by 1910. But the aggregate number of places remained everywhere small in relation to the size of the problem and their most helpful role, perhaps, was to segregate infectives from the wider community. In regard to preventive measures, some faltering progress was made in the setting and monitoring of quality standards for milk from the 1890s, probably with some beneficial effects on infant mortality rates. However, Britain and especially IRELAND were slower to take truly drastic action, entailing the systematic testing of cattle, slaughter with compensation, and accredited herd schemes, than were most American states, and Canada. Not until the 1940s and 1950s was tuberculosis finally overcome in the developed world—or so it seemed, 30 years ago, for there are now some disturbing signs of its resurgence—by the delayed adoption of BCG vaccination (bacille Calmette-Guerin, named after its French inventors) and the widespread use of streptomycin, devised at Rutgers University, and its successor drugs.

In the light of the tardiness of these developments in the medical sphere, and the fact that a decline in tuberculosis mortality rates was under way decades before their implementation, it is sometimes supposed that the disease, being a living organism, may have undergone a mutation, moving into a less virulent phase. Evidence of this is scant, but the possibility is there. More commonly, historians have pointed to a wide range of "social" factors that are likely to have had favorable effects in raising general standards of health and thus, resistance and recovery prospects. Thus, in the case of Britain, considerable significance has been attached to advances in nutrition as food prices fell and real wages rose, especially through 1873 to 1896; to improvements in average housing standards as a consequence of the clearance of some of the worst slums and, more important, controls on the quality of new additions to the housing stock; and a gradual decease in overcrowding. To a greater or lesser extent, parallels can be found in the experiences of other developed countries, so that a disease popularly thought of as a particularly nasty feature of Victorian times was also at least partially remedied by Victorian social progress.

See also DISEASES AND EPIDEMICS; MEDICAL PROFESSION; MEDICINE; VACCINATION.

FURTHER READING

Cronje, Gillian. "Tuberculosis and Mortality Decline in England and Wales, 1851–1910." In *Urban Disease and Mortality in Nineteenth Century England,* edited by Robert Woods and John Woodward, 79–101. New York: St. Martin's, 1984.
Dormandy, Thomas. *The White Death. A History of Tuberculosis.* London and Rio Grande, Ohio: Hambledon Press, 1999.
Dubos, René, and Jean Dubos. *The White Plague. Tuberculosis, Man and Society.* 1952. Reprint, with introduction by Barbara G. Rosenkrantz, New Brunswick: Rutgers University Press, 1987.
Smith, F. B. *The Retreat of Tuberculosis, 1850–1950.* London, New York, and Sydney: Croom Helm, 1988.

W. ALAN ARMSTRONG

TUPPER, MARTIN

Born: July 17, 1810; London, England
Died: November 29, 1889; London, England

Martin Farquhar Tupper was the best-selling poet of the early Victorian period. Through the many editions of his *Proverbial Philosophy*—a series of moral commentaries in blank verse first published in 1838—his name remained a household word for fifty years. His fall from favor was equally sensational, and he was to become the most parodied and ridiculed of British authors. His name now stands as a synonym for literary commonplace.

The son of an affluent London physician, Tupper left Oxford University in 1832 intending to train as a barrister, but soon turned to POETRY, publishing a volume of religious verse and two lengthy poems between 1832 and 1838. In the latter year, with a "Coronation Ode" addressed to QUEEN VICTORIA, he began his career as unofficial poet laureate during which he responded fulsomely to every patriotic occasion.

In 1828, inspired by his forthcoming marriage, Tupper had devised a highly original format of free, unrhymed, incantatory verses ("Rythmics," as he called them) in the manner of Solomon's Proverbs. In 1837 he extended his commentaries to cover a whole range of moral issues, resulting in the first series of *Proverbial Philosophy: A Book of Thoughts and Arguments, Originally Treated* (1838), followed by a second series in 1842.

Tupper's verses hit the prevailing mood. Animated by the fervent EVANGELICALISM that set the tone of the early Victorian period, they reinforced traditional Christian values in an age of rapid social and economic change. His topics had a universal appeal ("Sorrow," "Joy," "Love," "Matrimony," etc.). Pious and benign, couched in dignified language and fired with sincerity, his homilies brought comfort and inspiration to the hearts and minds of millions, high and low alike. Admirers included the queen and PRINCE ALBERT; the poets Robert Southey and WILLIAM WORDSWORTH; the future prime minister WILLIAM GLADSTONE, and GENERAL GORDON of Khartoum.

By 1860 the combined edition of the first two volumes had reached 38 editions; by 1866 more than 200,000 copies had been sold in Britain and around 1,000,000 in the UNITED STATES, where Tupper made successful tours in 1851 and 1876. Two further series of *Proverbial Philosophy* appeared in the late 1860s, but in the more sophisticated and increasingly agnostic High Victorian period, his fervent moral tone was already outdated. Ironically, given the derision which he earned amongst the intelligentsia, his free verse was to have a lasting influence on subsequent practitioners such as WALT WHITMAN and T. S. Eliot.

Whatever the adverse criticisms, Tupper was a man of learning and culture—an inventor, antiquarian, novelist, and translator as well as a poet, and a philanthropist whose many causes included the abolition of slavery and the promotion of ANGLO-AMERICAN RELATIONS. A regular attendant at court, Tupper played an active part in London society and retained the friendship and respect of many eminent people. He was elected fellow of the Royal Society in 1845 for his contributions to literature and archaeology, of which he was a keen amateur, and was granted a Civil List pension in 1871. Tupper died in 1889.

See also POETRY.

FURTHER READING

Hudson, Derek. *Martin Farquhar Tupper: His Rise and Fall.* London: Constable, 1949.

Scott, Patrick. "Martin F. Tupper." In *Victorian Poets before 1850,* 288-298. Volume 32 of *Dictionary of Literary Biography.* Detroit: Gale Group, 1984.

MARY COWLING

TURNER, J. M. W.

Born: April 23, 1775; Covent Garden, London
Died: December 19, 1851; Chelsea, London

Joseph Mallord William Turner is acknowledged as the greatest landscape painter of the Victorian period, perhaps of any period. Turner excelled in drawings, book illustrations, engravings, watercolors, and oil paintings. His subjects embraced landscapes and seascapes, but also ARCHITECTURE, genre scenes, and historical, religious, and mythological subjects. Although not immune from criticism, he is one of the few painters who have sustained a high reputation throughout his life and to the present time.

The son of a barber/wig maker and a severely disturbed mother, Turner spent his youth near Covent Garden and with relatives in Brentford. He became committed to art at an early age, selling drawings in his father's shop. Although self-educated, he became knowledgeable about history, art, poetry, and science. A short stocky man, often described as resembling a seaman, he earned lasting friendships, but lived a secretive life. He probably bore two daughters with the widow Sarah Danby; perhaps had relations with Hannah Danby, Sarah's niece and sometime housekeeper and gallery keeper; and, in his later years, lived with another widow, Sophia Booth. Many of his pornographic drawings were destroyed by Ruskin, an executor of his estate.

Turner began his career as a typographical artist, interested more in architecture than PAINTING. Under the tutelage of Dr. Thomas Monro he mastered watercolor techniques and produced many much-admired watercolors. After 1800 he used sketches and watercolors mainly to prepare for his work in oils and engravings. His early nineteenth-century work was influenced by the picturesque and sublime traditions, the teachings of Sir Joshua Reynolds (1723–1792), and the paintings of Richard Wilson, Nicolas Poussin, and Claude Lorrain, influences resulting in classic and ideal landscapes as *Dido Building Carthage; or the Rise of the Carthaginian Empire* (1815). His seascapes, such as *Dort, or Dordrecht, the Dort Packet-Boat from Rotterdam Becalmed* (1818), more closely resembled the Dutch school, particularly Aelbert Cuyp and Willem van de Velde, the Younger. At the same time he turned to engravings, producing series of views of specific places in England and the Continent based on his annual tours. In his *Liber Studiorum* (1807–1819) he produced 71 plates demonstrating the significance and range of landscape as a genre. His work was known, outside of LONDON, largely through his engravings.

Throughout his career, Turner was concerned to make his works express meanings beyond a literal transcription. Desiring to raise landscape painting to the level of history painting, he used accompanying poetry, including his own "Fallacies of Hope," and formal similarities, visual metaphors, and allusive clues to lead the viewer to contemplate past historical events, human emotions, and contemporary society. Through such associations he sought to jog the imagination to contemplate and imagine a world beyond the scene depicted. In *The Fighting Temeraire, Tugged to Her Last Berth to Be Broken Up* (1838), for example, he used an accompanying poem by Thomas Campbell and a glowing sunset in the background to reflect the end of the day for sailing ships. He also emphasized the ugliness and blackness of the steam-boat that would replace the elegant sailboat, thus evoking the tragic end of an era and the transience of human endeavors.

Turner's earlier canvasses tended to depict serene and somber scenes, as *Sun Rising through Vapour; Fishermen Cleaning and Selling Fish* (1807); later they focused on dazzling and luminous displays of color, light, and atmosphere, as in *The Fall of the Clyde* (circa 1835). A dark and apocalyptic tenor and sense of doom crept into the paintings of his last decade, as *Shade and Darkness: The Evening of the Deluge* (1843). Although he always retained a core of representation, his paintings became increasingly abstract. He seemed to be moving from depicting the appearance of a landscape to capturing the experience of nature's more violent moments, as in his 1842 *Snow Storm—Steam-Boat off a Harbour's Mouth*, for which Turner claimed that he was lashed to the mast to observe the storm.

These abstractions worried and confused some critics. Phrases like "fantastical absurdity" and "kaleidoscopic confusion," and comparisons of his paintings to "lobster salad," "eggs and spinach," and "soap-suds and whitewash" appeared in the periodical reviews. William Hazlitt called them "paintings of nothing, and very like." The Rev. John Eagles' scathing review in BLACKWOOD'S MAGAZINE moved noted critic JOHN RUSKIN (1819–1900) to Turner's defense, and eventually culminated in the critic's five-volume *Modern Painters* (1843–1860). Not only, Ruskin declared, were Turner's paintings the most true to nature, but they also were unprecedented in imagination and use

Chichester Canal (circa 1828) by J. M. W. Turner.

of symbolic elements. Ruskin's unswerving support helped greatly to counter Turner's sagging reputation and to educate the public to appreciate the originality and the complexities and grandeur of conception of his paintings.

The Royal Academy also provided support. Turner's lifetime loyalty to the ROYAL ACADEMY OF ART began when he was admitted to the Royal Academy Schools in 1789. Becoming an associate in 1799, a full R.A. in 1802, the professor of perspective from 1807 to 1838, a scrupulous auditor of the academy accounts from 1824 to 1846, and deputy president from to 1845 to 1846, he also served in a number of other ways. Although not very articulate in his lectures and critiques of student work, he was appreciated for his practical advice and demonstrations of techniques. He sent paintings to the annual exhibition almost every year, as well as exhibiting in his own gallery.

Throughout his career Turner had a number of loyal collectors and patrons including Sir John Leicester, Walter Fawkes, and the Earl of Egremont. Few British painters followed his style, but his later paintings, especially *Rain, Steam, and Speed—The Great Western Railway* (exhibited 1844) captured the attention of the French impressionists. In his will Turner attempted to leave the paintings in his possession to the nation, as well as money to house them. He also wished to provide a home for indigent male artists, and scholarships, lectureships, and prizes for the Royal Academy. His relatives, however, contested his will, and not until 1980 was his collection provided with its own gallery, the Clore Gallery, established by the Tate Gallery in London. The greatest number of his paintings and sketches are there, including 300 oils and 30,000 sketches and watercolors, but about 100 major works are in the United States. The Turner Prize for the best contemporary artist was established in Britain in 1984.

In Turner's own time, John Constable declared that he was "uncouth but has a wonderful range of mind." Ruskin placed him as "one with Byron and Goethe." While appreciating Turner's observant depictions of nature and his sublime evocations of light and atmosphere, modern scholars are also finding, through studying his use of history, classical themes, and poetry, new depth and complexity in Turner's works.

See also PAINTING; PAINTING, GENRES OF.

FURTHER READING

Butlin, Martin, and Evelyn Joll. *The Paintings of J. M. W. Turner.* 2 vols. New Haven and London: Yale University Press, 1984.

Finley, Gerald. *Angel in the Sun: Turner's Vision of History.* Montreal: McGill-Queen's University Press, 1999.
Gage, John. *Color in Turner; Poetry and Truth.* New York: Praeger, 1969.
Herrmann, Luke. *Turner Prints: The Engraved Work of J. M. W. Turner.* New York: New York University Press, 1990.
Joll, Evelyn, Martin Butlin, and Luke Herrmann. *The Oxford Companion to J. M. W. Turner.* Oxford: Oxford University Press, 2001.
Nicholson, Kathleen. *Turner's Classical Landscapes: Myth and Meaning.* Princeton, N.J.: Princeton University Press, 1990.
Shanes, Eric. *Turner's Human Landscape.* London: Heinemann, 1990.

HELENE E. ROBERTS

TWAIN, MARK

Born: November 30, 1835; Florida, Missouri
Died: April 21, 1910; Redding, Connecticut

Novelist and humorist Mark Twain (a pseudonym of Samuel Langhorne Clemens) is best known for his tales of life during the mid-1800s along the Mississippi River. The two young inhabitants of Twain's semi-fictional landscape, Tom Sawyer and Huckleberry Finn, have become twin icons of American everyday life during the nineteenth century for the way they embodied the aspirations and complexities of the nation during a period of unbridled expansion and horrific sectional conflict. While the characters and situations depicted in Twain's novels remain a source of contention—*The Adventures of Huckleberry Finn* (1884) was often pilloried after its 1885 publication for its use of crude language and situations, and it has been scorned in recent years for its controversial portrayal of interracial relations—Twain is almost universally regarded as one of the most astute commentators on the American character that the nation has ever produced.

More than a droll chronicler of boyhood idylls along the Mississippi, Twain excelled as a sometimes cantankerous social commentator who, like other Victorian-era essayists in the United States and Britain, took a broadly panoramic view of a culture that he lambasted for its pretentiousness and imperiousness. At a time when Americans were largely isolationist and self-absorbed, Twain set his sights on a global horizon, always maintaining a dim view of the excesses of an American Victorian-era culture that yielded a Gilded Age for the favored few while ignoring the crying needs of the many. In his later years he became active in the Anti-Imperialist League, an organization that frowned on American acquisition of overseas colonies after the Spanish-American War (1898). He lashed out against anti-Semitism and colonialism in FRANCE and also lent his support to groups that advocated an end to czarist rule in Russia. Essentially a humorist to the end, Twain ruthlessly mocked and satirized both the priggish and powerful with all the determination of more serious-minded Victorian-era critics such as JOHN RUSKIN and MATTHEW ARNOLD, and with a wryness and acerbity that had not been seen in English letters since the days of Jonathan Swift.

Twain's popularity extended beyond the borders of the UNITED STATES. Twain arguably did more than any other American writer to interpret the foibles of American life to the British, much as CHARLES DICKENS (1812–1870) had done in reverse a generation earlier. Even though he poked fun at British institutions in such novels as *A Connecticut Yankee in King Arthur's Court* (1889), Twain was widely read and admired in England. Commenting on the enthusiastic response of British readers to Twain, WILLIAM DEAN HOWELLS, his earliest biographer, wrote: "In England rank, fashion, and culture rejoiced in him. Lord mayors, lord chief justices, and magnates of many kinds were his hosts; he was desired in country houses, and his bold genius captivated the favor of periodicals which spurned the rest of our nation." Indeed, Twain was lionized in Britain: he was received by King Edward VII in 1907 and awarded an honorary degree at Oxford University.

Samuel Clemens was born in Florida, Missouri, and spent a rather idyllic childhood in the town of Hannibal, a thriving Mississippi River town that formed the backdrop for some of his later works. After working as a printer's apprentice and writing humorous sketches under a variety of names, he settled on the pseudonym "Mark Twain," a term used by local riverboat crews to indicate a depth of two fathoms. Twain himself worked as a steamboat pilot on the Mississippi until the CIVIL WAR (1861–1865) broke out. He deserted the Confederate Army after two weeks and made his way to Virginia City, Nevada, where his anti-slave brother had been appointed secretary to the territorial governor by President Abraham Lincoln. He wrote briefly for a local newspaper, where his contentious style of humor quickly earned him the enmity of rival journalists. After deeming it advisable to leave Nevada for safer ground, he made his way to a California mining camp via San Francisco where he wrote "The Celebrated Jumping Frog of Calaveras County," which won him fame back East when it was published in the New York *Saturday Press* in 1865. After traveling to the Sandwich Islands (Hawaii) as a newspaper correspondent, he returned East and quickly established himself as a lecturer and humorist. In 1867 he chronicled a celebrated voyage to the Holy Land in newspaper dispatches that were collected in his 1869 book *The Innocents Abroad*, which was a classic portrait of a group of naive, parvenu American tourists trying to make sense of the world of antiquity.

After his 1870 marriage to Olivia Langdon and a brief, unhappy stint as a newspaper editor in Buffalo, New York, Twain took up residence in Hartford, Connecticut, in a gaudy, gingerbread-style house that stands as a caricature of overwrought Victorian domestic ARCHITECTURE. Over the next two decades, he penned some of his most celebrated novels, including *The Adventures of Tom Sawyer* (1876), *The Prince and the Pauper* (1882), *Life on the Mississippi* (1883), *The Adventures of Huckleberry Finn* (1885), *A Connecticut Yankee in King Arthur's Court* (1889), and *Pudd'nhead Wilson* (1894). In these and other works, Twain helped establish an essentially American diction and style for a literature that was still often beholden to British models. If the Victorian era can be interpreted as a "coming of age" for American letters, Twain was one of its most prolific and robust contributors.

See also COMIC LITERATURE; NOVEL.

FURTHER READING

Emerson, Everett. *Mark Twain: A Literary Life.* Philadelphia: University of Pennsylvania Press, 2000.

Howells, William Dean. *My Mark Twain: Reminiscences and Criticisms.* New York: Harper and Brothers, 1910.

Twain, Mark. *Mark Twain's Sketches, New and Old.* New York: Oxford University Press, 1996.

SELECTED WEB SITE

Zwick, Jim, ed. *Mark Twain.* 2003.
http://www.boondocksnet.com/twainwww/index.html

EDWARD MORAN

TYLOR, EDWARD BURNETT

Born: October 2, 1832; London, England
Died: January 2, 1917; Wellington, England

Sir Edward Burnett Tylor was the most prominent among a group of scholars who, inspired by the achievements of historical linguists, geologists, archaeologists, and evolutionary biologists, defined the science of anthropology in the late nineteenth century. His book *Primitive Culture* (first edition, 1871) remains a classic introduction to the field as well as a lucid example of a theory of social evolution that relied heavily on the comparative method of analysis to explain the growth of human culture as a unilinear development from small-scale, relatively socially unstratified cultures to highly specialized, complex modern societies. In other writings he made major contributions to this new social science, especially in refining methods of collecting and analyzing data and in studies of the development of language and religion.

Tylor was raised as a member of the Society of Friends (the Quakers) and as a religious dissenter he could not enter an English university. He was educated privately in a Friends school where antidogmatic beliefs left him free to explore and adopt Enlightenment ideals and to learn the methods and conclusions of sciences. Tylor grew up among Benthamites (followers of JEREMY BENTHAM's utilitarian philosophy) philosophical radicals such as HERBERT SPENCER (1820–1903), Sir Henry Maine (1822–1888), James Clerk-Maxwell (1831–1879), George Grote (1794–1871), and JOHN STUART MILL (1806–1873), and he was deeply influenced by their beliefs in reason and progress and by their materialist methods of analysis.

After working in his father's brass foundry for seven years, Tylor developed tuberculosis and, in 1855, traveled to the UNITED STATES for his health. A year later he met Henry Christy, a fellow Quaker with an inter-

THE GRANGER COLLECTION

Edward Burnett Tylor is considered one of the fathers of modern anthropology.

est in ethnology, who convinced him to study the indigenous populations of Mexico. This visit and subsequent study changed the direction of Tylor's life and led to his first book, *Anahuac; Or Mexico and the Mexicans, Ancient and Modern* (1861). Tylor continued his research and writing and in 1865 published *Researches into the Early History of Mankind*, which used his highly original study of the development of gesture language by deaf mutes to shed light on the human capacity for language; its origins; the relation of language to thought, symbol and myth; and its function as an instrument of cultural development. This technique, of using research on a contemporary group to re-create the pre- and early history of humanity, is called the comparative method, and it became the formative orthodoxy of Tylor's studies and, indeed, of evolutionary anthropologists like Lewis Henry Morgan (1818–1881), Sir John Lubbock (1834–1913), and James G. Frazer (1854–1941).

The book made Tylor's reputation and was followed by *Primitive Culture*, in which Tylor defined anthropology as a more modest field than the kind of universal history that Herbert Spencer and others were writing. Anthropology, he wrote, studies not all history but a branch called "culture, the history not of tribes or nations, but of the conditions of knowledge, religion, art, custom and the like among them." Tylor argued that all human races had one origin (monogenesis) and that the history of different cultures would show substantially the same unilinear pattern of development, from, in his view, simple to complex, allowing for differences of climate and material surroundings. Archaeological studies of material culture (such as weapons, utensils, structures, and jewelry), particularly those done by Augustus Pitt-Rivers (1827–1900), suggested this pattern of development. In Tylor's study of nonmaterial culture (beliefs and practices), he used the comparative method to fill in the greater gaps of evidence in support of this hypothesis.

Aside from defining the field of anthropology, Tylor's research in many cultures ended the special attention given to the Aryan race and to Max Müller's (1823–1900) degenerationist thesis. But Tylor's most significant contribution in the book was his discussion of religion. Tylor suggests that all religion and philosophy began in animism, a belief in spiritual beings, ghosts and gods, and he found in contemporary tribes various stages of animism. Later he asserts that elements of animism became parts of ancient and even modern religions. He also introduced the concept of "survivals," the idea that ancient practices and rituals may survive as forms of play and games in later stages of social development. This concept figured powerfully in important works, such as James G. Frazer's landmark *The Golden Bough* (first edition, 1891) and Thorstein Veblen's work *The Theory of the Leisure Class* (1899).

Tylor's reputation and fame were secured by the critical reception of *Primitive Culture*. He became a fellow of the Royal Society the year it was published. By this time he had made most of his intellectual contributions to the science. He did write the entry on anthropology for the ninth edition of the *Encyclopaedia Britannica* (1878) and a handbook, *Anthropology* (1881), which became a widely used general introduction to the field. In 1883 he was appointed the keeper of the Pitt-Rivers Museum at Oxford, and he spent the rest of his professional career at the university, first as a reader, in 1884, and then as the first professor of anthropology in 1886. There remained, however, one further contribution, an article, "On a Method of Investigating the Development of Institutions, Applied to Laws of Marriage and Descent" (1889), often cited as the most important anthropological paper of the century, in which Tylor placed the comparative method on a statistical basis, using tabulation and classification to study the development of social institutions.

Tylor's last years were spent serving in professional organizations and receiving honors. In 1885 he became the first president of the anthropological section of the British Association, and he was twice president of the Anthropological Institute. He was awarded a Doctorate of Civil Laws degree from Oxford in 1875 and an honorary fellowship from Balliol College, Oxford, in 1903. He retired from the university in 1909, was knighted in 1912, and spent his remaining years in Wellington, Somerset, where he died.

While a reaction against the assumptions of evolutionary anthropology set in at the beginning of the twentieth century, especially concerning racial and cultural superiority and inferiority, Tylor's work has remained influential. Contemporary anthropologists such as Leslie White (1900–1975) and Marvin Harris (1927–2001) argued that there remains much of value in Tylor's writing and, more important, in the sophisticated methods he developed to pursue ethnological research.

See also AGNOSTICISM, ATHEISM, AND FREE THOUGHT; ANTHROPOLOGY AND ETHNOLOGY; EVOLUTION; SOCIAL DARWINISM.

FURTHER READING

Brew, J. C. *One Hundred Years of Anthropology.* Cambridge, Mass.: Harvard University Press, 1965.

Harris, Marvin. *The Rise of Anthropological Theory.* New York: Thomas Y. Crowell, 1968.
Lowie, Robert H. *The History of Ethnological Theory.* New York: Holt, Rinehart and Winston, 1937.
Marrett, Robert R. *Tylor.* New York: John Wiley and Sons, 1936.

MICHAEL S. HELFAND

TYPEWRITER

The typewriter was part of a technological revolution in Victorian business and office management in the last decades of the nineteenth century that included the introduction of the TELEGRAPH, the TELEPHONE, electric lights, carbon paper, duplicating machines, calculating machines, and dictating machines. The typewriter initially had more impact than these other technologies on the organization of commercial and government offices. The mechanism of the

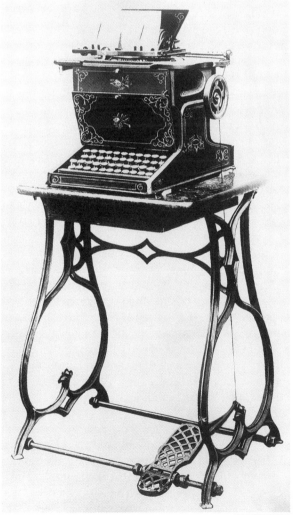

REMINGTON RAND

This first commercially produced typewriter, the Remington Rand, was sold in 1874 and revolutionized office work.

typewriter was comparatively simple and improvements in design progressed quickly. In addition the typewriter, unlike the telephone, which was commercially available about the same time, did not depend on established widespread adoption for its utility.

A Writing Machine

Patent records in the UNITED STATES, Britain, and Europe indicate that the idea of developing a "writing machine" dates back at least as far as the eighteenth century, but working prototypes of the typewriter did not appear until the 1830s and 1840s. Many of these early machines, some of which embossed letters rather than printing them, were developed as aids to the blind. Two such machines won prize medals at the GREAT EXHIBITION of 1851 and were subsequently used by institutes for the blind. By the middle of the nineteenth century, inventors were developing writing machines of varying design, some akin to a telegraph and others to a piano, but it was an American, Christopher Latham Sholes (1819–1890), who produced the version of the writing machine that was adopted as the typewriter.

Sholes's typewriter (a term he coined) had most of the features of the machines that were in use in offices around the world until the mid-twentieth century, when electric typewriters supplanted them. The type-bars in Sholes's machine were arranged in a semicircle and attached to keys that, when depressed, would swing the type bar against a platen to produce letters. Sholes also introduced the qwerty keyboard (named after the first six letters on the top row of keys), which was developed to reduce the jamming of type bars during the operation of the machine. Sholes's typewriter was first manufactured in 1873 by Remington, the major American producer of guns, farm equipment, and sewing machines, and appeared on the market in 1874. The original model typed only upper case letters; the shift key was introduced in 1878. Other models of typewriter were produced by manufacturers in the United States and Europe in the last two decades of the nineteenth century, but the Sholes model continued to dominate the market for many years.

The original market for the typewriter was conceived to be authors, lawyers, and clergymen, but the usefulness of typewriters in commercial and government offices quickly became apparent. The appearance of the typewriter was timely, coinciding with a period of rapid growth in trade and commerce and with the consequent expansion of the service sector of the economy, factors that undoubtedly contributed to the typewriter's immediate success as a business machine. Speed, efficiency, and legibility made the typewriter an attractive alternative to handwriting and copying, especially when an operator coupled typing skills with shorthand. Speed was further improved with the development of touch-typing in the 1880s. The two-finger, so-called hunt and peck system had been favored until speed-typing competitions made it clear that memorizing the keyboard and typing with all fingers were both feasible and practical expedients.

The Typewriter and the Employment of Women

The most dramatic effect of the typewriter in the late nineteenth century, besides its rapid adoption as a business machine, was the expansion of employment opportunities for women. Educated women in the middle and lower-middle classes who had to earn a living had few acceptable employment options available to them outside of teaching and NURSING. As a new and undersupplied occupation, typewriting offered an attractive alternative. Because it was new, typewriting was also not a gender specific occupation, which lowered social resistance to women entering this area of employment and allowed them to dominate it very quickly. (The telegraph and telephone offered similar opportunities for women). Despite the fact that male office clerks learned to type and that men dominated early speed-typing competitions, by the 1880s typewriting was perceived to be uniquely suited to women and was accordingly defined and described in terms of feminine characteristics and accomplishments. Parallels between touch-typing and piano playing—a standard part of a middle-class girl's education—were commonplace. Touch-typing was also assumed to be especially suited to women's smaller and supposedly more nimble fingers. The typewriter soon became literally synonymous with the young woman operating it: the term was used to designate both the machine and the operator (leading to the MUSIC HALL swell's joke about the difficulty of writing with his typewriter on his knee).

The association of women with typewriters probably had more to do with early production and marketing practices than with natural affinities. The first Remington model does in retrospect seem to have been designed with a Victorian lady in mind: it was decorated with painted flowers and mounted on the stand that the Remington factory was already producing in quantity—a sewing machine stand. Early marketing of typewriters often involved demonstrations of the machines, and the operators for these demonstrations were generally young women. Demographics and economics also played roles in women's predominance as typists. As the nineteenth century progressed, there were a growing number of single middle-class women who were unlikely or unwilling to marry—the so-called "odd women"—and who needed to earn their own livelihoods. The expanding service sector was a natural place to provide opportunities for these women, especially since clerical work was gradually opening up to women. The new phenomenon of the woman typist (or typewriter) had the advantage not only of being fast and efficient but also of being economical; she was cheaper to employ than her male counterpart, often earning less than half the salary paid to men for the same work. As a result of all these factors, the number of women employed as office clerks in Britain increased ninefold between 1881 and 1901, from 6,420 to 57,736. While it is impossible to know how many of these office clerks were typists because census records do not break these numbers down into specific types of work, advertisements and newspaper and periodical accounts of WOMEN'S WORK from the 1880s and 1890s suggest that a large percentage of these women were typists.

The typewriter was also at the center of changes in education and job training in the 1880s and 1890s. A number of enterprising women opened private offices that offered copying services; many of these offices also offered training in typing skills. The copying business provided work experience for the trainees. The changing face of the office and of the skills needed to work there led to the establishment of more formalized programs for commercial educa-

tion that included typewriting, shorthand, and bookkeeping. Commercial and business colleges were initially operated privately and their programs were unregulated and varied in quality. In the 1890s public school boards were eligible for government grants to establish commercial training programs that were typically offered as continuing education courses in the evening.

New business technologies and business education found their way into the fiction of the late Victorian period, the best know examples being GEORGE GISSING's *The Odd Women* (1893), in which Mary Barfoot and Rhoda Nunn run a typing office-*cum*-business training school, and BRAM STOKER's *Dracula* (1897), in which Mina Harker types up the records of the vampire hunters in triplicate and John Seward uses a primitive dictating machine to keep patient records.

See also TELEGRAPH; TELEPHONE; WOMEN'S WORK.

FURTHER READING

Beeching, Wilfred A. *Century of the Typewriter.* London: Heinemann, 1974.
Briggs, Asa. *Victorian Things.* Chicago: University of Chicago Press, 1988.
Holcombe, Lee. *Victorian Ladies at Work: Middle-Class Working Women in England and Wales 1850–1914.* Hamden, Conn.: Archon, 1973.
Silverstone, Rosalie. "Office Work for Women: An Historical Overview." *Business History* 18, no. 1 (January 1976): 98–110.

SELECTED WEB SITE

Rehr, Darryl. "The Typewriter." *Popular Mechanics.* August 1996. http://www.popularmechanics.com/popmech/spec/9608SFACM.html

ARLENE YOUNG

UNDERGROUND, THE

When QUEEN VICTORIA ascended to the throne in 1837, the streets of LONDON were heavily congested. The boom in Britain's POPULATION during the eighteenth century, sustained in the nineteenth century by the process of INDUSTRIALIZATION, meant that the inhabitants of London doubled between 1811 and 1851 from 1.1 million to 2.33 million. The city was so clogged that it was estimated that the short journey from a RAILWAY mainline terminus at Paddington to London Bridge took longer than the journey from Brighton on England's south coast. By 1850 there were roughly 7,500 journeys a day through the City by horse-drawn OMNIBUSES, CABS, wagons and goods vans, and ADVERTISING carts (whose particular, and no doubt annoying, task was to slow down traffic so that commercial slogans could be easily read).

Initial project proposals for a form of underground TRANSPORTATION in London were quashed due to fears that the pressure from traffic above ground along the route of the proposed system would collapse into the tunnels below. Property owners were also concerned that the vibrations from underground trains would shake and shudder houses so viciously that they would crumble or collapse. The general public was in opposition as well, seemingly startled by the concept of an underground railway. Somewhat oddly the Corporation of London was also opposed, although for financial reasons and limitations of building space, even though the system would dramatically improve the speed and efficiency of feeding the most important financial district in the world. In addition, the outbreak of the expensive CRIMEAN WAR in 1853 drew precious resources away from investing in the Underground. This broad front of opposition meant that, between 1845 and 1847 alone, speculators lost an estimated £10 million on lawsuits and submissions to parliamentary commissions in their quest to profit from the proposed Underground. One such lobbyist,

124

Charles Pearson (1793–1862), prepared no fewer than 20 proposals to parliamentary commissions promoting the extension of mainline railway termini into the city.

The pressures of this relentless lobbying and the clarity of the need for more effective transport in the British capital meant that the first work on the Underground was eventually started in 1860. The line was constructed by the "cut and cover" method by which a trench was dug to the proposed track level and covered with a roof that lay level with the previously existing road. Streets were closed off and the thrum of traffic dulled, having been diverted to the adjacent narrow side streets. The workers labored day and night, polluting the local area with noise, dirt, and fumes. A number of houses close to the work were made unstable and had to be propped-up with ad hoc wooden supports. Other families were displaced by the compulsory purchase of their homes in order to make way for the route. The accumulative effects resulted in considerable ire among the local inhabitants.

Although only 4 miles (6.4 kilometers) long, in January 1863 the world's first underground line opened to great fanfare. The route linked the mainline terminus at Paddington in the central west and Farringdon Street in the central east. Using steam power, the first train journey along this line was undertaken by a select group of dignitaries, although Prime Minister HENRY JOHN TEMPLE (Lord Palmerston) turned down an invitation to attend on the grounds that, "at my age I intend to remain above ground for as long as possible." Unfortunately, Pearson, the greatest advocate of the Underground, was also not among the privileged few; he died only four months before it was completed. When opened to the general public the line immediately experienced the equivalent of a rush hour, except that this was extended from open to close, with six engines carrying a total of 30,000 passengers on 120 journeys. Commercial companies immediately took advantage and advertised their proximity to the Underground and with good reason; in its first week alone almost 250,000 people traveled this short journey.

In its early phase the Underground had its fair share of problems. Enclosed stations meant that waiting

Workers excavating the Great Northern and City Tube Railway in 1901.

passengers choked on a combination of noxious gases both from locomotives and gas LIGHTING. Guards and Railway POLICE were compelled to request authority to grow beards in an attempt to combat the fumes. Bizarrely, some claimed that this cocktail of carbonic acid and carbonic oxide gases cured chest complaints, a conception that was soon put to rest when a jury concluded in 1867 that a female passenger's life was immaturely lost through the inhalation of the Underground's air. Consequently, glazing was taken away above some stations and "blow-holes" were cut into the roofs of tunnels to allow steam and fumes to escape into the streets above (although this greatly alarmed passing horses).

The first actual "tube" was opened in 1890 by the Prince of Wales and linked the City to South London. This project had the historical distinction of being the world's first fully electrified underground railway, although the TECHNOLOGY for electric traction was imported from Germany, having been developed by Dr. Werner von Siemens (1816–1892). This line moved beyond the disruptive and costly "cut and cover" method and kept the majority of works below ground. This was enabled through the invention in 1818, by Sir Marc Brunel, of a boring device using a "shield" with miners inside it to tunnel through the earth. This was used to dig the first tunnel under the River Thames in 1843 (later engineered by his son ISAMBARD K. BRUNEL). James Henry Greathead refined the shield to make it safer, more efficient, and suitable for Underground trains. His device became the standard for all of the tube railways and is still known as the "Greathead Shield." Yet the less sophisticated "cut and cover" approach remained the basic ENGINEERING approach to the construction of the majority of the rest of the world's tube railways. Owing to the fact that most of the first tubes traveled underground, the well-furnished carriages were built without windows; this earned them the popular distinction of being called "padded cells." The tube platforms were so deep underground that they had to be serviced by hydraulic lifts and escalators with a network of subways connecting the platforms.

The Central London Railway was the advent of the truly modern underground "tube." Opened in July 1900, it was fully electrified, popular, and economically viable. It was conceived as a service linking the middle-class residential areas of west London to the City. The route traveled along Oxford Street, thus providing access to London's principal shopping and entertainment district. Londoners immediately embraced the Central London and it proved a great commercial success. With its flat fare of twopence for all journeys, it earned the nickname of the "Twopenny Tube" and carried almost 15 million passengers in its first five months of service. By the last years of Queen Victoria's reign, underground travel had lost its novelty having become a day-to-day commuting experience for the capital's inhabitants. In the years immediately after her death, subsequent Underground routes began to spread out from the more central areas of London, feeding and making possible an ever-expanding suburbia. In fact, the reign of Victoria's son, King Edward VII, saw a sensational expansion of the Underground; it would take another 50 years for another underground line to be constructed underneath central London.

By the early twenty-first century, the London Underground had 245 stations linked by a network of 254 miles (409 kilometers) of line. Today, this hidden underworld, constantly humming beneath the feet of millions of city dwellers, covers an area of 620 square miles (1,606 square kilometers) and carries 784 million passengers per annum. Many of the original lines and stations have been abandoned or reworked, leaving as many as 40 "ghost stations" lurking in the darkness of contemporary London's subterranean world. Yet it was in the Victorian era that the foundation for modern city travel was laid, a model that would be replicated in cities throughout much of the industrialized world.

See also LONDON; RAILWAYS; RAILWAY STATIONS; TRANSPORTATION; URBANIZATION.

FURTHER READING

Ackroyd, Peter. *London: The Biography.* London: Chatto and Windus, 2000.
Day, John R., and John Reed. *The Story of London's Underground.* 8th ed. Middlesex: Capital Transport, 2001.
Douglas, Hugh. *The Underground Story.* London: Robert Hale, 1963.
Gorbutt, Paul. *World Metro Systems.* 2d ed. Middlesex: Capital Transport, 1997.
Green, Oliver. *The London Underground: An Illustrated History.* Shepperton, Surrey: Ian Allen, 1987.
Menear, Laurence. *London's Underground Stations: A Social and Architectural Study.* London: Midas, 1983.

SELECTED WEB SITES

London Transport Museum. 2003. http://www.ltmuseum.co.uk
thetube.com. 2003. http://www.thetube.com

LIAM CAMPLING

UNEMPLOYMENT

Unemployment was a marked feature of the British economy during Victorian era. There were three main types of unemployment, which are looked at in turn below: structural and technological unemployment; cyclical unemployment; and underemployment.

Unfortunately, we have little in the way of precise evidence to measure levels of unemployment in the nineteenth century. A number of unions of skilled workers reported the percentage of their members who were without jobs, but these are of doubtful reliability in the years before about 1870, though gradually becoming more reliable and more frequent in the later years of the century. For the period down to 1850 it is impossible to obtain more than general impressions, and in the earlier years of the union reports we have no certain knowledge of the numbers who failed to join the union or who preferred to drink away the funds that might have paid for membership. In 1886, a bad year for employment, the iron-founders reported an average of 13.9% unemployed; the blacksmiths 14.4%; and the boilermakers and iron shipbuilders 22.2%. These figures are alarming, but we cannot be sure what proportion of skilled men the unions represented. The further one goes back the more misleading the figures may be, for in the early years of the unions the members are likely to be the best in the trade, while it seems likely that the nonmembers were the first to be made unemployed. It might be argued that the figures suggested by union evidence, of perhaps 3% or 4% unemployment in good years, and 9% in bad ones, may be near the truth. There is, however, no way of being sure.

Furthermore, very large areas of employment were not covered at all by union records. There are no records that throw light on the growing numbers of textile workers or on the numerous outwork trades. There were no figures for the miners, and none for the whole fields of work covered by agricultural casual, unskilled, and women's labor. The textile mill owners met depressions by going on short time or by closing down altogether, but there are no ways of calculating the impact of either process. Contemporary observers spoke of new cotton mills being opened by men who possessed little knowledge of the trade but who were attracted by rising opportunities and the cheapness of capital. A subsequent depression led many of these to abandon the trade, so that in some cases the owners of mills changed rapidly. In trades that continued to be dominated by outwork, such as weaving, boots and shoes, nail and chain making, technological progress came in too slowly to create much unemployment, though it did create declining standards of work for remaining outworkers. The trades were overcrowded to begin with, and suffered from immigration of Irish hands and,

later, European Jews. The excess of workers made it easy for employers to meet bad times by giving out less work, and all of it rewarded with inadequate pay. Eventually the removal by death of the older hands, and the transfer to new production methods of the younger ones, favored the introduction of factory methods. The clothing industry, for example, became a factory one so gradually that it was never objected to by the women and girls who labored at the hand trades, for whom the change was a blessing.

It has to be remembered that employment in FACTORIES and in the hand trades was a remarkably uncertain matter. The workforce itself changed very rapidly, and in some factories the list of hands employed at the end of the year might be totally different from those engaged at the beginning of the year. Key workers whom the employer hated losing, like skilled engineers and managers, were too valued to be allowed to move on quickly, and in addition to high pay they were asked to sign long-term contracts designed to tie them down for a period of years.

The ordinary workforce in the factories and hand trades were affected, of course, by illness, MARRIAGE, and early death, but also by drunkenness and the failure to keep to factory hours or finish work given out. Even those who worked steadily for very long hours in poor conditions did not guarantee themselves good treatment; many, like factory spinners, were sacked permanently at the age of 40 or 45 when they were considered worked out, and their chances of getting another job were poor. There was a great deal of absenteeism in both factories and outwork. "Saint Monday" was celebrated as a holiday because in the hand trades it was the day for taking completed work back to the master, collecting new orders, and drinking some of the pay. Very often payment was made in inns, and this encouraged the survival of the holiday. The practice was also experienced in factories, and often on a Monday the factory was so thinly staffed that work was delayed, and full production might not be resumed until some time on Tuesday. The outwork trades tended to be busier toward the weekends when hands faced a shortage of time for completing their orders.

Other distractions that affected both factories and outwork arose from warm sunny days when hands did not turn up, sports meetings, parades and processions, and a circus arriving in town. Many workers took a haphazard and careless view of life, and if a busy period swelled their pay packets they were liable to go and spend it rather than turning up at the factory or workshop, despite the employer's penalties for lack of discipline and drunkenness. Toward the end of the century absenteeism in the height of summer was such that employers preferred to close down completely for a week rather than struggle on with few hands.

STRUCTURAL UNEMPLOYMENT

Structural unemployment arose from major changes in the methods of producing goods and services that made former ways uneconomic. The advent of the RAILWAYS had the greatest impact in terms of the movement of both goods and passengers. Two periods of rapid increase in railway construction, in the middle 1830s and the middle 1840s, meant that by 1850 over 6,000 route-miles had been completed. Further construction continued throughout the century, and by 1901 the railways had already nearly 19,000 miles of track. The cheapness and greater efficiency of railway transport brought a rapid end to the much more expensive coaches, with the numbers of rail passengers growing from 67 million per year to 1,146 million between 1850 and 1901. Once a railway route was completed the coach services collapsed. The coaches to Birmingham gave up as early as 1839 and many more died in the 1840s. The loss of jobs affected not only the booking office clerks, drivers, and guards but also the numerous innkeepers and waiters in the LONDON centers and the large inns where the coach stopped on route. The specialist horse breeders, harness makers, and repairers and builders of coaches gave up too. Fortunately, the majority of villages had no railway station, and consequently local carriers and coaches to railway centers survived, and it was very late in the century when these disappeared. The CANALS, covering some 4,000 route-miles, also gave way to the railways' superiority in the carriage of goods. Most canals were too old and unimproved, with varying depths, widths, and size of locks. Only the most favored were able to survive, and there resulted a fall in employment for canal boatmen, the horses and their tenders used for pulling the barges, the "leggers" who hauled the barges through tunnels, and the staffs of waterside inns. The railways, in due course, provided a far larger and more stable source of employment.

The building of steamships led to a much more gradual fall in the use of sailing vessels. The process was a longer one than with the railways because early steamboats still made use of sails, and it was many years before the gradual improvement of marine engines made it possible for steamships to tackle long-distance ocean routes. The numbers of steamships rose over fifteenfold during the Victorian era, from 624 in 1837 to 9,803 in 1901, while in the same period the number of sailing vessels in use fell from 19,900 to 10,572. The use of steamships developed first on coastal routes but eventually took over long-distance routes to other continents. Sailing ships continued on minor routes and carried large quantities of non-urgent goods all over the world. Many of them were sunk by German submarines in World War I (1914–1918). The use of iron in steamships created more work in IRON AND STEEL works, as well as for riveting in the shipyards, while the work of building sailing ships declined as their trade fell away.

The early arrival of cotton factories destroyed the work of hand spinsters. Delays in the development of successful weaving machines, however, meant that hand weavers were able to continue working down to about 1850. For a period cotton masters produced thread in their mills while also employing hand weavers to make the cloth. Other factories appeared later in the industries that made boots, shoes, and clothing, since they depended on adaptations to factory work of Singer's sewing machine, invented in 1851. For lengthy periods of time parts of the process of making boots and shoes continued to employ hand workers, while some parts of making shirts and clothing generally still gave some work to women and girls.

CYCLICAL UNEMPLOYMENT

Cyclical unemployment affected the work of textile factories and that of numerous hand workers, as well as cutting production in iron and steel works, ENGINEERING, metal working, shipbuilding, carpentry and woodworking, and construction. The slump years occurred periodically in 1841–1842, 1852, 1857–1858, 1861–1863 (arising from a severe shortage of raw cotton as a result of the CIVIL WAR in the United States), 1867–1869, 1878–1880, 1884–1887, 1892–1895, and—following the death of Victoria—in 1903–1905 and 1908–1909.

The effects of this cyclical unemployment were worsened by the concentration of the same kinds of work in a given town, so that some Lancashire towns were spinning centers and others were devoted to weaving. Iron and steel works, metal manufacturing, shipbuilding, and coal mining were all concentrated in limited geographic centers, so that a depression had a very strong local effect. In severe depressions workers were obliged to sell their possessions, even their furniture, to buy food, and in the last resort to appeal to the Poor Law. The situation was better in towns that enjoyed a more stable source of employment. Railway towns, for example, experience more limited effects because the work was less severely depressed, and the same is true of towns concerned with the production of food, clothing, and boots and shoes. In the later nineteenth century the decline in productivity made it possible for employers in some trades to have to hire more hands merely to maintain existing levels of output. Building work, for instance—one of the largest employers—was little affected by labor-saving machinery; indeed the London bricklayer maintained his average of laying 60 bricks an hour for a period of 30 years before 1911. In fact, the return in bricks and mortar for a given amount of labor and capital fell slightly over the period. In coal mining, too, physical efficiency was declining. Coal output per man employed had been rising up to 1881, but then fell from 403 tons per man in that year down to only 340 tons in 1901, and even down to only 309 tons in 1911. By that date 36% more miners were employed but to a production output of only 19% more coal.

UNDEREMPLOYMENT

There was of course a great deal of underemployment in Victorian Britain. The attitude to work displayed by both factory hands and outworkers was indifferent or even hostile. They stuck strongly to their usual holidays. In trades like building bad weather forced workers to down tools; and in major ports like London, Liverpool, Bristol, and Newcastle, there was a surplus of dock laborers and stevedores to take up the available work. The men affected by this lack of work might find odd jobs to do when they were not called to the docks, or they might work at home, cultivate a garden plot, or join their fellows in a PUBLIC HOUSE. In big cities there were innumerable street sellers, hawkers, costermongers (sellers of fruits and vegetables), knife grinders, rag and bone men, organ players, and many more such workers, and it is impossible to know the extent to which they were fully employed. Mrs. Pember Reeves found in her study of Lambeth, a central London suburb, that some of the unemployed had lost their jobs through illness or accidents. Many worked for very small businesses which closed, and were forced in due course to accept a job at a boy's rate of pay or turn to one of the street sellers trades. They tramped about to try and find their old sort of job, but were forced to take on petty work to bring in some income. Their wives and children were helped by neighbors' gifts of good or small loans to keep them from resorting to the parish. Mrs. Pember Reeves catalogued the detailed

spending of minute sums intended to put some food on the table, pointing to its insecurity as well as insufficiency. We do not know how many people struggled on from one odd job to another while, even in the center of London, finding it impossible to obtain a new job in their old trade as a carter, carpenter, or laborer. There was undoubtedly an abundance of workers in unskilled or semiskilled jobs who could not obtain a regular living, even at very low wages, and they have to be added to those experiencing unemployment in industrial towns where the causes are easier to find.

See also FACTORIES; POVERTY AND PAUPERISM.

FURTHER READING

Bagwell, Philip S. *The Transport Revolution from 1770.* London: Batsford, 1974.

Burnett, John. *Idle Hands: The Experience of Unemployment, 1790–1990.* London and New York: Routledge, 1994.

Clapham, John, Sir. *An Economic History of Modern Britain.* 3 vols. Cambridge: University Press, 1930–1938.

Reeves, Mrs. Pember. *Round about a Pound a Week.* London: G. Bell, 1913.

Whiteside, Noel. *Bad Times: Unemployment in British Social and Political History.* London and Boston: Faber and Faber, 1991.

G. E. MINGAY

UNIFORMS AND LIVERIES

A uniform is a type of clothing that displays an institutional affiliation; it is especially associated with the military, but its civilian use has a long history and tended to increase in the Victorian era. Modern uniforms began with medieval liveries, which were worn by noblemen's retainers in the Middle Ages, borrowing a Middle Eastern custom that the wearer dons a "coat of honor" given to him by his master, thus symbolizing its primary meanings of service and affiliation. But nobles' liverymen ceased being private warriors by the latter seventeenth century, though liveries continued for house servants. Military uniforms developed as a mid-seventeenth century offshoot, when large amounts of clothing were needed for newly raised regiments, and this easily identified, distinctive dress hindered desertion.

Military uniforms' bright colors and fancy trimmings celebrated the exalted ideals of soldiering: glory, bravery, self-sacrifice, brotherhood, solidarity, and defending the realm. The uniform was also believed to be sexually attractive, which enticed naive teenaged males to enlist in a profession notable for harsh, low-paid, dangerous conditions. The tight fit and regulation stiff posture helped instill discipline, enhanced by rigid distinctions in the quality of colors, trappings, trimmings and equipment, which were ever-present, visual reminders of hierarchy. Maintaining high standards of appearance also aided discipline, but the continual attention to petty details likewise encouraged morale and pride. These were thus instilled within soldiers—even those who hated the service—when paraded before cheering crowds, thereby tending to engineer soldiers' minds in a way useful to the commanders. The visual clothing aesthetic was thus an intrinsic managerial element. Officers, however, sometimes followed an elite British male custom of wearing mufti (civilian) dress, which likewise displayed the British gentleman's traditional sense of political independence.

The CRIMEAN WAR (1853–56) was the last European conflict that Britons fought wearing full parade dress, though its use continued in colonial wars against outgunned peoples of developing nations. Yet scarlet gradually diminished; last used for combat in 1885, it was reserved for domestic spectacle. *Khaki*, a South Asian Urdu word for "dust," became the camouflage color—to the regret of many soldiers. Nonprofessional defense forces (volunteers, militia and so on), modeled their uniforms on the regulars, and the Volunteer Movement from 1859 considerably expanded the presence of martial dress in society. ROYAL NAVY sailors got uniforms in 1857 (over a century after officers) to enhance morale, discipline, and cleanliness. These appeared much later than BRITISH ARMY uniforms because sailors could not desert as easily, were not normally paraded before civilians, and ships, not men, were the major focus of visual spectacle. Some captains had privately supplied uniforms for decades, but navy blue was less stiff and spectacular than army dress.

UNIFORMED CIVILIANS

Civilian uniforms flourished during VICTORIA's reign. Court dress was originally whatever was in high fashion; however, as the crown's political power decreased from the late seventeenth century, it exerted ever greater control over dress, not just for courtiers but also for many official and service positions. George III instituted the Windsor Uniform in 1778 for himself and male courtiers. By Victoria's reign, rigidly regulated, military-influenced uniformity was a proliferating pattern for a variety of court and civil service uniforms, and, in addition, it influenced servant liveries (including the royal rat catcher) in this bastion of elite conservatism amid a world of accelerating change.

Ministers of different denominations wore costumes that were essentially uniforms. The CHURCH OF ENGLAND's medieval styles were especially resistant to change, and in the early decades, large lawn sleeves especially symbolized venerability. UNIVERSITIES had always utilized churchmanlike academic gowns, and when women began to attend, the styles remained absolutely unaltered.

Some civic officials wore uniforms, and some private and public employees gradually acquired them, including postmen, undertakers, dustmen, lift boys and messenger boys. Regular POLICE forces proliferated in 1829–1856, and unlike many red government uniforms, wore dark blue to avoid enhancing public hostility. Fire brigades had long worn uniforms and badges, and railways put their more visible employees in uniform, with some sporting bullion braid. As a traditional British national color, red appeared in some occupational dress, such as the LONDON orphan shoeblacks; these "City Reds" from 1851 wore red coats and were organized into "brigades."

Occupational clothing often combined elements of uniforms, liveries, and/or traditional occupational garb. Over time, however, the latter two tended more toward uniforms in tone, as institutions proliferated and impersonal hierarchies replaced the older, family-based circles that had been central to trade, though this trend was later reversed for some groups, probably reacting against visual conformity. Over time, subdued military-inspired styles proliferated, making a much less flamboyant aesthetic tone, which became a modern institutional dress aesthetic.

Victorian male servants wore liveries in a variety of styles, each depending upon his duty. Upper servants dressed like gentlemen, with elements identifying their servile status, such as wearing an apron when serving drinks. For lower servants, archaic fancy dress clothed the very visible footmen and carriage attendants, and the vision of figures garbed in traditional garments symbolizing power and status was a pleasing fantasy, especially for newly rich businessmen eager to flaunt grandeur, veneration, and nobility. Hotel employees and waiters wore liveries derived from these. While nannies wore a more fashionable version of nurses' dress, other female servants initially had more freedom and were often criticized for dressing better than their mistresses. In mid-century they were forced into uniforms, and unlike male servants, they paid for their own dress. This probably reflects elite insecurities over controlling the lesser orders, as well as the status anxieties of the proliferating, social-climbing middle classes.

INSTITUTIONAL UNIFORMS

Uniforms for the institutionalized indigent, including orphans, elderly paupers, the infirm, and others, had existed for centuries. These emphasized humility and obedience, with old fashioned, quaint and often humiliating, archaic styles; large numbered badges were frequently mandatory, and orphans sometimes called each other by their numbers. Toward the latter nineteenth century, these styles came to conform more to contemporary dress, thus de-emphasizing the stigma of being without a family, as mass urban life became more impersonal for everyone. Uniformed almsmen, orphans, and poor schoolboys were paraded less often, and uniforms were increasingly reserved for special public events. Prison warders and convicts were also uniformed, the latter in drab colors symbolizing humiliation. Insane asylums likewise clad attendants in "forbidding uniform," and impoverished inmates frequently wore "prison uniform of sad coloured grey." The SALVATION ARMY likewise adopted martial dress to "campaign" against urban social evils.

Uniforms look best when massed together, thus displaying disciplined solidarity. In this vision, the social problems of POVERTY, orphans, crime, and the indigent, were transformed into a vision of discipline, order, modesty, cleanliness (and usually harmony) in a highly idealized, and oftentimes entertaining vision. As education became ever more important, elite PUBLIC SCHOOLS adopted uniforms and badges, which encouraged solidarity and esprit de corps, and "livery colors" for sports were also adopted, which aided identification and expressed teamwork. Long before 1837 uniforms were worn by elite sports clubs for golf, hunting (red prominent), cricket and archery (green prominent), although these uniforms were not always continued. Sporting shirts, sometimes collarless, appeared in the 1830s for rowing teams.

Women wore uniforms in increasing numbers in this era. Religious nursing sisters had long worn them, while FLORENCE NIGHTINGALE's efforts inspired greater acceptance of female nurses, with blue being a prominent color, while frills were discouraged (doctors adopted white gowns rather late). Girl's school uniforms appeared in late century; while women attempted then to adopt less constricting dress for sports, the public's insistence on very long skirts hindered lighter, less constraining costumes until very late in the century.

See also FASHION AND CLOTHING.

FURTHER READING

Cunnington, Phillis, and Catherine Lucas. *Charity Costumes of Children, Scholars Almsfolk, Pensioners.* London: Adams and Black, 1978.

Cunnington, Phillis. *Costume of Household Servants: From the Middle Ages to 1900.* London: Adam and Charles Black, 1974.

Ewing, Elizabeth. *Women in Uniform through the Centuries.* Totowa, N.J.: Roman and Littlefield, 1975.

Mansfield, Alan. *Ceremonial Costume Court, Civil and Civic Costume from 1660 to the Present Day.* London: Adam and Charles Black, 1980.

Myerly, Scott Hughes. *British Military Spectacle From the Napoleonic Wars through the Crimea.* Cambridge, Mass.: Harvard University Press, 1996.

SCOTT MYERLY

UNITED STATES OF AMERICA

When VICTORIA ascended the throne in 1837, Martin Van Buren had only recently been inaugurated as the eighth president of the United States, presiding over a nation of 26 states, only three of which were west of the Mississippi River. When she died in 1901, empress of an even vaster worldwide EMPIRE than the one she had inherited some 64 years earlier, William McKinley was about to be inaugurated for his second term as the 25th president. The United States he led now comprised 45 states, and the nation had just acquired its first overseas colonies after the war with Spain in 1898.

Properly speaking, the United States never had a Victorian period, since it never had Victoria as a monarch, having rejected the authority of her Hanoverian ancestor, George III, late in the eighteenth century. Victorian literature is a label more properly applied to the likes of authors such as CHARLES DICKENS, WILLIAM MAKEPEACE THACKERAY, or ALFRED, LORD TENNYSON, who critiqued British society at a time when most American writers were trying to figure out their own bearings on a continent-under-construction and fashion the language of the mother country to the needs of its busy, mobile, and more diverse population. In the United States, the term *Victorian* typically connotes a highly embellished style of vernacular ARCHITECTURE or crafts design, often with Gothic references, or an attitude of moral priggishness, stodginess, and propriety often associated with the pretensions of bourgeois (middle class) society. But as much as the United States had declared its independence from England, Americans did develop an affection for the Queen and the institutions she stood for. After all, Victoria, along with her beloved husband ALBERT, was a patron of the new industrial society that was emerging on both sides of the Atlantic.

In a very real sense, both of the great English-speaking nations of the nineteenth century were in the vanguard of all that was innovative and shared similar ideas about the role of culture and the individual in the new industrial order. It is in this sense that the United States can also be described as having a Victorian period.

In 1837, there were still Americans alive who remembered the Revolution of 1776 and the establishment of constitutional government. The nation had fought a second war with Britain from 1812 to 1814 to free itself of British restrictions on trade and expansion. Despite these animosities, for much of the century the United States looked across the ocean for cultural and spiritual affirmation. Writers such as James Fenimore Cooper and WASHINGTON IRVING attempted to develop a uniquely American literature, but Americans relied on models set largely in Britain. Even toward the end of the Victorian era, American authors such as HENRY JAMES and HENRY ADAMS still looked to British models of style, even as they strove to define themselves as writers for a new people. Part of this was simply because Americans in the early nineteenth century were still primarily of British stock. Irish immigrants did not begin arriving in large numbers until after the potato FAMINES of the 1840s, and immigration from southern and eastern Europe did not begin in earnest until about 1880. In the early Victorian era, many Americans still had fairly recent ancestral ties with Britain; even though they were preoccupied with building a new nation, they could not easily forget the language, the institutions, and the civic culture of the motherland. Though the American Revolution had severed ties with MONARCHY and Parliament, the framers of the Constitution were indebted to social institutions and common law that had been developing in Britain since the days of the Magna Carta (1215). Especially during the early Victorian era—and no matter how much its partisans tried to deny it—Americans still defined themselves in the shadow of Britain, though they may have thought of themselves more as unruly stepchildren than as dutiful sons or daughters.

A brief historical timeline will help frame the American context for these issues. In the 1830s, American political, cultural, and economic hegemony was centered on Boston and Philadelphia. New York City was just beginning its rise to power thanks to the recently completed Erie Canal, which opened significant commercial links to the American interior around the Great Lakes. The Northeast was beginning to prosper thanks to the Industrial Revolution, which began to develop around a well-integrated network of mechanized FACTORIES and RAILWAYS. Vast stretches of the continent west of the Mississippi were still inhabited primarily by Native Americans, who were already being displaced by the steady westward advance of the frontier. The agrarian South was still dominated by a slaveholding, agrarian ARISTOCRACY whose desire for expansion into the Western territories ignited serious sectional conflicts that culminated in the CIVIL WAR from 1861 to 1865. After the war, the defeated South struggled to recover during the Reconstruction Era (1865–1877), while the North continued to prosper, even while dealing with an influx of IMMIGRATION that crowded its large cities, whose rapid growth and deteriorating condition drew comparisons with the SLUMS of LONDON or MANCHESTER. In the Gilded Age of the 1880s and beyond, class divisions between Americans became more acute, especially after the closure of the American frontier in 1890. Although life on the frontier was not at all safe for Native Americans, or herds of buffalo, the frontier was long thought to have been an important safety valve for the pent-up conflicts back East. Separated from the rest of the world by two oceans and by relatively unthreatening neighbors to the north and south, the United States during the Victorian era was too preoccupied with its own internal development and its sectional conflicts to pay much attention to the rest of the world, except for a few intellectuals (such as Henry Adams) or artists (such as JAMES MCNEILL WHISTLER) or adventurers (such as Herman Melville) who were cosmopolitan enough to appreciate life abroad, whether in Chartres (France), Paris, or the South Seas.

EXPANDING EMPIRES

Both Britain and the United States participated in the unrelenting expansiveness that was a recurring theme of the Victorian era, but the historical and cultural experiences of the two English-speaking nations were often quite different. While the nineteenth century in England marked the zenith of a vast overseas empire that stood in stark contrast to its bleak urban slums and pinched farmscapes, America's empire was still essentially a domestic one, characterized by westward thrust across a vast continent, a nervous energy that poet WALT WHITMAN captured in his unorthodox cadences. Of course, America was a colonizing power, too, with native Americans and enslaved Africans among the colonized, but in the nineteenth century this was explained away by "manifest destiny," the belief that the nation had a divine mandate to expand across the North American continent and, by implication, to bring the benefits of Anglo-Saxon

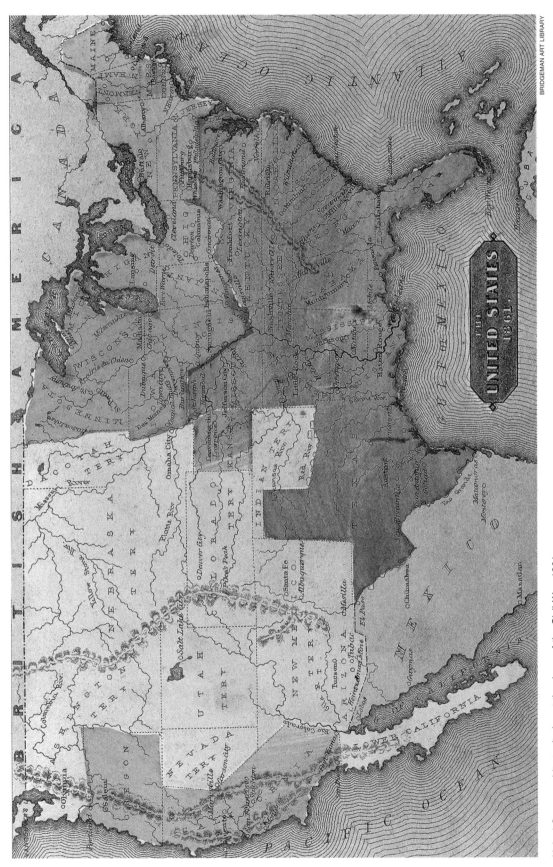

United States and its territories at the dawn of the Civil War, 1861.

civilization to those it encountered, even if it employed them as agricultural slaves in the South or industrial slaves in the North, or, in the case of Native Americans, place them in Indian schools or on reservations. The Victorian era in America thus saw a vast drama involving such issues as slavery, labor and capital, the role of women and immigrants, demands placed on land and resources by an expanding industrial civilization, and issues of self-identity.

The United States during the nineteenth century was still largely a nation of farms and small towns (it was not until 1920 that the population became predominantly nonrural). There were large cities, such as Boston, New York, and Philadelphia, but they did not really begin to teem with immigrants until later in the century. The modern institutions such as corporate conglomerates and labor unions both had their beginnings in the Victorian era as the United States lay the foundation to support itself as an industrialized power.

During the nineteenth century, and especially during the turbulent 1850s and 1860s, the national consciousness of Americans underwent a significant change. Whereas in the early half of the century, it was common to hear and read the expression "these United States are . . . ," the phrase "the United States is . . . " became almost universal by the end of the Victorian era. This was achieved at great cost, of course: sectional rivalries between North and South erupted into Civil War in 1861, a conflict in which the North (or Union) prevailed over the South (or Confederacy). For the rest of the century and well into the next, the defeated South languished while the victorious North enjoyed the fruits of the expanding capitalist system, a state of affairs that continues to have implications in American domestic policy and interracial relationships.

Geography played a major role in the divergent historical paths that the United States and Britain took during the Victorian era. In 1837, vast stretches of the American West were still unexplored and unsettled. In only 60 years, the nation had expanded from the original 13 colonies along the Atlantic seaboard over the Appalachians and west to the Mississippi and beyond. Most of Britain's population was concentrated on a small island nation of less than 100,000 square miles (259,000 square kilometers) (including Wales, Scotland, and northern IRELAND), an area roughly the size of the states of New York and Pennsylvania combined. The United States, by contrast, would expand across the North American continent, eventually claiming sovereignty of more than 3 million square miles (1.2 million hectares). The na-

tion's population grew from 3.9 million in 1790 to 17 million in 1840 and 76 million by 1900; Britain's population during the same period grew from about 8 million to 26 million to 41 million.

Despite the American myth that it is essentially a peace-loving nation that avoids foreign entanglements, westward expansion was marked with extreme violence against Native Americans and border conflicts with CANADA (over the Oregon territory) and Mexico (over Texas, California, and the American southwest). But Americans felt they had a divine mandate to expand from shore to shore, a "manifest destiny" that was typically Victorian in the way it justified aggressive actions as part of a grand, progressive, and benevolent scheme. At century's end, when dreams of British imperialism were fading and just as the American frontier was closing, it is not surprising that British poet RUDYARD KIPLING would challenge Americans to "take up the white man's burden" in a poem that recycled the notion of "manifest destiny" for another century.

The American frontier was not closed until 1890, when the admission of Idaho and Wyoming to the Union created an uninterrupted expanse from the Atlantic to the Pacific oceans. Historian Frederick Jackson Turner argued that it was the consciousness of an ever-expanding frontier that had inalterably shaped the American character and experience. In *The Significance of the Frontier in American History* (1893) he declared: "The existence of an area of free land, its continuous recession, and the advance of an American settlement westward, explain American development." Although his thesis is not as influential as it once was, it helps explain some of the ways that Americans were able to mitigate the effects of the Industrial Revolution during the Victorian era. While America certainly had its share of industrial cities and slums, urban blight seemed particularly acute in Britain, which had little room for expansion except through overseas colonization. In the United States by contrast, land and resources seemed inexhaustible, a consciousness that led to a culture of waste, conspicuous consumption, and environmental degradation. Americans in the nineteenth century were not worried about conservation because there were always new frontiers to claim just beyond the horizon. In contrast to today's tourists, who look for unspoiled beaches or remote mountain getaways, American tourists in the nineteenth century enjoyed visiting coal mines, factories, or logging operations in order to be stimulated by the verve and vitality of their fast-growing nation.

AMERICAN ART

This ambivalence toward the national environment was but one example of the cultural bipolarity that characterized American life during the Victorian era (other of these bipolarities involved issues of race, sex, class, and the conflicts between federal power and states' rights). But it was in the realm of artistic expression that American intellectuals first began grappling with issues that would later be characterized as environmental. Artists of the HUDSON RIVER SCHOOL, such as Albert Bierstadt, Frederick Edwin Church, THOMAS COLE, and Asher Durand, began to create works that idolized the sublime beauty of the unspoiled landscape, either of New York's Catskills (as in the case of Durand) or of the western Rockies (as in the case of Bierstadt). These artists did not merely create pretty landscapes on canvas; they infused their works with an attitude of transcendence that helped give Americans their first visual vocabulary of the "sublime," a uniquely American version of the Romantic-era mysticism that was at the heart of the PRE-RAPHAELITE movement in England. The two movements were very different, of course, but offered a critique of the new industrial society. In America, the landscapes were so vast and pristine that its artists created works that infused the natural environment with an almost pantheistic quality (an equating of God with the forces and laws of nature and the universe). The style of the artists of the Hudson River School—and of the transcendentalist notions that were emanating from the pens of such writers as Ralph Waldo Emerson and Henry David Thoreau—gave Americans a sense that their environment offered unlimited resources that would meet all their spiritual and material needs.

Even while developing a uniquely American style and subject matter, writers in the United States still looked to William Shakespeare, John Milton, and Alexander Pope as writers worthy of the highest emulation. Americans might have rejected the monarchy, the parliamentary system, and the exclusive university systems of Oxford or Cambridge, but they still spoke the queen's English and considered it their common tongue, even if it was acquiring a variety of regional accents. Noah Webster published the first American dictionary in 1806, greatly expanded into his 1828 *An American Dictionary of the English Language*. It had 70,000 words, some 12,000 more than the most comparable British example, the latest edition of Samuel Johnson's dictionary. Webster's work helped codify American usage and spelling for a new nation looking to be bound together by a uniquely local version of the language of their forebears. Webster's reference works, along with *McGuffey's Eclectic Readers*, helped create the prototypes of a mass society by linking millions of readers who had been exposed to the same word usages and (in the case of the readers) moralistic aphorisms and tales of PATRIOTISM and self-improvement.

Americans during the nineteenth century were stalwart advocates of the notion of universal free education. As Irish immigrants poured into American cities in the 1840s, nativists strongly resisted efforts on the part of Roman Catholics to establish a competitive parochial-school system. But separation of CHURCH AND STATE was not as rigid as it would become in the twentieth century. Even in the public schools (that is, state-administered schools, as opposed to the British PUBLIC SCHOOLS, which charged tuition and offered boarding), prayer and Bible reading (according to Protestant formulas, of course) were mandatory in schools, habituating children to forms of civic religion that formed the backdrop to public life, in which upper-class Protestant denominations like the Episcopalians and Presbyterians were given more prestige than lower-class Methodists or Baptists, or Roman Catholics of any social class.

It was not until mid-century that Americans began appreciating the writing of native-born writers, all of whom gave a uniquely American inflection to the issues and themes being discussed by their British Victorian cousins, as pointed out by F. O. Matthiessen in his classic study, *American Renaissance: Art and Expression in the Age of Emerson and Whitman*. The American writers most in vogue at the beginning of the Victorian era were Washington Irving, with his tales of the old days in Dutch New York; James Fenimore Cooper, with his novels of frontiersmen and Indians; and William Cullen Bryant, newspaper editor and poet whose style was most akin to that of the British Romanticist WILLIAM WORDSWORTH. Dickens, who had no real counterpart in the United States, attracted enthusiastic crowds to his lecture tours in America, and poets John Keats, Lord Byron, and P. B. Shelley were widely read, but American readers preferred Ralph Waldo Emerson for his combination of self-reliance and TRANSCENDENTALISM; Edgar Allan Poe for his macabre excursions into gothic fiction; NATHANIEL HAWTHORNE for his deft probing of the American mind as it shed its Puritan heritage; Herman Melville for the way he projected American aspirations onto an exotic seascape in his epic novels; WALT WHITMAN, the poet of American democracy and individualism who introduced new, freewheeling cadences into American poetry; and Emily Dickinson, the reclusive poet who at once undergirded and subverted Victorian propriety in her coded poems that appear devout and ethereal on the surface but that conceal a passionate assertiveness and even a fiery eroticism beneath. If the Victorian temperament was all about putting a presentable face on things, then Dickinson might be considered the quintessential American Victorian poet for her maidenly subterfuge.

REFORM

The United States in the nineteenth century was awash in reform movements that can be tied to a peculiarly Victorian sense of earnestness, modulated by evangelical fervor, that aimed to ameliorate unpleasant conditions. Religious reform has always been an important element in America, particularly so in the Victorian era when several channels began running together—new evangelical movements in the established churches, the traditional Quaker commitment to nonviolence, deistic (emphasis on morality and natural religion) and transcendentalist (emphasis on spirituality) thinking about humanity's relation to the environment, even utopian movements—to create a practical theology that had a significant impact on public policy and private charity. America was not yet a mass society, dominated by mass media, and social gatherings had a great impact on daily life. The annual pew-rental auctions in some important city churches were reported in the pages of the next day's newspapers, much as the play-by-play of a football game would be reported in today's sports columns. Churchgoing was an important social event and bonding ritual for many Victorian Americans, and it was not uncommon for them to warm to reform causes through religious sermons or tracts or CHAUTAUQUA lectures. While the religion of Puritan New England envisioned America as a "city set on a hill," the demanding requirements of strict Calvinist theology gave way in the nineteenth century to more inclusive religious practices. The religion experienced by many Victorian Americans emphasized the tender mercies of God rather than his harsh justice, and churches forged an easy alliance with movements designed to ameliorate the ills of society. The TEMPERANCE MOVEMENT was one of the most popular of these enthusiasms; unlike the prudish naysayers of popular stereotype, many temperance advocates forged alliances with abolitionists, feminists, and labor organizers to energize Victorian America with a humanitarian reform movement that significantly expanded the rights of African Americans, women, workers, the mentally ill, and paupers.

Class mobility was always more rigid in Britain than in United States. Although there was desperate poverty and discrimination in both countries, the masses did begin to enjoy a substantial rise in their standard of living during the Victorian era and into the twentieth century. But unlike their counterparts on the European continent, poorer or working-class Americans rarely developed an ideological solidarity with their fellows in the same station in life, looking instead to lift themselves into the ranks of at least the middle class. In the United States, the Horatio Alger myth of success through persistence, pluck, and hard work still resonates in the American psyche, and thus Americans reject the notion of being confined to a lower class forever. This aspect of American life was also fraught with paradox in Victorian America. On the surface, Americans have always shunned ostentation but they have always endowed the very rich, the very beautiful, and the very talented with the status of royalty or nobility. Thus Americans mythologized such presidential elections as that of 1828, when the uncouth frontiersman Andrew Jackson won the presidency; 1840, when the commoner William Henry ("Tippecanoe") Harrison defeated the aristocratic Martin Van Buren; or 1860, when rail-splitting Abraham Lincoln succeeded the uppity James Buchanan. But they could also elect scoundrels and grafters to high political office during the so-called Gilded Age at the end of the century, or secretly admire the vast wealth of John D. Rockefeller or Andrew Carnegie, while terming them robber barons and enemies of labor.

The Victorian era was a time of transition and transformation in both the United States and Great Britain, one in which the younger nation eventually outstripped its parent in population and wealth. At its close, Britain was unwittingly coming to the end of its 300-year domination as a world power while the United States was poised to begin its own. For Americans, the Victorian era marked the triumph of industrial capitalism over the old agrarian, yeoman-farmer models, as well as the beginning of a concentration of power in Washington, D.C., that would continue well into the next century. More important, it marked a coming-of-age period in which the United States settled, at least temporarily, its internecine quarrels long enough to take a major, if reluctant, place in world affairs.

FURTHER READING

Baron, Robert C., ed. *America, One Land, One People: Noted Historians Look at America.* Golden, Colo.: Fulcrum, 1987.
Douglas, Ann. *The Feminization of American Culture.* New York: Knopf, 1977.

Lears, T. J. Jackson. *No Place of Grace: Antimodernism and the Transformation of American Culture, 1880–1920.* New York: Pantheon, 1981.

Levine, Bruce, et al. *Who Built America?: Working People and the Nation's Economy, Politics, Culture, and Society.* New York: Pantheon Books, 1989–1992.

Mann, William Justin. *America in Its Relation to the Great Epochs of History.* Boston: Little, Brown, 1902.

Matthiessen, F. O. *American Renaissance: Art and Expression in the Age of Emerson and Whitman.* New York: Oxford University Press, 1941.

Simmons, James C. *Star-spangled Eden: 19th Century American through the Eyes of Dickens, Wilde, Frances Trollope, Frank Harris, and Other British Travelers.* New York: Carroll and Graf, 2000.

Whitman, Alden, ed. *American Reformers.* New York: H. W. Wilson, 1985.

EDWARD MORAN

UNIVERSITIES

In the course of the nineteenth century, British universities evolved from a handful of small, backward looking, socially exclusive centers of largely religious instruction into a large, dynamic collection of teaching and research institutions, open to both men and women, all religions and, increasingly, all social classes. This movement was painfully slow and incomplete—working class representation among students and staff remained pitifully small throughout this period, and women only gained access to the universities in the second half of the century. Nevertheless, the innovations that came so gradually and painfully in the nineteenth century laid the foundations for the enormous expansion of access in the twentieth. The universities could not avoid being touched by the great movements of the Victorian era: fuller citizenship rights for all social classes, religious pluralism, growth of the professions, and the emancipation of women.

In 1800, there were two universities in England (Oxford and Cambridge), four in Scotland (Edinburgh, Glasgow, St. Andrews, and Aberdeen), and Trinity College, Dublin and the small Roman Catholic Maynooth in Ireland. The two English universities, Oxford and Cambridge, required adherence to the 39 Articles of the CHURCH OF ENGLAND, while Trinity was still affiliated with the established Church of Ireland, and although it had recently removed its religious restric-

Kings College, Cambridge, founded in 1441 by King Henry VI.

137

tions, was still avoided by Roman Catholics. All the universities were closed to women, with those in England and Scotland alike bound by outdated statutes and customs. These limited their ability and their will to deploy their often considerable funds for such innovations as new subjects or broader access. In addition to statutory constraints, tradition and comfort weighed heavily with the teaching staff, or dons, of the two English universities in particular.

THE OXBRIDGE HERITAGE

The several separate colleges that made up the universities of Oxford and Cambridge enjoyed both wealth and autonomy within the universities themselves. Fellows, or dons as the teachers were (and are) called, enjoyed a comfortable standard of living and few responsibilities; students often led lives of intense dissipation while studiousness was a matter of individual choice and all too seldom a feature of a university education. Dons had little incentive to improve as teachers or develop as mentors to the young, since the celibacy requirement of their jobs ensured that they would quickly pass on from teaching to permanent careers as Church of England clergymen. Many parents, especially among the emerging business class, considered the two ancient universities to be nests of idleness and immoral living and saw little benefit in a university education for their sons. Students were drawn overwhelmingly from the ARISTOCRACY and the clergy. The curriculum also remained static in this early period, with Oxford the seat of CLASSICAL LANGUAGES AND LITERATURE and Cambridge of mathematics. Both subjects became self-perpetuating since fellowships tended to be linked to them and, having attained proficiency at one, a don would have little knowledge or experience of the other.

Although it did not appear so on the surface, preconditions for reform already existed in the recently adopted system of examinations at Oxbridge, as the two ancient English universities are collectively known. Cambridge had established its tripos, a strict examination, initially in mathematics, in 1780. In 1800, Oxford instituted a written examination, primarily in classics. The existence of examinations did not bring immediate change however, since there was no compulsion for students to attempt them and many did not—particularly the sons of aristocrats, who had little need of degrees. Nevertheless, the examinations at least set a standard of excellence in one discipline and created a mechanism for adding others. Indeed, Oxford did create a school of mathematics and physics in 1807 and Cambridge a classical tripos in 1824.

Beyond these measures, however, the institutions saw little change before mid-century.

By the 1820s it was obvious that Dissenters (non-Anglican Protestants) and other religious groups were going to have to look elsewhere for higher education for their children. Many went to the Scottish universities and others to the Continent, but as the dissenting middle class grew, so did the demand for a university closer to home. An alliance of dissenters—including Roman Catholics and Jews—broadly linked by their admiration for the principles of UTILITARIANISM, proposed a university for LONDON, modeled on those of Scotland, Prussia, and the new University of Virginia. Supporters included the historian THOMAS BABINGTON MACAULAY and the utilitarian politician and aristocrat HENRY BROUGHAM.

EXAMINATIONS

The University of London (later renamed University College) opened in 1828 and immediately a public outcry arose at the foreign concept of a "godless college," free of all religious ties. As an act of Anglican defiance, King's College opened in 1831 and in 1836 a royal charter was granted to a University of London that was centered neither on the godless college nor on the Anglican one but on an independent examining body, based in London, to which not only the two London rivals, but any college or institution could submit students for examination. This uneasy compromise proved to be the greatest innovation of the century in higher education, for it allowed students from any part of the country and, increasingly, from all reaches of the British EMPIRE, to take a degree of recognized standards regardless of the availability of universities in their area. The London external degree became an accepted standard for students and small educational institutions throughout the empire as the century progressed. At the same time, the two original colleges of the University of London were joined by others and increased in size and prestige, eventually to emerge as the teaching and examining body that is the University of London today.

The nineteenth-century preoccupation with examinations to certify competence produced the next great impetus to university expansion. Practical medical education was introduced in this period, although some medical instruction had existed previously at the two ancient universities and in Scotland. New regulations for training apothecaries and surgeons led to the establishment of medical schools in many of the large industrial cities in the 1820s and 1830s. Science, never previously a university subject, was now taught in an academic environment, much of it in London and in provincial towns where higher education had been previously lacking.

Despite the spectacular growth of population and increased prosperity in provincial cities, only one university was established outside London in the early nineteenth century. The diocese of Durham, well aware that the Ecclesiastical Commissioners were soon to redistribute part of its immense wealth in the church reforms of the 1830s, prudently invested the money in a university within the precincts of Durham Minster. With no clear educational mission, the new university provided a pallid imitation of an Oxford or Cambridge college, training mainly clergymen, and it was not until the twentieth century that the University of Durham matured into a university of distinction. Further exciting developments took place elsewhere. In 1846, the Manchester textile manufacturer John Owens left the city £100,000 to found a college. Owens College was free from religious criteria but, like all other British universities at this time, remained closed to women. Its students might attempt the London degree examination or attend other universities when their course at Owens was complete. The existence of the examining body in London allowed centers of higher education to develop in provincial cities and offered the assurance of uniform high quality that the British insisted on when conferring degrees. Other university colleges opened in the second half of the century. Some, such as Birmingham, Sheffield, and Southampton, were sponsored by one benefactor; others, notably Bristol and Leeds, were the creation of city guilds, and yet others, for example Liverpool, were the products of citywide effort. All began their existence poor, received their income from a combination of benefactors and student fees, and eventually responded to local demands for a higher education that would fit students for careers in local industry. Their founders' wishes often guaranteed a place for the traditional subjects in the curriculum. Despite fears that they would become purely technical colleges (another peculiarly British anxiety that did not feature in Continental or American education), new standards for the education of schoolteachers introduced late in the century guaranteed their arts faculties, which taught subjects such as literature, languages, and HISTORY, a steady flow of students.

Most of the students at these new universities were middle class, and this remained the case until well into the twentieth century. As universal PRIMARY EDUCATION for the working class was not instituted until 1870, the demand for higher education from this group was severely limited and was met in a fairly satisfactory way by the MECHANICS' INSTITUTES and university extension lectures, which catered to the needs of the working student. Thus, the real beneficiaries of the provincial university colleges were the middle classes, many of whom were moving into the new careers that appeared later in the century—engineering, the CIVIL SERVICE, and teaching in the new state schools. The other great beneficiaries were women. London University began admitting women in 1878, Owens College in 1883. After Owens, no civic college excluded women, who took an increasing part in civic college life as the century progressed. The colleges were largely nonresidential, which pleased middle-class parents who preferred their unmarried daughters to live at home.

THE ANCIENT UNIVERSITIES EVOLVE

The Oxbridge universities underwent changes that by mid-century allowed them to reassert their dominant position. Beginning in 1850 a succession of Royal Commissions reviewed the organization and finances of the ancient universities, removing archaic restrictions and diverting funds towards the teaching of new subjects. Sciences and such new subjects as History, POLITICAL ECONOMY, and English were added to the traditional curriculum. In 1871 religious tests were at last abolished, although it must be said that the universities continued to reflect a primarily Anglican stance. A change took place in the teaching staff, who became more professional and increasingly dedicated to both the intellectual and moral welfare of their students. The historian of Cambridge, Sheldon Rothblatt, has called this transformation "the revolution of the dons"—certainly it marked the evolution of a profession that was completed in the early 1880s when college fellows were allowed to marry, and promising young scholars could consider university teaching as a lifetime career. The new dons, influenced by such thinkers as THOMAS ARNOLD, took their role seriously as mentors to future leaders of the empire. In this period Balliol College, Oxford, in particular emerged as a nursery of statesmen and prime ministers under its master, BENJAMIN JOWETT. Balliol graduates included WILLIAM GLADSTONE, Herbert Asquith, Alfred Milner, and Lord Curzon. It has been estimated that Oxford approximately doubled the size of its student body in the nineteenth century. The ancient universities were lively and vital places to be in this period, offering a living and learning environment that was the envy of the poorer urban universities and their students.

The traditional subjects remained strong throughout the century, sustained by the belief that a classical education (or, at Cambridge, a mathematical one) cultivated the intellectual and moral faculties so that its possessor could turn his hand to any work in future life. Proponents of a liberal education believed that it was unnecessary for the universities to prepare their students for a particular career because the training they received in classics or mathematics gave them the breadth of character and flexibility of mind to master any future challenge. This concept of liberal education sat uneasily with more utilitarian ideas and failed to provide a rationale for such subjects as engineering and industrial chemistry that had become accepted university subjects by the end of the century. The university colleges, often staffed by Oxford and Cambridge graduates, suffered greatly from the tension induced by their desire to live up to the ancient universities' standard of liberal education and the increasing (and reasonable) demands of their home towns to devote their resources to studies useful to local industry. Fortunately for their survival and for British industry, scientific research, always strong in the civic universities, gained widespread respect and acceptance as the century progressed.

THE WOMAN QUESTION

With improvements in secondary education and the need for unmarried women to seek employment, demands for women's colleges grew throughout the century. Not only feminists but also men and women with more traditional views believed that education could be beneficial to women, although there were arguments about the permitted curriculum and the advisability of women attempting examinations. The first colleges for women were Queen's College and Bedford College in London, both founded in the late 1840s. Queen's aimed to improve the education of GOVERNESSES, then a pitifully insecure and ill-paid profession which many unmarried middle class women were forced by circumstance to pursue. The first Cambridge college for women, Girton, was founded in 1869. Its first head, Emily Davies (1830–1921), believed firmly in equal treatment of men and women in education and insisted her students complete the full degree course and sit the same examinations as men, although degrees remained closed to them. Newnham College, under the headship of Anne Jemima Clough, allowed women to take a partial course and avoid examinations, which were doubly difficult for women as they featured subjects such as

Greek that they were unlikely to have studied at school. Davies's first students did well and impressed the university with their ability, earning respect if not degrees. Oxford founded Lady Margaret Hall and Somerville College in 1879. The women's colleges drew students from all over the country and one of their earliest tasks was to convince parents that they offered a homelike environment to their students, providing adequate supervision and wholesome recreation. Generally poor but always respectable, the women's colleges set a standard for spartan domesticity that would be the model for women's residential education well into the next century.

By the 1880s, although their numbers were still small, women were fairly well integrated into the university system, although Oxford and Cambridge still declined to grant them degrees. Established professions proved the most resistant to female participation. In 1874, Sophia Jex-Blake became both the founder and one of the first students of the London School of Medicine for Women after she and several other women had been refused medical degrees by Edinburgh University. Medical education was the highest professional hurdle for women because of its perceived indecency, especially in the study of anatomy and the indelicacy of examining patients. Many of the early women practitioners distinguished themselves in the care of women and children.

The London and provincial colleges were at the outset empowered to teach but not to award degrees. Unlike the small colleges that proliferated in the United States and its territories, the British institutions were unable to certify the competence of their own graduates. Small colleges were tied to preparing candidates for the University of London degree examinations. This guaranteed a minimum and uniform standard and also prevented college teaching from veering too sharply toward the utilitarian, which the elite universities continued to associate with crass materialism. From the colleges' point of view, the London examination imposed a rigid curriculum on them that was often out of touch with the needs of the communities they served. In a study of federalism (colleges for teaching and a central examining body to certify the result), Rothblatt has suggested that this uneasy compromise represented the first steps toward coping with the foreign concept of pluralism, or the keeping of a balance between the idea of a liberal education for the cultivation of values and the increasing demand for practical and vocational education at university level. The federal system, based on the Cambridge model, combined the virtues of the college—where pupils worked and often lived in close proximity with their teachers, receiving both an academic and a moral education—with those of the university, which conducted examinations of an impartial and uniform standard and also provided the resources for research. The success of the University of London allowed new colleges to be founded without awakening the British fear of low standards, a problem that simply did not arise in the United States where the state exercised no control over college foundation and where the market determined success or failure.

THE QUESTION OF DEGREES

Inevitably the local colleges outgrew the dependent position in which the London degree examination had placed them. By the 1870s, Owens College was agitating for the right to confer its own degrees. The compromise of 1880 that allowed them to do so created a federation of the colleges of Manchester, Leeds, and Liverpool, known as the Victoria University. This compromise neatly expressed the government's respect for the maturing colleges and its desire to uphold standards by keeping degrees separate from local interest. The civic colleges had been a success and boasted strong departments that commanded international respect, for example the departments of chemistry under Henry Roscoe and history under T. F. Tout at Manchester. Tout's success proved that the Victoria University and its followers could excel in the humanities as well as in the sciences.

In both ancient and modern universities, the late nineteenth century was characterized by acceptance of original research as part of the modern university's function. This idea arose partly from advances in scholarship in all disciplines and partly from the fear that continental powers, most notably Germany, were surpassing Britain in science and technology. Although scientific and technical colleges had existed in Britain before this period, most of them had low status and only gained a foothold at university level when they joined forces with the civic universities and colleges. In London, Imperial College evolved out of the Government School of Mines (1831) to become a powerful center for scientific teaching and research. In the 1880s, the government offered a small grant to the struggling university colleges, and from this modest beginning grew the system of state funding that was to prove so useful for the expensive new scientific disciplines (and so irksome for university independence in the next century).

The nineteenth century also saw great developments in university education outside England. In Scotland, whose ancient universities possessed a strong independent tradition of their own, financial and curricular reforms brought them more into line with the needs of the rising Scottish middle class. Toward the end of the century, when the British civil services were opened to competitive examination, Scottish candidates found themselves at a disadvantage, for the examinations assumed a liberal education of the kind offered by the two ancient English universities. Curricular reform ironed out the differences in university preparation at the cost of some loss of the distinctive character of Scottish education, but there is little doubt that these changes were the will of Scottish parents and students, who recognized that the future lay in a certain amount of cultural integration with England. Late in the century, and after much debate, the Scottish universities admitted women to both study and degrees. Although the middle classes represented the largest part of the Scottish student body, there is evidence that Scotland admitted more students from the lower-middle and skilled working class than did the English universities in this period.

The situation in Ireland was more complex. Sectarian distrust pervaded the universities as it did every other level of society, leading the Roman Catholics to shun Trinity College, Dublin. Three new colleges were founded in 1849 with the idea of placating the Roman Catholic middle class, but these were distrusted by Catholics, who preferred the predominantly theological college at Maynooth. The Queen's Colleges at Cork, Galway, and Belfast were intended as nondenominational, but the first two faltered for lack of interest and only Belfast thrived. It became identified with the Protestants of the North, while University College in Dublin (1854) became the Catholic University of the South. Both Irish and Scottish university development was observed and debated by education reformers in London, and their experiences remained central to debates concerning university expansion in England throughout the second half of the century.

The Welsh universities movement came comparatively late and was influenced by both the Queen's Colleges in Ireland and the Victoria University in the north of England. Colleges were founded at Aberystwyth in 1872 and in the 1880s in Cardiff and Bangor. Initially they presented students for the London external examinations; after 1893 they were chartered as the University of Wales, with the right to award degrees. These Welsh colleges were small—in 1893 their combined student body was under 700—but they represented the beginning of a university system for a region that valued its own culture as well as the place of its own language and traditions within Great Britain.

By the end of the nineteenth century, then, British universities had undergone a thorough transformation and acquired many of the characteristics the twentieth century was to take for granted. On the one hand they were dedicated to teaching, character formation, and pastoral care; on the other they were centers of research in which original work was being carried out by teaching staff and advanced students in a dazzling variety of subjects. As was inevitable in a system that evolved piecemeal, there were inbuilt problems that would take a hundred years or more to solve. These concerned the role of both the state and industry in financing (and, by implication, controlling) academic institutions of higher learning; the ideals of a liberal, residential education so beautifully embodied by the ancient universities and so painfully out of reach of the new ones; and the place of working-class students in a system so exactly tailored to serving the needs of the middle class.

Certain features of the Victorian era universities disappeared after 1900, when the city of Birmingham obtained a charter for the University of Birmingham and the Victoria University broke up into the universities of Manchester, Leeds, and Liverpool. There never was another federal university in England. Other innovations came to flourish, with the proportion of women students increasing substantially and, although Oxford and Cambridge were the last to grant them full participation, they made great gains at the other universities. Finally, the size of the university system increased and the new universities became central to the enormous cultural confidence of the provincial towns in this era.

It would be a mistake to exaggerate the availability of higher education at the end of the nineteenth century. If we say that the percentage of 20- to 24-year-olds at university doubled between 1861 and 1901, this gives an idea of the expansion that had taken place, but the 1901 figures account for no more than 0.8% of that age group in the general population. For most people, especially for the working class, the changes brought about during the Victorian period represented only hopeful beginnings, not a finished system of higher education. In other ways, however, notably in the development of research; in setting examination standards respected and aspired to throughout the empire; and in producing talented graduates from the statesmen of Balliol to the schoolteachers of the civic universities, the British universities had earned high esteem and a place at the table

when the educational democratization of the twentieth century began.

See also EDUCATION OF WOMEN.

FURTHER READING

Anderson, R. D. *Education and Opportunity in Victorian Scotland.* Oxford: Clarendon Press, 1983.

Bender, Thomas, ed. *The University and the City: From Medieval Origins to the Present.* New York: Oxford University Press, 1988.

Dyhouse, Carol. *No Distinction of Sex? Women in British Universities, 1870–1939.* London: University College London Press, 1995.

Engel, A. J. *From Clergyman to Don: The Rise of the Academic Profession in Nineteenth-Century Oxford.* Oxford: Clarendon Press, 1983.

Jones, David R. *The Origins of Civic Universities: Manchester, Leeds & Liverpool.* London: Routledge, 1988.

McWilliams-Tullberg, Rita. *Women at Cambridge.* Revised ed. Cambridge: Cambridge University Press, 1998.

Rothblatt, Sheldon. *The Revolution of the Dons: Cambridge and Society in Victorian England.* Cambridge: Cambridge University Press, 1981.

Sanderson, Michael. *Education, Economic Change and Society in England, 1780–1870.* London: Macmillan, 1983.

Sanderson, Michael. *The Universities and British Industry 1850–1970.* London: Routledge and Kegan Paul, 1972.

Sanderson, Michael, ed. *The Universities in the Nineteenth Century.* London: Routledge & Kegan Paul, 1975.

Williams, J. Gwynn. *The University Movement in Wales.* Cardiff: University of Wales Press, 1993.

ELIZABETH J. MORSE

URBANIZATION

Through urbanization, the Victorians witnessed a cultural revolution unlike any that had come before. The shift in the late eighteenth century from an agrarian to an industrial society, of which the foundation lay in the emergence of modern capitalism, resulted in the transformation of physical space within and outside the nation's borders. As cities grew to meet the needs of industry and workers migrated to developing urban centers, the Victorian psyche evolved to embody the attributes of modernity and the creation of a newly urban consciousness.

Changing demographics serve to highlight the significance of the trend toward urbanization during the course of the nineteenth century. In 1837, the year QUEEN VICTORIA ascended to the throne, only five places in England and Wales had populations numbering more than 100,000; there were 23 in 1891. The POPULATION of LONDON grew from just under 2 million to over 4 million in the half-century between 1841 and 1891, and by the end of the century close to one-third of the population lived in London and other cities. The great provincial centers of England grew by leaps and bounds just prior to Victoria's ascension, with the populations of MANCHESTER, Leeds, Bradford, Birmingham, Liverpool, and Sheffield each increasing by 40% or more during the 1820s, and continuing to grow (albeit somewhat more slowly) during subsequent decades. The population of Glasgow grew from 5.1% of the total population of Scotland in 1801 to 19.4% 90 years later. Similarly, the relationship between the metropolis and the frontier in the British territories meant that the major cities in CANADA and AUSTRALIA AND NEW ZEALAND increased significantly in population during the mid- to late nineteenth century. In the latter case alone, for example, the population of Sydney, only 54,000 in 1851, numbered 383,000 by 1891; and Melbourne's population grew even more dramatically, from 23,000 in the early 1840s to almost half a million by the early 1890s. In the UNITED STATES, the major midwestern cities grew by 60% to 80% at minimum; from 1880 to 1890 Chicago's population doubled, while that of the Twin Cities, Minneapolis and St. Paul tripled. These figures alone can convey some sense of the dramatic changes to the nature of urban life during the Victorian period.

THE EFFECTS OF URBANIZATION UPON THE CITY

Clearly, to accommodate these increasing numbers of people, Victorian cities had to grow geographically as well. The very boundaries of the city were extended outwards at an unprecedented rate throughout the century. As Asa Briggs notes in his study *Victorian Cities*, citing a contemporary commentator, "The visitor to Birmingham could 'expect to find a street of houses in the autumn where he saw his horse at grass in the spring.'" Yet expansion on the edges of the city—the transformations of fields and open land into suburban and urban streets lined with residences and workplaces—initially resulted in a decline in population at the center. The number of inhabitants in London first began to decrease in the first decade of the nineteenth century, and many of the central wards of Liverpool, Birmingham, Leeds, and Bradford lost population as houses were torn down to make way for FACTORIES, warehouses, shops, and office buildings. Likewise, the RAILWAY boom of the 1830s and 1840s meant that large portions of formerly residential urban areas were cleared for tracks and yards. "A Country Architect," writing in *Architect* in 1873,

This illustration of the English city of Sheffield shows the extent of urbanization in the mid-nineteenth century.

argued that "A line of railway passing through a vast city such as London causes incalculable evil: it not only defaces existing thoroughfares, but renders the creation of good new ones impracticable for all time." As a result, nineteenth-century architects and urban planners seized the opportunity to create a new and iconic image of urban space. In the case of London, for instance, as the metropolis expanded away from the center, new axes such as Regent Street and Marylebone Road emerged, reorienting the city toward the burgeoning West End. Traffic patterns shifted accordingly; in 1838 the Select Committee on Metropolitan Improvements focused their energies on developing a new road network that would connect the City with Westminster and the West End in an effort to unify the metropolis. As Donald Olsen notes, many of the major thoroughfares in London today, such as Charing Cross Road, Shaftesbury Avenue, Holborn Viaduct, and the Thames Embankment, resulted from the Victorian enthusiasm for alleviating traffic congestion in the city. At the same time, new forms of TRANSPORTATION developed; in particular, the OMNIBUS and the hansom CAB allowed those without private carriages to travel trough the city with greater ease. And public parks, GARDENS, and other open spaces were created in an attempt to provide an ever greater number of urban denizens with opportunities for outdoor recreation.

Such rapid transformation of the urban landscape had its downside, however. Nineteenth-century cities found themselves plagued with modern societal ills: unsanitary living and working conditions, overcrowding, and the creation of new SLUMS that differed in character from neighborhoods that had historically served as low-income housing. In Asa Briggs's account of these "new slums," some of the most striking changes could be seen in once-elegant districts like the Saltmarket in Glasgow and formerly isolated villages that were newly absorbed into neighboring cities; Burmantofts and Quarry Hill, both once seen as pleasant locales outside Leeds, were soon drawn into its "insalubrious" atmosphere, and as a Bradford historian noted in 1886, the district of Horton had once been "a distinct place divided from the town by a long stretch of green fields." Slums were liable to be demolished with little or no regard for residents; in a study of London published in the 1840s, Charles Knight lamented, "We occasionally sweep away the wretched dens, hidden in back courts and alleys, where the poor are smothered: but far too rarely do we make provision for them." Overcrowding, particularly in working-class districts, remained a problem throughout the period; in 1884 there were sections

of Liverpool with 1,200 persons to the acre. Such conditions resulted in a strong push toward reform: the "Sanitary Idea" galvanized public interest in the 1840s, and official inquiries into living conditions amongst the poor in the 1860 and 1870s resulted in a series of Public Health acts that finally brought the conditions of urban districts under legislative control. The national death rate began to fall in the late 1870s, and although infant mortality rates remained relatively high until the end of the period—approximately 150 per 1,000 live births—the recognition of the significance of sanitary reform had wide-reaching effects. As the registrar-general observed in 1871, "The discovery of the laws of public health, the determination of the conditions of cleanliness, manners, water supply, food, exercise, isolation, medicine, most favorable to life in one city, in one country, is a boon to every city, to every country, for all can profit by the experience."

LONDON BECOMES A METROPOLIS

London crystallized both the positive and negative characteristics of the new metropolitan way of life in the Victorian era. THOMAS CARLYLE (1795–1881) wrote of "the fret and agitation of this Babylon," and JOHN RUSKIN (1819–1900) described "the great foul city of London" as "rattling, growling, smoking, stinking." Others, like Arthur Sherwell, saw London as a "great, hungry sea, which flows on and on, filling up every creek, and then overspreads its borders, flooding the plains beyond." Yet the metropolis exerted a powerful pull on the population of the nation. In CHARLES DICKENS's novel *Dombey and Son*, which was published serially from 1844 to 1846, Harriet Carker observes the numbers of people migrating toward the great metropolis:

> She often looked with compassion, at such a time, upon the stragglers who came wandering into London, by the great highway hard by, and who, footsore and weary, and gazing fearfully at the huge town before them, as if foreboding that their misery there would be but as a drop of water in the sea, or as a grain of sea-sand on the shore, went shrinking on [. . .] Day after day, such travelers crept past, but always, as she thought, in one direction—always towards the town. Swallowed up in one phase or other of its immensity, towards which they seemed impelled by a desperate fascination, they never returned. Food for the hospitals, the churchyards, the prisons, the river, fever, madness, vice, and death—they passed on to the monster, roaring in the distance, and were lost.

In the early Victorian period, London had declined in importance in comparison with the industrial cities of the north, but as the century progressed, the metropolis increasingly came to symbolize modern commercial interests, both domestic and international. Many extolled the virtues of London's role as a center of distribution and consumption; from the great DEPARTMENT STORES of the West End to the itinerant "costermongers," or street-sellers of fish and produce, described by HENRY MAYHEW in his *London Labour and the London Poor* (originally written as a series of articles for the *Morning Chronicle* in 1849 to 1850 and eventually published as part of a four-volume report in 1861 to 1862), seemingly anything and everything could be found for sale in London. The GREAT EXHIBITION OF 1851, held in the Crystal Palace in Hyde Park, celebrated Great Britain's role as a world power in the networks of international production. But there were drawbacks to this new culture of consumption; these were figured spatially through the distinction between the West End, a site of pleasure, leisure, and spectacle, and the East End, where workers toiled long hours in sweatshop conditions with little attention from the outside world. As Raymond Williams notes, the East End of London in effect became its own industrial city in the Victorian era, and social critics of the period studied the detrimental effects of industrial development of the urban masses living in tenements in the slums. Mayhew and others used their journalistic writings to explore and expose the living and working conditions of the East End in the 1850s and 1860s, and these texts were followed by a spate of writings in the following decades: John Hollingshead's *Ragged London in 1861*, James Greenwood's *A Night in a Workhouse* (1866) and *The Wilds of London* (1874), George Sims's *How the Poor Live* (1883), Andrew Mearns's *The Bitter Cry of Outcast London* (1883), and Arthur Morrison's *Tales of Mean Streets* (1894). Social investigators like CHARLES BOOTH (1840–1916) took up this cause in the 1890s; Booth's 17-volume work, *Life and Labour of the People of London* (1889–1903), mapped and categorized the population of the metropolis according to the modern sociological ideal of knowledge and vision of unexplored territory. Booth observed, "It is not in country but in town that 'terra incognita' needs to be written on our social map. In the country the machinery of human life is plainly to be seen and easily recognized: personal relations bind the whole together. The equipoise on which existing order rests, whether satisfactory or not, is palpable and evident. It is far otherwise with cities, where as to these questions we live in darkness, with doubting hearts and ignorant unnecessary fears." Other texts, such as SALVATION ARMY General William Booth's *In Darkest England and the Way Out* (1890), used the contrast between Stanley's "darkest Africa" and the spaces of "darkest London" to expose the sufferings of the urban poor, explicitly likening the project of urban MISSIONARY work to Britain's imperial efforts to colonize and control the globe. The scientist THOMAS HENRY HUXLEY (1825–1895) echoed this parallel in his comment that the Polynesian "savage," in his "primitive condition," was "not half so savage, so unclean, so irreclaimable as the tenant of a tenement in an East London slum." The sense of a vast chasm between the cultures of East and West, whether within London or beyond England's borders, suggests the connections between urbanization, INDUSTRIALIZATION, and IMPERIALISM, and underscores a sense of ignorance about the lives of others that came to characterize much of the differences within and between urban populations in the nineteenth century.

THE EXPANSION OF MANCHESTER

Manchester was seen as the second of England's "great cities" in the nineteenth century. It was officially incorporated as a town in 1838, but had long been recognized as an industrial and commercial capital, owing in large part to the explosion of the COTTON INDUSTRY in the late eighteenth century. The cotton mills provided the "din of machinery" that visitors and residents associated with economic PROGRESS on a grand scale. As *Chambers' Edinburgh Journal* noted in 1858, "Manchester streets may be irregular, and its trading inscriptions pretentious, its smoke may be dense, and its mud ultra-muddy, but not any or all of these things can prevent the image of a great city rising before us as the very symbol of civilization, foremost in the march of improvement, a grand incarnation of progress." However, writers did not fail to observe the mingling of squalor and wealth in a city that symbolized the inexorable nature of modern industrial growth. Alexis de Tocqueville thus described the city following his visit in 1835: "From this foul drain the greatest stream of human industry flows out to fertilize the whole world. From this filthy sewer pure gold flows. Here humanity attains its most complete development and its most brutish; here civilization works its miracles, and civilized man is turned back almost into a savage." Victorian cities such as Manchester grew according to economic demand, only afterward acquiring a social and political infrastructure and the institutions of culture. Marking it as a city ahead of its time, Manchester could boast the first national EXHIBITION of art from private collections, the first free LIBRARY in a city of its size, the first public parks in a major provincial city, the first railroad station in the world. As Josef Konvitz notes in his analysis of city-building in the nineteenth century, however, Manchester's greatest contribution was ideological, emphasizing the underpinnings of modern capitalism: "that active competition fostered the strength of the middle class; that such competition and the middle class were, in the long run, in the workers' interest; and that international trade and competition were good for the world." Yet not all nineteenth-century observers saw economic competition as beneficial to urban life; Henry Colman, an American visiting Manchester during this period, saw there only "Wretched, defrauded, oppressed, crushed human nature, lying in bleeding fragments all over the face of society . . . exhibitions of the most disgusting and loathsome forms of destitution, and utter vice and profligacy," and commented, "Every day I thank Heaven that I am not a poor man with a family in England." Indeed, EDWIN CHADWICK's *Report on the Sanitary Condition of the Labouring Population of Great Britain* (1842) and the Blue Books and other reports of the 1840s had demonstrated that Manchester was one of the most unhealthy cities in the country, where the average age of death for gentry and PROFESSIONAL persons was 38, for tradesmen and their families 20, and for mechanics and laborers 17, and where numbers of homeless children lived in extreme POVERTY. Friedrich Engels's *The Condition of the Working Class in England*, published in Germany in 1845 and first translated into English in 1892, gave an explicit account of the sufferings of the working population of Manchester housed in overcrowded dwellings filling ludicrously unplanned urban streets:

> Anyone who has never visited these courts and alleys [behind Long Millgate Street in the Old Town] can have no idea of the fantastic way in which the houses have been packed together in disorderly confusion in impudent defiance of all reasonable principles of town planning. . . . In the houses one seldom sees a wooden or a stone floor, while the doors and windows are nearly always broken and badly fitting. And the dirt! Everywhere one sees heaps of refuse, garbage, and filth. There are stagnant pools instead of gutters and the stench alone is so overpowering that no human being, even partially civilized, would find it bearable to live in such a district.

For Engels, as was the case for social investigators in London later in the century, Manchester's slums symbolized the worst effects of urbanization, which threatened to dehumanize the denizens of the city, stripping them of the most basic attributes of "civilization." With similar concerns in mind, the "CONDITION OF ENGLAND" novelists of the 1840s used their fictions to expose the troubling aspects of urbaniza-

tion, with particular attention to mill and factory labor: among these were FRANCES TROLLOPE's *Michael Armstrong* (1840), Charlotte Elizabeth Tonna's *Helen Fleetwood* (1841), BENJAMIN DISRAELI's *Coningsby* (1844) and *Sybil* (1845), ELIZABETH GASKELL's *Mary Barton* (1848) and *North and South* (1855), and Charles Dickens's critique of UTILITARIANISM, *Hard Times* (1854). Yet the troubling conditions of life for the working classes of Manchester had not gone unnoticed even before the publication of these widely read accounts; reform efforts were already underway in the late 1830s, and legislation such as the Borough Police Act (1844) and the Sanitary Improvement Act (1845) underscored the importance of local interest in again placing Manchester at the forefront of such efforts in cities across the country. The visit of Queen Victoria in 1851 marked a significant point in Manchester's history, as increasing prosperity and "respectability" resulted in a city that appeared far more ordered than it had during the preceding turbulent decades. The queen observed, "The streets were immensely full, and the cheering and enthusiasm most gratifying. The order and good behavior of the people, who were not placed behind any barriers, were the most complete we have seen in our many progressions through capitals and cities—London, Glasgow, Dublin, Edinburgh, etc.—for there never was a running crowd." In subsequent decades, Manchester ceased to embody controversy and gradually developed a civic and cultural infrastructure that suited its needs.

URBAN EXPANSION ACROSS GREAT BRITAIN

Other industrial cities experienced similar changes over the course of the century. The woolen and worsted towns of Leeds and Bradford grew significantly during the early Victorian period, and shared with Manchester many aspects of urbanization. As merchants and manufacturers grew wealthy from commerce, the divide between the rich and the poor became especially stark. In Leeds, for example, the working-class districts were described as crowded and unhealthy, while the prosperous districts of Headingley and Roundhay were filled with opulent villas. With its noxious canal, Bradford was called "the dirtiest, filthiest and worst regulated town in the Kingdom." Likewise, the metal towns of Birmingham and Sheffield embodied the best and the worst of urbanization; Léon Faucher commented that "Sheffield is the only city in England which presents as gloomy an appearance as Leeds," and Carlyle memorably described his view of early nineteenth-century Birmingham thus: "Torrents of thick smoke, with ever and anon a burst of dingy flame . . . the clank of innumerable steam engines, the rumbling of cars and vans, and the hum of men interrupted by the sharper rattle of some canal-boat loading or disloading . . . the whole is not without its attractions, as well as repulsions." Yet these provincial centers also strove to reflect what Asa Briggs has termed "civic pride," epitomized by the organization of LOCAL GOVERNMENT. The effort in Leeds to build a new Town Hall in the 1850s foundered in labor controversies, but on its completion was praised by the queen as a symbol of the "active industry and enterprising spirit" of the town. Birmingham, even more than Leeds, came to be seen as "the best-governed city in the world" by the late 1870s, owing in large parts to its efforts at social, political, and economic unity. Birmingham differed from other provincial cities as well in its range of trade occupations, its use of small workshops, its skilled labor force, and the greater degree of social mobility on the part of its population.

The provincial cities had much to offer the nation in their innovative approaches to industry, government, and reform, but with the increasingly strong influence of London on national identity in the late nineteenth century, these cities were not always recognized for their important contributions to modern British culture. The journalist T. Wemyss Reid lamented in 1888:

> The life of a provincial city presents no charms to the cultivated but superficial observer. Biography has nothing to say of the men who have had most to do with the building up of the fortunes of Birmingham and Manchester, of Liverpool and Leeds. The local reputation must acquire the stamp of metropolitan approbation before it is thought worthy of notice [. . .] Those who are diligent in observing and investigating the manners and customs of some tribe in the heart of Africa, or of the inhabitants of some island in the South Seas, are altogether ignorant of what is passing at their own doors, under their own eyes, in towns which, although they cannot boast of the historic glories of the great capitals of Europe, are even now superior to them in wealth and population, and are laying broad and deep the foundations of a future destiny which may vie in interest and importance with that of some of the most famous cities of the ancient world.

The sense that England's cities embodied both the spirit of the present and the promise of the future was at the heart of the trend toward urbanization during the Victorian period. Urbanization continued beyond the end of Victoria's reign in 1901, but the many of the cultural transformations wrought in the twentieth century—particularly the continued dual focus on industrial and technological innovation tempered by social reform—were founded on principles of urban development in the nineteenth century.

See also CONDITION OF ENGLAND QUESTION; FACTORIES; INDUSTRIALIZATION; LONDON; MANCHESTER; SANITATION; SLUMS; TRANSPORTATION.

FURTHER READING

Arnold, Dana. *Re-presenting the Metropolis: Architecture, Urban Experience and Social Life in London 1800–1840.* Aldershot, Hants, England: Ashgate, 2000.

Bairoch, Paul. *Cities and Economic Development: From the Dawn of History to the Present.* Translated by Christopher Braider. Chicago: University of Chicago Press, 1988.

Barth, Gunther. *City People: The Rise of Modern City Culture in Nineteenth-Century America.* New York and Oxford: Oxford University Press, 1980.

Briggs, Asa. *Victorian Cities.* 1963. New York and Evanston: Harper Colophon Books, 1970.

Cannadine, David, and David Reeder, eds. *Exploring the Urban Past: Essays in Urban History by H. J. Dyos.* Cambridge: Cambridge University Press, 1982.

Hamer, David. *New Towns in the New World: Images and Perceptions of the Nineteenth-Century Urban Frontier.* New York: Columbia University Press, 1990.

Konvitz, Josef W. *The Urban Millennium: The City-Building Process from the Early Middle Ages to the Present.* Carbondale, Ill.: Southern Illinois University Press, 1985.

Lees, Andrew. *Cities Perceived: Urban Society in European and American Thought, 1820–1940.* New York: Columbia University Press, 1985.

Nead, Lynda. *Victorian Babylon: People, Streets and Images in Nineteenth-Century London.* New Haven, CT: Yale University Press, 2000.

Olsen, Donald J. *The Growth of Victorian London.* New York: Holmes & Meier Publishers, 1976.

Schneer, Jonathan. *London 1900: The Imperial Metropolis.* New Haven and London: Yale University Press, 1999.

White, Dana F. *The Urbanists, 1865–1915.* New York: Greenwood Press, 1989.

Williams, Raymond. *The Country and the City.* New York: Oxford University Press, 1973.

LISE SHAPIRO SANDERS

UTILITARIANISM

Utilitarianism was one of the chief philosophies and practical avenues for public action in the Victorian period. It galvanized a whole generation to seek sociopolitical reforms, helping to transform British government from a disorganized, nepotistic, old-boy's network into an entity founded on the science of governing. Encouraging the establishment of the civil service and the practice of having legislative agendas, utilitarianism was in part responsible for turning governance from an avocation into a profession. The three major utilitarian philosophers of the Victorian period are JEREMY BENTHAM (1748–1832), JOHN STUART MILL (1806–1873), and HENRY SIDGWICK (1838–1900).

Bentham's leading adherent and father of John Stuart, James Mill (1773–1836), authored a treatise on associationist utilitarianism entitled *Analysis of the Phenomena of the Human Mind* (1829). He is known for being the organizer of Bentham's followers (who included David Ricardo and Joseph Hume). Bentham himself refers to David Hume, Helvetius, David Hartley, and especially Joseph Priestley, as the predecessors who influenced him in his systematization of utilitarianism.

Though Bentham died shortly before the beginning of the Victorian period, his writings were so dominant that they helped to establish utilitarianism as a formidable set of principles that influenced intellectual figures throughout the coming era. As Matti Häyry suggests, there are three principles central to Bentham's system: the greatest happiness principle, the hedonistic principle, and the principle of impartiality. Reading Joseph Priestley's *Treatise on Government*, Bentham was struck by the phrase "the greatest happiness of the greatest number." In *An Introduction to the Principles of Morals and Legislation* (1789), Bentham wrote the famous lines based upon this concept: "Nature has placed mankind under the governance of two sovereign masters, *pain* and *pleasure*. . . . On the one hand, the standard of right and wrong, on the other the chain of causes and effects, are fastened to their throne. They govern us in all we do, in all we say, in all we think." Believing that humans were motivated by self-interest—the urge to seek pleasure and avoid pain—utilitarians scientifically analyzed these two "sovereign masters."

The Greatest Happiness . . .

To Bentham the greatest quantity of happiness could be discovered through the scientific principles of induction and observation, as he notes in his "Article on Utilitarianism" (1829). In "Bentham" (1838), John Stuart Mill laid out Bentham's meticulous approach. "Bentham's method," he says, is one "of detail; of treating wholes by separating them into their parts, abstractions by resolving them into Things—classes and generalities by distinguishing them into the individuals of which they are made up; and breaking every question into pieces." Mill adds that Bentham's intellectual power came from his consistently practiced belief that "error lurks in generalities: . . . that abstractions are not realities per se, . . . and that the only practical mode of dealing with them is to trace them back to the facts."

This "just the facts" approach could lead to absurd forms of inhumanity, as CHARLES DICKENS so famously demonstrated through the characters of Mr. Gradgrind and McChoakumchild in his novel *Hard Times* (1854). Indeed, Bentham's factual system for studying the greatest happiness was incorporated into a simplistic mathematical formula called the "felicific calculus," which would seem laughably Dickensian if it had not been taken so seriously by the utilitarians. As Bentham remarks in his "Article on Utilitarianism," happiness is "a subject-matter of account and calculation, of profit and loss, just as money itself is." According to this formula, the utilitarian quantified the propinquity (nearness), intensity, purity, and degree of pleasure and pain. For example, in regard to the problem of crime, Victorian utilitarians might suggest measuring what level of intensity and duration of a particular punishment might in all probability produce the most consistent rehabilitation in the offender.

. . . to the Greatest Number

The idea of "the greatest number" was as important to Bentham as the notion of "the greatest pleasure." As Häyry points out, the principle of impartiality "requires that the pleasures and pains of all sentient beings ought to be taken equally into account when decisions are made." Interested in how the utilitarian philosopher could study human self-interest, Bentham wanted to train humans as sociopolitical groups to seek the good of the majority as the best means through which to achieve self-interest or hedonism for the whole. As P. J. Kelly explains, to Bentham, by scientifically "providing an account of the way individuals act, the legislator is able to determine the encouragements and punishments needed to bring" individual actions "into conformity with the requirements of duty" to the needs of the group.

In the "Principles of the Civil Code," Bentham argued that legislative principles were scientifically justified "If they may be employed by the legislator, as the foundation of his labours, with less inconvenience than any others." Focused on bringing the greatest happiness to the sociopolitical group, Bentham battled the common law, believing that, with the guidance of utilitarian philosophers, government officials could best decide what was most conducive to the happiness of society. Nancy L. Rosenblum writes that progress, according to Bentham, could only come about when legislation became "established as an ordinary and not extraordinary act," something that could be expected on a regular basis, not just in times of crisis.

UTILITARIANISM IN ACTION

The term *utilitarianism* comes from what Bentham referred to as the key question to be asked of all ideas, principles, and laws: What happiness, benefit, or usefulness does it provide? This question encapsulates J. S. Mill's reasons for believing Bentham to be one of the "two great seminal minds" in nineteenth-century England, the other being the poet and radical Samuel Coleridge. In "Bentham," Mill applauds the way his subject interrogated the British Constitution and British law to assess their effective correspondence with the needs of the people. Mill finds that Bentham voiced what a whole generation was feeling but could not articulate—that the government was not working for the greatest happiness of the greatest number. That utilitarian ideas brought about the NEW POOR LAW, the REFORM ACTS, and laws establishing prison and education reforms, as well as establishing the modern CIVIL SERVICE, is a testament to the ways that government changed during the Victorian period under the aegis of utilitarian philosophy.

An agnostic utilitarian and empiricist, James Mill believed that the Romantics placed too much emphasis on feelings. Raising his son as a kind of guinea pig to test utilitarian principles, Mill bred John Stuart to be a child prodigy who, for instance, started learning Greek at age three. Because his utilitarian education gave little room for human emotions or the appreciation of art, the child John was not allowed to read fairy tales or imaginative literature. In his *Autobiography* (1873), J. S. Mill writes about the dehumanizing effects of the utilitarian education that taught him through associations of pleasure and pain, with positive and negative reinforcements such as praise and punishment. These utilitarian educational strategies, he protests, turned him into an unfeeling, reasoning machine who could find no meaning in life.

As a result, Mill felt he had to find a way to invest utilitarian principles with human emotions. To understand how Mill humanized utilitarian principles, it is necessary to return to Bentham, who was not as concerned with the quality of pleasure as he was with measuring its quantity, the "greatest" happiness. Neither did he focus much on measuring the quality of the individual experiencing the pleasure. Likewise, in measuring the pleasure of "the greatest number," Bentham did not take account of the needs of the minority.

As Häyry points out, one of Mill's greatest contributions to classical utilitarianism was that "he amended the utilitarian axiology [criteria by which to judge ethical values] of value by stating that the quality of pleasures and pains should, contrary to Bentham's view, play a definite role in the happiness calculation." In keeping with this idea Mill did not accept, as did Bentham, that each person's pleasure should be viewed as equal. Thus Mill gives utilitarianism greater subtlety and the possibility of acknowledging the infinite range and levels of pleasure as well as the motivations for it. Believing that happiness included sensual and intellectual pleasures, Mill nonetheless asserted that humans have a sense of dignity that motivates them to choose the intellectual over the sensual.

Bentham noted five sanctions—physical, political, moral or popular, religious, and later, benevolence—that induced behavior. In "The Article on Utilitarianism" he said that a motive was "nothing but the fear of some pain, in the event of a certain mode of action which accordingly the will is urged to avoid, or the hope of a certain pleasure which accordingly the will is urged to put the individual in question in a condition to experience." Mill complicates this formula, recognizing the psychological power of what we call peer pressure and arguing that there are two types of motives. On the one hand are those that come from our desire to fulfill the expectations of external sources like God, parents, extended family, and associates, as well as larger venues, including religion, business, and social structures and the humans that represent them.

Mill believes that the internal desire to fulfill one's duty is the more important and authentic type of motive, one indicating the individual's natural unity and resulting desire for the good of all people. This internal sense of duty is produced from childhood onward from a combination of childhood experiences with religion, family, friends, and the feelings developed around them. This sense of duty compelled people not to act against the general happiness.

Mill both humanizes and complicates utilitarian principles by suggesting that individuals experiencing pain and pleasure are not all equal in their capacity for quality of experience. For example, in *Utilitarianism* (1861) he wrote, "It is better to be a human being dissatisfied than a pig satisfied; better to be Socrates dissatisfied than a fool satisfied." Likewise, in contrast to Bentham's statement that the game of "push pin" was more useful than literature, Mill regards the quality of pleasure as crucial. Noting that literature saved his life, Mill writes in the *Autobiography* that it offered him the emotions he needed to carry out his ethical sense of duty to others.

Though Mill insisted that utilitarianism be informed by emotions, he certainly never gave up his belief in scientific impartiality and the empirical method. This is made clear when Thomas Carlyle complains that Mill's supposedly emotional autobiography has the mechanical style of a "steam engine." Likewise, we should not completely discount Bentham's capacity for feeling, for he could write lyrically in a letter to the daughter of John Bowring on June 22, 1830, "Create all the happiness you are able to create; remove all the misery you are able to remove. . . . And for every grain of enjoyment you sow in the bosom of another, you shall find a harvest in your own bosom" leading to "joy in the sanctuary of your soul."

Finally, Mill moves away from the authoritarian implications of Bentham's pronounced belief in legislative power by strongly endorsing individual liberty and privacy as outlined in his essay *On Liberty* (1859). In this essay Mill argues, "the only purpose for which power can be rightfully exercised over any member of a civilized community, against his will, is to prevent harm to others."

PRACTICAL UTILITARIANISM

Henry Sidgwick, professor of philosophy at Cambridge University, focused his utilitarian principals in efforts to professionalize UNIVERSITIES. The changes he sought were wide-ranging and helped to establish the university as we know it today. As Stefan Collini asserts, rather than a generalist, Sidgwick was "one of the new breed of academic specialists." From the 1860s he worked to reform Cambridge by modernizing the curriculum and expanding its areas of interest; he also sought to make sure that university finances were used first and foremost for the purposes of research and teaching. Furthermore, he believed that in order for the professoriate to do its best work it had to be autonomous, especially independent of the influence of religion. An active participant in the administration of the university, Sidgwick also worked to establish Newnham College, the first college for women at Cambridge. Sidgwick's activism went beyond the university, for he served on four royal commissions, showing, as Collini remarks, "his strong sense of the possibility of deploying intellectual authority and expertise to help determine policy." Two of the commissions had to do with educational institutions, whereas the other two focused on finances and taxation in Britain.

As with many Victorian writers, Sidgwick's output was prodigious; he composed many works on education, literature, the history of political institutions, political theory, and philosophy. His most fa-

mous philosophical treatise is *Methods of Ethics* (1874), a defense of classical utilitarianism. In this work, as Häyry explains, Sidgwick argues that "valid moral theories must conform to certain clear and self-evident intuitions which form a coherent whole and which are accepted by all human beings who are capable of combining 'adequate intellectual enlightenment with a serious concern for morality.' " Analyzing what he calls the three most basic human intuitions of justice, prudence, and the universality of goodness alongside the three "methods of ethics"—dogmatic intuitionism, universalistic hedonism, and ethical egoism—Sidgwick compares the premises of these intuitions and methods with those of utilitarianism to show that utilitarianism was the most useful and correct. Nevertheless, he could not be as sanguine about utilitarianism as his earlier compatriots Mill and Bentham. Acknowledging that self-interest was a fragile premise upon which to base the happiness of the group unless there was a God to balance out injustices, Sidgwick admitted that it was scientifically impossible to test the existence of God.

Many Victorians vigorously opposed utilitarianism. Two of the more important complaints were that it did not acknowledge that moral choices were not always and only based upon the consequences of choosing pleasure over pain; and that the mechanistic, mathematical approach to social problems was heartless and immoral, particularly as manifested in the New Poor Law of 1834. Nevertheless, utilitarianism was without doubt one of the most influential philosophic movements of the century.

See also BENTHAM, JEREMY; MILL, JOHN STUART; PHILOSOPHY.

FURTHER READING

Bentham, Jeremy. Deontology *together with* A Table of the Springs of Action *and* The Article on Utilitarianism, edited by Amnon Goldworth. Oxford: Clarendon Press, 1983.
Collini, Stefan. "My Roles and Their Duties: Sidgwick as Philosopher, Professor and Public Moralist." In *Henry Sidgwick: Proceedings of the British Academy,* Vol. 109, 9–49. Oxford: Oxford University Press, 2001.
Häyry, Matti. *Liberal Utilitarianism and Applied Ethics.* London: Routledge, 1994.
Houghton, Walter E. *The Victorian Frame of Mind, 1830–1870.* New Haven: Yale University Press, 1956.
Kelly, P. J. *Utilitarianism and Distributive Justice: Jeremy Bentham and the Civil Law.* Oxford: Clarendon Press, 1990.
Rosenblum. Nancy L. *Bentham's Theory of the Modern State.* Cambridge: Harvard University Press, 1978.

GAIL TURLEY HOUSTON

VACCINATION

Vaccination, the process of administering vaccines—substances that protect from disease—was responsible for a dramatic decline in the spread of infectious disease during the Victorian era. In the eighteenth and nineteenth centuries communicable diseases such as smallpox, chicken pox, scarlet fever, and German measles raged among the populations of England and the rest of Europe. Such diseases were most dangerous to children and others with suppressed immune systems. If one could survive the initial exposure, however, then immunity usually was lifelong.

Infectious disease had been endemic in Europe since at least 500 A.D. Periodic outbreaks, though at times dangerous among vulnerable groups, usually had not been catastrophic among European peoples. Smallpox was a disease unknown in Mexico and Latin America, however, until Hernando Cortés arrived in

1518. By 1521 about one-half of the indigenous population had died from the disease. British travelers introduced smallpox into the aboriginal population of Australia in 1789. By the early 1800s, however, older children and adults increasingly were falling victim to smallpox, and infants were more seriously (often fatally) ill with the disease. No longer did one try to expose one's children to smallpox, as many parents previously had done, in order to confer immunity on them.

For at least 1,000 years before the outburst of virulent infectious disease among Europeans in the eighteenth century, physicians in Asia and the MIDDLE EAST had practiced inoculation. Inoculation—the introduction of a live form of human disease into a healthy patient—appeared to cause a milder form of the illness, which then conferred some immunity on the patient from further infection. In 1721 Lady Mary Wortley Montagu, the wife of the British ambassador to Turkey, sent back to England word of annual inoculations for smallpox—also known as "variolation." On her return to England Lady Mary used her contacts among the medical community and with the English ROYAL FAMILY to promote inoculation.

The medical community, however, was slow to embrace inoculation. Many physicians rightly feared that inoculated persons who were not quarantined would spread smallpox further. Also worrisome was the fact that between 3 and 5 persons of every 100 who were inoculated contracted a serious or even life-threatening version of smallpox.

English farmers had noticed for generations that exposure to the cowpox disease (well known among dairymaids) appeared to protect against smallpox. Faced with severe outbreaks of smallpox in the 1770s, several laypersons removed pus from the lymph nodes of infected cows and applied it to areas of broken skin in humans. The humans thus treated were made immune to smallpox. Edward Jenner (1749–1823), a physician in Gloucestershire, in 1796 used cowpox matter from a dairy worker's arm to apply to an eight-year-old boy, James Phipps. Phipps was protected from smallpox. Jenner published his findings in 1796, calling the cowpox from a human arm *variola vaccinae*.

Jenner's discovery was tested and confirmed in London by eminent medical practitioners. His "humanized" form of cowpox was called a vaccination. His method induced a form of disease in the patient that was milder than that caused through inoculation. Moreover patients vaccinated for smallpox did not spread the disease to others. Within a few years tens of thousands of persons were vaccinated for smallpox. In 1807 the Royal College of Physicians reported that vaccination—although not universally effective—was useful in preventing the infection of individuals and the spreading of smallpox to larger populations.

In 1835 England and Wales became the first areas of Europe to require vaccination against smallpox. Inoculation, on the other hand, fell out of favor with medical authorities and was made illegal in 1840. Compulsory vaccination in Scotland and IRELAND was established in 1845.

The requirement was effective in lessening the severity and breadth of smallpox outbreaks in Britain. After an epidemic from 1837 through 1840 smallpox tended to affect fewer children than adults (thus making it less deadly), and it most often appeared in crowded urban environments rather than on a widespread basis.

Under an act of Parliament in 1853 all infants had to be vaccinated—at government expense—before they reached the age of four months. The act made local NEW POOR LAW authorities responsible for arranging for vaccination. Among the complaints was that many residents had to travel to inconvenient locations in order to obtain the vaccine. Authorities were disappointed by the effect of the legislation; after about ten years smallpox still remained a threat. Vaccination alone was not sufficient to contain smallpox; it had to be coupled with a vigorous effort to isolate infected persons in hospitals designated as "lock hospitals."

The worst worldwide smallpox outbreak of the nineteenth century occurred in England between 1871 and 1873, where London was hit particularly hard. Especially disturbing was the infection of persons who previously had been vaccinated. Experts on smallpox concluded that some initial vaccination might not have been thorough enough—for example, there had not been enough skin-pricks on the arm of a vaccinated person. Patients who were admitted to London's Smallpox Hospital had a calamitous death rate—60% to 77%—during the epidemic.

Faced with such widespread mortality, the government tried to reorganize and centralize the vaccination program through the Vaccination and Local Governments Act of 1871. Those efforts bore some fruit; by the beginning of the 1900s smallpox noticeably had begun to recede as a widespread threat. As memories of the disease began to fade, however, resistance to vaccination appeared, especially among some poorer London residents who were most at risk for contagion.

Other diseases such as cholera, tuberculosis, typhus, and typhoid fever continued to be dangerous throughout most of the nineteenth century, but they affected most severely those populations who had limited or no immunity. Inoculation was a traditional practice in southern Africa and other locations, and vaccination along Jenner's model was introduced in areas of the empire in the 1800s, but there was practical difficulty in importing cowpox that was viable to faraway locales. The advent of fast steamships, meanwhile, meant that Europeans could transmit certain communicable diseases—such as measles, with an incubation period of just less than two weeks—to isolated populations with no natural immunity or access to medical help. British sailors brought catastrophic outbreaks of disease to the Hudson Bay Territory in Canada in 1846, South Africa and Mauritius in 1873, and Fiji in 1875.

See also CHOLERA; CONTAGIOUS DISEASES ACTS; DISEASES AND EPIDEMICS; HOSPITALS; MEDICAL PROFESSION; MEDICINE.

FURTHER READING

Cartwright, Frederick. *Disease and History*. New York: Dorset Press, 1972.

Hardy, Anne. *The Epidemic Streets: Infectious Diseases and the Rise of Preventive Medicine, 1856–1900*. Oxford: Clarendon Press, 1993.

Hopkins, Donald. *Princes and Paupers: Smallpox in History*. Chicago: University of Chicago Press, 1983.

Koplow, David. *Smallpox*. Berkeley: University of California Press, 2003.

Preston, Richard. *The Demon in the Freezer*. New York: Random House, 2002.

ELISABETH A. CAWTHON

VAUDEVILLE. *See* MUSIC HALLS.

VENEREAL DISEASE

Venereal disease was an endemic feature of Victorian society that affected men and women of all ages and classes. Within this context the two most significant diseases were gonorrhea and syphilis. Both remained medically problematic throughout the Victorian period with truly effective treatments not developed until the first decades of the twentieth century. Both were seen to have severe consequences not only for the infected individual but also for their families and society as a whole. In Britain, western Europe, and North America, between 10% and 15% of the male population was infected with syphilis, while gonorrhea was contracted by at least 50% of the male population at some point in their lives. Indeed, writing in 1901 America, moral reform author Prince Morrow argued that 80% of men in New York would be infected with gonorrhea at least once. Although exact figures for women are more problematic, rates of infection were likely similar during this period. In a culture where middle-class reformers were increasingly concerned with declining birth rates, which they regarded as an expression of "race suicide," the expanding medical knowledge about the rate of infection and long-term consequences of both gonorrhea and syphilis acted as a strong catalyst for social change. Consequently, during the last third of the nineteenth century, a campaign to gain medical control over and limit the social impact of these venereal diseases emerged. Although deeply associated with the campaign to repeal the Contagious Diseases Acts in Britain and its colonies, this campaign also reflected moral reformers' desire to impose a single standard of morality on late-Victorian society. This was evident through the campaigns of moral reformers and physicians for state regulation and increased public education to control contagion. An example of these efforts is the first International Conference for the Prophylaxis of Venereal Disease held in Brussels in 1899. However, in the colonial context calls for state regulation and reform campaigns continued to reflected racist preconceptions of the moral inferiority of nonwhite populations.

MEDICAL KNOWLEDGE ABOUT VENEREAL DISEASE

The key element within the transition of social attitudes toward venereal infection was the expansion of medical knowledge and the transformation of medical attitudes toward venereal diseases during the late Victorian period. Although Philippe Ricord had established the medical distinction between gonorrhea and syphilis in 1838, medical practice at mid-century still failed to fully recognize the seriousness of these conditions. Into the 1870s gonorrhea was often characterized as presenting no more danger than a severe cold, while syphilis continued to be viewed as a self-limiting disease that would subside of its own accord. These views, which were evident in respected medical textbooks and journals, reflect the poor medical knowledge of these diseases in the mid-Victorian period. Gonorrhea continued to be regarded within the established medical literature as an inflammatory disease triggered by irritability in the mucous membranes due to sexual excess or other overstimulation. This characterization was not fundamentally altered until after Albert Neisser identified the causative agent of gonorrhea in 1879. Medical understanding of syphilis was similarly problematic. Although in the 1870s Alfred Fournier linked syphilis to the development of long-term and severe illnesses that occurred decades after the initial infection, his work was not fully accepted until near the turn of the century. Further, medical understanding and the credibility of treatment continued to be undermined by the confusion between the primary stage of syphilis and chanceroid—an unrelated, milder, and localized venereal infection. This confusion encouraged the belief that syphilis could manifest as a mild and easily treatable disease. While the medical profession viewed syphilis with increasing seriousness in the 1880s and 1890s, these diagnostic problems were not solved until the early twentieth century. Research on venereal diseases was more advanced in Europe, particularly in France and Germany, but doctors in Britain, Canada, and the United States were quick to adopt new treatment methodologies. However, effective treatment remained dependent on the patient's willingness and ability to pay. In predominantly nonwhite colonies, medical treatment remained centered on the white population.

These difficulties were compounded by the problematic nature of medical treatment, which continued to be painful, ineffectual, expensive, and socially stigmatizing throughout the Victorian period. Consequently, patients frequently discontinued treatment soon after the initial symptoms had subsided and before a complete cure had been achieved. This was particularly the case concerning mercurial treatment for syphilis, which had harsh side effects, was expensive, and required the continuation of treatment over a prolonged period. The treatment of women and children, particularly among the middle and upper classes, was also complicated by the widespread practice of concealing the true nature of the disease. Supported by both reformers and medical professionals, this practice of concealment reflected the desire to protect women and children, if not from the disease itself, then at least from knowledge of it.

Despite these problems, as medical science uncovered the long-term consequences of gonorrhea and syphilis, doctors increasingly focused on the need to develop improved treatments. Success was first achieved with the introduction of efficacious treatments for gonorrhea in the 1880s and 1890s. However, syphilis remained difficult to treat, and despite various efforts to find alternatives, mercurial treatment remained the most beneficial. The important change during these decades was the recognition that mercurial treatment needed to be extended over a period of two to three years. Consequently, in their efforts to enforce this extended treatment, physicians joined moral reformers in an increasingly vocal campaign for state sponsored medical intervention to control venereal disease. These campaigns were particularly evident in western Europe, Britain, and North America. However, effective state sponsored medical treatment was not established until the World War I, after effective and relatively low-cost cures for both syphilis and gonorrhea had been developed.

SOCIAL ATTITUDES ABOUT VENEREAL DISEASE

These campaigns sponsored fundamental changes in social perceptions of venereal disease. While gonorrhea and syphilis had previously been characterized as fitting punishments for individuals who transgressed moral boundaries, these views were superseded by a growing concern with the impact of venereal disease on the innocent wives and children of men who contracted venereal disease through illicit sexual activity. Repeatedly, it was emphasized that the true victims were not these men but their wives who through no fault their own became victims of a loathsome disease. In this manner demands for reform were structured by Victorian assumptions that presented young women as pure and married women as virtuous. In this context the campaign for state intervention to control venereal disease was part of the larger reform effort to promote a single standard of sexuality and enforce moral regulation.

The transformation of venereal disease from a fitting punishment for sexual transgression to an epidemic that required state intervention was also sponsored by a rising discourse concerning the nonsexual transmission of venereal disease. Although medically unsound, the belief that venereal disease could be transmitted in a variety of nonsexual means legitimized the necessity for state intervention by distancing venereal disease from illicit sexuality. In this manner, venereal disease was compared to other contagious diseases such as tuberculosis or smallpox and its threat to society emphasized. Of course, while the idea of nonsexual transmission was used to justify increased medical regulation, it also acted as a social safety valve by allowing the venereal infections of "respectable" citizens to be explained in a manner that distanced the disease from any violation of Victorian sexual mores.

In conclusion, during the last third of the nineteenth century, Victorian conceptions of venereal disease were transformed by a growing appreciation within the medical community of the severity of these diseases and an increasingly vocal campaign to treat and contain the spread of venereal disease. This campaign transposed venereal disease from an individual punishment for sexual transgression to an epidemic that was seen to threaten the whole of society. Developing partially in response to the perceived crisis that faced Victorian society at the end of the century, the campaign to address venereal disease was an integral part of reformers' efforts to institute a single standard of morality and ensure the sanctity of marriage by protecting women and children from the dangers created by male sexual excess.

See also CONTAGIOUS DISEASES ACTS; PROSTITUTION.

FURTHER READING

Brandt, Allan M. *No Magic Bullet: A Social History of Venereal Disease in the United States since 1880.* New York: Oxford University Press, 1985.
Cassel, Jay. *The Secret Plague: Venereal Disease in Canada, 1838–1939.* Toronto: University of Toronto Press, 1987.

Davidson, Roger and Lesley A. Hall. *Sex, Sin, and Suffering: Venereal Disease and European Society since 1870.* London and New York: Routledge, 2001.

Haller, John S., and Robin M. Haller. *The Physician and Sexuality in Victorian America.* Urbana: University of Illinois Press, 1974.

Porter, Roy, and Lesley Hall. *The Facts of Life: The Creation of Sexual Knowledge in Britain, 1650–1950.* New Haven and London: Yale University Press, 1995.

Quétel, Claude. *History of Syphilis.* Translated by Judith Braddock and Brian Pike. Baltimore: Johns Hopkins University Press, 1990.

Walkowitz, Judith R. *Prostitution and Victorian Society: Women, Class, and the State.* Cambridge: Cambridge University Press, 1980.

CHRIS O'SHEA

VICTORIA, QUEEN

Born: May 24, 1819; London, England
Died: January 22, 1901; Isle of Wight, England

Queen Victoria not only lent her name to an age but also helped establish the particular cultural *zeitgeist* of her nation during her 64-year reign (1837–1901) through the very public nature of her unusual position as woman and monarch. Within the person of Queen Victoria existed a previously unknown blend of seemingly contradictory qualities: she was a woman who possessed great power, wealth, and prestige, but who also inhabited the ordinary roles of devoted wife/widow, mother, and grandmother. Victoria was keenly interested in the day-to-day running of her government and spent hours a day reading and signing official documents, yet by the time of Victoria's accession, British monarchs exerted influence, rather than direct control, over the government's specific workings and policy. By the end of Victoria's reign, for all intents and purposes, the MONARCHY's role in public life had settled into the largely symbolic position it holds in British life today, yet Queen Victoria remains a potent icon of domesticity, endurance, and empire.

THE INTRICACIES OF SUCCESSION

Queen Victoria's parentage and the circumstances surrounding her birth and youth are important to understanding her role in inflecting nineteenth-century British culture. In 1817 the English succession was thrown into confusion by the death in childbirth of the prince regent's (the future George IV, who ruled from 1820 to 1830) only legitimate heir, Princess Charlotte (1796–1817). Since the prince regent lacked an heir, at his death the crown would pass to the next son of George III (who ruled from 1760 to 1820) and

MANSELL/TIMEPIX/GETTY IMAGES

More than just the queen of England, Victoria was the symbolic center of the British Empire. She is shown here wearing the small imperial crown on her 66th birthday in 1885.

then to any legitimate child (sons preferred over daughters) of that line. Yet of the remaining sons of George III not one had a legitimate child (though it was calculated that at the time of his death in 1820, George III had 56 grandchildren), and thus in 1818 the bachelor royal dukes all scrambled to marry, some leaving mistresses of long-standing (and their children by a royal father) in the lurch. Given the close relationship between the British monarchy and the kingdom of Hanover (in northwest Germany)—a relationship that ultimately lasted for 123 years through five British kings (dating from the 1714 succession of George I, son of Ernest Augustus, elector of Hanover, and Sophia, granddaughter of James I)—it was natural that the sons of George III would look to the various minor kingdoms, duchies, and principalities of Germany to find wives. The Duke of Kent married the Dowager Princess Victoire (formerly of Coburg), widow of the Prince of Leiningen and the sister of the deceased Princess Charlotte's husband, Leopold. The duke of Clarence (the future William IV, who ruled from 1830 to 1837) married Princess Adelaide, a daughter of the duke of Saxe-Coburg-Meiningen, and the youngest duke, the duke of Cambridge, married Princess Augusta of Hesse-Cassel.

Princess Alexandrina Victoria was born at Kensington Palace on May 24, 1819. Her parents had raced to England from their rented accommodation in Amorbach when the duchess of Kent was seven months pregnant in order that their child should be born on English soil. The place of her birth would later become very important to Victoria's authority and claim to the throne. The duke and duchess of Kent were not especially popular with some members of the ROYAL FAMILY at the time, and to their chagrin the prince regent, de facto king while his father's long-standing illness continued unabated, was entirely ungracious in his role as godfather to the infant princess. He had the power to veto the names chosen for his niece and used that prerogative at the christening, refusing the traditional royal names of Charlotte, Augusta and Elizabeth. Alexandrina was chosen to honor one of the child's absent godfathers—the Tsar Alexander—who had loaned the duke of Kent money in the past, so only a second name was wanting. "Give her the mother's name," the regent said, and so a month after her birth the future queen of England was given the rather exotic name of Alexandrina Victoria.

After the ceremony the young family, still heavily in debt, retired to Sidmouth (Devonshire). There, only eight months after his daughter's birth, the duke of Kent succumbed to a bronchial illness and died, moving Victoria that much closer to the throne. Only a few days later old King George III was dead, and the prince regent was crowned king. By Victoria's tenth birthday it was clear that the subsequent king, William IV, and his wife Queen Adelaide would not produce any children (their two daughters had died in infancy), and thus at this uncle's death, Victoria would become queen. In 1830 the young future sovereign's training to become a monarch who would earn her people's approval began in earnest.

TRAINING A FUTURE QUEEN

Princess Victoria studied the same classic texts in history, religion, geography, literature, French, science, and math as other upper-class girls, but from an early age she also studied the laws of England. However, the duchess of Kent and her advisers were keenly aware that the degree of Victoria's popularity would be indexed not to her intelligence or worldliness but to the perception of her relative goodness and feminine virtue. To that end, during the years of Victoria's adolescence, the ambitious duchess of Kent organized several "royal progresses" through England and Wales to introduce Victoria to the nation, her future subjects, and the important Whig families at whose estates they would visit. She maintained a strict separation between her daughter and most of the royal family, refusing any contact between Victoria and the many royal illegitimate offspring who lived in the other palaces and shielding her from scandals that could and did erupt within the groups of "fashionables" at court.

The secluded young princess, who spent her days in the schoolroom and on the grounds of Kensington Palace under the watchful eyes of many, was passionate in her devotion to those she loved, in particular her half-sister Feodore (1807–1872) with whom she maintained an avid correspondence after Feodore's marriage to Prince Ernest of Hohenlohe-Langenburg in 1828 took her to far-off Germany; her governess, Louise Lehzen; her Uncle Leopold; and her visiting German relatives. She was an apt pupil both of her lessons and of human nature. Victoria realized from an early age that owing to her unique position she must exercise caution in all personal interactions, and so she rarely confided in anyone—including her mother—and never put private thoughts to paper: even her journal was an "open book" that the duchess of Kent and Lehzen read. This extreme care enabled Princess Victoria to remain truthful to all—a point of pride with her—yet also kept her from forming close ties with others.

Victoria's strong will and tenacity enabled her to withstand the pressures that would come to bear upon her when she was 16 years old in 1835 and suffering from a serious illness. While Victoria was still recovering, the duchess of Kent, with the encouragement of the power-hungry comptroller Sir John Conroy, whom Victoria despised, attempted to force Victoria to sign a paper indicating her desire to postpone her majority until she was 21, thus allowing the duchess of Kent a regency (in the event of William IV's death) that would end three years later than law allowed (Parliament had named the duchess the potential regent in 1830, and the legal age of majority was 18 years of age). Victoria refused again and again to sign the paper, risking her mother's and Conroy's wrath. Although there was never any danger that this document could have been legally enforced, even if signed by Victoria, in successfully blocking her mother the princess won a moral and personal victory. Although the experience hardened her against her mother and increased her suspicion of other people, it also gave the young and inexperienced Victoria confidence in her ability and authority to be queen.

EARLY SUCCESSES AS QUEEN

Soon after Victoria's 18th birthday, her uncle William IV's health began to fail for the last time. Victoria had just a few days to prepare for the inevitable change. When the archbishop of Canterbury and Lord Conyngham woke her early in the morning on June 20, 1837, to proclaim her queen, by all accounts she was calm and self-possessed. At her accession to the throne, her youth, gender, and inexperience were touted in the newspapers as both positive and negative characteristics of the new monarch. Certainly, the young Queen Victoria offered a very different image from that of the three elderly and dissolute Hanovers who had preceded her.

The duchess of Kent's "advertising campaign" and educational system had paid off: adjectives such as "simple," "modest," "innocent," "caring," and "lovely" were commonly applied to Victoria as evidence of her appropriate placement on the throne. Although there were missteps in her first years as queen—most notably in her almost slavish devotion to her first prime minister, WILLIAM LAMB (Lord Melbourne) (1779–1828), as well as her willingness to believe various scandal-mongers that the swelling abdomen of one of the ladies of her household was in fact due to an illicit liaison with Sir John Conroy rather than from the cancer that was killing her—for the most part Victoria was a popular, generous, and hardworking queen.

Victoria enjoyed her independence and her work as sovereign so much that she began to back away from the marriage plans that her uncle Leopold (now king of the Belgians, in which position he ruled from 1831 to 1865) had been urging. In the autumn of 1839 the queen reluctantly agreed to host a visit from her first cousins, Ernest and Albert of Saxe-Coburg Gotha. Once the princes arrived with their father (the duchess of Kent's brother), Victoria's attitude toward 20-year-old Albert, Leopold's first choice whom she had met only once three years earlier, changed irrevocably. "Albert is beautiful," she breathed to her journal. In love, five days later she nervously proposed marriage and was accepted by an equally anxious Albert. The decision to marry Albert, the decision that had the greatest impact on Victoria's life, would also influence the tenor of her reign, her eventual legacy, the changing role of the consort, diplomacy and foreign policy, and the establishment of educational, cultural, and scientific institutions. Albert would become Victoria's most trusted adviser and a leader in promoting Britain's interests and advances in the arts and technology.

After a short engagement during which the young couple were mostly apart, Victoria and Albert were married on February 10, 1840. The princess royal was born within a year of her parents' wedding and eight more children followed; the Prince of Wales (Albert Edward, who reigned as King Edward VII from 1901 to 1910) was born in 1841, and their last child, Princess Beatrice, was born in 1857. Although Victoria, with Albert increasingly at her side assuming ever more authority, was always diligent in performing her duties as monarch even throughout her many pregnancies, she greatly preferred the family's secluded visits and homely amusements at Osborne House (on the Isle of Wight), Balmoral Castle (in the Scottish highlands), and Windsor Castle to the exhausting state functions required by her office.

VICTORIAN AND ALBERT: MODELS FOR A NATION

Though punctuated by storms, the successful 20-year marriage of Queen Victoria and PRINCE ALBERT and their contented DOMESTICITY served as a model for the nation. The queen and consort initiated administrative reforms within the royal household that saved the government money (Albert's particular, early victory); set the fashion for the Highland retreat; enjoyed nature through picnics, sketching out-of-doors, and hunting wild animals while protecting domestic ones at home; supported traditional British industry and crafts; reintroduced the concept of medieval chivalry through their costume balls; helped to pioneer the use of chloroform as an anaesthesia for the pain of childbirth—among other actions and activities that encouraged the emulation of old-fashioned values of simplicity, efficiency, practicality, hard work, stability, and respectability. During the mid-Victorian era, in part owing to Victoria's influence—though it is perhaps ironic, given her unique placement of privilege and wealth—the home, whether a palace or a cottage, was elevated to a place of refuge and the locus of virtue. In 1851 Prince Albert's pet project, the GREAT EXHIBITION of the Industry of All Nations, opened to great success in the impressive Crystal Palace erected in Hyde Park. On her 18th wedding anniversary, Victoria boasted to King Leopold that her marriage "has brought . . . universal blessings on this country and Europe!"

The queen's domestic idyll came to an end when, only nine months after the death of her mother, with whom Victoria had reconciled, an exhausted and overburdened Prince Albert fell ill with a feverish cold in November 1861. He was soon diagnosed with typhoid fever (though his symptoms and the fact that he alone was sick suggests that his death may have been caused by a different disease). Albert died at Windsor Castle on December 14, his wife and five of his children around him. The hardy and healthy Victoria was cut down by sorrow and grief. She withdrew from London and public life and retreated to the Highlands. Victoria vowed to dedicate her remaining years to the preservation of the memory of Prince Albert. On Christmas Eve, 1861, Victoria wrote to King Leopold, "I am . . . anxious to repeat *one* thing, and *that one* is my *firm* resolve, my *irrevocable decision*, . . . that *his* wishes—*his* plans—about everything, *his* views about *every* thing are to be *my law*!" Victoria's attempt to fulfill this vow and her depression and overwhelming sense of loss, however, ultimately served to alienate her subjects and created tension between the government and the crown.

A QUEEN IN MOURNING

Queen Victoria had largely been a popular monarch in the years leading up to the prince consort's death. The assassination attempts of 1840, 1849, and 1850 (there were seven in all) galvanized the people in support of her; Albert's shortcomings due to his foreignness and extreme reticence were forgiven in the afterglow of the Great Exhibition; the Queen's conservatism on reforms such as the People's Charter (demanding, among other items, universal male suffrage) was generally shared by the middle upper classes; and patriotism surged during the CRIMEAN WAR (1853–1856). Yet after Prince Albert's death the queen receded into mourning so entirely that her subjects were insulted, and disapproving cartoons and editorials appeared in the media, goading or urging her to reappear and physically, visually, represent them once more. Her reliance on John Brown, a favorite Highland attendant of Albert's, was ridiculed in the press, the Queen's family and household hated his over-familiarity and influence with the Queen, and in some quarters insinuations were cast that the monarch and servant were lovers. In 1871, after her prime minister WILLIAM EWART GLADSTONE (1809–1898) had exhorted Victoria to emerge from her seclusion and take part in state functions, the depressed and frustrated queen threatened to abdicate the throne: " [The Queen] must solemnly repeat that unless her ministers support her & state the whole truth she cannot go on & must give her heavy burden up to younger hands." Victoria was first induced to appear in public early in 1872 in order to participate in the thanksgiving celebration of the Prince of Wales's recovery from typhoid. The event was a big success as enthu-

siastic crowds massed in the streets to cheer the procession. The queen came out of seclusion by degrees, frequently with ill grace and never more often than strictly necessary.

It was in the course of Queen Victoria's deepest period of mourning, from 1861–1871, however, that the most enduring images of the queen first emerged: a somber, staid widow in weeds whose visage and body language was read as denoting devotion, resignation, and virtue. Her name and features became recognizable the world over as symbols of mighty Britain, a monarch whose role as the "mother" of Britain was expanded to include the territories of the British Empire as her distant children. The ironies and disparities between Victoria's position as the most powerful person in Britain juxtaposed with her status as a woman (without the right to vote, subject to her husband, and so on) did not abate as she aged. As leader of a mighty nation and a grandmother (which she had become, by 1887, 30 times over), Victoria defied conventional expectations of womanhood. In 1876 the strong-willed and ambitious queen, who had pressed for some time for an alteration in her title, was formally named Empress of India to her great satisfaction.

THE QUEEN AS NATIONAL SYMBOL

Queen Victoria's wholly successful Golden and Diamond Jubilees (of 1887 and 1897) solidified her popularity and emphasized her role as the star of the spectacle of royalty. No one, including her cheering subjects, expected the queen to do much at this point in her life, beyond fulfilling ceremonial duties and representing Britain and British values to the rest of the world. After Prince Albert's death, Victoria no longer had a close ally with whom to discuss politics or receive advice, and thus her prime ministers, among them BENJAMIN DISRAELI (1804–81) who flattered the queen, Gladstone who infuriated her, and ROBERT CECIL (Lord Salisbury) (1830–1903) who agreed with her, bore the brunt of unmediated access to the queen's strong opinions on government matters such as foreign policy (especially in matters of war), the selection of cabinet members, proposed bills (such as HOME RULE and the Royal Titles Bill, which made her queen empress), the dismissal of ambassadors, or promotions of clergy.

For the young, Queen Victoria was less a political figure than a figurehead. For example, she was promoted as an exemplar for middle-class British girls in the popular girls' magazine *The Girl's Own Paper* in the 1887 Jubilee article "The Girl's Own Life of

Queen Victoria": "It is a great charm in the queen's life that what is best in it, and what has brought the greatest happiness, is within the reach of all of us. The true, pure loving family we can all strive after. . . . The queen's quiet and simple pleasures everyone can make her own, and whilst in matters of state Her Majesty may certainly be taken as an example for queens, she is thus in private life no less a pattern for people of every degree." In the March 1876, issue of the *Englishwoman's Domestic Magazine*, by contrast, middle-class adult women were coached to appreciate Queen Victoria as the head of Britain's imperial power and encouraged to identify with that dominance for the future: "It may not be that a future monarch of the country may add to the title 'Emperor of India' the words 'and Australasia,' for the colonies may be constitutionally independent; but they will be 'of us,' if not 'ours,' and the history of the world in the twentieth century will be really the history of the English-speaking people of the globe."

Although a sentimental interpretation of Queen Victoria's value such as that advanced by the *Girl's Own Paper* held true for a segment of her colonial subjects, Victoria's significance for the colonies of the British Empire is obviously complicated by British imperialism's economic, cultural, political, and religious domination of native peoples. Victoria herself asserted Britain's intentions concerning imperial control in her speech opening the Colonies and India Exhibition of 1886: she hoped that the exhibition would "strengthen the bonds of union which now exist in every portion of my empire." During her reign there were significant violent uprisings and conflicts in India (for example, the Sikh Wars of 1845–1849 that resulted in the annexation of the Punjab and the INDIAN MUTINY or "Sepoy Rebellion" of 1857–1858) and SOUTH AFRICA (the Zulu War of 1878–1879 and the BOER WAR of 1899–1902). For IRELAND, too (which Victoria visited only three times—in 1849, 1861, and 1900), the queen represented a government that denied Home Rule in 1866 (a political reform that Victoria was firmly against). The number of MONUMENTS of Queen Victoria, topographical features such as lakes (Lake Victoria in East Africa, for example), states (Victoria in South East Australia), and cities that bear her name in Australia, Canada, and Hong Kong attest, in part, to Victoria's impact. Queen Victoria was the "absent presence" that constructed the colonist's role as "subject" to a crown and "mother country" located far away and represented symbolically in the person of the queen.

Back in Britain, from the first moments after her death, commentators and historians sought to understand Queen Victoria's cultural significance. The earliest assessments were fulsome in their praise of the great and pure queen whose blameless conduct set a high standard for all succeeding monarchs. Not surprisingly, after her death from old age in January 1901, tributes to the queen praised her embodiment of traditional feminine virtues rather than acts of bravery, statesmanship, or guardianship. *The Girlhood of Queen Victoria: A Selection from Her Majesty's Diaries between the Years 1832 and 1840* (1912), Viscount Esher's two volume selections from Victoria's edited journals (at Victoria's request, all but the first 13 journals from her days as a princess were destroyed by Princess Beatrice, the queen's youngest daughter, after she had edited and transcribed them) offer a careful and respectful overview of the princess and young queen as a seemly and simple girl. While a tone of chivalrous loyalty inflects Esher's portrait of the queen in her own words, Lytton Strachey's 1921 biography of Queen Victoria views her through the powerful men who surrounded her, such as Prince Albert and her most significant prime ministers, including Lord Melbourne, Disraeli, and Gladstone. Every decade since the 1964 appearance of Elizabeth Longford's *Queen Victoria: Born to Succeed* has given rise to another large-scale biographical reassessment of Victoria.

Representations of the embodied queen—her image and the objects decorated by it or products advertised with it, as well as the queen's material possessions (her clothing, property, and homes)—all helped to create a culture in which the queen became a personality available to her subjects. Thus, Queen Victoria became a commodity to be bought, treasured, ignored, or despised, during the Victorian era and up to the present day. During her reign Queen Victoria's particular foibles and gestures were made immediately into caricatures of long standing: her dependence on the foreign Albert, the expense of the full nursery, her protracted mourning, her imperious nature and mishandling of the Prince of Wales, the accumulation of great wealth. Yet historian Dorothy Thompson persuasively argues that "If [Victoria] strengthened the moral authority of women in the family rather than making their presence in public more immediately acceptable, there must have been ways in which the presence of a woman at the head of the state worked at a deeper level to weaken prejudice and make change more possible in the century following her reign."

Citizens of the former colonies of the British Empire may have different interpretations of Victoria as a symbol of oppression and imperialism. No longer responsible for the awe, respect, and patriotism that images of Queen Victoria had at one time called forth in many, for people today, the image of Queen Victoria is often viewed with bemusement, detachment, or disregard; a misperception of the queen as prudish, dull, and irrelevant helps to sustain this attitude. It is no doubt true, however, that Queen Victoria remains one of the most easily recognized and known figures from world history whose legacy as a symbol of the monarchy, British Empire, and the Victorian era endures.

See also ALBERT, PRINCE; MONARCHY; ROYAL FAMILY.

FURTHER READING

Charlot, Monica. *Victoria: The Young Queen.* Oxford: Basil Blackwell, 1991.

Esher, Viscount. *The Girlhood of Queen Victoria: A Selection from Her Majesty's Diaries between the Years of 1832 and 1840.* 2 vols. London: John Murray, 1912.

Hibbert, Christopher. "The Girl's Own Life of Queen Victoria." *The Girl's Own Paper.* London, 1887.

Hibbert, Christopher. *Queen Victoria: A Personal History.* New York: HarperCollins, 2000.

Hibbert, Christopher. *Queen Victoria in Her Letters and Journals.* New York: Viking, 1985.

Homans, Margaret, and Adrienne Munich, eds. *Remaking Queen Victoria.* Cambridge: Cambridge University Press, 1997.

Longford, Elizabeth. *Queen Victoria: Born to Succeed.* New York: Harper and Row, 1964.

St. Aubyn, Giles. *Queen Victoria: A Portrait.* New York: Atheneum, 1992.

Strachey, Lytton. *Queen Victoria.* New York: Harcourt, Brace and Company, 1921.

Thompson, Dorothy. *Queen Victoria: The Woman, the Monarchy, and the People.* New York: Pantheon Books, 1990.

Tingsten, Herbert. *Victoria and the Victorians.* 1965. Trans. by David Grey and Eva Leckström Grey. New York: Delacorte Press, 1972.

Vallone, Lynne. *Becoming Victoria.* New Haven and London: Yale University Press, 2001.

Woodham-Smith, Cecil. *Queen Victoria: Her Life and Times, 1819–1861.* London: Penguin, 1972.

LYNNE VALLONE

VICTORIA AND ALBERT MUSEUM.

See SOUTH KENSINGTON MUSEUM.

WALLACE, ALFRED RUSSEL

Born: January 8, 1823; Usk, Wales
Died: November 7, 1913; Dorset, England

One of the most energetic and original thinkers of the nineteenth century, Alfred Russel Wallace was one of the first scientists to see that natural selection can explain evolutionary change. Sending his ideas in 1858 to CHARLES DARWIN (1809–1882), who had independently discovered the idea some 20 years earlier, Wallace stimulated Darwin to write his *On the Origin of Species*, published in 1859. Later, Wallace's work helped deepen and complicate scientific understanding of natural selection and pushed Darwin to explore the implications of the theory of EVOLUTION as it applied to humans.

Wallace was the child of a man whom he described as having no money worries, for his fortunes had sunk so low that there was no longer room for further descent. Apprenticed to an older brother, Wallace began life as a surveyor. The act of helping the ruling classes to mark and draw off land previously shared by all, together with a youthful attendance at a lecture given by the Scottish industrialist and utopian ROBERT OWEN, instilled in Wallace a lifelong commitment to SOCIALISM.

Socialism was but the first of a string of eccentric and outsider enthusiasms that motivated Wallace through his very long life—SPIRITUALISM, feminism, land reformism, and vegetarianism were among the others—but the enthusiasm for which he is justly famous is evolution. As a young man, Wallace read and was much impressed by ROBERT CHAMBERS's anonymously authored *Vestiges of the Natural History of Creation*. This determined Wallace to set off with a friend, Henry Walter Bates, to the Amazon basin, where they were to collect specimens (with an eye to selling to rich collectors) and at the same time look for evidence of evolution. No breakthroughs occurred and so Wallace returned to England, a trip marked by a fire on board ship and the loss of all of his specimens, an example of the ill fortune that seemed to dog him though life. (Wallace later lost all of his money through unwise investment; he was jilted without reason by his first fiancée; he got involved in a lawsuit with a madman over an unpaid debt about the impossibility of a proof that the earth is round, not realizing that in Britain debts from wagers are unenforceable; and even his middle name with its strangely missing final *l* was the result of an error on the birth certificate.)

Undeterred, Wallace set out again, this time going east to the Malay Peninsula. He was on the track of evolution and published work hinting at it, but it was not until the early part of 1858, lying in his hammock wracked with malaria, that Wallace had his big insight. Arguing in a way very similar to that of Charles Darwin some 20 years previously, Wallace saw that the ongoing struggle for existence would mean that there would be a differential survival and reproduction, and that since success in the struggle would be a function of the organism's own characteristics, there would therefore be a kind of natural selection, leading to adaptation. (Although Wallace referred to the struggle for existence by name, he did not then use the term "natural selection," and indeed would not have done so. Whereas Darwin stressed the similarity between the world of the breeder and the natural world, moving easily in concept and name from artificial selection to natural selection, Wallace stressed the dissimilarity between the world of the breeder and the natural world. For him, the key point is that although we cannot turn cows into pigs, nature can do something of this kind. Wallace always preferred HERBERT SPENCER's term of "survival of the fittest" for the idea of selection and urged it on Darwin, who accepted it for later editions of his *On the Origin of Species*.)

Wallace wrote up his ideas as a short essay and sent it to—of all people—Charles Darwin. Devastated that his ideas had been discovered independently, through the agency of friends CHARLES LYELL the geologist and Joseph Hooker the botanist, Darwin had Wallace's paper as well as some writings of his own delivered at and then published by the Linnaean Society of London. For the next 15 months Darwin wrote up his ideas, and at the end of 1859 they were published as *On the Origin of Species*. On the far side of the world, Wallace was out of touch with all of this and learned only of events very much after they had occurred. He never questioned the propriety of what Darwin and his friends had done (which was generous and just, for they certainly did act with integrity) and always regarded himself as the junior partner in the Darwin-Wallace "discovery" of the theory of evolution.

Returning to England in the early 1860s, he never did get paid employment as a scientist. Eventually the professional scientists (THOMAS H. HUXLEY particularly) got him a government pension, but there was no way in which they were going to give such an eccentric dreamer a position of authority or power. Wallace turned therefore to writing at the popular level and produced book after book on his various obsessions. He was, however, more than just a one-scientific-idea man, and through the 1860s he and Darwin carried on a very sophisticated discussion on the nature of selection. Whereas Darwin inclined always to an individualistic view of the selection process, Wallace (as a socialist) always inclined to see selection as working for the good of the group. In the 1870s Wallace wrote extensively on biogeography and produced definitive tomes on the distribution of organisms, especially on islands, particularly as they are found in the Far East. ("Wallace's line" refers to a division he found separating Asian-type specimens from Australasian-type specimens.)

In the late 1860s Wallace and Darwin fell out over the evolution of our own species, *Homo sapiens*. Originally they had agreed, but then Wallace (by now

MANSELL/TIMEPIX/GETTY IMAGES

Alfred Russel Wallace was one of the first scientists to realize that natural selection could explain evolutionary change.

taken up with spiritualism) argued that human evolution could not have been completely natural and had to have been guided by spirit forces. Appalled, Darwin struck back. He could not deny that natural selection seems inadequate to explain the kinds of features on which Wallace rested his case—human intelligence and hairlessness, for instance—so started to claim that it is sexual selection, the selection for mates, that is the key causal factor. Men and women are as they are because women and men are fussy about partners. Darwin wrote up his ideas in his work on our species, *The Descent of Man* (1871); his need to counter Wallace is the reason for the rather strange balance of the book, which is more than half a survey of sexual selection in the whole animal kingdom and less than half on the nature and causes of human evolution.

Late in life Wallace started to receive some of the respect that he merited, although fellowship in the Royal Society came over 30 years after that of Huxley, a younger man. He was awarded the Order of Merit, a gift from his sovereign (Edward the seventh), although modest and retiring to the end, he did not accept it in person. Yet, part genius, part crank, his modesty should not be confused with timidity. Wallace was fearless in his loyalty to the ideas he embraced. Scorn was a stimulus. It is the foundation of his deserved reputation that one of Wallace's ideas was evolution and that this led him to natural selection.

See also DARWIN, CHARLES; EVOLUTION; SOCIALISM; SPIRITUALISM.

FURTHER READING

Darwin, Charles, and Alfred Russel Wallace. *Evolution by Natural Selection.* Foreword by Gavin de Beer. Cambridge: Cambridge University Press, 1958.

Fichman, Martin. *Alfred Russel Wallace.* Boston, Mass.: Twayne, 1981.

Raby, Peter. *Alfred Russel Wallace: A Life.* Princeton, N.J.: Princeton University Press, 2001.

Ruse, Michael. *The Darwinian Revolution: Science Red in Tooth and Claw.* Chicago: University of Chicago Press, 1979.

Ruse, Michael. *Monad to Man: The Concept of Progress in Evolutionary Biology.* Cambridge, Mass.: Harvard University Press, 1996.

Shermer, Michael. *In Darwin's Shadow: The Life and Science of Alfred Russel Wallace.* New York: Oxford University Press, 2002.

Wallace, Alfred Russel. *My Life: A Record of Events and Opinions.* London: Chapman and Hall, 1905.

Wallace, Alfred Russel. *The Alfred Russel Wallace Reader: A Selection of Writings from the Field.* Edited by Jane R. Camerini. Baltimore, Md.: Johns Hopkins University Press, 2002.

MICHAEL RUSE

WARD, MARY AUGUSTA

Born: June 11, 1851; Hobart, Tasmania
Died: March 24, 1920; London, England

As a novelist, journalist, philanthropist, and anti-suffragist leader, Mary Augusta Ward—who published as Mrs. Humphry Ward—was a woman of note in her society, but because she was so much a person of her own time, she has not, perhaps, translated well to later generations. Also, she damaged her own reputation late in life by her strong stand as an anti-suffragist.

Ward was born into a distinguished Victorian family, with close ties both to education and to Oxford: her grandfather was the famous headmaster of Rugby, Dr. THOMAS ARNOLD; and her uncle, MATTHEW ARNOLD, was a poet and professor of poetry at Oxford University. Historian John Sutherland states that being an Arnold "was the most important single fact in Mary's life." Her childhood was marked by her father's indecision about his faith. Raised an Anglican, in 1847, in a quixotic search for a more democratic society, her father emigrated to New Zealand to farm. Failing at this, he secured a post as schools inspector in Tasmania, married, and converted to ROMAN CATHOLICISM. For this he was discharged, returned to England with his family in 1856, and then obtained a teaching post in Dublin, Ireland, through the influence of JOHN HENRY NEWMAN.

When the rest of her family moved to Dublin, Mary, age five, was left behind with her grandmother Arnold and Aunt Fan. For the next ten years she was virtually abandoned by her family; she was sent off to inadequate boarding schools for long periods of time, where, lonely and wretched, she gave way to ungovernable temper tantrums. Her father returned to Anglicanism in 1865; he moved the family, now consisting of seven siblings, to Oxford, and it was here that Mary's real life began.

BECOMING A WRITER

She relished the Oxford social scene, with its opportunities to meet the dons and their wives and famous guests, but most of all she was finally introduced to real education. She had, for many years, been writing fiction for her own pleasure, and now her first story, "A Westmoreland Story," was published in the *Churchman's Companion* (1870). Through the influence of Mark Pattison she received a pass to the Bodleian Library where she was free to read at will. She made herself an authority on Spanish literature and published two articles in *Macmillan's Magazine:*

MANSELL/TIMEPIX/GETTY IMAGES

Mary Augusta Ward, who published as Mrs. Humphry Ward.

Her husband's appointment as correspondent for the *Times* of London in 1881, where he eventually became the art critic, brought residence in Russell Square and the stimulation of life in the metropolis. After a family holiday in Switzerland, Ward translated Henri Amiel's *Journal Intime* (1883), followed in 1884 by the modest effort *Miss Bretherton*, the first of her 25 novels. However, Ward's career as a novelist really was launched in 1888, with publication of the vastly successful *Robert Elsmere* (1888), which brought her immediate fame and riches. Drawing on her own family experiences, this was a story of faith and doubt, poverty and wealth, and social responsibility. It captured the attention and imagination of her generation so powerfully that some declared it the "most popular novel of the century." Indeed, by 1889, 300,000 copies had been sold in England and 100,000 pirated copies in the United States.

David Grieve (1892) was less successful artistically but benefited from the new International Copyright Agreement (1891) by commanding the huge advance sum of £7,000 for the American rights. Henceforth, Ward published roughly one novel every couple of years for the rest of her life, some of the more memorable titles being *Marcella* (1894) and *Sir George Tressady* (1896), both social problem novels, and *Helbeck of Bannisdale* (1898), a sympathetic study of Catholicism. Her later books, less fresh and imaginative, include *Eleanor* (1900), *Lady Rose's Daughter*(1903), and *The Marriage of William Ashe* (1905), among others.

SOCIAL RESPONSIBILITY FUELS DIVERSE PROJECTS

Acting on her sense of social responsibility, Ward used some of her wealth in 1890 to establish a settlement (working people's center) in Bloomsbury named University House. This was later moved and renamed Passmore Edwards Center in 1897 after Edward's contribution of £14,000 toward its work. In 1908 the Wards toured North America, where Mary Ward's books had always been popular; she lectured on education and they were received by President Theodore Roosevelt and the governor general of CANADA. Upon her return, Ward was named to head the newly formed Women's Anti-Suffrage League. Ironically, she had fought hard in Oxford for women's education but now vigorously opposed their having the vote.

During World War I Ward and her daughter visited the trenches at Ypres, Belgium, in order to write "Letters" to be published in American newspapers to explain the war to Americans. These appeared as *England's Effort* (1916); a second volume, *Towards the Goal* (1917), was a huge success. The third of the

"The Poem of the *Cid*" (October 1871) and "Alfonso the Wise, King of Castile" (June 1872). This was the beginning of a distinguished career in JOURNALISM that would continue throughout her life and led her to contribute to such journals as CORNHILL MAGAZINE, *Dark Blue, Fortnightly Review, Manchester Guardian, New Review, Nineteenth Century, Oxford Spectator, Pall Mall Gazette, Quarterly Review, SATURDAY REVIEW,* the *TIMES,* plus a selection of 18 articles in *Macmillan's Magazine* between 1871 and 1885.

In 1872 she married Thomas Humphry Ward (1845–1926), a tutor at Brasenose College, by whom she had three children; oddly, after the birth of the second in 1876 her father reconverted to Catholicism. As a young Oxford matron, she became a founding member of Oxford Lectures for Ladies in 1873, which became the Association for the Education of Women in 1879; these early efforts resulted ultimately in the foundation of Somerville College (1879), Oxford's first college for women. She dabbled in scholarship by contributing more than 200 entries to Dean Wace's *Dictionary of Christian Biography* and produced a slender children's story, *Milly and Olly* (1880).

trilogy, *Fields of Victory* (1919), described a trip through the postwar battlefields of France and Belgium. Ward's autobiography, *A Writer's Recollections*, was published in 1918.

Ward's later years were plagued by ill health and financial worries. Her constitution had never been strong, and her ceaseless work had taken its toll. Financially, the Wards had overextended themselves with purchases of real estate and art for Humphry's collection. Their son ran up huge gambling losses for which they were responsible, and they incurred a heavy tax burden. Her husband became an invalid. These difficulties caused Ward to publish more frequently and hurriedly, and consequently much of her later work is less than her best. However, at the end she had the satisfaction of knowing she had produced a lasting classic, *Robert Elsmere*, which had once captured the attention of an admiring world.

See also EDUCATION OF WOMEN; NOVEL; WOMEN'S SUFFRAGE.

FURTHER READING

Peterson, William. *Victorian Heretic: Mrs. Humphry Ward's Robert Elsmere*. Leicester: University of Leicester Press, 1976.

Sutherland, John. *Mrs. Humphry Ward: Eminent Victorian, Pre-Eminent Edwardian*. Oxford and New York: Oxford University Press, 1990.

Trevelyan, Janet P. *The Life of Mrs. Humphry Ward*. London: Constable, 1923.

Ward, Mrs. Humphry. *Writer's Recollections*. London: Collins, 1918.

ROSEMARY T. VANARSDEL

WATERWAYS AND CANALS

Although the great era of canal building in Britain had finished by about 1840, absolute growth of traffic on navigable waterways continued during QUEEN VICTORIA's reign, as waterways remained viable for the movement of low-value bulk goods, such as coal, timber, and building materials. But through a mixture of the various private canal companies' own shortsightedness, government inaction, and the growing power of the railroad interests, the inland waterways fell far behind their main competitor: by 1898 the RAILWAYS carried nearly ten times greater tonnage of freight.

The improvement of rivers and the construction of canals, with their cuttings, embankments, tunnels, aqueducts, and pound locks, were techniques of long standing that, like water wheels, played an essential part in facilitating the innovations of the Industrial Revolution. A horse could tow between 30 and 50 times more by weight on a river or canal than it could

haul in a road wagon. But it proved difficult to apply back to the canals the innovations in iron making and steam power that were combined in the canals' formidable new competitor, the railroads. Iron troughs were sometimes used on canal aqueducts, and steam occasionally powered inclined planes used to transfer boats from one canal level to another, though these, like the vertical lifts employed for this purpose, more often operated hydraulically by counterbalancing their loads with caissons of water. Attempts to mechanize canal barges through steam power proved destructive to the banks of most canals and navigable rivers, and boats continued throughout the Victorian era to be towed by a horse or pair of donkeys, and sometimes by human gangs, with occasional supplement of sail. Steam tugs were, however, increasingly used in tunnels and on the larger waterways, especially in Scotland, where steam lighters (flat-bottomed barges) were also abundant.

Although the heyday of the canals had passed in Britain, there were some important developments in the Victorian era, especially overseas. Extensive irrigation canals were built in INDIA, notably the Ganges canal (1842–1857). Work continued on the improvement and connecting up of the great waterways of Europe and North America, where in particular the canals and navigations that linked the watery highway of the Great Lakes and the St. Lawrence River with the burgeoning cities of the middle and eastern UNITED STATES OF AMERICA made a huge contribution to rapid industrialization after the end of the CIVIL WAR (1861–1865). There was a vital new role for canals capable of carrying oceangoing ships; one such venture, the Manchester Ship Canal, which opened in 1894, made a striking contrast with the general

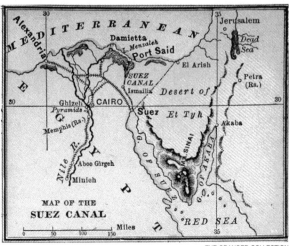

THE GRANGER COLLECTION

Nineteenth-century map of the Suez Canal.

BROWN BROS.

A ship moves through the Manchester Ship Canal.

decline of the inland waterway network, and soon made MANCHESTER, 36 miles (58 kilometers) from the sea, the country's fourth largest port. The completion in 1869 of the Suez Canal in EGYPT was a major contribution to the world's economic infrastructure, and the Kiel Canal, providing safe passage between the Baltic and North Seas from 1895, was to carry even more traffic than the cut at Suez.

The Victorian era saw the relative decline of British canals from their primary position as arteries of trade; their relegation to recreational backwaters would follow in the twentieth century. Unfolding alongside their economic malaise in the Victorian era was a human story of the declining wages and increasingly overcrowded and unsanitary conditions of the floating population of canal boat people, which prompted largely ineffective parliamentary measures in the 1870s and 1880s.

See also RAILWAYS; SHIPPING; TRANSPORTATION.

FURTHER READING

Bagwell, Philip S. *The Transport Revolution from 1770.* London: Batsford, 1974.

Farnie, D. A. *The Manchester Ship Canal and the Rise of the Port of Manchester, 1894–1975.* Manchester: Manchester University Press, 1980.

Hadfield, Charles. *British Canals: An Illustrated History.* 7th ed. Newton Abbot, Devon: David and Charles, 1984.

Harford, Ian. *Manchester and Its Ship Canal Movement: Class, Work, and Politics in Late-Victorian England.* London and Basingstoke: Macmillan Press, 1982.

Shaw, Ronald E. *Canals for a Nation: The Canal Era in the United States, 1790–1860.* Lexington: University Press of Kentucky, 1990.

COLIN CHANT

WATTS, GEORGE F.

Born: February 23, 1817; London, England
Died: July 1, 1904; London, England

In a career that spanned the entire Victorian period, artist George Frederick Watts never wavered in his aim to prove himself a worthy successor to the high idealism of ancient Greece and the Renaissance. A visionary who wanted "to paint ideas, not things," he hoped to do for an increasingly agnostic age what Michelangelo (1475–1564) had achieved in his own more religious time, by appealing to that spirituality that Watts believed to be instinctive in all mankind, independent of specific creed. Although he always strove for beauty and harmony, he believed above all that art should be morally purposeful and evolved a new kind of allegorical painting that he hoped would ennoble and uplift the hearts and minds of the nation.

Although humbly born, Watts was encouraged by his father and his first teacher, the sculptor William Behnes (1795–1864). Already a superb draftsman, he began at age 16 to make an income from portrait drawings, and from 1837 his clients included the Ionides family, the first of numerous wealthy and influential patrons. In 1835 he briefly attended the Royal Academy Schools but learned more from studying ancient Greek sculpture at the British Museum. His first visit to Italy (1843–1847) was financed by a first prize for his design of *King Caractacus* in the initial competition held for the decoration of the new Palace of Westminster. During a four-year stay in Florence, he was the guest of Lord and Lady Holland, accompanying them to Naples and Rome where he studied the Greeks and the great Renaissance masters, Michelangelo especially.

In Italy Watts painted portraits, landscapes, and literary subjects including *Paulo and Francesca* (1845, Victoria and Albert Museum)—an experiment in fresco—and the ambitious *Story from Boccaccio* (1847, Tate Gallery). In 1847 Watts's *King Alfred* won another first prize in the third Westminster competition. In 1848, in emulation of Michelangelo's Sistine ceiling, he conceived a plan to decorate a vast building ("The House of Life'") with paintings symbolizing the evolution of the world and human civilization from the first chaos to the Middle Ages. The scheme was impracticable and only odd pictures were completed. *Time and Oblivion* (1848, Eastnor Castle) was the first, and late examples include *Chaos* (1882, Tate Gallery) and *The Creation of Eve* (1899, Fogg Art Museum, Harvard). In 1850 Watts made a brief foray into social realism with paintings such as *The Irish Famine* and *The Bridge of Sighs* (both Watts Gallery, Compton) but soon returned to more congenial themes. In 1852 his offer to decorate without payment the hall of Euston Station on the theme of *The Progress of Cosmos* was refused; but an allegorical mural on *Justice*, for Lincoln's Inn, was completed in 1859.

In 1851 Watts was invited to live with Thoby and Sarah Prinsep (parents of the painter "Val") at Little Holland House, Kensington, where, for 24 years, he enjoyed the company of distinguished writers, artists, and statesmen—as well as generous patrons such

as Lord Eastnor, the Prinseps' brother-in-law. Portraiture and other commissions subsidized Watts's more ambitious subjects and enabled him to travel. On a second Italian trip in 1853 the richly coloured canvases of Titian and other Venetians had a profound effect on his artistic development. In Paris from 1855 to 1856, he portrayed members of the French aristocracy before proceeding to the excavations at Hallicarnassus in Greece on the invitation of the archaeologist Charles Newton.

In the 1860s Watts began working on a number of allegorical and classical themes, some of which took decades to complete. Among these are *Eve Repentant* (1897) and *Time, Death and Judgement* (1900, both Tate Gallery). Sitters for his portraits at this period range from Watts's fiancée, the actress Ellen Terry (1864), aged 16; to the venerable dramatist *Sir Henry Taylor* (1867, both National Portrait Gallery). Taylor's was one of a series of portraits of eminent men—the philosophers Thomas Carlyle and John Stuart Mill and the designer William Morris among them—which were presented to the nation from 1895 onward. In 1867 Watts was made both associate and full royal academician and in the same year turned seriously to sculpture, producing work as varied as the grace-

Hope (1885) by G. F. Watts.

ful bust of the nymph *Clytie* (1868, Guildhall Art Gallery) and the massive equestrian statues of *Hugh Lupus* (1883, Eaton Hall, Chesire) and *Physical Energy* (1904, Kensington Gardens).

The 1870s saw the completion of some of Watts's most important classical subjects: *Orpheus and Eurydice* (1872, Aberdeen Art Gallery); *Endymion* (1873, private collection); and *Ariadne in Naxos* (1875, Guildhall Art Gallery). Ariadne recalls Titian's own version of the subject (National Gallery), as well as the Parthenon sculptures in the British Museum, illustrating Watts's desire to combine the surface richness of the Venetians with the harmonious forms of the Greeks. Allegories include *The Spirit of Christianity* (1875, Tate Gallery), and one of Watts's most popular works, *Love and Death* (1877, University of Manchester), in which Love, a small winged boy, struggles vainly to prevent the ominous figure of Death from entering the house.

With the general public, Watts's greatest success was *Hope* (1886)—one of 22 spiritually edifying subjects intended as a gift to the nation, and which entered the Tate Gallery between 1897 and 1901. *Hope* sits, blindfolded, on the earth's globe, holding a wooden lyre with only one string remaining, listening intently for the faintest sound; the soft brushstrokes and color harmonies of blue, green, and gold creating a deeply spiritual mood. As one critic wrote in the *Art Annual*, 1896, it expressed "all the doubt and questioning . . . All the trouble and disquiet of modern times." But finding appropriate means of expressing modern allegories was a difficult task, and the results are sometimes trite, as in *Mammon* (1885)—an ugly, bloated figure personifying wealth as a source of evil (1886, Tate Gallery).

Watts's technique is often more innovatory than his iconography. The suggestive power of the picture surface played an increasingly important role in his art. He prized accidental effects created through multilayers of paint rubbed on with his fingers, or bits of rags and paper, to obtain a complex and suggestive web of color and texture; some later works including *After the Deluge* (1891) and the *Sower of the Systems* (1902, both Watts Gallery) verge on abstraction.

Watts exhibited at the Royal Academy from 1837, but it was his regular exhibits at the new Grosvenor Gallery, beginning in 1877 with *Love and Death* and three portraits, which made him famous. A one-man show of 56 works belonging to Watts's leading patron Charles Rickards, at the Manchester Institution in 1880, and 200 at the Grosvenor in 1881 to 1882, consolidated his reputation as one of the greatest and most original painters of the era. Another one-man exhibition staged in New York in 1884 to 1885 attracted 500,000 visitors. Watts regularly exhibited in Rome from 1886 and showed 22 works in Munich in 1893.

Watts's ill-advised marriage to Ellen Terry in 1864 lasted only 16 months; his second in 1886 to the painter and sculptor Mary Fraser Tytler was happy and productive. From 1891 their time was divided between the Melbury Road house that Watts had occupied since 1876 and their country home Limnerlease, at Compton, Surrey, with an adjacent gallery, which now houses a large collection of Watts's work. Unworldly to the end, Watts refused a baronetcy in 1885 and 1894 but in 1902 became one of the first holders of the Order of Merit.

See also PAINTING, GENRES OF; PAINTING; ROYAL ACADEMY OF ARTS.

FURTHER READING

Baliss, Wyke, Sir. *Five Great Painters of the Victorian Era: Leighton, Millais, Burne-Jones, Watts, Holman Hunt.* London: S. Low, Marston and Co., 1902.
Blunt, Wilfred. *England's Michelangelo: A Biography of George Frederic Watts, O.M., R.A.* London: Hamilton, 1975.
Chesterton, G. K. *G. F. Watts.* New York: Dutton, 1904.
Wilton, Andrew, and Robert Upstone, eds. *The Age of Rossetti, Burne-Jones and Watts: Symbolism in Britain, 1860–1910.* London: Tate Gallery, 1997.

MARY COWLING

WEALTHY, THE

The commercial and industrial revolutions of the Victorian era produced a substantial and growing class of newly rich men and families who have been identified and studied by historians, yet defining "the rich" in Victorian Britain is not straightforward. The commonly accepted definition of real wealth was £10,000 a year or more, although the wealthiest of the great LANDOWNERS and business magnates enjoyed incomes of 10 or 20 times this figure or even more.

NUMBER AND SCALE OF WEALTHY INCREASES

To the average man or woman, the sum of £10,000 a year was an extraordinary one. Most working-class men earned between £50 and £100 a year, a shipping clerk or Anglican vicar probably £300 or so, and a very successful barrister or solicitor only about £1,000. Because of the inadequacies of the income tax figures, only the roughest idea of how many persons enjoyed incomes of this level is known. In 1801 a total of 1,020 persons earned £5000 or more; in

1911 through 1912 this figure had risen to 13,134 persons, with 75 earning £100,000 or more. Virtually no reliable STATISTICS, however, exist for any of the intervening period. Much more is known of patterns of wealth holding from the probate records of wealth left at death. These clearly show the tremendous rise in the number of very wealthy persons in Britain during the Victorian era. The number of estates of £100,000 or more probated in Britain rose from about 30 per year during the 1830s to about 200 per year by 1900. (These figures include only personal property and exclude the capital value of LAND; had the value of land been included, these figures, especially the earlier ones, would be much higher.)

The scale of the very largest fortunes also rose. The wealthiest businessmen of the mid-Victorian period, such as the London warehouseman and the merchant banker James Morrison and the banker Samuel J. Loyd, Lord Overstone, were worth about £5 million. By the Edwardian era the upward limits of wealth had probably doubled, with Charles Morrison, James's son, leaving £11 million and the duke of Westminster reputedly worth £14 million, chiefly because of his vast London properties. Nevertheless compared with America's multimillionaires of the post–CIVIL WAR Gilded Age, Britain's wealth holders were not particularly rich: John D. Rockefeller, the richest American of the time, was probably worth $250 million by 1900 and about $1 billion at the peak of his wealth 15 years later.

EFFECT OF INDUSTRIALIZATION ON INCOME INEQUALITY

Economic historians have also examined the role of the Industrial Revolution on the distribution of income and wealth in Britain. Because population growth created so many impoverished workers, there is a general consensus that income inequality grew markedly during the nineteenth century, probably reaching its peak about 1870, and then narrowed slightly. This is consistent with the theories of Simon Kuznets, the American economic historian, that income inequality always widens during INDUSTRIALIZATION and then narrows. The pattern apparently found in Britain is, however, inconsistent with Marxist theory, which sees wealth as being held by ever-fewer persons and ever-increasing poverty. The British picture after 1870 provides no evidence for this view.

PROFESSIONS CHARACTERISTIC OF THE WEALTHY

What kind of person was likely to become rich in Victorian Britain? A detailed analysis of wealth hold-ers shows that a disproportionate number earned their fortunes in LONDON, especially in the City of London, as bankers, financiers, merchants, and in other financial and commercial pursuits rather than as manufacturers and industrialists in the new industrial towns in the north of England. Of course there were many wealthy manufacturers, such as Sir ROBERT PEEL, the father of the prime minister, who was the earliest authentic cotton-manufacturing millionaire, but they were outnumbered by commercial and financial wealth holders. This was most true at the very highest levels of wealth: at slightly lower levels, among businessmen who left between £100,000 and £300,000, there were proportionately more northern manufacturers. (About 11,000 persons left £100,000 or more in the century after 1809, when the valuation figures in the probate records began in a usable form.)

Large cities where commerce rather than manufacturing was predominant also produced more wealth holders than manufacturing towns: for example Liverpool produced more top wealth holders than MANCHESTER. There were also considerable numbers of those involved in the professions and public administration. Hundreds of barristers and solicitors, for example, left £100,000 or more during the nineteenth century. Especially during the earlier part of the Victorian era there were still many wealth holders who were the beneficiaries of "Old Corruption," having received phenomenal incomes as government placemen. There were also dozens of very wealthy Anglican clergymen. Consistently during the nineteenth century about 10% of all estates of £100,000 or more were left by women, almost invariably inheriting their fortunes as the daughters or widows of wealthy men. Only a tiny handful appeared to have played any active role in business life. Probably the best known of these was Harriet Mellon, the actress who married the famous banker Thomas Coutts and was actually the banker's active manager after his death. (She later married the much younger duke of St. Albans.) She left more than £600,000.

While there were a handful of genuine self-made millionaires who actually began life poor and built up a great fortune, their numbers were extremely rare in Victorian Britain. For example Edward Lloyd, founder of *The Daily Chronicle*, who left £800,000, began working at age 12. Nevertheless the great majority of the Victorian rich either inherited substantial fortunes or built up an already existing family firm into a large enterprise. Given the social class barriers that existed in Victorian Britain, it was, of course, all but impossible to obtain the capital to start a really successful business.

THE WEBER THESIS

In 1905 the German sociologist Max Weber (1864–1920) propounded the famous Weber Thesis, positing a salient causal connection between Protestantism and capitalism. The Weber Thesis has been discussed almost continuously ever since. In its British context many historians have looked at Protestant Nonconformists as having sparked the Industrial Revolution, noting how many famous inventors and innovators or industrialists were Dissenters. Taking the class of great wealth holders as a whole, however, there is less evidence for this view than one might expect. Most Victorian millionaires were Anglicans, and surprisingly few appear to have been Dissenters. This was probably because those mercantile and financial fields where money was to be made were entered by Anglicans, with Dissenters more prominent in the less lucrative factory capitalism. There were also considerable numbers of wealthy immigrants, especially JEWS, Greeks, and Germans, particularly in the City of London.

NEWLY RICH INDIFFERENT TO LAND OWNERSHIP

One subject that has been debated by historians of this subject is whether newly rich businessmen bought land in large amounts, attempting to join the landed gentry. To a surprising extent, no consensus has emerged on this question, whose ambiguity has revolved around which group of businessmen one examines, and what constitutes substantial land purchase. Nevertheless, given the enormous amount of wealth generated by the Industrial Revolution, much less land was purchased by newly rich businessmen than was potentially there to buy. Less than 10% of the major landowners listed in John Bateman's *Great Landowners of Great Britain and Ireland* (1883), based on the 1872 to 1875 official Return of Owners of Land, appear to have been members of families who earned their fortunes after 1780, while the great majority had owned their land for far longer. This is not inconsistent, however, with the fact that many hundreds of newly rich Victorian businessmen bought or built COUNTRY HOUSES, although their percentage among all notable Victorian businessmen remains unexplored.

See also ARISTOCRACY; COUNTRY HOUSE; INDUSTRIALIZATION; LAND AND LANDOWNERS; SOCIAL CLASSES.

FURTHER READING

Rubinstein, W. D. *Men of Property: The Very Wealthy in Britain since the Industrial Revolution.* London: Routledge, 1981.

Thompson, F. M. L. *Gentrification and the Enterprise Culture: Britain 1780–1980.* Oxford: Oxford University Press, 2001.

Williamson, Jeffrey G. *Did British Capitalism Breed Inequality?* Boston: Allen and Unwin, 1985.

W. D. RUBINSTEIN

WELLS, H. G.

Born: September 21, 1866; Bromley, England
Died: August 13, 1946; London, England

Few prominent Victorian writers devoted more attention to the future than the prolific novelist, journalist, and popular historian Herbert George Wells. An early adherent to SOCIALISM, H. G. Wells is perhaps best known for his science fiction works, which contained both implicit and explicit critiques of Victorian society. His lengthy career extended well into the twentieth century, but his initial fame developed in the last years of the Victorian era.

Wells spent much of his youth reading extensively, a habit he developed from a lengthy recovery from the complications of a leg fracture he sustained at age seven. Family financial difficulties required that he, like the protagonist in his NOVEL *Kipps* (1905), become an apprentice to a draper. He was able to continue to read voraciously by having access to the LIBRARY of an estate where his mother worked as a housekeeper. After studying at several schools in Bromley, he was admitted at age 17 to the Normal School of Science in LONDON where THOMAS HENRY HUXLEY was one of his instructors. Leaving his studies in 1887, he taught for several years at schools around London before earning his bachelor of science degree with honors in zoology. In the early 1890s, while working as a biology teacher, he developed health problems; during his recuperation he began his career as an author, writing several volumes of textbook material and preparing articles as a scientific journalist. He later returned to teaching and divorced his first wife, his cousin Isabel, in 1895; in the same year Wells married his student Amy Catherine Robbins, and they remained together until her death 32 years later.

Wells's writing career flourished in 1895 with the publications of a collection of short stories and his highly popular novel, *The Time Machine*, his initial "scientific romance." The book depicts a world 800,000 years in the future populated by the idle Eloi and the beastly Morlocks, who provide for the Eloi but also cannibalize them. Wells thus offers his pre-

In his works of science fiction, author H. G. Wells offered a searching critique of Victorian society.

diction of Victorian socioeconomic class divisions degenerating into a destructive split in the human species. This pessimistic portrayal of class-based Darwinian EVOLUTION was a critical and PUBLISHING success. A similar questioning of evolution and scientific PROGRESS was expressed in his shockingly gruesome novel *The Island of Doctor Moreau* (1896), where a prototypical mad scientist uses painful surgical techniques and unethical experiments to convert animals into humans. An evocative criticism of vivisectionists (those who practice animal experimentation that is perceived to cause harm to the animal) and immoral science, the novel offers a potent critique of the limits of science and its practitioners. Scientific advancement also is shown to lead to madness and criminality in Wells's *The Invisible Man* (1897), which contains a comic depiction of Victorian country life that Wells also satirizes in his fantasy *The Wonderful Visit* (1895). In *The War of the Worlds* (1898) Wells provides a fearful portrayal of England devastated by aliens invading from Mars—a subject of significant speculation by astronomers in the late Victorian period. This book not only evokes the horrors of war but also shows the inadequacy of science in defending England from superior TECHNOL-

OGY produced by a species that is nonetheless subsequently destroyed by terrestrial bacteria.

To address issues such as social ENGINEERING, monogamy, hunger and POVERTY, the need for world government, and dictatorships, Wells used other science fiction, futuristic, and fantasy works such as *The First Men in the Moon* (1901), *In the Days of the Comet* (1906), *When the Sleeper Wakes* (1899), *The War in the Air* (1908), *The Food of the Gods* (1904), *A Modern Utopia* (1905), *The World Set Free* (1914), and *The Shape of Things to Come* (1933), and short stories such as "The Man Who Could Work Miracles" (1937). These works anticipated such developments as the use of tanks and aircraft in warfare, the splitting of the atom and atomic power, lunar expeditions, urban expansion, and women's liberation, and several had Utopian themes.

Wells's numerous publications, however, were not in any way confined to the science fiction and fantasy works that brought him his early celebrity. His many short stories and novels such as *Kipps, The Wheels of Chance* (1896), *Love and Mr. Lewisham* (1900), and *The History of Mr. Polly* (1910) often focused on gentle portraits of the common people living in England and the problems of the lower middle class from which Wells himself had risen. His involvement with Fabian socialists (from whom he later broke when he was unable to influence their leadership) led to fictional works that included criticisms of class structure and hereditary ARISTOCRACY. Notorious for his extramarital affairs, Wells brought his own notions of sexual freedom into his romantic novels such as *Ann Veronica* (1909), *The Passionate Friends* (1913), and *The Research Magnificent* (1915). Other works such as *Mr. Britling Sees It Through* (1916) and *This Misery of Boots* (1907) addressed social and political issues. *Tono-Bungay* (1909) depicted irresponsible behavior in the BUSINESS world. In his later years Wells's fictional works took on an increasingly pessimistic tone.

Wells was equally prolific in authoring nonfiction and historical works. These reflected his ideas about social problems and the improvements in society that he believed to be necessary for human survival. Some of his early pamphlets criticized the social structure of Victorian England, and he often wrote for PERIODICALS ranging from *The Fortnightly Review* to *The New Republic*. His popular histories, *The Outline of History* (1920) and *A Short History of the World* (1922), were both publishing sensations.

Disillusioned with communism after conversations with Lenin and Trotsky, Wells wrote about the evolution of society and civilization, arguing that education rather than revolutionary actions would be the hope for a brighter future. He collaborated on a well-received scientific survey, *The Science of Life* (1929–1939), and wrote another textbook entitled *The Work, Wealth, and Happiness of Mankind* (1932), which summarized many of his beliefs. Following the death of his wife he wrote her biography and subsequently prepared his massive *Experiment in Autobiography* (1934); he also completed works on education and human rights.

Always interested in public issues, Wells worked during World War I (1914–1918) for the ministry of information and later supported the League of Nations. He twice ran unsuccessfully for Parliament in the early 1920s as a Labour candidate, and in the 1930s he traveled extensively to discuss world issues with such leaders as Joseph Stalin and Franklin Delano Roosevelt. Increasingly critical of political leadership and especially concerned with totalitarianism, *The Holy Terror* (1939) explored the psychological qualities of dictators such as Stalin, Adolf Hitler, and Benito Mussolini. At age 77 he was awarded a doctorate from the University of London for a study on personality, yet *Mind at the End of Its Tether* (1945) revealed his deep doubts about the survival of civilization. Suffering from diabetes and other maladies, Wells died at the outset of the Cold War at a time when his goal of a rational world order seemed as elusive as ever. Though often preoccupied with the future, H. G. Wells proved through his more than 100 different publications to be one of the most persistent critics of the Victorian society from which he came.

See also SOCIALISM.

FURTHER READING

Batchelor, John. *H. G. Wells.* New York: Cambridge University Press, 1985.

Brome, Vincent. *H. G. Wells.* Westport: Greenwood Press, 1970.

Foot, Michael. *H. G.: The History of Mr. Wells.* New York: Basic Books, 1995.

Haynes, R. D. *H. G. Wells—Discoverer of the Future: The Influence of Science on His Thought.* New York: New York University Press, 1980.

MacKenzie, Norman Ian, and Jeanne MacKenzie. *H. G. Wells.* New York: Simon and Schuster, 1973.

Smith, David C. *H. G. Wells, Desperately Mortal: A Biography.* New Haven: Yale University Press, 1986.

West, Anthony. *H. G. Wells: Aspects of a Life.* New York: Random House, 1984.

STEPHEN SHAFER

WESTMINSTER, PALACE OF

Originally constructed by King Canute (994–1035), the Palace of Westminster and its adjoining abbey were improved by Edward the Confessor (1003–1066). Subsequent Norman and Plantagenet kings made the palace their main royal residence in LONDON, pleased with its access to the River Thames. As Parliament grew in influence the House of Lords claimed the Chapter House, then the Painted Chamber for its meetings, while the Commons held its meeting in St. Stephen's Chapel. Henry VIII (1491–1547), who used Westminster Hall as a tennis court, finally abandoned Westminster for Whitehall as a royal residence in 1529, leaving the building complex for bureaucratic and parliamentary use.

On October 16, 1834, workmen burning medieval tally sticks as kindling overheated the palace furnace, causing a fire that quickly consumed the old building and most of its priceless archives. Only Westminster Hall was saved, by pumping in water from the Thames. Determined to rebuild on the site, a parliamentary committee of amateur architects offered a competition to design the new Westminster, specifying an Elizabethan or Gothic style, in contrast to the Greco-Roman style favored by American and European government buildings. The winning design by Sir Charles Barry (1795–1860) honored the English origins of Parliament with a Gothic design, meant to function as both a ceremonial center and working office complex.

Barry's contractors, Grissell and Petro, first drained the marshy Thames riverbank before laying a deep concrete foundation. Actual construction began in 1840 and exploited Victorian technological advances including cast iron girders, tram systems to deliver materials, and steam-powered winches. At any given time 200 craftsmen and up to 1,400 laborers, many of them Irish refugees, worked on the construction site. The interior decoration, overseen by a committed headed by PRINCE ALBERT (1819–1861), was handled by Augustus Pugin (1812–1852), who custom-designed every detail, down to specially fabricated door locks and floor grates, and used British textile mills and foundries in his orders for carpets and fixtures. The design preserved ancient parliamentary customs, such as the facing arrangement of seats, copying from the pews in St. Stephen's Chapel, and the safe distance of two sword lengths between the two banks of benches. All of the decoration stressed the continuity and dignity of the royal succession and the "British" identity of England, Scotland, Wales, and IRELAND.

BROWN BROS.

Westminster Abbey, the most famous church in the Commonwealth, is the focal point for the Palace of Westminster, the seat of the British government. The abbey is steeped in history and is the final resting place of numerous distinguished Britons and outstanding statesmen as well as many of England's monarchs.

The House of Lords met in their new chamber beginning in 1847, the Commons in 1850.

Neither Barry nor Pugin lived to see the building completed in 1870, Barry dying in 1860 and Pugin in 1852. ELECTRICITY was added to the House of Lords in 1883 and the Commons in 1912, while other modern conveniences, such as a parking garage and computer cabling, have since been blended into the original structure. Major reconstruction had to be done to repair bomb damage suffered in 1940–1941, while pollution and age make maintaining the details of Westminster's interior and exterior an ongoing process for the British government.

See also ARCHITECTURE; PARLIAMENTARY GOVERNMENT.

FURTHER READING

Atterbury, Paul, ed. *A. W. N. Pugin: Master of Gothic Revival.* New Haven: Yale University Press, 1995.

Cooke, Robert. *The Palace of Westminster.* New York: Burton Skira, 1987.

Jones, Christopher. *The Great Palace: The Story of Parliament.* London: British Broadcasting Company, 1983.

MARGARET SANKEY

WHEWELL, WILLIAM

Born: May 24, 1794; Lancaster, England
Died: March 6, 1866; Cambridge, England

William Whewell, recognized as a scientist, classicist, educator, and polymath (someone with many areas of skill and expertise), was one of the dominant figures in Victorian science and a leader in reforming the traditional curriculum of Cambridge University. The eldest child of a carpenter, his superior intellect took him to Trinity College, Cambridge, where he was elected a fellow in 1817. He subsequently served as assistant tutor (1818–1823), tutor (1823–1838), and master of the college (1841–1866). He was elected to the professorships of mineralogy (1825–

1832) and moral PHILOSOPHY (1838–55), and served two terms as university vice-chancellor (1842–1843 and 1856–1857).

Whewell's Cambridge friends and associates included the astronomers J. F. W. Herschel, Richard Sheepshanks, and George Biddell Airy; mathematicians CHARLES BABBAGE and George Peacock; economist Richard Jones; classicists Julius Hare and Connop Thirlwall; and geologist Adam Sedgwick. Together they introduced the teaching of advanced mathematics, mathematical science, and the philological and comparative approach to classical studies pioneered by continental European scholars.

Standing at the center of a network of Victorian scientists, Whewell was a member of more than 20 LEARNED SOCIETIES, and his wide-ranging contributions encompassed PHYSICS, ASTRONOMY, GEOLOGY, and mineralogy, as well as geophysics. He wrote and published best-selling textbooks on mechanics and dynamics, endeavored to measure the density of the earth, and pioneered the empirical study of tides. As a professor of mineralogy he formulated the basis of modern, mathematical crystallography, later known as the "law of rational indices." He was also the first to apply mathematics to the study of ECONOMICS, leading him to criticize the work of notable economists David Ricardo (1772–1823) and JOHN STUART MILL (1806–1873).

In his *History of the Inductive Sciences* (1837) and *Philosophy of the Inductive Sciences* (1840), Whewell developed a new philosophical explanation of the scientific method based upon the history of scientific research and discovery. A clergyman as well as a scientist, Whewell, like many other scientists of his generation, clung to the miraculous explanation of human origins. Nonetheless, his criticism of his friend CHARLES DARWIN's (1809–1882) major work on EVOLUTION was restrained and impersonal.

In addition to science and philosophy, Whewell published works on Gothic ARCHITECTURE, classical PHILOLOGY, economics, education, ethics, MORALITY, and theology. He composed POETRY and translated both Plato's dialogues and works of German literature into English. As master of Trinity, he modernized the college's statutes and endowed it with new buildings and scholarships. Although he spread his efforts thinly, as one of the last major scientists to shun specialization Whewell made enduring contributions, not least in the coining of a number of scientific terms, such as "physicist" and "scientist," demonstrating his immense influence on science in the Victorian period and after.

See also ASTRONOMY; ECONOMICS; GEOLOGY; LEARNED SOCIETIES; PHILOSOPHY; UNIVERSITIES.

FURTHER READING

Douglas, Janet Mary. *The Life and Selections from the Correspondence of William Whewell, D.D. Late Master of Trinity College Cambridge.* 1881. Reprint, Bristol: Thoemmes, 1991.

Fisch, Menachem. *William Whewell: Philosopher of Science.* Oxford: Clarendon Press, 1991.

Fisch, Menachem, and Simon Schaffer, eds. *William Whewell: A Composite Portrait.* Oxford: Clarendon Press, 1991.

Henderson, James. *Early Mathematical Economics: William Whewell and the British Case.* Lanham, Md.: Rowman and Littlefield, 1996.

Todhunter, Isaac. *William Whewell, D.D. Master of Trinity College, Cambridge: An Account of His Writings with Selections from His Literary and Scientific Correspondence.* 2 vols. London: Macmillan, 1876.

Yeo, Richard. *Defining Science: William Whewell, Natural Knowledge, and Public Debate in Early Victorian England.* Cambridge: Cambridge University Press, 1993.

MERRILL DISTAD

WHISTLER, JAMES MCNEILL

Born: July 10, 1834; Lowell, Massachusetts
Died: July 17, 1903; London, England

An innovative painter and graphic artist, an outspoken polemicist and self-publicist, and a pugnacious DANDY who sometimes resorted to fisticuffs, James Abbott McNeill Whistler courted controversy throughout his life. In his assumed role of leading exponent and spokesman on behalf of aestheticism, he fought a continuing battle against British insularity and philistinism (an attitude of ignorance toward artistic values). His commentaries on the nature and function of art and on the crucial matter of creative independence are among the most illuminating ever made by a practicing artist.

In Paris in 1855 Whistler was initially attracted by the realism of Gustave Courbet (1819–1877) but had abandoned it within a few years of moving to London in 1859. In Paris he had encountered the doctrine of "art for art's sake," which championed art as an autonomous, self-sufficient activity, serving no function beyond the creation of beauty. From Japanese prints Whistler learned how to express the essentials of form through summary, graceful strokes and subtle color harmonies; and Greek sculpture provided further lessons in formal perfection. Through his series of *White Girls* (1862–1867), he evolved a radical and sophisticated solution to the abstract, decorative treatment of the human figure, emphasizing his intentions by renaming them *Symphonies in White*. His later portraits were given similar titles: most famously the *Arrangement in Black and Grey: Portrait of the Painter's Mother* (1871, Musée d'Orsay).

Whistler's abstract tendencies climaxed with the *Nocturnes*. Largely inspired by the foggy atmosphere of the industrialized Thames, they enabled him to demonstrate the artist's command over nature, and his ability to transform any motif, however unpromising, into an object of beauty. At the opening of the Grosvenor Gallery in 1877, Whistler's *Nocturne in Black and Gold* (1874, Detroit Institute) was dismissed by Britain's leading critic, John Ruskin, as a mere daub—"a pot of paint [flung] in the public's face." Whistler sued for libel, using the ensuing trial as a platform for his artistic theories. He opposed the notion that art should serve a narrative or moral function, insisting that his *Nocturne* was primarily "an artistic arrangement" of line, form, and color. Although he won the case, the costs bankrupted him; but he soon recovered through the ready sale of etchings, pastels, and portraits. Beginning in 1885 Whistler renewed his war against philistinism in a series of witty, waspish lectures, pamphlets, and letters to the press.

Whistler was an inspired decorative designer, cultivating a minimalist style in the Tite Street House designed by the leading aesthetic architect E. W. Godwin. Although the house was destroyed, the blue and gold Peacock Room (1876–1877), which in its expressive linearism is an important precursor of ART NOUVEAU, is now in the Freer Gallery, Washington.

Despite his provocative behavior and cultivated posing, Whistler was passionately dedicated to the cause of art, seizing every opportunity in word and paint to proclaim its unique value. His originality and integrity, as both artist and theorist, have ensured his lasting reputation as one of the most important and influential artists of the nineteenth century.

See also AESTHETIC MOVEMENT; ART NOUVEAU.

FURTHER READING

Merrill, Linda. *A Pot of Paint: Aesthetics on Trial in Whistler v. Ruskin.* Washington, D.C.: Smithsonian Institution Press with the Freer Gallery, 1992.
Whistler, J. A. M. *The Gentle Art of Making Enemies.* New York: Dover, 1978.

MARY COWLING

WHITMAN, WALT

Born: May 31, 1819; West Hills, New York
Died: March 26, 1892; Camden, New Jersey

Poet, editor, and tenacious trumpeter of "these United States," Walt Whitman was a larger-than-life figure whose lifespan nearly paralleled that of QUEEN VICTO-

CHICAGO HISTORICAL SOCIETY
The American poet Walt Whitman.

RIA herself, but who came to represent a sensibility quite alien to that associated with the monarch who lent her name to an era they each defined in their own way. Whitman published several books during his lifetime, including *Drum-Taps* (CIVIL WAR memoirs, 1865), *Democratic Vistas* (political commentaries, 1871), and *Specimen Days & Collect* (travel pieces and memoirs, 1882–1883), but he is most universally renowned for his collection of poetry, *Leaves of Grass*, first published in 1855.

THE POET OF A SPRAWLING NATION

Though Victoria was unlikely to have been amused by this freewheeling poet of American democracy whose unconventional attitudes toward sexuality and social class flouted the stuffy bourgeois MORALITY and formalism she came to symbolize, he was appreciative enough to dedicate a transatlantic birthday verse to her in 1890, one "(smelling of countless blessings, prayers, and old-time thanks)—/ A bunch of white and pink arbutus, silent, spicy, shy, / From Hudson's, Delaware's, or Potomac's woody banks." But this was

175

not a mere sentimental gesture: in characteristic Whitmanesque fashion, he specified that it be "an American arbutus bunch" that was "to be put in a little vase of the royal breakfast table, May 24, 1890," in recognition of Victoria's "firm attitude" that forestalled Britain from joining the Civil War on behalf of the Confederacy some three decades earlier. On "this moment of a woman and queen," Whitman garrulously wrote in a footnote to the poem, "surely swung the grandest oscillation of modern history's pendulum."

This expression of Whitman's exuberance captures the fervent, bumptious temperament of a man who in so many ways shared the worldview of other Victorian-era writers on both sides of the Atlantic: a faith in PROGRESS, a belief that democratic values (especially of the American Jeffersonian and Jacksonian varieties) could help mitigate the harshness of industrial capitalism, and a fascination with scientific and technical innovation. (In "Song of the Exposition," a poem celebrating an industrial exposition not unlike the GREAT EXHIBITION OF 1851, he invoked a Muse "bluff'd not a bit by drain-pipe" and "install'd among the kitchen ware!") Whitman had long demonstrated an instinctive allegiance to working-class themes that resonated in the thinking of British utopian socialists such as Edward Carpenter and the Webbs, and an equally instinctive openness to a transcendental spirituality that included elements of Hindu and Buddhist thought, of the sort that might attract those aesthetes who were abandoning the established faith of which Victoria was a staunch defender. Not surprisingly, Dr. Richard Maurice Bucke, a Canadian, included Whitman in his 1901 tome, *Cosmic Consciousness*, among an array of highly evolved spiritual beings that included Buddha, Socrates, Jesus, and William Blake.

Without demeaning his considerable poetic talent, Whitman can be described as a cabinet of curiosities, a Victorian miscellany, arguably the most effusive village explainer the UNITED STATES had in the nineteenth or any other century. His far-ranging interests prompted him to include in his poetry and prose the great variety of Victorian life; he depicted phrenologists, the operas and popular entertainments of New York and Brooklyn, the Free Soil movement, "canker'd, crude, superstitious, and rotten" politics, the role of NEWSPAPERS, the camaraderie of mechanics and streetcar conductors, and the starry-eyed conceit of learned astronomers. In keeping with the spirit of a nation that was attempting to subdue a frontier wilderness, Whitman insisted that "I too am not a bit tamed—I too am untranslatable; I sound my barbaric yawp over the roofs of the world." But he is never a mere showman, like his countryman P. T. BARNUM; his poignant and elegiac lyrics on the death of Lincoln in "When Lilacs Last in the Door-yard Bloom'd" (included in *Drum-Taps*) are still considered by critics among the finest poetry America has ever produced, just as "O Captain! My Captain!" on the same theme is considered among the nation's most eminent doggerel.

LEAVES OF GRASS

Whitman was born in West Hills, on Long Island in New York, on May 31, 1819, the second of nine children of Walter Whitman, a carpenter of English stock, and his wife, Louisa Van Velsor, of Dutch and Welsh ancestry. Though neither of his parents had much formal education, they had a significant influence on young Walt's development. The elder Whitman, a Quaker in the liberal Hicksite tradition, was a supporter of the radical social ideas of Thomas Paine, whom he had met, and had further declared his faith in American democracy by naming three of his sons after George Washington, Thomas Jefferson, and Andrew Jackson. Walt worked with his father and brothers in the house-building trade in Brooklyn before taking on odd jobs as a typesetter and schoolteacher, all the while reading widely and voraciously. In the 1840s he wrote two temperance novels, began contributing pro–Democratic Party articles to local New York newspapers, and edited the *Brooklyn Eagle* from 1846 to 1848. For a brief period he edited the *New Orleans Crescent*, then returned home to found the *Brooklyn Freeman* and to edit the *Brooklyn Times* from 1857 to 1859.

In the meantime, in 1855 Whitman published *Leaves of Grass*, a poetry collection that he continued to revise over the years and that has come to be considered one of the landmarks of American literature. In it, he forged a unique poetical syntax of cadence and imagery that broke significantly with older models. His was arguably the first distinctly American verse, one that extolled the common man—even though the common man was often an undisguised personification of Whitman himself, as in "Song of Myself" (though modestly untitled as such until the 1882 edition), which famously begins "I celebrate myself, and sing myself. . . ." But he could also turn his approving gaze on vast, teeming crowds, either of Brooklyn ferry or a whole nation, as in his lines, "I hear America singing," a paean to the "varied carols" of carpenters, mechanics, and woodcutters. In a romantic tradition that had been transmuted into TRANSCENDENTALISM by midcentury, Whitman celebrated the sensuousness of the body (and all its enumerated parts) in "I Sing the Body Electric." Not surprisingly, the first significant critic to welcome the work's publication was the transcendentalist Ralph Waldo Emerson, who declared the collection "the most extraordinary piece of wit and wisdom that America has yet contributed."

After the Civil War broke out in 1861, Whitman went to Washington to seek out his brother, George, who was wounded in battle. The poet remained in Washington until 1873, working as a government clerk and, during the war years, spending his free time as a volunteer nurse and comrade to battle-scarred soldiers. (The letters he wrote to his mother about these experiences were edited by Dr. Bucke and published as *The Wound-Dresser* in 1897.) The Civil War years represented a vivid and highly charged period in Whitman's life, in which his spiritual gravity was vitalized by his humanitarian (and subliminal homoerotic) solidarity with the soldiers he tended, and in which he witnessed at close range the fast-moving drama that culminated in the assassination of Lincoln and the prevalence of the Union's cause.

When the war ended Whitman worked as a government clerk but was dismissed by the secretary of the interior after a copy of *Leaves of Grass*, considered obscene, was discovered in his desk. After suffering a stroke in 1873, Whitman left Washington for Camden, New Jersey, first taking up residence with his brother George and then buying his own house at 328 Mickle Street, where he remained until his death on March 26, 1892.

In Victorian America, Whitman was a larger-than-life witness to, and spokesman for, the bewildering social and cultural expansiveness that took place during the century. This man who came to be known as "the good, gray poet" was the literary interpreter of the dramatic shifts in American sense and sensibility during the nineteenth century. A child of the Jacksonian era—the period in which the common man of the frontier asserted his ascendancy over the colonial aristocracies of New England and Virginia—Whitman would come to be an ardent critic of the expansion of slavery, a worshipful supporter of Lincoln and the Union, a wound dresser to the young soldier-victims of the Civil War, an avatar of homophilia ostentatiously saluted by OSCAR WILDE on his American tour, and, in his later, wearier years, the sage of Camden, where he received visitors from around the world to a simple frame house on Mickle Street.

See also POETRY.

FURTHER READING

Allen, Gay Wilson. *The Solitary Singer: A Critical Biography of Walt Whitman.* New York: Macmillan, 1955.

Kaplan, Justin. *Walt Whitman: A Life.* New York: Simon and Schuster, 1980.

Loving, Jerome. *Walt Whitman: The Song of Himself.* Berkeley: University of California Press, 1999.

Myerson, Joel, ed. *Walt Whitman: A Documentary Volume.* Detroit: Gale Group, 2000.

Reynolds, David S. *Walt Whitman's America: A Cultural Biography.* New York: Knopf, 1995.

EDWARD MORAN

WILDE, OSCAR

Born: October 16, 1854; Dublin, Ireland
Died: November 30, 1900; Paris, France

"I am a man who stood in symbolic relations to the art and culture of my age," claimed Oscar Fingal O'Flahertie Wills Wilde in a remark that, though tainted by the egotism he made into a philosophy, contains a great deal of truth. For though Wilde is still sometimes seen as the most eloquently and flamboyantly outspoken Victorian exponent of Aestheticism and a fierce advocate for the autonomy of art, his writings—like his life—consistently engage with the values Victorian society held dear. Whether it be in turning earnestness and sincerity on their heads (*The Importance of Being Earnest*, 1895); in dramatizing the restless search for sensation and the satisfaction of untrammeled desire (*Salome*, 1892) or chronicling its consequences and those of vanity (*The Picture of Dorian Gray*, 1891); in his condemnation of British penal laws and judicial sanctimony (*The Ballad of Reading Gaol*, 1898); or in the critique of marriage conventions that runs through his society comedies, Wilde's works, without exception, subvert the dominant values of Victorian England. Dissidence runs through them like a leitmotif; and critics have pointed variously to Wilde's sexuality, his Irishness, his SOCIALISM, or simply to an indeterminate perversity as the root of that dissidence. Whatever the explanation, his writings paint the portrait of an artist-thinker in many ways at odds with his time, holding more in common with the Modernism he helped usher into being than with the Victorianism he eventually ran foul of.

A NAME OF HIGH DISTINCTION

Wilde was born in Dublin to highly accomplished middle-class parents with pronounced nationalist and literary ambitions. His mother was the Irish nationalist poet "Speranza." His father, an oculist and ear sur-

Author Oscar Wilde and his companion Lord Alfred Douglas posing in 1894.

geon of international repute, was also an accomplished amateur archaeologist, folklorist, and member of the Royal Irish Academy, whose many published works include a collection of Irish folk tales and a biography of Jonathan Swift. Justifiably, Wilde later claimed, "I inherited from my father and mother a name of high distinction in literature and art." But his parents' disregard for the conventional proprieties landed them both in court—Wilde's mother for publishing seditious POETRY, Wilde's father for allegedly raping a woman patient—and though both were found innocent, there can be little doubt that his parents' experiences at the hands of the British legal system helped shape the young Wilde's attitudes.

After an accomplished career at Trinity College, Dublin, where he won the Berkeley Gold Medal for Greek and fell under the spell of the brilliant classics professor John Pentland Mahaffy, Wilde entered Magdalen College, Oxford, on a classics demyship (a form of scholarship) in June 1874. Wilde excelled academically at Oxford, but his four years spent there were perhaps more remarkable for witnessing the beginnings of his career as a poet as well as his growing reputation, both in London and in Oxford, as an

aesthete and DANDY. His university rooms were filled with the blue china favored by the Pre-Raphaelites, and it was at Oxford that he quipped about how difficult it was to "live up to my blue china." As importantly, it was as a student that Wilde came under the influence of his tutors, the art critics JOHN RUSKIN and WALTER PATER, whose ideas discernibly affected his later writings.

POET, DANDY, AESTHETE

Wilde graduated in 1878 determined to pursue a literary and artistic career rather than the academic one he had seemed destined for. Both his poetry and his prose at this time speak of a fierce determination to occupy a position of authority within English cultural and literary traditions, and Wilde was satirized widely in PUNCH and on stage in these years as epitomizing the self-consciously aesthetic young man. His 1881 volume Poems was widely (though not always positively) reviewed and ran into several editions. Also in 1881 Richard D'Oyly Carte of the D'Oyly Carte opera company invited Wilde to give a series of lectures in the United States as an accompaniment to a tour of GILBERT AND SULLIVAN's operetta Patience, in which Wilde was satirized as the "fleshly poet" Bunthorne. Quickly dispensing with the knee breeches and velveteen jacket in which he delivered the first few lectures, Wilde used the tour to develop a sustained and nuanced platform for aesthetic ideas, with which he charmed American audiences. On his return, he spent three months in Paris, where he made important friendships among the French symbolists, before embarking on a career as a lecturer and journalist. In 1884 Wilde married Constance Lloyd (herself a keen aesthete), designing his wife's wedding dress himself and using the occasion to promote the aesthetic ideas with which his name was rapidly becoming associated.

In the mid-1880s the couple had two sons. For them Wilde created fairy stories which became the basis for his books A Happy Prince and Other Tales (1888) and A House of Pomegranates (1891) and which remain among the finest in all children's literature. Family responsibilities spurred Wilde's career as an author, and the late 1880s brought the publication of a number of ingenious short stories (gathered into the 1891 book Lord Arthur Savile's Crime and Other Stories) as well as the series of brilliant critical essays and dialogues that were republished in 1891 as Intentions. While not the most popular of his works, the latter rank among the most innovative works of critical theory produced in the Victorian era, prefiguring critical concepts now commonplace among post-structuralists and postmodernists.

WILDE'S HOMOSEXUALITY

The late 1880s were also marked for Wilde by a growing recognition of his HOMOSEXUALITY and his first sexual relations with men. His first homosexual relationship (with Robert Ross) began in 1886, the year of his son Cyril's birth. And though Wilde was to take many male lovers over the ensuing years, the relationship with Ross has some claims to rivaling that with Lord Alfred Douglas as the most important so far as his writing is concerned.

Wilde's emerging homosexuality began to affect his writing almost immediately—it can be sensed in the air of tragedy and secrecy that hangs over the characters of his children's stories—and in 1889 he published an essay ("The Portrait of Mr. W. H.") dedicated to proving (insofar as it can be proven) that the muse for Shakespeare's sonnets was a young male actor. This essay established convincing grounds for regarding the most iconic of English playwright/poets as a practicing homosexual, "queering the canon" as no other nineteenth-century critical text had done. However, from a literary standpoint, his only novel, *The Picture of Dorian Gray*, is the most interesting fruit of Wilde's incursions into London's homosexual subculture. Published in *Lippincott's Magazine* in 1890, the book scandalized English reviewers with its depictions of same-sex intimacy and infatuation (toned down for the 1891 book version), as well as by its apparent endorsement of a life of sensory fulfillment, and henceforth Wilde found himself increasingly at odds with a hostile critical establishment.

The initial reaction of *Dorian Gray*'s creator was to foreswear fiction and turn to playwriting, in which he had always been interested. But his first experiment in this vein (*Salome*), a symbolist drama written for the French actress SARAH BERNHARDT, only widened Wilde's disaffection with the Victorian establishment when it was banned in England. (It was performed in Paris, in French, in 1896.) Publicly Wilde announced that he would henceforth exile himself to France; and privately he devoted himself to writing a lengthy decadent poem ("The Sphinx") that he vowed "would destroy domesticity in England." But over the next few years the series of sparkling, brilliantly epigrammatic society comedies ensured his lasting place in the THEATER repertoire and brought the adjective "Wildean" into the language to indicate a particular style and quality of wit. This series of plays—*Lady Windermere's Fan* (1892), *A Woman of No Importance* (1893), *An Ideal Husband* (1895), and, supremely, *The Importance of Being Earnest*—constitutes a remarkable body of work by any standards and contributed greatly to the revival of interest in the drama as a serious literary form.

SCANDAL

The years of success as a dramatist were also those of greatest turbulence in Wilde's private life, owing largely to his unconquerable love for the vain Lord Alfred Douglas (1870–1945). Disaster struck in 1895 when Wilde allowed Douglas to persuade him into bringing a libel suit against his lover's father, the marquess of Queensberry. He lost the suit, Queensberry's lawyers having vindicated their client's claim that Wilde was a "posing somdomite" (sic), and Wilde was subsequently prosecuted to the fullest extent under England's harsh new anti-homosexual statutes. A two-year jail term resulted in the permanent breakdown of Wilde's health, estrangement from his family, and a major diminishing of his literary talent. Notwithstanding this last, the long autobiographical letter he wrote in jail in 1897, posthumously published as *De Profundis*, is a remarkable and painful document of self-reinvention; and imprisonment inspired *The Ballad of Reading Gaol,* a haunting and damning poetic indictment of man's inhumanity to man. Emerging from jail in 1897, he fled to exile in France, where he took the name Sebastian Melmoth, and died in Paris three years later, an impoverished and broken man.

See also AESTHETIC MOVEMENT; HOMOSEXUALITY; POETRY; THEATER.

FURTHER READING

Coakley, Davis. *Oscar Wilde: The Importance of Being Irish.* Dublin: Town House, 1994.

Ellmann, Richard. *Oscar Wilde.* London: Hamish Hamilton, 1987.

Frankel, Nicholas. *Oscar Wilde's Decorated Books.* Ann Arbor, Mich.: Univ. of Michigan Press, 2000.

Gagnier, Regenia. *Idylls of the Marketplace: Oscar Wilde and the Victorian Public.* Stanford: Stanford University Press, 1986.

Mikhail, E. H. *Oscar Wilde: An Annotated Bibliography of Criticism.* Totowa N.J.: Rowman and Littlefield, 1978.

Sinfield, Alan. *The Wilde Century: Effeminacy, Oscar Wilde, and the Queer Movement.* New York: Columbia University Press, 1994.

Small, Ian. *Oscar Wilde Revalued.* Greensboro, N.C.: ELT Press, 1993.

NICHOLAS FRANKEL

WILDERNESS AND PUBLIC LANDS

Ideas about the American wilderness, from New England's forests to the American West's mesas and canyons, changed dramatically between the 1840s and 1900s. Americans abandoned their Puritan beliefs about wilderness as the antithesis of PROGRESS and adopted a new one that stressed the spiritual and glorious side of nature. This new conception of wilderness, embodied by the Romantic writers and artists of the mid-nineteenth century, gave rise to the conservation of public lands in the UNITED STATES OF AMERICA, best illustrated by the nascent national parks movement of the late nineteenth century.

The experiences of English colonists in the seventeenth century generated Americans' first ideas of wilderness, or the belief that the forests harbored evil spirits and thwarted civilization. Colonists were biased against wilderness from the start, which is shown in three main sets of beliefs. The Enlightenment (the dominant intellectual movement of the seventeenth and eighteenth centuries) stressed Cartesian duality, where thinking became separate from material substance. Objective sciences thus became disembodied from the natural world, and nature separated from culture. Biblical ideas of reclaiming a fallen Canaan through industry inspired settlers to clear ancient forests, build towns, and destroy the Indian savages. On a physical level wilderness (and its indigenous populations) also constituted a direct threat to colonists' survival. It is thus not surprising that colonists equated wilderness with evil and savagery. Plymouth Colony governor William Bradford, for example, described the New England forest as a "hideous and desolate wilderness, full of wild beasts and wild men." Puritan writers such as NATHANIEL HAWTHORNE made the New England forest an allegory for evil, guilt, and fallen morality.

Over the next century Americans altered their views of wilderness in response to many factors. In the late 1700s and early 1800s, British poets and writers such as John Clare, John Keats, WILLIAM WORDSWORTH, and Samuel Taylor Coleridge began to see nature as a source of inspiration and celebration. They celebrated pastoral and wild landscapes at a time when the open English countryside was being divided up by the Enclosure Acts, which further spurred the growth of capitalist AGRICULTURE. Americans simultaneously saw the blossoming of literary ROMANTICISM. Poets and writers including William Cullen Bryant, James Fenimore Cooper, and Emily Dickinson celebrated, rather than denigrated, wilderness. The philosophers Ralph Waldo Emerson and Henry David Thoreau, as well as the landscape painters THOMAS COLE and Albert Bierstadt, among others, began to embrace a more spiritual view of nature that glorified its grandeur rather than its "hideous" qualities. Instead of Calvinist views of evil, Emerson, Thoreau, and their colleagues discerned a spark of divinity in nature.

Divine nature was fast disappearing from the North American continent. Writers' and artists' new ideas about wilderness reflected changing social, economic, and political conditions in the United States. By the late nineteenth century almost half of the nation's population lived in polluted, industrialized, and overcrowded cities on the East Coast, and much of the eastern forests had been cut to fuel the growth of the railroad, MINING, and tanning industries. Americans thus sought parks and wild areas as a refuge from the cities. The public lands were fast disappearing as well. Homesteading laws following the Louisiana Purchase and the exploration of the American western frontier distributed almost 2.5 million square miles (6.5 million square kilometers) to individuals and RAILWAYS, many of which abused loose land laws like the Homestead Act of 1862. Politicians were growing increasingly concerned about the management of the West's public lands, on which laid valuable mineral, timber, water, and grazing resources. The depletion of many of these resources (the mining industry, for example, deforested large swaths of western public lands) contributed to new ideas about conservation.

CONSERVATION MOVEMENT

The conservation movement was born in the late nineteenth century. It reflected a collection of beliefs about the governance, management, and use of public lands, stressing the wise use of the earth's resources. Conservation was also a scientific movement that sought to apply scientific principles to resource management. The formation of the U.S. Geological Survey in 1879, for example, was organized with the purpose of surveying and classifying natural resources on public lands.

Perhaps nothing embodies the conservation movement, and Americans' changing ideas of wilderness, better than the setting aside of public lands for state and national parks. The inspiration behind America's National Park System is often credited to the artist George Catlin, an American Romantic landscape painter. On a trip to the Dakotas in 1832, he wrote about the American West's disappearing wilderness and wildlife. Many artists, politicians, and writers over the next decades, including the famed landscape architect FREDERICK LAW OLMSTED and President Theodore Roosevelt, also mourned America's disappearing wilderness. The historian Frederick Jackson Turner argued in 1890 that the closing of the western frontier, and the disappearance of open space, threatened the American qualities of rugged individualism, independence, and democracy. Not until the late nineteenth century, however, did the United States formalize its commitment to wilderness conservation (and later preservation) with the creation of national parks. The motive behind the creation of national parks varied. Those such as the preservationist John Muir and his Sierra Club wanted to preserve wilderness for all time, while others such as the Southern Pacific Railroad barons wished to promote tourism in grand and scenic areas to make a profit. These early park movements set in place today's extensive National Park System, one of the first expressions of wilderness appreciation in the world.

NATIONAL PARKS

The first parcel of federal land to be designated as a park by the U.S. government was Yosemite Valley, which Congress ceded to the state of California as a state park in 1864. The setting aside of this land was unique in that up until this time most of the West had been open to unbridled resource exploitation, and few notions of conservation existed. The idea of what constituted a federally managed park, however, differed from later generations' ideal. The early Yosemite Valley and its environs were open to commercial development. Sheep grazed in the valley, and miners depleted the surrounding mountains of its little gold during the GOLD RUSHES. Still, it was set aside because it held many beautiful canyons, meadows, and natural curiosities. President Ulysses S. Grant designated land in the Wyoming and Montana territories eight years later, which became known as Yellowstone. It became a playground for the public benefit, one that retained its timber and mineral resources and natural wonders like geysers, intact. But because the territories had no state government to manage Yellowstone, the park remained in the custody of the U.S. Department of the Interior as a public resource and the world's first designated national park.

In the 1890s and 1900s Congress set aside other land it considered scenic, full of natural curiosities, and often of little or no commercial value. As a result of the efforts of the preservationist John Muir, Yosemite was designated as a national park in 1890. Most of the parks that were created in these early

years were in the West, including Sequoia, Mount Rainier, Crater Lake, and Glacier national parks. Congress also began to protect prehistoric Indian ruins and artifacts on public lands. In 1889 Congress designated Arizona's Casa Grande Ruin as a federal treasure, and in 1906 it created Mesa Verde National Park in southwestern Colorado. In the early 1900s Theodore Roosevelt and Congress passed the Antiquities Act, which authorized U.S. presidents to set aside historic structures in federal custody as national monuments. Roosevelt also set aside Pelican Island in Florida as the first national wildlife refuge in 1903. Before leaving the presidency, Roosevelt initiated the creation of 18 national monuments, including El Morro in New Mexico, the site of prehistoric petroglyphs, and Arizona's Petrified Forests and Grand Canyon. Many of the national monuments subsequently became national parks under later acts of Congress.

FURTHER READING

Allin, Craig W. *The Politics of Wilderness Preservation.* Westport, Conn.: Greenwood Press, 1982.
Cronon, William, ed. *Uncommon Ground: Toward Reinventing Nature.* New York: W. W. Norton & Co., 1995.
Fox, Steven. *John Muir and His Legacy: The American Conservation Movement.* Boston: Little, Brown, 1981.
Hays, Samuel P. *Conservation and the Gospel of Efficiency: The Progressive Conservation Movement, 1890–1920.* Cambridge, Mass.: Harvard University Press, 1959.
Merchant, Carolyn, ed. *Major Problems in American Environmental History.* Lexington, Mass.: D.C. Heath and Company, 1993.
Nash, Roderick. *Wilderness and the American Mind.* 3d ed. New Haven: Yale University Press, 1982.
Runte, Alfred. *National Parks: The American Experience.* 3d ed. Lincoln: University of Nebraska Press, 1997.
Williams, Raymond. *The Country and the City.* New York: Oxford University Press, 1973.

JESSICA B. TEISCH

WISEMAN, NICHOLAS PATRICK STEPHEN

Born: August 2, 1802; Seville, Spain
Died: February 15, 1865; London, England

Up until the autumn of 1850, English Roman Catholic priests operated in four districts, under the leadership of vicars apostolic. At the end of September, Pope Pius IX ("Pio Nono") announced that the Catholic hierarchy of England was to be restored. There would be 12 dioceses with bishops and suffragans, under the leadership of Nicholas Wiseman, who was to be cardinal archbishop of Westminster. Protestant England was horrified and the so-called Papal Aggression crisis ensued. Wiseman was undiplomatic and

Cardinal Nicholas Wiseman, the first archbishop of Westminster.

made a difficult start. By the time he died, however, he was widely admired as a great leader of the Catholic community.

Wiseman was born in Seville, of a Roman Catholic Irish family who had settled in Spain. After his father's death in 1805, the family moved to to England, initially, then to Waterford via London. Wiseman was educated at Ushaw from 1810, where he was influenced by the historian John Lingard and met George Errington. In 1818 he was sent to Rome, where he was first trained and then taught at the English College. He also became an authority on Roman antiquities and developed his remarkable gift for languages, mastering Hebrew, Greek, Latin, Syriac, Arabic, Persian, Sanskrit, French, Italian, German, Spanish, and Portuguese. He was made a doctor in divinity in 1825 and ordained priest the following year. By 1828 he was rector of the English College, which increased the frequency of his contact with the pope.

Having lectured at Moorfields Church in 1836—the first public presentation of Roman Catholic doctrines in industrial England—he moved to Oscott in 1840 as president, with the title of bishop of Melipotamus *in partibus*. (Before 1850 Roman Catholic bishops in England were given honorary titles based on defunct foreign sees.) Being insensitive to English

Roman Catholic traditions and strongly ultramontane (or Rome-centered), he was not popular among the laity at first. Yet he encouraged converts to the faith and laid the foundations of regular ecclesiastical life. Although English in identity—in his appreciation of fair play, for example—he loved to make return visits to Rome, which remained his spiritual home. He took the view that the English Oxford Movement (TRACTARIANISM) would come to nothing and that only the Roman church could lead a true Catholic revival in Protestant England. The conversion of JOHN HENRY NEWMAN (1801–1890) to Rome in 1845 appeared to prove him right. In 1847 he was in Rome advising the Holy See on the question of the restoration of the Catholic hierarchy, for which English Catholics had been pressing for some time.

In February 1849 Wiseman was made vicar apostolic of the London district. The following year, when the pope finally restored the hierarchy, Wiseman was made Archbishop of Westminster on September 29th and then a cardinal, with the title of St. Pudentiana, the following day. Wiseman, still in Rome, inflamed English sensibilities by sending a celebratory pastoral letter to English Catholics entitled "Without the Flaminian Gate of Rome" on October 7th. He was said to look like some Japanese god when he presided over grand ceremonial services in England, dressed in the full vestments of a cardinal, of which he was inordinately fond. So among the Roman Catholic clergy, the English cardinal archbishop looked more foreign than most.

Nevertheless, Wiseman was keen to reach out to the nation and published his *Appeal to the Reason and Good Feeling of the English People on the Subject of the Catholic Hierarchy* soon after becoming cardinal archbishop in 1850. His scholarly nature is reflected in the range of his publications, in an age in which religious issues were thrashed out in print. These include his *Discourse Delivered at St. John's, Catholic Church, Salford, on Sunday, July 28th, 1850, on the Gorham Controversy* (1850); *The Social and Intellectual State of England, Compared with Its Moral Condition: A Sermon Delivered in St. John's Catholic Church, Salford, on Sunday, July 28th 1850* (1850); *Three Lectures on the Catholic Hierarchy* (1850); *Essays on Various Subjects* (from the *Dublin Review*, 1853); his novel, *Fabiola; or, The Church of the Catacombs* (1854); *Recollections of the Last Four Popes* (1858); and *The Religious and Social Position of the Catholics in England: An Address Delivered to the Catholic Congress of Malines, August 21, 1863* (1864).

Wiseman was frequently ill during his years as cardinal archbishop and was an ineffective administrator who enjoyed the adulation of simple people. (The poor in the slums of the East End of London loved to touch his robes.) His feeling for the poor was, however, genuine, and he embraced modernity, seeing industry and the Roman church being on the march together. He was particularly keen to promote charitable work and education.   .

His funeral procession to the Kensal Green ceremony was said to have been almost regal in its pomp and was accompanied by national grief.

See also NEWMAN, JOHN HENRY; ROMAN CATHOLICISM; TRACTARIANISM.

FURTHER READING

Gwynn, Denis Rollecton. *Cardinal Wiseman.* London: Burns, Oates, 1929.
Jackman, Sydney Wayne. *Nicholas Wiseman: A Victorian Prelate and His Writings.* Dublin: Five Lamps, 1977.
Ward, Wilfrid. *The Life and Times of Cardinal Wiseman.* 2 vols. London: Longmans, Green, 1899.

MICHAEL WHEELER

WOMEN ARTISTS

Despite inadequate and discriminatory training, invidious comparisons to the work of male relatives, and patronizing assumptions about suitable "womanly" subjects, female Victorian artists began to enjoy some economic and critical success beginning in the 1850s. Clearly, given the Victorian identification of femininity with subordination and domesticity, and masculinity with worldly success and genius, women who professionally exhibited and sold their art, earning their livelihood—and possibly fame—by it, challenged their society's gender conservatism, whether or not they had a feminist agenda.

ART TRAINING FOR WOMEN

As early as the 1840s, British and American women needing to support themselves could attend government schools of design created to teach them artistic skills. However, such institutions—including London's Female School of Design (established 1842)—confined female students to the applied arts and to "ladylike" crafts such as china painting, while reserving the fine arts for men. Training was also available at Carey's and Leigh's, essentially preparatory schools for the ROYAL ACADEMY OF ARTS, which itself barred female students from its prestigious schools and elected no female members to its ranks, despite the fact that two women, Angelica Kauffmann (1741–1807) and the flower painter Mary Moser (1744–1819), had been among its founding artists in 1768. Only

one Victorian woman painter, the late PRE-RAPHAELITE Annie Louise Swynnerton (1844–1933), became an elected academician, and then only in 1922 did she become an associate member. Nevertheless, the Academy did include women's art in its exhibitions thanks to the anonymous selection of canvases worthy of recognition.

Not surprisingly, then, many women received their first valuable training at home, from fathers, brothers, or husbands in the arts; some worked under the tutelage of progressive male painters; some with sizable incomes went abroad to study. By 1859, however, when the progressive LANGHAM PLACE GROUP's petition for women's admittance failed to change the Academy's exclusionary policy, new support was available from the Society of Female Artists, founded in 1857 by Harriet Grote (1792–1878) to compensate for mainstream training deficits and to provide an alternate exhibition venue. The Society's first exhibition, with 358 works by 149 artists, initiated critical attention to women's talents, as well as their inequitable treatment, need for better schooling, and potential for genius. In 1861 the Academy finally opened its doors to women, though it limited their numbers drastically in the first coeducational decade and allowed them into its male-nude drawing classes only in 1893, even then burdening them with prudish restrictions.

Further progress came with the opening of the Slade School (1870), which set out to teach fine arts and grant scholarships coeducationally, and of the GROSVENOR GALLERY (1877), which welcomed women exhibitors from the first. In the same decade, such representations as the anonymous *Art Students at the Louvre* (1872) and George du Maurier's engraving *Varnishing Day at the Academy* (1877) for PUNCH portrayed women alongside their male colleagues without caricature or satire. Also, the 1875 *Academy Notes* found the notable art critic JOHN RUSKIN (1819–1900) publicly retracting his earlier pronouncement that "except in a graceful and minor way, women could not paint or draw."

PROMINENT WOMEN ARTISTS

The "Amazon work" that converted Ruskin came from the second of only two Victorian women artists who definitively asserted themselves on "male" terrain: Elizabeth Thompson, later Lady Butler (1846–1933). Initially working in watercolors, which were associated with feminine accomplishment and therefore commanded lower prices, Thompson devoted herself to military subjects after seeing pictures of the

Franco-Prussian War (1870–1871) at the 1870 Paris Salon. In 1874 she took the Academy by storm with *Calling the Roll after an Engagement, Crimea* (often known as *The Roll Call*), a grand-scale oil painting of the Grenadier Guards during the Crimean War. Stylistically traditional but new in its antiheroic sympathy for ordinary soldiers as well as in its female provenance, *The Roll Call* attracted such huge crowds that the Academy put up a barrier to protect it. Copies of the painting soon appeared in thousands of homes thanks to an engraving permitted by its eminent purchaser, QUEEN VICTORIA. By 1875 Thompson was England's most popular artist, though five years later she lost her appeal when pro–BOER WAR (1880–1881) NATIONALISM made her tragic view of battle and soldiering seem unpatriotic.

Thompson's success echoed an earlier incursion into large-scale painting by the best-known nineteenth-century woman artist, the animal painter Rosa Bonheur (1822–1899)—who, like Thompson, overcame gender stereotyping while practicing a conservative realism. Trained by her father, Bonheur impressed the 1855 Paris Salon with *The Horse Fair*, which then went on exhibition in England, where it won Queen Victoria's praise at a private viewing and led to Bonheur's immense popularity in the 1860s and 1870s, during intensified controversy over animal—and women's—rights. In her native France, she became the first female artist to win the Legion of Honor (1865), which Empress Eugénie presented to her in 1895 with a comment about genius having no gender.

A compatriot of Bonheur's, contemporaneously successful in England, was Sophie Anderson (1823–1903), a genre, landscape, and portrait painter who first exhibited at the Academy in 1855 and became known for sentimental images of Victorian children, such as *No Walk Today* (1890). Bonheur's fin-de-siècle successors included Lucy Kemp-Welch (1869–1958), an English animal painter who specialized in depicting heavy-breed horses and illustrated Anna Sewell's *Black Beauty* (1896).

In the mid-Victorian England that Bonheur visited, a handful of female contemporaries already had growing artistic reputations, although none would achieve the same enduring, international acclaim for female genius that she enjoyed. Probably the most famous of these was Henrietta Ward (1832–1924), the granddaughter, daughter, and wife of painters whose work critics invoked in relation to hers but also the recipient of favorable critical notices from her very first oil exhibition at the Academy in 1850. Starting traditionally with domestic scenes of her children and home,

Ward gradually moved to historical subjects, thereby eliciting censure for trespassing "upon the domain of her husband." Yet her compositional and technical skills in the more challenging historical genre earned praise for such paintings as *Queen Mary Quitting Stirling Castle . . .* (1863) and *Elizabeth Fry Visiting Newgate* (1876). Most popular between 1855 and 1870, Ward was a conservative middle-class acquaintance of Queen Victoria who nevertheless signed the 1859 petition to the Academy.

In midcentury America the prominent genre painter Lilly Martin Spencer (1822–1902) was likewise a conservative family woman, explicitly considering feminism a distraction from her art. Spencer's popularity began with an exhibition at New York's National Academy of Design in 1848 and spread when Cincinnati's Western Art Union purchased her *Life's Happy Hour* in 1849 for an engraving. By contrast, the sculptor Harriet Hosmer (1830–1908), one of many American female sculptors who studied and worked in Rome in the 1850s and 1860s, insisted that women artists could not afford the distraction of husband and children. In 1862, after a disappointing exhibition in England, Hosmer's *Zenobia in Chains* delighted the critics and drew record crowds back in the United States. Like her fellow antislavery feminist Anne Whitney (1821–1915), Hosmer also sculpted busts of America's leading abolitionists as well as life-size heroines.

Another signatory of the petition to the Academy, Emily Mary Osborn (1834–1898), lived the independent single life that Hosmer advocated for women artists. Like Ward, Osborn produced some historical paintings, including the well-received *The Escape of Lord Nithsdale from the Tower* (1861); unlike Ward, she added to the social realism established by Richard Redgrave (1804–1888) and WILLIAM POWELL FRITH (1819–1909) with contemporary paintings of female protagonists: a governess, for instance, in *Home Thoughts* (1856), nuns and child in *Lost* (1870). Most interestingly, perhaps, her *Nameless and Friendless* (1857) shows a needy widow standing in front of an art dealer who eyes her work skeptically while male customers covertly appraise the artist.

Emma Brownlow King (1832–1905) also explored social hardships—though with less technical skill than Osborn—in such canvases as *The Foundling Girl* (1852), her first Academy exhibit and the first in a series of paintings of and for the St. Pancras Foundling Hospital, and *Between the Acts* (1866), another sympathetic image of a widow's plight. Women's contributions to the "social conscience" tradition also included *The Seamstress: A Song of the Shirt* (1854), by Anna Blunden (1830–1915), criticized for her Pre-Raphaelite scrupulousness in detailing her landscapes.

PRE-RAPHAELITE CONNECTIONS

Indeed, association with the Pre-Raphaelites proved a mixed blessing for several women, both in the mid-Victorian era and afterwards. ELIZABETH SIDDAL (1829–1862), iconicized as the "stunner" model who became DANTE GABRIEL ROSSETTI's (1828–1882) wife, was virtually ignored as an artist in her own right. Between 1852 and 1861, under Rossetti's tutelage and with his encouragement, she produced over 100 pieces of art: oil paintings (*Self portrait*, 1853–54), watercolors (*Clerk Saunders*, 1857; *Lady Affixing a Pennant to a Knight's Spear*), and drawings (*The Lady of Shalott*). Her talent went largely unacknowledged. Similarly overlooked was the art of Rosa Brett (1829–1882), a gifted amateur watercolorist who exhibited at the Academy under the pseudonym Rosarius and whose brother, John, was championed by Ruskin. Rebecca Solomon (1832–1866), whose brother worked with the Pre-Raphaelites, became well known only to sink into obscurity after Simeon Solomon's career suffered from his 1873 disgrace for homosexuality. Initially JOHN EVERETT MILLAIS's studio assistant, she later produced such varied canvases as *The Governess* (1854), a Redgravian social commentary; *The Lovers* (1864), a romantic watercolor; and *The Wounded Dove* (1866), a genre painting with Christian symbolism.

The greatest acclaim came to the tenuously Pre-Raphaelite Joanna Boyce Wells (1831–1861), also the sister of an artist intimate with the Brotherhood. Boyce won critical esteem on a par with Ward's from her first Academy exhibit, *Elgiva* (1855), which drew plaudits from Ruskin and impressed FORD MADOX BROWN as "the best head in the rooms." While her laborers in *Our Servant* (1857) and *The Heathergatherer* (1859) and her individualized mother in the historical *The Child's Crusade* (1860) were as admirable, it was probably the title figure of *La Veneziana* (1861) that earned Boyce THE TIMES's praise for "paint[ing] with a manliness which there are few men to emulate!" Upon her early death, another critic eulogized her as "a real loss to the English school" without referring to gender.

Boyce was actually not the only woman artist to win Ruskin's approval even before his public "conversion" by Thompson. In the 1850s and 1860s, he (patronizingly) mentored Louisa Stuart, lady Waterford (1818–1891), an amateur Pre-Raphaelite who painted biblical scenes of children on the walls of a Northumberland schoolhouse; later, his protégées included "Slade girl" Kate Greenaway (1846–1901) and her friend Helen Paterson Allingham (1848–1926), watercolorists and illustrators whom he praised in his *Art of England* (1884). Greenaway with her immensely popular children's illustrations and Paterson with her watercolors of picturesque cottage scenes—as well as their fellow illustrator Beatrix Potter (1866–1943)—achieved far more renown than their predecessor Eleanor Vere Boyle (1825–1916), an amateur who signed her similar work only with E.V.B.

The most accomplished late Pre-Raphaelite was Evelyn Pickering de Morgan (1855–1919), a "Slade girl" inspired by Rossetti, Burne-Jones, and her studies in Italy with her uncle, John Roddam Spencer Stanhope (1829–1908). At the first Grosvenor Gallery exhibition, in 1877, she showed *Ariadne in Naxos*, which, like her Botticellian and Burne-Jonesian masterpiece *Flora* (1894), epitomizes her preference for large mythological or allegorical figures dominating a magical landscape. Pickering's colleague Marie Spartali Spillman (1844–1927), another "stunner," became a pupil of Ford Madox Brown (1821–1893) in the 1860s; however, she favored Rossettian flowers, subjects from Dante and Boccaccio, and allegory in her vibrant watercolors—one of her most ambitious being *Messer Ansaldo Showing Madonna Dianova His Enchanted Garden* (1889). Unfortunately, the tendency to diminish female Pre-Raphaelites as mere imitators or followers of the Brotherhood still hung over Pickering, Spartali, and the lesser-known Elizabeth Bunce (1858–1927) and Eleanor Fortescue Brickdale (1872–1945).

Like Pickering, Henrietta Rae (1859–1928) was one of the few women to specialize in classical subjects—and the foremost woman in that male-dominated area, the female nude. A scholarship student at the Academy schools and a yearly exhibitor from 1881, Rae enjoyed the privilege of having *Psyche at the Throne of Venus*, a large painting of thirteen women, hung in a special spot at the 1894 Academy exhibition. In 1896 it was Rae's friend Lord FREDERIC LEIGHTON (1830–1896) who awarded the sculptor Margaret Giles (1968–1949) the Academy's prize for another classical subject: Giles's triumph with *Hero*, her bronze statuette of a remarkably muscular, heroic mythological woman, marked the significant rise and success of fin-de-siècle women sculptors.

Sometimes considered an American Pre-Raphaelite, Anna Lea Merritt (1844–1930), a Philadelphian living in London, received institutional affirmation of her work on both sides of the Atlantic. Her most famous image, the allegorical *Love Locked Out* (1889)—her widow's design for a tombstone to be shared with her husband—became the first woman's painting bought by the Tate Gallery, in 1890. Then in 1893 she won medals for both her *Eve Overcome by Remorse* and her mural for the Women's Building at the World's Columbian Exposition in Chicago. Another mural contributor to this building was Mary Cassatt (1844–1926), likewise a Pennsylvanian expatriate abroad, established in Paris by 1866. Although arguably her Impressionist technique made Cassatt the most modern Victorian woman painter, she continued the middle-class domestic scenes of mothers and children so favored by such traditional genre painters as Jane Maria Bowkett (1837–1891), Edith (1860–1948), and Jessica Hayllar (1858–1940), Laura Alma-Tadema (1852–1909), and Louisa Goode Jopling (1843–1933)—also a portraitist and the first woman elected to the Royal Society of British Artists. Yet whatever their subjects, by century's end Victorian women had gained some visibility, popularity and even honor as artists. On the other hand, if the president of the Royal Society of British Artists could still, in 1890, welcome the Tate's purchase of *Love Locked Out* as "the formal, authoritative recognition of the fact that women can paint," obviously the struggle for equal respect was far from over.

See also ART EDUCATION; EDUCATION OF WOMEN; PAINTING, GENRES OF.

FURTHER READING

Casteras, Susan P., and Linda H. Peterson. *A Struggle for Fame: Victorian Women Artists and Authors.* New Haven: Yale Center for British Art, 1994.

Chadwick, Whitney. "Sex, Class, and Power in Victorian England." *Women, Art, and Society.* London: Thames and Hudson, 1990.

Cherry, Deborah. *Painting Women: Victorian Women Artists.* New York: Routledge, 1993.

Lambourne, Lionel. "Women Artists." *Victorian Painting.* London: Phaidon Press, 1999.

Nunn, Pamela Gerrish. *Canvassing: Recollections by Six Victorian Women Artists.* London: Camden Press, 1986.

Nunn, Pamela Gerrish. *Victorian Women Artists.* London: The Women's Press, 1987.

Wood, Christopher. "Women Artists." *Victorian Painting.* New York: Bulfinch Press, 1999.

MARGARET BOZENNA GOSCILO

WOMEN'S RIGHTS

The term *women's rights* is commonly associated with the WOMEN'S SUFFRAGE campaign of the late nineteenth-century. However, in reality it encompassed a wide range of social, economic, political, and educational issues throughout the Victorian era, including the lack of educational and employment opportunities for women, the legal inequities they suffered, and the nature of their property and divorce rights.

Debate over women's rights arose during the eighteenth-century Enlightenment and focused on a basic question: did the biological differences between men and women extend to other traits such as intelligence, character, and capability? The influential French philosopher Jean-Jacques Rousseau (1712–1778) argued that biology determined temperament, character, and capabilities, and in his popular novel *Emile* (1761), he asserted that nature created women only to function as wives and mothers, subservient to their men. This proposition was met with strong criticism from both sexes, with the English writer and early feminist Mary Wollstonecraft (1759–1797) arguing—in her *Vindication of the Rights of Woman* (1792)—that women's dependence on men was not the result of biological determinism but of a flawed educational system. She further suggested that women who paid taxes should be able to vote and thus became one of Britain's first advocates for women's suffrage.

Despite criticism, however, Rousseau's ideas were widely influential. Some claimed to see evidence in support of his views during the French Revolution, when many British observers believed that the political turmoil was due in part to the intervention of "unnatural" French women in politics. This image was so powerful that it figured prominently more than half a century later in CHARLES DICKENS's (1812–1870) highly sentimental and not too accurate account of the French Revolution in his novel *A Tale of Two Cities* (1859). Here, one of the novelist's most memorable creations is that of Madame Defarge, placidly knitting while enjoying the bloody spectator sport of watching innocent heads fall under the guillotine.

The fear of the consequences of giving women political power remained strong in the nineteenth century. For example, William Thompson found little support for his feminist tract, *Appeal of One Half of the Human Race, Women, against the Pretensions of the Other Half, Men, to Retain Them in Political and Thence in Civil and Domestic Slavery* (1825), which argued that women needed full political rights to protect them from male oppression. Those British politicians intent on expanding male suffrage dismissed this argument, and during the Reform Bill debates in 1832, a Yorkshire woman's petition for the right of female taxpayers to vote was greeted with derisive laughter. The Reform Bill intentionally disenfranchised women by using the word *men* to refer to eligible voters. (Although there is no evidence that eligible women actually did vote before 1832, technically they had the right to do so, since pre-1832 voting laws referred to "persons.") Even radicals and reformers were unwilling to demand political rights for women; in 1838, when the authors of the People's Charter demanded further political reform, they intentionally omitted any mention of women's suffrage. No large-scale debates about women's right to vote emerged again until the 1860s.

MARRIAGE, DIVORCE, AND THE NORTON AFFAIR

Yet even if suffrage was not widely debated in the early years of QUEEN VICTORIA's reign, other aspects of women's rights came under increasing scrutiny. MARRIAGE, divorce, and child custody issues were all raised in the 1830s. Under the NEW POOR LAW of 1834, single men were no longer pressed to marry women who charged them with having fathered their illegitimate children; under the new law women were held responsible for out-of-wedlock pregnancies, thus placing the financial burden as well as the social stigma entirely on their shoulders. The prominent socialist ROBERT OWEN (1771–1858) clearly had this law in mind when he published *Lectures on the Marriages of the Priesthood of the Old Immoral World* (1835). He alleged that the existing marriage system was oppressive to women and proposed substituting a civil contract that lasted only so long as both parties felt affection for each other. Either could obtain a divorce, and in order to make sure that economic dependence did not trap women in loveless marriages, Owen proposed higher wages for women and community support for all children, whether illegitimate or not.

Although some of Owen's proposals were enacted in his newly founded utopian community of New Harmony, Indiana, his work reached a relatively restricted audience in England. However, beginning in 1836 issues of marriage, divorce, marital property, and child custody became widely discussed in relation to the sensational case of the author CAROLINE NORTON (1808–1877). Jealous of her wit and intelligence, Caroline's husband George publicly charged the British prime minister, WILLIAM LAMB (Lord Melbourne), with having an affair with his wife. A jury rejected his suit, and, ironically, this legal decision that there had been no adultery made divorce impossible, since existing law only permitted the dissolution of marriage in cases of proven infidelity. George Norton subsequently removed his children from London and denied Caroline access to them. He finally offered to let her see them on the condition that she turn over her family property to him. A contract was drawn up between them, but he took the property and refused her access to the children. Caroline went to court to enforce

the agreement, whereupon the judge declared that as a married woman she had no legal existence separate from her husband and could not enter into contracts, even with him. Nevertheless, the court refused to return her property. In the final indignity, George Norton successfully argued in court that he had a right to her income as an author since husband and wife were considered one person in law.

Caroline Norton was not the first to suffer such abuses, but her case was well publicized. Not only was it widely reported in the press, but she also used her considerable literary talents to argue for reform in matters of marriage and divorce, women's property rights, and child custody. Even before publication in 1854 of her book *English Laws for Women in the Nineteenth Century*, her case inspired reform. In 1839 the Custody Act allowed women to petition for custody of children under the age of 7 in the event of a legal separation between the parents, thus ending the unquestioned right of fathers to retain absolute custody of their children. In 1878 the act was extended to children under the age of 16, but it was not until further legislation in 1886 that women automatically got custody of minor children upon the death of a father, even in cases where there had been no marital estrangement.

A number of people supported the idea of a woman retaining custody rights as being in the best interests of the child; however, no similar argument could be made about divorce. Since the late eighteenth century, certain American states had made it easier to obtain a divorce on the grounds of promoting social harmony (Napoleon had introduced civil divorce in FRANCE early in the nineteenth century), but Britons argued that to make divorce easier would be to undermine the whole institution of marriage. Nevertheless, a measure of reform was brought in 1857 with the Divorce and Matrimonial Causes Act, which established the first civil divorce court in Britain and made divorce cheaper and a little easier to obtain.

Previously, to end a marriage petitioners had had to go through a complex, expensive, and highly public process, which culminated in obtaining a parliamentary bill of dissolution. This state of affairs kept the divorce rate down to about 10 per year, but the number increased to nearly 150 per year during the decade from 1857. The new legislation, however, created a double standard: men could divorce their wives by proving adultery, but women could divorce their husbands only if they proved infidelity together with another serious cause such as cruelty, bigamy, incest, or bestiality. Nevertheless, the law did provide additional protection for women in that a deserted wife could apply for a judicial separation, which would legally restore to her sole control over her property. Additional acts were passed in 1878, 1886, and 1895. These extended powers to local magistrates to grant these legal separations, and they gave protection to more women by allowing them to seek a legal separation if they were victims of physical abuse or abandonment, or if their husbands failed to maintain them and their children.

These laws, however, did nothing to protect a woman's property during marriage, a point made in *A Brief Summary in Plain Language of the Most Important Laws Concerning Women* (1854) by BARBARA LEIGH SMITH BODICHON (1827–1891), who founded the Married Women's Property Committee in 1855 to agitate for laws to protect women's property and income during marriage. Despite intense lobbying it was not until 1870 that women secured the right to keep their own wages, and it was another 12 years before married women were given the right to retain property they held before and during marriage as their own "separate estate." As in divorce, Britain lagged behind the UNITED STATES where, by 1865, 29 states had adopted married women's property laws, with Mississippi passing the earliest of these in 1839.

THE FIGHT FOR EDUCATION

While reformers warmly greeted these developments, many believed that further changes were necessary. A group of young, educated feminists that included Bodichon, Bessie Parkes (1829–1925), and Emily Davies (1831–1921) emerged in the 1850s, committed to campaigning for further rights for women. Under the direction of Davies and Parkes, this group founded the *English Woman's Journal* in 1858 as the first periodical dedicated solely to a serious consideration of women's issues. Its offices were in Langham Place in central London, and the young feminists who gathered there founded the Langham Place Circle in 1859 to organize for women's legal, economic, and educational rights. They established the Society for Promoting the Employment of Women, which had a Ladies' Institute at the Langham Place offices that provided a job register, reading room, and lunchroom, as well as a postal address for women seeking work. Another member of the group, Emily Faithfull (1835–1895), founded the Victoria Press with the goal of training women to become compositors, and she went on to be named the printer and publisher in ordinary to the queen.

EDUCATING WOMEN

Many reformers realized that finding jobs for women was not enough; women needed access to better education as well. In 1848 Queen's College was founded in London as the first school to provide training and certificates of proficiency for governesses. One early Queen's student, Frances Mary Buss (1827–1894), was a dedicated education reformer who, in 1850, founded the North London Collegiate School for Girls where a rigorous curriculum, based on that used in boys' private secondary schools, made it a model for women's secondary day schools. When the Cambridge Local Examinations to prove subject proficiency were opened to women in 1863, Frances Buss's students were among the first to take the exams.

Reformers also turned their attention to higher education, possibly inspired by America where women had been first admitted to Oberlin College in 1837 and Antioch College in 1853, and where the first women's college, Vassar, was established in 1861. Emily Davies published *The Higher Education of Women* (1866), which argued that because there was no fundamental intellectual difference between women and men, both should receive the same rigorous education. In 1869 Davies and her supporters founded the institution that would formally become Girton College, Cambridge, in 1873, but although it was modeled on the other Cambridge colleges and required students to follow the same course of study, the university refused to give Girton official recognition. Other educational reformers took a different approach; Anne Jemima Clough (1820–1892) became the headmistress of another women's institution at Cambridge in 1871, which promoted better education for women but established a separate degree course for women different from that for men. This institution formally became Newnham College in 1880. Despite the founding of these two Cambridge colleges, as well as Lady Margaret Hall and Somerville at Oxford, both founded in 1879, professors at England's two most prestigious universities were under no obligation to accept female students into their lectures. While women were allowed to sit Oxbridge examinations, neither university granted degrees to women until the twentieth century. Other universities, however, were more adaptable, and Manchester New College, St. Andrew's University in Scotland, and London University all opened their doors to women in the late 1870s.

The EDUCATION ACT OF 1870 provided for national elementary education and reflected the debate over the EDUCATION OF WOMEN. While working-class boys and girls, who were the primary beneficiaries of these new publicly funded schools, followed the same academic curriculum for the most part (although in gender-segregated classrooms), in the vocational skills classes girls were required to learn sewing and domestic accomplishments, ostensibly to make them better mothers, but certainly with the objective of training them to become domestic servants.

These differences in the educational system reflect the Victorian ideal that women's place was in the domestic sphere. Many reformers who supported increased employment opportunities for women did so as a solution to the problem of so-called redundant or excess single women, who would never marry and had no other means of support. This reflected the middle-class view of many feminists and women's rights advocates who presumed that married women did not need paying jobs. When these reformers addressed the issue of working-class women, their perspective tended to emphasize the need to "rescue" and "protect" them to allow them to fill their true domestic place in the home. But this approach often meant legally restricting women's ability to work and showed little regard for what this would do to a struggling family's economy. Consequently, many working-class women were unenthusiastic about women's rights campaigns, since their concerns were often quite different from those of the middle classes; instead of divorce, property rights, and access to higher education, they focused on such issues as higher wages, job protection, and better working conditions.

MIDDLE-CLASS MORALITY

By the middle of the century, however, even those women whose wealth freed them from the necessity to earn a living found domesticity mind numbing and confining; some agreed with reformers such as author ANNA JAMESON (1794–1860), who argued in *Communion of Labour* (1856) that the extension of women's influence into every aspect of public life would help society's progress. These women became volunteers for a variety of causes, using their social and economic positions to agitate for social or political change. For example, FLORENCE NIGHTINGALE (1820–1910) actively campaigned for sanitary reform in the army after her CRIMEAN WAR experiences; establishing nursing as a respectable profession for women and improving sanitation in civilian hospitals were secondary goals. FRANCES POWER COBBE (1822–1904), known for her work with "ragged schools" for poverty-stricken and neglected children, also founded the British Union for the Abolition of Vivisection, which

lobbied Parliament to legislate against medical experimentation on live animals. Sophia Jex-Blake (1840–1912), frustrated in her efforts to obtain a medical degree, founded the first women's medical college in London and successfully pushed Parliament to pass legislation in 1876 that empowered all educational examining boards to give exams to women. Isabella Somerset ((1851–1921) and Rosalind Howard, ninth countess of Carlisle (1845–1921), were leaders of the British TEMPERANCE MOVEMENT, while Catherine Booth (1829–1890), wife of SALVATION ARMY founder William Booth (1829–1912), successfully convinced her husband's organization that women should be welcomed as officers and other workers. ANGELA BURDETT-COUTTS (1814–1906), possibly the wealthiest woman of the Victorian age, devoted herself to philanthropy, founding both "ragged schools" and technical training schools for older students and establishing "rescue" houses for women engaged in PROSTITUTION in order to teach them marketable skills.

Many people, including some of these women, viewed their charitable work as an extension of women's natural moral influence. This attitude made their efforts more easily acceptable, since they did not seem to challenge established gender roles, but the emphasis on women's innate morality sometimes created difficulties when they addressed issues related to sexuality. For example, in 1866 few criticized JOSEPHINE BUTLER (1828–1906), the wife of an Anglican clergyman, when she established a "house of rest" in Liverpool for women attempting to escape prostitution and poverty. Three years later, however, Butler was vilified when she became the leader of the Ladies' National Association for the Repeal of the CONTAGIOUS DISEASES ACTS. This legislation (three acts passed in 1864, 1866, and 1869) aimed to reduce venereal disease in port cities among soldiers and sailors, not by placing restrictions on the men but by targeting the women. Officials were empowered to inspect—by force if necessary—any woman suspected of engaging in prostitution and incarcerating without trial those infected with venereal disease until they were judged to be cured. Butler and her supporters argued that this denied poor women their constitutional rights and pointed out the double standard of morality that obtained by punishing only the women. Further, they alleged that the legislation effectively legalized prostitution by giving it tacit government sanction. Despite much public hostility, these reformers persevered, and when the acts were rescinded in 1886 Butler's campaign was credited with pushing through the repeal.

Butler's campaign came at a time of increased debate about women's sexuality and the desirability of greater sex education. So-called experts such as Dr. WILLIAM ACTON (1813–1875), a prominent physician, wrote extensively about prostitution and venereal disease, but he based his conclusions largely on the work of other male physicians. While he did not deny that women had sexual urges, he proposed that they did not naturally act on those impulses and were not overtly interested in sex except as a means of being a dutiful wife and becoming a mother. This had a significant impact on public attitudes toward birth control, since women who sought to avoid pregnancy were thought to take an "unnatural" pleasure from sex. But proponents of increased access to contraception argued that women's health would improve if they could control the number and timing of their pregnancies. Members of the Malthusian League, named after political economist Thomas Malthus, an early nineteenth-century author on population, also argued that birth control was good for society as a whole, suggesting that unplanned births created poverty among the poor and hardship among the middle classes. Officials found this argument unconvincing, and in 1877, when ANNIE BESANT (1847–1933) and CHARLES BRADLAUGH (1833–1891) reprinted Charles Knowlton's *The Fruits of Philosophy* (1832), one of the first reliable discussions of birth control methods, they were tried under the Obscene Publications Act. Subsequently, Besant was judged to be an unfit mother and lost custody of her daughter. Nevertheless, members of the Malthusian League persevered and in 1881 opened the first women's clinic to offer instruction on birth control.

Thus, by the second half of Victoria's reign women were involved in a wide range of reform campaigns aimed at broadening women's rights; many activists learned organizational skills and formed networks through their work on these issues. This would serve them well when women's suffrage became the dominant women's issue late in the century. In hindsight, however, feminists recognized that the World Anti-Slavery Convention held in London in 1840 was the catalyst that stirred debate about women's suffrage. Despite the considerable contribution of American women delegates to the ANTISLAVERY MOVEMENT, their British convention hosts refused to seat them in the assembly hall. A compromise kept a large section of the American delegation from withdrawing: the women were allowed to stay, but they had to sit behind a screen and remain silent. This indignity spurred them into action on their own behalf, and after several years of correspondence and planning, these ad-

vocates met in SENECA FALLS, New York, in 1848 for the first women's rights convention. The result was the "Declaration of Sentiments," which stated their wide-ranging grievances, ranging from lack of access to education and employment to property rights and child custody.

The "Declaration of Sentiments" was a clarion call for women's rights activists, both in the United States and in Europe. Suffrage was by no means the only point in the document, and many people who approved of some of its critiques of contemporary education, employment, and domestic conditions questioned the wisdom of giving women the vote. Yet in the 1850s and 1860s, when reformers faced constant criticism from the public and evasion and delay from politicians, many came to the conclusion that their other grievances would be fully addressed only when women, as voters, could put political pressure on elected officials to enact changes.

VOTES FOR WOMEN

Feminist organizations promoting women's suffrage in Britain began to emerge in the 1860s. In 1865 the *Englishwoman's Review of Social and Industrial Questions* (1866–1910) replaced the *English Woman's Journal* as the center of a feminist communications network dedicated to women's rights, particularly to female suffrage. It supported women's causes and provided its readership with a wealth of relevant information that included summaries of political debates, lists of parliamentary votes, reports of court proceedings, and the names and degrees of women students. A considerable number of the Langham Place Circle became involved in the suffrage movement; most prominent was Barbara Leigh Smith Bodichon, who organized the first WOMEN'S SUFFRAGE committee in 1865 to gather signatures in support of adding women's suffrage to a voting rights bill currently being debated. In 1866 Emily Davies delivered the petition to JOHN STUART MILL, who subsequently argued (unsuccessfully) that the word "man" in the bill be changed to "person." Similar unsuccessful attempts to change the wording and thus allow women to vote in national elections were made in 1870, 1883, and 1892.

Even while women could not vote for members of Parliament, they were slowly gaining local voting rights. In 1869 unmarried women who paid taxes gained the right to vote in municipal elections, while the Education Act in the following year created elected school boards and allowed women taxpayers to both vote for board members and to run for the positions themselves. In 1888 the right to vote in county and municipal elections was extended to all adult single and married women, and in 1894 this was extended to district and parish elections.

Not everyone viewed the extension of women's voting rights with complacency, and this included many prominent women. QUEEN VICTORIA opposed women's suffrage as, surprisingly, did the Victorian era's foremost female intellectual GEORGE ELIOT. The novelist and reformer MARY WARD (Mrs. Humphrey) organized an anti-suffrage campaign, publishing in the *Nineteenth Century* magazine an anti-suffrage letter signed by more than 100 prominent women. *PUNCH* and other periodicals attacked pro-suffrage women, suggesting that they were unnatural and masculine for wanting access to public life. However, many of those working for votes for women—among them Frances Power Cobbe, Barbara Bodichon, Emily Davies, and Josephine Butler—were undeterred by such opposition; they were veteran political activists who had faced condemnation of their various women's causes for years. Millicent Garret Fawcett (1847–1929), who became the first president of the National Union of Women's Suffrage Societies (NUWSS) in 1897, had been an outspoken supporter of women's suffrage since the 1860s. The NUWSS was an umbrella group that brought together various pro-suffrage organizations to undertake intensive lobbying

of members of Parliament to extend universal suffrage to women without regard to marital status or property qualifications.

Early in the twentieth century the suffrage movement split over the question of how best to attain its ends. Fawcett headed the "constitutionalist" party, or suffragists, which attempted to persuade through petitions and lobbying, while the "militant" party, or suffragettes, under the leadership of Emmeline Pankhurst (1858–1929) resorted to demonstrations, civil disobedience, and occasional violence. Both sides suspended their activities during World War I (1914–1918), and in 1918 the Representation of the People Act granted women over the age of 30 the right to vote in national elections (in 1928, the voting age for women was lowered to 21); the United States followed suit in 1920 for federal elections.

Neither country could claim to be innovative: the British Commonwealth countries of New Zealand, AUSTRALIA, and CANADA had been ahead of both on the franchise issue. New Zealand had granted women the right to vote in 1893, Australia followed suit with restricted voting rights in 1902, and Canada granted women limited national voting rights in 1917. In Europe, Finland granted women's suffrage in 1906, Norway in 1913, and Denmark and Iceland in 1915. But in Britain, as in many of these other countries, this was the last major achievement of the initial wom-

Marchers demanding that women gain the right to vote demonstrate in the streets of London, circa 1900.

en's movement. After universal suffrage was achieved, many activists turned to other projects, and no unified approach to women's issues would arise again until the 1960s.

See also EDUCATION OF WOMEN; MARRIAGE AND DIVORCE; WOMEN'S SUFFRAGE; WOMEN'S WORK.

FURTHER READING

Blackburn, Helen. *Women's Suffrage: A Record of the Women's Suffrage Movement in the British Isles.* 1902. Reprint, New York: Source Book Press, 1971.

Caine, Barbara. *Victorian Feminists.* New York and Oxford: Oxford University Press, 1992.

Frawley, Maria. "The Editor as Advocate: Emily Faithfull and the Victoria Magazine." *Victorian Periodicals Review* 31 (1998): 87–104.

Gleadle, Kathryn. *The Early Feminists: Radical Unitarians and the Emergence of the Women's Rights Movements, 1831–51.* New York: St. Martin's Press, 1998.

Gleadle, Kathryn. *British Women in the Nineteenth Century.* New York: Palgrave, 2001.

Herstein, Sheila R. *A Mid-Victorian Feminist, Barbara Leigh Smith Bodichon.* New Haven: Yale University Press, 1985.

Holcombe, Lee. *Wives and Property: Reform of the Married Women's Property Law in Nineteenth Century England.* Toronto: University of Toronto Press, 1983.

Lacey, Candida Ann, ed. *Barbara Leigh Smith Bodichon and the Langham Place Group.* New York: Routledge, 1986.

Levine, Philippa. *Feminist Lives in Victorian England: Private Roles and Public Commitment.* New York: Basil Blackwell, 1990.

Rosen, Andrew. "Emily Davies and the Women's Movement, 1862–1867." *Journal of British Studies* 19 (1979): 101–121.

Rover, Constance. *Women's Suffrage and Party Politics in Britain, 1866–1914.* London: Routledge and Kegan Paul, 1967.

Shanley, Mary Lyndon. *Feminism, Marriage and the Law in England, 1850–1895.* Princeton: Princeton University Press, 1989.

Smith, Harold L. *The British Women's Suffrage Campaign, 1866–1928.* London: Longman, 1998.

Strachey, Ray. *The Cause.* London: G. Bell, 1928; reprinted Port Washington, NY: Kennikat Press, 1978.

Vicinus, Martha. *Independent Women: Work and Community for Single Women, 1850–1920.* Chicago: University of Chicago Press, 1985.

TAMARA L. HUNT

WOMEN'S SUFFRAGE

A significant aspect of the Victorian era's sociopolitical landscape, the movement for women's suffrage emerged in the nineteenth century as a critical component of nation- and empire-building and in response to the growing political mobilization of women on behalf of WOMEN'S RIGHTS. Over a period of some 60 years, thousands of women worked together in numerous organizations to secure political rights at both local and national levels. In some contexts women's suffrage was granted by governing bodies with little or no agitation on the part of women themselves, as in the 1881 extension of the parliamentary franchise to female householders on the Isle of Man. Sustained, but relatively brief campaigns, led to parliamentary enfranchisement of both indigenous and European women in New Zealand in 1893, while in AUSTRALIA, women—excluding Aborigine women—acquired such rights in 1902. In contrast, the women of Britain struggled long and hard for the right to the parliamentary vote. The British suffrage movement took root in the 1860s and continued until 1918 when women succeeded in gaining partial enfranchisement, but it was not until 1928 that full enfranchisement was granted to British women.

FIRST RUMBLINGS OF A WOMEN'S SUFFRAGE MOVEMENT

The nineteenth-century Anglo-American women's suffrage movement is frequently regarded as having begun with the 1848 SENECA FALLS CONVENTION at which American suffragette Elizabeth Cady Stanton (1815–1902) presented her "Declaration of Sentiments," which set out women's rights on the model of the Declaration of Independence and championed the right of women to vote. The Seneca Falls meeting, however, had been inspired by the experiences of British and American women delegates to the 1840 World Anti-Slavery Convention in LONDON, where their sex precluded them from taking part in the proceedings. The antislavery antecedents of the Seneca Falls Convention are critical to understanding the emergence of movements for women's suffrage in the Victorian era. Many British and American suffragettes were active in campaigns to abolish slavery in the UNITED STATES, and women's suffrage movements borrowed personnel and ideas from abolitionist campaigns.

The first expressly political demand for female enfranchisement in Britain grew out of working-class protests in the early nineteenth century. In 1818 and 1819 women and men in the Lancashire cotton towns of the north of England campaigned for a universal parliamentary franchise but failed to have their have their demands considered by Parliament. In 1831 the first petition for women's suffrage was presented to Parliament, requesting that the parliamentary franchise be expanded to include all women who met existing property qualifications—in other words, demanding equal rights of franchise for middle-class women as those enjoyed by middle-class men. The 1832 REFORM ACT passed by Parliament, however, was worded in such a way that for the first time the word "elector" was qualified as "male." The act increased the number of males eligible to vote by about half a million, primarily drawn from the middle and landowning classes. By stipulating that electors were men, the act removed from previous legislation any ambiguity that might have been advantageous to women. By thus identifying them as a group excluded from franchise rights, women found a cause and, with it, a political identity. In the decades following the passage of the Reform Act, the issue of women's suffrage was actively discussed among those committed to challenging the status quo. Unitarian and socialist feminists debated the merits of suffrage in the 1830s and 1840s, laying the groundwork for liberal feminists' adoption of the cause in the 1860s.

Expansion of the electorate reemerged as an important political question in the mid-1860s when pressure from working men's organizations and growing public interest in democracy combined to bring franchise reform to the attention of Parliament. The nineteenth-century movement for women's suffrage entered the public agenda in the context of debate over the passage of the second Reform Act. During 1866 and 1867, feminists gathered signatures on multiple petitions as evidence of women's desire to be included in the proposed electoral reforms. In May 1867 JOHN STUART MILL (1806–1873), then the radical Liberal member of Parliament for Westminster, introduced an amendment to the bill that would substitute the word "person" for the word "man." Mill was supported in Parliament by a loose coalition of liberals and radicals, but his amendment was defeated by 73 votes to 196. The Reform Act of 1867 gave the vote in boroughs to adult male owners and ten male lodgers, who were required to have been resident for one year and to pay at least ten pounds per year in rent. The electorate in England and Wales increased from 20% to 36%, leaving roughly two-thirds of the adult male population—and all women—disenfranchised.

AN ORGANIZED CAMPAIGN

Out of the failure of Mill's amendment came the organized campaign for women's parliamentary enfranchisement. The Victorian women's suffrage movement was characterized by loose groupings of suffragists working together under the aegis of national umbrella organizations. No single organization or individual dominated the nineteenth-century movement. In 1868 regional suffrage committees in

Women sign up for the National Woman Suffrage Association in this 1869 illustration.

London, Birmingham, Bristol, Manchester, and Edinburgh federated to form the National Society for Women's Suffrage (NSWS). The NSWS split into two organizations between 1872 and 1877 over disagreement about whether members ought to participate in the international campaign to repeal the CONTAGIOUS DISEASES ACTS, legislation that empowered the POLICE to incarcerate and examine women suspected of engaging in PROSTITUTION. The two organizations reunited in 1877 as the Central Committee of the NSWS. A further schism occurred in 1888, however, when members disagreed over whether to allow the women's sections of political parties to participate in its organization. Despite these differences, the movement agreed to a remarkable extent on the strategies to be employed in agitating for the vote. These included lobbying members of Parliament and presenting petitions to Parliament or to deputations of government ministers. The primary area of disagreement was over whether their campaign should focus on single women only or allow the inclusion of married women.

The 1870s and 1880s were crucial decades in the shaping of suffragettes' demand for the vote in Britain. Four developments in particular must be highlighted. First was the growing number of opportunities that arose for middle-class women to vote in elections other than parliamentary ones. While unable to pass a measure for women's parliamentary enfranchisement, in 1869 member of Parliament (M.P.) JOHN BRIGHT (1811–1889) did manage to pass a bill giving women ratepayers in England and Wales the borough franchise, which permitted them to vote in local government elections; Scottish women received this right in 1882. Further franchise extensions came with the EDUCATION ACT OF 1870, which allowed those women entitled to the municipal vote in England and Wales both to stand for election to school boards and to vote in such elections. Single or widowed female ratepayers in England and Wales could vote for, and stand as, Poor Law Guardians, while qualified Irish women could vote for, but not stand as, Poor Law Guardians. By 1888 women ratepayers were empowered to vote for county councils in England and Wales, and Scotland followed suit a year later. The second development was reform in the laws pertaining to married women's rights to own property in their own names. In 1870, and again in 1882, Parliament passed MARRIED WOMEN'S PROPERTY ACTS that allowed women to retain control of their own property upon MARRIAGE. These acts, while marking a significant improvement in the legal status of women, nonetheless made clear to a number of men and women that further politi-

cal change would be necessary if women were to obtain the legal means to control their own destinies. The third development was the change in women's philanthropic activities. A growing number of middle-class women undertook settlement work, living among the working poor in industrial areas with the aim of improving workers' lives through personal interaction and the introduction of HYGIENE and culture. Settlement work politicized many middle-class women, who came to see that they could only effect real social change by possessing the parliamentary vote. The fourth development was the passage in 1883 of the Corrupt Practices Act, which outlawed payment of political party canvassers and led to the creation of women's auxiliaries to the main political parties, which came to serve as reservoirs of volunteer election workers. Conservative women formed the Primrose League in 1884, and Liberal women formed the Women's Liberal Federation in 1887 (with groups splitting off as the Women's Liberal Unionist Association in 1888 and the Women's National Liberal Association in 1892).

THE HEIGHT OF THE MOVEMENT

The suffrage movement peaked with passage of the 1884 Reform Bill, which provided for the enfranchisement of a large number of male AGRICULTURAL WORKERS. After 1884 approximately 5 million men—about two-thirds of the adult male population in Britain—held the parliamentary franchise, while no women could vote in general elections. The 1884 campaign was especially disillusioning for women's suffrage organizers because it made clear that further expansion of the franchise would not be given Parliament's consideration for some years. The 1890s, however, became a significant decade for the suffragettes. New organizations and strategies emerged in the campaign, and the growing involvement of working-class women, socialists, and progressives brought fresh ideas and constituencies into play. Three organizations in particular, the Women's Emancipation Union, the Women's Franchise League, and the Union of Practical Suffragists within the Women's Liberal Federation, pointed towards new strategies for the acquisition of the vote. These organizations emphasized the justice of women's claims and introduced a new idealism into their campaigning, while their willingness to break ranks with party to secure political rights laid the groundwork for innovative working strategies in the twentieth-century movement.

Around the turn of the century, three organizations emerged that transformed the organized campaign for women's political rights. In 1897 some 20 suffragist organizations across England, Scotland, and Wales joined to form the National Union of Women's Suffrage Societies (NUWSS). These women became known as the suffragettes and as "constitutionalists," because they advocated the use of middle-class, constitutionally approved methods of agitation by means of lectures, public meetings, distribution of pamphlets, and petitioning and putting pressure on Parliament and its members. This was a continuation and expansion of campaigning activities that had begun in the 1860s, and the NUWSS activities generated a great deal of attention and activity. However, they failed to raise general public awareness of the women's suffrage issue. In 1903 the Lancashire and Cheshire Women Textile and Other Workers Representation Committee, a ginger group within the North of England Society for Women's Suffrage (NESWS), emerged as the first predominantly working-class suffragette organization. The Women's Social and Political Union (WSPU), founded in Manchester in 1903 by Emmeline and Christabel Pankhurst, the most famous and influential leaders of the British suffragette movement, had its origins in the Pankhursts' affiliation with both the NESWS and the fledgling Independent Labour Party. The WSPU pioneered what it called militant methods, the systematic refusal to grant legitimacy to government as long as women remained without the parliamentary vote. Members of the WSPU, and other later militant organizations such as the Women's Freedom League (formed 1907) and the Men's Political Union (1910), took the issue of women's suffrage before the public and into the streets. By 1910 the Edwardian suffrage movement was split between militants and nonmilitants, and militants themselves were divided on the use of violence. Members of militant and nonmilitant organizations alike formed processions, held demonstrations, and staged pageants to make women's suffrage as public an issue as possible. WSPU protests escalated from public demonstrations to mass window-breaking of government and private offices, arson, slashing of paintings, other forms of property damage, and, notoriously, women chaining themselves to the railings of Hyde Park and even Buckingham Palace. Violent militancy ceased with the outbreak of war in 1914, but other forms of militant protest, such as tax resistance, continued until a measure of women's suffrage was granted in 1918.

The Representation of the People Act (1918) gave the parliamentary vote to women over the age of 30 who already were, or whose husbands were, local government electors on the basis of the property qualification, while simultaneously enfranchising all men at the age of 21. Historians see this inequity arising from the politicians' desire to reward soldiers and sailors with the vote and, in so doing, to retain a predominantly male electorate. Contemporary estimates suggested that had women been enfranchised equally with men in 1918, there would have been five million more female voters than male. Within a decade, however, a second Representation of the People Act (1928) had enfranchised women on the same terms as men. That act, passed with relatively little controversy, finally gave women the political rights for which they had fought for over six decades.

See also ELECTIONS AND ELECTIONEERING; SENECA FALLS CONVENTION; WOMEN'S RIGHTS.

FURTHER READING

Caine, Barbara. *Victorian Feminists.* Oxford: Oxford University Press, 1992.
Crawford, Elizabeth. *The Women's Suffrage Movement: A Reference Guide, 1866–1928.* London: UCL Press, 1999.
Daley, Caroline, and Melanie Nolan, eds. *Suffrage and Beyond: International Feminist Perspectives.* New York: New York University Press, 1994.
Holton, Sandra Stanley. *Feminism and Democracy: Women's Suffrage and Reform Politics in Britain, 1900–1918.* Cambridge, England: Cambridge University Press, 1986.
Liddington, Jill, and Jill Norris. *One Hand Tied behind Us: The Rise of the Women's Suffrage Movement.* London: Virago, 1978.
Pugh, Martin. *The March of the Women: A Revisionist Analysis of the Campaign for Women's Suffrage, 1866–1914.* Oxford: Oxford University Press, 2000.
Rosen, Andrew. *"Rise Up, Women!" The Militant Campaign of the Women's Social and Political Union, 1903–1914.* London: Routledge and Kegan Paul, 1974.
Tickner, Lisa. *The Spectacle of Women: Imagery of the Suffrage Campaign 1907–1914.* London: Chatto and Windus, 1987.
Vicinus, Martha. *Independent Women: Work & Community for Single Women, 1850–1920.* Chicago: University of Chicago Press, 1985.
Vickery, Amanda, ed. *Women, Privilege, and Power: British Politics, 1750 to the Present.* Palo Alto: Stanford University Press, 2001.

LAURA E. NYM MAYHALL

WOMEN'S WORK

The term *women's work* has several meanings in the context of the Victorian era. Some define it as the domestic ideal of middle-class Victorians, others as duties and tasks assigned to women based on assumptions about female character and abilities; still others see it merely as women's paid labor. Whatever the definition, women's labor was transformed during the rapidly industrializing nineteenth century, as a result of a changing economic system, new technologies, and new ideologies about gender.

Before widespread industrialization every family member was expected to contribute to the household economy. Thus, while women cared for the house, they often did other kinds of income-earning labor as well, including outdoor work. For example, although men generally did the heavy work such as plowing, their wives and daughters did paid farm work such as dairying or seasonal jobs such as planting, weeding crops, and haymaking. To raise extra money, many women sold eggs or produce from their gardens or worked alone or as part of a family unit spinning thread or weaving textiles. Merchants supplied them with the raw materials and then returned to pick up the finished cloth, allowing them to complete the work at home at their own pace. In urban areas women without skills or who came from families too poor to operate a shop supplemented the family income by sewing, taking in laundry, or selling goods in the streets. However, many young women learned skilled trades through apprenticeship; while some worked in clothing-related workshops, girls were also apprenticed in such diverse trades as bookbinding, printing, shoemaking, and cutlery production. Daughters of artisans or shopkeepers often learned the family business, making them desirable marriage (and business) partners. Further, because early death was a constant possibility, a widow's ability to run the family business herself was vital, and widows carried on their late husbands' businesses in many trades, ranging from tailoring to meat cutting to iron production.

CHANGES FOR A NEW ECONOMY

This traditional economy was transformed in the late eighteenth century. Enclosure of land, new agricultural technology, and the trend toward large-scale market agriculture dramatically changed rural life in many areas. In southern and eastern England and some areas of Ireland, enclosure and larger-scale farming decreased the number of agricultural jobs and claimed the small plots and common pastures

Eyre Crowe's painting *The Dinner Hour, Wigan* (1874) depicts women working in an industrial setting.

that were vital for supporting individual families. Day labor replaced live-in help, favoring the employment of men who could do heavy farm work. These changes excluded women from many of the traditional means of supplementing the family income, and young unmarried women often were forced to leave the parental home to seek domestic service or factory work in the cities. But in urban areas traditional employment opportunities for women also declined. Successful merchants rented or bought residences outside of the business districts instead of living above or behind the shop, and the exclusion of women and children from the family business became a tangible symbol of middle-class success (although a number of women continued to work behind the scenes as bookkeepers and advisers). Without their wives on the premises, employers turned to independent journeymen who lived elsewhere rather than apprentices who lived with the family, thereby reducing employment opportunities for women. Independent businesswomen found it increasingly difficult to succeed. Greater competition (even in traditional "women's trades" such as millinery and dressmaking) required a larger capital investment, and lone women often found it difficult to secure financing. Further, they were excluded from the educational system and new professional organizations that were available to their male rivals.

These changes, however, often generated other sorts of work for women, and in some instances the demand for traditional women's labor actually increased, such as in dairy farming. The NEW POOR LAW of 1834 also increased the demand for female farm labor in some areas. This law primarily provided relief for able-bodied males, and farmers feared hiring men for seasonal or casual labor that might qualify them later on for local relief and thus increase poor rates. Consequently, some entrepreneurs organized traveling "gangs" of women and girls who performed seasonal labor during planting and at harvest time.

New textile technology also increased opportunities for some women; in the late eighteenth century, the multiple-spindled spinning jenny substantially increased thread output, which in turn led to a greater demand for domestic hand-loom weavers. Later developments in the early nineteenth century, such as the introduction of the steam-driven spinning mule and the power loom in factories, undercut domestic spinning and removed one source of women's employment, although demand for home spinning and weaving did not completely disappear. New technologies in other industries also opened opportunities for women, especially those that called for more delicate or intricate work, including the production of gloves, buttons, lace, and toys. Women found employment in the burgeoning pottery industries in the Midlands as painters and decorators and were prominent in the lacquer and japanning trades. They also operated metal-stamping machinery to produce clocks, buckles, lamps, and ornamental bronze work.

INCREASING NUMBERS OF WORKING WOMEN

Despite the obstacles and challenges faced by working women, their numbers continued to increase throughout the century. The 1851 CENSUS was the first to give a more reliable indication of the number of employed women, since earlier censuses listed only the occupation of the head of the household. This revealed that nearly 3 million women were engaged in paid labor, although the actual number was probably larger since the census takers and the women themselves often did not include certain types of jobs, such as part-time labor or working in the family business. Just over 40% were employed as domestic servants, 20% worked in textile production, 18% sewed clothing, 8% were agricultural laborers, and the remainder worked in occupations ranging from construction to teaching. Within three decades, the number of working women had increased by a third, to more than 4 million. The census of 1881 shows that 45% were employed as domestic servants, 19% worked in textile manufacture, and 17% sewed clothing. Women's employment increased in virtually every other occupation as well, ranging from pottery and glass production to transport and communications.

This was comparable to the United States, where census figures for 1890 show that women worked all but 9 of the 369 occupations listed, and nearly 20% of U.S. women worked for wages outside the home. The slightly later census of 1910 shows that 37% of American women employed outside the home worked as domestic servants, nearly 30% were employed in manufacturing, 18% were employed in agricultural labor, and the remainder were found in clerical, professional, and service positions. However, as was the case with British figures, it is likely that women's work was underrepresented in American and Canadian censuses, which generally excluded women working at home or part time. Further, the frontier nature of large portions of each of these countries meant that women recognized only as housewives by themselves and the census takers frequently did whatever labor was required to allow the family to survive.

Thus, women's employment was increasing in virtually every category in the second half of the nineteenth century with two notable exceptions: agriculture and coal mining. Changes in agricultural methods by 1881 reduced the number of women to half of the midcentury figure (although women's seasonal and casual labor continued to be underreported). Mining, however, was a different case, for women had virtually disappeared from the industry. In the 1840s public reports of extremely harsh conditions in coal mines had inspired an official inquiry, which revealed that barely-clothed women performed grueling physical labor alongside the men. Newspaper editors and members of Parliament expressed shock at these potentially immoral and degrading conditions, voicing concern that these women were incapable of performing their moral duties as wives and mothers. Over the protests of miners and their families who would suffer from the loss of the women's income, Parliament banned women from virtually all aspects of mining under the Mines Act of 1842, the first legislation that recognized women as a distinct group of laborers.

PROTECTING WOMEN WORKERS

Two years later, in the Factory Act of 1844, the ban on minors working in factories at night or for more than 12 hours a shift was extended to women, indicating that legislators had come to believe that women, like children, formed a special category of workers that needed protection. But few officials argued for this on the basis of biology or physical capabilities; instead, their concerns reflected the ideal of Victorian domesticity, which emphasized the central moral role of wives and mothers in the family as "angels in the house." Thus, officials made no effort to improve conditions for those in "proper" women's work, such as domestic service or piecework sewing in the so-called sweated trades, despite the long hours and heavy tasks they performed. Most domestic servants, especially the large number who worked for the lower middle class, were underpaid and ill-housed. They performed the most laborious tasks in the household, toiling up stairs numerous times a day with heavy buckets of water or coal. Since domestic servants usually lived with their employers, they were on duty virtually 24 hours a day, and they were vulnerable to seduction or even rape by the men in the household. For women who worked sewing clothing in the sweated trades, conditions could be even worse. For miserably low pay, these women endured overcrowded and unsanitary conditions, long hours

of unremitting and monotonous labor, and irregular employment. After the sewing machine was introduced in 1851, the volume of home-sewing increased, but neither wages nor conditions improved. HENRY MAYHEW and other contemporary investigators noted that these women were those most likely to turn to part-time PROSTITUTION, joining the ranks of other destitute and underemployed women who relied upon the sex trades for survival.

Since many women in the sweated trades were homeworkers, they found it difficult to organize to improve conditions. However, even women in factories and workshops faced difficulty organizing. Many women left work at or shortly after marriage and viewed paid positions as temporary employment, but union organizing suggested a much longer-term commitment. Further, women who wanted to form or join unions not only faced hostility from their employers but also from their male colleagues. Because women generally earned one-half to two-thirds the pay of their male counterparts, male workers feared that women's employment would lead to underemployment for men or a cut in their wages. Further, unions tended to be all-male; in cases where women were allowed to join, they formed their own separate sections within the union. It was not until 1874 that Emma Paterson founded the Women's Protective and Provident League as a benefit society for the sweated trades; in the following year, under its auspices, the first women delegates attended the Trades Union Congress.

EDUCATING WOMEN

The situation was also changing for middle-class women who sought or needed employment. Before midcentury, impoverished middle-class women were limited to posts as teachers, governesses, or paid companions for wealthy women; domestic service, working in factories, or appearing in public on stage or in music halls would result in a loss of social status. Even those who had talent and sufficient education to become successful authors, reviewers, translators, or editors, such as HARRIET MARTINEAU or MARGARET OLIPHANT, ran this risk. Reformers sought to improve middle-class women's opportunities in several ways. First, they emphasized education, establishing the first girls' secondary schools in the 1840s, followed by government-funded endowed girls' schools in the 1860s, and the first boarding schools in the 1870s. By the end of the century, St. Andrew's and London universities were granting degrees to women, although Cambridge and Oxford did not follow suit until the twentieth century, despite the founding of women's colleges there in the 1870s.

To some extent Britain lagged behind the United States in the area of higher education for women; Oberlin College had begun admitting women in 1837, while Antioch College followed suit in 1853. Following the American CIVIL WAR (1861–1865), a number of women's colleges and seminaries opened, especially in the northeastern states; meanwhile, in the American Midwest and West, state colleges also began admitting women. As was the case in Britain, however, the elite male institutions refused to admit women, and as a result a number of elite female colleges were founded, including Vassar (1861), Wellesley (1870), Smith (1871), and Bryn Mawr (1885). On another front, middle-class feminists founded the Society for Promoting the Employment of Women in 1859, which provided a job register, reading room, lunchroom, and postal address for women seeking employment in London.

Reform in the medical profession also led to new opportunities for women. From the 1850s, owing in large part to the efforts of FLORENCE NIGHTINGALE, nursing became a respectable, middle-class profession rather than merely a form of domestic service, but women had a more difficult time establishing themselves as physicians. Sophia Jex-Blake, one of the leading proponents of medical education for women, founded the London School of Medicine for Women in the 1870s after she had successfully completed the course of study for physicians at Edinburgh University but was denied her degree.

The increased education available to all women by the late Victorian Period also prepared them for new nondomestic service-sector positions. Although shop assistants in the earlier nineteenth century usually were men, the dominance of the female consumer led shops and the new department stores to hire polite, well-groomed young women who could read, write, and count, to serve their female clientele. Women also replaced men in clerical positions, especially after the introduction of the typewriter in the 1880s; many employers believed that typing skills, like playing the piano, came naturally to women. For similar reasons the government employed female TELEGRAPH and TELEPHONE operators; however, in most positions, strict gender segregation was enforced on the job.

MAINTAINING RESPECTABILITY

One reason why employers were anxious to provide separate work spaces for women was to convince the public that it was respectable for working- and middle-class women to be employed in these new positions. This reflected a changed attitude toward the propriety of women's work, which was partially in response to a changing economic situation. By the end of the century, the pace of economic expansion slowed, and many working- and middle-class families found it increasingly difficult to make ends meet on a single salary. New educational opportunities were not without expense, and married women often returned to work to provide adequate education and other opportunities for their children. Thus, despite earlier fears that working mothers undermined the public morality by neglecting their domestic duties, employment to secure better educational opportunities for their children was accepted as an extension of the maternal role. This led to a change in attitude toward married women's work and provided greater possibilities for long-term employment. Yet despite more job opportunities, women's labor continued to be considered as only temporary or merely supplemental to the family income, therefore justifying women's lower pay. Further, this kept women out of managerial positions and the higher ranks of the civil service. Only the dramatic impact of World War I and II in the twentieth century began to break down these barriers.

See also EDUCATION OF WOMEN; FACTORY LEGISLATION; INDUSTRIALIZATION; NEW WOMAN; TEN HOURS MOVEMENT; TRADE UNIONS; URBANIZATION; WOMEN'S RIGHTS.

FURTHER READING

Davidoff, Leonore, and Catherine Hall. *Family Fortunes: Men and Women of the English Middle Classes, 1780–1850.* London: Hutchinson, 1987.

Holcombe, Lee. *Victorian Ladies at Work: Middle Class Working Women in England and Wales.* Hamden, Conn: Archon Books, 1973.

John, Angela, ed. *Unequal Opportunities: Women's Employment in England, 1800–1918.* Oxford: Basil Blackwell, 1985.

Lewenhak, Sheila. *Women and Trade Unions: An Outline History of Women in the British Trade Union Movement.* London: Earnest Benn, 1977.

Pinchbeck, Ivy. *Women Workers and the Industrial Revolution, 1750–1850.* 1930. Reprint, London: Cass, 1969.

Rendall, Jane. *Women in an Industrializing Society: England 1750–1880.* Oxford: Basil Blackwell, 1990.

Schmiechen, James. *Sweated Industries and Sweated Labor: The London Clothing Trades, 1860–1914.* Urbana: University of Illinois Press, 1984.

Tilly, Louise, and Joan Scott. *Women, Work and Family.* New York: Methuen, 1978.

TAMARA L. HUNT

A portrait of the poet William Wordsworth.

WORDSWORTH, WILLIAM

Born: April 7, 1770; Cockermouth, England
Died: April 23, 1850; Rydal Mount, England

William Wordsworth's poetry heavily influenced writers during the Victorian period. Chronologically speaking, William Wordsworth can just barely be considered a Victorian writer. He was already in his 67th year when VICTORIA ascended to the throne in 1837, serving as her poet laureate for the final seven years of his life, from 1843 to 1850. He was of the generation of Romantics in England and on the Continent that came of age during the final decade of the eighteenth century, the era of the French Revolution, which Wordsworth had aptly characterized in the lines "bliss was it in that dawn to be alive, but to be young was very heaven!" Thematically, a stronger case can be made for characterizing Wordsworth as a Victorian: though his best work had been written and published decades before 1837, his nature-idealizing poetry gave Victorian writers and critics the spiritual ammunition they needed to critique the new industrial society that had emerged in England. MATTHEW ARNOLD, arguably the quintessential critic of the late Victorian era, was an admirer and published an influential edition of the older man's shorter lyrics, *Poems of Wordsworth* (1879). It is generally agreed that

Wordsworth, William Blake, and Samuel Taylor Coleridge were the seminal figures in English literary ROMANTICISM, the forebears of other poets (John Keats, Lord Byron, and Percy Bysshe Shelley) whose writings served as an important counterforce to the social dehumanization and moral prudishness that has come to be synonymous with the Victorian era. Even the scientific progress so prized by the later Victorians can in a way be seen as a secularization of the spiritual energies unleashed by Wordsworth in *Lyrical Ballads*, his most famous collection, published with Coleridge in 1798.

Wordsworth's poetical credo, crystallized in the expression "emotion recollected in tranquillity," aimed to counter the prevailing schools that looked to classic models and that thus denied the validity of personal feelings and the spontaneous expressions of ordinary folk. The Romantic sensibility, which privileged natural (and supernatural) experience over intellectual study, became the worldview of a generation eager to cast off the old tyrannical orders of church and state. This sensibility as embraced by Wordsworth reechoed during the long Victorian era in a variety of guises: the PRE-RAPHAELITE BROTHERHOOD and the GOTHIC REVIVAL movement; the social reform movements that drew their sustenance, however indirect, from the beginning of the French Revolution in the Paris of 1789; even in the idyllic mythography of ALFRED, LORD TENNYSON or the religious lyrics of GERARD MANLEY HOPKINS, both of which idealized a remote past.

William Wordsworth was the second son born into an upper-middle-class household headed by John and Ann Cookson Wordsworth. His father was steward to the wealthy Sir James Lowther, who became the earl of Lonsdale, and his mother was the daughter of a draper. Also born to this union was Dorothy Wordsworth, who remained especially close to her brother; their correspondence, which shed much light on Wordsworth's life and thinking, was published in six volumes from 1935 to 1939. Both his parents nourished young William's bent toward literature: his father encouraged him to memorize long passages from William Shakespeare, John Milton, Alexander Pope, and other English writers while his mother taught him at home, exposing him to classic works such as *Gulliver's Travels* and the *Arabian Nights*. He later studied at a "dame's school" (a private school headed by a mistress) in Penrith before boarding at the Hawkshead grammar school, whose influential headmaster William Taylor was a poetry lover as well as a progressive educator.

Both of Wordsworth's parents died before he reached 13 years, and William was supported by a small trust fund administered by two parsimonious uncles who became his guardians. A more generous uncle, William Cookson, enabled his nephew to obtain a scholarship to St. John's College, Cambridge, to which William removed in 1787. He was not a zealous student and preferred his time spent in a *Wanderjahr* (a year of traveling) on the Continent in 1790, when he visited France, Switzerland, Germany, and Italy. He went back to FRANCE in 1791 to learn the language and fell in love with a barber's daughter named Annette Vallon, four years his senior, who bore him a child, Anne Caroline. During this period he became a fervent partisan of the revolutionists in France, defending the execution of Louis XVI in a 1793 pamphlet, *Letter to the Bishop of Llandaff*, that was considered too provocative to be published. He was soon forced to return home when his funds ran out. (It has been suggested by biographer Kenneth R. Johnston that Wordsworth acted as a spy on behalf of the newly formed British Secret Service, informing the crown about revolutionary fellow travelers in England.) He did not see Annette again until 1802, shortly before he married Mary Hutchinson, who bore him five children.

ESTABLISHING HIS REPUTATION AS A ROMANTIC

In the meantime, in England Wordsworth was writing the poetry that would forever establish his reputation as a Romantic. Though he had penned noteworthy verse in his school days at Hawkshead and Cambridge, it was not until 1793 that his poetry began attracting the attention of literary figures such as Coleridge. After receiving a bequest from a friend he had nursed through an illness, he settled, with Dorothy, at a house in Dorset. Over the next few years the poet spent a great deal of time hiking through England and Wales, garnering material for some of his best-regarded poems such as "Lines Composed a Few Miles above Tintern Abbey, on Revisiting the Banks of the Wye during a Tour, July 13, 1798." Also published during this period were "Salisbury Plain," "The Borderers," and "The Ruined Cottage." His most productive period began in the middle of 1797, yielding works published in his *Lyrical Ballads* collection in September 1798. Immediately afterwards the Wordsworths, accompanied by Coleridge, embarked on a tour of Germany, where William wrote some of his best poems, some of which formed the basis for *The Prelude*; completed in 1805 he would not allow it to be published until after his death. Epic in scope and conception, *The Prelude* is an autobiographical poem that traces the spiritual evolution of a child who grew up in the Lake District at the same time Wordsworth did, who witnessed the French Revolution, and who reflects on all these mighty experiences "of genius, power/Creation and divinity itself." Among the other collections that followed were *Poems in Two Volumes* (1807), which included such classics as "Ode: Intimations of Immortality," "Ode to Duty," and "Resolution and Independence"; *The Excursion* (1814); and *Poems* (1815), a collection of many short poems that had already seen print.

Back in England by 1799, William and Dorothy Wordsworth settled at Dove Cottage, Grasmere, in Westmorland, in the Lake District. In 1813, the year he and his wife moved to Rydal Mount, Wordsworth was named the official distributor of stamps for Westmorland. His revolutionary fervor long since dissipated, much to the derision of Shelley and, later, Robert Browning, who pilloried the old man as a sellout in his poem "The Lost Leader" ("Just for a handful of silver he left us . . . "). To the chagrin of even some of his ardent supporters, Wordsworth spent his remaining years more in tranquility than in emotion. He published a few good poems after this time, but his best work was essentially behind him. Still, that work is considered among the finest and most forceful in English literature, one that signaled a new age in life and letters and that helped define the parameters of the Victorian soul.

See also ROMANTICISM.

FURTHER READING
Johnston, Kenneth R. *The Hidden Wordsworth: Poet, Lover, Rebel, Spy*. New York: W. W. Norton, 1998.
Mahoney, John L. *William Wordsworth: A Poetic Life*. New York: Fordham, 1997.

EDWARD MORAN

WORKHOUSE, THE

The bleak iniquities of the workhouse, vividly portrayed by, among others, CHARLES DICKENS in *Oliver Twist*, remains one of the less attractive emblems of the English social order during the Victorian era. Workhouses were institutions for housing paupers, that is poor persons in receipt of state welfare. They were the central mechanism of the NEW POOR LAW of 1834, whose commissioners had concluded in their report on the law that, in order to enforce "less eligibility" (the principle that those on welfare benefits must be seen to be worse off than those in work on the lowest wages), the only offer of assistance to the unemployed male should be by entry into a "well-regulated workhouse." By this definition they envisaged a deterrent institution that would propel the able-bodied poor back into the labor market. To achieve this the workhouse was conceived as a repellent and inhumane institution, designed to deter all but the truly destitute from applying for relief. Although the principle of less eligibility was mainly aimed at the able-bodied, the decision in the mid-1830s to adopt the general mixed workhouse meant its application to all categories of "indoor pauper," as workhouse inmates were known.

The workhouse was intended to enforce less eligibility by psychological means rather than through physical cruelty (though, in practice, there was sometimes a fine line between the different forms of abuse). The institutions were run with an emphasis on uniformity and discipline, and the inmates subjected to a monotony of routine, useless task work, and segregation in all corners of the building. "Receiving wards," work rooms, exercise yards, dormitories, and sick wards were all segregated by gender and by age. Since able-bodied but poverty-stricken adults could not receive aid without their families entering the workhouse, this meant the separation of husband and wife, parents and children. The workhouse deprived inmates of identity and dignity. Although there were later additions and exceptions to workhouse rules, such as provision for elderly married couples and imbeciles and the introduction of fever and lying-in wards, the system of classification and segregation introduced in the 1830s remained the basis of workhouse organization for the rest of the century.

However, some myths about the Victorian workhouse can be dispelled. Firstly, only a minority of paupers were ever housed there, and even after 1834 out-relief—welfare benefits that did not require the recipient to enter a workhouse—remained the main source of poor relief. In 1849, of the recorded total of over a million recipients of relief, 88% were assisted without having to enter the workhouse. Twenty years later, in 1869, the position was similar, with 84% on out-relief. By 1900, after a period of declining out-relief rolls, the proportion of outdoor to total paupers was nevertheless still as high as 73%. Secondly, the workhouse was not a static institution. Increasing specialization, at least in the larger urban workhouses, saw the development of designated accommodation for the sick and the infirm, children, and the elderly. Indeed, following much public criticism of workhouse provision for the sick, reforms in the 1860s went some way to creating a public hospital system in LONDON and certain other larger cities.

However, the smaller rural workhouses remained largely unreformed. Moreover, even in the cities workhouse conditions did not follow a simple path to improvement. This is most clearly illustrated in the widespread building of casual or "tramp" wards for vagrants, a class of pauper that faced increasingly harsh treatment as the century wore on. It is with some justification that the workhouse remains a potent symbol of the Victorian treatment of poverty.

See also NEW POOR LAW; POVERTY AND PAUPERISM.

FURTHER READING

Crowther, Margaret A. *The Workhouse System: The History of an English Social Institution, 1834–1929.* London: Methuen, 1981.

Digby, Anne. *Pauper Palaces.* London: Routledge & Kegan Paul, 1978.

Driver, Felix. *Power and Pauperism: The Workhouse System, 1834–1884.* Cambridge: Cambridge University Press, 1993.

Kidd, Alan J. *State, Society and the Poor in Nineteenth Century England.* London & New York: Macmillan, 1999.

ALAN J. KIDD

WORKING-CLASS EDUCATION

In the Victorian period education was explicitly conceived of in class terms. The core of working-class education consisted of primary and SUNDAY SCHOOLS. However, throughout the nineteenth century efforts were made to provide a more extensive education for manual workers. Although only a small minority of the working classes actually participated, these extended instructional efforts were significant barometers of the evolution of class relationships throughout the century. Not only did Victorian efforts at adult education for the manual classes influence subsequent twentieth-century developments, but a number of the institutions established during the Victorian era for this purpose have survived to the present day.

EDUCATION OUTSIDE SCHOOLS

Although education has long been most commonly associated with the school classroom, in seventeenth- and eighteenth-century England much of the process of educating the working classes to function within society took place outside of school, chiefly by means of apprenticeship to a trade in urban areas, to farmers in rural areas, and in household service to the middle and upper classes throughout the country. Apprenticeship was conceived as providing acculturation into the general society of the day, but by the early nineteenth century it began to decline. In 1814 the Statute of Artificers, which had set rules concerning apprenticeships and the labor supply, was officially repealed by Parliament, but apprenticeship nonetheless persisted throughout the remainder of the nineteenth century.

The late eighteenth and early nineteenth century saw the emergence of institutions that undertook working-class adult educational activity, frequently instigated by middle-class and intellectual reformers who viewed education as a way of ameliorating the social conditions faced by the working class and thereby defusing class tensions. Radical members of the working class viewed education as a means of empowerment, of obtaining and protecting their rights, and of overturning existing power structures— a vision that fed the gradual growth and eventual influence of TRADE UNIONS on working practices. Working-class educational schemes thus often encompassed a mix of social agitation, efforts at personal self-improvement, and the promotion of social cooperation. Education that went beyond the basics of reading, writing, and mathematics frequently entailed pursuing middle-class values and aspirations. However, many people were aware of the tensions between the elevated education that was offered and the actual social position of working-class students. Extended working-class education was opposed by certain elitist writers on the grounds that it would serve only to propagate useless literary knowledge that would make manual workers unsuited for practical work.

POLITICS AND EDUCATION

The French Revolution of 1789 had an important influence on late-eighteenth- and early-nineteenth-century adult working-class education. In the 1790s the LONDON Corresponding Society and associated provincial societies were formed in order to exchange ideas about the egalitarian concept of society emerging in France and to discuss the work of radical thinkers such as Thomas Paine. While these societies were political, they also sponsored educational activities on the grounds that knowledge of new social principles was required in order to mobilize working-class support for social change.

In contrast, the MECHANICS' INSTITUTES that sprouted up in the first half of the nineteenth century were, at least overtly, nonpolitical. During the eighteenth century, lecture series on scientific subjects aimed at a relatively educated audience had been held in London and other large cities. Some mechanics' institutes had their origins in efforts to adapt such scien-

tific lectures for a more working-class audience, many of whom might have a call for applied science in their daily work. However, as they evolved, the institutes generally held lectures and classes on a broad range of topics of popular interest and provided recreational activities rather than maintaining a focus on applied science. Mechanics' institutes were established and supported by both middle- and working-class sponsors, and conflicts arose over the extent of working-class control. This was especially notable in the case of the London Mechanics' Institution, founded in 1823, where efforts by some supporters to shift control into working-class hands were thwarted by Francis Place, the prominent working-class organizer, and George Birkbeck, founding lecturer, who managed to maintain middle-class control. By the mid-nineteenth century, many observers opined that despite the founding of hundreds of mechanics' institutes throughout Britain, the movement was in decline and was primarily patronized by a lower-middle rather than working-class clientele.

Middle-class reformers were concerned about both insurrectionary working-class political activity and degenerate working-class leisure habits. One significant response was the formation of the Society for the Diffusion of Useful Knowledge (SDUK), founded in London in 1826 and disbanded in 1846. It was essentially a publishing clearinghouse for material aimed at the working-class autodidact. It aimed to provide publications that would be enlightening and moral rather than either practical or merely amusing and entertaining. By the late 1830s publications from other sources, which reached a more even balance between amusement and enlightenment, gained in popularity. Consequently, the SDUK lost momentum, particularly as its establishment political connections made it suspect among purely working-class elements.

Working-class leaders who wanted to retain control and to pursue more radical reforms of society formed alternative organizations for this purpose. One such organization was the Halls of Science, influenced by the educational ideas of ROBERT OWEN. Halls of Science formed in a number of cities in the 1840s and sponsored lectures advocating egalitarian visions of society. From the 1830s the CHARTISM movement was also an important influence in this regard and sponsored evening classes aimed at workers.

An organization that came to have great impact on adult education was the YOUNG MEN'S CHRISTIAN ASSOCIATION (YMCA), founded in London by George Williams and his fellow drapers' assistants in 1844. Although initially formed as a nondenominational moral and religious support group, the YMCA soon sponsored lectures and other educational activities. Although its initial clientele was primarily from the lower middle class, by the early twentieth century there was also extensive working-class participation. By the early 1850s YMCAs had been established in the UNITED STATES OF AMERICA, and by the end of the nineteenth century thousands of branches had been established throughout the world. In 1855 two organizations that were to form the Young Women's Christian Association were established in separate locations in the greater London area. The YWCA quickly achieved similar international influence to the YMCA. The rapid spread and enduring presence of both the YMCA and YWCA suggests the widespread demand for such community associations in modern industrial societies.

While mechanics institutes, YMCAs, and similar adult educational institutions also spread to the United States at this time, American activities did not arise from the same foundations of class difference. Further, with the far more rapid spread of access to education in the United States, they played a much lesser role in extended educational activity for the manual classes of the country.

CHRISTIAN SOCIALISM AND SETTLEMENTS

A key impetus to educational activities aimed at the working classes was the rise of the Christian Socialist movement in England during the 1840s. In contrast to the laissez-faire approach of leaving the poor to fend for themselves, the Christian Socialists set out to cultivate a concern for the poorer classes based on Christian principles of communal responsibility. Figures associated with CHRISTIAN SOCIALISM established workingmen's colleges. One early but relatively short-lived venture was the Sheffield People's College, founded in 1842. In 1854 the prominent Christian Socialist FREDERICK DENISON MAURICE (1805–1872) founded the Working Men's College in London. The Working Men's College initially offered evening courses in politics, science, languages and literature, and art. Such prominent figures in arts and letters as DANTE GABRIEL ROSSETTI, JOHN RUSKIN, EDWARD BURNE-JONES, CHARLES KINGSLEY, and LESLIE STEPHEN served at times as instructors. Enrollments grew from 145 in 1854 to 588 in 1903. The college issued certificates and encouraged students to sit for outside examinations. It represented an advance over mechanics' institutes in the extent of social fellowship that it provided; it also conceived education for the working classes based on general liberal principles aimed at developing the whole person rather than focused instruction in a particular set of subjects, whether scientific, technical, or political.

Despite the increasing incorporation of scientific principles into manufacturing practice in the later nineteenth century, there was no serious effort to extend technical training into working-class education. The various government schemes for technical education from the 1850s onwards never developed very far and, if anything, stood to attract a primarily lower-middle-class clientele.

If, by the last quarter of the nineteenth century, concerns of revolutionary upheaval by the working classes in England were dissipated, there was a growing perception that large segments of the working classes were isolated from the civilizing influences of religion. Here again the Christian Socialist movement had an important influence in the development of the SETTLEMENT movement in the 1880s. The central figure in this movement was Samuel Barnett, vicar of St. Judas in the London working-class district of Whitechapel from 1873. Under Barnett's leadership Toynbee Hall was established in 1884 in the East End of London. Toynbee Hall was named after the prominent Oxford reformer and philanthropist Arnold Toynbee and brought Oxford undergraduates to live in the East End and engage in friendly relationships with the working classes there. This initiative aimed to observe working-class living situations at first hand and to tailor efforts at ameliorating the local social conditions the observers found. Toynbee Hall sponsored numerous activities such as the workingman's club—an alternative to leisure time being spent in PUBLIC HOUSES, or pubs—and a wide range of social and educational activities that included lectures, reading parties, concerts, and literary society meetings. Prominent working-class leaders such as Ben Tillet, Tom Mann, and the socialist campaigner, crusader, politician, and reformer George Lansbury were brought in to lecture, and prominent industrialists and philanthropists attended debates. Toynbee Hall also sponsored investigations into social conditions and problems.

Following Barnett's lead with Toynbee Hall in 1884, a number of similar settlements were established in London. Some were concerned about the lack of religion associated with Toynbee Hall, and in 1885 Anglo-Catholics from Oxford set up Oxford House in Bethnal Green. Subsequently, Cambridge colleges sponsored a number of missions and settlements. Nonconformists also became active in this area, forming Mansfield House in Canning Town (1890), the Bermondsey Settlement (1891), and the Robert Browning Settlement in Walworth (1895). In addition to those in London, Glasgow University set up a settlement in 1889 and Manchester University one at Ancoats in 1895.

The settlement movement probably influenced only a tiny segment of the working classes and many of its activities drew in lower-middle-class rather than working-class elements. However, the movement does indicate how some members of the more privileged classes in Britain undertook to understand and alleviate social unrest and squalor in urban areas.

UNIVERSITY EDUCATION

External university courses were developed and offered to the working classes beginning in the 1870s. The first were sponsored by Cambridge University in response to requests from mechanics' institutes and cooperative societies. Subsequent efforts by Oxford and other universities followed. In the early 1880s thousands of miners attended lectures in POLITICAL ECONOMY and a range of other scientific and literary topics given in the Northeast Coal Fields. The great miners' strike of 1887 put an end to this activity, and interest in intellectual leadership turned to more socialist sources. However, university extension education continued to flourish through the 1890s, when it is estimated that as many as 60,000 students attended these classes. However, as with the settlement movement, it appears that much of the real audience for these activities was lower-middle rather than working-class.

In 1903 a major force for adult education activity arrived on the scene with the establishment of the Workers Educational Association (WEA), formed by Albert Mansbridge. The WEA aimed to establish a link between trade union activity and night schools. By the early 1920s it was widespread throughout England. Initially, the emphasis was on social and economic subjects in an effort to promote social activism. However, in its early decades much of the activity

shifted to more general academic teaching and evening extension work, which brought it in more direct competition with universities. The formation of Ruskin College in Oxford with trade union sponsorship, along with the involvement of some Oxford University faculty members in the early 1900s, also represented an attempt to retain trade union influence in extending working-class political activity.

Whatever the limited immediate impact during the Victorian era of such higher order working-class educational activity, it did leave a lasting legacy for various working-class organizing activities and extramural university activities. The Working Men's College, founded 1854, and Toynbee Hall, founded 1884, remain in existence in the twenty-first century, and London University's Birkbeck College traces its origins back to the London Mechanics Institution, founded in 1823.

See also EDUCATION ACT OF 1870; PRIMARY EDUCATION; UNIVERSITIES.

FURTHER READING

Briggs, Asa, and Anne Macartney. *Toynbee Hall: The First Hundred Years.* London and New York: Routledge and Kegan Paul, 1984.
Harrison, J. F. C. *A History of the Working Men's College, 1854–1954.* London: Routledge and Kegan Paul, 1954.
Harrison, J. F. C. *Learning and Living, 1790–1960: A Study in the History of the English Adult Education Movement.* London: Routledge and Kegan Paul, 1961.
Kelly, Thomas. *A History of Adult Education in Great Britain.* 3d ed. Liverpool: Liverpool University Press, 1961.
Kett, Joseph F. *The Pursuit of Knowledge under Difficulties: From Self-Improvement to Adult Education in America, 1750–1990.* Stanford: Stanford University Press, 1994.
Meachem, Standish. *Toynbee Hall and Social Reform, 1880–1914: The Search for Community.* New Haven: Yale University Press, 1987.
Simon, Brian. *Education and the Labour Movement, 1870–1920.* London: Lawrence and Wishart, 1965.
Simon, Brian. *The Two Nations and the Educational Structure, 1780–1870.* London: Lawrence and Wishart, 1974.

DAVID MITCH

Y

YMCA. *See* YOUNG MEN'S CHRISTIAN ASSOCIATION.

YONGE, CHARLOTTE MARY

Born: August 11, 1823; Otterbourne, England
Died: March 24, 1901; Otterbourne, England

Although today she is primarily recognized as an author of novels for girls, Charlotte Mary Yonge was one of the best-known authors of the mid- to late-Victorian era. One young Sunday school scholar of Yonge's opined with reverence that Miss Yonge looked like QUEEN VICTORIA herself.

The shy, modest, and deeply religious Yonge wrote more than 160 novels, histories, and biographies, including the best-selling *The Heir of Redclyffe* (1853), on which her reputation was made. This serious romance contrasted the conduct and beliefs of two cousins—Guy and Philip Morville—and promoted submission to authority, piety, and self-discipline as deeply desirable masculine behaviors. Guy, who embodies true goodness in the face of daily temptations as well as the treachery of his cousin Philip, marries his beloved; however, while on his honeymoon Guy learns that his cousin is dangerously ill with a fever. In nursing Philip, Guy catches the fever and dies. Jo March, in LOUISA MAY ALCOTT's *Little Women* (1868–1869), would later weep and sigh over Yonge's *The Heir of Redclyffe*. Biographer Georgina Battiscombe notes that Yonge's great contribution lies in the effect her novels had on the readers in creating "the longing to be good."

Yonge shared this longing. She dedicated her life to promoting the good works of the Anglican church, to serving her community through teaching Sunday school, and donating to church-related causes the money she earned by her writing. For example, Yonge funded missionary ventures in the Melanesian Islands

206

Charlotte Mary Yonge wrote 160 novels, most of them for young girls.

and New Zealand with the considerable profits gained from her books.

Yonge is generally classified as a novelist of the Oxford Movement (also known as TRACTARIANISM), a revitalizing movement within the Anglican church begun in 1833 by clergy at Oxford University such as JOHN KEBLE (1792–1866), which restored certain Roman Catholic doctrines and rituals to the CHURCH OF ENGLAND. The ideals of this movement can be found throughout Yonge's fiction. The Oxford Movement reverberated within British life through its emphasis on social reform, education, church-building, and the revival of Anglican religious communities. The two greatest influences on Yonge's life were her father, who taught her at home, and Keble, who left Oxford to become vicar of Hursley, to which the Yonge family's parish at Otterbourne was then joined. The lessons of Yonge's confirmation at age 15 under the spiritual guidance of Keble would influence both the tenor and conduct of Yonge's public and private life in all the years of fame to come.

Yonge's great talent lay in creating memorable, lifelike personalities and in writing realistic dialogue. Indeed, conversations create much of the plots of her domestic stories. Yonge's most famous work of domestic realism for young readers, *The Daisy Chain* (1856), chronicles the family life, parish work, and emotional and spiritual crises of Dr. May and his 11 children. Enthusiastic, intelligent, and clumsy Ethel May—a precursor to Alcott's Jo March, and a similarly autobiographical character—is one of Yonge's most beloved creations. Although the audience for *The Daisy Chain* was primarily adolescent girls, GEORGE ELIOT (1819–1880), for one, found the long novel to be both absorbing and satisfying and read it to George Henry Lewes in Florence. Yonge's work was popular in America as well as Britain: for example, by the time of the publication of *Little Women*, *The Daisy Chain* was in its ninth edition.

As the long-standing editor and contributor to *The Monthly Packet* (1851–1890), a magazine for girls, Charlotte Yonge helped to construct middle- and upper-class girls' reading through two generations. Called "a Maidens' Manual" by Yonge's first biographer Christabel Coleridge, this high-church periodical had a small circulation and ran on a shoestring budget without an office or staff, yet in its attempt to mold the characters of its girl readers through moral tales, articles on history, and papers on parish work and foreign missions, its persuasive impact exceeded its modest circumstances. One enthusiastic set of Yonge's admirers formed a group called The Goslings whose purpose was to improve the minds of its members by modeling themselves after the virtuous heroines of Yonge's fiction. For 15 years Yonge guided this group of girls and oversaw the production of their manuscript magazine, *The Barnacle*.

The sales figures of her works, which rivaled CHARLES DICKENS'S, and the fanaticism of some of her readers such as The Goslings, attest to Yonge's popularity during her lifetime. Yet today her oeuvre is largely unknown and most of her books are out of print. The high-minded religious principles that inform all of Yonge's works may account for this phenomenon. As Yonge advised aspiring women writers in *Womankind* (1877), "the rule of only writing as a Christian with the glory of God in view, needs to be kept in mind. . . . " Other contemporary Victorian women novelists who wrote about the family in society or an individual woman's struggle both to fulfill her duty and find personal happiness, such as George Eliot or CHARLOTTE BRONTË (1816–1855), were not so narrowly constrained. One has only to contrast the figure of St. John Rivers, the missionary in *Jane Eyre* (1847) whose cold perfection horrifies Jane, with Yonge's hero, the brilliant missionary-priest Norman May (from *The Daisy Chain*) who repudiates the glories of the scholar's life and valiantly goes off to the South Seas with his bride, to understand the differences between the romances of Yonge the Tractarian and the secular novelists. Although she was publishing during the so-called Golden Age of children's literature of the later Victorian era, which gave rise to British classics (LEWIS CARROLL's *Alice* books [1865 and 1871], George Macdonald's *The Princess and the Goblin* [1872], and ROBERT LOUIS STEVENSON's *Treasure Island* [1883]), Yonge's domestic sagas, historical romances, inspirational biographical sketches (such as *A Book of Golden Deeds* [1864]), and schoolroom texts (such as *Aunt Charlotte's Stories of English History for the Little Ones* [1873]) can be distinguished from these works of fantasy and adventure that either dispense with didacticism entirely, or wear it lightly. Through their realism, well-developed characters, and psychological insights, Yonge's children's books are also distinct from the myriad Evangelical stories of conversion published by the Religious Tract Society during the nineteenth century such as Hesba Stretton's *Jessica's First Prayer* (1867).

See also CHILDREN'S LITERATURE; TRACTARIANISM.

FURTHER READING

Battiscombe, Georgina. *Charlotte Mary Yonge: The Story of an Uneventful Life.* London: Constable, 1943.
Battiscombe, Georgina, and Marghanita Laski, eds. *A Chaplet for Charlotte Yonge.* London: The Cresset Press, 1965.
Coleridge, Christabel. *Charlotte Mary Yonge: Her Life and Letters.* London: Macmillan, 1903.
Dennis, Barbara. *Charlotte Yonge: Novelist of the Oxford Movement.* Lewiston, NY: The Edwin Mellen Press, 1992.
Sturrock, June. *"Heaven and Home": Charlotte M. Yonge's Domestic Fiction and the Victorian Debate Over Women.* Victoria, British Columbia: ELS Monograph Series 66, 1995.
Yonge, Charlotte Mary. *Womankind.* London: Mozeley and Smith, 1877.

LYNNE VALLONE

YOUNG ENGLAND

Young England was a small political cadre within the Tory party in the 1840s. Its leader was BENJAMIN DISRAELI (1804–1881) whose evident ambition and sense of romance inspired other young Tory members of Parliament to join him in a crusade against what they believed was the prevailing UTILITARIANISM of the day. They saw their leader and the prime minister, ROBERT PEEL (1788–1850), as utilitarianism's agent within the Tory party, the consequences of which were political compromise and a profound weakening of the

party's historical traditions, especially its foundation in the landed classes.

Disraeli, first elected to the House of Commons in 1837, expected to be named to Peel's cabinet in 1841. He was not, and one of the results of this apparent prime ministerial neglect was Disraeli's founding of an opposition group within the Tories comprising similarly disaffected members of Parliament (M.P.s). Young England, as it called itself, was galvanized by Disraeli's belief in the organic nature of medieval Catholic English society where church and state had existed in apparent harmony. Disraeli's romantic creed fit nicely with the emerging and reactionary medievalism of English society in the 1830s and 1840s, and he quickly captured two ardent parliamentary supporters: Lord John Manners (1818–1906) and George Smythe (1818–1857). Beginning in the fall of 1843 these men and others sat together on the backbenches of the government side, speaking and voting in concert, often in opposition to Peel. In addition, Disraeli, who had established himself as an author of some note in the late 1820s, began publishing expressly political novels. The first of three books that came to be known as Disraeli's "political trilogy" was published in 1844. *Coningsby; or, The New Generation*, was interpreted to be a political manifesto about regenerating the aristocracy. Next, came *Sybil; or, The Two Nations* (1845), regarded as probably Disraeli's best novel and written as an allegory about how church and state might best be unified to bind together the nation. In 1847 the final book in the trilogy was published, *Tancred; or The New Crusade*, a continuation of the themes found in *Sybil* but without either its literary merit or its social vision.

Two years earlier in 1845, however, Young England had foundered over a bill introduced by Peel's government to grant a permanent annual subsidy to the Roman Catholic seminary in Maynooth, Ireland. The rhetoric of Young England with its praise of medieval English Catholicism might have made voting for this piece of legislation logical. But Disraeli forgot both logic and his colleagues and voted against the measure in order to oppose Peel. The bill passed, and from that moment on Young England lost its initiative.

For Victorian romantics Young England was an inspiration. Drawing on influences such as the Oxford Movement (TRACTARIANISM), the social theory of Samuel Taylor Coleridge, and the novels of Walter Scott, Young England presented a compelling case for what ailed industrializing England but was hopelessly anachronistic in suggesting a cure. As Disraeli's most comprehensive biographer, Sir Robert Blake, puts it: "The history of Young England has all the charm and nostalgia which attend tales of forlorn hopes and lost causes . . . ."

See also DISRAELI, BENJAMIN; UTILITARIANISM.

FURTHER READING

Blake, Robert. *Disraeli.* London: Eyre and Spottiswoode, 1966.
Faber, Richard. *Young England.* London: Faber and Faber, 1987.
Feuchtwanger, Edgar. *Disraeli.* London: Arnold, 2000.

C. BRAD FAUGHT

YOUNG MEN'S CHRISTIAN ASSOCIATION

A response to the social and religious problems caused by urbanization, the Young Men's Christian Association (YMCA) was by the end of the century a great Victorian institution whose impact was global. From humble origins, it developed by the end of Victoria's reign into an international network of societies performing a range of religious, educational, recreational, and welfare functions. Like so much philanthropic activity in the Victorian age, the YMCA was inspired by EVANGELICALISM and was concerned with both winning souls and improving minds and bodies. It was instrumental in the propagation of what have come to be seen as key Victorian values such as respectability, moral earnestness, and MUSCULAR CHRISTIANITY.

PROVIDING MORAL GUIDANCE FOR YOUNG MEN

The association was founded by a small group of assistant drapers in the LONDON firm of Hitchcock and Rogers. Economic expansion had undermined the paternalistic living-in system practiced by firms that was meant to safeguard the morals of workers. At Hitchcock and Rogers over 100 young men lived above the premises, where, after long working hours, they endured cramped conditions, often having to share beds. To feed expansion the firm relied on bringing in new employees from rural areas. One of these was George Williams, son of a Somerset farmer. A committed evangelical from 1837, on arriving in London four years later he began energetic missionary and ragged school (informal education) activity. At work he was particularly shocked by the "language, the immorality, the drunkenness" that he witnessed, and he helped to establish prayer meetings and bible classes in an attempt to convert his colleagues. George Hitchcock, the men's employer, was impressed with these efforts, and he hired a firm chaplain and established daily "family prayers."

Word of the religious activity at Hitchcock and Rogers began to spread, and this encouraged the men to extend their activities. In a meeting in Williams's bedroom on June 6, 1844, they agreed to form a "Society for Improving the Spiritual Condition of Young Men Engaged in the Drapery and other Trades." The object, according to the diary of Edward Valentine, who attended the meeting, was "to influence religious young men to spread the Redeemer's Kingdom amongst those by whom they are surrounded." The name "Young Men's Christian Association" was adopted soon afterwards.

RAPID EXPANSION

The YMCA was not the first religious society for young men. What set the YMCA apart was its aggressive evangelical expansionism. A rule adopted early in the association's history (though not followed by YMCAs in the rest of the world) stated that only converts could enjoy full membership, a rule designed, in the words of Williams, "to keep the spiritual temperature of the Association high, its efforts earnest, and its methods aggressive." The expansionist urge was also exhibited by the appointment in 1845 of T. H. Tarlton as the association's first paid secretary-missionary, briefed to oversee the formation of branch associations in the large towns and cities.

The early YMCA displayed another trait that was to contribute to its long-term success: a willingness to minister to more than just the religious needs of young men. Tapping into the popular enthusiasm for self-help, from 1845 the London YMCA ran seasons of lectures on an eclectic range of topics. These were so well attended that they soon had to be held in EXETER HALL, where they became a prominent feature of the cultural life of the capital. Though bible classes remained important, several branches diversified by holding educational classes in subjects such as languages, arithmetic, and English literature. Many YMCAs also offered LIBRARIES and reading rooms. The *Athenaeum* praised the range of facilities available for just a guinea per annum at Aldersgate, the headquarters of the London branch, and judged it "a good Club House" for any city clerk.

But several members regarded the educational and recreational facilities offered by the YMCA as distractions from the primary religious function of the organization, or worse, as actual obstacles to the salvation of souls. W. E. Shipton, secretary of the London branch, worried that the associations were coming to be seen as little more than "places of amusement for young people," while at the end of the century, another old stalwart was perturbed to learn that significant numbers of members wanted "smoking and billiards." Even the encouragement of seemingly harmless pursuits such as boating could prove problematic: in the 1890s the Sunderland Boat Club was locally renamed the "Floating Fornication Club" after it became known that members were using the club's craft to entertain female companions. Nevertheless the willingness of the YMCA to cater for its members' mental, social, and physical needs was a crucial factor in its domestic expansion.

Another factor was the generous backing it received from rich donors. Fortunately, Williams and his cofounders proved adept at cultivating interest in the association among those with the money to finance its operations. Hitchcock was first in a long line of patrons that included lord Shaftesbury, president of the YMCA for 34 years, from 1851 to 1885 the wealthy banker R. C. L. Bevan, and Samuel Morley, the Liberal mill owner. These benefactors not only provided the resources necessary for expansion but also helped to increase both the profile and the respectability of the association.

AN INTERNATIONAL MOVEMENT

Fittingly, it was the 1850s, the decade of the GREAT EXHIBITION OF 1851, that saw the YMCA develop into an international movement. Indeed, the exhibition itself provided a useful opportunity to encourage the formation of new branches, with members distributing over 300,000 tracts to visitors. Organizations calling themselves YMCAs were beginning to form in AUSTRALIA AND NEW ZEALAND, the UNITED STATES, and across Europe. Ninety-seven representatives of seven YMCAs met in Paris in 1855 and established the World's Alliance of YMCAs. At this stage most YMCAs were happy to look to London for a lead: indeed George Williams, at 34 the oldest representative at Paris, was already the "grand old man" of the movement. London became the headquarters of the alliance, and Shipton became the de facto world secretary. Thirteen more World's Conferences were to be held in Victoria's reign.

The YMCA was from the start interdenominational, a factor which clearly aided its rapid spread. Initially dominated by DISSENTERS, the Anglican influence was stronger from the 1850s. Accompanying this trend was a tendency to avoid controversy, preferring to refrain from expressing views on issues such as TEMPERANCE or HOME RULE. But the YMCA was not immune from the increasingly democratic climate of the later Victorian period, and, appropriately enough, it was in the reform-minded 1870s that the YMCA became a more democratic institution. The natural right of the "old men" of the YMCA to govern was increasingly challenged in the 1870s, with the result that the London Committee's rule on the world stage was replaced in 1878 by a Central International Committee for the World's Alliance and on the national level, four years later, by an English National Council.

By this time the YMCA was truly a Victorian institution, and it was apt that in 1894, sandwiched in between Victoria's golden and diamond jubilees, came the YMCA's own golden jubilee. Williams was knighted and granted the Freedom of the City of London. By now there were 405 associations in Britain with 60,000 members, while world membership totaled half a million. As historian Clyde Binfield has noted, the YMCA "encircled the world rather more successfully than the British Empire did." It has also proved somewhat more durable than this latter institution.

See also EVANGELICALISM.

FURTHER READING

Binfield, Clyde. *George Williams and the YMCA: A Study in Victorian Social Attitudes.* London: Heinemann, 1973.
Garnham, Neal. "Both Praying and Playing: 'Muscular Christianity' and the YMCA in North-East County Durham." *Journal of Social History* 35 (Winter 2001): 397–407.
Shedd, Clarence Prouty, ed. *History of the World's Alliance of Young Men's Christian Associations.* London: SPCK, 1955.
Williams, J. E. Hodder. *The Life of Sir George Williams.* London: Hodder and Stoughton, 1906.

JAMES TAYLOR

ZANGWILL, ISRAEL

Born: February 14, 1864; Bristol, England
Died: August 1, 1926; Preston, England

Israel Zangwill, nicknamed the "Jewish Dickens" for his representations of Jewish slums and ghettos, was a prolific writer of books, plays, short stories, and journal articles and an active supporter of political causes such as pacifism, Zionism, and WOMEN'S SUF-FRAGE. He was a well-known figure in London's Victorian literary scene, and his fame extended to the UNITED STATES, where his play *The Melting Pot* was successfully represented, providing a forceful metaphor for the American character.

Born in Bristol to poor Russian immigrants, Israel Zangwill was educated at the Jewish Free School of London's East End and later taught there. While in East End Jewry, Zangwill recorded his thoughts about the community in notebooks, which later became the basis of his novels. Zangwill was a member of The

Wanderers of Kilburn, a circle of educated Jews who gathered in LONDON in the 1880s. These intellectuals were concerned with the nature of Jewish identity in British society and tried to reconcile the demands of traditional Judaism with assimilation and modernity required by an increasingly secular society. Members of the group included scholars such as Solomon Schechter; journalists such as Asher Myers, editor of the *Jewish Chronicle*; and the artist Solomon J. Solomon. They played a leading role in establishing the Maccabæans and Jewish Historical Society and established the cultural foundations of modern Anglo-Jewish community. Although his writings depict ghetto life in humorous and nostalgic terms, Zangwill thought that traditional Judaism was an anachronism in Victorian society. The dilemma between the choices of Judaism and modernity is mirrored by Zangwill's characters, who are stuck between the familiar and safe, if unexciting, ghetto life and the charms of the outer world.

Although Zangwill supported Zionism, he changed his mind several times as to where a Jewish state was to be established. After visiting Eretz Yisrael in 1897, he became a vocal advocate of Jewish nationalism, arguing that this could be realized in any area and not exclusively in Eretz Yisrael. Following the Zionist Congress's rejection of the Uganda proposal in 1905, Zangwill became disillusioned with the mainstream Zionist movement and contributed to the founding of the Jewish Territorialist Organization, whose aim was to gain territory for a Jewish settlement. Yet the group was largely unsuccessful. Following the Balfour Declaration, Zangwill rejoined the official Zionist movement, but the pioneers' difficulties in colonizing the land and in resolving the conflicts with the Arabs prompted him to return to his earlier opinion that a different territory would present a more feasible option.

Zangwill's writing covered many subjects that ranged from East End Jewish life in *Children of the Ghetto* (the first work of fiction to be published by the Jewish Publication Society of America in 1895) to detective fiction in *The Big Bow Mystery* and translations of Hebrew prayers. His play *The Melting Pot*, which was widely acclaimed in the United States and was appreciated by reformers such as Theodore Roosevelt (1858–1919) and Jane Addams (1860–1935), shaped the ethnic debate well beyond the Victorian era. The play focuses on the love affair between David Quixano, a young Jewish composer, and Vera Revendal, the daughter of a renowned anti-Semite who was responsible for the pogrom (massacre of Jews) where David's parents and brother were killed. Although the story takes place in New York, Vera's parents are still linked to Old World beliefs, and they oppose the relationship between David and their daughter. Despite this, their romance triumphs, and the play ends with a vision of America's ability to act as God's crucible where all the races are "melting and reforming."

FURTHER READING

Leftwich, Joseph. *Israel Zangwill.* New York: Thomas Yoseloff, 1957.

Sollors, Werner. *Beyond Ethnicity. Consent and Descent in American Culture.* New York: Oxford University Press, 1986.

Udelson, Joseph H. *Dreamer of the Ghetto: The Life and Works of Israel Zangwill.* Tuscaloosa: University of Alabama Press, 1990.

Zangwill, Israel. *Children of the Ghetto. A Study of a Peculiar People.* Introduction, Notes, and Biography by Meri-Jane Rochelson. Detroit: Wayne State University Press, 1998.

LUCA PRONO

ZOOLOGICAL GARDENS

Zoological gardens were collections of exotic animals situated in a park setting within a largely urban context. The origins of these attractions can be found in the great courtly menageries from the twelfth century onward, when a passion for collecting exotic animals was a favorite courtly pastime in Europe. By the eighteenth century traveling beast SHOWS or menageries were exhibited on fairgrounds, with Bostock and Wombwell's Royal Menagerie established from the late 1780s onward.

One of the earliest menagerie collections open to the public was the Royal Menagerie of Louis XI, founded at Versailles in 1664. This was open to the public and the scientific community until the French Revolution, when opposition to princely collections resulted in the animals being sent to the Jardin des Plantes, a botanical garden in Paris. The combination of a public botanical and animal collection within an area of parkland formed the model for zoological gardens throughout Europe and America, and many were situated within former PLEASURE GARDENS. The first zoological collection opened as a commercial venture in the United Kingdom was Edward Cross's Menagerie (1773–1829). Cross's Menagerie featured animals and animal acts that were exhibited in a building on the Strand. It was one of the first opportunities for people in London to see lions, tigers, monkeys, a hippopotamus, and a sloth. One of the most popular animals was a 5-ton elephant named Chunee, who in 1825 achieved notoriety when he became enraged and killed his keeper. Following the closure of the menagerie building in 1829, Cross moved his collection to the newly opened Surrey Zoological Gardens, located on a 13-acre (5-hectare) site near the famous Vauxhall Pleasure Gardens. Unlike their earlier rival at Regent's Park, the Surrey gardens were a commercial venture, charging admission. They featured flower shows, EXHIBITIONS, fireworks, volcanic eruptions, and the dramatic enactments of the Siege of Gibraltar, in addition to animals. Their popularity continued unabated until 1851, when competition from the GREAT EXHIBITION OF 1851 resulted in a severe loss of revenue and drop in visitor numbers.

REGENT'S PARK

The Zoological Society of London founded the oldest zoological gardens in continual use in Regent's Park in 1828. Based on the Jardin des Plantes model, the purpose of the society was scientific study, and the collection was intended to be a research center for studying animals in the comparative freedom of a leased site in Regent's Park. The establishment of a museum for comparative zoology, the research publications and library collection, and its policy of exhibiting as wide a range of species as possible, both common and exotic, set Regent's Park apart from comparable collections in Madrid, Paris, and Vienna. Unlike Cross's earlier menagerie it was to be a collection of living animals, a museum with prepared specimens, and a library primarily for scientists. The public was admitted by entrance fee as a means to finance its research. After the closure of the King's menagerie in the Tower of London, which had originally been founded in the twelfth century, many of the animals moved to Regent's Park in 1832. Over the course of the nineteenth century, Regent's Park Zoo became the home of the world's largest animal collection. The first elephant was acquired in 1831, followed by an Indian rhinoceros in 1834, giraffes in 1836, and a 4-ton hippopotamus named Obaysch in 1850. Perhaps its most famous inmate was Jumbo the African elephant, who first came to the zoo in 1865 and acquired international fame in 1882 following his sale to P. T. BARNUM, the American showman who then exhibited him in his great show. The col-

lection also featured reptiles that were housed in their own buildings in 1849, and in 1853 the Zoological Society commissioned the world's first public aquarium.

Zoological gardens became increasingly popular in the United Kingdom and Europe throughout the nineteenth century. One of the largest collections outside London was to be found in Belle Vue Pleasure Gardens near Manchester, founded in 1836. Zoos opened throughout Europe as cities competed against each other to follow the examples of Paris and London. Collections were open to the public in Amsterdam (1838), Antwerp (1843) Brussels (1851), and Rotterdam (1857). According to Eric Baratay and Elizabeth Hardouin-Fugier in *Zoo: A History of Zoological Gardens in the West:* "The spread of the zoological gardens was so rapid and extensive because of the added political dimensions of competition between nations. . . . This was also a case of urban elites emulating each other, a zoological garden being seen as an indispensable tool in the confirmation or maintenance of a city's status." The craze for entertainment often outweighed the pretensions of research, with many cities combining the commercial aspect

Visitors to a zoological garden, circa 1881.

of the pleasure garden with the fascination for the exotic, where one would promenade around the landscaped gardens and be both educated and amused.

Although the history of zoological gardens is largely seen as a European phenomenon, zoological parks began to appear in the UNITED STATES OF AMERICA after 1865. Many of these zoological parks were conceived in the 1860s and opened in the years following the CIVIL WAR. Early collections open to the public included New York's Central Park, opened in 1868; some 20 zoos opened between 1885 and 1900, including the Smithsonian National Zoological Park in Rock Creek Park, in Washington, D.C., which was established by an act of Congress in 1889. These parks were based largely on the European model but later changed their development and evolution to mirror the developments in Germany, especially those pioneered by Carl Hagenbeck.

THE MODERN ZOO

One of the most significant developments in the history of zoos was the emergence of zoological collections in Germany. Many of the major German towns opened a zoological garden between 1860 to 1880, including inaugurations in Cologne (1860), Hamburg (1863), and Stuttgart (1870), to name but a few. One of the major figures in the development of zoological gardens in Germany and Europe was Carl Hagenbeck (1844–1913), who acted as a wild animal dealer, CIRCUS proprietor, and founder of zoological gardens. Hagenbeck started his small menagerie with two performing seals and by the 1870s was one of the largest animal dealers in Europe. He developed the idea of a menagerie and *Volkerschauen* (native show) to be exhibited alongside each other in his new quarters at Neuer Pferdemarkt in Hamburg. In his autobiography, translated into English in 1910, Hagenbeck recalls that he first introduced native exhibitions into his menagerie when it was suggested that he import a family of Lapps to accompany the reindeers. The scenes of simplicity and domesticity with the Laplanders sitting in their encampments within the Zoological Gardens, preparing their food, were an instant success.

By the late nineteenth century Hagenbeck had emerged as the world's undisputed leader in the capture and transport of exotic animals. His business included the *Volkerschauen* and the training of exotic animals without the use of force. Quickly known as the Hagenbeck method, he first exhibited his animals

in the Cirque d'Hiver in Paris in 1889. In 1896 he patented the concept of a "zoo of the future with open enclosure without bars," which is credited as being one of the cornerstones of modern zoos. When the Hagenbeck Animal Park opened in 1907 in Stellingen, Germany, Hagenbeck brought together all his business interests in a revolutionary zoological park. The animals were placed in enclosures that were designed to reflect the indigenous landscape of the animals. Caging and artificial enclosures were replaced by natural ones, such as water, dry moats, ditches, and plants. The Stellingen effect revolutionized zoological collections throughout the world, and according to Baratay and Hardouin-Fugier, "Stellingen had left every other zoo looking outdated." The nineteenth-century zoological garden, with its landscaped settings, caged enclosures, and entertainment arenas, soon appeared outdated and restrictive to the animals on display. Zoos with naturalistic effects became the norm.

Although modern zoological gardens continued to evolve from Hagenbeck's revolutionary techniques, zoological gardens and to some extent the earlier pleasure gardens of the eighteenth century can be linked to the renaissance of urban industrial centers. They were part of the urban renovation programs that occurred throughout Europe and the United Kingdom from the 1860s onward. Often set up on the outskirts of towns, the gardens were seen as improving the landscape of the city, regenerating urban spaces, and providing a domesticated and idealized view of nature. These landscaped wonderlands were the means by which the Victorian public first saw or encountered wild or exotic animals from across the world and formed the basis for scientific study and research centers that are still in existence today.

See also CIRCUS; PLEASURE GARDENS; SHOWS.

FURTHER READING

Altick, Richard D. *Shows of London: A Panoramic History of Exhibitions, 1600–1862.* Cambridge, Mass.: Harvard University Press, 1978.

Baratay, Eric, and Elizabeth Hardouin-Fugier. *Zoo: A History of Zoological Gardens in the West.* London: Reaktion Books, 2002.

Habn, Emily. *Zoos.* London: Secker and Warburg, 1968.

Hagenbeck, Carl. *Beasts and Men: Being Carl Hagenbeck's Experiences for Half a Century among Wild Animals.* London: Longman, Green, 1910.

VANESSA TOULMIN

ENCYCLOPEDIA OF THE
VICTORIAN ERA

Back Matter

Appendix I: Map of the British Isles

Appendix II
Primary Documents

DOMESTIC LIFE AND SOCIAL CONDITIONS

Life at the beginning of Queen Victoria's reign in 1837 was much different from life at the end of her reign in 1901. The social changes caused by industrialization had an impact on where people lived (with many moving from agricultural lands to cramped cities); how they lived (with members of working class living in unsanitary conditions where disease ran rampant); and who they worked for (with the increase in wealth allowing members of the growing middle class greater independence, yet also increasing the number of people living as domestic servants).

The excerpts in this section highlight the changes to domestic life during the Victorian era. Despite general improvements in living standards as the era progressed, the working class suffered the brunt of the crowded, hazardous conditions caused by the growing number of people and factories in cities. In his novel *Sybil* (1845) Benjamin Disraeli detailed the results of increasing urbanization and industrialization in the fictional rural town of Marney, England; health reformer William Acton documented the impact of venereal disease on the health of prostitutes and their clients, as well as the efficacy of the Contagious Diseases Act in midcentury; George Godwin described the horrific conditions of the Thames river that oozed through London sloshing contaminated muck and grime along its banks.

The life of the more privileged classes is also documented here. The improvements in transportation offered many opportunities to explore the world as tourists. Tourist journals became popular reading, and Sir Francis Galton offers here a description of his own trip to Spain in 1860. Life at home, for the wealthy and the middle class, became increasingly filled with ritual. Domestic servants became necessary to maintain appropriate living standards among the well-to-do. Instructions for how to treat domestic servants could be found in *Cassell's Household Guide* (1869–

1871), the first published step-by-step guidance on all areas of household maintenance and social etiquette.

A DIFFICULT LIFE FOR THE WORKING CLASSES

As a novelist Benjamin Disraeli (1804–1881) illustrated the vast differences of experience between rich and poor. As a politician he worked to better the lives of the working classes by insisting that doing so was the duty of the upper class. In his 1845 novel, Sybil, *subtitled* The Two Nations, *Disraeli detailed the plight of the working classes as they coped with the difficult living conditions industrialization forced on them.*

EXCERPT FROM *SYBIL; OR, THE TWO NATIONS.*

The situation of the rural town of Marney was one of the most delightful easily to be imagined. In a spreading dale, contiguous to the margin of a clear and lively stream, surrounded by meadows and gardens, and backed by lofty hills, undulating and richly wooded, the traveller on the opposite heights of the dale would often stop to admire the merry prospect that recalled to him the traditional epithet of his country.

Beautiful illusion! For behind that laughing landscape, penury and disease fed upon the vitals of a miserable population.

The contrast between the interior of the town and its external aspect was as striking as it was full of pain. With the exception of the dull high street, which had the usual characteristics of a small agricultural market town, some sombre mansions, a dingy inn, and a petty bourse, Marney mainly consisted of a variety of narrow and crowded lanes formed by cottages built of rubble, or unhewn stones without cement, and, from age or badness of the material, looking as if they could scarcely hold together. The gaping chinks admitted every blast; the leaning chimneys had lost half their original height; the rotten rafters were evidently misplaced; while in many instances the thatch, yawning in some parts to admit the wind and wet, and in all utterly unfit for its original purpose of giving protection from the weather, looked more like the top of a dunghill than a cottage. Before the doors of these dwellings, and often surrounding them, ran open drains full of animal and vegetable refuse, decomposing into disease, or sometimes in their imperfect course filling foul pits or spreading into stagnant pools, while a concentrated solution of every species of dissolving filth was allowed to soak through, and thoroughly impregnate, the walls and ground adjoining.

These wretched tenements seldom consisted of more than two rooms, in one of which the whole family, however numerous, were obliged to sleep, without distinction of age, or sex, or suffering. With the water streaming down the walls, the light distinguished through the roof, with no hearth even in winter, the virtuous mother in the sacred pangs of childbirth gives forth another victim to our thoughtless civilisation; surrounded by three generations whose inevitable presence is more painful than her sufferings in that hour of travail; while the father of her coming child, in another corner of the sordid chamber, lies stricken by that typhus which his contaminating dwelling has breathed into his veins, and for whose next prey is perhaps destined his new-born child. These swarming walls had neither windows nor doors sufficient to keep out the weather, or admit the sun, or supply the means of ventilation; the humid and putrid roof of thatch exhaling malaria like all other decaying vegetable matter. The dwelling-rooms were neither boarded nor paved; and whether it were that some were situate in low and damp places, occasionally flooded the river, and usually much below the level of the road; that the springs, as was often the case, would burst through the mud floor; the ground was at no time better than so much clay, while sometimes you might see little channels cut from the centre under the doorways to carry off the water, the door itself removed from its hinges: a resting-place for infancy in its deluged home. These hovels were in many instances not provided with the commonest conveniences of the rudest police; contiguous to every door might be observed the dung-heap on which every kind of filth was accumulated, for the purpose of being disposed of for manure, so that, when the poor man opened his narrow habitation in

the hope of refreshing it with the breeze of summer, he was met with a mixture gases from reeking dung-hills.

This town of Marney was a metropolis of agricultural labour, for the proprietors of the neighbourhood having for last half century acted on the system of destroying the cottages on their estates, in order to become exempted from maintenance of the population, the expelled people had flocked to Marney, where, during the war, a manufactory had afforded them some relief, though its wheels had long ceased disturb the waters of the Mar.

Deprived of this resource, they had again gradually spread themselves over that land which had, as it were, rejected them; and obtained from its churlish breast a niggardly subsistence. Their re-entrance into the surrounding parishes was viewed with great suspicion; their renewed settlement opposed every ingenious contrivance; those who availed themselves of their labour were careful that they should not become dwellers on the soil; and though, from the excessive competition, there were few districts in the kingdom where the rate of wages was more depressed, those who were fortunate enough to obtain the scant remuneration, had, in addition to their toil, to endure, each morn and even, a weary journey before they could reach the scene of their labour, or return to the squalid hovel which profaned the name of home. To that home, over which malaria hovered, and round whose shivering hearth were clustered other guests beside the exhausted family of toil—Fever, in every form, pale Consumption, exhausting Synochus, and trembling Ague,—returned after cultivating the broad fields of merry England, the bold British peasant, returned to encounter the worst of diseases, with a frame the least qualified to oppose them; a frame that, subdued by toil, was never sustained by animal food; drenched by the tempest, could not change its dripping rags; and was indebted for its scanty fuel to the windfalls of the woods.

The eyes of this unhappy race might have been raised to the solitary spire that sprang up in the midst of them, the bearer of present consolation, the harbinger of future equality; but Holy Church at Marney had forgotten her sacred mission. We have introduced the reader to the vicar, an orderly man, who deemed he did his duty if he preached each week two sermons, and enforced humility on his congregation, and gratitude for the blessings of this life. The high street and some neighbouring gentry were the staple of his hearers. Lord and Lady Marney, attended by Captain Grouse, came every Sunday morning, with commendable regularity, and were ushered into the invisible interior of a vast pew, that occupied half of the gallery, was lined with crimson damask, and furnished with easy chairs, and, for those who chose them, well-padded stools of prayer. The people of Marney took refuge in conventicles, which abounded; little plain buildings of pale brick with the names painted on them, of Sion, Bethel, Bethesda; names of a distant land, and the language of a persecuted and ancient race; yet such is the mysterious power of their divine quality, breathing consolation in the nineteenth century to the harassed forms and the harrowed souls of a Saxon peasantry.

But, however devoted to his flock might have been the Vicar of Marney, his exertions for their well-being, under any circumstances, must have been mainly limited to spiritual consolation.

[See also: DISRAELI, BENJAMIN; DISEASES AND EPIDEMICS; HOUSES AND HOUSING; INDUSTRIALIZATION; LIVING STANDARDS; URBANIZATION.]

SOURCE

Disraeli, Benjamin. *Sybil; or, the Two Nations.* London: Frederick Warne, 1845. Reprint, London and New York: Oxford University Press, 1964.

REGULATING VENEREAL DISEASE AND PROSTITUTION

Venereal disease proved to be a vexing problem during the Victorian era. The consequences, both moral and social, became a principal concern for Victorians. William Acton (1813–1875) dedicated himself to the study of sexuality and its associated diseases and wrote several influential reports on the treatment of sexually transmitted diseases and prostitution. A supporter of legalized prostitution in London, he published a detailed survey of English prostitution in 1857, comparing it to the systems found on the Continent, such as in France.

The following excerpt is from Acton's second edition of Prostitution, Considered in its Moral, Social, and Sanitary Aspects, *published in 1870, in which he explains the social circumstances that led to the Contagious Diseases Acts of 1864 and 1866 and describes the treatment offered to diseased women, mostly prostitutes, at Lock Hospital in London.*

EXCERPT FROM *PROSTITUTION, CONSIDERED IN ITS MORAL, SOCIAL, AND SANITARY ASPECTS.*

Contagious Diseases Act

However much it may be the duty of the State to leave for settlement to the individual conscience all ques-

tions of morals and religion, it can hardly be seriously contended that it is right to abandon to the care of the improvident and profligate the restraining of contagious maladies, yet this, except in a few military and naval stations, is virtually the case in England. A woman who knows herself to be diseased, is free to invite all corners to the enjoyment of her person, and to spread among them deadly contagion. The total of venereal beds is, as we have seen, in St Bartholomew's, 75; in Guy's, 58; in Middlesex, 20; in the Royal Free, 26; in the Lock, exclusive of those required by Government, 30. Thus, although the population of London numbers over 3,000,000, there are only 155 beds given up to females labouring under venereal affections, if we deduct the 120 beds at the Lock Hospital devoted to the Government patients sent there from Woolwich, Aldershot, and other garrison towns.

These figures speak for themselves, and when we remember the deadly character of the disease with which we have to contend, the strong temptations that lead to its contraction, and the vast numbers who yield to that temptation, and compare them with the means at our disposal for supplying an antidote to the poison, we may well marvel at the indifference of society and the supineness of Government. But if we can ill excuse the laws, which afford no protection to those who, after all, are comparatively free agents, what shall we say of them, if we find them placing thousands of men every year in the utmost jeopardy, compelling them almost, for the convenience of the State, to have recourse to the prostitution by which they are surrounded, and yet providing for them no means of safety or adequate relief? It is hardly credible that, until a few years ago, this was the case in England. At length in 1864 the injury inflicted by this apathy on our soldiers and sailors, and the loss sustained by the public purse, seem to have touched the conscience or the cupidity of the legislature, and in that year an act was passed, . . . having for its object the remedy of the evils to which the army and navy are exposed; its provisions, however, proved totally inadequate to meet the requirements of the case, and it was followed in 1866 by a more comprehensive measure, . . . commonly called the Contagious Diseases Act.

This act now extends its operation to Canterbury, Dover, Gravesend, Maidstone, Southampton, Winchester, Portsmouth, Plymouth and Devonport, Woolwich, Chatham, Sheerness, Aldershot, Windsor, Colchester, Shorncliffe, the Curragh, Cork, and Queenstown. By the 15th and 16th sections, a justice of the peace, on information being laid before him that a woman, living in any place to which the act extends, is a common prostitute, and on oath before him substantiating such information, may, if he thinks fit, order that the woman be subject to a periodical medical examination by the visiting surgeon appointed under the provisions of the act, for any period not exceeding one year, for the purpose of ascertaining at each such examination whether she is affected with a contagious disease; and thereupon she shall be subject to such a periodical medical examination, and the order shall be a sufficient warrant for the visiting surgeon to conduct such examination accordingly; and by the 17th section any woman, in any place to which the act applies, may, by a submission signed by her, in the presence of, and attested by the superintendent of police, subject herself to a periodical examination under this act for any period not exceeding one year. Any woman found on examination to be diseased, may either go herself, or will be apprehended and sent, to some hospital certified for the reception and detention of government patients. The reception of a woman in a certified hospital by the managers or persons having the management or control thereof shall be deemed to be an undertaking by them to provide for her care, treatment, lodging, clothing and food during her detention in hospital. This period of detention is limited to three months, or, on the certificate prescribed by the act that further detention is necessary, to a further period of six months, making nine months in the whole. If a woman considers herself detained in hospital too long, she may apply to a justice for an order of discharge. Prostitutes refusing to conform to the provisions of this act are liable to be punished by imprisonment, and anyone permitting a woman who to his knowledge is suffering from a contagious disease, to use his house for the purpose of prostitution shall, in addition to the other consequences to which he may be liable for keeping a disorderly house, be liable to six months imprisonment with or without hard labour. The appointment of the necessary surgeons, inspectors of hospitals, and other officers, is intrusted to the Admiralty and War Offices, by whom also hospitals may be provided and certified for use, and all expenses incurred in the execution of the act must be defrayed. The carrying out of the act in the minor details is of course intrusted to the police. It is also provided that adequate provision must be made by the several hospitals for the moral and religious instruction of the women detained in them under this act. We have already seen that a considerable number of beds have been secured at the Lock Hospital for the use of Government patients. The most admirable arrangements have been adopted at this institution for the examination and treatment of the patients committed to its care, and as the possibility of carrying out an act having for its object the diminution of disease forms an important element in considering the advisability of further extending its sphere of usefulness, I shall offer no apology for relating pretty fully the method pursued in this institution.

Lock Hospital

I was anxious to see the working of the existing Government Lock Hospital, and Mr. J. Lane kindly allowed me to accompany him, and explained everything on my visit in October, 1868.

The patients (female) are lodged in a new wing; the wards are lofty, and kept scrupulously clean. Each inmate has a separate bed, provided with three blankets, and a hair mattress, an extra blanket being given in winter. Each patient has two pannikins, a half-pint and a pint tin can, with a pewter spoon and a steel knife and fork, and a little box in which she may keep her things, is placed near her bed. The patients are not allowed to go into other wards, but there is an open court in which they take exercise, and they have a sort of hospital dress in place of their own clothes, which are left under the care of the matron. At the head of the bed hangs a towel.

In a little room at the end of the ward water is laid on, and copper basins are hung by a chain to the wall; these basins are kept for the women to wash their faces. This arrangement is specially made to prevent any possible contagion. Fixed to the floor is a bidet, across which the female sits. There is here an admirable device for facilitating the cleansing of the private parts; by which means, a brass syringe, with a long pewter ball, and holding, say six ounces, she injects the lotion, and the waste fluid runs away on opening a plug fixed in the bottom of the bidet. The only improvement I could suggest was that each patient be furnished with two small napkins to dry the organs after injection. The patient always uses an injection before presenting herself to the surgeon, in order that the organs may be in a proper condition for examination, and I must say the cleanliness shown does great credit to the nurses who manage the wards.

The inspections are conducted in the following manner:—The women are introduced one at a time from the wards by one nurse into a special room, containing a properly-raised bed, with feet, similar to the one in use on the Continent. The patient ascends the steps placed by the side of the bed, lays down, places her feet in the slippers arranged for the purpose, and the house surgeon separates the labia to see if there are any sores. If no suspicion of these exists, and if the female is suffering from discharge, the speculum is at once employed. In this institution several sizes are used, and they are silvered and covered with India-rubber. The head nurse after each examination washes the speculum in a solution of permanganate of potash, then wipes it carefully, oils it ready for the next examination, so that the surgeon loses no time, and the examinations are conducted with great rapidity. In the course of one hour and three-quarters I assisted in the thorough examination of 58 women with the speculum.

In this institution the house surgeon examines the women; the surgeon superintending and prescribing the remedies.

[. . .]

The medical officers told me, in reply to my enquiries, that there had been occasional disturbances among the patients. The nurse first tries to stop any outbreak of temper; if unsuccessful, the house surgeon is appealed to, and if he fails, the girl is conveyed to the police station by the hospital porter, who is empowered to act as a police constable in relation to these patients, who are then liable to two months' imprisonment.

I have little to say about the patients; in appearance they are not generally prepossessing; a few among those whom I saw were young, and looked middle-aged and plain. The primary syphilitic affections were few, but the diseases of the uterus numerous, similar to those I witness in private practice . . .

The following is the scale of dietary at the hospital:

DIETARY

ORDINARY

Breakfast: 8 oz. Bread; ½ pint Cocoa.
Dinner:
Five days— ½ lb. Meat; ½ lb. Potatoes.
Two days— 1 pint Soup; Soup Meat. 1½ oz. Rice.
Tea: 6 oz. Bread; ½ pint Tea.
Supper: 1 pint Gruel.

MEAT DIET

Breakfast: As above.
Dinner: ½ lb. Meat; ½ lb. Potatoes, every day.
Tea: 6 oz. Bread; ½ pint Tea.
Supper: 1 pint Gruel.

BEEF TEA AND PUDDING DIET

Breakfast: As above, and 1 pint of Milk.
Dinner: 1 pint Beef Tea; 2 oz. Rice in a pudding.
Tea: As above.
Supper: 1 pint Gruel.
Mutton Chop or Fish, when ordered, instead of Meat Diet or ordinary. Rice occasionally instead of Potatoes.
Extras— Porter, Wine, Spirits and Milk.

SOURCE

Acton, William. *Prostitution, Considered in its Moral, Social, and Sanitary Aspects, in London and Other Large Cities and Garrison Towns, with Proposals for the Control and Prevention of Its Attendant Evils.* 1857. 2nd ed., 1870. Reprint of 2nd ed., London: Frank Cass, 1972.

SANITATION IN THE CITY

The rapid industrialization and urbanization during the Victorian era caused enormous strain on the traditional systems for disposing of waste in urban areas, most notably in London. Sanitary conditions in London declined so quickly as a result of urban growth that sanitation became a hotly debated topic of the day and new systems of sanitation were vigorously pursued.

George Godwin (1813–1881), the editor of The Builder *(the leading English architectural and building periodical of the nineteenth century), used his journal to campaign for a number of social issues, especially those concerned with the housing and sanitary conditions of the working classes. A prolific writer, Godwin combined his training as an architect with his intense energy and varied interests to create many different books on architecture, social conditions, and even a play. The following excerpt is taken from Godwin's 1859 book,* Town Swamps and Social Bridges, *in which he describes the devastating effects urban and industrial growth had on the Thames, which flowed through London as both the major source of "fresh" water and waste removal for the city.*

EXCERPT FROM *TOWN SWAMPS AND SOCIAL BRIDGES.*

[. . .] For years past the deterioration of the [Thames] river has been noticed; and from time to time endeavours have been made to direct attention to the subject as one of great public interest. Every day increases the evil. Without taking into consideration the immense annual growth of London, it must be borne in mind that other large districts give their refuse to the river. There are also gas-works, most unwholesome manufactories, slaughter-houses, cow-sheds, stables, breweries, and the drainage of thickly-filled graveyards, to aid the mischief; and yet intelligent men can be found to maintain the salubrity of the Thames. The health of thousands must be affected by it, and what may occur cannot be calmly contemplated.

[. . .]

Many of our readers may have noticed time black, offensive, and dangerous matter which is taken from choked drains in the neighbourhood of cesspools. There are many thousands of tons of equally poisonous stuff on the shore of the Thames. A considerable quantity of such matter is kept in solution by the action of the tide and the steam-vessels, which adds materially to the bad state of the water.

While wandering along this putrid shore, which is both a shame and a wonder in the nineteenth century, thoughts arise, in spite of some overpowering feelings, of other days, of processions of stately barges, full of the influential citizens in whose hands the protection of Father Thames was placed. This body found the stream clean and wholesome; the apprentices and citizens came from long distances to avail themselves of the water-supply. For years festive bands of citizens, at stated intervals, mingling pleasure with business, went forth to survey the important charge, which was in a healthy condition, intrusted to their care : now Father Thames has become such a castaway that the Lord Mayor has declared that he cannot again venture on a visit. The days of "swan-hopping" and river perambulation are at an end.

One Sunday evening last summer, just after low water, we passed along the shore. And all who would have an idea of time extent to which the Thames is used, should visit the landing-place at Hunger ford-bridge on a fine Sunday evening. The day had been cooler than some days previously; nevertheless, the stench at the different points was frightful, and produced a sickness which lasted till the next morning. Bad as was the state of affairs at the time referred to, the watermen at the landing-places said the air w as "lavender" to what it had been. Early in the morning, they continued, when the first steam-packets begin to move about, the smell is enough to strike down strong men. During a few hours of the night, when there is but little traffic, the heavy matter sinks, and the renewed agitation in the morning causes the escape of pungent gases, of a most poisonous description. Even the dipping of time oars, at early hours, produces a sickening sensation. The weight of the impure portion of Thames water is a peculiarity which formerly caused the water to be held in much favour

by sailors for long foreign voyages. Large establishments were formed for the purpose of filtering it; but even so lately as 1840 and 1841, many ships took it without this process from the outside of the docks. A person who has sailed from the Thames, but who is now a waterman, described how that he had been twelve months and upwards on board ship with Thames water, obtained in the manner just mentioned, and that it remained good all the time: the heavy earthy matters settled firmly to the bottom of the casks; but on the bung being started, it was necessary to give time water "a wide berth," for the smell was almost unbearable—sometimes the force of the gas had burst out the bungs with a report like that of a pistol. A similar process, on a large scale, is going on daily on the Thames. The soil, put in motion by the action of the water, is now more considerable than formerly; and the amount of poisonous gases which is thrown off is proportionate to the increase of the sewage which is passed into the stream. Fifteen or sixteen years ago the Thames water was not so bad, and persons on the river did not hesitate at dipping in a vessel and drinking the contents. Such a thing now would be like an act of insanity; and yet we are told, on good authority, that in a part of Rotherhithe a number of poor persons, who have no proper water-supply, are obliged to use, for drinking and other purposes, the Thames water in its present abominable condition, unfiltered. This is a matter which should receive immediate attention.

In order to form a proper notion of the condition of the Thames shore, it is necessary not to restrict the examination to the landing-places alone—for care is taken at these points to remove the slimy matter as much as possible ; but even here, as we found at one place by an excavation, there is a depth of more than four feet of poisonous soil; and it is certain that a large portion of this is cesspool refuse.

In considering the effect of time condition of the Thames on the health of the metropolis, it must be borne in mind that the actual number of those who dwell on the shore is small in comparison with those who merely remain all day in the neighbourhood. Thousands are employed during the day only, in the docks, the canals, and in the large manufactories, warehouses, and other establishments which line the river; most of these workmen travel long distances to closer neighbourhoods after the labours of the day are ended, so that there may be a difficulty in clearly tracing the amount of mischief which is actually caused by the pestilential condition of the Thames. The docks especially are a fertile source of disease.

When in this district, we glanced at the basin and other parts of the Regent's Canal, and found that a large quantity of water is daily passed from this important work into the river. The water was very cloudy, and of a brownish colour; but, compared with that of the Thames, its purity looked remarkable, and there is not a large amount of animal refuse in this tributary. Complaints are, however, made of certain offensive manufactures which drain into one of the branches. "But, in order to show you that we do good rather than harm," said a superintendent on duty, "please to look here, where the Thames is just beginning to flow into the entrance-lock of the canal." And truly the effect was a startling one. The stream of the Thames, of a sable hue, "thick and slab," could be seen meeting and invading the canal, presenting such an appearance as might be expected by the bursting close by of several hogsheads of Warren's blacking, [. . .]

[. . .] The sides and bottoms of boats become covered with solid matter; objects are not visible at even an inch below the surface; the reflection of ships is very faint, but shadows almost as strong as those on land are thrown on the face of the water by the sunshine. When gravely pondering these things, De Foe's description of the neglected condition of London at the time of the visit of the Great Plague of 1665 comes to mind; and we think, with Byron, of "ships rotting, sailorless," and other uncomfortable associations.

[. . .]

In passing along the foul shore, we came to one of the Thames tributaries, and the scene so clearly illustrates an existing evil [. . . .] This place is a creek which extends some distance inland, similar to that which has been so much complained of near Blackfriars-bridge. At the north end is a large sewer, which drains Bow-common, and all buildings in that direction. The mouth is partly covered by a loose iron flap, which, when the tide is out, allows the sewage-water to flow in a rapid stream. Dwelling-houses are built on the sewer wall, and around it. The people living about here have, in most instances, sickly children, who in a measure resemble the poor plants observable in some of the windows about. Everything around is bad. The bank, when. the tide goes out, is covered with filth; and when the number of the similar tributaries which flow to Father Thames, both night and day, is recollected, his state is not to be wondered at.

Both Houses of Parliament were loud last session in their condemnation of the existing state of things. They have the evil at their own door—a retribution,—

for it is certain that the present conditions are in a great measure the result of want of forethought and consideration of the subject. And let our provincial cities and towns take warning in time, and avoid the transformation of their rivers into reeking sewers and decomposing cess-banks, which act upon health, and degrade character.

During the discussion of the mode to be adopted in draining London, the assertion that sewage-matter is washed backwards and forwards by the tide, and is long before it gets out to sea, was derided. The fact, however, is unquestionable. Look at the next sketch. It shows the way in which a dead dog, under our own eyes, travelled. We thought he would get away: however, after a time, and after whirling and resting amongst the posts and barges, the dead dog came again in sight, moving against the tide, but much nearer to the shore; he turns off again towards the sea, and returns this time much sooner than the last ; and after describing various circles, as shown by the arrows in the sketch, he is deposited in the slime, together with other specimens of his own and allied families.

[*See also:* LONDON; POPULATION; SANITATION; URBANIZATION.]

SOURCE

Godwin, George. *Town Swamps and Social Bridges.* London: Routledge, 1859.

A TOURIST'S JOURNAL

Traveling in order to understand different parts of the world and its people was a popular endeavor during the Victorian era. Advances in technology made such travel possible for the rising middle class. Trains and new steamships increased the speed, ease, comfort, and affordability of traveling for pleasure. By the end of the Victorian era, all but the most impoverished workers could at least enjoy the pleasure of a holiday at the seaside.

Notes travelers took of their new surroundings were sometimes published and would often become enormously popular. Sir Francis Galton published the accounts of several travelers in 1861. Volume 1 of Vacation Tourists, Notes of Travel in 1860 *records detailed accounts of several different individuals' travel notes from a tour of Croatia to a description of life in Iceland. The following excerpt is from Chapter 12, in which Galton describes his personal experiences in the Basque country of Spain.*

EXCERPT FROM *VACATION TOURISTS, AND NOTES OF TRAVEL IN 1860.*

A Visit to North Spain at the Time of the Eclipse, By Francis Galton, F.R.S.

A direction was given to my summer rambles by the desire of witnessing the solar eclipse of last June, and by the fact that the path of its totality, where nearest to England, lay across a country which I ardently longed to visit. The result was, that I applied for permission, and obtained it, to form one of the party of astronomers who, under the leadership of the Astronomer-Royal, were taken by H. M.S. *Himalaya* to Spain.

The *Himalaya* is truly a noble vessel, and we were right imperially treated. Those whose experience has been drawn from coasting passenger-steamers, in English or Mediterranean water, would hardly credit that anything floated comparable in spaciousness and luxury to this magnificent ship. And she is as fast and easy, excepting a tendency to roll, as she is spacious and comfortable; we steamed out of Plymouth Sound on a Saturday forenoon, so steadily, that I hardly knew we were moving; and on the Sunday night we were going at half-power, because we were too near the Spanish coast, whose bold outlines lay in full view on the early Monday morning.

It was therefore with one of those feelings of contrast so often enjoyed by travellers, that I, with my eyes still toned to that dim English daylight in which we had just bade farewell to our shores, found myself paddling up the Bilbao river in a small shore-going craft, under a full flood of southern sunshine, by the side of suburbs and quays crowded with people— where every incident, shape, colour, and sound, assured me that I was in a new country, and amidst a civilization that was neither English, French, nor Italian, nor resembling that of any other country I knew, buy something wholly peculiar.

[. . .]

The thoughtful arrangements for our comfort on landing, and the energy with which Mr. Vignolles fulfilled the self-imposed duty of host and guardian to our large party, were such as made us feel an almost painful debt of gratitude. I and my friends were billeted as guests in a capital house, belonging to a Spanish merchant, who tended us like infants. Even a packet of tea, provided by Mr. Vignolles, was in readiness for our use. Our luggage was looked after, our money was changed, our plans were settled, introductions to the authorities at Logroño were given to us, and every difficulty was smoothed away as soon as it was discovered. [. . .]

For my part, I do not profess to do more in this place than to give a brief account of two or three appearances which made considerable impression on me at the time, and which do not seem to have been so fully, if at all, observed by others, either in the present eclipse or in previous ones, and which I am glad of an opportunity of putting upon record. To these I will recur. At present, I will endeavour to describe a few of my general recollections of that rapidly improving part of Spain which I had the opportunity of seeing. I think I may be excused for doing so, although my stay was a very short one, because I have not found any book that gives a recent, and at the same time what appears to me to be a fair account of this portion of the Basque provinces. They are usually described as different from Spain only in being less Spanish, and by having a strong infusion of the Basque mountaineer element; yet I found it [. . .] with none of the airs of an outlying province of a larger and vivifying central kingdom. Bilbao is becoming exceedingly wealthy; the provinces to which it and Santander are the outlets, are being cut into by railways. There is every sign of abundant local activity; no beggary, or apparent poverty, or listless indolence; added to all this, there is a remarkable picturesqueness in its social life. In short, this portion of the Basque provinces did not appear to me as I had been led to expect.

Almost the first thing that arrested my attention on Spanish land was the chiaro-oscuro (veiled) tint of everything I saw. It was especially remarkable in the soil and in the buildings. There was an abundance of bright colour, but it seemed to have none of the garish effect which is so remarkable under a French sky. The exquisite mellowness and depths of shading surpassed anything I had previously seen, and explained at once that possibility and the truthfulness of Murillo's treatment. It also showed me that the universal black dresses of the upper class of cither sex were in no way incongruous or dismal when seen through a Spanish atmosphere, and with Spanish surroundings. The eye soon becomes used to a new influence, and while I always recognized its effect, I afterwards tried in vain to recall the vividness of that first impression of novelty. [. . .]

It was a great delight to me to find that the Spanish ways of life appeared thoroughly characteristic, and wholly uncopied from other nations of modern Europe. There is a common cant phrase used sometimes in respect to France, and sometime to England, of "advancing in the van [sic] of European civilization." Yet, however flattering to our vanities, it would be a matter of deep regret if European civilization should ever become so far one and indivisible, that nations, whose instincts and geographical conditions of life are different, should make it a point of fashion or of education to live on the same model. One longs to see a freer development than exists at present, of the immense variety of aptitudes and peculiarities that are found in the human race, and are fostered by different geographical circumstances. Let us, at least, hope that a united Italy may develop a vigorous and high-class, but an autogenous form of social life. If she did so, it would be as welcome to that majority of educated Europe, as a new face and a new mind to a small provincial society. Yet an exception to this statement must be made on behalf of the French, to whom any hope of the kind would be wholly unintelligible. They are strangely unconscious of their own monotony, and seem honestly convinced of the doctrine they subscribe,—that all which is not Frenchified is pagan, that there is but one path of perfection, and that the panacea for afflicted aliens is French influence and the Code Napoleon.

[*See also:* TRAVEL AND TOURISM.]

SOURCE

Galton, Francis. "A Visit to North Spain at the Time of the Eclipse." In *Vacation Tourists, and Notes of Travel in 1860.* Vol. 1. Cambridge, England: Macmillan, 1861[permission must be received for subsequent distribution in print or electronically. Please contact umdl-info@umich.edu for more information].

MANAGING HOUSEHOLD HELP

Cassell's Household Guide, *published in England during the late 1800s, promised in its introduction to "to set out accurately, and in something like scientific order, the laws which govern, and the rules which should regulate, that most necessary and most important of all institutions, THE HOUSEHOLD." Within its four comprehensive volumes, the* Guide *offered practical advice to help homeowners in all areas of domestic life, from how to play popular parlor games to how to manage household servants.*

Domestic workers had been an important part of running wealthy households for many years, but during the Victorian era more and more people earned enough money to employ servants. The engagement of domestic help soon became an increasingly important symbol of social status. The following excerpt from Cassell's Household Guide *offers homeowners instruction on how to divide duties among different types of servants and provides insight into what duties a housemaid in an English household would be expected to*

perform, including practical instruction on how she would do the required work.

EXCERPT FROM *CASSELL'S HOUSEHOLD GUIDE.*

Servants of the House. IV.

The Housemaid

IN many English households two servants only are kept—cook and housemaid—a small domestic staff, but one capable, under able supervision, of getting through a considerable amount of work. In order to effect this, it is necessary that each servant should be efficient in her duties, and that a regular plan of household labour be laid down, by which, instead of impeding each other's progress, mutual help may be rendered to facilitate a thorough dispatch of work. As a general rule, however, the less a cook has to do out of her kitchen the better will she be enabled to cook, and the more time a housemaid bestows on house cleaning, the greater will be the comfort of the family. Dusty furniture and a close atmosphere are evils which are apt to generate ailments in establishments where sufficient domestic labour cannot be afforded. Ailments of the kind should have no existence where sufficient servants are employed to keep every part of a house clean and wholesome.

One of the chief obstacles to the better discharge of housemaids' work than generally obtains is, not only the notion on the part of the servant herself, that her duties are of a semi-laborious nature, but the too ready acquiescence in this view by employers. Many ladies, when engaging a housemaid, hold out the "lightness of the work" as an inducement to get the place filled. Consequently, no sphere of domestic service is so crowded with young women in delicate health as that of the housemaid. Good health is, nevertheless, indispensable to the fit discharge of all kinds of labour.

[. . .]

As the duties of a housemaid are very numerous, and liable to vary in different households, it is advisable in this place to explain only those which are of general application.

A good housemaid will rise at six, and have her grates cleaned and rooms swept by seven. She will then go upstairs, wash her hands, and make herself tidy for taking to the bedroom hot water if required to do so. In the meanwhile the dust will have settled, and the rooms will be ready on her return to be finished by eight. By nine o'clock breakfast ought to be cleared away and the housemaid ready to strip the beds, empty slops, and set the bedrooms in order. By eleven o'clock the up-stairs work ought to be done, unless extra cleaning is in question. Washing up china and glass, dusting the drawing-room, and other light labour of the kind may take till twelve or one o'clock, by which time a housemaid ought to be dressed for the day, fit to answer the door, wait on the family, and do needlework. Any work required of the servant after mid-day should be of a nature not to soil her garments. At dusk, it is a housemaid's place to close all the windows at the upper part of the house. Before going to bed she has to turn down all the beds of the family, replenish ewers [pitchers] and water bottles, empty slops, and put everything in its place. If she has the charge of the plate-basket she carries it to the master's room, together with hot water. Considerate employers will dispense with a housemaid's attendance by ten o'clock, bearing in mind her morning duties.

The usual plan of housemaid's work, when no washing is done at home, is to clean the drawing-room thoroughly on Mondays, and one or two other rooms, according to their size, on each successive day during the week. Saturday should be a tolerably clear day from housecleaning, beyond general dusting and setting in order for Sunday, cleaning plate, airing clean linen from the wash, &c. Any spare time left beyond these duties is generally allowed the housemaid for repairing or making her own clothes. If washing is done at home, the household work must necessarily be delayed in its course.

The following directions are written for the guidance of housemaids.

Sweeping and Dusting.—Before sweeping a room remove all light articles of furniture out of the way, and cover up those which would be spoiled by dust. Draw back the window-curtains and pin them up as high as you can reach. Open the windows a few inches top and bottom, and shut the door. Turn the front of picture-frames to the wall, hang a sweeping-sheet over looking-glass frames, mirrors, &c. Then sprinkle tea-leaves, drained, but not dry, all over the carpet, especially in the corners. Sweep all carpets the way of the pile, whether it be in one direction or in another. If the fireplace is in use, all the ashes should be removed from the grate before sweeping the carpet. Whilst the dust settles, clean the grate. Having done so, tie a soft clean cloth over a hair broom and sweep the cornice and ceiling, also the walls. A turk's-head broom answers better for this purpose, if you have one. In like manner sweep the curtain-poles, hangings, &c. In the absence of tea-leaves, some pieces of coarse brown paper, moistened with clean water, will answer the purpose. Without something of the kind you simply drive the dust from one part of the room to another.

Dusting.—Remove all articles from the place to be dusted, and do not wipe round them. Put everything back in its place. Use a painter's brush for dusting skirtings, and wipe glass and china ornaments with a fine soft cloth. White dusters are best for chintz furniture. A small feather broom should be used for raised china and gilt work. Never wipe picture frames with a duster. Carved woodwork should be dusted with a short-haired furniture brush, which likewise polishes. Pianoforte keys should be dusted with an old silk pocket-handkerchief; kept for the purpose.

Scrubbing.—Neglected boards will not come clean without extra pains. If of a very bad colour a mixture of three parts of powdered pipeclay with one of chloride of lime, about the thickness of cream, will be useful. This should be laid on to dry in some time before scrubbing. Or some white sand laid on the brush when scrubbing will remove the dirt. Grease will only yield to fuller's earth spread on the spots for several hours. Well kept boards, especially in country houses, require nothing but cold water. Soap and soda in hot water make boards black. In scrubbing, only arm's length should be wetted at the time, taking care that the flannel is wrung each time dry of the soiled water. Good bass scrubbing-brushes are more cleansing than those of hair. Vulcanised india-rubber scrubbing-brushes are the best of all, but are rather expensive at the first outlay.[The article goes on to describe the proper methods for cleaning grates, brass and copper, ormolu (gilded bronze or brass), lacquered work, marble, glass, oil cloth, paint, and wallpaper.]The above are some of the chief daily duties of a housemaid. Directions for other portions of her work, sometimes performed by the parlour-maid, page, and laundry-maid, will be considered in subsequent chapters.

[See also: DOMESTIC WORKERS.]

SOURCE

Cassell's Household Guide: Being A Complete Encyclopedia Of Domestic And Social Economy, And Forming A Guide To Every Department Of Practical Life. 4 vols. London: Cassell, Petter, and Galpin, Ludgate Hill, E.C., 1869–1871.

LITERATURE

The literature of the Victorian period was as various as the age itself. Novels, poetry, essays, biography, travel literature, and more poured forth from the pens of the Victorians and were avidly consumed throughout the English-speaking world. In the days before radio, film, and television, reading was perhaps the most important leisure activity of the era. Fiction writers often published their works in installments in popular magazines like *Blackwood's* or *Macmillan's Magazine*. This serialization allowed the books to grow to great lengths, and many such works, when published in book form, filled several volumes. The Victorian novel is famous for its rambling quality; American novelist Henry James (1843–1916) referred to such novels as "large loose baggy monsters." Among the most notable of the Victorian novelists are Charles Dickens, George Eliot, William Makepeace Thackeray, Anthony Trollope, and the Brontë sisters, Anne, Charlotte, and Emily.

Though the Victorian age is often heralded as the golden age of the novel, poetry was also very popular with readers. Poets such as Robert Browning and Alfred Tennyson were among the best known writers of the period, and many others also found large audiences. Breaking with the Romantic tradition of the late seventeenth and early eighteenth centuries, Victorian poets moved their art in many different directions. Women poets—such as Elizabeth Barrett Browning and Amy Levy—also produced important work during the period. Finally, criticism of literature and the arts also matured dramatically during the nineteenth century. Walter Pater, John Ruskin, and Matthew Arnold were the century's most heralded critics, and they brought new esteem to the critical arts.

The selections that follow give just a taste of the approaches adopted by novelists, poets, and critics during the Victorian era. Included are excerpts from Charles Dickens's novel *A Tale of Two Cities* (1859) and Mary Elizabeth Braddon's novel *Lady Audley's Secret* (1862); selected poems by Robert Browning, Elizabeth Barrett Browning, Alfred Tennyson, Rudyard Kipling, and Oscar Wilde; and excerpts from Matthew Arnold's essay "The Function of Criticism at the Present Time" (1865).

DICKENS, THE ERA'S GREAT NOVELIST

Charles Dickens (1812–1870) was the most popular and important novelist of the Victorian era. In such works as Oliver Twist *(1839),* A Christmas Carol *(1843),* David Copperfield *(1850),* Bleak House *(1853),* Hard Times *(1854),* Little Dorrit *(1857),* A Tale of Two Cities *(1859), and* Great Expectations *(1860), Dickens painted a complex portrait of the industrializing and modernizing British landscape. The opening scene from* A Tale of Two Cities *(excerpted below), though set in an earlier age, is often thought to capture the conflicted and paradoxical tenor of Dickens's own time.*

EXCERPT FROM *A TALE OF TWO CITIES*.

The Period

IT WAS the best of times, it was the worst of times, it was the age of wisdom, it was the age of foolishness, it was the epoch of belief, it was the epoch of incredulity, it was the season of Light, it was the season of Darkness, it was the spring of hope, it was the winter of despair, we had everything before us, we had nothing before us, we were all going direct to Heaven, we were all going direct the other way—in short, the period was so far like the present period, that some of its noisiest authorities insisted on its being received, for good or for evil, in the superlative degree of comparison only.

There were a king with a large jaw and a queen with a plain face, on the throne of England; there were a king with a large jaw and a queen with a fair face, on the throne of France. In both countries it was clearer than crystal to the lords of the State preserves of loaves and fishes, that things in general were settled for ever.

It was the year of Our Lord one thousand seven hundred and seventy-five. Spiritual revelations were conceded to England at that favoured period, as at this. Mrs. Southcott had recently attained her five-and-twentieth blessed birthday, of whom a prophetic private in the Life Guards had heralded the sublime appearance by announcing that arrangements were made for the swallowing up of London and Westminster. Even the Cock-lane ghost had been laid only a round dozen of years, after rapping out its messages, as the spirits of this very year last past (supernaturally deficient in originality) rapped out theirs. Mere messages in the earthly order of events had lately come to the English Crown and People, from a congress of British subjects in America: which, strange to relate, have proved more important to the human race than any communications yet received through any of the chickens of the Cock-lane brood.

France, less favoured on the whole as to matters spiritual than her sister of the shield and trident, rolled with exceeding smoothness down hill, making paper money and spending it. Under the guidance of her Christian pastors, she entertained herself, besides, with such humane achievements as sentencing a youth to have his hands cut off, his tongue torn out with pincers, and his body burned alive, because he had not kneeled down in the rain to do honour to a dirty procession of monks which passed within his view, at a distance of some fifty or sixty yards. It is likely enough that, rooted in the woods of France and Norway, there were growing trees, when that sufferer was put to death, already marked by the Woodman, Fate, to come down and be sawn into boards, to make a certain movable framework with a sack and a knife in it, terrible in history. It is likely enough that in the rough outhouses of some tillers of the heavy lands adjacent to Paris, there were sheltered from the weather that very day, rude carts, bespattered with rustic mire, snuffed about by pigs, and roosted in by poultry, which the Farmer, Death, had already set apart to be his tumbrels of the Revolution. But that Woodman and that Farmer, though they work unceasingly, work silently, and no one heard them as they went about with muffled tread: the rather, forasmuch as to entertain any suspicion that they were awake, was to be atheistical and traitorous.

In England, there was scarcely an amount of order and protection to justify much national boasting. Daring burglaries by armed men, and highway robberies, took place in the capital itself every night; families were publicly cautioned not to go out of town without removing their furniture to upholsterers' warehouses for security; the highwayman in the dark was a City tradesman in the light, and, being recognised and challenged by his fellow-tradesman whom he stopped in his character of "the Captain," gallantly shot him through the head and rode away; the mall was waylaid by seven robbers, and the guard shot three dead, and then got shot dead himself by the other four, "in consequence of the failure of his ammunition:" after which the mall was robbed in peace; that magnificent potentate, the Lord Mayor of London, was made to stand and deliver on Turnham Green, by one highwayman, who despoiled the illustrious creature in sight of all his retinue; prisoners in London gaols [jails] fought battles with their turnkeys, and the majesty of the law fired blunderbusses in among them, loaded with rounds of shot and ball; thieves snipped off diamond crosses from the necks of noble lords at Court drawing-rooms; musketeers went into St. Giles's, to search for contraband goods, and the mob fired on the musketeers, and the musketeers fired on the mob, and nobody thought any

of these occurrences much out of the common way. In the midst of them, the hangman, ever busy and ever worse than useless, was in constant requisition; now, stringing up long rows of miscellaneous criminals; now, hanging a housebreaker on Saturday who had been taken on Tuesday; now, burning people in the hand at Newgate by the dozen, and now burning pamphlets at the door of Westminster Hall; to-day, taking the life of an atrocious murderer, and to-morrow of a wretched pilferer who had robbed a farmer's boy of sixpence.

All these things, and a thousand like them, came to pass in and close upon the dear old year one thousand seven hundred and seventy-five. Environed by them, while the Woodman and the Farmer worked unheeded, those two of the large jaws, and those other two of the plain and the fair faces, trod with stir enough, and carried their divine rights with a high hand. Thus did the year one thousand seven hundred and seventy-five conduct their Greatnesses, and myriads of small creatures—the creatures of this chronicle among the rest—along the roads that lay before them.

[See also: DICKENS, CHARLES; LONDON; NOVEL.]

SOURCE

Dickens, Charles. *A Tale of Two Cities.* London: Chapman and Hall, 1859; Philadelphia: Peterson, 1859. Reprint, with introduction by Andrew Sanders. New York and Oxford: Oxford University Press, 1988.

THE SENSATION NOVEL

Sensation novels were the Victorian equivalent of the Harlequin romance: lurid, sensational novels with fast-paced plots that promised readers escape into a more dramatic world. Work's such as Wilkie Collins's The Woman in White *(1860), Mary Ellen Wood's* East Lynne *(1861), and Mary Elizabeth Braddon's* Lady Audley's Secret *(1862) were labeled "sensation novels" in 1863 by philosopher H. L. Mansel, who claimed in the* Quarterly Review *in 1863 that they were a moral poison that was "moulding the minds and forming the habits and tastes of its generation." Though the claim was overstated, it is clear that the novels reflected well the shifting terrain of Victorian gender and class relations. In this excerpt from Braddon's (1835–1915)* Lady Audley's Secret, *the devious Lady Audley—who has already faked her own death and plotted the murder of her first husband—plots to murder her aristocratic husband, Sir Michael, and his nephew, who happens to be her first husband's best friend. Lady Audley is finally found out and sent off to a Belgian madhouse, where she ends her life.*

EXCERPT FROM *LADY AUDLEY'S SECRET.*

Chapter XXXII.
The Red Light in the Sky

[. . .]

MY lady crushed the letter fiercely in her hand, and flung it from her into the flames.

"If he stood before me now, and I could kill him," she muttered in a strange, inward whisper, "I would do it—I would do it!" She snatched up the lamp and rushed into the adjoining room. She shut the door behind her. She could not endure any witness of her horrible despair—she could endure nothing, neither herself nor her surroundings.

The door between my lady's dressing-room and the bedchamber in which Sir Michael lay, had been left open. The baronet slept peacefully, his noble face plainly visible in the subdued lamplight. His breathing was low and regular, his lips curved in a half smile—a smile of tender happiness which he often wore when he looked at his beautiful wife, the smile of an all-indulgent father, who looked admiringly at his favorite child.

Some touch of womanly feeling, some sentiment of compassion softened Lady Audley's glance as it fell upon that noble reposing figure. For a moment the horrible egotism of her own misery yielded to her pitying tenderness for another. It was perhaps only a semi-selfish tenderness after all, in which pity for herself was as powerful as pity for her husband; but for once, in a way, her thoughts ran out of the narrow groove of her own terrors and her own troubles to dwell with prophetic grief upon the coming sorrows of another.

"If they make him believe, how wretched he will be," she thought.

But intermingled with that thought there was another—there was the thought of her lovely face, her bewitching manner, her arch smile, her low musical laugh, which was like a peal of silvery bells ringing across a broad expanse of flat meadow-land and a rippling river in the misty summer evening. She thought of all these things with a transient thrill of triumph, which was stronger even than her terror.

If Sir Michael Audley lived to be a hundred years old, whatever he might learn to believe of her, however he might grow to despise her, would he ever be able to disassociate her from these attributes? No; a thousand times no. To the last hour of his life his memory would present her to him invested with the loveliness that had first won his enthusiastic admiration, his devoted affection. Her worst enemies could not rob her of that fairy dower which had been so fatal in its influence upon her frivolous mind.

She paced up and down the dressing-room in the silvery lamplight, pondering upon the strange letter which she had received from Robert Audley. She walked backwards and forwards in that monotonous wandering for some time before she was able to steady her thoughts—before she was able to bring the scattered forces of her narrow intellect to bear upon the one all-important subject of the threat contained in the barrister's letter.

"He will do it," she said, between her set teeth—"he will do it, unless I get him into a lunatic asylum first; or unless—"

She did not finish the thought in words. She did not even think out the sentence; but some new and unnatural impulse in her heart seemed to beat out each syllable against her breast.

The thought was this: "He will do it, unless some strange calamity befalls him, and silences him forever." The red blood flashed up into my lady's face with as sudden and transient a blaze as the flickering flame of a fire, and died as suddenly away, leaving her more pale than winter snow. Her hands, which had before been locked convulsively together, fell apart and dropped heavily at her sides. She stopped in her rapid pacing to and fro—stopped as Lot's wife may have stopped, after that fatal backward glance at the perishing city—with every pulse slackening, with every drop of blood congealing in her veins, in the terrible process that was to transform her from a woman into a statue.

Lady Audley stood still for about five minutes in that strangely statuesque attitude, her head erect, her eyes staring straight before her—staring far beyond the narrow boundary of her chamber wall, into dark distances of peril and horror.

But by and by she started from that rigid attitude almost as abruptly as she had fallen into it. She roused herself from that semi-lethargy. She walked rapidly to her dressing-table, and, seating herself before it, pushed away the litter of golden-stoppered bottles, and delicate china essence-boxes, and looked at her reflection in the large oval glass. She was very pale; but there was no other trace of agitation visible in her girlish face. The lines of her exquisitely molded lips were so beautiful, that it was only a very close observer who could have perceived a certain rigidity that was unusual to them. She saw this herself, and tried to smile away that statue-like immobility; but to-night the rosy lips refused to obey her; they were firmly locked, and were no longer the slaves of her will and pleasure. All the latent forces of her character concentrated themselves in this one feature. She might command her eyes; but she could not control the muscles of her mouth. She rose from before her dressing-table, and took a dark velvet cloak and bonnet from the recesses of her ward-robe, and dressed herself for walking. The little ormolu clock on the chimney-piece struck the quarter after eleven while Lady Audley was employed in this manner; five minutes afterwards she re-entered the room in which she had left Phoebe Marks.

The innkeeper's wife was sitting before the low fender [hearth] very much in the same attitude as that in which her late mistress had brooded over that lonely hearth earlier in the evening. Phoebe had replenished the fire, and had reassumed her bonnet and shawl. She was anxious to get home to that brutal husband, who was only too apt to fall into some mischief in her absence. She looked up as Lady Audley entered the room, and uttered an exclamation of surprise at seeing her late mistress in a walking-costume.

"My lady," she cried, "you are not going out to-night?"

"Yes, I am Phoebe," Lady Audley answered, very quietly; "I am going to Mount Stanning with you to see this bailiff, and to pay and dismiss him myself."

[. . .]

[See also: ASYLUMS; BRADDON, MARY ELIZABETH; MELODRAMA; NOVEL; SENSATION NOVEL.]

SOURCE

Braddon, Mary Elizabeth. *Lady Audley's Secret.* 3 vols. London: Tinsley, 1862. 1 vol. New York: Federal Book Co., n.d. Reprint, with introduction by David Skilton, New York and Oxford: Oxford University Press, 1987.

THE DRAMATIC MONOLOGUE

Robert Browning (1812–1889) was, after Alfred Tennyson, the most acclaimed poet of the Victorian era. Browning was a poetic pioneer, exploring psychological states and new metrical schemes in ways that at first confused many. Yet the world eventually caught up with Browning and lauded him for his poetic achievements. Perhaps Browning's greatest innovation was the dramatic monologue, a poem in which a fully dramatized character addresses an audience within the poem. In "My Last Duchess" (1842), excerpted below, the speaker's address to an envoy from his next duchess suggests far more about his character than he might wish

to reveal—including the intimation that he may have murdered his wife.

"MY LAST DUCHESS."

Ferrara

That's my last Duchess painted on the wall,
Looking as if she were alive. I call
That piece a wonder, now: Frà Pandolf's hands
Worked busily a day, and there she stands.
Will 't please you sit and look at her? I said
"Frà Pandolf" by design, for never read
Strangers like you that pictured countenance,
The depth and passion of its earnest glance,
But to myself they turned (since none puts by
The curtain I have drawn for you, but I)
And seemed as they would ask me, if they durst,
How such a glance came there; so, not the first
Are you to turn and ask thus. Sir, 't was not
Her husband's presence only, called that spot
Of joy into the Duchess' cheek: perhaps
Frà Pandolf chanced to say, "Her mantle laps
Over my Lady's wrist too much," or "Paint
Must never hope to reproduce the faint
Half-flush that dies along her throat"; such stuff
Was courtesy, she thought, and cause enough
For calling up that spot of joy. She had
A heart—how shall I say?—too soon made glad,
Too easily impressed; she liked whate'er
She looked on, and her looks went everywhere.
Sir, 't was all one! My favor at her breast,
The dropping of the daylight in the West,
The bough of cherries some officious fool
Broke in the orchard for her, the white mule
She rode with round the terrace—all and each
Would draw from her alike the approving speech,
Or blush, at least. She thanked men,—good! but thanked
Somehow—I know not how—as if she ranked
My gift of a nine-hundred-years-old name
With anybody's gift. Who'd stoop to blame
This sort of trifling? Even had you skill
In speech—(which I have not)—to make your will
Quite clear to such an one, and say, "Just this
Or that in you disgusts me; here you miss,
Or there exceed the mark"—and if she let
Herself be lessoned so, nor plainly set
Her wits to yours, forsooth, and made excuse,
—E'en then would be some stooping; and I choose
Never to stoop. Oh, sir, she smiled, no doubt,
Whene'er I passed her; but who passed without
Much the same smile? This grew; I gave commands;
Then all smiles stopped together. There she stands
As if alive. Will 't please you rise? We'll meet
The company below, then. I repeat,
The Count your Master's known munificence
Is ample warrant that no just pretence
Of mine for dowry will be disallowed;
Though his fair daughter's self, as I avowed
At starting, is my object. Nay, we'll go
Together down, Sir! Notice Neptune, though,

Taming a sea-horse, thought a rarity,
Which Claus of Innsbruck cast in bronze for me.

[*See also:* BROWNING, ROBERT; DRAMATIC MONOLOGUE; POETRY.]

SOURCE

Browning, Robert. "My Last Duchess." *Dramatic Lyrics.* London: Moxon, 1842. Collected in *The Poetry of Robert Browning,* edited by Jacob Korg. Indianapolis and New York: Bobbs-Merrill, 1971.

THE WOMAN POET

Elizabeth Barrett Browning (1806–1861) was the most prominent woman poet of the Victorian era. In an era in which women were too rarely recognized for their achievements, she was suggested as the successor to William Wordsworth as the nation's poet laureate. Barrett Browning's poetry encompassed a wide range of topics and forms, from politics to romance, lyrics to hymns. Among her most acclaimed works is the verse-novel Aurora Leigh *(1859), which narrates a woman poet's struggle to attain her voice and gain acceptance for her work, issues that are hinted at in the excerpt below.*

EXCERPT FROM *AURORA LEIGH.*

Fifth Book

[. . .]
Aurora Leigh, be humble. Shall I hope
To speak my poems in mysterious tune
With man and nature?—with the lava-lymph
That trickles from successive galaxies
Still drop by drop adown the finger of God
In still new worlds?—with summer-days in this
That scarce dare breathe they are so beautiful?
With spring's delicious trouble in the ground,
Tormented by the quickened blood of roots,
And softly pricked by golden crocus-sheaves
In token of the harvest-time of flowers?
With winters and with autumns,—and beyond,
With the human heart's large seasons, when it hopes
And fears, joys, grieves, and loves?—with all that strain
Of sexual passion, which devours the flesh
In a sacrament of souls? with mother's breasts
Which, round the new-made creatures hanging there,
Throb luminous and harmonious like pure spheres?—
With multitudinous life, and finally
With the great escapings of ecstatic souls,
Who, in a rush of too long prisoned flame,
Their radiant faces upward, burn away
This dark of the body, issuing on a world,
Beyond our mortal?—can I speak my verse
So plainly in tune to these things and the rest,
That men shall feel it catch them on the quick,
As having the same warrant over them
To hold and move them if they will or no,

Alike imperious as the primal rhythm
Of that theurgic nature?—I must fail,
Who fail at the beginning to hold and move
One man,—and he my cousin, and he my friend,
And he born tender, made intelligent,
Inclined to ponder the precipitous sides
Of difficult questions ; yet, obtuse to *me*,
Of *me*, incurious! likes me very well,
And wishes me a paradise of good,
Good looks, good means, and good digestion,—ay,
But otherwise evades me, puts me off
With kindness, with a tolerant gentleness,—
Too light a book for a grave man's reading ! Go,
Aurora Leigh : be humble.

There it is,
We women are too apt to look to one,
Which proves a certain impotence in art.
We strain our natures at doing something great,
Far less because it 's something great to do,
Than haply that we, so, commend ourselves
As being not small, and more appreciable
To some one friend. We must have mediators
Betwixt our highest conscience and the judge;
Some sweet saint's blood must quicken in our palms
Or all the life in heaven seems slow and cold:
Good only being perceived as the end of good,
And God alone pleased,—that 's too poor, we think,
And not enough for us by any means.
Ay—Romney, I remember, told me once
We miss the abstract when we comprehend.
We miss it most when we aspire,—and fail.

Yet, so, I will not.—This vile woman's way
Of trailing garments, shall not trip me up :
I'll have no traffic with the personal thought
In Art's pure temple. Must I work in vain,
Without the approbation of a man?
It cannot be; it shall not. Fame itself,
That approbation of the general race,
Presents a poor end (though the arrow speed
Shot straight with vigorous finger to the white),
And the highest fame was never reached except
By what was aimed above it. Art for art,
And good for God Himself, the essential Good!
We'll keep our aims sublime, our eyes erect,
Although our woman-hands should shake and fail;
And if we fail . . . But must we?—

Shall I fail?
The Greeks said grandly in their tragic phrase,
"Let no one be called happy till his death."
To which I add,—Let no one till his death
Be called unhappy. Measure not the work
Until the day 's out and the labor done,
Then bring your gauges. If the day's work 's scant,
Why, call it scant; affect no compromise;
And, in that we have nobly striven at least,
Deal with us nobly, women though we be.
And honor us with truth if not with praise.
[. . .]

[*See also:* BROWNING, ELIZABETH BARRETT; POETRY; WOMEN'S RIGHTS.]

SOURCE

Browning, Elizabeth Barrett. *Aurora Leigh.* London: Chapman and Hall, 1857, revised, 1859; New York: C. S. Francis, 1857. Collected in *The Complete Poetical Works of Elizabeth Barrett Browning,* edited by Harriet Waters Preston. 1900. Revised as *The Poetical Works of Elizabeth Barrett Browning,* with new introduction by Ruth M. Adams. Boston: Houghton Mifflin, 1974.

THE GREATEST POET OF HIS AGE

Poet Laureate from 1850 to his death in 1892, Alfred Tennyson (1809–1892) is often hailed as the greatest poet of his age. Tennyson's poetry is complex and emotionally charged. While on the surface much of his work seems to reflect the conventional morality of the era, a deeper reading often reveals untold depths. Twentieth-century poet T. S. Eliot once wrote that Tennyson was "the most instinctive rebel against the society in which he was the most perfect conformist." The two poems printed below reveal some of the range of Tennyson's poetry. "The Charge of the Light Brigade" was written to commemorate British military action in the Crimean War (1853–1856). "Ulysses," a dramatic monologue that is considered one of the poet's greatest works, speaks to the value of pushing forward despite loss and sorrow, and was one of several poems that echoed with the sadness of the loss of Tennyson's great friend, Arthur Hallam, in 1833.

"THE CHARGE OF THE LIGHT BRIGADE."

I

Half a league, half a league,
Half a league onward,
All in the valley of Death
Rode the six hundred.
"Forward, the Light Brigade!
Charge for the guns!" he said.
Into the valley of Death
Rode the six hundred.

II

"Forward, the Light Brigade!"
Was there a man dismay'd?
Not tho' the soldier knew
Some one had blunder'd.
Theirs not to make reply,
Theirs not to reason why,
Theirs but to do and die:
Into the valley of Death
Rode the six hundred.

III

Cannon to right of them,
Cannon to left of them,

Cannon in front of them
Volley'd and thunder'd;
Storm'd at with shot and shell,
Boldly they rode and well,
Into the jaws of Death,
Into the mouth of Hell
Rode the six hundred.

IV

Flash'd all their sabres bare,
Flash'd as they turn'd in air
Sabring the gunners there,
Charging an army, while
All the world wonder'd:
Plunged in the battery-smoke
Right thro' the line they broke;
Cossack and Russian
Reel'd from the sabre-stroke
Shatter'd and sunder'd.
Then they rode back, but not,
Not the six hundred.

V

Cannon to right of them,
Cannon to left of them,
Cannon behind them
Volley'd and thunder'd;
Storm'd at with shot and shell,
While horse and hero fell,
They that had fought so well
Came thro' the jaws of Death,
Back from the mouth of Hell,
All that was left of them,
Left of six hundred.

VI

When can their glory fade?
O the wild charge they made!
All the world wonder'd.
Honor the charge they made!
Honor the Light Brigade,
Noble six hundred!

"ULYSSES."

It little profits that an idle king,
By this still hearth, among these barren crags,
Match'd with an aged wife, I mete and dole
Unequal laws unto a savage race,
That hoard, and sleep, and feed, and know not me.
I cannot rest from travel: I will drink
Life to the lees: All times I have enjoy'd
Greatly, have suffer'd greatly, both with those
That loved me, and alone; on shore, and when
Thro' scudding drifts the rainy Hyades
Vext the dim sea: I am become a name;
For always roaming with a hungry heart
Much have I seen and known,—cities of men
And manners, climates, councils, governments,
Myself not least, but honour'd of them all,—
And drunk delight of battle with my peers,
Far on the ringing plains of windy Troy.
I am a part of all that I have met;
Yet all experience is an arch wherethro'

Gleams that untravell'd world whose margin fades
For ever and for ever when I move.
How dull it is to pause, to make an end,
To rust unburnish'd, not to shine in use!
As tho' to breathe were life! Life piled on life
Were all too little, and of one to me
Little remains; but every hour is saved
From that eternal silence, something more,
A bringer of new things; and vile it were
For some three suns to store and hoard myself,
And this gray spirit yearning in desire
To follow knowledge like a sinking star,
Beyond the utmost bound of human thought.

This is my son, mine own Telemachus,
To whom I leave the sceptre and the isle,—
Well-loved of me, discerning to fulfil
This labor, by slow prudence to make mild
A rugged people, and thro' soft degrees
Subdue them to the useful and the good.
Most blameless is he, centred in the sphere
Of common duties, decent not to fail
In offices of tenderness, and pay
Meet adoration to my household gods,
When I am gone. He works his work, I mine.

There lies the port; the vessel puffs her sail;
There gloom the dark, broad seas. My mariners,
Souls that have toil'd, and wrought, and thought with
    me,—
That ever with a frolic welcome took
The thunder and the sunshine, and opposed
Free hearts, free foreheads,—you and I are old;
Old age hath yet his honor and his toil.
Death closes all: but something ere the end,
Some work of noble note, may yet be done,
Not unbecoming men that strove with Gods.
The lights begin to twinkle from the rocks;
The long day wanes; the slow moon climbs; the deep
Moans round with many voices. Come, my friends.
'T is not too late to seek a newer world.
Push off, and sitting well in order smite
The sounding furrows; for my purpose holds
To sail beyond the sunset, and the baths
Of all the western stars, until I die.
It may be that the gulfs will wash us down;
It may be we shall touch the Happy Isles,
And see the great Achilles, whom we knew.
Tho' much is taken, much abides; and tho'
We are not now that strength which in old days
Moved earth and heaven, that which we are, we are,—
One equal temper of heroic hearts,
Made weak by time and fate, but strong in will
To strive, to seek, to find, and not to yield.

[See also: CRIMEAN WAR; POETRY; TENNYSON, ALFRED.]

SOURCE

Tennyson, Alfred. "The Charge of the Light Brigade." *The Examiner* (December 9, 1854). Collected in *The Poems of Tennyson,* edited by Jerome Hamilton Buckley. Cambridge, Mass.: Riverside Press, 1958.

Tennyson, Alfred. "Ulysses." In *Poems.* 2 vols. London: Moxon, 1842; Boston: Ticknor, 1842. Collected in *The Poems of Tennyson,* edited by Jerome Hamilton Buckley. Cambridge, Mass.: Riverside Press, 1958.

THE CONTRARY VICTORIAN

Playwright, poet, novelist, and critic Oscar Wilde (1854–1900) was in many ways the anti-Victorian. At nearly every turn he rejected and publicly railed against the conventional mores of Victorian society. In his art he rejected moralism and adhered to the aesthetic of "art for art's sake"; in politics he was a committed socialist. Perhaps most radically, he was a known homosexual, a "crime" for which he was imprisoned for two years, from 1895 to 1897. His imprisonment led Wilde to write the following poem, "The Ballad of Reading Gaol," lamenting the inhumanity of British prisons.

EXCERPT FROM "THE BALLAD OF READING GAOL" (1898), BY OSCAR WILDE.

In Debtors' Yard the stones are hard,
And the dripping wall is high,
So it was there he took the air
Beneath the leaden sky,
And by each side a Warder walked,
For fear the man might die.

Or else he sat with those who watched
His anguish night and day;
Who watched him when he rose to weep,
And when he crouched to pray;
Who watched him lest himself should rob
Their scaffold of its prey.

The Governor was strong upon
The Regulations Act:
The Doctor said that Death was but
A scientific fact:
And twice a day the Chaplain called,
And left a little tract.

And twice a day he smoked his pipe,
And drank his quart of beer:
His soul was resolute, and held
No hiding-place for fear;
He often said that he was glad
The hangman's hands were near.

But why he said so strange a thing
No Warder dared to ask:
For he to whom a watcher's doom
Is given as his task,
Must set a lock upon his lips,
And make his face a mask.

Or else he might be moved, and try
To comfort or console:

237

And what should Human Pity do
Pent up in Murderer's Hole?
What word of grace in such a place
Could help a brother's soul?

With slouch and swing around the ring
We trod the Fools' Parade!
We did not care: we knew we were
The Devil's Own Brigade:
And shaven head and feet of lead
Make a merry masquerade.

We tore the tarry rope to shreds
With blunt and bleeding nails;
We rubbed the doors, and scrubbed the floors,
And cleaned the shining rails:
And, rank by rank, we soaped the plank,
And clattered with the pails.

We sewed the sacks, we broke the stones,
We turned the dusty drill:
We banged the tins, and bawled the hymns,
And sweated on the mill:
But in the heart of every man
Terror was lying still.

So still it lay that every day
Crawled like a weed-clogged wave:
And we forgot the bitter lot
That waits for fool and knave,
Till once, as we tramped in from work,
We passed an open grave.

With yawning mouth the yellow hole
Gaped for a living thing;
The very mud cried out for blood
To the thirsty asphalte ring:
And we knew that ere one dawn grew fair
Some prisoner had to swing.

Right in we went, with soul intent
On Death and Dread and Doom:
The hangman, with his little bag,
Went shuffling through the gloom:
And each man trembled as he crept
Into his numbered tomb.

That night the empty corridors
Were full of forms of Fear,
And up and down the iron town
Stole feet we could not hear,
And through the bars that hide the stars
White faces seemed to peer.

He lay as one who lies and dreams
In a pleasant meadow-land,
The watchers watched him as he slept,
And could not understand
How one could sleep so sweet a sleep
With a hangman close at hand.

But there is no sleep when men must weep
Who never yet have wept:

So we—the fool, the fraud, the knave—
That endless vigil kept,
And through each brain on hands of pain
Another's terror crept.

Alas! it is a fearful thing
To feel another's guilt!
For, right within, the sword of Sin
Pierced to its poisoned hilt,
And as molten lead were the tears we shed
For the blood we had not spilt.

The Warders with their shoes of felt
Crept by each padlocked door,
And peeped and saw, with eyes of awe,
Gray figures on the floor,
And wondered why men knelt to pray
Who never prayed before.

All through the night we knelt and prayed,
Mad mourners of a corse!
The troubled plumes of midnight were
The plumes upon a hearse:
And bitter wine upon a sponge
Was the savour of Remorse.

The gray cock crew, the red cock crew,
But never came the day:
And crooked shapes of Terror crouched,
In the corners where we lay:
And each evil sprite that walks by night
Before us seemed to play.

They glided past, they glided fast,
Like travellers through a mist:
They mocked the moon in a rigadoon [a lively dance]
Of delicate turn and twist,
And with formal pace and loathsome grace
The phantoms kept their tryst.

With mop and mow, we saw them go,
Slim shadows hand in hand:
About, about, in ghostly rout
They trod a saraband [a court dance]:
And damned grotesques made arabesques,
Like the wind upon the sand!

With the pirouettes of marionettes,
They tripped on pointed tread:
But with flutes of Fear they filled the ear,
As their grisly masque they led,
And loud they sang, and long they sang,
For they sang to wake the dead.

"Oho!" they cried, "the world is wide,
But fettered limbs go lame!
And once, or twice, to throw the dice
Is a gentlemanly game,
But he does not win who plays with Sin
In the Secret House of Shame."

No things of air these antics were,
That frolicked with such glee:

To men whose lives were held in gyves,
And whose feet might not go free,
Ah! wounds of Christ! they were living things,
Most terrible to see.

Around, around, they waltzed and wound;
Some wheeled in smirking pairs;
With the mincing step of a
demirep [classy prostitute]
Some sidled up the stairs:
And with subtle sneer, and fawning leer,
Each helped us at our prayers.

The morning wind began to moan,
But still the night went on:
Through its giant loom the web of gloom
Crept till each thread was spun:
And, as we prayed, we grew afraid
Of the Justice of the Sun.

The moaning wind went wandering round
The weeping prison-wall:
Till like a wheel of turning steel
We felt the minutes crawl:
O moaning wind! what had we done
To have such a seneschal [steward]?

At last I saw the shadowed bars,
Like a lattice wrought in lead,
Move right across the whitewashed wall
That faced my three-plank bed,
And I knew that somewhere in the world
God's dreadful dawn was red.

At six o'clock we cleaned our cells,
At seven all was still,
But the sough and swing of a mighty wing
The prison seemed to fill,
For the Lord of Death with icy breath
Had entered in to kill.

He did not pass in purple pomp,
Nor ride a moon-white steed.
Three yards of cord and a sliding board
Are all the gallows' need:
So with rope of shame the Herald came
To do the secret deed.

We were as men who through a fen
Of filthy darkness grope:
We did not dare to breathe a prayer,
Or to give our anguish scope:
Something was dead in each of us,
And what was dead was Hope.

For Man's grim Justice goes its way
And will not swerve aside:
It slays the weak, it slays the strong,
It has a deadly stride:
With iron heel it slays the strong,
The monstrous parricide!

We waited for the stroke of eight:

Each tongue was thick with thirst:
For the stroke of eight is the stroke of Fate
That makes a man accursed,
And Fate will use a running noose
For the best man and the worst.

We had no other thing to do,
Save to wait for the sign to come:
So, like things of stone in a valley lone,
Quiet we sat and dumb:
But each man's heart beat thick and quick,
Like a madman on a drum!

With sudden shock the prison-clock
Smote on the shivering air,
And from all the gaol rose up a wail
Of impotent despair,
Like the sound the frightened marshes hear
From some leper in his lair.

And as one sees most fearful things
In the crystal of a dream,
We saw the greasy hempen rope
Hooked to the blackened beam,
And heard the prayer the hangman's snare
Strangled into a scream.

And all the woe that moved him so
That he gave that bitter cry,
And the wild regrets, and the bloody sweats,
None knew so well as I:
For he who lives more lives than one
More deaths than one must die.

[*See also:* AESTHETIC MOVEMENT; CAPITAL PUNISHMENT; HOMOSEXUALITY; POETRY; WILDE, OSCAR.]

SOURCE

Wilde, Oscar. *The Ballad of Reading Gaol.* London: Smithers, 1898. Reprint, in *The Poems of Oscar Wilde,* edited by Robert Ross. London: Dawsons of Pall Mall, 1969.

THE WHITE MAN'S BURDEN

Rudyard Kipling (1865–1936) was one of the rising literary stars of the 1890s. His stories from India and the Orient fascinated readers across the globe, and such tales as The Jungle Book *(1894–1895) and* Kim *(1901) remain much-loved to this day. During the decade he also published six collections of short stories and several collections of poetry. The poem printed below, "The White Man's Burden," was written on the occasion of America's obtaining the Philippines after its victory in the Spanish-American War of 1898. It was symbolic of Kipling's belief that the expanding British and American empires had a duty to "civilize" the people of the colonies that they claimed, views that were widely embraced by many in the colonizing nations. Yet Kipling's poem—and especially its patronizing and racist title—were seized upon by critics of imperialism, helping to* contribute to the downfall of Kipling's reputation. Kipling is often remembered today as the spokesman for chauvinistic imperialism, though a close reading of the poem reveals that his views were not as simplistic as critics might claim.

"THE WHITE MAN'S BURDEN."

The United States and the Philippine Islands

Take up the White Man's burden—
Send forth the best ye breed—
Go bind your sons to exile
To serve your captives' need;
To wait in heavy harness,
On fluttered folk and wild—
Your new-caught, sullen peoples,
Half-devil and half-child.

Take up the White Man's burden—
In patience to abide,
To veil the threat of terror
And check the show of pride;
By open speech and simple,
An hundred times made plain
To seek another's profit,
And work another's gain.

Take up the White Man's burden—
The savage wars of peace—
Fill full the mouth of Famine
And bid the sickness cease;
And when your goal is nearest
The end for others sought,
Watch sloth and heathen Folly
Bring all your hopes to nought.

Take up the White Man's burden—
No tawdry rule of kings,
But toil of serf and sweeper—
The tale of common things.
The ports ye shall not enter,
The roads ye shall not tread,
Go mark them with your living,
And mark them with your dead!

Take up the White Man's burden—
And reap his old reward:
The blame of those ye better,
The hate of those ye guard—
The cry of hosts ye humour
(Ah, slowly!) toward the light:—
"Why brought he us from bondage,
Our loved Egyptian night?"

Take up the White Man's burden—
Ye dare not stoop to less—
Nor call too loud on Freedom
To cloke your weariness;
By all ye cry or whisper,
By all ye leave or do,
The silent, sullen peoples

Shall weigh your gods and you.

Take up the White Man's burden—
Have done with childish days—
The lightly proferred laurel,
The easy, ungrudged praise.
Comes now, to search your manhood
Through all the thankless years
Cold, edged with dear-bought wisdom,
The judgment of your peers!

[See also: EMPIRE; IMPERIALISM; KIPLING, RUDYARD; POETRY.]

SOURCE

Kipling, Rudyard. "The White Man's Burden." *McClure's Magazine* (February 1899). Collected in *Collected Verse*. New York: Doubleday, Page, 1907; London: Hodder and Stoughton, 1912.

THE ROLE OF THE CRITIC

One of the towering figures in the Victorian literary world, Matthew Arnold (1822–1888) was an acclaimed poet and one of the most influential literary critics of all time. Arnold published several important collections of verse in the 1840s and 1850s. He struggled in his poetry to find a stable philosophical stance from which to base his work, and eventually concluded that in the rapidly shifting intellectual winds of midcentury no such position was possible. It was this insight that fed into some of his greatest criticism, for he found in the study of the classics and the Bible—what the termed "the best that is known and thought in the world"—a port in a stormy world of ideas. In 'The Function of Criticism at the Present Time" (excerpted below), Arnold argues for the role that criticism should play in the modern world. His arguments helped provide the rationale for liberal education in the West, and remain influential to this day.

EXCERPT FROM "THE FUNCTION OF CRITICISM AT THE PRESENT TIME."

The Function of Criticism at the Present Time

MANY objections have been made to a proposition which, in some remarks of mine on translating Homer, I ventured to put forth; a proposition about criticism, and its importance at the present day. I said: "Of the literature of France and Germany, as of the intellect of Europe in general, the main effort, for now many years, has been a critical effort; the endeavour, in all branches of knowledge, theology, philosophy, history, art, science, to see the object as in itself it really is." I added, that owing to the operation in English literature of certain causes, "almost the last thing for which one would come to English literature is just that very thing which now Europe most desires—criticism;" and that the power and value of English literature was thereby impaired. More than one rejoinder declared that the importance I here assigned to criticism was excessive, and asserted the inherent superiority of the creative effort of the human spirit over its critical effort.

[. . .]

[. . .] Everybody, too, would be willing to admit, as a general proposition, that the critical faculty is lower than the inventive. But is it true that criticism is really, in itself, a baneful and injurious employment; is it true that all time given to writing critiques on the works of others would be much better employed if it were given to original composition, of whatever kind this may be?[. . .]

[. . .]

The critical power is of lower rank than the creative. True; but in assenting to this proposition, one or two things are to be kept in mind. It is undeniable that the exercise of a creative power, that a free creative activity, is the highest function of man; it is proved to be so by man's finding in it his true happiness. But it is undeniable, also, that men may have the sense of exercising this free creative activity in other ways than in producing great works of literature or art; if it were not so, all but a very few men would be shut out from the true happiness of all men. They may have it in well-doing, they may have it in learning, they may have it even in criticising. This is one thing to be kept in mind. Another is, that the exercise of the creative power in the production of great works of literature or art, however high this exercise of it may rank, is not at all epochs and under all conditions possible; and that therefore labour may be vainly spent in attempting it, which might with more fruit be used in preparing for it, in rendering it possible. [. . .] This is why great creative epochs in literature are so rare, this is why there is so much that is unsatisfactory in the productions of many men of real genius; because for the creation of a masterwork of literature two powers must concur, the power of the man and the power of the moment, and the man is not enough without the moment; the creative power has, for its happy exercise, appointed elements, and those elements are not in its own control.

Nay, they are more within the control of the critical power. It is the business of the critical power, as I said in the words already quoted, "in all branches of knowledge, theology, philosophy, history, art, science, to see the object as in itself it really is." Thus it tends, at last, to make an intellectual situation of which the creative power can profitably avail itself.

It tends to establish an order of ideas, if not absolutely true, yet true by comparison with that which it displaces; to make the best ideas prevail. Presently these new ideas reach society, the touch of truth is the touch of life, and there is a stir and growth everywhere; out of this stir and growth come the creative epochs of literature.

[. . .]

For the Englishman in general is like my friend the Member of Parliament, and believes, point-blank, that for a thing to be an anomaly is absolutely no objection to it whatever. He is like the Lord Auckland of Burke's day, who, in a memorandum on the French Revolution, talks of "certain miscreants, assuming the name of philosophers, who have presumed themselves capable of establishing a new system of society." The Englishman has been called a political animal, and he values what is political and practical so much that ideas easily become objects of dislike in his eyes, and thinkers "miscreants," because ideas and thinkers have rashly meddled with politics and practice. This would be all very well if the dislike and neglect confined themselves to ideas transported out of their own sphere, and meddling rashly with practice; but they are inevitably extended to ideas as such, and to the whole life of intelligence; practice is everything, a free play of the mind is nothing. The notion of the free play of the mind upon all subjects being a pleasure in itself, being an object of desire, being an essential provider of elements without which a nation's spirit, whatever compensations it may have for them, must, in the long run, die of inanition, hardly enters into an Englishman's thoughts. It is noticeable that the word *curiosity*, which in other languages is used in a good sense, to mean, as a high and fine quality of man's nature, just this disinterested love of a free play of the mind on all subjects, for its own sake,—it is noticeable, I say, that this word has in our language no sense of the kind, no sense but a rather bad and disparaging one. But criticism, real criticism, is essentially the exercise of this very quality; it obeys an instinct prompting it to try to know the best that is known and thought in the world, irrespectively of practice, politics, and everything of the kind; and to value knowledge and thought as they approach this best, without the intrusion of any other considerations whatever. This is an instinct for which there is, I think, little original sympathy in the practical English nature, and what there was of it has undergone a long benumbing period of blight and suppression in the epoch of concentration which followed the French Revolution.

241

But epochs of concentration cannot well endure for ever; epochs of expansion, in the due course of things, follow them. Such an epoch of expansion seems to be opening in this country. In the first place all danger of a hostile forcible pressure of foreign ideas upon our practice has long disappeared; like the traveller in the fable, therefore, we begin to wear our cloak a little more loosely. Then, with a long peace, the ideas of Europe steal gradually and amicably in, and mingle, though in infinitesimally small quantities at a time, with our own notions. Then, too, in spite of all that is said about the absorbing and brutalising influence of our passionate material progress, it seems to me indisputable that this progress is likely, though not certain, to lead in the end to an apparition of intellectual life; and that man, after he has made himself perfectly comfortable and has now to determine what to do with himself next, may begin to remember that he has a mind, and that the mind may be made the source of great pleasure. I grant it is mainly the privilege of faith, at present, to discern this end to our railways, our business, and our fortune-making; but we shall see if, here as elsewhere, faith is not in the end the true prophet. Our ease, our travelling, and our unbounded liberty to hold just as hard and securely as we please to the practice to which our notions have given birth, all tend to beget an inclination to deal a little more freely with these notions themselves, to canvass them a little, to penetrate a little into their real nature. Flutterings of curiosity, in the foreign sense of the word, appear amongst us, and it is in these that criticism must look to find its account. Criticism first; a time of true creative activity, perhaps,—which, as I have said, must inevitably be preceded amongst us by a time of criticism,—hereafter, when criticism has done its work.

It is of the last importance that English criticism should clearly discern what rule for its course, in order to avail itself of the field now opening to it, and to produce fruit for the future, it ought to take. The rule may be summed up in one word,—*disinterestedness*. And how is criticism to show disinterestedness? By keeping aloof from what is called "the practical view of things;" by resolutely following the law of its own nature, which is to be a free play of the mind on all subjects which it touches. By steadily refusing to lend itself to any of those ulterior, political, practical considerations about ideas, which plenty of people will be sure to attach to them, which perhaps ought often to be attached to them, which in this country at any rate are certain to be attached to them quite sufficiently, but which criticism has really nothing to do with. Its business is, as I have said, simply to know the best that is known and thought in the world, and by in its turn making this known, to create a current of true and fresh ideas. Its business is to do this with inflexible honesty, with due ability; but its business is to do no more, and to leave alone all questions of practical consequences and applications, questions which will never fail to have due prominence given to them. Else criticism, besides being really false to its own nature, merely continues in the old rut which it has hitherto followed in this country, and will certainly miss the chance now given to it. For what is at present the bane of criticism in this country? It is that practical considerations cling to it and stifle it. It subserves interests not its own. Our organs of criticism are organs of men and parties having practical ends to serve, and with them those practical ends are the first thing and the play of mind the second; so much play of mind as is compatible with the prosecution of those practical ends is all that is wanted. An organ like the *Revue des Deux Mondes*, having for its main function to understand and utter the best that is known and thought in the world, existing, it may be said, as just an organ for a free play of the mind, we have not. But we have the *Edinburgh Review*, existing as an organ of the old Whigs, and for as much play of mind as may suit its being that; we have the *Quarterly Review*, existing as an organ of the Tories, and for as much play of mind as may suit its being that; we have the *British Quarterly Review*, existing as an organ of the political Dissenters, and for as much play of mind as may suit its being that; we have the *Times*, existing as an organ of the common, satisfied, well-to-do Englishman, and for as much play of mind as may suit its being that. And so on through all the various fractions, political and religious, of our society; every fraction has, as such, its organ of criticism, but the notion of combining all fractions in the common pleasure of a free disinterested play of mind meets with no favour. Directly this play of mind wants to have more scope, and to forget the pressure of practical considerations a little, it is checked, it is made to feel the chain. We saw this the other day in the extinction, so much to be regretted, of the *Home and Foreign Review*. Perhaps in no organ of criticism in this country was there so much knowledge, so much play of mind; but these could not save it. The *Dublin Review* subordinates play of mind to the practical business of English and Irish Catholicism, and lives. It must needs be that men should act in sects and parties, that each of these sects and parties should have its organ, and should make this organ subserve the interests of its action; but it would be well, too, that there should be a criticism, not the minister of these interests, not their enemy, but absolutely and entirely independent of them. No other criticism will ever attain any real authority or make any real way towards its end,—the creating a current of true and fresh ideas.

[. . .]

It will be said that it is a very subtle and indirect action which I am thus prescribing for criticism, and that, by embracing in this manner the Indian virtue of detachment and abandoning the sphere of practical life, it condemns itself to a slow and obscure work. Slow and obscure it may be, but it is the only proper work of criticism. The mass of mankind will never have any ardent zeal for seeing things as they are; very inadequate ideas will always satisfy them. On these inadequate ideas reposes, and must repose, the general practice of the world. That is as much as saying that whoever sets himself to see things as they are will find himself one of a very small circle; but it is only by this small circle resolutely doing its own work that adequate ideas will ever get current at all. The rush and roar of practical life will always have a dizzying and attracting effect upon the most collected spectator, and tend to draw him into its vortex; most of all will this be the case where that life is so powerful as it is in England. But it is only by remaining collected, and refusing to lend himself to the point of view of the practical man, that the critic can do the practical man any service; and it is only by the greatest sincerity in pursuing his own course, and by at last convincing even the practical man of his sincerity, that he can escape misunderstandings which perpetually threaten him.

[. . . .]

[. . .] Criticism must maintain its independence of the practical spirit and its aims. Even with well-meant efforts of the practical spirit it must express dissatisfaction, if in the sphere of the ideal they seem impoverishing and limiting. It must not hurry on to the goal because of its practical importance. It must be patient, and know how to wait; and flexible, and know how to attach itself to things and how to withdraw from them. It must be apt to study and praise elements that for the fulness of spiritual perfection are wanted, even though they belong to a power which in the practical sphere may be maleficent. It must be apt to discern the spiritual shortcomings or illusions of powers that in the practical sphere may be beneficent. And this with out any notion of favouring or injuring, in the practical sphere, one power or the other; without any notion of playing off, in this sphere, one power against the other.

[. . .]

If I have insisted so much on the course which criticism must take where politics and religion are concerned, it is because, where these burning matters are in question, it is most likely to go astray. I have wished, above all, to insist on the attitude which criticism should adopt towards things in general; on its right tone and temper of mind. But then comes another questions as to the subject-matter which literary criticism must seek. Here, in general, its course is determined for it by the idea which is the law of its being; the idea of a disinterested endeavour to learn and propagate the best that is known and thought in the world, and thus to establish a current of fresh and true ideas. By the very nature of things, as England is not all the world, much of the best that is known and thought in the world cannot be of English growth, must be foreign; by the nature of things, again, it is just this that we are least likely to know, while English thought is streaming in upon us from all sides, and takes excellent care that we shall not be ignorant of its existence. The English critic of literature, therefore, must dwell much on foreign thought, and with particular heed on any part of it, which, while significant and fruitful in itself, is for any reason specially likely to escape him. Again, judging is often spoken of as the critic's one business, and so in some sense it is; but the judgment which almost insensibly forms itself in a fair and clear mind, along with fresh knowledge, is the valuable one; and thus knowledge, and ever fresh knowledge, must be the critic's great concern for himself. And it is by communicating fresh knowledge, and letting his own judgment pass along with it,—but insensibly, and in the second place not the first, as a sort of companion and clue, not as an abstract law-giver,—that he will generally do most good to his readers. Sometimes, no doubt, for the sake of establishing an author's place in literature, and his relation to a central standard (and if this is not done how are we to get at our *best in the world*?), criticism may have to deal with a subject-matter so familiar that fresh knowledge is out of the question, and then it must be all judgment; an enunciation and detailed application of principles. Here the great safeguard is never to let oneself become abstract, always to retain an intimate and lively consciousness of the truth of what one is saying, and, the moment this fails us, to be sure that something is wrong. Still, under all circumstances, this mere judgment and application of principles is, in itself, not the most satisfactory work to the critic; like mathematics it is tautological, and cannot well give us, like fresh learning, the sense of creative activity.

But stop, some one will say; all this talk is of no practical use to us whatever; this criticism of yours is not what we have in our minds when we speak of criticism; when we speak of critics and criticism, we mean critics and criticism of the current English literature of the day; when you offer to tell criticism its function, it is to this criticism that we expect you to address yourself. I am sorry for it, for I am afraid I must disappoint these expectations. I am bound by my own definition of criticism: *a disinterested endeavour to learn and propagate the best that is known and thought in the world*. How much of current English literature comes into this "best that is known and thought in the world"? Not very much, I fear; certainly less, at this moment, than of the current literature of France or Germany. Well, then, am I to alter my definition of criticism, in order to meet the requirements of a number of practising English critics, who, after all, are free in their choice of a business? That would be making criticism lend itself just to one of those alien practical considerations, which, I have said, are so fatal to it. One may say, indeed, to those who have to deal with the mass—so much better disregarded—of current English literature, that they may at all events endeavour, in dealing with this, to try it, so far as they can, by the standard of the best that is known and thought in the world; one may say, that to get anywhere near this standard, every critic should try and possess one great literature, at least, besides his own; and the more unlike his own, the better. But, after all, the criticism I am really concerned with— the criticism which alone can much help us for the future, the criticism which, throughout Europe, is at the present day meant, when so much stress is laid on the importance of criticism and the critical spirit— is a criticism which regards Europe as being, for intellectual and spiritual purposes, one great confederation, bound to a joint action and working to a common result; and whose members have, for their proper outfit, a knowledge of Greek, Roman, and Eastern antiquity, and of one another. Special, local, and temporary advantages being put out of account, that modern nation will in the intellectual and spiritual sphere make most progress, which most thoroughly carries out this programme. And what is that but saying that we too, all of us, as individuals, the more thoroughly we carry it out, shall make the more progress?

[. . .]

I conclude with what I said at the beginning: to have the sense of creative activity is the great happiness and the great proof of being alive, and it is not denied to criticism to have it; but then criticism must be sincere, simple, flexible, ardent, ever widening its knowledge. Then it may have, in no contemptible measure, a joyful sense of creative activity; a sense which a man of insight and conscience will prefer to what he might derive from a poor, starved, fragmentary, inadequate creation. And at some epochs no other creation is possible.

Still, in full measure, the sense of creative activity belongs only to genuine creation; in literature we must never forget that. But what true man of letters ever can forget it? It is no such common matter for a gifted nature to come into possession of a current of true and living ideas, and to produce amidst the inspiration of them, that we are likely to underrate it. The epochs of Æschylus and Shakspeare [sic] make us feel their pre-eminence. In an epoch like those is, no doubt, the true life of a literature; there is the promised land, towards which criticism can only beckon. That promised land it will not be ours to enter, and we shall die in the wilderness: but to have desired to enter it, to have saluted it from afar, is already, perhaps, the best distinction among contemporaries; it will certainly be the best title to esteem with posterity.

[*See also:* ARNOLD, MATTHEW; LITERARY CRITICISM.]

SOURCE

Matthew Arnold. "The Function of Criticism at the Present Time." *Essays in Criticism*. London: Macmillan, 1865.

POLITICS AND ECONOMICS

The political and economic changes occurring during the Victorian era had an impact on life in profound ways. Never before had so many people earned so much money. With their new wealth, many began to question the old sources of political power and privilege and pushed to open the political arena to more people. Who should be able to vote, how the government should work, and the broader topic of whether or not British imperialism benefited society were hotly debated topics during the period.

This collection of primary sources offers samples of documents that provide a window into the economic and political changes of the time. The following excerpts include the first effective legislation to protect children from mistreatment at the hands of employers; the People's Charter of 1839, which served as a guide for the Chartist's cause; powerful insight into the conflict between Ireland and Great Britain regarding Home Rule, as described by Irish activist Daniel O'Connell, who worked tirelessly to repeal the Act of Union that subsumed Ireland into greater Britain; Sir Robert Peel's Tamworth Manifesto, in which he articulated what would soon be considered the foundation of the Conservative party; and John A. Hobson's assessment of British imperialism at the end of the era, which became one of the most influential critiques of the economic policies that prevailed during that time.

REGULATING CHILD LABOR

The proliferation of factories in urban areas during the Industrial Revolution brought the plight of factory workers, especially child laborers, to the public's attention. Concerned citizens soon organized humanitarian reform efforts in order to stop the abuses that were caused by unregulated labor. Their efforts led directly to legislative action on the part of the British Parliament. The first Factory Act, passed in 1802, was entitled the Health and Morals of Apprentices Act and targeted the harsh conditions that "apprentices" (pauper children from the age of seven) suffered under the supervision of cotton-mill owners. Although this act detailed improvements for labor, it did not provide for the enforcement of its regulation. In the following decades factory legislation would become increasingly specific and methods for effective enforcement would be designed.

The following excerpt is from the Factory Act of 1833. This act was the first piece of effective factory legislation and was entitled the Regulation of Child Labor Law. This law limited the hours for child laborers, and al-

though it repeated some of the earlier legislation, the 1833 act provided for the enforcement of the law. A small number of factory inspectors oversaw factories in designated counties and reported their findings to the House of Commons.

EXCERPT FROM THE FACTORY ACT OF 1833.

Whereas it is necessary that the Hours of Labour of Children and young Persons employed in Mills and Factories, of whatever description, should be regulated, inasmuch as it has become a practice in many such Mills and Factories to employ a great number of Children and young Persons of both Sexes an unreasonable length of time, and late at Night, and in many instances all Night, to the great and manifest injury of the Health and Morals of such Children and young Persons;

Be it therefore enacted, by The King's most Excellent Majesty by and with the Advice and Consent of the Lords Spiritual and Temporal, and Commons, in this present Parliament assembled, and by the Authority of the same, THAT from and after the First day of July One thousand eight hundred and Thirty-three no Person under the age of Twenty-one Years shall be allowed to work in or during the Night, (that is to say) between the Hours of Seven of the clock in the Evening and Six of the clock in the Morning (except as hereinafter provided) in or about any Cotton, Woollen, Worsted, Hemp, Flax, Tow, Linen, Lace or Silk Mill or Factory wherein Steam or Water or any other Power in or shall be used to propel or work the Machinery in such Mill or Factory of Cotton, Wool, Worsted, Hemp, Flax, Tow or Silk, either separately or mixed, in any such Mill or Factory, situate in any part of the United Kingdom of Great Britain and Ireland.

And be it further Enacted, That no Person under the age of *Eighteen Years* shall be employed or allowed to work in any such Mill or Factory, in or upon any description of Work or Employment as aforesaid, or in any way preparing or manufacturing or finishing the aforesaid Materials, either separately or mixed, or in cleaning any Machinery or Mill-work therein, or belonging thereunto, or in repairing the same, more than *Ten Hours* in any one day, nor more than *Eight Hours* one Saturday, exclusive of the times to be allowed for Meals and Refreshment, as hereinafter mentioned: Provided always, That nothing in this Act shall apply or extend to the working of any Steam or other Engine, Water-wheel or other Power in or belonging to any Mill or Building or Machinery, when used in that part of the process or work commonly called Fulling of Woollens, nor to any Apprentices or other Persons employed therein.

And be it further Enacted, That, [. . .] there shall be allowed to every such Child or young Person so employed in any such Mill or Factory as aforesaid, *Two full hours,* (that is to say) *One half hour* for Breakfast-time, *One hour* for Dinner-time, and *Half an hour* for Afternoon Refreshment, at such times of the day as the Employer or Employers, and the Parents or natural or legal Guardians of such Children and young Persons so employed shall agree upon [. . .]

[. . .]

Be it enacted, That said Labour or Employment, from its commencement in the Morning to its termination in the Evening shall be continuous, excepting during Meal-times, and shall not in any case exceed *Twelve Hours,* including Three Meals, or *Eleven hours and a half,* including Two Meals, or *Eleven Hours,* including One Meal, as hereinbefore provided.

[. . .]

And be it further Enacted, That from and after the passing of this Act, no Child being under the age of *Nine Years* shall be employed in any manner or description of Work in any Cotton, Woollen, Worsted, Flax, Hemp, Tow, Linen, Lace, Netting, Weaving, or Silk Mill or Factory whatsoever.

[. . .]

BE it Enacted, That any Occupier or Occupiers of any such Mill or Factory who shall employ Children and young Persons for any purposes whatever on the Sabbath Day, shall on conviction, forfeit and pay for every such Individual so employed, any sum not exceeding *Ten Pounds,* nor less than *Five Pounds,* at the discretion of the Justices of the Peace before whom such Offender or Offenders shall be convicted.

[. . .]

And be it further Enacted, That no Justice of the Peace being also a Proprietor or Occupier of, or otherwise interested in, any such Mill or Factory as aforesaid, or the Father, Son or Brother of any such Proprietor or Occupier or interested Person, shall act as a Justice of the Peace in the execution of this Act.

[. . .]

And whereas a practice is known to exist in certain Mills or Factories of using Two or more different Clocks or Time-pieces, one of which is a Clock or Time-piece regulated by the velocity of the Steam Engine or Machinery, and often called a Speed Clock, by the alternate use of which different Clocks the period of daily labour, though nominally limited to a certain duration, is often increased much beyond the time professedly fixed, and by which practice also

the provisions of this Act for the regulation of the time and labour of Children and young Persons in Mills and Factories might and could be evaded; BE it therefore Enacted, That the times and duration of the labour or employment of Children and young Persons employed in any such Mill or Factory as aforesaid shall be determined by the nearest principal public Clock of the Parish, Township or Neighbourhood.

[*See also:* CHILD LABOR; FACTORIES; LAW AND LEGAL REFORM.]

SOURCE

Great Britain House of Commons Parliamentary Papers. Vol II. London: H.M.S.O., 1833.

CHARTIST HOPES FOR PARLIAMENTARY REFORM

In 1832 the British Parliament enfranchised much of the English middle class, but even though working-class people had worked diligently for legal reform, they were not granted voting rights. From about 1837 to the mid-1850s, workers united into what came to be called the Chartist movement in hopes of passing democratic reforms through Parliament that eliminated what they considered "class legislation," such as the New Poor Law of 1834.

The People's Charter, written in 1837 by a committee of the London Working Men's Association led by William Lovett, articulated the workers' hopes, including universal male suffrage; payment for members of Parliament; no property qualifications for members of Parliament; equal electoral districts; the secret ballot; and annual parliaments. If the Chartists could get these issues through Parliament, working people could freely participate in politics, both as voters and as legislators.

Chartists labored for 11 years to achieve the Charter. Chartists used petitioning, rather than violence, as a central tactic. In hopes of forcing Parliament to consider the People's Charter, Chartists circulated petitions in 1839, 1842, and 1848. Although hundreds of thousands of signatures were collected, the House of Commons found fraudulent and duplicated signatures and tabled the petitions. Continued government resistance to the Chartists' petition effort and the failure of the movement's Land Company led to the disintegration of the movement by the mid-1800s. The ideas of the Chartist movement lingered in the minds of politicians, however, and by the end of the nineteenth century many of the issues raised in the People's Charter were made into law.

EXCERPT FROM THE PEOPLE'S CHARTER.

Being the Outline of an Act to provide for the just Representation of the People of Great Britain and Ireland in the Commons' House of Parliament: embracing the Principles of Universal Suffrage, no Property Qualification, Annual Parliaments, Equal Representation, Payment of Members, and Vote by Ballot.

Prepared by a Committee of twelve persons, six Members of Parliament and six Members of the London Working Men's Association, and addressed to the People of the United Kingdom.

An Act to provide for the just Representation of the People of Great Britain and Ireland, in the Commons' House of Parliament.

Whereas, to insure, in as far as it is best possible by human forethought and wisdom, the just government of the people, it is necessary to subject those who have the power of making the laws to a wholesome and strict responsibility to those whose duty it is to obey them when made:

And, whereas, this responsibility is best enforced through the instrumentality of a body which emanates directly from, and is itself immediately subject to, the whole people, and which completely represents their feelings and their interests:

And, whereas, as the Common's House of Parliament now exercises in the name and on the supposed behalf of the people, the power of making the laws, it ought, in order to fulfil with wisdom and with honesty the great duties imposed in it, to be made the faithful and accurate representation of the people's wishes, feelings, and interests.

Be it therefore Enacted,

That from and after the passing of this Act, every male inhabitant of these realms be entitled to vote for the election of a Member of Parliament, subject however to the following conditions.

(1) That he be a native of these realms, or a foreigner who has lived in this country upwards of two years, and been naturalised..

(2) That he be twenty-one years of age.

(3) That he be not proved insane when the list of voters are revised.

(4) That he be not convicted of felony within six months from and after the passing of this Act.

(5) That his electoral rights be not suspended for bribery at elections, or for personation, or for forgery of election certificates, according to the penalties of this Act.

Electoral Districts

I. Be it enacted, that for the purpose of obtaining an equal representation of the people in the Commons' House of Parliament, the United Kingdom be divided into 300 electoral districts.

II. That each such district contain, as nearly as may be, an equal number of inhabitants.

III. That the number of inhabitants be taken from the last census, and as soon as possible after the next ensuing decennial census shall have been taken, the electoral districts be made to conform thereto.

IV. That each electoral district be named after the principal city or borough within its limits.

V. That each electoral district return one representative to sit in the Commons' House of Parliament, and no more. [. . .].

Arrangement for Nominations

I. Be it enacted, that for the purpose of guarding against too great a number of candidates, who might otherwise be heedlessly proposed, as well as for giving time for the electors to enquire into the merits of the persons who may be nominated for Members of Parliament, as well as for returning officers, that all nominations be taken as herinafter directed.

II. That for all general elections of Members of Parliament, a requisition of the following form, signed by at least one hundred qualified electors of the district, be delivered to the returning officer of the district between the first and 10th day of May in each year; and that such requisition constitute the nomination of such person as a candidate for the district. [. . .].

XI. That no other qualification shall be required for members to serve in the Commons' House of Parliament, than the choice of the electors. [. . .].

Duration of Parliament

I. Be it enacted, that the Members of the House of Commons chosen as aforesaid, shall meet on the first Monday in June in each year, and continue their sittings from time to time as they may deem it convenient, till the first Monday in June the following, when the next new Parliament is to be chosen: they shall be eligible to be re-elected.

II. That during an adjournment, they be liable to be called together by the executive, in cases of emergency.

III. That a register be kept of the daily attendance of each member, which at the close of the session shall be printed as a sessional paper, showing how the members have attended.

Payment of Members

I. Be it enacted, that every Member of the House of Commons by entitles, at the close of the session, to a writ of expenses on the Treasury, for his legislative duties in the public service, and shall be paid £500 per annum.

[. . .]

[*See also:* CHARTISM; PARLIAMENTARY GOVERNMENT.]

SOURCE

The Chartist Circular. September 28, 1839.

HOME RULE

A heated debate raged in Ireland over Home Rule. The Act of Union in 1801, which united Ireland with Great Britain under a single Parliament as a way of quelling the religious turmoil in the country, marked the beginning of the controversy. Irish political groups soon formed to push for the repeal of the Act of Union. Irish nationalist Daniel O'Connell (1775-1847) and others formed the Catholic Association in 1823 to campaign for the repeal of the Act of Union, Catholic Emancipation, the abolishment of the Irish tithe system, universal suffrage, and a secret ballot for parliamentary elections. The Association had some success in 1829 when Catholic Emancipation was granted. To increase pressure for the repeal of the Act of Union, O'Connell formed the Repeal Association in 1840 and declared 1843 to be "the year of the great repeal." Despite O'Connell's and the Association's vigorous efforts, the Act of Union remained in place. O'Connell, however, remained steadfast in his conviction that Ireland should have Home Rule. In the following excerpt from a letter O'Connell wrote in 1844 to Mr. Charles Buller, a liberal politician and, at the time of O'Connell's letter, M.P. for Liskeard, O'Connell explains the basis for Irish discontent with English rule.

EXCERPT FROM DANIEL O'CONNELL'S LETTER TO MR. CHARLES BULLER JANUARY 9, 1844

My dear Buller,

[. . .] I begin by expressing my total dissent from your opinion that there is a *great* or *strong* party in England favourable to justice to Ireland. The utter weakness of the British Government in relation to foreign powers, whilst Ireland continues justly dissatisfied, has, I admit, created a species of restlessness amongst a number of the English. They would fain be doing *something* for Ireland in order to lessen their own apprehensions. There is no *heart* in it. If they

were made to believe that coercion would serve their purposes they would prefer coercion. There are, to be sure, a chosen few, augmented in number by recent events and present circumstances, who would join you and Mr. Hawes [Benjamin Hawes, M.P. for Lambeth, 1832-1847] in doing substantial justice to Ireland.

Let us, however, not wrangle about the strength of the "Justice to Ireland" party in England. I will take for granted that it is strong enough to be useful. Upon that supposition I meet at once and candidly your demand to suggest measures that would be satisfactory to the Irish people. I am not telling you what would satisfy me personally but I will tell you what I know would deprive me of many of my present adherents. As for myself, you admit that the slightest shrinking from the Repeal is at the present moment impracticable. Even my usual doctrine of instalments would under existing circumstances have the appearance of cowardice or at least of paltry timidity. But as I have no notion of keeping up a party at the expense of sacrificing any measure useful to Ireland, I will candidly tell you what I think would mitigate the present ardent desire for Repeal. These are the measures which in my deliberate and well informed judgment would have that effect.

Firstly. Establishing perfect religious equality which could be done in either of two ways: the one would be the paying all religious instructors of Catholics and Episcopalian Protestants: the *second* way would be by paying neither [. . .] [The second way] is the right one—the paying neither clergy, the having no state church.

Secondly. The second measure which I should propose is one that ought easily to be acceded to. It is to restore the law of landlord and tenant to the state it was in at the time of the Union. There have been since the Union (I think) *seven* Statutes passed enhancing the landlord's power of distraint and eviction, enabling the landlord to ruin the tenant at a very trifling expense to himself, enabling the landlord to distraint growing crops which before the Union he could not do in Ireland, augmenting the expenses of distraint upon the tenant etc. [. . .]

Thirdly. The county franchise is becoming totally extinct. [. . .] The basis of the franchise must be extended to the people at large. It is a matter of difficulty how they shall be saved from the oppressive power of the landlord. The ballot would do; but as that won't be conceded, something else must. [. . .]

Fourthly. The Corporate Reform Bill for Ireland should be made equally potential with the corporate reform for England and Scotland. [. . .]

Fifthly. Our town constituencies should be rendered more extensive; and the old Freemen—an ancient Protestant nuisance—should be abolished. [. . .]

Sixthly. The income tax upon Irish absentees should be increased five-fold.

Seventhly. The question of fixity of tenure should be taken into the most deliberate consideration. [. . .] [A]nd the commission entrusted with that enquiry should be composed of tenants as well as landlords.

I have thus, my dear Buller, candidly given you the elements of the destruction of my political power and for the diminishing the demand for the Repeal. [. . .] But I do not expect any important result from your exertions. The British people will think of doing justice to Ireland, as they did to America, when too late. [. . .] But the important thing now is to see how you can make up a party sufficiently strong to give respectability to any exertions in favour of Ireland. The Whigs won't do it. The principal part of them will necessarily be under the control of Lord John Russell and he will never permit anything like justice to be done to the Catholic people of this country. I know him well. He has a thorough, contemptuous, Whig hatred of the Irish. He has a strong and I believe a conscientious abhorrence of Popery everywhere but I believe particularly of Irish Popery. His conduct since he came into opposition in shielding the present ministry against my demand to have the Catholic clergy allowed to *look after* Catholics in prisons and workhouses bespeaks a foregone conclusion of anticatholicity in his mind. In fact you have not the least chance of doing anything to conciliate Ireland. [. . .] I am sure chains of iron or of adamant cannot bind us much longer.

[. . .] You cannot succeed—it is impossible—your countrymen are too deeply imbued in national antipathy to the Irish. You have injured us too deeply, too cruelly, ever to forgive us. And then there is a **bigoted anti-catholic** spirit embittering, enhancing and augmenting the English hatred of the Irish nation. [. . .]

[*See also:* HOME RULE; IRELAND.]

SOURCE

O'Connell, Maurice R., ed. *The Correspondence of Daniel O'Connell*, vol. VII, 1841–1845. Dublin: Blackwater, 1973; from Russell Papers, Public Record Office, London, P.R.O. 30/22/4C, ff. 132–7.

THE POLITICAL POWER OF SIR ROBERT PEEL

Sir Robert Peel (1788–1850) was the leading parliamentarian of his age. His influence was so great that the years between 1830 and 1850 are often referred to as the "Age of Peel." Peel's letter to his electors in 1834, now called the Tamworth Manifesto, illustrates Peel's political might and is considered the first election manifesto issued in Britain.

When Peel accepted the post of prime minister on December 9, 1834, the Tory party was in the minority in Parliament and an election would soon be called. To bolster support for his views in the General Election of January 1835, Peel wrote a letter to his electors in Tamworth. In the statement, Peel reversed his previous view and declared support for the Reform Act of 1832. He also determined that the rights of landed interests and trade, among others, should be safeguarded. Peel's effort added about 100 Conservative votes in the subsequent election. Even though Peel had not garnered enough support to win the election, his Tamworth Manifesto would be remembered as the foundation for the modern-day Conservative party.

EXCERPT FROM THE TAMWORTH MANIFESTO.

To the Electors of the Borough of Tamworth.

Gentlemen,

On the 26th of November last, being then at Rome, I received from His Majesty a summons, wholly unforeseen and unexpected by me, to return to England without delay, for the purpose of assisting His Majesty in the formation of a new government. I instantly obeyed the command for my return; and on my arrival, I did not hesitate, after an anxious review of the position of public affairs, to place at the disposal of my Sovereign any services which I might be thought capable of rendering.

My acceptance of the first office in the Government terminates, for the present, my political connection with you. In seeking the renewal of it, whenever you shall be called upon to perform the duty of electing a representative in Parliament, I feel it incumbent on me to enter into a declaration of my views of public policy, as full and unreserved as I can make it, consistently with my duty as a Minister of the Crown.

You are entitled to this, from the nature of the trust which I again solicit, from the long habits of friendly intercourse in which we have lived, and from your tried adherence to me in times of difficulty, when the demonstration of unabated confidence was of peculiar value. I gladly avail myself also of this, a legitimate opportunity, of making a more public appeal— of addressing, through you, to that great and intelligent class of society of which you are a portion, and a fair and unexceptionable representative—to that class which is much less interested in the contentions of party, than in the maintenance of order and the cause of good government, that frank exposition of general principles and views which appears to be anxiously expected, and which it ought not to be the inclination, and cannot be the interest, of a Minister of this country to withhold.

Gentlemen, the arduous duties in which I am engaged have been imposed upon me through no act of mine. Whether they were an object of ambition coveted by me—whether I regard the power and distinction they confer as of any sufficient compensation for the heavy sacrifices they involve—are matters of mere personal concern, on which I will not waste a word. The King, in a crisis of great difficulty, required my services. The question I had to decide was this—Shall I obey the call? or shall I shrink from the responsibility, alleging as the reason, that I consider myself, in consequence of the Reform Bill, as labouring under a sort of moral disqualification, which must preclude me, and all who think with me, both now and for ever, from entering into the official service of the Crown? Would it, I ask, be becoming in any public man to act upon such a principle? Was it fit that I should assume that either the object or the effect of the Reform Bill has been to preclude all hope of a successful appeal to the good sense and calm judgment of the people, and so fetter the prerogative of the Crown, that the King has no free choice among his subjects, but must select his Ministers from one section, and from one section only, of public men?

I have taken another course, but I have not taken it without deep and anxious consideration as to the probability that my opinions are so far in unison with those of the constituent body of the United Kingdom as to enable me, and those with whom I am about to act, and whose sentiments are in entire concurrence with my own, to establish such a claim upon public confidence as shall enable us to conduct with vigour and success the Government of this country.

I have the firmest convictions that that confidence cannot be secured by any other course than that of a frank and explicit declaration of principle; that vague and unmeaning professions of popular opinions may quiet distrust for a time, may influence this or that election; but that such professions must ultimately and signally fail, if, being made, they are not adhered to, or if they are inconsistent with the honour and character of those who made them.

Now I say at once that I will not accept power on the condition of declaring myself an apostate from the principles on which I have heretofore acted. At the same time, I never will admit that I have been, either before or after the Reform Bill, the defender of abuses, or the enemy of judicious reforms. I appeal with confidence, in denial of the charge, to the active part I took in the great question of the Currency—in the consolidation and amendment of the Criminal Law—in the revisal of the whole system of Trial by Jury—to the opinions I have professed, and uniformly acted on, with regard to other branches of the jurisprudence of this country—I appeal to this as a proof that I have not been disposed to acquiesce in acknowledged evils, either from the mere superstitious reverence for ancient usages, or from the dread of labour or responsibility in the application of a remedy.

But the Reform Bill, it is said, constitutes a new era, and it is the duty of a Minister to declare explicitly—first, whether he will maintain the Bill itself, and, secondly, whether he will act on the spirit in which it was conceived.

With respect to the Reform Bill itself, I will repeat now the declaration which I made when I entered the House of Commons as a Member of the Reformed Parliament, that I consider the Reform Bill a final and irrevocable settlement of a great Constitutional question—a settlement which no friend to the peace and welfare of this country would attempt to disturb, either by direct or by insidious means.

Then, as to the spirit of the Reform Bill, and the willingness to adopt and enforce it as a rule of government: if, by adopting the spirit of the Reform Bill, it be meant that we are to live in a perpetual vortex of agitation; that public men can only support themselves in public estimation by adopting every popular impression of the day,—by promising the instant redress of anything which anybody may call an abuse,—by abandoning altogether that great aid of government—more powerful than either law or reason—the respect for ancient rights, and the deference to prescriptive authority; if this be the spirit of the Reform Bill, I will not undertake to adopt it. But if the spirit of the Reform Bill implies merely a careful review of institutions, civil and ecclesiastical, undertaken in a friendly temper, combining, with the firm maintenance of established rights, the correction of proved abuses and the redress of real grievances,—in that case, I can for myself and colleagues undertake to act in such a spirit and with such intentions.

Such declarations of general principle are, I am aware, necessarily vague: but in order to be more explicit, I will endeavour to apply them practically to some of those questions which have of late attracted the greater share of public interest and attention.

I take, first, the inquiry into Municipal Corporations:

It is not my intention to advise the Crown to interrupt the process of that inquiry, nor to transfer the conduct of it from those to whom it was committed by the late Government. For myself, I gave the best proof that I was not unfriendly to the principle of inquiry, by consenting to be a member of that Committee of the House of Commons on which it was originally devolved. No report has yet been made by the Commissioners to whom the inquiry was afterwards referred; and, until that report by made, I cannot be expected to give, on the part of the Government, any other pledge than that they will bestow on the suggestions it may contain, and the evidence on which they may be founded, a full and unprejudiced consideration.

I will, in the next place, address myself to the questions in which those of our fellow-countrymen who dissent from the doctrines of the Established Church take an especial interest.

Instead of making new professions, I will refer to the course which I took upon those subjects when out of power.

In the first place, I supported the measure brought forward by Lord Althorp, the object of which was to exempt all classes from the payment of Church-rates, applying in lieu thereof, out of a branch of revenue, a certain sum for the building and repair of churches. I never expressed, nor did I entertain, the slightest objection to the principle of a bill of which Lord John Russell was the author, intended to relieve the conscientious scruples of Dissenters in respect to the ceremony of marriage. I give no opinion now on the particular measures themselves: they were proposed by Ministers in whom the Dissenters had confidence; they were intended to give relief; and it is sufficient for my present purposes to state that I supported the principle of them.

I opposed—and I am bound to state that my opinions in that respect have undergone no change—the admission of Dissenters, as a claim of right, into the Universities; but I expressly declared that if regulations, enforced by public authorities superintending the professions of law and medicine, and the studies connected with them, had the effect of conferring advantages of the nature of civil privileges on one class of the King's subjects from which another was excluded—those regulations ought to undergo modification, with the view of placing all the King's subjects, whatever their religious creeds, upon a footing of perfect equality with respect to any civil privilege.

I appeal to the course which I pursued on those several questions, when office must have been out of contemplation; and I ask, with confidence, does that course imply that I was actuated by any illiberal or intolerant spirit towards the Dissenting body, or by an unwillingness to consider fairly the redress of any real grievances?

In the examination of other questions which excited the public feeling, I will not omit the Pension List. I resisted—and, with the opinions I entertain, I should again resist—a retrospective inquiry into pensions granted by the Crown at a time when the discretion of the Crown was neither fettered by law nor by the expression of any opinion on the part of the House of Commons; but I voted for the Resolution, moved by Lord Althorp, that pensions on the Civil List ought, for the future, to be confined to such persons only as have just claims to the Royal beneficence, or are entitled to consideration on account either of their personal services to the Crown, or of performance of duties to the public, or their scientific or literary eminence. On the Resolution which I thus supported as a private Member of Parliament, I shall scrupulously act as a Minister of the Crown, and shall advise the grant of no pension which is not in conformity with the spirit and intention of the vote to which I was a party.

Then, as to the great question of Church Reform. On that head I have no new professions to make. I cannot give my consent to the alienating of Church property, in any part of the United Kingdom, from strictly Ecclesiastical purposes. But I repeat now the opinions that I have already expressed in Parliament in regard to the Church Establishment in Ireland—that if, by an improved distribution of the revenues of the Church, its just influence can be extended, and the true interests of the Established religion promoted, all other considerations should be made subordinate to the advancement of objects of such paramount importance.

As to Church property in this country, no person has expressed a more earnest wish than I have done that the question of tithe, complicated and difficult as I acknowledge it to be, should, if possible, be satisfactorily settled by means of a commutation, founded upon just principles, and proposed after mature consideration.

With regard to alterations in the laws which govern our Ecclesiastical Establishment, I have had no recent opportunity of giving that grave consideration to a subject of the deepest interest, which could alone justify me in making any public declaration of opinion. It is a subject which must undergo the fullest deliberation, and into that deliberation the Government will enter, with the sincerest desire to remove every abuse that can impair the efficiency of the Establishment, to extend the sphere of its usefulness, and to strengthen and confirm its just claims upon the respect and affection of the people.

It is unnecessary for my purpose to enter into any further details. I have said enough, with respect to general principles and their practical application to public measures, to indicate the spirit in which the King's Government is prepared to act. Our object will be—the maintenance of peace—the scrupulous and honourable fulfilment, without reference to their original policy, of all existing engagements with Foreign Powers,—the support of public credit—the enforcement of strict economy—and the just and impartial consideration of what is due to all interests—agricultural, manufacturing, and commercial.

Whatever may be the issue of the undertaking in which I am engaged, I feel assured that you will mark, by a renewal of your confidence, your approbation of the course I have pursued in accepting office. I enter upon the arduous duties assigned to me with the deepest sense of the responsibility they involve, with great distrust of my own qualifications for their adequate discharge, but at the same time with a resolution to persevere, which nothing could inspire but the strong impulse of public duty, the consciousness of upright motives, and the firm belief that the people of this country will so far maintain the prerogative of the King, as to give to the Ministers of his choice, not an implicit confidence, but a fair trial.

I am, Gentlemen,

With affectionate regard,

Most faithfully yours,

Robert Peel.

[See also: PARLIAMENTARY GOVERNMENT; PEEL, ROBERT; REFORM ACTS.]

SOURCE

"The Tamworth Manifesto," December 18, 1834, as quoted in *Memoirs by the Right Honourable Sir Robert Peel, BART., M.P., &c. Part I, The Roman Catholic Question, 1828–9.* 1856. Reprint, New York: Kraus Reprint Co., 1969.

A CRITIQUE OF IMPERIALISM

John A. Hobson's (1858–1940) Imperialism: A Study, *published at the end of the Victorian era, became one of the most famous critiques of British imperial expansion. A Liberal economist and writer, Hobson taught English literature and economics for the Oxford University Extension Delegacy and the London Society for the Extension of University Teaching before becoming a freelance writer. His many books include* Problems of Poverty *(1891),* The Evolution of Modern Capitalism *(1894),* The Problem of the Unemployed *(1896),* The Economics of Distribution *(1900), and* John Ruskin, Social Reformer *(1898). His work influenced such influential people as the economist John Maynard Keynes and Russian leader Vladimir Lenin.*

The following excerpt from Imperialism: A Study *illustrates Hobson's view of British imperialism at the end of the Victorian era.*

EXCERPT FROM *IMPERIALISM: A STUDY.*

Part II, Chapter VII

The Outcome

I

If Imperialism may no longer be regarded as a blind inevitable destiny, is it certain that imperial expansion as a deliberately chosen line of public policy can be stopped?

We have seen that it is motived, not by the interests of the nation as a whole, but by those of certain classes, who impose the policy upon the nation for their own advantage. The amalgam of economic and political forces which exercises this pressure has been submitted to close analysis. But will the detection of this confederacy of vicious forces destroy or any wise abate their operative power? For this power is a natural outcome of an unsound theory in our foreign policy. Put into plain language, the theory is this, that any British subject choosing, for his own private pleasure or profit, to venture his person or his property in the territory of a foreign State can call upon this nation to protect or avenge him in case he or his property is injured either by the Government or by any inhabitant of this foreign State. Now this is a perilous doctrine: It places the entire military, political, and financial resources of this nation at the beck and call of any missionary society which considers it has a peculiar duty to attack the religious sentiments or observances of some savage people, or of some reckless explorer who chooses just those spots of earth known to be inhabited by hostile peoples ignorant of British power; the speculative trader or the mining prospector gravitates naturally towards dangerous and unexplored countries, where the gains of a successful venture will be quick and large. All these men, missionaries, travellers, sportsmen, scientists, traders, in no proper sense the accredited representatives of this country, but actuated by private personal motives, are at liberty to call upon the British nation to spend millions of money and thousands of lives to defend them against risks which the nation has not sanctioned. It is only right to add that unscrupulous statesmen have deliberately utilised these insidious methods of encroachment, seizing upon every alleged outrage inflicted on these private adventurers or marauders as a pretext for a punitive expedition which results in the British flag waving over some new tract of territory. Thus the most reckless and irresponsible individual members of our nation are permitted to direct our foreign policy. Now that we have some four hundred million British subjects, any one of whom in theory or in practice may call upon the British arms to extricate him from the results of his private folly, the prospects of a genuine pax Britannica are not particularly bright.

But those sporadic risks, grave though they have sometimes proved, are insignificant when compared with the dangers associated with modern methods of international capitalism and finance. It is not long since industry was virtually restricted by political boundaries, the economic intercourse of nations being almost wholly confined to commercial exchanges of goods. The recent habit of investing capital in a foreign country has now grown to such an extent that the well-to-do and politically powerful classes in Great Britain to-day derive a large and ever larger proportion of their incomes from capital invested outside the British Empire. This growing stake of our wealthy classes in countries over which they have no political control is a revolutionary force in modern politics; it means a constantly growing tendency to use their political power as citizens of this State to interfere with the political condition of those States where they have an industrial stake.

The essentially illicit nature of this use of the public resources of the nation to safeguard and improve private investments should be clearly recognised. If I put my savings in a home investment, I take into consideration all the chances and changes to which the business is liable, including the possibilities of political changes of tariff, taxation, or industrial legislation which may affect its profits. In the case of such investment, I am quite aware that I have no right to call upon the public to protect me from loss or depreciation of my capital due to any of these causes. The political conditions of my country are taken into calculation at the time of my investment. If I invest in consols, I fully recognise that no right of political interference with foreign policy affecting my investment is accorded to me in virtue of my interest as a fund-holder. But, if I invest either in the public funds or in some private industrial venture in a foreign country for the benefit of my private purse, getting specially favourable terms to cover risks arising from the political insecurity of the country or the deficiencies of its Government, I am entitled to call upon my Government to use its political and military force to secure me against those very risks which I have already discounted in the terms of my investment. Can anything be more palpably unfair?

It may be said that no such claim of the individual investor upon State aid is admitted. But while the theory may not have been openly avowed, recent history shows a growth of consistent practice based upon its tacit acceptance. I need not retrace the clear chain of evidence, consisting chiefly of the admissions of the mining capitalists, by which this claim to use public resources for their private profit has been enforced by the financiers who seduced our Government and people into our latest and most costly exploit. This is but the clearest and most dramatic instance of the operation of the world-wide forces of international finance: These forces are commonly described as capitalistic, but the gravest danger arises not from genuine industrial investments in foreign lands, but from the handling of stocks and shares based upon these investments by financiers. Those who own a genuine stake in the natural resources or the industry of a foreign land have at least some substantial interest in the peace and good government of that land; but the stock speculator has no such stake: his interest lies in the oscillations of paper values, which require fluctuation and insecurity of political conditions as their instrument.

As these forms of international investment and finance are wider spread and better organised for economic and political purposes, these demands for political and military interference with foreign countries, on the ground of protecting the property of British subjects, will be more frequent and more effective; the demands of investors will commonly be backed by personal grievances of British outlanders, and we shall be drawn into a series of interferences with foreign Governments, which, if we can conduct them successfully, will lead to annexation of territory as the only security for the lives and property of our subjects.

That this policy marks a straight road to ruin there can be no doubt. But how to stop it. What principle of safety can we lay down? Only one an absolute repudiation of the right of British subjects to call upon their Government to protect their persons or property from injuries or dangers incurred on their private initiative. This principle is just and expedient. If we send an emissary on a public mission into a foreign country, let us support and protect him by our public purse and arms; if a private person, or a company of private persons, place their lives or property in a foreign land, seeking their own ends, let them clearly understand that they do so at their own risk, and that the State will not act for their protection.

If so complete a reversal of our consistent policy be regarded as a counsel of perfection involving a definite abandonment of domiciliary, trading, and other rights secured by existing treaties or conventions with foreign States, upon the observance of which we are entitled to insist, let us at any rate lay down two plain rules of policy. First, never to sanction any interference on the part of our foreign representatives on general grounds of foreign misgovernment outside the strict limits of our treaty rights, submitting interpretation of such treaty rights to arbitration. Secondly, if in any case armed force is applied to secure the observance of these treaty rights, to confine such force to the attainment of the specific object which justifies its use.

[*See also:* EMPIRE; IMPERIALISM; INTERNATIONAL TRADE.]

SOURCE

Hobson, John A. *Imperialism: A Study.* New York: James Pott and Co., 1902.

RELIGION, PHILOSOPHY, AND SCIENCE

From what source do human actions draw their authority? How are we to understand the origins of life? On what basis can humans commit themselves to belief, and from there to action? How do we know right from wrong? These and other fundamental questions were debated openly and avidly in the Victorian era. In an era in which the once-unchallenged source of authority, the Church of England, came increasingly to be seen as a fallible tool of earthly interests, theologians, philosophers, scientists, and other thinkers stepped forth to offer new ways to understand the most basic of human questions.

The source of primary religious authority in Great Britain, the Church of England, came under attack from a variety of directions—from Dissenters, Evangelicals, Catholics, atheists, agnostics, and so forth. Perhaps the most damaging attacks came from within, from Anglicans who began to question whether the Church of England was an appropriate home for true believers. Many such churchmen, known as Tractarians, or members of the Oxford Movement, eventually converted to Roman Catholicism. But more fundamental challenges came from those who began openly to doubt whether religious faith even offered access to truth.

Armed with new evidence, scientists from a variety of fields—including geology, anthropology, astronomy, physics—also proposed theories to explain fundamental questions about the nature of life on earth. No theory was more revolutionary or controversial than the theory of natural selection proposed by Charles Darwin in his *On the Origin of Species* (1859). As he predicted, it utterly reshaped the study of the development of life on earth and, in the process, helped unseat the Biblical story of creation as the dominant explanation.

The documents that follow are excerpted from some of the most famous and controversial writings of the period: John Henry Newman's 1833 tract "The Catholic Church"; Thomas Henry Huxley's 1889 essay "Agnosticism and Christianity"; Charles Darwin's *On the Origin of the Species* (1859); and John Stuart Mill's *Utilitarianism* (1861).

CHALLENGING THE ESTABLISHED CHURCH

Beginning in the 1830s a number of members of the Church of England sought to renew in the church the sense of reverence, history, and authority that they felt had been challenged by the increasing religious tolerance and pluralism of the late eighteenth and earlier nineteenth century. These churchmen, centered at Oxford University, feared that the church was becoming a tool of secular, political interests. Beginning in 1833 they began to issue a series of religious tracts calling for reforms in the church, thus earning for themselves the nickname "Tractarians." The following tract, written by Tractarian leader John Henry Newman (1801-1890), calls on followers to serve the interests of the church before those of the state. Newman eventually converted to Roman Catholicism in 1845 and was made a cardinal in 1879.

"THE CATHOLIC CHURCH."

THE CATHOLIC CHURCH

No weapon that is formed against thee shall prosper, and every tongue that shall rise against thee in judgment THOU SHALT CONDEMN.

It is sometimes said, that the Clergy should abstain from politics; and that, if a Minister of CHRIST is political, he is not a follower of him who said, "My kingdom is not of this world." Now there is a sense in which this is true, but, as it is commonly taken, it is very false.

It is true that the mere affairs of this world should not engage a Clergyman; but it is absurd to say that the affairs of this world should not at all engage his attention. If so, this world is not a preparation for another. Are we to speak when individuals sin, and not when a nation, which is but a collection of individuals? Must we speak to the poor, but not to the rich and powerful? In vain does St. James warn us against having the faith of our LORD JESUS CHRIST with respect of persons. In vain does the Prophet declare to us the word of the LORD, that if the watchmen of Israel "speak not to warn the wicked from his way," "his blood will be required at the watchman's hand."

Complete our LORD's declaration concerning the nature of His kingdom, and you will see it is not at all inconsistent with the duty of our active and zealous interference in matters of this world. "If My kingdom were of this world," He says, *"then would My servants fight."*—Here He has vouchsafed so to explain Himself, that there is no room for misunderstanding His meaning. No one contends that His ministers ought to use the weapons of a carnal warfare; but surely to protest, to warn, to threaten, to excommunicate, are not such weapons. Let us not be scared from a plain duty, by the mere force of a misapplied text. There is an unexceptionable sense in which a clergyman may, nay, must be *political*. And above all, when the Nation interferes with the rights and possessions of the Church, it can with even less grace complain of the Church interfering with the Nation.

With this introduction let me call your attention to what seems a most dangerous infringement on our rights, on the part of the State. The Legislature has lately taken upon itself to remodel the dioceses of Ireland; a proceeding which involves the appointment of certain Bishops over certain Clergy, and of certain clergy under certain Bishops, without the Church being consulted in the matter. I do not say whether or not harm will follow from this particular act with reference to Ireland; but consider whether it be not in itself an interference with things spiritual.

Are we content to be accounted the mere creation of the State, as schoolmasters and teachers may be, or soldiers, or magistrates, or other public officers? Did the State make us? can it unmake us? can it send out missionaries? can it arrange dioceses? Surely all these are spiritual functions; and Laymen may as well set about preaching, and consecrating the LORD's Supper, as assume these. I do not say the guilt is equal; but that, if the latter is guilt, the former is. Would St. Paul, with his good will, have suffered the Roman power to appoint Timothy, Bishop of Miletus, as well as of Ephesus? Would Timothy at such a bidding have undertaken the charge? Is not the notion of such an order, such an obedience, absurd? Yet has it not been realized in what has lately happened? For in what is the English state at present different from the Roman formerly? Neither can be accounted members of the Church of CHRIST. No one can say the British Legislature is in our communion, or that its members are necessarily even Christians. What pretence then has it for not merely advising, but superseding the Ecclesiastical power?

Bear with me, which I express my fear, that we do not, as much as we ought, consider the force of that article of our Belief, "The One Catholic and Apostolic Church." This is a tenet so important as to have been in the Creed from the beginning. It is mentioned there as a *fact*, and a fact *to be believed*, and therefore practical. Now what do we conceive is meant by it? As people vaguely take it in the present day, it seems only an assertion that there is a number of sincere Christians scattered through the world. But is not this a truism? who doubts it? who can deny that there are people in various places who are sincere believers? what comes of this? how is it important? why should it be placed as an article of faith, after the belief in the HOLY GHOST? Doubtless the only true and satisfactory meaning is that which our Divines have ever taken, that there is on earth an existing Society, Apostolic as founded by the Apostles, Catholic because it spreads its branches in every place; i.e. the Church Visible with its Bishops, Priests, and Deacons. And this surely *is* a most important doctrine; for what can be better news to the bulk of mankind than to be told that CHRIST when He ascended, did not leave us orphans, but appointed representatives of Himself to the end of time?

"The necessity of believing the Holy Catholic Church," says Bishop Pearson in this Exposition of the Creed, "appeareth first in this, that CHRIST hath appointed it as the only way to eternal life . . . . CHRIST never appointed two ways to heaven, nor did He build a Church to save some, and make another institution for other men's salvation. There is none other name under heaven given among men whereby we must be saved, but the name of JESUS; and that name is no otherwise given under heaven than in the Church." "This is the congregation of those persons here on earth which shall hereafter meet in heaven . . . . There is a necessity of believing the Catholic Church, because except a man be of that he can be of none. Whatsoever Church pretendeth to a new beginning, pretendeth at the same time to a new Churchdom, and whatsoever is so new is none." This indeed is the unanimous opinion of our divines, that, as the Sacraments, so Communion with the Church, is "generally necessary to salvation," in the case of those who can obtain it.

If then we express our belief in the existence of One Church on earth from CHRIST's coming to the end of all things, if there is a promise it shall continue, and if it is our duty to do our part in our generation towards it continuance, how can we with a safe conscience countenance the interference of the Nation in its concerns? Does not such interference tend to destroy it? Would it not destroy it, if consistently followed up? Now, may we sit still and keep silence, when efforts are making to break up, or at least materially to weaken that Ecclesiastical Body which we know is intended to last while the world endures, and the safely of which is committed to our keeping in our day? How shall we answer for it, if we transmit that Ordinance of GOD less entire than it came to us?

Now what am I calling on you to do? You cannot help what has been done in Ireland; but you may protest against it. You may as a duty protest against it in public and private; you may keep a jealous watch on the proceedings of the Nation, lest a second act of the same kind be attempted. You may keep it before you as a desirable object that the Irish Church should at some future day meet in Synod and protest herself against what has been done; and then proceed to establish or rescind the State injunction, as may be thought expedient.

I know it is too much the fashion of the times to think any earnestness for ecclesiastical rights unseasonable and absurd, as if it were the feeling of those who live among books and not in the world. But it is our *duty* to live among books, especially to live by ONE BOOK, and a very old one; and therein we are enjoined to "keep that good thing which is committed unto us," to "neglect not our gift." And when men talk, as they sometime do, as if in opposing them we were standing on technical difficulties instead of welcoming great and extensive benefits which would be the result of their measures, I would ask them, (letting alone the question of their beneficial nature, which *is* a question,) whether this is not being wise above that is written, whether it is not doing evil that good may come. We cannot know the effects which will follow certain alterations; but we can decide that the means by which it is proposed to attain them are unprecedented and disrespectful to the Church. And when men say, *"the day is past* for stickling about ecclesiastical rights," let them see to it, lest they use substantially the same arguments to maintain their position as those who say, "The day is past for being a Christian."

Lastly, is it not plain that by showing a bold front and defending the rights of the Church, we are taking the only course which can make us respected? Yielding will not persuade our enemies to desist from their efforts to destroy us root and branch. We cannot hope by giving something to keep the rest. Of this surely we have had of late years sufficient experience. But by resisting strenuously, and contemplating and providing against the worst, we may actually prevent the very evils we fear. To prepare for persecution may be the best way to avert it.

[*See also:* CHURCH OF ENGLAND; NEWMAN, JOHN HENRY; TRACTARIANISM.]

SOURCE

Newman, John Henry. "The Catholic Church." In *Tracts for the Times* (September 9, 1933); *Tracts for the Times*. Vol. 1. London: Rivington and Parker, 1840.

DARING TO DISBELIEVE

Thomas Henry Huxley was simply one of the most controversial figures of his era. A scientist, educator, and reformer, Huxley was an avid promoter of Charles Darwin's theories of evolution—so much so that he earned the nickname "Darwin's Bulldog." Huxley publicly applied Darwin's theories to the descent of man well before Darwin dared to, and he set himself in opposition to religious claims to knowledge. In order to clarify the nature of his objections to religious reasoning, Huxley coined the term "agnosticism." In the excerpts from his famous 1889 essay "Agnosticism and Christianity," Huxley spells out the differences between the way agnostics and Christians claim to know truth.

EXCERPT FROM "AGNOSTICISM AND CHRISTIANITY."

[. . .] The present discussion has arisen out of the use, which has become general in the last few years, of the terms "Agnostic" and "Agnosticism."

The people who call themselves "Agnostics" have been charged with doing so because they have not the courage to declare themselves "Infidels." It has been insinuated that they have adopted a new name in order to escape the unpleasantness which attaches to their proper denomination. To this wholly erroneous imputation, I have replied by showing that the term "Agnostic" did, as a matter of fact, arise in a manner which negatives it; and my statement has not been, and cannot be, refuted. Moreover, speaking for myself, and without impugning the right of any other person to use the term in another sense, I further say that Agnosticism is not properly described as a "negative" creed, nor indeed as a creed of any kind, except in so far as it expresses absolute faith in the validity of a principle, which is as much ethical as intellectual. This principle may be stated in various ways, but they all amount to this: that it is wrong for a man to say that he is certain of the objective truth of any proposition unless he can produce evidence which logically justifies that certainty. This is what Agnosticism asserts; and, in my opinion, it is all that is essential to Agnosticism. That which Agnostics deny and repudiate, as immoral, is the contrary doctrine, that there are propositions which men ought to believe, without logically satisfactory evidence; and that reprobation ought to attach to the profession of disbelief in such inadequately supported propositions. The justification of the Agnostic principle lies in the success which follows upon its application, whether in the field of natural, or in that of civil, history; and in the fact that, so far as these topics are concerned, no sane man thinks of denying its validity.

Still speaking for myself, I add, that though Agnosticism is not, and cannot be, a creed, except in so far as its general principle is concerned; yet that the application of that principle results in the denial of, or the suspension of judgment concerning, a number of propositions respecting which our contemporary ecclesiastical "gnostics" profess entire certainty. And, in so far as these ecclesiastical persons can be justified in their old-established custom (which many nowadays think more honoured in the breach than the observance) of using opprobrious names to those who differ from them, I fully admit their right to call me and those who think with me "Infidels"; all I have ventured to urge is that they must not expect us to speak of ourselves by that title.

The extent of the region of the uncertain, the number of the problems the investigation of which ends in a verdict of not proven, will vary according to the knowledge and the intellectual habits of the individual Agnostic. I do not very much care to speak of anything as "unknowable."[1] What I am sure about is that there are many topics about which I know nothing; and which, so far as I can see, are out of reach of my faculties. But whether these things are knowable by any one else is exactly one of those matters which is beyond my knowledge, though I may have a tolerably strong opinion as to the probabilities of the case. Relatively to myself, I am quite sure that the region of uncertainty—the nebulous country in which words play the part of realities—is far more extensive than I could wish. Materialism and Idealism; Theism and Atheism; the doctrine of the soul and its mortality or immortality—appear in the history of philosophy like the shades of Scandinavian heroes, eternally slaying one another and eternally coming to life again in a metaphysical "Nifelheim." It is getting on for twenty-five centuries, at least, since mankind began seriously to give their minds to these topics. Generation after generation, philosophy has been doomed to roll the stone uphill; and, just as all the world swore it was at the top, down it has rolled to the bottom again. All this is written in innumerable books; and he who will toil through them will discover that the stone is just where it was when the work began. Hume saw this; Kant saw it; since their time, more and more eyes have been cleansed of the films which prevented them from seeing it; until now the weight and number of those who refuse to be the prey of verbal mystifications has begun to tell in practical life.

It was inevitable that a conflict should arise between Agnosticism and Theology; or rather, I ought to say, between Agnosticism and Ecclesiasticism. For Theology, the science, is one thing; and Ecclesiasticism, the championship of a foregone conclusion[2] as to the truth of a particular form of Theology, is another. With scientific Theology, Agnosticism has no quarrel.

[. . .]

But, as between Agnosticism and Ecclesiasticism, or, as our neighbours across the Channel call it, Clericalism, there can be neither peace nor truce. The Cleric asserts that it is morally wrong not to believe certain propositions, whatever the results of a strict scientific investigation of the evidence of these propositions. He tells us "that religious error is, in itself, of an immoral nature."[3] He declares that he has prejudged certain conclusions, and looks upon those who show cause for arrest of judgment as emissaries of Satan. It necessarily follows that, for him, the attainment of faith, not the ascertainment of truth, is the highest aim of mental life. And, on careful analysis of the nature of this faith, it will too often be found to be, not the mystic process of unity with the Divine, understood by the religious enthusiast; but that which the candid simplicity of a Sunday scholar once defined it to be. "Faith," said this unconscious plagiarist of Tertullian, "is the power of saying you believe things which are incredible."

Now I, and many other Agnostics, believe that faith, in this sense, is an abomination; and though we do not indulge in the luxury of self-righteousness so far as to call those who are not of our way of thinking hard names, we do feel that the disagreement between ourselves and those who hold this doctrine is even more moral than intellectual. It is desirable there should be an end of any mistakes on this topic. If our clerical opponents were clearly aware of the real state of the case, there would be an end of the curious delusion, which often appears between the lines of their writings, that those whom they are so fond of calling "Infidels" are people who not only ought to be, but in their hearts are, ashamed of themselves. It would be discourteous to do more than hint the antipodal opposition of this pleasant dream of theirs to facts.

The clerics and their lay allies commonly tell us, that if we refuse to admit that there is good ground for expressing definite convictions about certain topics, the bonds of human society will dissolve and mankind lapse into savagery. There are several answers to this assertion. One is that the bonds of human society were formed without the aid of their theology; and, in the opinion of not a few competent judges, have been weakened rather than strengthened by a good deal of it. Greek science, Greek art, the ethics of old Israel, the social organisation of old

Rome, contrived to come into being, without the help of any one who believed in a single distinctive article of the simplest of the Christian creeds. The science, the art, the jurisprudence, the chief political and social theories, of the modern world have grown out of those of Greece and Rome—not by favour of, but in the teeth of, the fundamental teachings of early Christianity, to which science, art, and any serious occupation with the things of this world, were alike despicable.

[. . .]

I trust that I have now made amends for any ambiguity, or want of fulness, in my previous exposition of that which I hold to be the essence of the Agnostic doctrine. Henceforward, I might hope to hear no more of the assertion that we are necessarily Materialists, Idealists, Atheists, Theists, or any other *ists,* if experience had led me to think that the proved falsity of a statement was any guarantee against its repetition. And those who appreciate the nature of our position will see, at once, that when Ecclesiasticism declares that we ought to believe this, that, and the other, and are very wicked if we don't, it is impossible for us to give any answer but this: We have not the slightest objection to believe anything you like, if you will give us good grounds for belief; but, if you cannot, we must respectfully refuse, even if that refusal should wreck morality and insure our own damnation several times over. We are quite content to leave that to the decision of the future. The course of the past has impressed us with the firm conviction that no good ever comes of falsehood, and we feel warranted in refusing even to experiment in that direction.

[. . .]

[*See also:* AGNOSTICISM, ATHEISM, AND FREE THOUGHT; EVOLUTION; HUXLEY, THOMAS HENRY.]

[1] 'I confess that, long ago, I once or twice made this mistake; even to the waste of a capital 'U.' 1893.

[2] "Let us maintain, before we have proved. This seeming paradox is the secret of happiness" (Dr. Newman: Tract 85, p. 85).

[3] Dr. Newman, Essay on Development, p. 357.

SOURCE

Huxley, Thomas Henry. "Agnosticism and Christianity." In *Christianity and Agnosticism: A Controversy.* New York: D. Appleton, 1889. Collected in *Collected Essays.* 9 vols. New York: Greenwood Press, 1968.

EVOLUTION

Evolution, it is safe to say, was the most challenging and transformative idea of the nineteenth century. Emerging out of the combined work of a variety of geologists, historians, botanists, and philosophers, and

given its first full expression in Charles Darwin's 1859 On the Origin of Species by Means of Natural Selection, or the Preservation of Favoured Races in the Struggle for Life, *the explanation that life of earth came to take its present forms through a lengthy process of natural selection and evolution utterly transformed scientific discourse. More than this, it challenged people from all walks of life to examine the most fundamental elements of their thinking and thus took part in the larger reexamination of ideas that characterized the era. The excerpts from the concluding chapter of* On the Origin of Species *give some idea of the revolutionary quality of Darwin's thinking.*

EXCERPT FROM *ON THE ORIGIN OF SPECIES.*

CHAPTER XIV.
RECAPITULATION AND CONCLUSION

[. . .]

As this whole volume is one long argument, it may be convenient to the reader to have the leading facts and inferences briefly recapitulated.

That many and grave objections may be advanced against the theory of descent with modification through natural selection, I do not deny. I have endeavoured to give to them their full force. Nothing at first can appear more difficult to believe than that the more complex organs and instincts should have been perfected not by means superior to, though analogous with, human reason, but by the accumulation of innumerable slight variations, each good for the individual possessor. Nevertheless, this difficulty, though appearing to our imagination insuperably great, cannot be considered real if we admit the following propositions, namely,—that gradations in the perfection of any organ or instinct, which we may consider, either do now exist or could have existed, each good of its kind,—that all organs and instincts are, in ever so slight a degree, variable,—and, lastly, that there is a struggle for existence leading to the preservation of each profitable deviation of structure or instinct. The truth of these propositions cannot, I think, be disputed.

[Darwin refutes some of the most important objections to his theories, then offers a summation of his thinking on the process of natural selection, drawing on the most compelling of the examples offered in the body of his work, before moving on to his conclusion.]

[. . .]

I have now recapitulated the chief facts and considerations which have thoroughly convinced me that species have changed, and are still slowly changing by the preservation and accumulation of successive slight favourable variations. Why, it may be asked, have all the most eminent living naturalists and geologists rejected this view of the mutability of species? It cannot be asserted that organic beings in a state of nature are subject to no variation; it cannot be proved that the amount of variation in the course of long ages is a limited quantity; no clear distinction has been, or can be, drawn between species and well-marked varieties. It cannot be maintained that species when intercrossed are invariably sterile, and varieties invariably fertile; or that sterility is a special endowment and sign of creation. The belief that species were immutable productions was almost unavoidable as long as the history of the world was thought to be of short duration; and now that we have acquired some idea of the lapse of time, we are too apt to assume, without proof, that the geological record is so perfect that it would have afforded us plain evidence of the mutation of species, if they had undergone mutation.

But the chief cause of our natural unwillingness to admit that one species has given birth to other and distinct species, is that we are always slow in admitting any great change of which we do not see the intermediate steps. The difficulty is the same as that felt by so many geologists, when Lyell first insisted that long lines of inland cliffs had been formed, and great valleys excavated, by the slow action of the coast-waves. The mind cannot possibly grasp the full meaning of the term of a hundred million years; it cannot add up and perceive the full effects of many slight variations, accumulated during an almost infinite number of generations.

Although I am fully convinced of the truth of the views given in this volume under the form of an abstract, I by no means expect to convince experienced naturalists whose minds are stocked with a multitude of facts all viewed, during a long course of years, from a point of view directly opposite to mine. It is so easy to hide our ignorance under such expressions as the "plan of creation," "unity of design," &c., and to think that we give an explanation when we only restate a fact. Any one whose disposition leads him to attach more weight to unexplained difficulties than to the explanation of a certain number of facts will certainly reject my theory. A few naturalists, endowed with much flexibility of mind, and who have already begun to doubt on the immutability of species, may be influenced by this volume; but I look

with confidence to the future, to young and rising naturalists, who will be able to view both sides of the question with impartiality. Whoever is led to believe that species are mutable will do good service by conscientiously expressing his conviction; for only thus can the load of prejudice by which this subject is overwhelmed be removed.

[. . .]

It may be asked how far I extend the doctrine of the modification of species. The question is difficult to answer, because the more distinct the forms are which we may consider, by so much the arguments fall away in force. But some arguments of the greatest weight extend very far. All the members of whole classes can be connected together by chains of affinities, and all can be classified on the same principle, in groups subordinate to groups. Fossil remains sometimes tend to fill up very wide intervals between existing orders. Organs in a rudimentary condition plainly show that an early progenitor had the organ in a fully developed state; and this in some instances necessarily implies an enormous amount of modification in the descendants. Throughout whole classes various structures are formed on the same pattern, and at an embryonic age the species closely resemble each other. Therefore I cannot doubt that the theory of descent with modification embraces all the members of the same class. I believe that animals have descended from at most only four or five progenitors, and plants from an equal or lesser number.

Analogy would lead me one step further, namely, to the belief that all animals and plants have descended from some one prototype. But analogy may be a deceitful guide. Nevertheless all living things have much in common, in their chemical composition, their germinal vesicles, their cellular structure, and their laws of growth and reproduction. We see this even in so trifling a circumstance as that the same poison often similarly affects plants and animals; or that the poison secreted by the gall-fly produces monstrous growths on the wild rose or oak-tree. Therefore I should infer from analogy that probably all the organic beings which have ever lived on this earth have descended from some one primordial form, into which life was first breathed.

[. . .]

Authors of the highest eminence seem to be fully satisfied with the view that each species has been independently created. To my mind it accords better with what we know of the laws impressed on matter by the Creator, that the production and extinction of the past and present inhabitants of the world should have been due to secondary causes, like those determining the birth and death of the individual. When I view all beings not as special creations, but as the lineal descendants of some few beings which lived long before the first bed of the Silurian system was deposited, they seem to me to become ennobled. Judging from the past, we may safely infer that not one living species will transmit its unaltered likeness to a distant futurity. And of the species now living very few will transmit progeny of any kind to a far distant futurity; for the manner in which all organic beings are grouped, shows that the greater number of species of each genus, and all the species of many genera, have left no descendants, but have become utterly extinct. We can so far take a prophetic glance into futurity as to foretel that it will be the common and widely-spread species, belonging to the larger and dominant groups, which will ultimately prevail and procreate new and dominant species. As all the living forms of life are the lineal descendants of those which lived long before the Silurian epoch, we may feel certain that the ordinary succession by generation has never once been broken, and that no cataclysm has desolated the whole world. Hence we may look with some confidence to a secure future of equally inappreciable length. And as natural selection works solely by and for the good of each being, all corporeal and mental endowments will tend to progress towards perfection.

It is interesting to contemplate an entangled bank, clothed with many plants of many kinds, with birds singing on the bushes, with various insects flitting about, and with worms crawling through the damp earth, and to reflect that these elaborately constructed forms, so different from each other, and dependent on each other in so complex a manner, have all been produced by laws acting around us. These laws, taken in the largest sense, being Growth with Reproduction; Inheritance which is almost implied by Reproduction; Variability from the indirect and direct action of the external conditions of life, and from use and disuse; a Ratio of Increase so high as to lead to a Struggle for Life, and as a consequence to Natural Selection, entailing Divergence of Character and the Extinction of less-improved forms. Thus, from the war of nature, from famine and death, the most exalted object which we are capable of conceiving, namely, the production of the higher animals, directly follows. There is grandeur in this view of life, with its several powers, having been originally breathed into a few forms or into one; and that, whilst this planet has gone cycling on according to the fixed law of gravity, from so simple a beginning endless forms most beautiful and most wonderful have been, and are being, evolved.

[*See also:* DARWIN, CHARLES; EVOLUTION.]

SOURCE

Darwin, Charles. *On the Origin of Species by Means of Natural Selection, or the Preservation of Favoured Races in the Struggle for Life.* London: J. Murray, 1859. Reprint, with an introduction by Ernst Mayr, Cambridge, Mass.: Harvard University Press, 1964.

THE GREATEST HAPPINESS . . .

If there was a philosophy behind the reforms in government and civil service that characterized the Victorian era, that philosophy was Utilitarianism. First championed by English philosopher Jeremy Bentham (1748–1832), and later taken up most notably by James Mill (1773–1836) and his son, John Stuart Mill (1806–1873), Utilitarianism provided a form of rational calculus by which reformers could determine how best to make improvements in such areas as voting rights, sanitation, the courts and prisons, and myriad other areas. The following excerpt from John Stuart Mill's essay Utilitarianism *(1861) outlines some of the major concepts of the philosophy.*

EXCERPT FROM *UTILITARIANISM.*

GENERAL REMARKS

[. . .] On the present occasion, I shall [. . .] attempt to contribute something towards the understanding and appreciation of the "utilitarian" or "happiness" theory, and towards such proof as it is susceptible of. It is evident that this cannot be proof in the ordinary and popular meaning of the term. Questions of ultimate ends are not amenable to direct proof. Whatever can be proved to be good must be so by being shown to be a means to something admitted to be good without proof. The medical art is proved to be good by its conducing to health; but how is it possible to prove that health is good? The art of music is good, for the reason, among others, that it produces pleasure; but what proof is it possible to give that pleasure is good? If, then, it is asserted that there is a comprehensive formula, including all things which are in themselves good, and that whatever else is good, is not so as an end but as a means, the formula may be accepted or rejected, but is not a subject of what is commonly understood by proof. We are not, however, to infer that its acceptance or rejection must depend on blind impulse or arbitrary choice. There is a larger meaning of the word "proof," in which this question is as amenable to it as any other of the disputed questions of philosophy. The subject is within the cognizance of the rational faculty; and neither does that faculty deal with it solely in the way of intuition. Considerations may be presented capable of determining the intellect either to give or withhold its assent to the doctrine; and this is equivalent to proof.

We shall examine presently of what nature are these considerations; in what manner they apply to the case, and what rational grounds, therefore, can be given for accepting or rejecting the utilitarian formula. But it is a preliminary condition of rational acceptance or rejection, that the formula should be correctly understood. I believe that the very imperfect notion ordinarily formed of its meaning is the chief obstacle which impedes its reception; and that, could it be cleared even from only the grosser misconceptions, the question would be greatly simplified and a large proportion of its difficulties removed. Before, therefore, I attempt to enter into the philosophical grounds which can be given for assenting to the utilitarian standard, I shall offer some illustrations of the doctrine itself; with the view of showing more clearly what it is, distinguishing it from what it is not, and disposing of such of the practical objections to it as either originate in, or are closely connected with, mistaken interpretations of its meaning. Having thus prepared the ground, I shall afterwards endeavor to throw such light as I can upon the question considered as one of philosophical theory.

[. . .]

WHAT UTILITARIANISM IS

[. . .]

The creed which accepts as the foundation of morals "utility" or the "greatest happiness principle" holds that actions are right in proportion as they tend to promote happiness; wrong as they tend to produce the reverse of happiness. By happiness is intended pleasure and the absence of pain; by unhappiness, pain and the privation of pleasure. To give a clear view of the moral standard set up by the theory, much more requires to be said; in particular, what things it includes in the ideas of pain and pleasure, and to what extent this is left an open question. But these supplementary explanations do not affect the theory of life on which this theory of morality is grounded—namely, that pleasure and freedom from pain are the only things desirable as ends; and that all desirable things (which are as numerous in the utilitarian as in any other scheme) are desirable either for the plea-

sure inherent in themselves or as means to the promotion of pleasure and the prevention of pain.

Now, such a theory of life excites in many minds, and among them in some of the most estimable in feeling and purpose, inveterate dislike. To suppose that life has (as they express it) no higher end than pleasure—no better and nobler object of desire and pursuit—they designate as utterly mean and groveling, as a doctrine worthy only of swine, to whom the followers of Epicurus were, at a very early period, contemptuously likened; and modern holders of the doctrine are occasionally made the subject of equally polite comparisons by its German, French, and English assailants.

When thus attacked, the Epicureans have always answered that it is not they, but their accusers, who represent human nature in a degrading light, since the accusation supposes human beings to be capable of no pleasures except those of which swine are capable. If this supposition were true, the charge could not be gainsaid, but would then be no longer an imputation; for if the sources of pleasure were precisely the same to human beings and to swine, the rule of life which is good enough for the one would be good enough for the other. The comparison of the Epicurean life to that of beasts is felt as degrading, precisely because a beast's pleasures do not satisfy a human being's conceptions of happiness. Human beings have faculties more elevated than the animal appetites and, when once made conscious of them, do not regard anything as happiness which does not include their gratification. I do not, indeed, consider the Epicureans to have been by any means faultless in drawing out their scheme of consequences from the utilitarian principle. To do this in any sufficient manner, many Stoic, as well as Christian, elements require to be included. But there is no known Epicurean theory of life which does not assign to the pleasures of the intellect, of the feelings and imagination, and of the moral sentiments a much higher value as pleasures than to those of mere sensation. It must be admitted, however, that utilitarian writers in general have placed the superiority of mental over bodily pleasures chiefly in the greater permanency, safety, uncostliness, etc., of the former—that is, in their circumstantial advantages rather than in their intrinsic nature. And on all these points utilitarians have fully proved their case; but they might have taken the other and, as it may be called, higher ground with entire consistency. It is quite compatible with the principle of utility to recognize the fact that some kinds of pleasure are more desirable and more valuable than others. It would be absurd that while, in estimating all other things quality is considered as well as quantity, the estimation of pleasures should be supposed to depend on quantity alone.

[. . .]

I must again repeat what the assailants of utilitarianism seldom have the justice to acknowledge, that the happiness which forms the utilitarian standard of what is right in conduct is not the agent's own happiness but that of all concerned. As between his own happiness and that of others, utilitarianism requires him to be as strictly impartial as a disinterested and benevolent spectator. In the golden rule of Jesus of Nazareth, we read the complete spirit of the ethics of utility. "To do as you would be done by," and "to love your neighbor as yourself," constitute the ideal perfection of utilitarian morality. As the means of making the nearest approach to this ideal, utility would enjoin, first, that laws and social arrangements should place the happiness or (as speaking practically, it may be called) the interest of every individual as nearly as possible in harmony with the interest of the whole; and secondly, that education and opinion, which have so vast a power over human character, should so use that power as to establish in the mind of every individual an indissoluble association between his own happiness and the good of the whole, especially between his own happiness and the practice of such modes of conduct, negative and positive, as regard for the universal happiness prescribes; so that not only he may be unable to conceive the possibility of happiness to himself, consistently with conduct opposed to the general good, but also that a direct impulse to promote the general good may be in every individual one of the habitual motives of action, and the sentiments connected therewith may fill a large and prominent place in every human being's sentient existence. If the impugners of the utilitarian morality represented it to their own minds in this its true character, I know not what recommendation possessed by any other morality they could possibly affirm to be wanting to it; what more beautiful or more exalted developments of human nature any other ethical system can be supposed to foster, or what springs of action, not accessible to the utilitarian, such systems rely on for giving effect to their mandates.

[*See also:* BENTHAM, JEREMY; MILL, JOHN STUART; PHILOSOPHY; UTILITARIANISM.]

SOURCE

Mill, John Stuart. "Utilitarianism." *Fraser's Magazine* (October–December, 1861). As *Utilitarianism*. London: Parker and Brown, 1863. Reprint, *Utilitarianism and Other Essays,* edited by Alan Ryan. Harmondsworth, England, and New York: Penguin, 1987.

Appendix III
Selected Web Resources

WORLD WIDE WEB RESOURCES

The following list of Web sites may be of particular interest to students and readers interested in learning more about the Victorian era. This is by no means a comprehensive list of Web sites dedicated to the time period; one can easily find additional sites dedicated to specific events or authors, for instance. The sites detailed below are some of the most comprehensive and thoroughly researched sites the editors have encountered during their work on this project. The sites are maintained by universities or by scholars who have created sites of particular quality.

Halsall, Paul. *Internet Modern History Sourcebook.*
http://www.fordham.edu/halsall/mod/ modsbook.html

A compilation of historical texts and links to related sites. A rich source for information about nineteenth-century British and Irish history, as well as detailed information about the Industrial Revolution.

Jackson, Lee. *Victorian London.*
http://www.victorianlondon.org

A Web site that includes a vast array of primary source material and information about the social history of Victorian London.

Landow, George P. *The Victorian Web.*
http://www.victorianweb.org

A comprehensive Web site funded by the National University of Singapore, offering essays on important people, events, and ideas related to the Victorian era, as well as excerpts from various primary sources. This is the key Web site for Victorian studies, with many links to other sources.

Leary, Patrick. *Victorian Research Web.*
http://www.indiana.edu/˜victoria/

A collection of resources for the scholarly researcher of nineteenth-century Britain, maintained by the manager of the VICTORIA discussion list.

Maginnis, Tara. "Victorian Fashion Links." *The Costumer's Manifesto.*
http://www.costumes.org/pages/victlinks.htm

A rich source of links to fashion and costume throughout the Victorian era.

The 19th Century London Stage: An Exploration.
http://ascc.artsci.washington.edu/drama-phd/ melodram.html

A site dedicated to the theatrical and social history of the nineteenth century, created by the departments of Theatre History and Dramatic Theory at the University of Washington, Seattle.

Willet, Perry, ed. *The Victorian Women Writers Project.*
http://www.indiana.edu/˜letrs/vwwp/

A collection of transcriptions of works—including anthologies, novels, political pamphlets, religious tracts, children's books, and volumes of poetry and verse drama—selected by an advisory board.

Synoptic Table of Contents

Biographies (cont.)

COMMERCE AND ECONOMICS

EDUCATION

POLITICS, DIPLOMACY, AND WAR

Visual Arts and Architecture (cont.)

Directory of Contributors

TIMOTHY ALBORN
Lehman College, City University of New York
Business and Corporate Structure; The Census; Empire; Gold Rushes; Gold Standard; Insurance; Railways

ELIZABETH ALDRICH
Dance Heritage Coalition, Washington, D.C.
Social Dance

ROBERT D. AGUIRRE
Wayne State University, Detroit, Michigan
Anthropology and Ethnology

ANNE ANDERSON
Southampton Institute, England
Art Criticism; Art Market and Collecting; Art Nouveau; Arts and Crafts Movement; Walter Besant; Decorative Arts and Design; Gothic Revival; Eliza Lynn Linton; William Morris

FIONA ANDERSON
Edinburgh College of Art, Scotland
Tailoring

NANCY FIX ANDERSON
Loyola University, New Orleans, Louisiana
Annie Besant

STEPHEN ARATA
University of Virginia, Charlottesville
Henry James

W. ALAN ARMSTRONG
University of Kent at Canterbury, England
Emigration and Immigration; Population; Tuberculosis

WALTER L. ARNSTEIN
University of Illinois at Urbana-Champaign
Monarchy; Royal Family

ZARENA ASLAMI
University of Chicago, Illinois
Afghan Wars

PETER BAILEY
University of Manitoba, Canada
Dan Leno; Marie Lloyd; Pleasure Gardens; Public Houses; Street Performers; Tea

WILLIAM BAKER
Northern Illinois University, DeKalb
Samuel Butler; Wilkie Collins; George Henry Lewes; Philosophy

COLIN BARR
National University of Ireland, Maynooth
Paul Cardinal Cullen; Irish Catholicism

BARBARA J. BLACK
Skidmore College, Saratoga Springs, New York
British Museum; Gentlemen's Clubs

ANDREAS BLÜHM
Van Gogh Museum, Amsterdam, The Netherlands
Lighting

SAMMANTHA BREMER
University of South Carolina, Columbia
Country Pastimes and Rituals

G. W. E. BRIGHTWELL
University of Glasgow, Scotland
Musical Institutions

JAMIE L. BRONSTEIN
New Mexico State University, Las Cruces
Anglo-American Relations; Chartism

ANTHONY BRUNDAGE
California State Polytechnic University, Pomona
Edwin Chadwick; New Poor Law; Regulatory State

LIAM CAMPLING
Seychelles Polytechnic, University of Manchester Twinning Program
Antislavery Movement; Industrialization; Middle East; Red Cross; The Underground

ANTOINE CAPET
University of Rouen, France
> Arthur Balfour; Joseph Chamberlain;
> Poverty and Pauperism

PETER CARR
Caribbean Historical and Genealogical Journal
> Thomas Cook

ELISABETH A. CAWTHON
University of Texas at Arlington
> Asylums; Isambard K. Brunel; Vaccination

COLIN CHANT
The Open University, Milton Keynes, United Kingdom
> Astronomy; Cabs and Omnibuses; Internal
> Combustion Engine; Iron and Steel
> Industry; Shipping; Transportation;
> Waterways and Canals

ALISON CHAPMAN
University of Glasgow, Scotland
> Julia Margaret Cameron; Italy; Mesmerism;
> Napoleon III; Spiritualism

JULIE F. CODELL
Arizona State University, Tempe
> Ford Madox Brown

SUZANNE FAGENCE COOPER
Victoria and Albert Museum, London, England
> Edward Burne-Jones

JAMES M. CORNELIUS
University of Illinois at Urbana-Champaign
> Robert Cecil; Edward Stanley; Henry John
> Temple

RICHARD A. COSGROVE
University of Arizona, Tucson
> Law and Legal Reform

CASEY A. COTHRAN
College of William and Mary, Williamsburg, Virginia
> Bread; Soap

JOHN COUTTS
The University of Greenwich, England
> Church of Scotland; William Lamb; Henry
> Wadsworth Longfellow; Coventry Kersey
> Dighton Patmore

MARY COWLING
University of London, England
> Aesthetic Movement; Charles Eastlake;
> Edwin Landseer; Frederic Leighton;
> Painting; Physiognomy and Phrenology;
> Pre-Raphaelite Brotherhood; Martin
> Tupper; G. F. Watts; James McNeill
> Whistler

TERRY CROWLEY
University of Guelph, Ontario, Canada
> Agriculture; Alexander Graham Bell;
> Chautauqua; Rural Laborers

CYNTHIA CURRAN
College of St.Benedict/St. John's University, St. Joseph, Minnesota
> Birth Control; Hair; Pets; Charles Trevelyan

NEIL DAVIE
Université Paris 7, France
> Criminology

RICHARD W. DAVIS
Washington University, St. Louis, Missouri
> Church and State; Benjamin Disraeli;
> Dissent; Parliamentary Government;
> Rothschild Family

CAROL MARGARET DAVISON
University of Windsor, Ontario, Canada
> Alcohol; Dogs; Gothic Novel

HAMID DEBBAH
Seychelles Polytechnic
> Middle East

JUILEE DECKER
Case Western Reserve University and Cleveland Museum of Art, Ohio
> Chocolate and Candy Industry; Historic
> Preservation

JEREMY DIBBLE
University of Durham, England
> Edward Elgar; George Grove; Musical
> Criticism; Musical Education; Musical
> Festivals; Oratorio and Choral Music;
> Charles Hubert Hastings Parry; John
> Stainer; Charles Stanford

STEVEN DILLON
Bates College, Lewiston, Maine
> Archaeology; Thomas Carlyle; Thomas
> Cooper; Literary Criticism; Karl Marx

ROBERT DINGLEY
University of New England, New South Wales, Australia
> Sporting Novel

MERRILL DISTAD
University of Alberta, Canada
> Automobile; Broad Church; Exploration; Frederick Denison Maurice; Pornography; Postal Services; Potatoes; Smith, W. H., Booksellers; Travel and Tourism; William Whewell

C. R. B. DUNLOP
University of Alberta, Canada
> Debtors

BRADFORD LEE EDEN
University Libraries, University of Nevada, Las Vegas
> Concert Life; Folklore; Folksong; Linguistics and Philology; Medievalism; The Music Profession; Musicology; Parlor Ballad; Piano and Piano Music; Royal Academy of Arts

CLIVE EMSLEY
The Open University, United Kingdom
> Crime and Punishment; Police

CAROL MARIE ENGELHARDT
Wright State University, Dayton, Ohio
> Anti-Catholicism; Charles Bradlaugh; Edward Bouverie Pusey

GLENN EVERETT
Stonehill College, Easton, Massachusetts
> Agnosticism, Atheism, and Free Thought; Positivism

DAVID M. FAHEY
Miami University, Oxford, Ohio
> Temperance Movement

C. BRAD FAUGHT
Ontario, Canada
> African Colonialism; Anglo-Russian Relations; Boer War; Cotton Industry; Dining; Edward, Prince of Wales; Exeter Hall; William Gladstone; Golf; Horses and Equestrian Sport; Jamaica and the West Indies; David Livingstone; Methodism; Missionaries; Daniel O'Connell; Progress; Romanticism; Royal Geographical Society; Tennis; Young England

ALAN FISCHLER
Le Moyne College, Syracuse, New York
> Dion Boucicault; Gilbert and Sullivan

JOHN FISHER
Newcastle University, New South Wales, Australia
> Land and Landowners; Livestock and Animal Husbandry

MICHAEL FLAVIN
Rochester Independent College, Kent, United Kingdom
> Gambling

PAMELA M. FLETCHER
Bowdoin College, Brunswick, Maine
> Genres of Painting

LEWIS FOREMAN
Rickmansworth, England
> Music Printing and Publishing; Symphonies

RUSSELL FOWLER
University of Tennessee at Chattanooga
> Courts

E. FRANCES FRAME
The Citadel, Charleston, South Carolina
> Thomas Arnold; Isabella Bird; The British Army; Christian Socialism; Morality; Rugby

NICHOLAS FRANKEL
Virginia Commonwealth University, Richmond
> Aubrey Beardsley; Illustration; Poetry; Oscar Wilde

W. HAMISH FRASER
University of Strathclyde, Glasgow, Scotland
> Department Stores; Robert Owen; Retail Trade; Trade Unions

MARK FREEMAN
University of Glasgow, Scotland
> Brewing and Distilling; Settlements; Taxation; William Thomson

GILLIAN GANE
Hamilton College, Clinton, New York
> Cecil Rhodes; Southern Africa

JOHN GARDINER
> Autobiographies and Memoirs; Homosexuality; Nationalism and Patriotism; Orchestral Music

PAULA GILLETT
San Jose State University, California
Grosvenor Gallery

SHELDON GOLDFARB
Edward Bulwer-Lytton; Daguerreotype;
William Charles Macready; William
Makepeace Thackeray

MARGARET BOZENNA GOSCILO
University of Pittsburgh, Pennsylvania
William Archer; William Powell Frith; John
Singer Sargent; Women Artists

KEVIN GRANT
Hamilton College, Clinton, New York
Henry Morton Stanley

F. ELIZABETH GRAY
University of Virginia, Charlottesville
Angel of the House; Charlotte Brontë and
Emily Brontë; Letitia Landon; Amy Levy;
Tractarianism

ERIK GRAY
*Harvard University, Cambridge,
Massachusetts*
Dramatic Monologue

JENNIFER GREEN-LEWIS
*George Washington University, Washington,
D.C.*
William Henry Fox Talbot

PETER GROSVENOR
*Pacific Lutheran University, Tacoma,
Washington*
Canada

MARAH GUBAR
University of Pittsburgh, Pennsylvania
Lewis Carroll; Childhood

GARY HAINES
Contemporary British History Journal
Charles Booth; Henry Mayhew; Newgate;
Robert Peel

DONALD S. HAIR
University of Western Ontario, Canada
Romance

CHARLES HAJDAMACH
Broadfield House Glass Museum, England
Glass

MARK HAMPTON
*Wesleyan University, Middletown,
Connecticut*
Daily Telegraph; Journalism; Newspapers;
Reuters News Agency; W. T. Stead; *The
Times*

JANINE C. HARTMAN
University of Cincinnati, Ohio
Etiquette; France

I. LEEAN HAWKINS
University of South Carolina, Columbia
Elizabeth Blackwell; Michael Faraday;
Mary Somerville

MICHAEL HAWKINS
Kingston University, England
Social Darwinism; Herbert Spencer

MICHAEL HELFAND
University of Pittsburgh, Pennsylvania
China; James Frazer; Psychology; Edward
Burnett Tylor

ANNE HELMREICH
Texas Christian University, Fort Worth
Gardens and Garden Design; Edward Lear;
John Everett Millais

TREVOR HERBERT
Open University, United Kingdom
Brass Bands; Military Bands

NICOLE HERZ
University of Virginia, Charlottesville
Anglo-French Relations; Engineering;
Holidays; Learned Societies

ANN R. HIGGINBOTHAM
*Eastern Connecticut State University,
Willimantic*
Illegitimacy

MATTHEW HILTON
University of Birmingham, United Kingdom
Tobacco

PETER HORTON
Royal College of Music, London, England
Cathedral and Church Music

GAIL TURLEY HOUSTON
University of New Mexico, Albuquerque
"Condition of England" Question; Diet;
Economic Cycles; Grand Tour; Houses and
Housing; Insanity; William Stanley Jevons;
George Meredith; Utilitarianism

ANNE HUMPHERYS
Lehman College, New York
Melodrama

AERON HUNT
University of Chicago, Illinois
Sarah Stickney Ellis; Married Women's
Property Act; Railway Literature

KIMBERLEY HUNT
Lyceums

TAMARA HUNT
Loyola Marymount University, Los Angeles
Henry Peter Brougham; Cartoons;
Copyright Law; George Cruikshank;
Education of Women; Famines; Fenianism;
Godey's Lady's Book; Governesses; Home
Rule; Ireland; Douglas Jerrold; Literary
Annuals; Harriet Martineau; James
Martineau; Charles S. Parnell; Women's
Work; Women's Rights

JENNINE HURL-EAMON
Carleton University, Ottawa, Canada
Capital Punishment; Hygiene

MARY M. HUSEMANN
University of South Carolina, Columbia
Blackwood's Magazine

CAROL JENKINS
Bath Spa University College, United Kingdom
Smithsonian Institution

ELLEN J. JENKINS
Arkansas Tech University, Russellville
Cemeteries; Horatio Herbert Kitchener

DALE A. JOHNSON
Vanderbilt University, Nashville, Tennessee
Test Acts

BETH A. KATTELMAN
Ohio State University, Columbus
Actors and Acting; P. T. Barnum; Cinema;
Henry Irving; Washington Irving; Music
Halls; Arthur Wing Pinero; Theater

ROBYN KARNEY
London, England
George Eliot

SUZANNE KEEN
Washington and Lee University, Lexington, Virginia
Thomas Hardy; Quakers; Anthony Trollope

ALAN J. KIDD
Manchester Metropolitan University, Manchester, England
Manchester; The Workhouse

J. M. IVO KLAVER
University of Urbino, Italy
Muscular Christianity

JUDITH KNELMAN
University of Western Ontario, Canada
Civil Service; Literacy and the Reading
Public; James Fitzjames Stephen

DANIEL J. KNICKREHM
University of Iowa, Iowa City
South Pacific

ARUNA KRISHNAMURTHY
York College, CUNY, Jamaica, New York
James Kay-Shuttleworth; Mechanics'
Institutes; Richard Owen; Ten Hours
Movement

TODD KUCHTA
Indiana University, Bloomington
Suburbia

TODD E. A. LARSON
University of Illinois at Urbana-Champaign
Anglo-German Relations; Otto von
Bismarck; Fishing; Hunting; Alfred Thayer
Mahan; The Royal Navy; Bram Stoker

NANCY LOPATIN-LUMMIS
University of Wisconsin-Stevens Point
John Bright; Richard Cobden; Corn Laws;
Reform Acts

CORY LOWN
Hamilton College, Clinton, New York
Decadence

JOHN E. LUEBERING
University of Chicago, Illinois
Bridges; Railway Stations; Charles Haddon
Spurgeon; Tom Taylor

JOHN LOWERSON
University of Sussex, United Kingdom
Amateur Theatricals; Opera; Social
Classes; Sports

FRANCIS MACDONNELL
Southern Virginia University, Buena Vista
Civil War

PATRICIA MARKS
Valdosta State University, Georgia
Sarah Bernhardt

JAN MARSH
Christina Rossetti; Dante Gabriel Rossetti;
Elizabeth Siddal

LAURA E. NYM MAYHALL
The Catholic University of America,
Washington, D.C.
The New Woman; Women's Suffrage

KENNETH MCCONKEY
University of Northumbria at Newcastle,
United Kingdom
Impressionism

JOHN M. MACKENZIE
University of St. Andrews, Scotland
Orientalism

IAIN MCLEAN
Oxford University, England
Elections and Electioneering

GLENN MELANCON
Southeastern Oklahoma State University,
Durant
Opium Wars

JULIE MELNYK
The Honors College, University of Missouri,
Columbia
Elizabeth Barrett Browning;
Evangelicalism; Felicia Hemans; Hymns
and Sacred Songs; Religious Orders

BARRY MILLIGAN
Wright State University, Dayton, Ohio
Medical Profession

G. E. MINGAY
University of Kent at Canterbury, United
Kingdom
Agricultural Workers; The Country House;
Factories; International Trade; Living
Standards; Unemployment

DAVID MITCH
University of Maryland Baltimore County
Primary Education; Sunday Schools;
Working-Class Education

EDWARD MORAN
Long Island University, New York
Henry Adams; Henry George; Nathaniel
Hawthorne; Gerard Manley Hopkins;
Dwight Moody; Organs and Organists;
George Stephenson; Mark Twain; United
States of America; Walt Whitman; William
Wordsworth

ELIZABETH JEAN MORSE
University of California, Berkeley
Alfred Marshall; Universities

IWAN RHYS MORUS
Queen's University of Belfast, Ireland
Electricity; Inventions; Telegraph

NORMAN H. MURDOCH
University of Cincinnati, Ohio
Salvation Army

ANN MURPHY
Assumption College, Worcester,
Massachusetts
Henry Sidgwick

SCOTT HUGHES MYERLY
Crimean War; Fashion and Clothing;
Uniforms and Liveries

DAVID NASH
Oxford Brookes University, United Kingdom
Republicanism

CLAUDIA NELSON
Southwest Texas State University, San Marcos
Children's Literature; Domesticity; Gender

RACHEL OBERTER
Yale University, New Haven, Connecticut
Anna Jameson

ROBERT O'KELL
University of Manitoba, Winnipeg, Canada
Advertising

DAVID OLDROYD
The University of New South Wales, Australia;
International Commission on the History of
Geological Sciences
Geology

PATRICIA O'NEILL
Hamilton College, Clinton, New York
Egypt; Kodak Cameras; Olive Schreiner

CAROL A. OSBORNE
University of Lancaster, England
Mountaineering

CHRISTOPHER D. O'SHEA
University of Guelph, Canada
Chess; The Dandy; Diseases and
Epidemics; Drugs; Environment; History
and Historiography; Hospitals;
Organization of Labor; Medicine; Physics;
Resorts; Socialism; Venereal Disease

ROBERT PATTISON
*Southampton College of Long Island
University, New York*
Walter Bagehot; Evolution; Football;
Edmund Gosse; A. E. Housman; John
Russell; Leslie Stephen

JOYCE SENDERS PEDERSEN
University of Southern Denmark at Odense
Dorothea Beale

JOHN PERKINS
Macquarie University, Sydney, Australia
Sugar

CHARLES R. PERRY
*The University of the South, Sewanee,
Tennessee*
Telephone

PAUL T. PHILLIPS
*St. Francis Xavier University, Antigonish,
Nova Scotia, Canada*
Goldwin Smith

MARY POOVEY
New York University, New York City
Banking, Money, and Credit; Bankruptcy;
Cholera; East India Company; Edinburgh
Review; Financial Scandals; Free Trade;
India; Investments; Limited Liability;
Florence Nightingale; Caroline Norton;
Political Economy; Sanitation; Statistics;
Stock Markets

CHRISTOPHER J. PROM
University of Illinois at Urbana-Champaign
Friendly Societies; Libraries; Samuel
Smiles

LUCA PRONO
Independent scholar
Thomas Cole; Eugenics; Hudson River
School; Slums; Sociology; Israel Zangwill

DEIRDRE RAFTERY
University College Dublin, Ireland
Frances Power Cobbe

ANNIE RAVENHILL-JOHNSON
University of Central England, Birmingham
Industrial Workers

DARA ROSSMAN REGAIGNON
Princeton University, Princeton, New Jersey
Angela Burdett-Coutts; Frances Trollope

CAROLINE REITZ
Saint Louis University, St. Louis, Missouri
The Detective; Newgate Novel

HARRY RICKETTS
*Victoria University of Wellington, Wellington,
New Zealand*
Rudyard Kipling

JAMIESON RIDENHOUR
University of South Carolina, Columbia
Charles Dickens; London; Robert Louis
Stevenson

DAVID G. RIEDE
Ohio State University, Columbus
Matthew Arnold; Biblical Criticism; Robert
Browning; Richard Burton; Arthur Hugh
Clough; Dinosaurs; Havelock Ellis; Essays
and Reviews; Edward FitzGerald; The
Novel; Walter Pater; Sensation Novel;
Algernon Swinburne; John Addington
Symonds; Arthur Symons; Tennyson,
Alfred

HELENE E. ROBERTS
*An International Journal of Documentation,
and The Encyclopedia of Comparative
Iconography*
Margaret Oliphant; J. M. W. Turner

SOLVEIG C. ROBINSON
*Pacific Lutheran University, Seattle,
Washington*
Mary Elizabeth Braddon; Indian Mutiny;
Langham Place Group; Mudie's Select
Circulating Library; Print Technology;
William Howard Russell

ELLEN BAYUK ROSENMAN
University of Kentucky, Lexington
Ballet

287

CHRISTINE ROTH
University of Wisconsin Oshkosh
Domestic Workers; London "Season"

WILLIAM D. RUBINSTEIN
University of Wales-Aberystwyth, United Kingdom
Aristocracy; Jews and Judaism; The Wealthy

MICHAEL RUSE
Florida State University, Tallahassee; Royal Society of Canada
Louis Agassiz; Robert Chambers; Thomas Henry Huxley; Charles Lyell; Alfred Russel Wallace

JENNIFER RUTH
Portland State University, Oregon
Professionals and Professionalism

MICHAEL T. SALER
University of California, Davis
Adventure Fiction

LISE SHAPIRO SANDERS
Hampshire College, Amherst, Massachusetts
Bicycling; Marriage and Divorce; Retail Clerks; Spinsters; Urbanization

MARGARET SANKEY
Minnesota State University—Moorhead
Alexander Campbell Mackenzie; Palace of Westminster

CANNON SCHMITT
Duke University, Durham, North Carolina
Central and South America; Natural History

ANGELA SCHWARZ
University of Duisburg-Essen, Germany
Charles Darwin; Seaside

STEPHEN C. SHAFER
University of Illinois at Urbana-Champaign
Arthur Conan Doyle; George Bernard Shaw; H.G. Wells

VICTOR SHEA
York University, Toronto, Canada
Classical Languages and Literature; Education Act of 1870; James Anthony Froude; Charles George Gordon; Thomas Hughes; Imperialism; Oxford English Dictionary; Penny Dreadfuls; John Robert Seeley

MICHAEL SHIRLEY
Eastern Illinois University, Charleston
Cricket; W. G. Grace; Thomas Babington Macaulay; G. W. M. Reynolds

MICHAEL SLETCHER
Benjamin Franklin Papers, Yale University, New Haven, Connecticut
John Alexander Macdonald; Rowing

TABITHA SPARKS
Center for Humanistic Inquiry, Emory University, Atlanta, Georgia
Economics; Sarah Grand

DAVID SPURR
University of Geneva, Switzerland
Architecture

ROY STARRS
Otago University, New Zealand
Australia and New Zealand; Japan

ANDREW M. STAUFFER
Boston University, Massachusetts
Punch

MARK STOCKER
University of Canterbury, Christchurch, New Zealand
Coins; Monuments; Sculpture

CHRISTOPHER STRAY
University of Wales Swansea, United Kingdom
Public Schools

YASUKO SUGA
Saitama University, Japan
Art Education; Liberty and Company; National Gallery of Art ; Joseph Paxton; South Kensington Museum

HERBERT SUSSMAN
Northeastern University, Boston, Massachusetts
Charles Babbage; Gentleman; Industrial Novel; Technology

JAMES TAYLOR
Institute of Historical Research, London, England
Office Workers; Young Men's Christian Association (YMCA)

ERNIE TEAGARDEN
Dakota State University, Madison, South Dakota
Thomas Alva Edison; Prisons

JESSICA B. TEISCH
University of California, Berkeley
Horatio Alger; John James Audubon; William Dean Howells; Frederic Law Olmsted; Transcendentalism; Wilderness and Public Lands

WILLIAM B. THESING
University of South Carolina, Columbia
Mining

VANESSA TOULMIN
National Fairground Archive, University of Sheffield Library, United Kingdom
Circus; Buffalo Bill Cody and His Wild West Show; Exhibitions; Freak Shows; Great Exhibition of 1851; Shows; Traveling Fairs; Zoological Gardens

CAROLYN TUTTLE
Lake Forest College, Lake Forest, Illinois
Child Labor; Factory Legislation

LARRY K. UFFELMAN
Mansfield University of Pennsylvania, Mansfield
Frederick Douglass; Elizabeth Gaskell; Charles Kingsley; Jenny Lind

LYNNE VALLONE
Texas A & M University
Louisa May Alcott; Victoria, Queen; Charlotte Mary Yonge

ROSEMARY T. VANARSDEL
University of Puget Sound, Tacoma, Washington
John Campbell Gordon; John Stuart Mill; John Morley; Arthur Penrhyn Stanley; Mary Augusta Ward; Susan B. Anthony; Barbara Leigh Smith Bodichon; Henry Cole; Dinah Mulock Craik; Macmillan's Magazine; Periodicals; Seneca Falls Convention

FRANCESCA VANKE ALTMAN
London Institute and Birkbeck College, University of London, England
William Holman Hunt; Ceramics; Race and Racism

DIANE WAGGONER
The Huntington Library, Art Collections, and Botanical Gardens, San Marino, California
Ellen Terry

CHRIS WALSH
Chester College of Higher Education, United Kingdom
Jeremy Bentham; The Cornhill Magazine; Fraser's Magazine

ALEXIS WEEDON
University of Luton, United Kingdom
Publishing and Publishers

NANCY MARTHA WEST
University of Missouri-Columbia
Photography

MICHAEL WHEELER
Visiting Professor of English, Universities of Southampton and Surrey Roehampton, United Kingdom
Church of England; John Keble; Henry Edward Manning; John Henry Newman; Religious Literature; Roman Catholicism; John Ruskin; Nicholas Patrick Stephen Wiseman

BARBARA WHITE
American Junior Year Abroad Programme, Bath, England
Censorship

WILLIAM WHITLA
York University, Toronto, Canada
William Acton; Albert, Prince Consort; Josephine Butler; Classical Languages and Literature; Contagious Disease Acts; Benjamin Jowett; Prostitution; George Gilbert Scott

AMY WOODSON-BOULTON
University of California, Los Angeles
Local Government; Museums

MARTIN MORSE WOOSTER
Capital Research Center, Washington, D.C.
Philanthropy

DEBORAH WYNNE
Chester College of Higher Education, United Kingdom
Comic Literature; Charles Lever; The Saturday Review

ARLENE YOUNG
University of Manitoba, Winnipeg, Canada
George Gissing; Jack the Ripper; Nursing;
Typewriter

BENNETT ZON
University of Durham, United Kingdom
Ethnomusicology

Index

Page numbers in **boldface** type indicate article titles. Page numbers in *italic* type indicate illustrations. Volume numbers are in **boldface** type.

ATC. *See* American Telegraph Company
atheism. *See* agnosticism, atheism, and free thought
Athenaeum (Glasgow school). *See* National Scottish Academy of Music
Athenaeum (London club) **2:**150, 151
Athenaeum (weekly periodical) **2:**302, 315, 374, 381; **3:**15, 37, 89, 91, 188; **4:**2
   Rossetti's (Christina) poetry published in **3:**331
   on Young Men's Christian Association facilities **4:**209
Athenian constitution **1:**279
Athlete Wrestling with a Python (Leighton sculpture) **3:**372
Atkins, Ivor **3:**95
Atkinson, Henry G. **3:**10
Atkinson, Lucy **4:**105
Atlanta, fall of (1864) **1:**276
Atlantic cable. *See* transatlantic cable
Atlantic Monthly **2:**382; **3:**189
   on American mediums **4:**2
   Howell's editorship **2:**220, 221
Atlantic Telegraph Company **4:**85
Atlas (periodical) **3:**89
Attempt to Discriminate the Styles of English Architecture (T. Rickman) **2:**178
Attempt to Establish Physiognomy upon Scientific Principles (Cross) **3:**208
Attwood, Thomas **3:**302
Aubrey, John **1:**61
Auburn Correctional Facility (New York) **3:**252, 254
Auckland, Lord **1:**14
Auden, W. H. **2:**330
audiences **1:**4; **3:**83
audiometer **1:**125
Audubon, John James **1:93–95**
Audubon, John Woodhouse (son) **1:**93, 94
Audubon, Victor Gifford (son) **1:**93, 94
Audubon Society **1:**94
Augusta, Princess of Hesse-Cassel **4:**155
Augusta Ada, Countess of Lovelace **1:**105
Auguste Comte and the Positivists (J. S. Mill) **3:**47, 231
Augustine, Saint **1:**98
Aukland, Lord **2:**250
Aunt Charlotte's Stories of English History for the Little Ones (Yonge) **4:**208
Aurora Floyd (Braddon) **1:**151
Aurora Leigh (Barrett Browning) **1:**173, 174; **2:**302, 345; **3:**217, 218, 266, 329
Austen, Jane **1:**292; **2:**70; **3:**127, 130, 426
   Gaskell compared with **2:**140, 141
Austin, Alfred **2:**137
Austin, Charles **3:**46
Austin, Herbert **1:**102
Austin, John (jurist) **2:**349; **3:**187
Austin, John Turnell (organ maker) **3:**150
Australia and New Zealand **1:95–98**
   aboriginal smallpox deaths **4:**151
   African colonialism and **1:**17
   agricultural worker immigrants in **3:**350
   agriculture and **1:**25, 28, 29; **2:**267; **3:**351

alcohol and **1:**34
Anglicanism and **1:**265
anti-Catholicism and **1:**58
art education and **1:**80
Bernhardt's tour of **1:**128
birthrates **3:**228
Boer War troops from **1:**145
brass bands **1:**155
British army action in **1:**163
as British book export market **3:**279
as British cotton export market **1:**309
Britons' images of **1:**97–98
business organization and **1:**187–88
Butler (Samuel) sheep ranching experience in **1:**98, 192
capital punishment **1:**204
Cecil and **1:**215
census **1:**223
children's periodicals **1:**249
coins **1:**286–87
as Commonwealth member **1:**95
Contagious Diseases Acts and **1:**301
courts **1:**317
cricket and **1:**320; **2:**182; **4:**9
criminal code **4:**23
Dickens novels' portrayals of **1:**97–98
Divorce Bill (1890) **3:**6
electoral system **2:**42
emigration to **2:**52, 55, 56, 57, 59, 267, 338
Empire and **1:**95–98; **2:**59; **3:**356
exhibitions held in **2:**84
exploration of **2:**89, 93
Fabian Society in **3:**411
folklore **2:**115
football and **4:**9
fossils found in **2:**154
gender theories and **2:**141–42
gold rush **1:**96, 287; **2:**52, 56, 167, 168, 169, 170, 286; **3:**53, 252
immigrants. *See subhead* emigration to *above*
indigenous peoples **1:**97; **2:**59, 61, 144; **3:**293
industrial production **2:**268
insurance companies **2:**275
Irish emigration to **2:**289
juvenile smoking ban **4:**89
labor organization **2:**337, 338
labor parties **2:**339
land system abolishment **2:**344
libraries **2:**366, 367, 368
livestock produce **2:**390
London dock strike and **2:**263
male gender models **2:**142
map of **1:**96
missionaries from **3:**54
monarchy and **3:**55, 58
monuments exported to **3:**62
mortality rate **3:**228
mountaineering in **3:**75
museums **3:**78, 79
musical festivals **3:**96
New Imperialism and **2:**243
penal colonies **1:**97, 98, 324; **2:**52, 56, 59, 391; **3:**66, 251, 252, 328
penal colony image of **1:**98
periodicals **3:**189
population **1:**96; **3:**228
public health reforms **2:**233
railways **1:**96; **2:**267, 277, 286; **3:**299
Reuters News Agency and **3:**321

Russell (John) and **3:**356
Salvation Army **3:**361–62
Scotch whiskey exports to **1:**34
Seeley on **3:**377
sheep farming **1:**98, 192; **2:**256, 390–91
sports exports to **4:**9
suburbia **4:**33
sugar consumption **4:**38, 39
tea consumption **4:**39
telegraph **3:**206
telephones **4:**65
temperance movement **4:**67
tuberculosis cases **4:**115
urban population growth **4:**143
Victoria as queen of **3:**58
Victoria monuments and place-names in **1:**95; **3:**61
women's suffrage **4:**191, 192
wool industry **2:**390–91
Young Men's Christian Association **4:**210
Australia and New Zealand (A. Trollope) **1:**98
Austria (Austria-Hungary)
   Anglo-French relations and **1:**44, 45, 46
   Anglo-German relations and **1:**47, 49
   Art Nouveau and **1:**84, 85
   beet sugar industry **4:**37
   Crimean War results and **1:**329
   emigration **2:**53
   eugenic sterilization law **2:**75
   exhibitions held in **2:**84
   glass products **2:**164, 165
   trade with **2:**248
Austro-Italian War **4:**70
Austro-Prussian War **1:**370
Author (journal) **1:**131
Authoress of the "Odyssey," The (S. Butler) **1:**193
authorial ownership. *See* copyright law
autobiographies and memoirs **1:98–100**
   Barnum and **1:**118
   Cooper (Thomas) and **1:**303
   Darwin (Charles) and **1:**99, 339, 341
   Douglass and **2:**10
   Gosse and **1:**99; **2:**175
   Grant and **1:**99, 337
   Kipling and **2:**330
   Leno and **2:**359
   Martineau (Harriet) and **3:**9, 10, 11
   Mill (John Stuart) and **1:**99; **3:**47; **4:**149, 150
   Newman and **1:**58, 99; **2:**328; **3:**308
   Oliphant and **3:**140
   Roosevelt (Theodore) **1:**249
   Ruskin and **1:**99; **3:**352, 353, 355
   Spencer and **3:**424
   spiritual **1:**58, 98–99; **2:**328; **3:**308
   Symonds and **4:**42, 43
   Trollope (Anthony) and **1:**99, 272; **2:**382; **4:**112
   Victorians' distrust of **1:**99
   Ward and **4:**165
Autobiography and Selected Letters (C. Darwin) **1:**99, 339, 341
Autocar, The (periodical) **1:**102
automatic loom. *See* power loom
automatic writing **4:**1
automobile **1:100–102**; **2:**276, 281; **4:**100
   first gasoline-powered **1:**101; **2:**275, 276

first steam-powered **4:**99
holidays and **2:**203
red flag rule **1:**100, *101*, 102; **2:**275; **4:**99
suburbia and **4:**34
women and **4:**101
Autumn Leaves (Millais painting) **1:**12; **3:**50, 240
Aveling, Edward **1:**130; **3:**15
aviation **1:**125; **2:**276
Awadh (India). *See* Oudh
"Awake, Awake; Put on Thy Strength" (Stainer anthem) **1:**213
Awakening Conscience, The (Hunt painting) **1:**82; **2:**225, *225*, 226; **3:**161–62, 240, 266
Awful Disclosures of the Hotel Dieu Nunnery (M. Monk) **1:**57
Awkward Age, The (H. James) **2:**310
Axminster pile carpet **2:**97
Ayala's Angel (A. Trollope) **4:**112
Ayling, Mary **3:**69
Ayrton, William (music journalist) **3:**91
Ayton, William (inventor) **1:**101
Aytoun, William (writer) **3:**216; **4:**2
Azeth the Egyptian (Linton) **2:**378
Aztec civilization **1:**226

B

Bab Ballads, The (W. S. Gilbert) **1:**294; **2:**156
Babbage, Charles **1:103–5**
   anti-street performer campaign and **4:**32
   computational machine designs **1:**103, 104; **4:**58, 60
   on industrial technology **4:**59
   on roots of invention **2:**279
   Somerville and **3:**414
   statistical movement and **1:**104, 222; **4:**19
   Whewell and **4:**174
Babcock, C. **3:**338
Baboo Jabberjee, B. A. (Anstey) **1:**293
Babylonian Marriage Market (Long painting) **1:**82
Baccarat (glass manufacture) **2:**165
Bacchus of Birmingham (glass manufacture) **2:**165
Bach, Johann Sebastian **3:**95, 150, 151, 178
Bach Choir **3:**178
bachelors **2:**141, 150
Bachman, John **1:**94
back-to-backs (housing design) **1:**233; **2:**214–15
Bacon, Francis **2:**81; **3:**257
Bacon, John, Jr. and Sr. **3:**60
Bacon, R. M. **3:**91
"bad boy" stories **1:**249
Baden-Baden (Germany) **4:**103
Badham, Richard J. **3:**412
badminton **4:**9
Baedeker, Karl **4:**106
Baedeker travel guides **2:**201; **4:**106
Baekeland, Leo **2:**100
Baeyer, Adolf von **2:**64
Bagehot, Walter **1:105–7**; **2:**22; **3:**389
   literary essays by **2:**387
   on monarchy **3:**55, 56
   on political evolution **2:**82–83
   on royal family **3:**341, 401
   as *Saturday Review* contributor **3:**367

dogs (cont.)
emotional connections with **3:**192
humane treatment laws **3:**190
hunting and **2:**227; **3:**191
kidnapping of **3:**191
Landseer's paintings of **1:**377;
  2:*345*, 346; **3:**165, 168
as pets **1:**376–78; **3:**190–93
rabies controversy and **3:**192
showing of **1:**377; **3:**191
Doll's House, A (Ibsen) **2:**144; **3:**111;
  4:83
"dollymops" (prostitutes) **3:**265
"Dolores" (Swinburne) **4:**41
Dombey and Son (Dickens) **1:**110,
  356; **2:**142; **3:**296; **4:**144
domestic comedy **1:**291, 292–93, 294
Domestic Manners of the Americans (F.
  Trollope) **4:**104, 113
domestic violence
Cobbe's reports on **1:**282–83; **3:**65
as legal separation cause **4:**188
domestic workers **2:**1–6, 259–60
cost of keeping **2:**395
country houses and **1:**312
domesticity and **2:**1, 7, 8
dress and **2:**109; **3:**404; **4:**130
etiquette and **2:**70, 72; **3:**404
factories and **2:**6, 97
farm women as **3:**351
governess status and **2:**2, 179, 181
hand washing by **3:**399
hunting and **2:**227
illegitimate births and **2:**236, 237
income basis for keeping **2:**395
internal ranking of **2:**2, 4–5
living standards and **2:**2, 395
prostitution and **2:**2; **3:**262
social class of **3:**402
sports and **4:**8
tea habit and **4:**35, 56
uniforms and liveries for **4:**130
wages of **2:**5–6, 395
women's education and **2:**6, 33,
  35; **4:**189
women's employment as **2:**2–3, 4,
  5–6, 259–60; **3:**351, 402;
  4:35, 197, 198
working conditions **2:**4, 5–6, 395
domesticity **2:**6–9
Albert and **1:**32
Angel of the House ideal and **1:**40;
  2:6, 7; **4:**198
Blackwell's endorsement of **1:**143
child socialization and **1:**249; **2:**7
as children's literature theme
  1:248
convent life vs. **3:**309
cottages and **2:**218
Ellis's (Sarah) popularization of
  2:51
garden as symbol of **2:**139
gender and **2:**142–43
gentlemen's clubs and **2:**150
Godey's Lady's Book and **2:**167
home cooking and **1:**360
House Beautiful movement and
  1:349
literary depictions of **2:**7–8
missionaries and **3:**54
morality and **2:**6–7; **3:**63
organ music and **3:**151
parlor ballad and **3:**175
pet dogs associated with **3:**190–91,
  192
piano and **3:**210, 212
royal family and **1:**32; **2:**6, 144;
  3:341; **4:**155, 156, 157, 159

separate spheres and **1:**190;
  2:143–44, 216
servants and **2:**1, 7
suburban living and **2:**216; **4:**33,
  101
tea linked with **4:**55, 57
women social reformers and **4:**189
women's educational path reflect-
  ing **2:**32, 33, 35; **4:**189
as women's work **1:**40; **2:**6–9;
  4:195, 198
Dominion Lands Act (1872) **1:**29
"Dominus regit me" (Dykes hymn)
  1:214
Don Juan (Byron) **2:**302, 370
Don Quixote (Cervantes) **1:**205
Donkin, Bryan **3:**250
Donne, John **2:**175
Donovan, Edward **1:**93
"Dora" (Tennyson) **4:**74
Doré, Gustave **1:**128; **2:**240, *406*;
  3:237
Dorion, Antoine-Aimé **1:**199
*Dort or Dordrecht, the Dort Packet-
  Boat from Rotterdam
  Becalmed* (Turner painting)
  4:117
Douay Bible **3:**307
Double Indemnity (film) **3:**33
double standard
Acton (William) and **1:**2, 221–22
Blackwell's opposition to **1:**143
Butler (Josephine) campaign
  against **1:**190, 191
Contagious Disease Acts and
  1:300; **3:**66; **4:**189–90
divorce law and **2:**7, 143; **3:**3–4;
  4:187–88
dramatic monologue exposure of
  3:217
Grand's novel attacking **2:**182, 183
Hardy's novels exposing **2:**192
illegitimate births and **2:**237; **4:**187
marriage and **2:**8; **3:**3–4, 6,
  64; **4:**187–88
morality and **3:**64
prostitution and **3:**66, 263, 265
sexuality and **2:**143; **3:**64
venereal disease and **4:**153, 154
Doughty, Charles **2:**92; **3:**154; **4:**105
Douglas, Alfred **1:**343; **2:**208; **4:***178*,
  179
Douglas, Bloomfield **1:**137
Douglas Jerrold's Shilling Magazine
  (periodical) **2:**315
Douglas Jerrold's Weekly Newspaper
  (periodical) **2:**315
Douglass, Frederick **2:**9–11
Douglass's Monthly (periodical) **2:**10
Doulton ceramics **1:**229
Dove in the Eagle's Nest, A (Yonge)
  2:421
"Dover Beach" (M. Arnold) **1:**72;
  3:220
Dover-Calais telegraph cable **2:**322;
  4:64
Dowden, Edward **2:**387
Down, John Langdon **1:**92
Downing, Andrew Jackson **2:**137–38;
  3:142
Down's syndrome **1:**92
Downside (public school) **3:**273
Downton castle **1:**312
Dowson, Ernest **1:**246, 343; **4:**44
Doyle, Arthur Conan **2:**11–13
adventure fiction and **1:**7, 8, 366;
  3:131
detective story and **1:**354; **2:**11–12,
  70, 73; **3:**278, 288

gentlemen's club portrayal by
  2:151
India portrayal by **2:**254
Meredith and **3:**35
"philosophy" of smoking and **4:**88
phrenological terms and **3:**288
serialization and **3:**278
on social class and etiquette **2:**70,
  73
suburbia setting **4:**34
Doyle, George **3:**282
Doyle, Innes **2:**13
Doyle, John ("HB") **1:**210; **2:**11
Doyle, Kingsley Conan **2:**13
Doyle, Richard ("Dickey") **1:**210, 211
D'Oyly Carte. *See* Carte, Richard
  D'Oyly
D'Oyly Carte opera company **4:**178
Dr. Jekyll and Mr. Hyde (Stevenson).
  *See Strange Case of Dr. Jekyll
  and Mr. Hyde*
Dracula (Stoker) **2:**176; **3:**131; **4:**3,
  30, 31, 123
draft, military **1:**276
Drais von Sauerbronn, Karl Friedrich
  1:134
Drake, Francis **1:**225, 226
Dramatic Lyrics (R. Browning) **1:**176;
  3:216
dramatic monologue **2:**13–14
Browning (Robert) and **1:**176;
  3:216; **4:**2
Levy and **2:**14, 360–61; **3:**217
mesmerism and **3:**37
Rossetti (Christina) and **2:**14; **3:**331
Rossetti (Dante Gabriel) and **2:**14;
  3:217, 335
Dramatic Romances and Lyrics (R.
  Browning) **1:**176; **3:**216
Dreadnought (battleship) **3:**347
Dream and Other Poems, The (Norton)
  3:125
Dream of Gerontius, The (Elgar orato-
  rio) **2:**46; **3:**147
Dream of Gerontius, The (J. H. New-
  man) **3:**118, 308
Dream of John Ball, A (Morris) **3:**28
Dreams (Schreiner) **3:**369
Dresden Exposition (1897) **2:**86
Dresser, Christopher **1:**87, 229, 346,
  348, 350; **2:**165; **3:**153, 416
dressmaking and clothing trade **2:**99,
  100, 107, 259, 260; **4:**196,
  197
Drimmer, Thomas **2:**124
Drink and the Victorians (Harrison)
  3:65
drinking. *See* alcohol; public houses
drinking water. *See* water supply
Drop Down Ye Heavens from Above
  (Stainer anthem) **4:**11
druggist chains **3:**319
drugs **2:**14–16; **3:**47
alcohol and **1:**33–34
Collins's novels and **1:**290, 291,
  354
London traffic in **2:**406
medicine and **3:**23
Opium War and **3:**145–46
pharmaceutical standardization
  2:15–16
Rossetti (Dante Gabriel) and **1:**33;
  3:335
sugar and **4:**34
Druitt, Montague **2:**306–7
Drum-Taps (Whitman) **4:**175, 176
Drummond, Henry **1:**267
Drunkard's Children, The (Cruikshank
  illustrations) **1:**332

drunkenness. *See* alcohol
Drury, Alfred **3:**372
Drury Lane theatre (Theatre Royal)
  1:3, 4; **2:**358–59, 398, 405;
  3:31, 33
interior **4:**81
Macready management **2:**422
royal patent **4:**79
dry-plate process **2:**333–34
Du Cane, Edmund **1:**325–26
Du Maurier, George **1:**13, 211; **2:**319;
  3:37; **4:**183
as *Punch* contributor **3:**280, 282
spiritualism and **4:**3
Du Mont, Henry **1:**212
Dublin **2:**84; **3:**98
Abbey Theatre, as Gaelic cultural
  center **2:**293
bridges **1:**161
as ecclesiastical province **2:**294,
  295
Guinness's brewery **1:**157
Metropolitan Police **3:**221, 223
Dublin Stock Exchange **4:**29
Dublin University Magazine **1:**318;
  2:360
Duckham, Helen and Baron **3:**52
Duckworth, Robinson **1:**208; **3:**274
*Due West, or Round the World in Ten
  Months* (Ballou) **1:**254
Dufay and His Contemporaries
  (Stainer, ed.) **3:**89, 99; **4:**12
Duffield, Alexander James **1:**226
Dugdale, Florence. *See* Hardy, Flor-
  ence Dugdale
Dugdale, William **3:**229, 230
Duke, James Buchanan **4:**88–89
Duke of Wellington Monument (Lon-
  don) **3:**59
Duke's Children, The (A. Trollope)
  2:148; **4:**111
Dulles, Foster Rhea **3:**194
Dulong, René **2:**86
Dunant, Henry **3:**300
Duncombe, Edward **3:**229
Dundee Stock Exchange **4:**29
Dunfermline public park **3:**181
Dunlop, John Boyd **1:**135; **4:**100
Dunning, Eric **3:**348
Dupont-Sommer, André **2:**355
Dupotet, Charles **3:**36
Durand, Asher **2:**222; **4:**135
Durand-Ruel, Paul **2:**244
Durban Museum **3:**79
Durham, John George Lambton **1:**199
Durham, Joseph **3:**371
Durham Architectural Society **2:**355
Durham Report (1839) **1:**199; **2:**242
Durham University. *See* University of
  Durham
Durkheim, Émile **3:**412
Duryea, Charles **1:**101
Duse, Eleonora **1:**3, 128
Dusik, Jan Ladislav **3:**212
Dutch East India Company **3:**419, 421
Dutch settlers. *See* Afrikaners
duties. *See* stamp tax; tariffs
Dutton, Clarence **2:**153
Duty (Smiles) **3:**394
Dvořák, Antonín **3:**92, 95, 98, 148,
  149, 150; **4:**12
dwarfs **2:**124, 126
Dwight, John S. **3:**100; **4:**96
Dyce, William **1:**32, 287; **2:**19, 312;
  3:160, 164, 241
dye
artificial **2:**64, 280
international trade in **2:**277
Morris natural products **3:**71

G

H

adventure fiction and **1:**7
advertising and **1:**11
aesthetic movement and **1:**13
Art Nouveau and **1:**83, 85
Audubon and **1:**93–94
Beardsley and **1:**85, 121–23; **2:**240, 241
Bible editions and **3:**307
botanical **3:**181
of British icons **1:**98, 211; **3:**281
Brown (Ford Madox) and **1:**171–72
Burne-Jones and 1; **1:**182, 183
Cameron's photographic **1:**197
censorship and **1:**219
children's literature and **1:**208, 211, 247; **3:**282; **4:**184, 185
in color **3:**277
Cruikshank and **1:**34, 332, 356; **2:**240; **3:**189
du Maurier and **3:**282
garden treatises and **2:**137, 138
Godey's Lady's Book and **2:**167
Lear and **1:**211; **2:**352–53; **3:**167
Leech and **3:**280, 281–82
literary annuals and 0; **1:**210; **2:**238, 384, 385
Millais and **3:**50
Morris and **2:**239, 241
music publishing and **3:**85, 86
natural history **1:**93–94; **2:**352–53
newspapers and **3:**120
novel serialization and **2:**240–41; **3:**250
penny dreadfuls and **3:**185
periodicals and **1:**210–11; **2:**238, 239, 313, 315; **3:**187, 189
"Phiz" and **1:**210–11, 294
photography as **2:**238–39, 241; **3:**250, 275; **4:**52
pornography and **3:**64, 229, 230
Pre-Raphaelites and **2:**241
print technology and **2:**238–39, 241; **3:**250–51, 275, 277
Punch and **3:**280, 281–82
Royal Academy training in **3:**340
Ruskin and **2:**238; **3:**354
Tenniel and **1:**208, 211; **2:**238, *239*; **3:**280, 282
Thackeray and **3:**281
travel literature and **2:**353, 354
by women **4:**185
See also cartoons
Illustrations of Political Economy (H. Martineau) **3:**10; **4:**59
Illustrations of the Family of Psitt-acidae, or Parrots (Lear) **2:**353
Illustrators of the Sixties (F. Reid) **2:**238
Image, Selwyn **1:**86
"Imaginative Woman, An" (Hardy) **3:**202
immigration. *See* emigration and immigration
Immigration Act (1901; Australia) **2:**56
Immigration and Public Works Act (1871; New Zealand) **2:**56
"Immortality Ode" (Wordsworth) **1:**245
Impeachment of the House of Brunswick, The (Bradlaugh) **3:**312
Imperial College (London) **2:**186; **4:**141
Imperial Federation League **2:**243; **3:**377
Imperial Gothic genre **2:**176
Imperial March (Elgar composition) **2:**46; **3:**90
Imperial Museum (Japan) 3, 416

Imperial Odes (Sullivan composition) **3:**148
Imperial Preference (trade policy) **1:**232, 234; **2:**357
Imperial Tobacco conglomerate **4:**89
imperialism **2:242–43**
adventure fiction and **1:**7, 8; **3:**186
African colonialism and **1:**15, 16, 17, 145; **2:**37–39, 171–72; **3:**260–61
Anglo-French relations and **1:**44, 45, 46
Anglo-German relations and **1:**48, 50, 141
antislavery movement and **1:**59
Australian and New Zealand **1:**97
Balfour and **1:**108
Besant (Annie) as critic of **1:**130–31
Bird's travel experiences and **1:**137, 138
Blackwood Magazine's support for **1:**144
Boer War and **1:**145–47; **2:**243; **3:**419
British army and **1:**163
British Museum treasures and **1:**164, 165
Burton and **1:**184–85
Cecil and **1:**214, 216
Central and South America and **1:**225, 226, 228; **2:**58
as central to Victorian culture **2:**58
Chamberlain and **1:**234
China and **1:**253
as Collins topic **1:**290
Conservatives and **2:**41, 61
critics of **1:**130–31; **2:**26, 61, 221–22, 243; **3:**260, 285, 367, 368–69; **4:**118–19
Daily Telegraph's popularization of **1:**336
Darwinian evolution as bolstering **2:**142
Disraeli and 2; **1:**371; **2:**61, 203, 318–19; **3:**259
East India Company and **2:**17
Edward (Prince of Wales) and **2:**37
Egypt and **2:**37–39, 60, 61
Evangelical paternalism and **2:**77
exploration and **2:**88; **4:**104, 105
free trade and **2:**242
genre painting and **3:**167
Gladstone's policies and **2:**171, 172; **3:**261
Gordon ("Chinese") and **2:**171–73; **3:**261
"Great White Hunter" image and **2:**226, 227–28, 229
as Hemans poetic theme **2:**195
Howells's campaign against **2:**221–22
India and **2:**254
industrialization and **2:**265, 270; **4:**145
insurance and **2:**274–75
investments and **2:**284, 285–86
Kidd and **3:**409
Kipling and 3; **2:**254, 329, 330; **3:**293
Kitchener and **2:**331–32
Mahan and **2:**423
manliness equated with **2:**42
Methodism and **3:**40
Middle East and **3:**40–44
military uniforms and **4:**130
missionaries and **2:**77; **3:**54, 55
morality and **3:**64–65, 68
museums and **1:**165

Napoleon III and **3:**101–2
New Imperialism **2:**242–43; **3:**261
orientalism and **3:**152–53, 154
photography and **3:**204
progress ideal and **3:**260–61
racial justifications for **2:**242, 243; **3:**288–89, 292–93; **4:**134
Rothschilds and **3:**337
Royal Navy and **3:**260, 345–46
sanitary reform and **3:**365
Schreiner's writings on **3:**367, 368–69
Seeley and **1:**226; **3:**261, 376–77
shipping and **3:**383, 385
Smith (Adam) and **3:**418
Smith (Goldwin) and **3:**395
social Darwinism and 3; **3:**65, 292, 408–9; **4:**5
Southern Africa and **3:**419–22
Spencer and **3:**409, 424
sports and **4:**5
tailoring as visual identity of **4:**49
Tennyson's poetry and **3:**217
Thomson (Lord Kelvin) and **4:**85
Twain's campaign against **2:**221; **4:**118–19
United States and **2:**221–22; **3:**261; **4:**132, 134, 136
urbanization parallel with **4:**145
Victoria and **4:**159–60
Victoria Memorial and **3:**61
See also Empire
Imperialism (Lenin) **2:**243
Imperialism: A Study (Hobson) **2:**61, 243; **3:**337
Importance of Being Earnest, The (Wilde) **1:**4, 180, 207, 294; **2:**72; **4:**84, 177, 179
Gilbert's *Engaged* and **2:**156
imports. *See* international trade
impressionism **2:243–47**; **3:**296
art criticism and **1:**78; **2:**244–45
Cassatt and **4:**186
Debussy's music and **3:**154
Japanese influence on **1:**348
as landscape painting influence **3:**167
Sargent and **2:**246–47; **3:**365
Turner and **2:**246, 247; **4:**118
Whistler and **2:**245–46; **3:**164
impressment **3:**344
Improvisatrice, And Other Poems, The (Landon) **2:**345
In Darkest Africa (H. M. Stanley) **4:**105
In Darkest England and the Way Out (W. Booth) **3:**237, 362; **4:**145
In Ghostly Japan (Hearn) **2:**314
In Memoriam (Paton painting) **3:**162
In Memoriam: A.H.H. (Tennyson) **1:**237, 364; **2:**82, 206; **3:**216, 217, 308; **4:**74, 75
"In the Bleak Mid-Winter" (C. Rossetti) **3:**331
"In the Cage" (H. James) **4:**3
In the Days of the Comet (Wells) **4:**171
"In the Depths of a Coal Mine" (S. Crane) **3:**52
"In the Gloaming" (Hill song) **3:**175
In the South (Elgar composition) **2:**46
In the Year of the Jubilee (Gissing) **2:**160, 161
Inaugural Lecture on the Utility of Anglo-Saxon Literature (Ingram) **2:**376
Inca civilization **1:**226
incandescent bulb **2:**29, 30, 370–71; **3:**207; **4:**62
incest **2:**121; **3:**65
Inchbold, John William **3:**166

Incidents of Travel in Central American, Chiapas, and Yucatán (J. L. Stephens) **1:**61, 226; **4:**105
Incidents of Travel in Egypt, Arabia Patraea, and the Holy Land (Stephens) **4:**105
income tax **2:**395
Bagehot's opposition to **1:**107
as direct taxation **4:**53
in India **2:**253
industrialization and **2:**269
Peel reintroduction of **2:**392; **3:**184; **4:**53, 54
rate of (1900) **4:**54
surtax and **4:**53–54
Incondita (R. Browning) **1:**175
indentured labor **4:**36
Independent Irish Party **2:**294
Independent Labour Party **2:**339; **3:**411; **4:**54, 195
Independent Order of Oddfellows **2:**128
Independent Theatre Society **3:**382
Indes Librorum Prohibitorum (Ashbee) **3:**230
India **2:247–54**
acquisition of **2:**58, 61
Afghan Wars and **1:**13, 14, 15
African colonialism and **1:**16, 17; **3:**419, 421
agriculture and **1:**25, 27–28, 30; **2:**250, 252
amateur theatricals and **1:**38, 39
Anglican presence in **1:**265
Anglo-French relations and **1:**44, 46
Anglo-Indian War and **1:**27
Anglo-Russian relations and **1:**50, 52; **2:**332
antislavery movement and **1:**58
archaeology and **1:**63
architecture and **1:**65
Besant (Annie) and **1:**130–31
big-game hunting in 9; **2:**226–27, 229, *253*
Bird's travels in **1:**138
as book export market **3:**279
British American Tobacco and **4:**89
British army in **1:**163; **2:**247–48, 256, 332
British territorial expansion in **2:**250, 254
Burton and **1:**184, 185
business structure **1:**188
Cameron photographs of **1:**197
Cecil and **1:**214, 215, 216
census **1:**223, 224
cholera epidemic and **1:**256, 367; **2:**406
cinchona cultivation **2:**90
civil service and **3:**275; **4:**110–11
coins **1:**287
Contagious Diseases Acts and **1:**191, 301
Cook tours of **1:**302
cotton production **1:**27, 309; **2:**61, 128, 248, 253
cricket and **1:**320; **2:**182; **4:**9
criminal code **4:**23
decorative arts and **1:**347–48
East India Company and **2:**17–18, 59, 61, 128, 248–50, 252–54; **3:**225; **4:**16
educational system **2:**250; **4:**109
electoral system **2:**42
emigration **2:**57
Empire and **2:**58, 59, 61; **3:**259, 261; **4:**16

N

P

temporal and spiritual **3:**328
Trollope (Anthony) and **4:**112
Young England and **4:**208–9
Romance of Natural History, The (P. H. Gosse) **3:**107
romantic ballet **1:**108–9
Romanticism **3:329–31**
archaeology and **1:**61
autobiographies as legacy of **1:**98
ballet and **1:**108–9
Browning's (Robert) move from **1:**175
on child's innocence **1:**244, 245
critics of Bentham and **1:**126
demise of **3:**215
dramatic monologue and **2:**13, 14
French writers and **2:**120–21
Gothic Revival and **2:**178; **3:**330–31
Hemans's poetry and **2:**195
Hudson River School and **2:**222; **4:**135
India locale and **2:**253
as industrialization backlash **1:**311; **3:**257
landscape idealization and **2:**184; **3:**329–30
landscape painting and **3:**164, 330; **4:**135, 180
Mill's (James) reaction against **4:**149
Morris and **3:**71
opera and **3:**143
orchestral music and **3:**149
pastoral cemeteries and **1:**218
Pater and **2:**388; **3:**180
piano music and **3:**211, 212
poetry and **3:**215, 216, 217, 218, 220, 330; **4:**95, 180
realism as reaction to **2:**220
seminal literary figures in **4:**200
Swinburne and **4:**39
Tennyson and **4:**73–74
transcendentalism and **4:**95–96
United States and **4:**180
vitalism and **3:**267
wilderness concept in **4:**180
Wordsworth and **3:**330; **4:**95, 96, 135, 200, 201
Rome
as Grand Tour centerpiece **2:**183
Hawthorne in **2:**195
Lear's paintings and **2:**353
tourist travel to **4:**102
Watts exhibitions in **4:**168
Rome, ancient. *See* antiquities; classical languages and literature; Roman Empire
Romilly, Samuel **1:**353
Romola (G. Eliot) **1:**308; **2:**48, 303
Ronalds, Francis **4:**62
Rooke, Thomas **1:**184
"rookeries" (London slums) **2:**405, 406
Rookwood (Ainsworth) **3:**114
Roosevelt, Franklin Delano **1:**277; **4:**172
Roosevelt, Theodore **1:**224, 277; **4:**164, 212
autobiography of **1:**249
conservationism and **4:**181
dandyism and **1:**337
manhood images and **2:**141
Root, J. W. **1:**67
Root, Waverley **1:**360
Rope, Ellen Mary **3:**373
"Rope, The" (cotillion figure) **3:**406
Rosa Triplex (D. G. Rossetti painting) **3:***241*

Rosamunde (Schubert composition) **2:**188
Rosarius (pseudonym) **4:**185
Rosary Cemetery (Norwich) **1:**218–19
Roscoe, Henry **4:**141
Rose, H. J. **3:**116
Rose, Jonathan **1:**8; **3:**47
Rose, Michael **3:**67
Rose Blanche and Violet (Lewes) **2:**362
Rose of Life, The (Braddon) **1:**151
Rose of Sharon, The (Mackenzie oratorio) **2:**420; **3:**147
Rosebery, Lord. *See* Primrose, Archibald Philip
Rosenblum, Nancy L. **4:**148
Rosenbusch, Harry **2:**153
Rosetta Stone **1:**164; **2:**37
Ross, Alexander **2:***63*
Ross, James Clark **2:**90–91
Ross, John **2:**90
Ross, Martin (Violet Martin) **4:**4
Ross, Robert **4:**179
Rossa, Jeremiah O'Donovan **2:**110
Rosse, earl of. *See* Parsons, William
Rossetti, Christina **2:**303; **3:331–33**
brother Dante Gabriel and **3:**331, 333, *334*
Brown (Ford Maddox) and **1:**172
Carroll and **1:**208; **3:**332, *334*
children's poetry and **1:**248; **3:**332
dramatic monologue and **2:**14; **3:**331
hymns by **2:**235
Landon (L. E. L.) and **2:**345; **3:**331
as Levy influence **2:**360
Macmillan's Magazine and **2:**421
poetry by **3:**218, 219, 331–33; **4:**91
posthumous reputation of **3:**334
sonnet sequences **3:**218, 331, 332
Tractarianism and **3:**331, 332; **4:**91
Rossetti, Dante Gabriel **4:333–35**
aesthetic movement and **1:**12, 13; **3:**162, 333
archaeology and **1:**61
art criticism and **1:**76, 77
art market and **1:**82; **3:**333–34, 335
beautiful woman "fancy head" paintings by **3:**334, 335
Brown (Ford Madox) friendship **1:**171, 172
Burne-Jones and **1:**182; **4:**333
classical influences on **1:**279
criticisms of **3:**240
dramatic monologue and **2:**14; **3:**217, 335
fallen woman theme and **3:**166, 335
Fitzgerald (Edward) and **2:**113
genre painting and **3:**161, 162
historic preservation and **2:**196
Hunt friendship **2:**225
as illustrator **2:**238
influence of **3:**333
Italy and **2:**303
Jameson's art criticism and **2:**312
laudanum use by **1:**33; **3:**335
literary criticism and **2:**387
medievalism and **3:**28, 30, 333
Millais and **3:**49
Morley and **3:**69
Morris association **3:**71, 333, 334, 335
Morris's wife and **3:**334, 335
muses of **3:**334, 335
poem on prostitution by **3:**266
Pre-Raphaelites and **3:**30, 161, 239, 240, 333–35, 340
retrospective exhibit (2003) **3:**335

Rosa Triplex **3:***241*
Royal Academy training **1:**77; **3:**333, 340
Ruskin and **3:**333–34, 353
Siddal and **3:**388–89; **4:**185, 334, 335
sister Christina and **3:**219, 331, 333, *334*
sonnet sequences **3:**218, 334–35
as Swinburne influence **3:**335; **4:**40, 41
as Working Men's College instructor **4:**204
Rossetti, William Michael **3:**239, 371
art criticism and **1:**76
Brown (Lucy Madox) marriage **1:**172
Rossini, Gioacchino **3:**91, 143, 144
Rostand, Edmond **1:**3
rotary printing press **1:**8; **3:**185, *248*, 249, 278; **4:**58
Rothblatt, Sheldon **4:**139, 140
Rothenstein, John **2:**247
Rothschild, Hannah (granddaughter) *See* Primrose, Hannah Rothschild
Rothschild, Hannah Barent Cohen (mother) **3:**336, 337
Rothschild, Lionel de (son) **2:**318; **3:**336, 337
Rothschild, Mayer (son) **3:**336–37
Rothschild, Nathan Mayer (father) **2:**187; **3:**336
Rothschild, Nathan Mayer ("Natty"; Lord Rothschild of Tring) **3:**337
Rothschild family **2:**317, 319; **3:335–37**
art collection **1:**81
first Jewish peer and **2:**318; **3:**337
international investment and **2:**285
Russell (John) and **3:**356
Suez Canal shares and **1:**370
Rotten Row (London society parade) **2:**408
Rotterdam (Netherlands), zoological garden **4:**212
Rotundo, Anthony **2:**142
Roughing It (Twain) **2:**201
Rougon-Macquart book series **2:**120–21
Round, John Horace **2:**350; **3:**29
Round Reading Room (British Library) **2:**365, *366*
roundabouts (steam-powered carousels) **4:**108–9
Rousseau (J. Morley) **3:**69
Rousseau, Jean-Jacques **1:**241, 244; **3:**30
as autobiography exemplar **1:**99; **4:**43
belief in women's inferiority of **4:**186
Roussel, Theodore **2:**246
Routledge (publisher) **3:**275
Routledge's "Railway Library" **3:**294, 396
Rover automobile manufacture **4:**100
Rover safety bicycle **1:**135; **4:**100
row houses **2:***216*, 218
Rowan, Charles **3:**222
rowing **1:**314; **3:337–38**; **4:**5, *7*
amateur status and **4:**8
American Henley Regatta winners **4:**10
Henley Rules (1879) **4:**8
shirts **4:**131
Rowland, Alexander **2:**190
Rowlandson, Thomas **1:**210; **2:**385

Rowntree (chocolatier) **1:**255, 256; **3:**238
Rowntree, Henry Isaac **1:**255
Rowntree, Joseph **2:**129
Rowntree, Seebohm **1:**223; **2:**392, 393–95; **3:**238–39, 403
Royal Academy of Arts **2:**355, 405; **3:**103, **338–41**
annual exhibition **1:**75; **3:**339, 340
art criticism and **1:**75
art market and **1:**81; **3:**340
Brown (Ford Madox) exhibitions **1:**171
Burne-Jones resignation from **1:**183
Eastlake (Charles Lock) and **2:**19
Frith and **2:**130
Grosvenor Gallery contrasted with **2:**187; **3:**162
history of **3:**339
Hunt and **2:**226
impressionism and **2:**244, 245, 246; **3:**164; **4:**5
inaugural exhibition **3:**338
Landseer and **2:**346
Lear and **2:**353
Leighton and **2:**357; **3:**339, 372
Millais and **3:**49, 50, 240
painting genres and **3:**159, 163, 165, 166
painting hanging policies **3:**340
Pre-Raphaelites' critique of **3:**239, 240
Rossetti (Dante Gabriel) and **1:**77; **3:**333, 340
Sargent and **3:**365
Scott (George Gilbert) and **3:**370
sculpture and **3:**370
South Kensington System design schools and **1:**79, 84
"Summer Shows" of **1:**75, 77
Turner's loyalty to **4:**118
Watts and **4:**167, 168
women's 1859 petition to **4:**183, 184
Royal Academy of Music **3:**88, 90, 94, 97, 98, 149; **4:**46, 47
Mackenzie and **2:**420
See also Royal College of Music
Royal Academy Pictures series **1:**75
Royal Adelaide Gallery **2:**44
Royal Agricultural Hall **3:**386, 387
Royal Agriculture Society **1:**26
Royal Albert Bridge (Saltash) **1:**160, 178
Royal Albert Hall (London) **1:**32, 288
Royal Albert Memorial. *See* Albert Memorial
Royal and Ancient Golf Club (Scotland). *See* St. Andrews Royal and Ancient Golf Club
Royal Artillery Band **3:**44
Royal Association **2:**354–55
Royal Botanical Gardens **1:**130; **2:**89; **3:**109
Royal British Bank **1:**115
Royal British Nursing Association **3:**122
Royal Cape Golf Club **2:**171
royal charter **1:**187
new companies and **2:**110
professionals and **3:**255, 256
See also East India Company
Royal Circus (London) **1:**270
Royal College of Art **1:**80; **3:**372
Royal College of Music **1:**288; **3:**88–90, 342; **4:**47
Grove as first director **2:**188; **3:**88, 90, 94, 97, 149

S

sanitation (cont.)
  alcohol and **1:**34
  automobiles and **1:**102
  Booth (Charles) London maps and **1:**148
  British army and **1:**163, 164
  Chadwick report and reforms **1:**218, 231, 257; **2:**260; **3:**132, 305, 362, 363, 363–64
  cholera and **1:**256, 257; **2:**406; **3:**362, 363, 403
  diseases and epidemics and **1:**32, 218, 231, 366–67; **2:**212, 231–32, 407; **3:**362–65; **4:**58
  environment and **2:**65–66
  Faraday and **2:**105
  graveyard burial and **1:**217–18, 231
  horse waste pollution and **1:**102; **2:**265–66
  hospitals and **2:**212, 213
  housing and **1:**366; **2:**214, 215, 218, 262, 394
  hygiene and **2:**231–33; **3:**67–68
  in India **2:**128; **3:**122, 123, 365
  local vs. central government and **2:**399, 401, 402; **3:**305–6
  London sewer system and **2:**407
  London system for **3:**67–68
  morality linked with **2:**233
  mortality rate and **1:**231; **2:**212; **3:**226
  Nightingale reform campaign **4:**189
  nursing reforms and **3:**132, 134
  poverty and **1:**218, 231; **2:**233, 394
  Public Health Act (1875) and **1:**187; **2:**212; **3:**68, 306; **4:**33, 144
  public health oversight of **2:**233, 402
  statistics and **3:**362–64, 403; **4:**19
  as urbanization problem **1:**34, 231, 298, 367; **2:**212, 231, 232; **4:**144, 146
  water supply and **2:**232, 406, 407; **3:**67
Sankey, Ira **1:**267; **3:**62
Sanskrit **2:**114
Sappho **2:**345; **4:**41, 43
Sara Crewe (Burnett) **1:**249
Saratoga Springs (New York) **2:**201; **3:**314
Sargent, John Singer **2:**174; **3:**164, 168, **365–66**
  impressionism and **2:**246–47; **3:**365
Sartor Resartus (Carlyle) **1:**205; **2:**122; **3:**188
Sartre, Jean-Paul **1:**22
Sarum Gradual (Frere, ed.) **3:**99
Saskatchewan (Canada) **1:**201
Sassoon, Siegfried **1:**49; **2:**121, 227
satire. *See* cartoons; comic literature
Satirist, or Censor of the Times (periodical) **3:**230
Satow, Ernest **2:**314
Saturday Concerts (Crystal Palace) **4:**47
Saturday Evening Post (U.S. monthly magazine) **3:**189
Saturday half-holiday legislation (1850s) **2:**201
Saturday Review, The **3:366–67**
  on Contagious Disease Acts repeal activists **1:**300
  on Kingley's muscular Christianity **3:**76
  Linton published in **2:**144, 378
  Morley and **3:**68
  musical criticism in **3:**91, 92

readership **2:**381
Shaw's drama criticism in **3:**382
on Sidgwick **3:**390
Smith (Goldwin) published in **3:**394
Stephen (James Fitzjames) published in **4:**22
Stephen (Leslie) published in **4:**24
Symonds published in **4:**42
Ward published in **4:**165
as weekly **3:**188
Saunders, David **1:**220
Savage, Frederick **4:**108
Savage, Henri **1:**85
Savage, William **3:**250
Savage State, The (T. Cole painting) **1:**289
savages. *See* indigenous peoples
Savile Row tailors (London) **4:**50
Savoy (London theatre) **2:**158, 159
Savoy, The (literary magazine) **1:**344; **4:**43, 44
Savoy Company (Philadelphia theatrical troupe) **1:**40
sawdust **2:**66
Sawyer, Herbert **1:**138
Sax, Adolphe **1:**154
Saxons in England, a History of the English Commonwealth, The (Kemble) **2:**376
saxophone **1:**155
Say, J. B. **2:**22
Sayers, Dorothy L. **1:**68; **2:**70, 72
"Scandal in Bohemia, A" (A. C. Doyle) **2:**12
Scandinavian Symphony (Cowen) **3:**149; **4:**47
Scapegoat, The (Hunt painting) **2:**226; **3:**240
Scarborough (seaside resort) **2:**201; **3:**374
scarlet fever **1:**366; **4:**151
Scarlet Letter, The (Hawthorne) **2:**194
Scenes and Hymns of Life (Hemans) **2:**195
Scenes from King Olaf (Elgar composition) **2:**45
Scenes from Prometheus Unbound (Parry cantata) **3:**148, 178
Scenes from the Saga of King Olaf (Elgar choral work) **3:**148
Scenes of Clerical Life (G. Eliot) **2:**48
Schechter, Solomon **4:**211
Schelling, Friedrich **1:**18
Schiller, Friedrich von **3:**30–31
Schinkle, Karl Friedrich **2:**178
Schlegel, August Wilhelm von **1:**31
Schleiermacher, Friedrich **1:**132, 166
Schleswig-Holstein affair (1864) **1:**45
"Scholar-Gipsy, The" (M. Arnold) **1:**72
Schomburg, Richard **1:**228
School and Guild of Handicrafts **1:**87, 88, 347
school boards **2:**30, 31, 33–35, 402
  tax levying power and **3:**245; **4:**53
  women's enfranchisement and **2:**9; **4:**190–91, 194
Schoolcraft, Henry **2:**92
Schoolmistress, The (Pinero) **3:**213
schools. *See* education; education of women; primary education; public schools
Schools of Design **1:**78, 84, 288, 346
schottische (dance) **3:**406
Schreiber, Lady Charlotte **1:**83
Schreiner, Olive **3:**111, **367–69**, 426
  Decadence and **1:**344
  Ellis (Havelock) and **2:**50; **3:**368

gender roles and **2:**146; **3:**367, 368, 369
  Levy friendship **2:**361
Schubert, Franz **1:**32; **2:**188; **3:**87
Schumann, Clara **2:**188
Schumann, Robert **1:**32; **2:**188; **3:**89, 91, 178; **4:**45, 47
Schwatka, Frederick **2:**92
Schwechten, Franz **3:**295
Schweitzer, Albert **3:**150
science
  Agassiz and **1:**18–20
  agriculture and **1:**25, 26, 32
  antivivisection movement and **3:**191–92
  astronomy and **1:**89–90
  Babbage and **1:**103
  Bell and **1:**125
  biblical creation story vs. **1:**132, 341; **2:**153, 175; **3:**198
  categories of **3:**81
  Cecil and **1:**216
  Chambers and **1:**235–37
  chemical engineering and **2:**64
  criminology as **1:**330–32
  Darwin and **1:**338–41; **3:**198
  detective story and **1:**354
  exploration and **2:**88–90; **4:**104, 105
  Faraday's popularization of **2:**105–6
  Fortnightly Review articles on **3:**68
  Frazer's (James) view of **2:**123–24
  geology and **2:**151–54
  as Great Exhibition of 1851 theme **2:**185
  Huxley and **2:**229–31
  learned societies and **2:**354–56, 405
  Lewes's writings on **2:**362, 363
  mechanics' institutes and **3:**18, 19
  medical profession and **3:**??
  medicine and **3:**23–24, 25
  Meredith and **3:**34
  mesmerism and **3:**36
  Millais use of **3:**50–51
  Morley and **3:**68
  mountaineering and **3:**73
  museums of **3:**78, 81
  natural resource management and **4:**180
  Owen (Richard) and **3:**155
  phrenology classified as **3:**208–9, 288
  physics and **3:**205–8
  political economy as **2:**24
  positivist hierarchy of disciplines **3:**231
  progress ideal and **3:**258, 259
  psychology and **3:**269
  public health movement and **3:**306
  in public school curricula **3:**273
  racist theories and **3:**290
  religion and **2:**153, 356
  Somerville and **3:**414
  Spencer as champion of **3:**423
  statistical movement and **1:**222; **2:**74
  Thomson (Lord Kelvin) and 85
  in university curricula **4:**138–39, 141
  utility principle as **4:**148, 150
  Wells and **4:**170, 172
  Whewell and **3:**197; **4:**173–74
  See also British Association for the Advancement of Science; evolution; natural history; *specific disciplines*
Science (magazine) **1:**125

science fiction
  Bulwer-Lytton and **1:**179
  Gothic novel and **2:**175
  Wells and **3:**131; **4:**170–71
Science Museum (South Kensington Museum) **1:**105; **3:**78, 80
Science of Ethics (L. Stephen) **2:**83; **4:**25
Science of Life, The (Wells) **4:**172
scientific historiography **2:**199–200
scientific instruments **2:**277; **4:**85
scientific materialism **1:**279
scientific method **3:**208, 231, 232
scientific philanthropists **3:**194–95
scientist, Whewell's coining of term **3:**197; **4:**174
Scopes monkey trial (1925) **2:**81
Scotch Reel **3:**406
"Scotch Rhapsody" (Mackenzie composition) **2:**420
Scotch whiskey **1:**34
  "Victorian heydey" of **1:**158
Scotland
  Act of Union **1:**260; **2:**351; **3:**55
  actuaries abd **3:**255
  Agassiz and **1:**18–19
  Art Nouveau and **1:**84, 85
  asylums **1:**92
  banknote issuance **1:**111
  banks **1:**112–13, 115, 187
  Bird's travels in **1:**136
  brewing industry **1:**157
  bridges **1:**159, 160–61
  census **1:**222
  Cook tour of **1:**301–2
  cooperative industrial movement **3:**155–56
  cotton industry **1:**309; **4:**92
  department store **1:**352
  divorce and **3:**6
  Edinburgh Review **2:**26
  electorate **2:**40
  emigration **2:**52, 53, 55, 56
  Empire and **3:**105
  established church **1:**260, 265–68
  famines **2:**103
  fishing **4:**9
  folklore **2:**114, 115
  football **2:**117, 118
  geology **2:**153
  gin palaces **1:**34
  Glen Roy parallel roads **1:**18–19; **2:**413
  golf **2:**170; **4:**6
  Great Reform Act of 1832 and **2:**39, 40
  hunting and shooting **2:**227; **4:**6
  illegitimacy ratio **2:**237
  kilts and **2:**109
  landscape painting and **3:**165
  learned societies **2:**355
  legal system **2:**351–52
  Liberal Party and **2:**42
  libraries **2:**366, 367
  life insurance companies **2:**274
  Mackenzie and **2:**420
  mechanics' institutes **2:**411; **3:**18–19
  medical schools **4:**138
  medicine **3:**25
  Millais and **3:**50
  national education system **2:**32
  nationalism and, l **3:**105
  oat cakes as diet staple **1:**156
  painting and **3:**163–64
  parliamentary seat redistribution **2:**39
  philosophy and **3:**196–97
  police force **3:**221, 224

steel industry. *See* iron and steel industry
steel-plate engraving **3:**250
Steele, Anne **2:**234
steeplechasing **2:**210, 211; **3:**77
Steer, Philip Wilson **2:**244, 246–47; **3:**164, 168
Steggall, Charles **1:**214
Stein, Edouard **2:**420
Stein, Gertrude **2:**309
Stein, Heinrich Friedrich Karl von **3:**377
Steinitz, Wilhelm **1:**241
Stepan, Nancy **1:**226
Stephen, James (father) **4:**22, 24
Stephen, James Fitzjames **4:22–24**
Stephen, Leslie **3:**389; **4:24–26**
  agnosticism and **1:**21, 22; **4:**24, 25
  biography and **1:**280; **3:**69; **4:**24, 25, 26
  brother James Fitzjames and **4:**22
  on Clough **1:**280
  Cornhill Magazine editorship **1:**308; **2:**192, 320; **4:**24–25
  daughter Virgina Woolf and **1:**308; **2:**387; **4:**25–26
  Dictionary of National Biography and **1:**280; **4:**24, 25
  family background **4:**22, 24
  Hardy and **2:**192, 193
  literary criticism **2:**387; **4:**24
  on memoirs' value **1:**100
  natural selection theory and **2:**83
  as *Saturday Review* contributor **3:**367
  Thackeray relationship **1:**308
  travel literature and **4:**104
  as Working Men's College instructor **4:**204
Stephens, Charles **4:**47
Stephens, Frederic George **1:**76; **3:**239, 240
Stephens, James Fitzjames **2:**109, 110
Stephens, John Lloyd **1:**61, 226; **4:**105
Stephenson, George **1:**177; **2:**265; **4:26,** 60
  steam locomotive and **2:**279–80, 282; **4:**26
Stephenson, Robert **1:**177; **2:**188, 282
  bridges and **1:**159, 160
  engineering and **2:**62, *63*
  steam locomotive and **2:**279–80; **3:**297; **4:**26
Stepney Fair **4:**108
stereoplates **3:**277, 278
stereoscope **3:**204
"Stereotypes of Femininity in a Theory of Sexual Evolution" (J. Conway) **2:**141
sterilization, involuntary **2:**73, 74, 75, 237
sterling **2:**277
Sterling, John **1:**166; **3:**15
Sterling Club **1:**166
Sterne, Laurence **1:**205; **2:**387; **3:**166
Stetson, Dorothy M. **3:**3, 5
Stevens, Alfred **3:**59, 61, 371
Stevens, F. W. **3:**296
Stevens, John Lloyd **1:**226
Stevens, R. J. S. **3:**99
Stevenson, Fanny Osbourne **4:**27, 28
Stevenson, J. J. **1:**67
Stevenson, Robert Louis **2:**151; **4:26–28**
  adventure fiction and **1:**7–8; **3:**131, 329; **4:**26, 27
  Besant (Walter) and **1:**131
  Braddon as influence on **1:**151

children's literature and **1:**35; **4:**26, 27, 28, 208
children's poetry and **1:**248
as *Cornhill Magazine* contributor **1:**308; **4:**24
on electric light **2:**370
gin palaces and **1:**34
Gothic genre and **2:**176; **4:**27, 28
Meredith and **3:**35
romance and **3:**328, 329
Stewart, A. T. **1:**350
Stewart, Dugald **3:**196, 197; **4:**69
Stewart, Robert Prescott **1:**212; **3:**94
Stickley, Gustav **1:**88
stilt walkers **4:**31
Stingle, Richard **3:**329
Stirling, Elizabeth **3:**151
stock markets **4:28–30**
  Bagehot theory **1:**106
  brewery shares **1:**158
  British foreign loans and **2:**128
  business and corporate structure **1:**187
  East India Company shares **2:**248–49
  foreign enterprises and **4:**29
  fraud and **2:**110, 111
  international links **4:**30
  jobbers vs. brokers and **4:**28–29
  London Exchange and **1:**110, 187; **2:**128; **4:**28–29, 30
  provincial **4:**29–30
  railway shares **3:**297–98, 299; **4:**29
  wealth and **4:**29
  See also joint-stock companies
stock tickers **2:**28
Stockdale, John **3:**229–30
stocking frame **2:**99
Stockley, William **3:**150
Stockton and Darlington Railway **4:**26
Stoke-on-Trent **1:**229, 285, 339
Stoke Rochford Hall **3:**318
Stoker, Bram **3:**131; **4:**3, 30–31, 123
  Gothic genre and **2:**176; **4:**30, 31
  Irving (Henry) and **2:**298
Stone, Marcus **3:**163
stone bridges **1:**159
Stonebreaker (Brett) **3:**164
Stonehenge **1:**61; **2:**196; **3:**70
Stones of Venice, The (Ruskin) **1:**66; **2:**165, 179; **3:**28, 353
Stonyhurst (public school) **3:**273
Stoppard, Tom **2:**219
Storey, Joseph **1:**317
Stories, Dreams and Allegories (Schreiner) **3:**369
Stories of Ohio (Howells) **2:**221
"Stories of the Seen and Unseen" (M. Oliphant) **3:**139
Storks, Henry **1:**190, 300
Storm-Cloud of the Nineteenth Century, The (Ruskin) **3:**354–55
Story from Boccaccio (Watts painting) **4:**167
Story of a Bad Boy (Aldrich) **1:**36, 249
Story of an African Farm, The (Schreiner) **2:**50; **3:**111, 367–68, 369
Story of Organ Music, The (C. F. A. Williams) **3:**152
"Story of Sayid" (Mackenzie composition) **2:**420
Stott, Edward **2:**244
Stott of Oldham, William **2:**244, 247
Stourbridge glass district **2:**164, 165, 166
Stowe, Harriet Beecher **1:**282, 332; **2:**166; **3:**294; **4:**55

on divinity of childhood **1:**245
melodrama and **3:**31
novel's sales in England **3:**129
portrayal of Quakers by **3:**285
See also Uncle Tom's Cabin
Strachan, Hew **1:**164
Strachey, Lytton **3:**389
  on Bernhardt **1:**128
  biography of Queen Victoria by **4:**159
  on Gordon ("Chinese") **2:**173
Strachey, Ray **3:**122
Strafford (R. Browning) **1:**175
Strahorn, Carrie **4:**105
Straits Convention (1841) **4:**69
Strand (magazine) **2:**12, 382; **3:**189, 278
Strand, The (London area) **2:**405; **3:**318; **4:**212
Strange, William **3:**230
Strange Case of Dr. Jekyll and Mr. Hyde, The (Stevenson) **1:**34; **2:**176; **3:**329; **4:**27, 28
stratigraphy **2:**152, 153, 154
Stratton, Charles Sherwood. *See* Tom Thumb
Stratton, Lavinia **2:**126
Strauss, David Friedrich **1:**133, 166, 281; **2:**47; **3:**376
Strauss, Levi **2:**169
Strauss, Richard **2:**46
"Straussianism" **1:**166
Strawberry Thief (Morris textile design) **3:**71
Strayed Reveller, and Other Poems, The (M. Arnold) **1:**71, 72
Strayed Sheep (Hunt painting) **3:**164
Street, George Edmund **2:**178, 179; **3:**30, 370
Street, Joseph **3:**87
Street, Matthew **1:**221
street lighting **2:**369–70, *371*; **3:**207
street literature **3:**235
street performers **1:**4; **4:31–32**
street sellers **3:**235, 317, 318; **4:**145
  underemployment and **4:**129
street thieves **2:**406
Streets of Philadelphia, The (Boucicault) **1:**150
streetwalkers. *See* prostitution
Stretton, Hesba **1:**245, 250; **4:**208
Strickland, Agnes **3:**161
Stride, Elizabeth **2:**305
strikes
  bread prices and **1:**156
  Chartist **1:**239
  industrial unionization and **2:**337–38
  legal system and **2:**350, 351; **4:**94
  technological unemployment and **4:**58
  trade unions and **4:**92, 94
  U.S. railroads and **3:**300
  variety artists and **2:**398
  women match workers **1:**130; **2:**260
String of Pearls, The (T. P. Prest) **3:**185
strip cartoons **1:**211
Strudwick, J. M. **1:**12
Strutt family **2:**342
Stuart, Louisa (Lady Waterford) **4:**185
Stuart dynasty **3:**356; **4:**41
Stuart of Dunleath (Norton) **3:**125
Stubbs, William **2:**199, 350; **3:**29
Student's Marx, The: An Introduction to His "Capital" (Aveling) **3:**15
Studies in Animal Life (Lewes) **2:**362
Studies in Modern Music (Hadow) **3:**91

Studies in the History of the Renaissance (Pater) **1:**12, 13, 343–44; **2:**206, 303
Studies in the Psychology of Sex (H. Ellis) **2:**49, 50, 51; **4:**42, 43
Studies in Two Literatures (Symons) **4:**45
Studies of a Biographer (L. Stephen) **4:**25
Studies on Homer and the Homeric Age (Gladstone) **1:**279
Studio, The (periodical) **1:**76, 83; **3:**373
Study of Ecclesiastical History, The (A. P. Stanley) **4:**14
Study of Psychology, The (Lewes and Eliot) **2:**362; **3:**199
Study of Religion, A (J. Martineau) **3:**12
Study of Shakespeare (Swinburne) **2:**388
Stumpf, Carl Friederich **2:**68
Sturge, John **3:**286
Sturgeon, William **2:**44
Sturt, Charles **2:**93
Stuttgart zoological garden **4:**214
Style in Musical Art (Parry) **3:**91, 178
style manuals (typesetting) **3:**250
Subjection of Women, The (J. S. Mill) **2:**143; **3:**47, 48; **4:**22
submarines **3:**347
subscription libraries **2:**365, 383, 405
Subscription No Bondage (Maurice) **3:**15–16
Suburban Gardener and Villa Companion, The (Loudon) **2:**136, 138–39
Suburban Sketches (Howells) **2:**221
suburbia **4:32–34**
  automobile and **1:**102
  as Brown (Ford Madox) painting subject **1:**171
  conservatories and **2:**136
  criticisms of **4:**34
  department stores and **1:**352
  diet and dining habits and **1:**359
  domestic comedy on **1:**293; **4:**34
  explosion of (1861-1901) **4:32–33**
  franchise extension and **2:**42
  garden city movement and **2:**139; **4:**33
  garden design and gardening and **2:**135, 138–39
  housing **2:**215–17; **4:**33, 34, 100
  London and **2:**215, 216–17, 405; **4:32–34**
  pleasure gardens and **3:**214–15
  population growth **1:**265; **4:**33
  railways and **4:**99, 101
  reputation of **4:**33
  social classes and **3:**403
  transportation and **1:**194; **3:**403; **4:**33–34, 99, 101, 126
  Underground and **4:**126
  urban expansion and **4:**143
  white-collar workers and **3:**402
subway system. *See* Underground
Sudan **3:**43
  Anglo-French relations and **1:**44, 46
  civil service and **3:**275
  Egypt and **2:**37, 38
  Empire and **2:**60, 62
  Gordon ("Chinese") and **2:**163, 171–72, 331; **3:**174, 261
  Kitchener and **2:**331; **3:**69
  Stanley (Henry Morton) and **4:**18
Sudan Interior Mission **3:**54

telegraph (cont.)
Thomson (Lord Kelvin) and **4:**85
travel and **2:**201
typewriter and **4:**121, 122
underseas cable and **1:**178; **2:**322; **3:**206, 207; **4:**30, 61, 64, 85
war journalism and **3:**358
warfare and **3:**207
women workers and **4:**122, 199
telepathy **4:**2–3
telephone **2:**86; **3:**207; **4:64–66**
Bell's invention of **1:**123, 124–25; **2:**280, 284; **3:**207; **4:**64–65
Britons' lag in use of **4:**65
in department stores **1:**352
electricity and **3:**206; **4:**65
nationalization of **4:**66
post office and **3:**233; **4:**66
stock exchanges and **4:**30
typewriter and **4:**121, 122
women as operators **2:**144; **4:**65, 122, 199
worldwide adoption of **4:**66
telescope **1:**89–90
televangelists **3:**62
Telford, Thomas **1:**159, 160, 178; **2:**279
temperance movement **4:66–68**
alcohol and **1:**33, 34
Alcott and **1:**36
Anthony and **1:**53, 54
antitobacco movement and **4:**89
Blackwell and **1:**148
breweries and **1:**157, 158
British women leaders of **4:**189
Chautauqua and **1:**240
Cruikshank and **1:**332
hymns of **2:**234
in Ireland **2:**289; **4:**67, 68
magic lantern shows and **3:**387
Methodism and **3:**39
morality and **3:**66; **4:**66–68
organization of **4:**68
prohibitionist wing **4:**68
public houses as targets **3:**269, 271; **4:**67
Seneca Falls Convention and **3:**378
statistical movement and **1:**222
as tea consumption influence **4:**35, 55, 57
teetotalers and **1:**34; **3:**271; **4:**57, 67, 68
U.S. social reform and **4:**67, 68, 136
U.S. Sunday schools and **4:**39
women's rights activists and **3:**378
Temperance Society **2:**83; **4:**68
temperature scale **4:**85
Temple, Emily Cowper (Lady Palmerston) **4:**70
Temple, Frederick **1:**167, 264; **2:**68, 324
Temple, Henry John (Lord Palmerston) **4:68–71**
American Civil War and **1:**275; **4:**70
Anglo-French relations and **1:**44; **3:**102, 172; **4:**69, 70
Anglo-Russian relations and **1:**50, 51, 52; **4:**69
architecture and **1:**65; **3:**370
aristocracy and **1:**68
child labor and **4:**71
cholera epidemic and **1:**257
Crimean War and **4:**69–70
decorative arts and **1:**346
as foreign secretary **4:**69–70
Gladstone and **2:**162; **4:**70

Liberal leadership **2:**40; **3:**172; **4:**68–70
personal style of **4:**70
as prime minister **3:**173; **4:**16, 68, 70
Russell (John) conflicts with **3:**172, 173; **4:**70
Russell (John) in cabinet of **3:**356
Stanley (Edward) and **4:**16
Times and **3:**118
Temple Bar (monthly periodical) **1:**131; **2:**382; **3:**189
Temple of Bassae (Lear) **2:**353
Temple of Industry (France) **2:**84, 185
Temple of Karnak (Egypt) **2:**38
Ten Hours Act (1847) **1:**247; **2:**76, 101, 201; **3:**356
Ten Hours Movement **4:71**
child labor and **1:**247
coal mining and **3:**52
Recordite Evangelicalism and **2:**76
Ten Years Conflict (1833-1843) **1:**266
tenant farmers **2:**52, 103, 342, 343, 344
former slaves as **2:**344; **3:**351
Irish Land War and **3:**176, 177
Irish potato crop and **3:**234
Mill's (John Stuart) land reform efforts and **3:**48
Tenant of Wildfell Hall, The (A. Brontë) **1:**34
tenements. *See* slums
Tenniel, John
Alice's Adventures in Wonderland illustrations **1:**208; **2:**238, 239; **3:**282
career of **1:**211
Punch cartoons **1:**210, 211; **3:**280, 282
tennis **2:**107, 139; **4:**6, 8, 9, **71–73**
women players **2:**145; **4:**9, 71, 72, 73
Tennis Party (Lavery painting) **3:**164
Tennyson, Alfred **2:**158, 298, 386; **3:**148, 218, 326, 389; **4:73–75**
as aristocrat **1:**69
Arnold (Matthew) and **1:**72
Bulwer-Lytton and **1:**179
Cameron and **1:**197
Carroll and **1:**208
Chambers and **1:**237
classical studies and **1:**278, 279
Cobbe and **1:**283
as *Cornhill Magazine* contributor **1:**308
Crimean War poem by **1:**327
Darwinian view of nature and **2:**82
dinosaur image used by **1:**364
dramatic monologue and **2:**13, 14; **3:**217
evolution theories and **1:**237; **3:**35
Fitzgerald (Edward) and **2:**113
garden portrayals by **2:**139
Gordon ("Chinese") epigraph by **2:**172–73
greatness as poet **1:**174; **3:**217
Hallam's poetic views and **3:**215, 216, 217; **4:**74
Hemans as influence on **2:**195
homoerotic elegy and **2:**206
illustration of *Poems* and **2:**241
Lear's illustrations and **2:**354
literary annuals and **2:**385
Longfellow visit with **2:**410
Macmillan's Magazine and **2:**421
Macready poetic tribute by **2:**423
medievalism and **3:**27, 161
melancholy of **4:**73

mesmerism and **3:**37
Millais illustrations and **3:**50
as poet laureate **3:**217, 356; **4:**73
religious poetry and **3:**308
Rossetti (Dante Gabriel) and **3:**333
Saturday Review praise for **3:**367
spasmodic poetry and **3:**217
Swinburne's poetry ranked with **4:**41
Symons's appreciation of **4:**44
Watts portrait of **3:**168
Wordsworthian sensibility and **4:**200
works as painting subjects **1:**81
Tenth Symphony (Potter) **4:**46
Ternan, Ellen **1:**357
terraces **2:**136
Terre, La (Zola) **1:**220; **3:**230
Terry, Ellen **1:**3; **2:**130; **4:75–77**
Beardsley's pen-and-ink portraits of **1:**121
international stardom of **1:**128
Irving (Henry) and **2:**298
Shaw correspondence with **4:**77
Watts marriage to **4:**76, 167, 168
Watts's portrait of **3:**164; **4:**167
Terry, Kate **4:**75–76
Tesla, Nikola **2:**283
Tess of the D'Urbervilles (Hardy) **2:**72, 192, 422; **3:**31, 129, 130, 266
Test Acts **4:77–78**
Bradlaugh and **1:**152–53
church and state and **1:**153, 260, 261, 371; **3:**285; **4:**77–78
Dissent and **1:**371, 372; **4:**77
Jews and **1:**153; **2:**317; **3:**336; **4:**77
repeal of **1:**260, 372–73, 376; **2:**400; **3:**172; **4:**77
requirements of **3:**285
Tractarian opposition to **1:**166
Tewfik Pasha **2:**38; **3:**42
Tewkesbury Abbey **3:**370
Texas **1:**42; **2:**391; **4:**134
textbooks **3:**276
textile design **1:**344, 345, 347
collections of **3:**80
Morris and **1:**345; **3:**71
textile industry
business structure of **1:**186
chemical dyes and **2:**64
child labor and **1:**186, 241, 242; **3:**304; **4:**58, 71
child labor laws and **2:**98, 101
cyclical unemployment and **4:**128–29
decline of **1:**311
Dickens's writings on **2:**261
economic cycles and **2:**20, 21
environmental pollution and **2:**64, 65; **4:**58
immigrants and **2:**53
India and **1:**188; **2:**248
industrialization and **2:**264–65
"informal empire" trade and **2:**59, 60
in Ireland **2:**289
Luddite antimechnization protests and **2:**99; **4:**59
mechanization and **1:**308; **2:**96–97, 297; **4:**47, 58
Peel and **3:**182, 184
quality decline **1:**78
steam engine and **2:**62, 65, 95; **4:**58
strikes and **4:**92
technology and **4:**58, 60
Ten Hours Movement **4:**71
trade unions and **2:**96, 98; **4:**92, 94
United States **1:**188

urbanization and **4:**146–47
women workers **1:**186, 188; **2:**260; **4:**197
women's low wages **3:**265
wool and worsted **4:**146
See also cotton industry; wool
Thackeray, William Makepeace **2:**49, 71, 120, 181, 254; **4:78–79**
art criticism by **1:**76
Brontë (Charlotte) and **1:**168
as Bulwer-Lytton critic **1:**179
capital punishment views of **1:**203
comic literature and **1:**291, 292, 293
on compensation for writers **3:**255
Cornhill Magazine editorship **1:**307, 308; **2:**122, 382; **3:**189, 354
on Doyle's (John) *Political Sketches* **1:**210
Fitzgerald (Edward) and **2:**113
Fraser's magazine and **2:**122, 385
illustrations and **3:**281
influence of **2:**220
James (Henry) and **2:**310
Jerrold friendship **2:**315
Lewes and **2:**362, 363
literary annuals and **2:**385
literary criticism and **2:**386
Mayhew and **3:**16
novel and **2:**382; **3:**126; **4:**78, 79
novel serialization and **3:**128, 278; **4:**78
periodicals and **2:**381, 382
portrayal of debtors by **1:**342
portrayal of gentlemen's club by **2:**141
portrayal of India by **2:**248, 254
portrayal of social conditions by **2:**208, 221
portrayal of social etiquette by **2:**71
portrayal of social snobbery by **3:**404
portrayal of tobacco use by **4:**88
prison novels of **3:**113, 114
Punch contributions by **1:**292; **3:**280, 281; **4:**78
realist novels of **3:**128; **4:**79
romance and **3:**328
on Russell's (William) war reports **3:**358
Saturday Review praise for **3:**367
sporting novel and **4:**4
Thames Embankment (London) **4:**144
Thames Ironworks Football Club **2:**117
Thames River
boating races **3:**337–38; **4:**8
bridges and tunnel **1:**159, 161, 177; **2:**282
docks **2:**404
as drinking water source **2:**232, 407
paddle steamers **4:**99
sewage pollution of **2:**105, 407; **3:**67–68
Westminster and **4:**172
Thames Tunnel **1:**17
Thanksgiving Day (U.S.) **2:**167
Thatcher, Margaret **2:**243; **4:**66
theater **2:**405, 422; **4:79–85**
actor-managers and **4:**83–84
actors and **1:**2–5; **4:**83–84
amateur productions **1:**37, 40, 356
Archer and **1:**63–64
aristocrats' box seats **4:**80
audience behavior **4:**80
auditorium lighting **4:**80
ballet and **1:**108–9